CALIFORNIA REAL ESTATE PRACTICE

FOURTH EDITION

Sherry Shindler Price • *Leigh Conway*

This publication is designed to provide accurate and current information regarding the subject matter covered. The principles and conclusions presented are subject to local, state and federal laws and regulations, court cases, and revisions of same. If legal advice or other expert assistance is required, the reader is urged to consult a competent professional in that field.

Real Estate Publisher
Leigh Conway

Academic Information Analyst
Laura King

Writer
Sue Carlson

Technical Writer
Ben Hernandez

Copyeditor
Stephanie Pratap

Graphic Designer
Susan Mackessy Richmond

©2013 by Ashley Crown Systems, Inc., a division of Allied Business Schools, Inc.
Fourth Edition

Published by:
Ashley Crown Systems, Inc.
22952 Alcalde Drive
Laguna Hills, California 92653

Printed in the United States of America

ISBN 978-0-934772-66-2

CONTENTS

Preface .... *v*
About the Authors .... *vi*
Acknowledgements .... *vi*

Unit 1: Your Real Estate Career 1
   Introduction 1
   Getting Started in Real Estate 2
   What Do New Salespeople Do? 4
   Why Go Into Residential Real Estate Sales? 9
   How Does Real Estate Differ From Other Jobs? ... 10
   What is the Job Outlook? 11
   The Interview 14
   Choose the Right Brokerage Company 16
   Summary 30
   Unit 1 Review 31

Unit 2: Prepare for Success 35
   Introduction 35
   Prepare Your Finances 36
   Put Your Best Foot Forward 45
   Perfect Your Communication Skills 50
   Summary 53
   Unit 2 Review 54

Unit 3: Goal Setting & Productivity 57
   Introduction 57
   Business Plan 58
   Personal Marketing Plan 64
   Time Management Plan 72
   Summary 77
   Unit 3 Review 78

Unit 4: Product Knowledge 81

Introduction 81
Know the Neighborhoods 82
Know What Creates Architectural Styles 86
Know the Architectural Styles 97
Assigning a Style to a House 113
Summary 114
Unit 4 Review 117

Unit 5: Completing the Seller's Forms 121

Introduction 121
Case Study 122
Agency Relationships and Disclosure 125
Residential Listing Agreement – Exclusive 130
Estimated Seller's Proceeds 143
Seller Instruction to Exclude Listing From the Multiple Listing Service 143
Seller's Advisory 147
Real Estate Transfer Disclosure Statement (TDS) 152
Supplemental Statutory and Contractual Disclosures 156
Natural Hazard Disclosure Statement (NHD) 159
Combined Hazards Book 164
Water Heaters, Smoke Detectors, and Carbon Monoxide Detectors 165
Homeowner Association Information Request 165
Seller's Affidavit of Nonforeign Status and/or California Withholding Exemption . . 169
Unit 5 Review 171

Unit 6: Completing the Buyer's Forms 175

Introduction 175
Case Study 176
Disclosing the Agency Relationship 179
California Residential Purchase Agreement and Joint Escrow Instructions 183
Estimated Buyer's Closing Costs 209
Buyer's Inspection Advisory 211
Unit 6 Review 214

Unit 7: How Will You Get Your Business? 217

Introduction 217
Who are Likely Prospects? 218
Prospecting Laws 221
Prospecting Strategy 224
Always Ask for Referrals 239
Summary 240
Unit 7 Review 241

Unit 8: Advertising & Marketing Listings 245
Introduction 245
Create a Property Marketing Plan 246
Advertising 249
Advertising Media 255
Summary 265
Unit 8 Review 266

Unit 9: The Listing Presentation 269
Introduction 269
Preparing for the Listing Appointment 270
The Listing Presentation 276
Top Reasons Homes Fail To Sell 283
NAR Code of Ethics—Listings 284
Summary 286
Unit 9 Review 287

Unit 10: Servicing the Listing 291
Introduction 291
Servicing the Listing 292
Steps In Servicing the Listing 293
Holding a Successful Open House 301
Summary 316
Unit 10 Review 318

Unit 11: Working with Buyers 321
Introduction 321
Buyer Representation 322
Prospecting for Buyers 324
Qualifying Buyers 329
Showing Properties 334
Buying Signs 338
Ask for the Sale 340
Due Diligence and Disclosure 341
Summary 343
Unit 11 Review 344

Unit 12: Writing and Presenting an Offer 347
Introduction 347
Writing the Offer 348
Presenting the Offer 355
Counteroffers 363
After Acceptance 366
Summary 367
Unit 12 Review 368

Unit 13: Financing the Purchase **371**

    Introduction 371

    Fundamentals of Real Estate Finance 372

    The Loan Process 390

    What if a Loan is Denied? 401

    Summary 406

    Unit 13 Review 408

Unit 14: From Acceptance to Close **413**

    Introduction 413

    Opening Escrow 414

    Who Does What During Escrow? 415

    Summary 432

    Unit 14 Review 433

Unit 15: Putting it all Together **437**

    Introduction 437

    Working with Sellers 438

    Working with Buyers 443

    Required Transaction Documents 447

    Required Disclosures 448

    Summary 450

    Unit 15 Review 451

    Appendix A: Answer Key 455

    Glossary 473

    Index 489

PREFACE

Whether your purpose is to increase your knowledge as a buyer, seller, or a real estate salesperson, you will find the information in this text to be useful. Although this text was written primarily for the beginning real estate salesperson, inquiring consumers and investors will also find answers to their real estate questions.

This text is unique in that it gives a practical day-to-day description of the "nuts and bolts" of a real estate salesperson's professional life. Students will learn secrets of the trade which will help them succeed in their chosen field of residential real estate. They will learn the value of professionalism and ethics. Other skills students will acquire include identifying prospective buyers and sellers, recognizing product information, and completing the necessary forms in a real estate transaction. While earning a sizable commission is important, students will learn that helping clients successfully navigate their way through the real estate transaction is ultimately the most rewarding aspect of the profession.

Each unit in this textbook has been divided into topics. Topic content is reinforced through real-life examples, photographs, illustrations, charts, and tables. Important terms are highlighted in **bold** type in each unit.

Review exercises have been designed for each unit. The quiz exercises feature real estate terms and multiple-choice questions. The multiple-choice questions at the end of each unit will help students prepare for their career in real estate. These questions were designed to test concepts and will require students to combine the information they have learned in different units.

After completing a quiz exercise, students can check their answers by reviewing the Answer Key in the Appendix. Students should be encouraged to review their work often to make sure they understand what they have read.

ABOUT THE AUTHORS

SHERRY SHINDLER PRICE

Sherry Shindler Price has been a California Community College real estate instructor since 1986. She has over twenty-five years in the real estate profession, including eight years of specialization in investment properties and residential sales. She has authored *California Real Estate Principles* and *Escrow Principles and Practices*. In addition, Ms. Shindler Price has reviewed numerous real estate textbooks for major publishers and has written a series of continuing education courses for private real estate schools. Her extensive knowledge in real estate was used to write test questions for state licensing examinations in Nevada, Wisconsin, Minnesota, Maryland, and Iowa. Ms. Shindler Price has a Bachelor of Science degree in Education from Long Beach State College.

LEIGH CONWAY

Leigh Conway brings a rich background in real estate to the creation and production of this text. She is a licensed real estate broker in California with experience in commercial brokerage, residential and commercial property management, syndication, and real estate development. With over ten years of experience in real estate education, she has taught various statutory and continuing education courses. In addition, she co-authored a number of real estate textbooks and wrote several continuing education courses for private real estate schools. Ms. Conway has a Bachelor's Degree from the University of California at Los Angeles.

ACKNOWLEDGEMENTS

The authors would like to thank Dr. Thomas W. Paradis for his gracious use of personal photographs of historical american housing styles found in Unit 4 on page 109. His knowledge in historic preservation, geography, and landscape studies have helped to illustrate architectural concepts in this text. Professor Paradis teaches courses in geography, design and preservation at Northern Arizona University. His area of interest focuses on downtown redevelopment, cultural landscapes, small town growth and change.

In addition, special thanks to Laura King who brings practical and useful insights into the content using her years of experience as a multi-state licensed real estate broker. The authors would also like to acknowledge Ben Hernandez who was responsible for the completed forms found in Units 5 and 6. Mr. Hernandez brings years of experience dealing with real estate subject matter, not only in California, but other states, such as Texas, Florida, and Virginia.

Finally, the authors would like to acknowledge the California Department of Real Estate, California Association of REALTORS®, and others for the forms and contracts printed throughout the text.

Your Real Estate Career

Unit 1

INTRODUCTION

The real estate industry is one of the largest sectors of the U.S. economy. Almost two trillion dollars worth of new and existing homes are sold each year, according to the **National Association of REALTORS® (NAR)**. The term **REALTOR®** is a registered trade name that only may be used by active members of the National Association of REALTORS® (NAR), its state and local associations. These real estate transactions provide millions of Americans with jobs and result in hundreds of billions of dollars of economic activity each year. The housing sector accounts for about 22% of the **annual gross domestic product (GDP)**. In short, the real estate industry, increases income flow, creates net worth, and offers consumers and practitioners alike the opportunity to achieve financial success. This huge segment of the economy offers a variety of employment opportunities—from development and finance through home improvements and residential sales.

You have made a good decision to become a part of this vibrant industry. As a licensed salesperson working in a brokerage, you will be in a unique position to help people with their real estate transactions because you have knowledge and experience that most buyers and sellers do not possess. Consumers depend on you, the real estate professional, to guide them through the complex world of real estate sales. Knowing that consumers will turn to you to help make their real estate dreams a reality can appear overwhelming.

New real estate salespeople usually have an abundance of questions about a career in real estate, such as "How much money can I make?", "What is so great about a career in real estate?", "Now that I have my license, what else do I need to know?", "What does a real estate salesperson do all day?", "How do I choose an office?"

People commonly refer to a real estate firm as a real estate agency, but the firm is actually a brokerage. The term **brokerage** generally refers to an activity involving the sale of something through an intermediary who negotiates the transaction for payment. In the case of a real estate brokerage, the sale involves real property, with the broker acting as an agent for a principal, earning a commission at the end when the transaction closes. The purpose of a real estate brokerage is to help people buy and sell real property. A brokerage firm must have a licensed real estate broker who may work alone or with the help of hundreds of salespeople.

The ways a brokerage may be operated, the people you may find working at a real estate brokerage, your role as a salesperson in a brokerage, and the various brokerage activities you will perform will be discussed later in this unit.

Learning Objectives

After reading this unit, you should be able to:

- recognize the advantages of pursuing a career in real estate.
- identify the daily activities of a real estate sales associate.
- describe the transition to a career in real estate, including earnings and the employment relationship with the broker.
- list the types of brokerages available to a new salesperson.
- identify the brokerage employees and their roles.

GETTING STARTED IN REAL ESTATE

Many new licensees begin their real estate careers by starting out as a trainee, with a mentor to guide them through their first few transactions as salespeople. A **mentor** is a person providing quality support, advice, and counseling. Others prefer to start out as an assistant to a successful salesperson, and receive a small salary and perhaps a small commission, based on the sales price of each transaction. Still others may choose a starting position, usually based on a salary, as an office assistant or transaction coordinator.

Many different real estate career opportunities are available to a licensed real estate salesperson. You may decide to specialize in residential, commercial, or industrial brokerage, or become a mortgage loan agent or leasing agent. However, the majority of new licensees begin as sales trainees in a residential brokerage firm.

Residential property is where the majority of new licensees begin their real estate careers.

As a result, the focus of this book will be on the sale of residential property within a brokerage.

Residential Sales

Residential brokerage is the business of helping homeowners sell and home buyers purchase homes. Most new licensees choose this segment of the industry. In order to be successful in this area, a licensee must have knowledge of available inventory and financing options. In addition, the new salesperson must know how to complete all necessary paperwork, and be able to guide the transaction through to a successful close. The better the agent is prepared, the better he or she will be able to facilitate the transaction, saving his or her clients time, trouble, and money. Licensees who choose residential brokerage need to have knowledge of the local economic trends, disclosure requirements, real estate and fair housing laws, and available financing. In addition, they must be willing and able to work weekends and even some evenings. Experienced salespeople can advance in many large firms to sales manager or general manager. A person with a broker license may also open his or her own brokerage office.

Mortgage Loan Agent

A **mortgage loan agent** is in the business of helping borrowers qualify for and get loans to purchase homes. Well-informed buyers get pre-qualified by a lender before looking for a home. Once the home is selected, the loan agent takes information from the borrower and prepares the actual loan application, which is sent to the lender for processing. Loan agents must have a California real estate salesperson license if they work for a loan brokerage licensed by the California Department of Real Estate.

Commercial/Industrial Sales

Licensees interested in income-producing properties such as apartments, office buildings, retail stores, shopping centers, industrial parks, and ware-houses should consider a career in **commercial brokerage**. Due to the complexity of these transactions, however, most new licensees begin their career in residential brokerage and then move into commercial/industrial as they learn more about the industry. It is important to know about any economic trends because clients will expect their broker to know why a particular property would be a good investment. Even though real estate licensees do not give tax advice, it is also important to understand current income tax regulations because they could affect the buyer's return on his or her investment. Just like residential brokers, commercial brokers should have financing sources for the prospective buyer. Sometimes, the new owner will ask the broker to help lease any remaining vacant space and take over ongoing management of the property.

Leasing Agent or Property Manager

The main goal of **property management** is to protect the owner's investment in order to produce the highest possible financial return over the longest period of time. Leasing agents usually work for large apartment complexes, showing the apartments to prospective renters. Property managers usually work for real estate firms that manage homes, condominiums, duplexes, and apartments.

Real Estate Appraiser

Real estate appraisers determine the value of properties. To become a real estate **appraiser**, a person must meet education requirements, experience requirements, and pass an examination administered by the California Office of Real Estate Appraisers.

WHAT DO NEW SALESPEOPLE DO?

New real estate salespeople wonder what they will be doing all day. Initially, most new licensees go through a training program. Once it is completed, they talk to homeowners to get listings to sell the homeowner's property. Salespeople talk to buyers to help them find available properties. Finally, they handle the paperwork necessary to close the transaction.

In the beginning of your career, you will have very little paperwork to complete. You will most likely schedule time to prepare marketing materials, and consider that as part of your administrative duties. However, as you become more involved on the job, you will need to schedule time to follow-up on outstanding requirements from each of your transactions. This time may include making phone calls to buyers, sellers, escrow parties, and other salespeople, and making sure all paperwork is in order. When your business begins to expand, making time for administrative duties will help to keep you caught up on transactions, and allow you to close deals as quickly and smoothly as possible.

Salespeople focus on the following activities in order to produce and maintain a consistent flow of business: training, improving product knowledge, previewing properties, prospecting, obtaining listings, marketing properties, working with buyers, handling paperwork, closing sales, attending sales meetings, and keeping current with market trends. All of these topics will be discussed in further detail as you progress through the book.

A brokerage may offer a new salesperson training or a mentoring program.

Training

After passing the state exam and getting your license, you will probably enter one of the new license training programs offered by larger real estate firms. You may get good, indifferent, or no training, depending on the brokerage. Many real estate brokerages provide sales training, and on the job training, or a combination of both. Sometimes brokers, managers, or mentors accompany new salespeople to their first appointments. Remember, the broker is responsible for everything a salesperson does. He or she does not want anyone making costly mistakes that may affect the reputation of the brokerage or lead to a lawsuit.

Depending on what your brokerage provides, scheduling time for training, seminars, and continuing education should be a weekly priority for you as a real estate salesperson. Take advantage of all training and educational opportunities throughout your career. Even the most accomplished salesperson requires ongoing training to keep his or her skills current.

Mentoring Program

Most new salespeople feel anxious and overwhelmed by the job ahead of them and have no idea where to start. Some brokerage firms give new salespeople a head start by introducing a mentoring program, where a seasoned salesperson will act as a mentor, guiding the inexperienced salesperson through the first few transactions or first few months.

Mentoring develops a new salesperson's confidence as well as professional abilities. In addition, the mentor gains personal and professional rewards from the association. Generally, the mentor guides the new salesperson by accompanying him or her on listing appointments, helping to write up offers, and suggesting profitable activities.

A mentor and protégé should have a written agreement about the direction of the mentoring. Details such as how often they meet, their goals, the duration of the mentoring relationship, and the compensation agreement should all be in writing. Some brokerage firms pay mentors directly, while in others, experienced salespeople make their own arrangements to mentor new salespeople. Salespeople commonly pay their mentor 40% of their commissions.

Mentors and protégés form strong professional and personal bonds. The challenge of a mentorship is to help a new salesperson become a strong, independent, real estate professional without the salesperson holding on too long to the mentor's knowledge and experience.

Learn About the Product

Without product knowledge, a real estate salesperson will not be able to have a successful career. Product knowledge for licensees specializing in residential real estate sales includes knowing about architectural styles, housing features, and current inventory of homes that are for sale in the community. Product knowledge is learned by previewing as many new listings as possible. If you, as the salesperson, have been inside most of the homes, you will be able to better present the property to potential buyers.

Prospecting

The bottom line for every salesperson is building future business. The process of developing business, through any number of activities, is called **prospecting**. Prospecting encompasses the activities a salesperson performs in order to seek out potential clients. Past customers, open houses, for-sale-by-owners (FSBOs), expired listings, social spheres, local business networks, introductory calls, and your neighborhood or area of specialty, are all good places to connect with prospects.

Obtain Listings

Salespeople and brokers must have properties to sell. Consequently, to obtain listings, they set appointments with prospective sellers to give presentations that will encourage the seller(s) to sign a listing agreement. A **listing agreement** is a bilateral contract between the property owner and the broker to place properties for sale with the broker. When listing a property for sale, brokers and salespeople compare the listed property with similar properties that have been recently sold to determine its competitive market value.

Match Prospective Buyers with Homes

Before showing properties to potential buyers, salespeople try to pre-qualify the buyers. In this pre-qualifying phase, the salesperson will meet with potential buyers to define the type of home in which the buyer is interested. In addition, the salesperson, working with a lender, will determine how much the buyer(s) can afford to spend. Then, the salesperson prepares a list of properties for sale, including locations and descriptions, that are comparable to the buyer's requirements determined in the pre-qualifying phase.

Matching people to homes that meet their requirements is important.

Real estate salespeople may meet many times with prospective buyers to discuss and visit available properties. Salespeople should identify and emphasize the most pertinent selling points. When meeting with a young family looking for a house, they may emphasize the convenient floor plan, the area's low crime rate, and the close proximity to schools and shopping centers. When meeting with a potential investor, they may point out the tax advantages of owning a rental property and the ease of finding a renter. If price negotiations become necessary, salespeople must carefully follow their client's instructions and may present counteroffers to get the best price. A **counteroffer** is the rejection of an original purchase offer and the submission of a new and different offer.

Write Up Purchase Offers

Hopefully, prospective buyers will want to make an offer on one of the properties the salesperson has shown them. If so, the salesperson prepares a **purchase offer** according to the buyer's terms and has the buyer sign it. The signed purchase contract is delivered to the listing broker, along with an earnest money deposit. If the seller signs the purchase offer, a contract is made between the buyer and seller.

Once the buyer and seller have signed the purchase contract, the real estate broker or salesperson must be sure that all special terms of the contract are met so that escrow can close. For example, the salesperson must be sure that mandatory disclosures and agreed-upon inspections take place. If the seller agrees to any repairs, the broker or salesperson must be sure the repairs are made. While loan officers, attorneys, or other people may be involved, the real estate salesperson must ensure that all parts of a real estate transaction are completed.

Handle the Paperwork

When selling real estate, the salesperson begins the transaction by writing an offer on the property chosen by a buyer and then submitting that offer to the seller for approval. If the seller dislikes the offer, he or she can counter the buyer's offer by writing and submitting a counteroffer to the buyer. The process continues until both parties reach an agreement on a final purchase price, or reject the offer altogether.

Close Escrow

Once the buyer and seller agree on price and terms, escrow opens. **Escrow** is the period of time when all parties are held accountable for the terms of the agreement such as disclosures, financing, property inspection, title search, etc. When escrow closes, the new owners receive a deed, the seller receives his or her proceeds, and the real estate brokers receive their commissions.

Attend Meetings

Depending on the brokerage you choose, you will need to schedule time for weekly or monthly meetings. Many brokerages hold weekly sales meetings to discuss such items as sales techniques and important upcoming events, and to acknowledge the accomplishments made by salespeople in the brokerage. It is important to attend these meetings to learn the latest information, provide feedback, and show team spirit.

Follow Economic Trends

It is important to pay attention to swings in the economy because they affect the employment of real estate brokers and salespeople. During periods of declining economic activity and tight credit, the volume of sales, and the resulting demand for salespeople, falls. The earnings of brokers and salespeople decline during these times, and many work fewer hours or leave this field of employment.

WHY GO INTO RESIDENTIAL REAL ESTATE SALES?

Real estate is an attractive and rewarding career. It offers the opportunity to build a secure future for yourself and to help shape the future of your community. A career in real estate also offers real estate salespeople high earning potential, career opportunities, independence, flexible work schedule, and an unlimited inventory.

High Earning Potential

Your **earning potential** as a real estate salesperson is in your own hands, and is not based on a pay scale established by your employer. Have you ever had a job where you worked harder and more diligently than your co-workers did, but they were paid more because they had worked there longer? Well, as a real estate salesperson, your pay is based solely on the results you produce— closed transactions. You are in control of your success and your income is limited only by the amount of energy you use to pursue that success. If you are working harder, smarter, and more diligently, you will make more money and see more results than someone who is not. "Real estate is the best paying hard work and the worst paying easy work." Think about that statement. It is an important principle to understand if you are interested in a career as a real estate salesperson.

Independence

A career in real estate offers independence and freedom to set your own schedule. Real estate salespeople decide how and when they will perform the duties of their job. Performing to your highest potential is an advantage for the individual who does not enjoy sitting at a desk doing the same boring work day after day. For a salesperson in real estate, no two days are exactly alike. You meet different people, make new sales, and discover new beginnings and challenges each day.

Flexible Work Schedule

In the past, many homemakers and retired people were attracted to real estate sales because of the flexible and part-time work schedules that are characteristic of this field. They could enter, leave, and then later re-enter the occupation, depending on the strength of the real estate market, family responsibilities, or personal circumstances. Recently, however, the attractiveness of part-time work has declined as the increasingly complex legal and technological requirements raise the start-up time and costs associated with becoming a salesperson.

Unlimited Inventory

One of the unique things about residential real estate sales is that you have access not only to your own listings, or your firm's listings, but also to all of the listings in the Multiple Listing Service (MLS). In California, you can sell any house in town due to the Multiple Listing Service (MLS). The **Multiple Listing Service (MLS)** is a cooperative listing service conducted by a group of brokers, usually members of a real estate association. Salespeople and brokers submit listings to a central bureau. The listings are then entered into a computerized system available for all MLS members to see. The MLS affords salespeople and brokers the ability to help people find the perfect property rather than selling them on a single property.

HOW DOES REAL ESTATE DIFFER FROM OTHER JOBS?

All of the reasons for starting a career in real estate—potential high earnings, independence, and flexibility—are the differences from the typical 9 to 5 job. A career as a real estate salesperson is rewarding; offering flexibility, freedom, and the opportunity to build a secure future.

High Potential Earnings

Real estate salespeople act as independent contractors. An **independent contractor** is a person who chooses the method to use in completing the work under contract, and is accountable for the results. Instead of salaries, real estate agents earn commissions when transactions close. A **commission** is a fee charged by the broker that is based on a percentage of the property's sales price. The advantage is that you can earn an excellent living if you work hard and work smart. However, a disadvantage of being an independent contractor is that you do not collect a salary and you do not receive your commission until an escrow closes. Commissions on sales are the main source of earnings for real estate salespeople and brokers.

A beginner's earnings are often irregular because weeks or months may pass without a sale. A beginner should have enough money to live on for at least six months, or until commissions begin to flow regularly. Since a commission is based on a certain percentage of the sales price, you can give yourself a raise by selling more properties or selling properties that are more expensive. By doing this, you will have a constant cost-of-living increase since the appreciation of real property usually is greater than inflation.

A beginner in real estate needs to have enough money for at least six months or until commissions begin producing a steady income.

Independence & Flexibility

You are responsible for your career, so being a self-starter is essential. Learning to be a self-starter in real estate is especially important for those who have spent most of their life working in an environment where someone else made the decisions and told them what to do. Since you are your own boss, you must decide how to get results.

The successful salesperson knows not only how to work hard, but how to work smart. **Working smarter** means developing a strategy that will help you complete more tasks in a shorter amount of time. This means planning your day, week, month, and year ahead of time and following that plan to avoid crises, rather than confronting one crisis after another. Working smart, above all else, means setting goals and creating a plan to help you reach those goals.

WHAT IS THE JOB OUTLOOK?

The California housing market is one of the largest in the nation. Every year, California typically gains more new households, but does not build enough new housing units, thus creating a shortfall. This continuing housing shortage will create an ongoing demand for homes.

Employment in this field will come primarily from increased demand for home purchases and rental units. Shifts in the age distribution of the population over the next decade will result in a growing number of retirees and these people will be moving to smaller accommodations, often in quieter, smaller cities, towns, or retirement communities. At the same time, younger families are expected to move out of apartments or smaller houses to larger accommodations. Real estate sales take place in all areas, but employment is concentrated in large urban areas and in smaller, rapidly growing communities.

In 2011, membership in the California Association of REALTORS® (C.A.R.) reached approximately 165,000 members. The **California Association of REALTORS® (C.A.R.)** is one of the largest state trade organizations in the United States. Each year, thousands of real estate agents become new members of C.A.R.

The large number of real estate licensees creates a very competitive industry. If the number of residential transactions is divided by the number of C.A.R. members, the result is nearly three transactions. Since each transaction has two sides (buyer side and seller side), this equates to approximately six **transaction sides** per member. This is the lowest productivity among C.A.R. members since the mid-1990s.

This lowered productivity has made it difficult for the seasoned brokers and salespeople to earn a living, and even more so for the new licensees in the industry. Studies show that due to the competitive nature of the business, by the fifth year, fewer than one-half of new licensees remain in the real estate field. Not everyone is successful in this highly competitive field. Many beginners become discouraged by their inability to get listings and close a sufficient number of sales. Those who are successful attribute their success to strong determination combined with effective training, mentoring, and marketing.

Will the Internet Make Real Estate Licensees Obsolete?

The Internet has been used extensively in real estate transactions for the past few years. Many people in the business say the Internet has complemented, not diminished, the licensee's role in the real estate transaction. Home sellers appreciate the increased visual marketing and instant access to their properties. Both buyers and sellers like the photos, maps, virtual tours, and neighborhood information available online. After researching neighborhoods, properties, financing options, and brokerage offices online, homebuyers choose a real estate licensee to finalize the home-buying process. The Internet speeds up the process because it gives the prospective buyer the information to make a more informed choice. Prospective buyers view the Internet as a tool to help them research the real estate market, not as a replacement for the salesperson's expertise in the field.

Opportunities for Real Estate Assistants

As mentioned previously, you may want to begin your real estate career as a **real estate assistant** to a successful salesperson or broker. This will help you gain the experience and knowledge needed to succeed in your own real estate sales career.

Some people obtain career experience and knowledge in real estate as an assistant to a successful salesperson or broker.

Real estate assistants are able to free up a large portion of the real estate professional's time by handling a major portion of the paperwork. This allows the salesperson to spend more time getting new business that will generate commissions, such as prospecting, following-up on leads, competing for listings, and showing property. An efficient salesperson/assistant team offers more service to clients and customers than one salesperson working alone.

What Makes A Great Assistant?

Ideally, a real estate assistant should have the business skills of an administrative assistant and the attitude of a partner. An assistant tracks the paperwork through escrow, sets appointments to show property, helps prepare for listing presentations, and oversees advertising. Some successful salespeople only hire an assistant who has a real estate license; others will hire a non-licensee and train that person.

How Much Will You Earn?

Most real estate assistants usually receive a fixed salary. In addition, many receive a percentage or an incentive bonus on each closed transaction. This mix of salary and bonus combines the security of a known income with the incentive of additional income based on performance.

Specialized Training

You can get training and improve your skills by attending the National Association of REALTORS® (NAR) two-day, professional assistant course.

The **Real Estate Professional Assistant**^{sm} (REPA^{sm}) is a quick-start two-day certificate course that introduces you to the business side of real estate. The course covers such topics as listing and sales forms, MLS input forms, types of agency, mandatory disclosures, marketing concepts, and professional ethics.

THE INTERVIEW

Remember that choosing a brokerage is a very important step in your real estate career. It is important to take the necessary steps to prepare for your interview. Present yourself well; dress professionally and do not wear heavy cologne or perfume. Be sure to leave early, allowing enough time so that you

can arrive ten to fifteen minutes early. If you are going to an area with which you are not familiar, it is a good idea to double check directions before leaving. Turn off your cell phone before you begin the interview.

When considering a brokerage, both you and the broker must be convinced that your association will be mutually beneficial, long lasting, and compatible with regard to both the broker's and your objectives. You must persuade a prospective broker that you have good organizational and communication skills, and are committed to being successful in the real estate profession. In an interview, remember that the employer is not the only one performing an evaluation. You are also evaluating them to see if you would like to work for that particular company. In this business, brokers need you as much as you need them.

What to Ask During the Interview

Your success as a new real estate salesperson is largely dependent on your skills, background, motivation, and drive. It is helpful to know which questions to ask to help you determine which brokerage to choose. The answers to these questions will help you discover if you and the broker can work together in a mutually beneficial manner.

Typical Questions to Ask During an Interview

- What types of training and/or educational seminars does the brokerage offer? Who pays for the training?

- Is there a mentor program? Are any commissions shared?

- Does the brokerage offer "up-desk time" or "floor time" where phone leads and walk-in customers are handled by the salesperson on duty?

- What commission rates do they offer? Is the commission on a sliding scale, with the percentage increasing as more income is brought into the firm?

- What membership expenses are required with associations that the brokerage requires salespeople to join? (Associations such as Multiple Listing Service, or California Association of REALTORS®.)

- What type of advertising does the brokerage use? (Such as yellow pages, Internet, newspaper and magazine ads, etc.) Who pays for the advertisement of the listings – brokerage or salesperson? Does the brokerage pay for any portion of personal ads? Is there a marketing/advertising coordinator? Read the real estate ads in the weekend newspaper, or check the Internet to evaluate the advertising efforts made by the brokerage.

- Does the brokerage hire a receptionist or coordinators to help with the transactions?

- What are the costs associated with signs, flags, business cards, Internet websites, e-mail addresses, and forms? Will the brokerage assist with these costs?

- Who pays for long-distance telephone calls, stamps, stationery, photocopies, office supplies, and other business expenses? Does the brokerage charge a flat monthly desk fee or a percentage of certain expenses?

- Does the brokerage have computer equipment for all salespeople to use? Is any software pertinent to the real estate profession provided?

- What other start-up costs, ongoing expenses, or new salesperson requirements should be expected?

- Does the firm carry E&O Insurance for its salespeople? How much does it cost?

- How long have the other salespeople been working there and how successful have they been?

CHOOSE THE RIGHT BROKERAGE COMPANY

When considering a career in real estate, it is important for you to choose the right real estate brokerage. A real estate brokerage relies heavily on its reputation. A brokerage with a steady history and positive reputation in the community will be able to offer you the resources to become successful and take your career in a positive direction.

Word-of-mouth is a powerful source in every community, and most consumers have heard which real estate companies to avoid and which to embrace. Prospective clients will have formed an opinion of you based on your company. Consider the appearance of the reception area, receptionist, and other associates. The concept of business attire differs with geographic location and the expectations of the clientele. In any event, being clean and polished is always essential.

Both beginning and experienced real estate professionals have various choices about which type of office environment they prefer, such as a small independent office, a large franchise, or a national real estate company. Most real estate firms are relatively small. Some larger real estate firms have several hundred salespeople operating out of various branch offices, and others have franchise agreements with national or regional real estate organizations.

The receptionist represents the brokerage. A professional appearance and attitude is essential to project the appropriate message to the clientele.

You may find several different types of real estate companies in the area where you will work. After making a list of the real estate offices in your area, narrow the list to only those offices that would best suit your personality and career goals.

The Mode of Operation

A licensed real estate broker creates a brokerage to bring together parties who want to make transactions in real estate. The broker who creates the real estate brokerage firm is the **broker-owner** and sets all policies for the firm. A broker does not have to own a brokerage firm to be in business; they can opt to work for another firm or even work from home. The broker may operate as an independent firm or as a franchise.

Small Independent Firms

Many newly licensed salespeople choose to work in a small independent firm. **Small independent firms** usually have one or two office locations and offer the greatest amount of flexibility for a new associate. A higher commission split is also possible. The office environment may be more personal, with fewer salespeople and fewer time commitments required of the new associate. Training opportunities are determined by the broker's attitude toward teaching and mentoring new associates until they learn the business. In some cases, the broker is the office manager and is available to new associates at any time. In other agencies, the broker lists and sells alongside the other salespeople, which leaves the new associates to learn the business on their own.

Large Independent Firms

Large independent firms do not have an affiliation with national franchises. **Large independent firms** are usually owned by private parties or partnerships, and may have many offices in one area. These companies usually operate like franchised companies and offer management opportunities as well.

One advantage of working for a large independent company is that an associate will have the local name recognition of a well-established firm without having to pay a franchise fee. Salespeople who work for franchised companies will have to pay a share of their commissions for the "use" of the franchise's name. In addition, customers may desire the perceived benefit of a local office rather than that of a national franchise.

Franchises

According to the recent National Association of REALTORS® Member Profile, over half of all REALTORS® are affiliated with a national franchise. A **franchise** is a business organization (franchisor) that enters into a contract with other businesses (franchisees) for a fee in order to operate under the franchisor's name and guidance. Each franchisee is an independent brokerage that is affiliated via the franchise's network to other brokerages. The heart of national franchise loyalty lies with its brand name recognition among consumers. For this increased exposure, the franchisee pays an agreed-upon percentage of their profits to the franchisors. Some of the well-known real estate franchises are Century 21®, Coldwell Banker®, ERA®, GMAC, Help-U-Sell, RE/MAX®, Realty Executives, Realty World America, Inc., and Red Carpet Real Estate.

Generally, a national franchise real estate company offers the greatest opportunity for training. These national franchises want their salespeople to be successful, and they understand that training plays a major role in helping their new associates to succeed. By sponsoring classes, the owner of a franchise ensures that the investment of hiring a new salesperson is in their best interest. Although franchised brokers often receive help in training their salespeople and running their offices, they bear the ultimate responsibility for the success or failure of their firm.

Business activities usually have more structure in a national franchise than in an independent company. Some factors a salesperson should think about when considering a national franchise office are sales meetings, training, the availability of floor time (the time period during which salespeople get new leads or customers from ads or walk-in buyers or sellers) or other regularly scheduled events that may be required. Scheduled mandatory events, while beneficial, do tend to interrupt an associate's planned activities.

National franchises may also offer to pay for certain business expenses such as business cards, flyer printing, signs, and advertising. National franchises have the ability to buy in bulk and therefore pay lower rates, making it easier to supplement their employee's business needs.

The People in the Brokerage

In order to be in business, a residential brokerage must have a licensed real estate broker. The brokerage does not have to employ anyone; however, brokers usually make more money when they have licensed salespeople who help get new listings and market existing listings. As the  number of sales associates increases, most brokers hire sales managers and/or coordinators to help generate new business and complete the transactions.

The Broker & Salesperson Relationship

A licensed broker employs licensed salespeople to conduct real estate business. The broker is the agent of the buyer or seller, whereas a salesperson (also known as sales associate or associate licensee) is employed and is the agent of a broker. As you may recall, an **agent** is someone who represents a principal in negotiating with a **third party**.

Review - Agency Relationships

Agent	Principal	Third Party
(*Broker*)	(*Client*)	(*Customer*)
Listing Agent	Seller	Buyer
Buyer's Agent	Buyer	Seller
Selling Agent	Seller or Buyer	Buyer or Seller

In a broker-salesperson relationship, the licensed salesperson is the agent of his or her employing broker (principal) and must deal fairly with third parties (broker's clients). The real estate salesperson employed by the broker is an agent for the broker. The broker bears the final responsibility for any agency relationships created by a salesperson in the broker's employ.

Example: Dan is a salesperson in the employ of broker Rosa. Dan listed a property owned by Kim. Under the law, the agency relationship is between Kim, the seller and Rosa, the broker. Dan is bound by the agency because, as Rosa's employee, he represents Rosa with every action he makes as a real estate salesperson.

Review - Real Estate Broker

- Person holding a broker license and permitted by law to employ those holding either a salesperson or a broker license
- Agent of the principal - may negotiate for other people
- Acts as an independent contractor for income tax, workers' compensation, and unemployment insurance purposes

Review - Real Estate Salesperson

- Person holding a salesperson license and employed by a real estate broker, for pay, to perform real estate activities
- Agent of the broker—not the buyer or the seller
- Employed by the broker, under real estate license law
- Acts as an independent contractor for income tax purposes

The real estate license law considers a licensed salesperson an employee of a broker for purposes of supervision. An **employee** is someone who is under the control and direction of an employer. For all other purposes, he or she is an **independent contractor**: a person who is hired to do work for another person but who is not an employee of that person. Independent contractors are responsible for the results of their labor, unlike employees who must follow employers' directions in completing the work.

The broker-salesperson relationship is viewed in this manner only by the license law, not by other agencies. A salesperson's status under one law does not establish what that status is under different circumstances, such as federal and state income tax, workers' compensation, unemployment insurance, or other matters not covered by the real estate law. Except for purposes of supervision under the license law, a salesperson is an independent contractor.

Determining Independent Contractor Status

Three basic requirements are used to determine independent contractor status, and must comply with both federal and state laws.

1. The first requirement is that the salesperson must have a valid real estate license. In California, the California Department of Real Estate must issue the license.

2. Next, the salesperson must be compensated based on the number of sales closed and commissions earned, not based on the number of hours worked.

3. Finally, for both federal and California tax purposes, there must be a written contract between the employing broker and the salesperson specifying that the salesperson is an independent contractor. Fortunately, the same contract can cover both federal and California requirements.

A broker can create and use his or her own employment contract; however, be advised that the C.A.R. Broker-Associate Licensee Contract contains the required language. When the employment agreement has the correct language, a real estate salesperson is an independent contractor for income tax purposes; therefore, tax is generally not taken out of the commission check.

Employment Agreement

The real estate law requires that every broker have a written employment agreement with each of his or her salespeople. Although the **employment agreement** does not have to be on a form approved by the Commissioner, it must cover the important aspects of the employment relationship, including supervision of licensed activities, licensee's duties, and the compensation arrangement. Additionally, in order to protect the independent contractor status of the salespeople, the contract must include the required language as discussed in the previous two paragraphs.

CALIFORNIA
ASSOCIATION
OF REALTORS®

INDEPENDENT CONTRACTOR AGREEMENT
(Between Broker and Associate-Licensee)
(C.A.R. Form ICA, Revised 6/11)

This Agreement, dated _____ , is made between _____
_____ ("Broker") and
_____ ("Associate-Licensee").

In consideration of the covenants and representations contained in this Agreement, Broker and Associate-Licensee agree as follows:

1. **BROKER:** Broker represents that Broker is duly licensed as a real estate broker by the State of California, ☐ doing business as _____ (firm name), ☐ a sole proprietorship, ☐ a partnership, or ☐ a corporation. Broker is a member of the _____ Association(s) of REALTORS®, and a subscriber to the _____ Multiple Listing Service(s). Broker shall keep Broker's license current during the term of this Agreement.

2. **ASSOCIATE-LICENSEE:** Associate-Licensee represents that: **(i)** he/she is duly licensed by the State of California as a ☐ real estate broker, ☐ real estate salesperson, and **(ii)** he/she has not used any other names within the past five years, except _____ .
Associate-Licensee shall keep his/her license current during the term of this Agreement, including satisfying all applicable continuing education and provisional license requirements.

3. **INDEPENDENT CONTRACTOR RELATIONSHIP:**
   A. Broker and Associate-Licensee intend that, to the maximum extent permissible by law: **(i)** This Agreement does not constitute an employment agreement by either party; **(ii)** Broker and Associate-Licensee are independent contracting parties with respect to all services rendered under this Agreement; and **(iii)** This Agreement shall not be construed as a partnership.
   B. Broker shall not: **(i)** restrict Associate-Licensee's activities to particular geographical areas, or **(ii)** dictate Associate-Licensee's activities with regard to hours, leads, open houses, opportunity or floor time, production, prospects, sales meetings, schedule, inventory, time off, vacation, or similar activities, except to the extent required by law.
   C. Associate-Licensee shall not be required to accept an assignment by Broker to service any particular current or prospective listing or parties.
   D. Except as required by law: **(i)** Associate-Licensee retains sole and absolute discretion and judgment in the methods, techniques, and procedures to be used in soliciting and obtaining listings, sales, exchanges, leases, rentals, or other transactions, and in carrying out Associate-Licensee's selling and soliciting activities; **(ii)** Associate-Licensee is under the control of Broker as to the results of Associate-Licensee's work only, and not as to the means by which those results are accomplished; **(iii)** Associate-Licensee has no authority to bind Broker by any promise or representation; and **(iv)** Broker shall not be liable for any obligation or liability incurred by Associate-Licensee.
   E. Associate-Licensee's only remuneration shall be the compensation specified in paragraph 8.
   F. Associate-Licensee who only performs as a real estate sales agent, shall not be treated as an employee for state and federal tax purposes. However, an Associate-Licensee who performs loan activity shall be treated as an employee for state and federal tax purposes unless the activity satisfies the legal requirements to establish an independent contractor relationship.
   G. The fact the Broker may carry workers' compensation insurance for Broker's own benefit and for the mutual benefit of Broker and licensees associated with Broker, including Associate-Licensee, shall not create an inference of employment.
   (Workers' Compensation Advisory: Even though a Real Estate sales person may be treated as independent contractors for tax and other purposes, the California Labor and Workforce Development Agency considers them to be employees for workers' compensation purposes. According to that Agency: **(i)** Broker must obtain workers' compensation insurance for a Real Estate sales person and **(ii)** Broker, not a Real Estate sales person, must bear the cost of workers' compensation insurance. Penalties for failure to carry workers' compensation include, among others, the issuance of stop-work orders and fines of up to $1,000 per agent, not to exceed $100,000 per company.)

4. **LICENSED ACTIVITY:**
   A. All listings of property, and all agreements, acts or actions for performance of licensed acts, which are taken or performed in connection with this Agreement, shall be taken and performed in the name of Broker. Associate-Licensee agrees to and does hereby contribute all right and title to such listings to Broker for the benefit and use of Broker, Associate-Licensee, and other licensees associated with Broker.

Broker's Initials (_____) (_____)

ICA REVISED 6/11 (PAGE 1 OF 4)

Associate-Licensee's Initials (_____) (_____)

Reviewed by _____ Date _____

EQUAL HOUSING
OPPORTUNITY

INDEPENDENT CONTRACTOR AGREEMENT (ICA PAGE 1 OF 4)

| Agent: | Phone: | Fax: | Prepared using zipForm® software |
| Broker: | | | |

B. Broker shall make available to Associate-Licensee, equally with other licensees associated with Broker, all current listings in Broker's office, except any listing which Broker may choose to place in the exclusive servicing of Associate-Licensee or one or more other specific licensees associated with Broker.

C. Associate-Licensee shall provide and pay for all professional licenses, supplies, services, and other items required in connection with Associate-Licensee's activities under this Agreement, or any listing or transaction, without reimbursement from Broker except as required by law.

D. Associate-Licensee shall work diligently and with his/her best efforts to: **(i)** sell, exchange, lease, or rent properties listed with Broker or other cooperating Brokers; **(ii)** solicit additional listings, clients, and customers; and **(iii)** otherwise promote the business of serving the public in real estate transactions to the end that Broker and Associate-Licensee may derive the greatest benefit possible, in accordance with law.

E. Associate-Licensee shall not commit any unlawful act under federal, state or local law or regulation while conducting licensed activity. Associate-Licensee shall at all times be familiar, and comply, with all applicable federal, state and local laws, including, but not limited to, anti-discrimination laws and restrictions against the giving or accepting a fee, or other thing of value, for the referral of business to title companies, escrow companies, home inspection companies, pest control companies and other settlement service providers pursuant to the California Business and Professions Code and the Real Estate Settlement Procedures Acts (RESPA).

F. Broker shall make available for Associate-Licensee's use, along with other licensees associated with Broker, the facilities of the real estate office operated by Broker at _____ and the facilities of any other office locations made available by Broker pursuant to this Agreement.

G. PROHIBITED ACTIVITIES: Associate-Licensee agrees not to engage in any of the following Real Estate licensed activities without the express written consent of Broker:
☐ Property Management;
☐ Loan Brokerage
☐ _____ ;
☐ _____

However, if Associate-Licensee has a Real Estate Broker's License, Associate-Licensee may nonetheless engage in the following prohibited activity(ies) only: _____
provided that **(1)** such prohibited activities are not done under the Broker's License, **(2)** no facilities of Broker (including but not limited to phones, fax, computers, and office space) are used for any such prohibited activities, **(3)** Associate-Licensee shall not use any marketing, solicitation or contact information that include Broker's name (including business cards) for such prohibited activities, **(4)** Associate-Licensee informs any actual or intended Principal for whom Associate-Licensee performs or intends to perform such prohibited activities the name of the broker under whose license the prohibited activities are performed, and **(5)** if Associate-Licensee is performing other permitted licensed activity for that Principal under Broker's license, then Associate-Licensee shall inform any actual or intended Principal for whom the prohibited activities are performed that the prohibited activities are not performed under Broker's license.

5. PROPRIETARY INFORMATION AND FILES:

A. All files and documents pertaining to listings, leads and transactions are the property of Broker and shall be delivered to Broker by Associate-Licensee immediately upon request or termination of this Agreement.

B. Associate-Licensee acknowledges that Broker's method of conducting business is a protected trade secret.

C. Associate-Licensee shall not use to his/her own advantage, or the advantage of any other person, business, or entity, except as specifically agreed in writing, either during Associate-Licensee's association with Broker, or thereafter, any information gained for or from the business, or files of Broker.

6. SUPERVISION: Associate-Licensee, within 24 hours (or ☐ _____) after preparing, signing, or receiving same, shall submit to Broker, or Broker's designated licensee: **(i)** all documents which may have a material effect upon the rights and duties of principals in a transaction; **(ii)** any documents or other items connected with a transaction pursuant to this Agreement in the possession of or available to Associate-Licensee; and **(iii)** all documents associated with any real estate transaction in which Associate-Licensee is a principal.

7. TRUST FUNDS: All trust funds shall be handled in compliance with the Business and Professions Code, and other applicable laws.

8. COMPENSATION:

A. TO BROKER: Compensation shall be charged to parties who enter into listing or other agreements for services requiring a real estate license:
☐ as shown in "Exhibit A" attached, which is incorporated as a part of this Agreement by reference, or
☐ as follows: _____
_____

Any deviation which is not approved in writing in advance by Broker, shall be: **(1)** deducted from Associate-Licensee's compensation, if lower than the amount or rate approved above; and, **(2)** subject to Broker approval, if higher than the amount approved above. Any permanent change in commission schedule shall be disseminated by Broker to Associate-Licensee.

Broker's Initials (_____)(_____)

Associate-Licensee's Initials (_____)(_____)

ICA REVISED 6/11 (PAGE 2 OF 4)

| Reviewed by _____ Date _____ |

EQUAL HOUSING
OPPORTUNITY

INDEPENDENT CONTRACTOR AGREEMENT (ICA PAGE 2 OF 4)

B. TO ASSOCIATE-LICENSEE: Associate-Licensee shall receive a share of compensation actually collected by Broker, on listings or other agreements for services requiring a real estate license, which are solicited and obtained by Associate-Licensee, and on transactions of which Associate-Licensee's activities are the procuring cause, as follows:

☐ as shown in "Exhibit B" attached, which is incorporated as a part of this Agreement by reference, or

☐ other: _____

_____

C. PARTNERS, TEAMS, AND AGREEMENTS WITH OTHER ASSOCIATE-LICENSEES IN OFFICE: If Associate-Licensee and one or more other Associate-Licensees affiliated with Broker participate on the same side (either listing or selling) of a transaction, the commission allocated to their combined activities shall be divided by Broker and paid to them according to their written agreement. Broker shall have the right to withhold total compensation if there is a dispute between associate-licensees, or if there is no written agreement, or if no written agreement has been provided to Broker.

D. EXPENSES AND OFFSETS: If Broker elects to advance funds to pay expenses or liabilities of Associate-Licensee, or for an advance payment of, or draw upon, future compensation, Broker may deduct the full amount advanced from compensation payable to Associate-Licensee on any transaction without notice. If Associate-Licensee's compensation is subject to a lien, garnishment or other restriction on payment, Broker shall charge Associate-Licensee a fee for complying with such restriction.

E. PAYMENT: (i) All compensation collected by Broker and due to Associate-Licensee shall be paid to Associate-Licensee, after deduction of expenses and offsets, immediately or as soon thereafter as practicable, except as otherwise provided in this Agreement, or a separate written agreement between Broker and Associate-Licensee. **(ii)** Compensation shall not be paid to Associate-Licensee until both the transaction and file are complete. **(iii)** Broker is under no obligation to pursue collection of compensation from any person or entity responsible for payment. Associate-Licensee does not have the independent right to pursue collection of compensation for activities which require a real estate license which were done in the name of Broker. **(iv)** Expenses which are incurred in the attempt to collect compensation shall be paid by Broker and Associate-Licensee in the same proportion as set forth for the division of compensation (paragraph 8(B)). **(v)** If there is a known or pending claim against Broker or Associate-Licensee on transactions for which Associate-Licensee has not yet been paid, Broker may withhold from compensation due Associate-Licensee on that transaction amounts for which Associate-Licensee could be responsible under paragraph 14, until such claim is resolved. **(vi)** Associate-Licensee shall not be entitled to any advance payment from Broker upon future compensation.

F. UPON OR AFTER TERMINATION: If this Agreement is terminated while Associate-Licensee has listings or pending transactions that require further work normally rendered by Associate-Licensee, Broker shall make arrangements with another associate-licensee to perform the required work, or Broker shall perform the work him/herself. The licensee performing the work shall be reasonably compensated for completing work on those listings or transactions, and such reasonable compensation shall be deducted from Associate-Licensee's share of compensation. Except for such offset, Associate-Licensee shall receive the compensation due as specified above.

9. TERMINATION OF RELATIONSHIP: Broker or Associate-Licensee may terminate their relationship under this Agreement at any time, with or without cause. After termination, Associate-Licensee shall not solicit: **(i)** prospective or existing clients or customers based upon company-generated leads obtained during the time Associate-Licensee was affiliated with Broker; **(ii)** any principal with existing contractual obligations to Broker; or **(iii)** any principal with a contractual transactional obligation for which Broker is entitled to be compensated. Even after termination, this Agreement shall govern all disputes and claims between Broker and Associate-Licensee connected with their relationship under this Agreement, including obligations and liabilities arising from existing and completed listings, transactions, and services.

10. DISPUTE RESOLUTION:
Broker and Associate-Licensee agree to mediate all disputes and claims between them arising from or connected in any way with this Agreement before resorting to court action. If any dispute or claim is not resolved through mediation, or otherwise, instead of resolving the matter in court, Broker and Associate-Licensee may mutually agree to submit the dispute to arbitration at, and pursuant to the rules and bylaws of, the Association of REALTORS® to which both parties belong.

11. AUTOMOBILE: Associate-Licensee shall maintain automobile insurance coverage for liability and property damage in the following amounts $ _____ /$ _____ . Broker shall be named as an additional insured party on Associate-Licensee's policies. A copy of the endorsement showing Broker as an additional insured shall be provided to Broker.

Broker's Initials (_____) (_____)   Associate-Licensee's Initials (_____) (_____)

ICA REVISED 6/11 (PAGE 3 OF 4)

Reviewed by _____ Date _____

EQUAL HOUSING OPPORTUNITY

INDEPENDENT CONTRACTOR AGREEMENT (ICA PAGE 3 OF 4)

12. **PERSONAL ASSISTANTS:** Associate-Licensee may make use of a personal assistant, provided the following requirements are satisfied. Associate-Licensee shall have a written agreement with the personal assistant which establishes the terms and responsibilities of the parties to the employment agreement, including, but not limited to, compensation, supervision and compliance with applicable law. The agreement shall be subject to Broker's review and approval. Unless otherwise agreed, if the personal assistant has a real estate license, that license must be provided to the Broker. Both Associate-Licensee and personal assistant must sign any agreement that Broker has established for such purposes.

13. **OFFICE POLICY MANUAL:** If Broker's office policy manual, now or as modified in the future, conflicts with or differs from the terms of this Agreement, the terms of the office policy manual shall govern the relationship between Broker and Associate-Licensee.

14. **INDEMNITY AND HOLD HARMLESS; NOTICE OF CLAIMS:**
    A. Regarding any action taken or omitted by Associate-Licensee, or others working through, or on behalf of Associate-Licensee in connection with services rendered or to be rendered pursuant to this Agreement or Real Estate licensed activity prohibited by this agreement: (i) Associate-Licensee agrees to indemnify, defend and hold Broker harmless from all claims, disputes, litigation, judgments, awards, costs and attorney's fees, arising therefrom and (ii) Associate-Licensee shall immediately notify Broker if Associate-Licensee is served with or becomes aware of a lawsuit or claim regarding any such action.
    B. Any such claims or costs payable pursuant to this Agreement, are due as follows:
    ☐ Paid in full by Associate-Licensee, who hereby agrees to indemnify and hold harmless Broker for all such sums, or
    ☐ In the same ratio as the compensation split as it existed at the time the compensation was earned by Associate-Licensee ☐ Other: _____
    Payment from Associate-Licensee is due at the time Broker makes such payment and can be offset from any compensation due Associate-Licensee as above. Broker retains the authority to settle claims or disputes, whether or not Associate-Licensee consents to such settlement.

15. **ADDITIONAL PROVISIONS:** _____
_____

16. **DEFINITIONS:** As used in this Agreement, the following terms have the meanings indicated:
    A. "Listing" means an agreement with a property owner or other party to locate a buyer, exchange party, lessee, or other party to a transaction involving real property, a mobile home, or other property or transaction which may be brokered by a real estate licensee, or an agreement with a party to locate or negotiate for any such property or transaction.
    B. "Compensation" means compensation for acts requiring a real estate license, regardless of whether calculated as a percentage of transaction price, flat fee, hourly rate, or in any other manner.
    C. "Transaction" means a sale, exchange, lease, or rental of real property, a business opportunity, or a manufactured home, which may lawfully be brokered by a real estate licensee.

17. **ATTORNEY FEES:** In any action, proceeding, or arbitration between Broker and Associate-Licensee arising from or related to this Agreement, the prevailing Broker or Associate-Licensee shall be entitled to reasonable attorney fees and costs.

18. **ENTIRE AGREEMENT:** All prior agreements between the parties concerning their relationship as Broker and Associate-Licensee are incorporated in this Agreement, which constitutes the entire contract. Its terms are intended by the parties as a final and complete expression of their agreement with respect to its subject matter, and may not be contradicted by evidence of any prior agreement or contemporaneous oral agreement. This Agreement may not be amended, modified, altered, or changed except by a further agreement in writing executed by Broker and Associate-Licensee.

Broker: Associate-Licensee:

_____   _____
(Brokerage firm name)   (Signature)
By
Its ☐ Broker ☐ Office manager (check one)   _____
                                                                 (Print name)
_____
(Print name)   _____
                                                                 (Address)
_____
(Address)   _____
                                                                 (City, State, Zip)
_____
(City, State, Zip)   _____
                                                                 (Telephone)   (Fax)
_____
(Telephone)   (Fax)

THIS FORM HAS BEEN APPROVED BY THE CALIFORNIA ASSOCIATION OF REALTORS® (C.A.R.). NO REPRESENTATION IS MADE AS TO THE LEGAL VALIDITY OR ADEQUACY OF ANY PROVISION IN ANY SPECIFIC TRANSACTION. A REAL ESTATE BROKER IS THE PERSON QUALIFIED TO ADVISE ON REAL ESTATE TRANSACTIONS. IF YOU DESIRE LEGAL OR TAX ADVICE, CONSULT AN APPROPRIATE PROFESSIONAL.

This form is available for use by the entire real estate industry. It is not intended to identify the user as a REALTOR®. REALTOR® is a registered collective membership mark which may be used only by members of the NATIONAL ASSOCIATION OF REALTORS® who subscribe to its Code of Ethics.

Published and Distributed by:
REAL ESTATE BUSINESS SERVICES, INC.
a subsidiary of the California Association of REALTORS®
525 South Virgil Avenue, Los Angeles, California 90020

Reviewed by _____ Date _____

ICA REVISED 6/11 (PAGE 4 OF 4)

INDEPENDENT CONTRACTOR AGREEMENT (ICA PAGE 4 OF 4)

Both parties must sign and date the agreement and if employment is terminated, the broker must keep copies of it for three years after the date of termination. A salesperson may receive compensation from his or her employing broker and may not receive compensation or referral fees from a lender, developer, or seller.

Commissions

Commissions may be divided among several brokers and their salespeople. The broker and salesperson on each side of the transaction share their commission when the transaction closes escrow. Commissions are based on a certain percentage of the property's sale price. The amount is not set by law, and must be decided between the broker and seller.

At the transaction closing, the seller is debited the amount he or she has agreed to pay the listing broker as commission on the sale. The escrow officer divides the amount between the listing broker and the selling broker, according to the commission split agreement between the brokers. Each broker then splits his or her share with the listing salesperson or selling salesperson. The escrow office never pays a commission directly to a salesperson. Salespeople may receive their commissions only from their employing brokers.

Commission Split

Your **commission split** will be a certain percentage of the commission that comes to the brokerage from your sales. The percentage is based on the commission split agreement you have with your broker as written in the employment agreement. The rate of commission varies according to broker and salesperson agreement, the type of property, and its value. Although a salesperson's share varies greatly from firm to firm, a beginning salesperson's split usually is 50% of the total amount received by the broker. That means that the broker gets 50% and you get 50% of the commission on any sale you make. For example, if the agreed-upon commission split is 50% and the commission paid to the brokerage by the seller on one of your sales was $15,000, the broker gets $7,500 and you get $7,500. As a salesperson gains more experience and develops a clientele, it is common to negotiate a higher commission rate.

Example: Calculating Commissions

A home sold for $200,000 with a 6% commission paid by the seller. Best Real Estate Company was the listing broker and Better Realty was the selling broker. Individual salespeople for each company were on a 60-40 split with their brokers.

1. First calculate the total commission paid by the seller.
   $200,000 (selling price) x 6% (rate) = $12,000 (commission)

2. Calculate the amount of each broker's commission. They have a 50/50 split: each broker will get $6,000 ($12,000 ÷ 2).

3. Finally, calculate the amount each salesperson will receive. Each salesperson has a 60/40 split with their broker. The broker will keep 60% of their $6,000 which is $3,600 ($6,000 x .60) and will pay their salesperson 40% of the $6,000 earned by the company. Each salesperson will receive $2,400 ($6,000 x .40) from his or her broker.

Most brokerages that offer a higher commission split upfront do not provide as many services, such as training, to their salespeople. Remember, the more support the brokerage provides to you as a new salesperson, the more opportunities you will have to become a successful salesperson. It is more important, as a new salesperson, to look for support and services from a brokerage rather than higher commission splits.

Commission Disputes

If a commission disagreement occurs between a broker and a salesperson, the Real Estate Commissioner does not have the authority to resolve the dispute. Any commission dispute between brokers or salespeople is a civil matter, and must be resolved in court. A salesperson or broker involved in a commission dispute should contact the Labor Commissioner who will determine whether the salesperson is an independent contractor or an employee. If the salesperson is an independent contractor, the dispute settlement must take place in a court of law or through arbitration.

Income Taxes on Commissions

As a real estate licensee, you receive commissions that have no taxes deducted. Your income will be reported to the IRS on a form called the 1099-misc. form. This 1099 form is used because all of the money you earn is paid on an untaxed basis. You are responsible for filing the proper forms and paying any federal and state income taxes you owe. By January 30th, your brokerage firm will send you a 1099 form showing your total earnings for the prior year. If you have never filed your federal and state income taxes with the 1099 form, it is a good idea to get help from a tax professional or accountant.

CALIFORNIA ASSOCIATION OF REALTORS®

COMMISSION AGREEMENT
(C.A.R. Form CA, Revised 11/12)

1. **COMPENSATION: Notice:** The amount or rate of real estate commissions is not fixed by law. They are set by each broker individually and may be negotiable between the Seller/Buyer/Landlord/Tenant/Optionor/Optionee ("Principal") and Broker.

_____ ("Principal"),
agrees to pay to _____, ("Broker(s)"),
as compensation for services, irrespective of agency relationships, the sum of either ☐ _____ percent of the transaction price, or
☐
_____
Dollars ($_____), for property situated in the City of _____, County of
_____, California, described as _____.
Compensation is payable if Principal accepts an offer on the above described property no later than _____ (date) payable **as follows:**
(i) On recordation of the deed or other evidence of title or, if a lease, on execution of the lease, or if an option, on execution of the option agreement; or **(ii)** If completion of the transaction is prevented by default of Principal, then upon such default; or **(iii)** If completion of the transaction is prevented by a party to the transaction other than Principal, then only if and when Principal collects damages by suit, settlement, or otherwise, and then in an amount equal to the lesser of one-half of the damages recovered, or the above compensation, after first deducting title and escrow expenses and the expenses of collection, if any. Broker may cooperate with other brokers, and divide with other brokers such compensation in any manner acceptable to Broker. Principal hereby irrevocably assigns to Broker the above compensation from Principal's funds and proceeds in escrow.

2. **ATTORNEY FEES:** In any action, proceeding, or arbitration between Principal and Broker(s) arising out of this Agreement, the prevailing party shall be entitled to reasonable attorney fees and costs.

3. **DISPUTE RESOLUTION:**
   A. **MEDIATION:** Principal and Broker agree to mediate any dispute or claim arising between them out of this Agreement, or any resulting transaction, before resorting to arbitration or court action: exclusions from this mediation agreement are specified in paragraph 3C below. Mediation fees, if any, shall be divided equally among the parties involved. If any party commences an action based on a dispute or claim to which this paragraph applies, without first attempting to resolve the matter through mediation, then that party shall not be entitled to recover attorney fees, even if they would otherwise be available to that party in any such action. THIS MEDIATION PROVISION APPLIES WHETHER OR NOT THE ARBITRATION PROVISION IS INITIALED.
   B. **ARBITRATION OF DISPUTES:** Principal and Broker agree that any dispute or claim in law or equity arising between them regarding the obligation to pay compensation under this Agreement, which is not settled through mediation, shall be decided by neutral, binding arbitration. Exclusions from this arbitration agreement are specified in paragraph 3C below. The arbitrator shall be a retired judge or justice, or an attorney with at least five years of residential real estate law experience, unless the parties mutually agree to a different arbitrator, who shall render an award in accordance with substantive California Law. In all other respects, the arbitration shall be conducted in accordance with Part III, Title 9 of the California Code of Civil Procedure. Judgment upon the award of the arbitrator(s) may be entered in any court having jurisdiction. The parties shall have the right to discovery in accordance with Code of Civil Procedure §1283.05.

   "NOTICE: BY INITIALING IN THE SPACE BELOW YOU ARE AGREEING TO HAVE ANY DISPUTE ARISING OUT OF THE MATTERS INCLUDED IN THE 'ARBITRATION OF DISPUTES' PROVISION DECIDED BY NEUTRAL ARBITRATION AS PROVIDED BY CALIFORNIA LAW AND YOU ARE GIVING UP ANY RIGHTS YOU MIGHT POSSESS TO HAVE THE DISPUTE LITIGATED IN A COURT OR JURY TRIAL. BY INITIALING IN THE SPACE BELOW YOU ARE GIVING UP YOUR JUDICIAL RIGHTS TO DISCOVERY AND APPEAL, UNLESS THOSE RIGHTS ARE SPECIFICALLY INCLUDED IN THE 'ARBITRATION OF DISPUTES' PROVISION. IF YOU REFUSE TO SUBMIT TO ARBITRATION AFTER AGREEING TO THIS PROVISION, YOU MAY BE COMPELLED TO ARBITRATE UNDER THE AUTHORITY OF THE CALIFORNIA CODE OF CIVIL PROCEDURE. YOUR AGREEMENT TO THIS ARBITRATION PROVISION IS VOLUNTARY."

   "WE HAVE READ AND UNDERSTAND THE FOREGOING AND AGREE TO SUBMIT DISPUTES ARISING OUT OF THE MATTERS INCLUDED IN THE 'ARBITRATION OF DISPUTES' PROVISION TO NEUTRAL ARBITRATION."

   Principal's Initials _____ / _____   Broker's Initials _____ / _____

   C. ADDITIONAL **MEDIATION AND ARBITRATION** TERMS: The following matters are excluded from Mediation and Arbitration hereunder: **(a)** A judicial or non-judicial foreclosure or other action or proceeding to enforce a deed of trust, mortgage, or installment land sale contract as defined in Civil Code §2985; **(b)** An unlawful detainer action; **(c)** The filing or enforcement of a mechanic's lien; **(d)** Any matter that is within the jurisdiction of a probate, small claims, or bankruptcy court; and **(e)** An action for bodily injury or wrongful death, or for latent or patent defects to which Code of Civil Procedure §337.1 or §337.15 applies. The filing of a court action to enable the recording of a notice of pending action, for order of attachment, receivership, injunction, or other provisional remedies, shall not constitute a violation of the mediation and arbitration provisions.

4. **OTHER TERMS AND CONDITIONS:** _____
Principal has read and acknowledges receipt of a copy of this Agreement.

Principal _____   Principal _____
_____   _____
(Print name)   (Print name)
Address _____   Address _____
_____   _____
Date _____ Phone/Fax/Email _____   Date _____ Phone/Fax/Email _____
Real Estate Broker agrees to the foregoing:
Broker_____   By _____ Date _____
DRE Lic. #_____

Reviewed by _____ Date _____

CA REVISED 4/09 (PAGE 1 OF 1)

Who Pays for Workers' Compensation Insurance

As you have learned, for federal and state income tax purposes, salespeople (salespeople and broker associates) are independent contractors. However, due to their employee status, a broker must provide **workers' compensation insurance** to all salespeople as well as any non-licensee employees of the firm. The Employment Development Department enforces compliance with workers' compensation insurance requirements. Failure to provide workers' compensation coverage for their real estate salespeople could result in fines up to $100,000.

Sales Managers

Sales managers are responsible for hiring and motivating the sales team. They work directly with the broker/owner to create training programs and to develop marketing strategies. An understanding of the real estate brokerage business from prospecting through closing is essential for a sales manager. Sales managers work closely with coordinators (if any) to ensure that transactions close as quickly and smoothly as possible.

Brokerage Coordinators

Salespeople are responsible for coordinating all of the paperwork involved in a transaction. You may be fortunate enough to find a brokerage that employs **coordinators** for several specialized areas to help their salespeople. These specialized areas include advertising, transactions, and prospecting. Coordinators keep the files of each transaction or listing current and active.

The entire team benefits from the efforts of coordinators who become the authority in their specialized subject. Each team member relies on the coordinators to maintain the framework that supports the income-generating activities of the salespeople as they work with buyers and sellers. Coordinators are usually salaried and may receive a small percentage of the team's commission income.

Advertising Coordinator

Advertising is an essential ingredient for the success of any business. The **advertising coordinator** for a team makes sure every listing gets its share of advertising time and creates flyers and brochures for team listings. Advertising coordinators might post new listings on the Internet and MLS or in various print media such as glossy magazines or in newspaper ads. An advertising coordinator must be creative as well as technically skilled and have the ability to promote the goals of the team.

Transaction Coordinator

Many brokerage firms employ a transaction coordinator to whom salespeople give the paperwork for a transaction just after a buyer and seller sign the offer to purchase. The **transaction coordinator** must be organized and manage information effectively. The success of the brokerage, as well as the income of the salesperson, lies in the capable hands of this person. He or she has the qualities and skills that lead each transaction to a successful and timely close.

Not all brokerage firms employ transaction coordinators, but having someone to help with the details of a transaction will provide salespeople more time to pursue new business. A transaction coordinator may be paid a salary by the brokerage, and then paid independently by the salespeople, or be strictly an independent contractor dealing directly with the salespeople. The charge to the salesperson is usually $250 to $500 per transaction, depending on the coordinator.

Listing Coordinator

The **listing coordinator** manages all required paperwork for listings. Duties may include preparing a pre-listing package and competitive market analysis (CMA) for each seller, communicating with sellers regarding the marketing of their property, following-up with salespeople who show the property, arranging office and MLS previews, and completing any task required to take the listing from potential sale to closed transaction.

Listing coordinators may also be asked to put up and remove signs, install lock boxes, and deliver flyers and documents to help balance the jobs of other team members.

Escrow Coordinator

When a seller accepts an offer, the salesperson or the listing coordinator gives the file to the escrow coordinator who guides the transaction through to closing. The **escrow coordinator** manages all earnest money deposits, inspections, disclosures, financing, title, and escrow issues. During the escrow process, anything that needs to be resolved prior to closing is the responsibility of the escrow coordinator. This may include the buyer's approval of the property inspection, pest control inspection, geological report and other disclosures required by law or by agreement of the buyer and seller.

Prospecting Coordinator

Salespeople tend to put off prospecting for new business. The primary responsibility of a **prospecting coordinator** is to be on the telephone seeking new business at least six hours a day, to generate leads and set up appointments for the lead listing salesperson. The task of creating new leads day in and day out can be a challenge for any salesperson and it takes a special attitude to perform this job. The coordinator may organize a wide range of prospecting activities, such as door-knocking campaigns, e-mail communication with prospects, contacting For-Sale-By-Owners (FSBOs), contacting expired listings, arranging holiday giveaways, or open house contacts.

SUMMARY

A **career in real estate** allows licensed real estate salespeople to help consumers realize their dreams. Buyers and sellers rely on the salesperson to provide the knowledge that will guide them through the complex world of real estate sales.

Several advantages of pursuing a career in the real estate profession include high earning potential, independence, and a flexible work schedule.

Beginning a real estate career is different for all individuals depending on their work experience. However, everyone must obtain the licensing and education necessary to enter the field. Achieving success in this highly competitive field is possible for those who are willing to work hard.

A real estate salesperson who specializes in **residential sales** prospect, preview properties, obtain listings, work with buyers, handle paperwork, and attend meetings. Brokers and salespeople often work evenings and weekends, and are always on call to suit the needs of clients.

The **interview process** is an opportunity for the newly licensed salesperson to select a brokerage that meets his or her needs regarding training, commissions, and flexibility.

The purpose of a real estate brokerage is to help people buy and sell real property. A brokerage firm includes a licensed real estate broker who may work alone or with the help of as many as several hundred licensed real estate sales associates. A real estate brokerage is primarily concerned with securing **listings**, finding **buyers**, and closing **transactions**.

Some brokerages have coordinators and mentoring programs. **Coordinators** provide services to their agents in areas such as listing, escrow, prospecting, advertising, and transaction coordination. New salespeople are helped by mentors who guide the inexperienced salesperson through the first few transactions.

UNIT 1 REVIEW

Matching Exercise

Instructions: Write the letter of the matching term on the blank line before its definition. Answers are in Appendix A.

Terms

A. appraiser

B. advertising coordinator

C. broker-owner

D. commission

E. counteroffer

F. escrow coordinator

G. earning potential

H. franchise

I. independent contractor

J. independent firms

K. job outlook

L. listing agreement

M. listing coordinator

N. mentor

O. Multiple Listing Service (MLS)

P. offer to purchase

Q. property management

R. prospecting

S. prospecting coordinator

T. Real Estate Professional Assistant[sm] (REPA)

U. third party

V. transaction sides

W. transaction coordinator

X. working smarter

Definitions

1. _____ A person who guides a trainee through the first few months or transactions as a salesperson

2. _____ The operation and maintenance of rental properties

3. _____ A person who estimates property value

4. _____ The act of seeking out potential clients

5. _____ A contract between the property owner and the broker to place properties for sale with the brokerage

6. _____ The proposal made by a potential buyer to an owner of property to purchase the property under stated terms

7. _____ The rejection of an original purchase and the submission of a new and different offer

8. _____ A cooperative listing service conducted by a group of brokers, usually members of a real estate association

9. _____ A person who chooses the method to use in completing the work under contract, and is accountable for the results

10. _____ The main source of earnings for real estate salespeople and brokers based on a certain percentage of the property's sales price

11. _____ Buyer and seller sides to a transaction

12. _____ A comprehensive two-day certificate course that introduces the real estate business and the specific ways support staff can become valuable assets to their employers

13. _____ A broker who creates a firm and sets all the policies of the firm

14. _____ A national real estate company that generally offers the greatest opportunity for training

15. _____ The customer in an agency relationship

16. _____ A brokerage worker who manages all required paperwork for listings

17. _____ A brokerage worker who guides the transaction through to closing and manages all earnest money deposits, inspections, disclosures, financing, title, and escrow issues

18. _____ A brokerage worker who seeks new business to generate leads and set up appointments for the lead listing salesperson

19. _____ A brokerage worker who makes sure every listing gets its share of ad time as well as making up flyers and brochures for team listings

20. _____ Brokerage worker to whom salespeople give the paperwork for a transaction just after a buyer and seller sign the offer to purchase

▨ Multiple Choice Questions

Instructions: Circle your response and go to Appendix A to read the complete explanation for each question.

1. Why do people go into real estate sales?
    a. High earning potential
    b. Independence
    c. Flexible schedule
    d. All of the above

2. Real estate salespeople are paid when:
    a. they obtain a listing.
    b. one of their transactions closes.
    c. the broker receives the earnest money deposits from the buyer.
    d. the buyer and seller open escrow.

3. The main source of earnings for real estate salespeople and brokers are:
    a. referral fees.
    b. commissions.
    c. desk fees.
    d. salaries.

4. Who determines the amount of commission a broker receives?
    a. The broker and the seller
    b. The broker and the buyer
    c. The Real Estate Commissioner
    d. The National Association of REALTORS®

5. Someone who is under the control and direction of an employer is:
    a. an independent contractor.
    b. a broker.
    c. an employee.
    d. none of the above

6. An activity involving the sale of something through an intermediary who negotiates the transaction for payment is a:
    a. brokerage.
    b. listing.
    c. deposit.
    d. funding.

7. A listing agreement is an employment contract between a seller and a:
   a. prospecting coordinator.
   b. buyer.
   c. broker.
   d. salesperson.

8. Prospecting for listings and selling properties are the main activities of:
   a. sellers.
   b. salespeople.
   c. real estate assistants.
   d. transaction coordinators.

9. Preparing CMAs and arranging office previews might be performed by the:
   a. listing coordinator.
   b. escrow coordinator.
   c. property coordinator.
   d. property manager.

10. The _____ coordinator is responsible for paperwork regarding property inspections while the transaction is in escrow.
    a. listing
    b. escrow
    c. appraisal
    d. disclosure

Prepare for Success

Unit 2

INTRODUCTION

As you enter the real estate profession, you may wonder what it takes to become successful. Just knowing enough to pass the state licensing exam is not enough. Many successful California Association of REALTORS® members attribute their success to determination, good training, and mentoring. Of course, as a new real estate salesperson, success is not possible without the financial reserves to keep you going until you develop a steady commission stream.

The competitive nature of the real estate profession can be the invisible deal breaker for those who are surprised to find that they are not the only optimistic sales associate in their area trying to list or sell a house. New sales associates must be willing to work longer hours. In fact, NAR statistics show that a majority of new members work more than 40 hours per week. Competition is part of the career, and willingness to seek out a challenge is basic to the real estate sales associate. The accomplishment of becoming a successful real estate professional is only achieved by the sales associate who acquires a competitive edge and learns to prevail in a demanding profession.

Learning Objectives

After reading this unit, you should be able to:

- identify the various costs and expenses in starting a real estate sales career.
- identify the start-up equipment needed to begin a real estate sales career.
- describe the personal attributes and factors that help real estate licensees become successful.
- list steps to improve your communication skills.

PREPARE YOUR FINANCES

Many new salespeople leave the real estate business within the first year. Some put their licenses on inactive status, whereas others leave the field completely. Why isn't the success rate higher for new salespeople? The main reason is not being prepared. Frequently new salespeople think selling real estate is easy money and end up turning in their licenses once they find out the difficulty and competitiveness of the profession.

Salespeople who make it in this business have determination, financial staying power, and product knowledge. They know how to manage their time, market themselves, and advertise their services and listings.

What Do You Expect to Earn?

Based on the sales price of homes in California, most new agents expect to earn several thousand dollars in their first year. Although it is not impossible, it is highly unlikely. Since it takes a while to build your business and establish yourself, new salespeople do not earn as much as salespeople with years of experience.

Income usually increases as an agent gains experience. According to the 2012 NAR Member Profile, the nationwide median income for REALTORS® with over 15 years of experience is $50,200. **Median income** is the middle income in a series of incomes ranked from lowest to highest.

As you can see from the following chart, the most recent median income for salespeople nationwide was $27,200. To calculate their pre-tax net income, subtract the $4,520 in annual business expenses. After expenses, the median income for salespeople was $22,680 or $2,268 for each transaction side.

Profile of NAR Members

Year	2009	2010	2011
Number of NAR Members	1,128,895	1,088,919	1,024,669
Number of hours worked per week	40	40	40
Median income (broker & salesperson)	$35,700	$34,100	$34,900
Median salesperson income	$26,600	$24,900	$27,200
Median broker income	$49,100	$48,700	$48,400
Number of transaction sides per year	7	8	10
Residential brokerage	80%	79%	80%
Regularly use email with clients	93%	92%	93%
Have personal websites	60%	62%	66%
Annual business expenses	$5,480	$4,270	$4,520
Percentage of independent contractors	81%	82%	81%
Length of time with a firm	5 years	5 years	6 years

The first few years in real estate sales are financially challenging. However, REALTORS® who have been in the business for a long time have only one regret—they did not start sooner.

Get Your Finances in Order

Sales associates need to have sufficient cash reserves set aside before making even one sale. It can take six months or longer before your real estate career will provide financial support for you and your family. Before starting your sales career, get your finances in order. Write a monthly household budget for your household expenses. Be as conservative as possible. It is vital to your success that you have savings or other resources to maintain your household expenses while your real estate business is growing. Any strain on your personal budget will put the financial success of your new career at risk.

You will also need money to purchase the necessary equipment and supplies to start your new real estate career. Essentially, as a real estate salesperson, you are starting your own business. It is important to be aware of the expenses involved in starting and maintaining a real estate business. Starting a business is costly, especially when it comes to equipment, supplies, marketing, and advertising. Owners do not make any money until a transaction is complete.

Until your income is steady, anticipate business expenses to be a frequent drain on your financial resources. The first year is critical for new salespeople, and because of these unanticipated expenses, many do not make it to the second year.

To determine how much money you will need, identify all of the business costs and expenses you can expect to incur as a real estate salesperson. Decide which are essential or optional; then estimate what it will cost each month for the first several months. Some of these expenses will be one-time costs (start-up costs) such as computer equipment. Others are ongoing expenses that recur every month like your cell phone bill, car maintenance, postage, printing, advertising, and insurance premiums.

A realistic start-up **budget** should only include those things that are necessary to get started. When business picks up, you can always add the optional items on your list. Expect to incur the following expenses when starting your career in real estate:

List of Items Needed to Start a Career in Real Estate

Start-Up Costs

- Basic equipment (cell phone, computer, fax, GPS)
- Lockbox key
- Business cards
- Letterhead & envelopes
- Preprinted forms
- Business supplies (maps, pens, paper, etc.)
- Open house supplies
- Marketing materials
- Presentation materials
- Signs and sign riders

Ongoing Expenses

- Cell phone bill
- Car maintenance
- Internet and email account
- Printing costs
- Advertising
- Automobile insurance
- Photos
- Postage
- Association dues & MLS fees
- Coordinator fees
- E&O & liability insurance
- Continuing education
- License renewal

Get Your License and Join the Board

Your first expense after passing the state exam will be to pay for your salesperson license, which you must have before you can work in a brokerage.

Next, you will probably pay the fees to join the local Association of REALTORS®. This includes membership in the California Association of REALTORS® (C.A.R.) and the National Association of REALTORS® (NAR). As a member, you will be able to access the free ZipForm® software or go to the local board office and purchase the standard printed forms and other supplies you may need. ZipForm® is a free software program that allows members to download, complete, and print transaction forms from their computers.

Membership in the local association also includes access to the Multiple Listing Service (MLS). In order to show properties listed in the MLS you will need a lockbox key. The **lockbox** is a box that holds the key to a listed property and is hung on or near the front door of the property. Only licensees who are members of the local real estate boards have the key or combination to open the lockbox and get the property key.

Lockboxes are either mechanical or electronic. Electronic lockboxes use a special "electronic key" to open them. The **electronic lockbox key** looks like a small remote and can be updated by placing it in the special HotSync cradle. There is a charge for the key, and depending on the board it is paid monthly, quarterly, or annually. Since each broker and salesperson is issued an individual "key" code, electronic lockboxes record who has opened them, the date and time opened, and the office and phone number. In addition, listing agents have an audit trail so if anything is missing or damaged they will know who has entered the home.

Get the Necessary Equipment

Investing in technology is crucial to remain competitive in today's real estate profession. Consumers today require better service and more value from real estate professionals than in the past. In addition to traditional skills, a competitive associate must use technology effectively. While friendliness, style, and a quick wit are assets, in order to compete in the real estate market today, a professional must use the computer and communication devices currently available.

Technology provides countless benefits and conveniences to real estate salespeople; however, the vast number of products available that promise to make our lives easier can be overwhelming. How do you figure out which products will be of most use to you? Before investing in the latest "gadgets", do a little research and consider your needs. Find out what brands are available and which have the best reviews based upon consumer use. The following sections provide information on the latest products used by real estate professionals today.

Smartphones

Communication is the "lifeblood" of real estate sales, and the "smart" cell phone is your primary point of contact. In fact, smartphones are almost pocket computers. It is nearly impossible to imagine a real estate agent without a cell phone.

The latest smartphones have multiple features which you may want to consider when selecting your phone:

- **Bluetooth Technology** – Since your car is your second office, a phone with Bluetooth connectivity and a Bluetooth enabled headset allows you to drive and speak simultaneously.
- **Email** – An email feature will help you stay connected to your office and clients. Most smartphones have a keyboard or use touch screen technology to send text messages or emails.
- **Internet Access** – Access to the Internet is great for quick searches or accessing your company's website.
- **Apps** – Apps are small, downloadable programs developed primarily for smartphones. There are hundreds of useful apps designed for real estate professionals to help increase productivity.
- **Camera** – A camera is a practical option on your smartphone. Quickly snap a photo and email it to a client.
- **GPS** – If you do not have a Global Positioning System (GPS) navigation system, consider a phone with this feature.

Computer System

Real estate salespeople need a computer system with the appropriate software and Internet access to succeed. Real estate sales associates are able to stay in contact with clients, access current MLS data, download zipForm®, and create presentations. Your brokerage may or may not provide a computer and its essential components for sales associates to use.

If you do not already have a computer, consider a notebook computer because its small, thin design allows for increased portability. Consider a WiFi (wireless fidelity) model, in order to access the Internet wirelessly while on the road. Many airports, hotels, restaurants, and other businesses offer public access, called **hotspots**, to WiFi networks so people can log onto the Internet.

Real estate sales associates are able to work from an office, automobile, hotel room, or a seller's home. A laptop computer is versatile and convenient for real estate professionals.

Contact Management Software

Today, contact management is essential for effective listing, selling, and marketing. **Contact management software** is a database program that allows you to manage and track all your client information and activities, including names, phone numbers, addresses, websites, email addresses, last meeting dates, and more.

You can choose from generic off-the-shelf programs, real estate productivity programs, or a hybrid that adds real estate features to an existing generic program.

Generic Programs

Several generic programs such as Microsoft® Outlook, Act!®, GoldMine®, and AnyTime™ Organizer are available from retail stores. These all give you the latest features in contact management, but you will need to spend some time adapting them to the real estate business.

Real Estate Productivity Software

Contact management software that is specifically designed for real estate has predefined fields relevant to real estate listing and sales activities. The built-in real estate letters, emails, flyers, and brochures make marketing tasks easy. Some of the well-known real estate productivity programs used by real estate professionals include Top Producer®, RealFuture™ Solutions, AgentOffice™, and Maximizer™.

Hybrid Software Solutions

The third option is software add-ons such as Trans/ACT! for Residential Real Estate and ACTiveAgent. These allow you to customize programs such as ACT!® or Microsoft® Outlook for real estate special needs. Both ACTive Agent and Trans/ACT! for Residential Real Estate are used with ACT!® software. Real Estate Management System is a software add-on used with Microsoft® Outlook.

Be Internet Savvy

To be competitive in this market, you must be competent in using the Internet. Most buyers and sellers use the Internet to search for property. Once the Internet homebuyer has researched the neighborhood and price range of homes, he or she is ready to look at the actual homes. In fact, many homebuyers found a sales associate to represent them on the Internet. The average Internet homebuyer looks at six houses and takes only two weeks to purchase, compared to traditional real estate buyers who look at multiple houses and take weeks to purchase.

Most prospective sellers and Internet homebuyers will not even consider hiring you if you do not have Internet access. Therefore, if you do not already have regular access to the Internet and your brokerage does not provide an account for its sales associates, you will need to pay for an account. You will need Internet access so you can have an email address and maybe even your own website.

Websites

Websites are essential for businesses to stay competitive with other companies. A **website** is the place (address) an individual or company has on the World Wide Web. Your brokerage company will have a website, but you may want to have your own personal website as well. With your own website, you will announce that you are a consumer-oriented, technologically informed sales associate. In addition, you can make marketing your name a top priority by choosing the domain name to be your own name. Then your email address will be even more personalized.

> Example: Susan Sails, who works for one of the large, national franchises, wants to market herself and create a stronger image in the community. She decides to create her own website using www.SuzySellsRealEstate.com as the domain name. To personalize her image further, her email address could be susansails@SuzySellsRealEstate.com. Since she owns the domain name, regardless of which brokerage company she works for, her name, telephone number, and email address follow her wherever she goes.

A well-designed website focuses on the needs of its readers. It should provide all the data a consumer might seek such as information about financing, home inspectors, community and school statistics, moving information, a local map, and property profiles. Site visitors will quickly learn that you are an informed real estate professional who will provide the products and services they desire.

A mailed marketing piece should direct prospects to your website. While there, they can select their preferred method of communication and let you know if they are interested in buying, selling, or refinancing. You could list addresses and telephone numbers of local services such as dry cleaners, veterinarians, athletic clubs, and pre-schools. The information you provide on your website is dependent on the demographics of your target audience.

Your website should also include your qualifications and contact information. It should reflect your professional image: a photo, your resume, a logo, and the services you will provide. In addition, customer testimonials are a good way for prospects to learn more about you and the level of service you will provide. All the information you provide should allow a visitor to navigate your website easily. Studies show that Internet real estate leads are an excellent source of real estate leads overall, second only to "For Sale" signs.

Presentation Hardware

Be sure your computer system has a DVD (digital videodisc) drive. With this feature, you will be able to create presentations with video, graphics, and photographs for websites or simply for potential clients. Software such as Microsoft® PowerPoint will allow you to display graphics, charts, and tables in these presentations.

Mobile Printer

With a mobile printer, you can be the true road warrior and have the convenience of printing right from your laptop. Mobile printers are convenient for printing contracts, CMAs, and even color photos.

Digital Cameras

Digital cameras are affordable, user-friendly, and compact. A digital camera provides numerous avenues for increasing your productivity, such as emailing photos to clients, or adding photos to your website and brochures. A competitive sales associate will use photos to win over reluctant prospects, whether buyers or sellers, by showing instead of telling them what they want to know. Remember, "A picture is worth a thousand words."

Global Positioning System (GPS)

A **global positioning system (GPS)** is a device that uses satellite technology to track your location and map out driving directions to a desired destination. GPS and/or navigation systems are nice options for people who spend much of their professional lives on the road. Options range from handheld to built-in models in your automobile's dashboard. Many models available are voice activated which allow you to keep your eyes on the road.

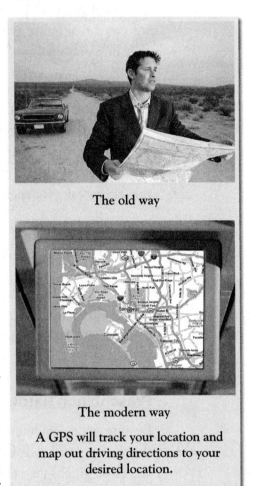

The old way

The modern way

A GPS will track your location and map out driving directions to your desired location.

Risk Management

In order to minimize risk and help protect themselves in the event of a lawsuit, real estate sales associates must carefully document every event in a transaction. For example, be sure to have the seller sign a waiver if the seller declines the purchase of a home warranty on behalf of the buyer. If a termite inspection is required, make sure to give the seller a list of good companies. Do not recommend a specific company. This avoids being at fault if the seller feels injured by the report. If a seller and buyer agree to skip a termite inspection, refuse to complete recommended repairs or seek pest control, the sales associate should have both parties sign a disclaimer stating it was their decision to decline having the work done.

Automobile Insurance

As a real estate salesperson, part of your time will be spent driving clients around to show them properties. Your personal auto policy should be sufficient; however, you may want to increase your liability coverage. If you cause an accident, the injured parties can go after your personal and business assets. Higher liability limits are recommended in order to minimize risk.

Errors and Omissions Insurance

Claims against real estate brokerage firms have been on the rise for at least the last 15 years. Some claimants consider the "deep pockets" of large real estate companies to be the obvious choice for a lawsuit. As part of ongoing risk management, brokerage firms purchase errors and omissions insurance. **Errors and omissions insurance** (E&O) is a policy that covers various claims for errors, mistakes, neglect, or carelessness in the normal business activities of a real estate brokerage.

Each brokerage has different requirements for errors and omissions insurance. Some companies charge sales associates by the transaction, taking a certain percentage out of each commission check at the close of escrow. Others require sales associates to pay the insurance premiums as an annual payment or as monthly installments. The amount companies charge associates may vary due to the amount of the deductible. Sales associates who only do a few transactions a year prefer the per-transaction method, while busier sales associates like the annual fee. Either way, as a licensee, you will be required to purchase E&O insurance to protect yourself against possible lawsuits.

Many times, an easily solved problem becomes an enormous crisis and the only solution seems to be a lawsuit. The reason could stem from a variety of issues such as poor brokerage management, a poorly trained sales associate, or lack of disclosure.

PUT YOUR BEST FOOT FORWARD

The first impression you make is very important to the success or failure of your real estate career. How prospective clients perceive you could mean the difference between making a sale and needing a new line of work. Real estate knowledge and customer service may be what matters most when concluding a successful sale, but an excellent first impression, professional appearance, and positive attitude are initially what gets you through the door.

Professional Appearance

It is important to be aware of your personal appearance. You only have one chance to make a good first impression. The way you dress and present yourself is a powerful business tool. If you were interested in buying or selling property, would you prefer a salesperson wearing freshly pressed, clean clothes or someone wearing old jeans, running shoes, and a wrinkled T-shirt? Usually, the salesperson wearing the clean, freshly pressed clothing and clean shoes appears more professional and makes the best impression.

Dress for Success

The image you present helps you build rapport with prospective clients. When connecting with a client, if you remind them of someone they like or mirror their own taste, they are more likely to respond to you positively.

These styles of dressing are not recommended if you want a successful career.

When considering how to dress, the best strategy is to mirror the style of your clients. If you are selling million dollar homes to older buyers, dress conservatively in a suit. If you were selling starter homes to new families, a suit might be "overdressing", and perhaps intimidating. What is most appropriate to wear depends on the age and income of your clients and whether they are urban, suburban, or rural.

Employees who dress appropriately leave a lasting impression of professionalism.

Wardrobe Tips

When choosing an outfit, avoid anything that is too flashy or provocative. Some salespeople strive for the "business casual" look. This can be a bit confusing because everyone defines it differently. In general, business casual for men means a jacket or a sports coat without a tie. For women, it means sweater sets with pants or skirts. It does not mean a sweat suit, denim jeans, and running shoes.

Buy a wardrobe that is flexible and easy to take care of so you will not have to spend time and money on wardrobe upkeep. Buy good quality fabrics that will last. Linen, silk, and some synthetics can look tired in a hurry. Be sure jackets have pockets to hold keys and business cards. Choose friendly, approachable colors—browns, blues, burgundies, and olives. If you wear black, try mixing it with a softer color.

Keep accessories and jewelry simple and useful. Avoid wearing strong colognes or perfumes because certain scents may trigger allergies.

Your Vehicle

A clean and tidy environment, whether it is your office, home, or car shows that you are organized and that you care about yourself as well as others. In addition to your personal appearance, your vehicle is another important part of your image as a real estate professional.

You will be responsible for driving clients to locations to show them properties. Keep your vehicle neat, clean, and free from unpleasant odors caused by food, cigarettes, pets, and strong perfumes or colognes. Files, signs, and all personal items should be kept in the trunk. Remember to have your vehicle washed and serviced regularly.

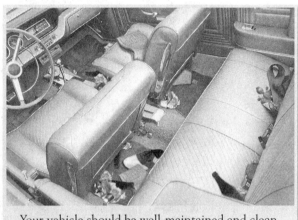

Your vehicle should be well-maintained and clean. It should not look like this.

Professional Attitude

Professional appearance often refers only to the physical, but the mental picture you project to prospective clients is equally important. Your attitude has an effect on your overall image. When you have a good attitude and are confident, you appear trustworthy and reliable. As a real estate salesperson, it is especially important to be trustworthy because people will feel more comfortable working with and depending on you.

You must always project a positive, professional attitude regardless of the circumstances. Everyone has good and bad days; however, real estate sales associates have to smile every day, no matter what is going on in their personal lives. The moment you allow your personal feelings to influence how you interact with clients, your undisciplined behavior will suggest an unprofessional sales associate. No one wants to hear about your personal problems. Even if sales are down, you must remember not to let it affect you. The trick is how you choose to perceive the person or event. If you can make the shift in your thinking from "problem" to "opportunity", you will actually enhance your creativity and your ability to solve problems.

> Example: It would be easy to feel negative if you had just spent the last three days showing buyers 12 homes—none of which they liked. But instead of saying, "I am never going to find a home for these people; this is hopeless," you can turn your problem into an opportunity by saying, "Based on the responses to the homes they have looked at so far, I have a much better understanding of what these buyers want. Tomorrow, I will do my best to show them homes they are sure to like."

If at that moment you do not feel self-confident, fake it until you feel it. Even if you do not feel it at that moment just smile, put out your hand and give a firm handshake, put your shoulders back, and have some energy in your step. If you do this, you will find that the customer will often start responding to you positively, and your self-confidence will be boosted.

As a real estate professional, set definite boundaries between your professional and personal life. The sales associate who is secure in his or her professionalism knows how to lead communication with clients toward the sale without becoming overly personal or too chummy. This does not mean the sales associate should avoid a personal connection with their clients; a personal connection with buyers and sellers is desirable. A good sense of humor, a smile on your face, and a conscious effort to keep conversation positive and directed toward the common goal of finding a property will benefit you and your clients.

PERFECT YOUR COMMUNICATION SKILLS

Communication, the effective exchange of information, is a basic component for any real estate transaction. Your **communication skills** affect how you connect with the people who rely on you. If you are not connecting, then you are not communicating. It takes practice to know when to say the right thing or to understand someone who has a hard time explaining things well.

Your job as a sales associate is to answer questions and explain the complexities of real estate transactions. Sales associates need to be problem solvers because the nature of real estate transactions creates many opportunities for miscommunication.

In the process of communicating, it is important to know when to stop talking. Every experienced sales associate knows when to be quiet and when to let the client speak. The skilled communicator is sensitive to whether he or she is connecting with the listener and if they are building the desired relationship.

Listening Skills

Listening skills are active listening techniques used to improve your ability to understand and comprehend verbal information. These skills will help you communicate ideas and knowledge more effectively. Skills such as these are gained from experience in closing a sale, knowing the timing and techniques to help a buyer come to a decision about a property, showing just the right amount of warmth and friendliness to convey caring, and having a desire to help buyers and sellers achieve their goals.

A good sales associate tries to hear what is being said, even if the buyer does not communicate well. That is what listening is all about. A sales associate's job includes:

- listening to people's dreams.
- determining how those dreams define the kind of house that will provide the desired lifestyle.
- finding a way to make those dreams come true.

It is safe to assume that most successful sales associates are the ones who do the least amount of talking. How will you know what the buyer wants if you do not listen and hear what they are saying? When you give them the freedom to speak and you actively listen to them, you will earn their respect as well as a commission check when the sale is made.

Listening is a skill that you can learn by asking questions and listening to the answers you are given. To assess your listening skills, take the following listening quiz. If you are able to answer the majority of the statements with a "yes", you are on your way to being a great listener.

Listening Quiz

- Do you make eye contact with the speaker?
- Do you use physical or verbal cues to show that you are listening?
- Do you ask clarification questions?
- Do you give the speaker your undivided attention?
- Do you avoid interrupting or contradicting?
- Can you tolerate brief moments of silence?
- Can you restate what people say to you?

Tips to improve your listening skills:

- Maintain a relaxed, unhurried mood and concentrate on what the speaker is saying.
- Watch the speaker's face for clues that may show approval, excitement, boredom, a need for security, or some other need that may help you understand what the buyer wants.
- Do not let your personal prejudice influence what you hear.
- Try to focus on the buyer's most important issues.
- Keep a written record of what a buyer wants and does not want.
- Summarize what you think you hear and repeat it back to the buyer.
- Never interrupt if a story is being told or a question answered.

Ability to Work with a Variety of People

A good personality attracts people; however, attracting people is not enough. A real estate sales associate must be able to work with them. All types of people want to buy real estate, and you must be able to deal appropriately with them if you plan to have referral business. Make the effort to see the potential in every individual and you will be on the right track to achieve your goals for success.

Respect Other Cultures

Respecting other cultures is an important part of dealing with and understanding people. America has become increasingly diverse, and having a knowledge and interest in other cultures is important. It demonstrates respect and consideration for the diverse clientele you may serve and lets your clients know that you are a professional who is sensitive to cultural differences.

Respect Other Lifestyles

You may not have the same lifestyle as your clients and co-workers; however, you need to treat them with respect. For example, you may not have children, but many of your clients may. The attention you give to their children can go a long way to show the parents you care for them and their needs. Try to pay special attention to the needs of your clients. For example, if you have children visiting your office, have books or toys on hand and offer them to the children or parents.

Clients represent different cultures and lifestyles. It's important to pay attention to their needs.

Dealing with Difficult Clients

Put on a smile and accept the challenge of helping people who may be unpleasant or difficult. The first step in dealing with difficult clients is to listen to them. Do not make any statements before they have said what they need to say, even though it may take some time. Try to be empathetic toward their situation.

Dealing with Difficult Clients

- Listen carefully to the client's criticism.
- Calmly ask questions to find out more information and to determine the main issue bothering the client.
- Do not interrupt the client. If the client becomes abusive, politely ask them to tone down their language.

- Become sympathetic. Try to see things from the client's point of view, no matter how unreasonable or irrational he or she may seem.

- Avoid arguing with the client. Acknowledge differing viewpoints if necessary. Remember, the goal is to come to an understanding, not to win an argument.

- Remain encouraging. People often become hostile when frustrated or confused.

- Stay calm. If you cannot remain calm, end the call or meeting until you can respond calmly.

Dealing with difficult or hostile people can be a challenge. Listen to them, and calmly determine what is bothering them.

SUMMARY

Financial reserves, a **professional appearance**, and good **communication skills** are all extremely important factors to take into consideration before entering the real estate profession. Success in this profession requires hard work. The successful sales associate must be prepared to work 40 or more hours per week.

It is prudent to have at least six months to a year of savings set aside as a new salesperson for **living expenses**, **start-up costs**, and **ongoing business expenses**. Investing in the necessary equipment is crucial if you are to remain competitive in today's real estate profession. Sales associates depend on smartphones, computers, digital cameras, and navigation systems.

The salesperson's **personal appearance** and **attitude** must be professional. Although different geographic areas enjoy varied styles and dress codes, being clean and polished is always essential.

Communication is a basic component of any real estate transaction. Some real estate sales associates who have a good personality may fall short on communication skills. Your job is to answer questions, explain the complicated world of real estate, and make communication possible between buyers and sellers. As a good communicator and problem solver, a real estate salesperson must be able to work with all types of people.

UNIT 2 REVIEW

◻ Matching Exercise

Instructions: Write the letter of the matching term on the blank line before its definition. Answers are in Appendix A.

Terms

A. business casual

B. communication

C. contact management software

D. electronic lockbox key

E. errors and omissions

F. global positioning system

G. hotspots

H. lockbox

I. median income

J. ongoing expenses

K. presentation hardware

L. start-up costs

M. website

N. WiFi

O. ZipForm®

Definitions

1. _____ The middle income in a series of incomes ranked from lowest to highest

2. _____ A software program available to C.A.R.® members that allows transaction forms to be downloaded and completed

3. _____ The box that holds the key to a listed property and is hung on or near the front door of the property

4. _____ The electronic device that looks like a small remote used to open a lockbox

5. _____ Database program that manages and tracks your client information and activities

6. _____ Businesses that offer public access to wireless Internet networks

7. _____ The place (address) an individual or company has on the Word Wide Web

8. _____ A type of insurance that covers various claims for errors, mistakes, neglect, or carelessness in the normal business activities of a real estate brokerage

9. _____ Attire that is a jacket or a sports coat without a tie for men and sweater sets with pants or skirts for women. It does not mean a sweat suit, denim jeans, and running shoes

10. _____ A basic component for any real estate transaction, which affects how a sales associate connects with other people

◻ Multiple Choice Questions

Instructions: Circle your response and go to Appendix A to read the complete explanation for each question.

1. What are important factors to take into consideration before entering the real estate profession?
    a. Financial reserves
    b. Professional attitude
    c. Good communication skills
    d. All of the above

2. A salesperson should have _____ months of cash reserves to allow enough time and money to build a substantial client base.
    a. 6 to 12
    b. 4 to 6
    c. 3 or 4
    d. 1 to 3

3. Expenses that recur every month like your cell phone bill and car maintenance are called:
    a. start-up costs.
    b. ongoing expenses.
    c. tax write-offs.
    d. unanticipated expenses.

4. One of the first things you will have to buy before you can start your career is:
    a. business cards.
    b. a smartphone.
    c. a WiFi-enabled computer system.
    d. your real estate license.

5. Which device is probably the least used by real estate professionals today?
    a. WiFi laptop
    b. Cell phone or smartphone
    c. Typewriter
    d. GPS

6. A well-designed website should focus on:
    a. flashy graphics.
    b. catchy theme music.
    c. the needs of its readers.
    d. leaving out commonly asked questions.

7. Real estate professionals can minimize risk by:
    a. denying the incident.
    b. documenting every event in a transaction.
    c. blaming the incident on another sales associate.
    d. obtaining a highly-paid attorney.

8. Why is a professional appearance important?
    a. It shows you respect yourself and your clients.
    b. You represent yourself and your firm with the way you dress.
    c. You only have one chance to make a good first impression.
    d. All of the above statements are true.

9. What is one way that can help improve your listening skills?
    a. Pay attention to other tasks while speaking with a client.
    b. Speak to the client in a noisy environment.
    c. Focus on the buyer's most important issues.
    d. Allow your personal prejudice to influence what you hear.

10. John, a sales associate, is on the phone with an angry client who is obviously frustrated. In this case, John should:
    a. lash back at the client.
    b. listen carefully to the client's criticism.
    c. hang up the phone and let the client cool off.
    d. transfer the call to the next available agent.

Goal Setting & Productivity

Unit 3

INTRODUCTION

You are probably wondering how salespeople find the time to get everything done. When will you prepare all of your marketing materials and find time to hold an open house? Is it possible to prospect, show property, and preview listings all in one day? You can successfully do all this and more and manage your time by using your time productively.

Productivity management incorporates creating a business plan, using a personal marketing plan, and following a time management plan to help you be productive and quickly reach your goals. By making and following a plan, you will know what activities must be done to get the desired results. A productivity management plan involves goal setting, prioritizing, and most importantly, the actual practice of managing time. The plan should be specific and include long-term and short-term goals, marketing strategies, and detailed daily, weekly, and monthly activities that lead to meeting yearly goals.

As your career progresses, your productivity management plan will need to be adjusted. It will change depending on the insights you gain from your experiences. It is important to monitor and modify the activities in your productivity management plan. After you have been in business for a year, ask yourself, "Where did my business come from, what worked, and what did not?" If 80% of your business comes from an activity that takes 20% of your time, then increasing the time spent on that activity could increase your business. Working smart by spending your time wisely will help you reach your goals more quickly.

Learning Objectives

After reading this unit, you should be able to:

- identify the components of productivity management.
- differentiate between long-term and short-term goals.
- recognize marketing activities included in an income funnel.
- recall time management guidelines.

BUSINESS PLAN

Very few new salespeople take the time to put together a quality business plan. Your broker or sales manager should help you to create a business plan. A business plan should be written to answer the following questions.

- "How much do I want to earn in gross commission?" This figure includes not only the income you want but also the taxes and expense income that must be generated in order to achieve the bottom line.
- "Where will my business come from?"
- "What is the target market?"
- "What will be my average sales price and the average commission generated?" You need to know how many transactions must close to reach your financial goal.
- "What are the average expenses associated with each transaction?"
- "How many hours per day am I going to work?"
- "How many days am I going to work this year?"
- "When is vacation time scheduled and how do I manage my workweek?"
- "What education and training will I need to take my business to the next level?" You should work as hard on yourself as you work on your business, and time has to be scheduled in order for it to happen.

A business plan is not a static document. It is dynamic and changes while at the same time providing a road map of the business' direction. You must review and renew the plan on a regular basis or it loses any impact it might have had on business productivity.

Setting Priorities

The key to setting priorities begins with deciding what is most important in life and then organizing the time and activities needed to achieve those objectives. Many new sales associates think that if they work hard enough to get enough money, everything else will fall into place. Unfortunately, with that mindset, they will never have enough money, and if they are not careful, they will work too hard trying to get there.

Successful real estate sales associates know how to balance personal and real estate activities. Real estate could become your whole life, leaving you with little time for anything else. This extreme focus is shortsighted because you cannot keep up a frenzied pace indefinitely and may burn out. If you burn out, you will have no revenue.

Balance is important. Make sure that financial goals are not your only objectives; overall balance and harmony for all "pieces of the pie" in life contribute to your success. Remember to include the activities you enjoy and create a balance between your personal and professional lives. Look at life as a pie, divided into sections by subject. By doing so, you may be able to better visualize and commit to balance and harmony. Make a list of categories for each piece in the pie and decide what you need to do to give equal time to each of your commitments.

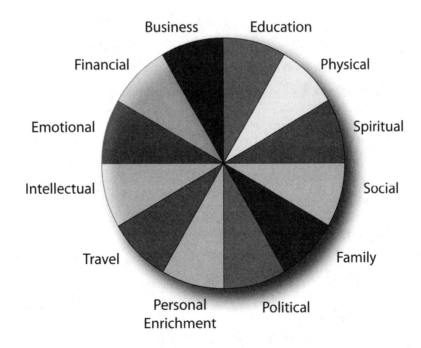

Long-Term Goals

The Importance of Goals

Goals are the driving force behind productivity. A **goal** is the measurable accomplishment that an individual strives to achieve in order to produce a desired outcome. Goals should be SMART (specific, measurable, attainable, relevant, and timely). Individuals differ in what goals they want to achieve and how they will accomplish them. Their goals are not necessarily your goals. Therefore, it is important to become aware of what you want and how you intend to get it.

Long-Term and Short-Term Goals

Typically, goals are either long term or short term. **Long-term goals** refer to the major areas of life, such as career, family, and lifestyle. **Short-term goals** are the stepping-stones used to meet the long-term goals. Short-term goals can be met in hours, days, or weeks.

Long-Term Goals

Determine which goals are long-term and list them separately. Listing long-term goals is a powerful tool for success. First, create headings from the categories in the Long-Term Goals Chart. Then, list each long-term goal beneath the appropriate heading.

Headings for Long-Term Goals		
Business	Family	Personal Enrichment
Financial	Physical	Intellectual
Social/Networking	Emotional	Travel
Education	Spiritual	Political

It is beneficial to set long-term goals at the beginning of each calendar year. You should make a list of what you would like to accomplish within the year. Then, reflection and consistent monitoring of your goals throughout the year helps keep you focused.

Short-Term Goals

Long-term goals determine the short-term goals. Therefore, it is helpful to break long-term goals into easier, short-term goals. A practical way to do this is to make daily activities consistent with the daily, weekly, and monthly goals.

> Example: A new licensee has a long-term financial goal to make $30,000 in the first year. By dividing that amount by 12, the short-term, monthly goal is $2,500.

If the goal in the preceding example were changed to $75,000, this figure can be broken down into monthly, weekly, daily, and even hourly goals and activities. You will have to make a certain number of average sales to reach your desired income. Break down how many sales are needed into yearly, monthly, and weekly goals. Realistically, the more prospecting you do, the better your chances are to make a sale.

Short-term goals are based on daily, weekly, and monthly activities.

Setting Goals

Goal setting is an activity that requires making a list of things you want to achieve, acquire, or attract in a certain amount of time. Setting goals should be a lifelong process. Success in any career may be measured by a person's ability to set and achieve goals. Therefore, you need to set clear goals and expectations so that you can stay focused and realize your goals.

Setting daily, weekly, and monthly goals allows you to stay grounded in activities that lead to successful real estate sales. You should keep your list of daily goals where you can read it at least twice a day. You should look at your weekly goals before planning each week, and your monthly goals as you plan your activities for the coming month. In doing this, you will be aware of your successes and failures and have time to make any necessary changes to your long-term goals.

To be valid, goals must be measurable. If they are not measurable, how will you know when you have achieved them? How will you know what "successful" is if you do not define what must be done to be successful? Your goals must be well defined and tangible.

Articulating goals involves creating a detailed set of instructions on how to reach that goal. Ineffective statements such as "I want to be successful." or "I want to be rich." will not achieve the desired results, because those statements are not action-specific. Instead, be precise about what is desired by making a statement, such as "I want to earn $75,000 next year." along with the steps that must be taken to earn that amount. In addition, determine a specific timeframe in which to achieve the goals.

Ambitious sales associates set **financial goals** and decide how much money they want to make and then create a plan to achieve that goal. For example, if your goal is to earn $75,000 this year, you know you would have to list or sell a certain amount of properties per year to guarantee the $75,000.

> Example: Assume you have a 50/50 commission split with your broker and the median price for a home in your area is $250,000. The median home price is the price that is midway between the least expensive and most expensive home sold in an area during a given period. The average commission in the area is 6% split between the listing and selling brokers. If your goal is to make $45,000 your first year, you will have to close 12 transactions within the first year annually to make that amount.
>
> $250,000 sales price
>
> x   .030 average % commission to listing or selling broker
>
> $ 7,500 dollar amount to listing or selling broker
>
> x   50% commission split to sales associate
>
> $ 3,750 dollar amount to new sales associate after splitting with broker
>
> $45,000 divided by $3,750 = 12 sales annually
>
> The example shows that by consistently listing or selling one property every four weeks the sales associate would meet the financial goal of $45,000.

Remember, as a sales associate you are in business for yourself and will have ongoing business expenses that you must pay. The first thing you need to do is set aside money to pay your quarterly estimated federal and state income taxes. Then, you need to have money to pay for professional organizations, Multiple Listing Service, supplies, advertising, education and training, automobile expenses, taxes, insurance, and any other costs that may be incurred. The money that remains, you use to pay your personal expenses.

The Career Goal Chart will help you break down your career goals based on your desired annual income. This will help you determine how much activity you will need on a weekly, monthly, and yearly basis in order to reach that income goal.

ABC Realty Group
Career Goals

Place this chart in a visible area for daily review

Goal	Amount
Yearly Income	$
Monthly Income	$
Weekly Income	$
Target Average Sale Price	$
Target Average Commission Per Sale	$
Transaction Goal For The Year	
Total Transactions Per Month	
Total Transactions Per Week	
Listings Needed Per Year	
Listings Needed Per Month	
Listings Needed Per Week	
Buyers Needed Per Year	
Buyers Needed Per Month	
Buyers Needed Per Week	

Write the Goals Down

Be sure to write down everything you want to accomplish, both personally and professionally. In that way the plan can be referenced throughout the year. This is an important step in the goal setting process because once goals are on paper it is easier to determine if you are realistic. Writing down goals also creates a visual reminder of what you would like to achieve, acquire, or attract.

Create a Timeframe

A realistic timeframe is necessary to accomplish goals. The operative word is realistic. The timeframe should include all necessary steps and a deadline for accomplishing the goal. When setting a deadline, include activities that can be started and finished within a reasonable amount of time. Accomplishing each step creates a sense of completion, success, and achievement.

Failure to accomplish goals within a realistic timeframe may mean that the timeframe should be re-evaluated, not the goals. The real estate business can be stressful and demanding; activities that are impossible to complete in any given period will only add to the level of frustration if you fail to accomplish them.

Stay Focused

Maintaining a focus on your commitments and priorities is vital to success. Sometimes it is difficult for a salesperson to decide what or who has priority each day because it seems you have more than one boss. As a result, some salespeople develop the bad habit of working only on what is in front of you. As a result, you forget planned activities, neglect goals, and wonder why you feel stressed or are always running late.

The solution is to prioritize everything and stick to your plan whenever possible. Urgent requests or requirements will occur, and when they do, they need to be dealt with in a timely manner. The needs and wants of buyers and sellers drive real estate activity. Each client believes that their needs should come first and wants to claim more than their fair share of a salesperson's time. Learn when to say "no" and remain focused on your priorities.

Evaluate Your Progress

It is important to continually analyze and evaluate your progress to see if you are achieving the appropriate results. When considering your goals, ask yourself, "Am I halfway there, not even close, or somewhere in between?" Modify any behavior that is not leading to the desired results.

PERSONAL MARKETING PLAN

Now that you have determined your priorities, set your financial goals, and calculated how many sales are needed to reach the goal, you need to market yourself. **Personal marketing**, or reminding people to think of you when they need real estate brokerage services, is what separates you, a top producer, from the average salesperson.

There are many different ways you can market yourself as the best possible real estate salesperson. This begins with your personal marketing plan and continues with your daily and weekly activities. A **personal marketing plan** describes the marketing efforts you will make to reach your target market. A **target market** is an identified group of people who are most likely to seek your services or buy your product. The purpose of personal marketing is to remind

Remind people to think of you when they need real estate brokerage services.

people to think of you when they need real estate brokerage services. Personal marketing is what separates a top producer from the average sales associate.

You must find a way to inspire buyers and sellers to choose you instead of one of your competitors. The more effective your personal marketing campaign, the better your chance of success. Wherever you go—the gas station, the cleaners, or the line at the ATM—keep in mind that almost everyone you meet owns or wants to own property. Your ability to present yourself as the best real estate professional in the business will determine a large degree of your success. If you create an effective marketing campaign, people are more likely to remember you when they are ready to buy or sell property. Even if your company does not have a strong influence in the real estate community, a good personal marketing plan will help you establish yourself in the real estate community.

Personal Marketing Pieces

A first impression is a lasting one. When preparing and presenting marketing pieces, it is important to be professional. If your marketing pieces are of poor quality, they may have a negative effect on a prospect. However, this does not mean you need to spend a fortune to attract your prospects by creating marketing pieces in color. Your **marketing pieces** should include business cards, stationery and envelopes, flyers, door-hangers and brochures, promotional or giveaway items, newsletters, and presentation binders. According to the Department of Real Estate, these marketing pieces are **solicitation materials** and licensees are required to include their license identification number on them.

Your business card is your most important marketing piece. Create a good first impression by having it printed on quality card stock. Include your name, license identification number, photo, logo, slogan, broker's name and address, business telephone number and cell phone number, email address, and personal website. Use the back of the business card to provide a home buying checklist, emergency phone numbers, or a calendar that will encourage potential clients to keep your card.

Your brochure should focus on your abilities and commitment to your target market. Look at other salespeople's brochures and analyze what makes them effective. Do not limit yourself to what you find in other real estate brochures, because good ideas can come from anywhere. Make a list of the ideas and points you want to consider for your own brochure.

Customize your brochures with a personal or company logo, a slogan, color printing, and photos. Be consistent. If, for example, you create a logo that is maroon and is printed on a light grey background, use the same color scheme for every marketing piece that carries that logo. Also, be sure to keep the same slogan, style, and format for all your printed materials.

Develop a branding strategy so that when prospective clients see your name or your company, they know exactly who you are. **Branding** is a process in which a product is given a distinctive logo, image, name, or style. As a sales associate, you are your own product.

> Example: If you go to the store to buy Kleenex®, you may not actually buy the Kleenex® brand, but you will use the name Kleenex® to find and purchase the facial tissues.

The logo on your business cards, brochures, stationery, and envelopes should all match. Stay away from dark colors. Use the four key colors that make people feel confident from the start—white, beige, green, and blue. White or beige signifies credibility. Light green is the color of money. Pale grey-blue implies "trust me" (such as the stationery used by your local banker or attorney).

Career Book

A **career book** is another marketing piece that identifies the salesperson and highlights his or her qualifications. This marketing piece is solely about you—your credentials and successes.

A career book can be a loose-leaf binder or a photo album.

The career book is usually a loose-leaf binder or a photo album, but going through it page by page with the prospect may be too tedious for you and boring for the prospect. Instead, the career book may be sent to the prospect with the pre-listing package or hand-carried to the listing appointment. Leaving the book with the prospect to look over at his or her leisure provides a good excuse for a return visit in a few days to pick it up.

Your market, budget, and personal style will determine what you include in your pre-listing package. Suggested inclusions are listed below:

Introduction

- The front page should be a letter of introduction.
- List your telephone, cell phone, and fax numbers, as well as your e-mail and personal and company websites.
- Add a friendly photograph of you with a happy seller. Indicate your desire to meet with the seller to discuss marketing their property.

Qualifications

- Briefly list your qualifications. You should explain your selling philosophy, code of ethics, marketing approach, and commitment to first-rate service.
- Include your education, training, and seminars you have attended.
- Show any awards and certificates of achievement you have received.

Satisfied Clients

- Referrals. Show copies of complimentary notes from clients about successful listings, sales, and closings.

- Show just-listed and just-sold properties with you pictured or designated as the sales associate.
- Keep a file of photographs of homes you have listed or sold along with addresses, sales prices and, if possible, photographs of the pleased sellers (with their permission). Include those photographs in the career book to create the impression of a busy, productive salesperson who works with satisfied sellers.

Information about the brokerage

- Include company listings and listings with "sold" riders on them.
- If you are working with a team of assistants or a partner, highlight each person's experience and qualifications.

Sample Marketing Plans

Part of the start-up expense for new licensees is marketing. However, before creating a personal marketing plan, you must determine how much money is available for marketing and advertising. Creating a budget for marketing costs is one of the most demanding and yet necessary tasks for any sales associate.

You should not wait for your first commission before allocating anything to marketing because it may be too late by then. For experienced sales associates, a common rule-of-thumb is to budget at least 10% of each commission income for marketing.

Use two or three types of media when communicating with the target group. Traditionally, the marketing activities that produce income are networking, regular mailings, floor time, website leads, open houses, referrals, repeat business, and other sources.

Be sure to consider market and economic conditions when developing the marketing plan. Knowing whether current economic conditions favor a sellers' market or a buyers' market will give customers and clients exactly what they deserve—a knowledgeable sales associate working in their best interests.

Sensible ways to connect with target markets include email communications, mail-out campaigns, and newsletters. When communicating to your target market the cost of postage, envelope, paper and labor is approximately $1 per person; an email is about 3 cents per person. Repeated and consistent marketing for at least six months makes your name recognizable.

Although there are many marketing plans available, we are describing a plan for new sales associates and one for more seasoned sales associates.

Marketing Plan One – Limited Budget

Plan One is for new sales associates with a $200 to $500 monthly marketing budget. A new licensee may only be able to afford business cards and a website. Therefore, this plan focuses on networking, passing out business cards to as many prospects as possible, and setting up a website.

The purpose of this plan is to obtain and increase business, which will establish a steady cash flow and allow expansion into a longer-term marketing approach shown in Plan Two.

Business Cards

Print plenty of business cards because handing out business cards is an inexpensive way to generate business. Remember to give or email business cards to everyone in your sphere of influence. At a minimum, you should hand out at least ten business cards per day to new people. Always have your business cards ready to give out. When eating in restaurants, put the server's tip on top of your business card when you leave. Be active in community service organizations, such as Soroptimist International, Rotary International, or others. Let the members know you are in the real estate business and do not forget to hand out a business card.

Website

Even with a small budget, allow for a good website with a personal domain name. A **domain name** is a unique address of a website. Do not make the mistake of not getting a domain name. They are not expensive and are easy to obtain. Depending on the budget, the website should have at least a few pages of text and photos.

As emails and requests are received on the website, develop two mailing lists for lead follow-up—an email list and a list for future print mailings. Be sure to assign a code to different online articles to see which ones get the most hits.

Open Houses

New sales associates should hold an open house every Saturday and Sunday. You should be friendly, greet everyone who walks in the door, and hand visitors a flyer on the property along with your business card. You

should spend the next day following up with phone calls to everyone who signed the guest book at the open house. Remember to code and rate the quality of leads before adding them to your database.

Marketing Plan Two - Consistent Monthly Investment

Plan Two requires a regular investment of about $1,500 per month for at least nine months. However, you could use this marketing plan for the rest of your career. In addition to networking, referrals, and repeat business, this plan focuses on repeated mailings of a strong, direct-mail piece because it consistently produces one of the highest rates of return for real estate agents with a mid-sized marketing budget. The purpose of Plan Two is to establish consistent and permanent name recognition, which will generate new and repeat business. This plan will work very well by itself, but additional activities, such as a supporting website and face-to-face marketing will increase the plan's overall effectiveness.

Printed Materials

Determine the size of the target market. Is it large enough to reach the financial goals? To make Plan Two economically viable, the target market should be at least 1,000 homes, but 3,000 homes are ideal. To carry out this program between 10,000 and 12,000 marketing pieces will be needed every 90 days.

Regular mailings over a period of at least six months build the level of name recognition, generate referrals and repeat business, and allow you to achieve a major market share in your area. Typically, 95% of all experienced real estate agents generate between two and five transactions in the first 30 days after a mailing and ten or more transactions within 90 days after a mailing.

Create high-quality personal marketing pieces. The marketing pieces should promote you—not the company or listings. Look at each piece for fifteen seconds, and then write down what you remember. If you remember anything other than your name or marketing slogan, new marketing pieces need to be created.

Suggested Marketing Pieces
- A 4-inch by 6-inch, four-color postcard printed with an image on one side and a different promotional message on the other
- A four-color brochure, with envelope if needed
- Business cards with the same design elements and marketing theme as your brochure and postcards

Postcards

Every month, postcards with different messages should be mailed to the target market. Useful information should be printed on promotional postcards. Homeowners are interested in the average selling price of homes in their area, tips for improving their homes for sale, suggestions for winterizing their homes, and remodeling options that add the most value to their homes. Sometimes, the postcard could include personal information, such as award ceremonies, speaking engagements, educational achievements, or closed listings.

Brochures

Brochures are effective when consistently mailed monthly to each resident in your target market. In addition, you should mail a brochure with a well-written cover letter to all of the expired listings and FSBO properties.

Website

You should create or redesign your website to reflect your new marketing identity. You should contact a web hosting company to discuss the needs for the new site and to ensure that there is enough server space for the newly enhanced site.

Select a web designer to help develop your site and to build a template into the site that will allow a new copy to be added with little or no coding. The template will also allow changes to be made in certain areas, saving the expense of additional web design.

A straightforward website design of 25 to 30 pages will require approximately 125 to 150 hours of work. Allow two to four months for the site to be completed. Always be sure that all images and links on the website are working correctly before promoting it to the public.

Analyze Marketing Activities

The results of the marketing must be measured to determine whether you are getting your money's worth for the marketing dollar. You should keep track of the advertising responses and notice what is making the telephone ring. You should use a prospect management system to track the source of leads. By assigning codes to each promotion, the responses can be tracked and entered in the prospect database. The quality of each lead can be rated as "A" (hot prospect), "B" (medium interest), or "C" (marginal interest). By running reports using the marketing method, you will know the number of prospects generated by each campaign. This will help to determine which marketing campaigns are effective. It is easier and more accurate to determine the number of prospects generated from a website. This is tracked through the website statistics.

The purpose of analyzing the market activities and creating an income funnel is to determine the effectiveness of the marketing plan. This list of possible sources of income is called an **income funnel**. The income funnel quantifies the number of prospects from each activity that must be contacted in order to complete a sale.

The shape of a funnel (wide at the top, narrow at the bottom) is used to monitor the process. All new prospects, regardless of the prospecting activity that generated them, are initially placed into the top of the funnel. These prospects

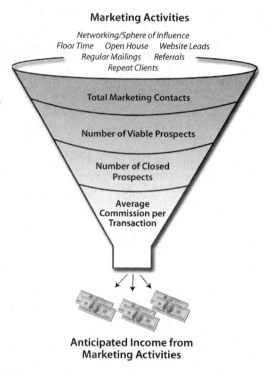

Marketing Activities

Networking/Sphere of Influence
Floor Time   Open House   Website Leads
Regular Mailings   Referrals
Repeat Clients

Total Marketing Contacts

Number of Viable Prospects

Number of Closed Prospects

Average Commission per Transaction

Anticipated Income from Marketing Activities

may or may not translate into a closed transaction. At the bottom of the funnel, you have the closed transactions. The funnel image shows that the number of resulting sales is usually significantly less than the number of total prospects.

TIME MANAGEMENT PLAN

The third part of a productivity management plan is to create and follow a time management plan. It is easy to feel burdened by the numerous activities that take place during a business day. The first step in learning to manage your time is to analyze how you currently spend each day. After keeping a daily chart of every activity for at least a week, you may be surprised to discover how much time is wasted. This tendency to waste time includes the time spent reading e-mail, visiting the coffee shop, talking with co-workers, going to lunch, keeping a friend company while he or she previews a listing, or dealing with various distractions.

A logical way to stay focused on the priority of numerous commitments and activities is to make a time management plan and commit to it. A **time management plan** schedules all of the required activities necessary to reach your goals.

Action Plans and Task Lists

An **action plan** lists the tasks that you must perform to accomplish a particular long-term goal. Your goals are the basis and act as a guide when creating an action plan. By focusing on the completion of a single goal rather than a number of objectives, an action plan leads you progressively toward achieving each goal. You can track your progress, or lack thereof, by referring to the action plan.

An action plan differs from a task list in that it focuses on the achievement of a single goal. A **task list** is a prioritized list of every task that must be done within a certain period. It is different from an action plan because it combines everything into one list—not just the tasks needed to meet one goal.

A task list should be made daily to ensure it is current and the tasks are relevant. Important or difficult tasks should be at the top of the list because it helps prevent procrastination. If there are three or four large tasks for that day, divide them into smaller tasks. That way, larger tasks that once seemed overwhelming may be worked on as smaller steps or tasks, without stress. Be sure to finish each project and handle each piece of paper only once.

Scheduling

Scheduling is the process of determining to use the available time to achieve identified goals. A successful schedule is a written log, which has the activities crossed off as they are completed. Therefore, you should use some type of scheduling system, such as a paper-based organizer, electronic organizer, or a software package like MS Outlook. A daily or weekly schedule lists every activity, including non-job related tasks. A well thought out schedule allows you to manage your business and personal commitments, leave time for yourself, and avoid work overload.

The first step is to determine what time to start work each day. Each workday should start at a standard time that is not dictated by whim. Next, determine which activities have priority and enter them into the daily planner. The highest priority activities and goals should be scheduled first. For example, if you pick your children up from school every day, that is scheduled first. If a priority is to work out at the gym every other day for an hour, block off that time. When preparing a schedule, priorities are scheduled before other activities. Regularly scheduled office meetings and commitments are added next. Then, schedule the business and prospecting activities for the week and items from the prioritized task list that need to be completed.

Finally, block in some contingency time. Real estate is an unpredictable career filled with constant interruptions. Many interruptions could lead to a commission, so you should leave a little space in your schedules to take care of urgent issues.

Analyze how you spend your time to see if your daily activities line up with your priorities and goals. Try to accomplish as much as you can in one day, but you should set realistic goals with realistic deadlines. Efficient scheduling reduces stress and maximizes effectiveness.

Review - Time Management Tips
- Plan each day the night before. Make weekly plans prior to each week, make monthly plans at the beginning of each month, and make yearly plans at the beginning of each year.
- Start work at a regular hour each day.
- Identify the available time.
- Block in the essential tasks necessary to reach financial goals.
- Set realistic goals with realistic deadlines.
- Allow sufficient time to complete each activity.
- Schedule in high priority tasks.
- Schedule regularly occurring meetings.
- Block in contingency time.
- Learn when to say "no".

ABC Realty Group, Inc.

Daily Plan

Date___/___/___	Today's Plan	Actual	Results (Time Spent)
6:00 AM			Listing Contracts_____
6:30 AM			Listing Sales_____
7:00 AM			Buyer Sales_____
7:30 AM			Escrows Closed_____
8:00 AM			**SALES ACTIVITIES**
8:30 AM			Listing Presentations_____
9:00 AM			Offers Prepared_____
9:30 AM			Properties Shown_____
10:00 AM			Open Houses Held_____
10:30 AM			**PREPARATION ACTIVITIES**
11:00 AM			Properties Previewed_____
12:00 PM			CMAs Prepared_____
12:30 PM			Offers Written_____
1:00 PM			Ads/Highlights Written_____
1:30 PM			**MARKETING ACTIVITIES**
2:00 PM			Prospecting Calls_____
2:30 PM			In-Person Prospecting_____
3:00 PM			Mass Mailing_____
3:30 PM			Personal Notes_____
4:00 PM			Open House Follow-Up_____
4:30 PM			FSBO Contact_____
5:00 PM			Expired Contracts_____
5:30 PM			Drive Listing Bank_____
6:00 PM			**BUSINESS ACTIVITIES**
6:30 PM			Calling Agents/Vendors_____
7:00 PM			Meeting Agents/Vendors_____
7:30 PM			Paperwork_____
8:00 PM			Training_____
8:30 PM			Planning_____

Priorities:

Development (Check all that apply):

Listen more than I talk____   Use "you" instead of "I"____   Pause after making points, answering objections____

Write a personal note____   Read a chapter from a book on selling or motivation____   Do something extra for client____

EXPENSES: Car: $_____   Phone: $_____   Meals: $_____   Other: $_____

WEEKLY REVIEW

Name:_____

Week of: RESULTS	Sunday	Monday	Tuesday	Wednesday	Thursday	Friday	Saturday	Total
Listing Contracts								
Listing Sales								
Buyer Sales								
Escrows Closed								
SALES ACTIVITIES								
Listing Presentations								
Offers Presented								
Properties Shown								
Open Houses Held								
PREPARATION ACTIVITIES								
Properties Previewed								
C.M.A.'s Prepared								
Offers Written								
Ads/Highlights Written								
MARKETING/ACTIVITIES								
Prospecting Calls								
In-Person Prospecting								
Mass Mailing								
Personal Notes								
Open House Follow up								
FSBO Contact								
Expireds Contact								
Drive Listing Bank								
BUSINESS ACTIVITIES (Time Spent)								
Calling Agents/Vendors								
Meeting Agents/Vendors								
Board/Office Meetings								
Paperwork								
Training/Reading								
Planning								

WASTED TIME

What Worked Well This Week:

Plans for Improving Next Week:

Monthly Action Plan			
	Daily	Days/week	Days/month
1. Days worked			
2. Hours prospected			
3. Contacts			
4. Leads generated			
5. Appointments set			
6. Listing appointments			
7. Listing taken			
8. Listing sold			
9. Buyer's appointments			
10. Buyer's sales made			
11. Price reduction			
12. Transaction fees			
13. Listing Exp/Cxl'd			
14. Listing inventory			
15. Income earned			

SUMMARY

Productivity management incorporates business planning techniques, personal marketing strategies, and time management skills to help agents be productive and quickly reach their goals. A **goal** is the measurable accomplishment that an individual strives to achieve in order to produce a desired outcome. **Long-term goals** refer to the major areas of life, such as career, family, and lifestyle. **Short-term goals** are the stepping-stones used to meet the long-term goals. Short-term goals can be met in hours, days, or weeks.

Be sure to write down long-term goals and create a **business plan**. Setting **financial goals** and creating a business plan should be a lifelong process and carrying them out will determine success in both personal and professional life.

You will need to create a **personal marketing plan** to market yourself to buyers and sellers. To create a personal marketing plan, you must develop a unique selling proposition that will separate you from your competition.

The results of the marketing activities must be measured to determine whether you are getting your money's worth for the marketing dollar. You should keep track of the advertising responses and notice what is making the telephone ring, then modify the marketing strategy as necessary.

One way to analyze the marketing plan is to use an income funnel. The **income funnel** quantifies the number of prospects from each activity that must be contacted in order to complete a sale.

The third part of a productivity management plan is to create and follow a time management plan. When implementing a **time management plan**, you should use some type of scheduling system, such as a paper-based organizer or a computer program (e.g., MS Outlook). A well thought out schedule allows you to manage your business and personal commitments, leave time for yourself, and avoid work overload.

UNIT 3 REVIEW

■ Matching Exercise

Instructions: Write the letter of the matching term on the blank line before its definition. Answers are in Appendix A.

Terms

A. action plan
B. domain name
C. income funnel
D. long-term goals
E. median home price

F. scheduling
G. short-term goals
H. target market
I. task list
J. time management plan

Definitions

1. _____ Goals for the major areas of life, such as career, family, and lifestyle

2. _____ Goals that can be met in hours, days, or weeks

3. _____ Midway price between the least expensive and most expensive home sold in an area during a given period

4. _____ Identified group of people who are most likely to seek your services or buy your product

5. _____ Unique address of a website

6. _____ List of possible sources of income arranged by marketing activity

7. _____ Schedule all of the required activities necessary to reach a person's goals

8. _____ All tasks that an associate must perform to accomplish a particular goal

9. _____ Prioritized list of every task that must be done within a certain period

10. _____ Process of determining to use the available time to achieve identified goals

▣ **Multiple Choice Questions**

Instructions: Circle your response and go to Appendix A to read the complete explanation for each question.

1. Productivity management involves:
    a. business planning.
    b. personal marketing strategies.
    c. practicing time management.
    d. all of the above.

2. When creating a business plan, keep in mind that it:
    a. should always remain the same.
    b. is not necessarily important.
    c. is not a static document.
    d. need not be reviewed on a regular basis.

3. Goals should be SMART. This acronym stands for:
    a. specific, measurable, attainable, irrelevant, and timeless.
    b. specific, imprecise, attainable, unrelated, and timely.
    c. specific, measurable, unattainable, relevant, and timeless.
    d. specific, measurable, attainable, relevant, and timely.

4. Sales associate Sam is prioritizing the areas in his life in order to set his annual long-term goals. Which of the following is not considered a long-term goal?
    a. Allocating more family time
    b. Closing the Lake Street transaction
    c. Planning to spend more time traveling
    d. Setting financial goals

5. A practical way to keep sight of long-term goals is to:
    a. break them down into mid-term goals.
    b. set short-term goals.
    c. focus on financial goals only.
    d. make travel goals a priority.

6. In order to attract buyers and sellers, a sales associate must create and use a(n):

    a. company marketing plan.
    b. institutional marketing plan.
    c. personal marketing plan.
    d. time management plan.

7. The best way for a sales associate to get name recognition in his or her target market is to:

    a. infrequently mail 4-color postcards to the target group.
    b. only use television advertising.
    c. repeatedly mail marketing pieces to the target group.
    d. rely on the marketing done by the broker.

8. What is the purpose of a prospect management system?

    a. Record marketing costs
    b. Report marketing results to prospects
    c. Track the source of leads
    d. Verify institutional prospects

9. The income funnel quantifies the number of prospects from each marketing activity that must be contacted in order to complete a sale. Which of the following is a marketing activity?

    a. Open houses
    b. Regular mailings
    c. Website leads
    d. All of the above

10. Scheduling the available time when creating a time management plan includes all of the following, except:

    a. determining what time to start work each day.
    b. putting activities with high priority first.
    c. allowing for no contingency time.
    d. scheduling the weekly business and prospecting activities.

Product Knowledge

Unit 4

INTRODUCTION

Housing styles follow trends, and as with any trend, they come and they go. New building materials, technological advances, the state of the economy, and changes in the expectations of homebuyers influence housing trends.

In the past, those who built houses used the supplies that were readily available. At one time, the size of a Cape Cod house was determined by the length of the tallest trees. Now, contemporary houses can be any shape and size using steel girders and glass. Today's houses have electrical, heating, and plumbing systems that are far superior to their predecessors.

The late 1800s brought machines and the railroad, which had an impact on the diversity and availability of building supplies, as well as the expansion of communities. After the Great Depression in the 1930s and 1940s, houses became very small and utilitarian. However, since the 1950s, houses have doubled in size and the type of amenities included in the design has increased.

Learning Objectives

After reading this unit, you should be able to:
- name the benefits of both older and newer neighborhoods.
- recall the components that create the various architectural styles.
- recognize the various styles of architecture.
- assign a particular architectural style to a house.

KNOW THE NEIGHBORHOODS

In order to list and show property, you must know the neighborhoods in your area. Whether older, newer, custom-built, or tract-built, buyers have preferences regarding the houses and nearby amenities in a neighborhood. Every neighborhood will have good selling points. For example, an older, more established neighborhood offers stability and an existing community infrastructure. While it may be easier to sell the houses in a brand new neighborhood, the location of the development may be far from work, services, and community amenities.

The typical new house has approximately 2,400 square feet, three or more bedrooms, two-and-one-half baths, and larger garages. This is more than twice the size of a house built in the 1950s.

Not only are houses getting larger, better insulated, and safer, homebuyers expect the latest amenities. Whether it is a new house or a remodeled older house, granite countertops, high-end kitchen appliances, designer paint, and large walk-in closets are expected. Older houses (unless remodeled) do not have these amenities and features, whereas they are standard features in new developments. In order to help buyers decide on the neighborhood that suits them best, you need to know the neighborhoods in your community.

Selling Points for Established Neighborhoods

By understanding the strong points of older, established neighborhoods, you will be able to more readily list and sell houses. Find out about the things that make an established neighborhood interesting, such as quaint restaurants, specialty shops, excellent schools, marvelous views, great hospitals, or good security.

Older neighborhoods with mature trees and landscaping have an added charm not usually seen in new neighborhoods. In an older neighborhood, there

Older neighborhoods have established schools, stores, parks, landscaping, and trees.

are no surprises because everything is already built—the stores, parks, schools, houses of worship, police and fire stations, public buildings, and restaurants. Just by driving through the neighborhood, it is often easy to see if neighbors exhibit pride of ownership with well-maintained houses and yards and if the city keeps the roads repaired and the trees properly trimmed. Whereas, in a new development, a buyer can only hope the neighbors will have pride of ownership, that the planned shopping centers and schools will be built, and that the city will maintain the public roads and facilities. In spite of this uncertainty, the lure of a new house is strong because newer houses have many advantages.

Selling Points for New Neighborhoods

The obvious selling point for new neighborhoods is that everything is new, modern, and sought-after. The houses are larger with up-to-date floor plans and amenities. The houses are safer, easier to maintain, and energy efficient.

A new neighborhood has homes that are easier to maintain, energy efficient, and safer. However, the neighborhood has not been built and scheduled improvements can change.

Size and Floor Plan

As mentioned earlier, newer houses are larger than those built between the 1950s and the 1990s. Currently the average house size is approximately 2,400 square feet. Obviously, new homebuyers are looking for larger houses.

What type of floor plan is the most popular? Nearly all homebuyers look for large kitchens, open, informal space that offers flexibility, more bedrooms, and two-and-one-half to three bathrooms. Precious square footage is gained if there are fewer hallways. The trend is toward a small living room and larger informal area that combines the family room and dining area. Many times the kitchen is separated by a half-wall or counter.

Many buyers want houses that can accommodate family members with mobility problems. That means fewer (or no) stairs, wider doors and hallways, and larger bathrooms. One-story houses and two-story houses with a master bedroom suite on the main floor are becoming more popular.

Everyone looks for ample storage space. A small house that has good storage space will usually sell as easily as a larger house that has inadequate closets and storage space. Plenty of cabinets, cupboards, and storage closets help a house to be functional. A house usually would appeal to any homebuyer if it has adequate kitchen pantries, easy-to-reach kitchen cabinets, walk-in closets, dressing rooms, linen closets in all bathrooms, guest closets, and cabinets for cleaning equipment and laundry supplies.

Increase in space includes other areas of the house. For example, it is always better to have a conveniently located laundry room rather than an area in the drafty garage. If large enough, the laundry room can be used for crafts and other hobbies. As vehicles get larger, many homebuyers want wider garages for their SUVs and other large vehicles.

Amenities

New houses feature the amenities that are in vogue. Currently, granite or marble countertops, travertine floors, and stainless steel appliances are very desirable. However, in a few years, these amenities will be looked at the way we currently view Formica™ countertops, shag carpet, and avocado green appliances. It may be less expensive and easier for a buyer to purchase a house with these features already installed rather than remodel an older house.

Energy Efficient

New houses are designed and built to conserve energy. The use of dual and triple-glazed windows, increased insulation in walls and roofs, more efficient heating and cooling equipment, and Energy Star® appliances have helped to decrease energy consumption. These houses not only save the homeowner money, but they are less drafty and more comfortable.

The Energy Star® program even rates an entire house—not just the appliances—for overall efficiency. A new house certified by the Energy Star®

program performs at least 30% more efficiently than houses built to the 1993 Model Energy Code. The Energy Star® designation is displayed on the inside of the circuit breaker.

Windows

Depending on the climate and total glass area in the house, windows account for 10% of the heat loss. However, dual and triple-glazing increases the insulating ability for windows. **Glazing** refers to the glass panes used in windows and doors.

Insulation

Air leaking through the roof, floor, walls, and windows can waste 25-40% of the energy used to heat or cool a house. If the insulation in the house meets or exceeds local standards, be sure to mention that to a potential buyer. In addition, call attention to proper weatherization such as caulked and sealed windows, weather stripping around doors, and rubber gaskets installed behind outlets and switch plates. A properly weatherized house reduces energy costs and is quieter.

Heating and Cooling Systems

Energy-efficient heating, ventilation, and air conditioning equipment uses less fuel and needs less maintenance. Ask if the house has programmable thermostats or zoned systems that heat or cool different areas of the house separately. Ceiling fans circulate air and cut down on more expensive air conditioning or heating.

The house may have a solar water heater, a solar heating system, and even a solar system to create electricity in the residence. Another means to increase energy efficiency is to use a heat pump or geothermal heat pump heating and cooling system to exchange hot and cool air with the soil in the ground.

Appliances

Look for the blue and white Energy Star® label on kitchen appliances, laundry equipment, and water heaters to confirm that they are among the most efficient on the market. Tankless water heaters are more economical, reducing water heating costs by up to 50% and providing an endless supply of hot water. The tankless water heater unit lasts twice as long as the standard water heater.

Lower Maintenance

The materials used in new houses require less maintenance. Some siding and trim never need to be painted and windows have been designed to be self-cleaning.

Safer Building Materials

A ground fault circuit interrupter (GFCI)

Many building materials that were standard in older houses, like asbestos, lead, or formaldehyde, are no longer used in new construction. In areas where radon gas is a problem, builders install systems to control it.

New houses are pre-wired for data, cable, and phone, in addition to meeting the wiring needs for the heavy electrical demands. Gone are the old fuse boxes, being replaced by circuit breakers. Ground fault circuit interrupters (GFCI) are standard in bathrooms, kitchens, and outside receptacles. A GFCI will reduce the chance of fire and electrocution.

KNOW WHAT CREATES ARCHITECTURAL STYLES

When you arrive at a house, one of the first things you notice is the number of stories, the shape, and the architectural influence or style of the house.

Every house has a style, which will be discussed later. Many older houses were built with an exact style in mind, like Craftsman, Queen Anne, or Cape Cod. Many newer houses are an eclectic mix of a variety of styles. These houses are described with phrases like "Victorian accents", "Art Deco inspired", or "Tudor detailing". Other houses are a mix of historic periods and cultures. The Mediterranean style is a mix of Spanish, Moorish, Byzantine, and Pueblo styles combined with modern construction techniques and materials.

To help you learn the different styles, first examine key characteristics and features. Then determine how those key features combine to create distinctive architectural styles. Initially, the features to look for include housing types, roof shapes and embellishments, wall materials, window types and arrangements, door shapes, and exterior ornamental details.

House Types

In the United States, the five basic types of houses are one-story, one-and-one-half story, two-story, split-level, and multiple-story.

One-Story

The one-story house is typically the easiest to maintain and is the most common type of single-family house in the United States. The obvious appeal to the one-story design is that there are no stairs to climb. Typical one-story house styles include Ranch, Pueblo, Bungalow, Art Moderne, and Neo-Eclectic.

A Ranch is an example of a one story house.

One-and-One-Half Story

The one-and-one half-story house is technically a one-story house with an expanded attic, which allows an occupant the benefits of living in a Ranch style house. Sometimes the attic/second floor is without insulation, furnishings, etc., but often it is finished like the rest of the house to provide extra living space. Typical one-and-one-half story house styles include Cape Cod, Craftsman, Contemporary, A-Frame, and Neo-Eclectic.

A Ranch with dormers is an example of a one-and-a-half story house.

Two-Story

Two-story houses may cost less to heat, cool, and build because the plumbing and other interior fixtures are aligned. Other advantages include separation of living areas on the first floor from the sleeping quarters on the second, which contributes to quieter, more private areas. Typical two-story house styles include Colonial, Mission, Monterey, American Foursquare, French Provincial, French Normandy, Art Deco, International, and Neo-Eclectic.

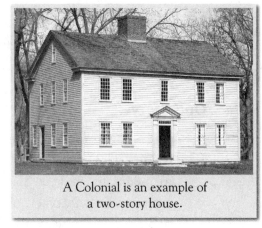

A Colonial is an example of a two-story house.

Split-Level

A split-level house has benefits similar to those of a two-story house. The split-level usually has the garage and major appliances like an air conditioning unit and a washer and dryer on the ground floor. The second level is typically offset one-half floor above the garage area and contains the living areas. The sleeping quarters are one-half floor above the living area and directly above the garage area. This floor plan offers more design possibilities than either the single or the two-story plan. Typical split-level house styles include Raised Ranch, Contemporary, and Neo-Eclectic.

A Contemporary is an example of a split-level house.

Multi-Level

Multi-level houses—typical of Victorian, Queen Anne, Second Empire, Tudor, and Contemporary styles—have complex floor plans and multiple stairwells.

A Victorian is an example of a multi-level house.

House Shapes

The shape of the house indicates the architectural style. For example, a rectangular, symmetrical shape is typical of the Cape Cod, Colonial, Mission, Monterey, and some Mediterranean styles. A square, box-like shape indicates California Bungalow, American Foursquare, and Art Deco. If the box-like shape has rounded corners, the style would be Pueblo or Art Moderne. L-shaped houses indicate a Ranch or National style. If the house is complicated and asymmetrical, it is probably a Queen Anne or Elizabethan Tudor style.

Roofs

Roof lines also indicate the architectural style of a house. A real estate sales associate should be able to distinguish the different roof types. Roof types are determined by the direction, steepness, and number of roof planes. The **pitch** of a roof is how steep it is. A roof with an unusually steep pitch indicates Tudor, Victorian, Shed, and A-frame styles. A roof with an unusually low pitch indicates Craftsman, Prairie, Ranch, Monterey, and Spanish styles. Flat roofs are found on Pueblo, Art Moderne, Contemporary, Mediterranean, and Modernistic styles.

Gable and hip roofs are popular and are featured in many different architectural styles. A **gable roof** is pitched with two sloping sides. A **hip roof** is pitched with sloping sides and ends (all four sides). A **gambrel roof**, typically seen in Dutch Colonial architecture, is curbed with a steep lower slope and a flatter one above. A **mansard roof** has four nearly vertical sides with a flat top; it is featured in Second Empire and other French-inspired styles.

Other features found on roofs can help a new salesperson determine the architectural style of a house.

- Flared eaves: Craftsman, Prairie, French-inspired styles
- Round towers: Queen Anne, French Normandy
- Rounded parapets: Mission

Flat

The **flat roof** is popular in the Southwestern house styles, such as Pueblo and Spanish Eclectic, and modern styles, such as International, Art Moderne, and Art Deco.

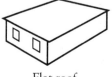

Flat roof

Gable

The triangular shape of a gable roof is featured in many American housing styles, from Cape Cod and Colonial, to Contemporary.

Front-gabled roofs are used in Cape Cod and Colonial styles.

Side-gabled roofs are used in Cape Cod, Colonial, National, and Ranch styles.

Cross-gabled roofs are used on Cape Cod and Tudor styles.

Front-gabled roof

Side-gabled roof

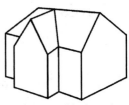

Cross-gabled roof

Gambrel

A **gambrel roof** is a gable roof that has a slight bend on each side and is the distinctive characteristic of the Dutch Colonial style.

Gambrel roof

Shed

The streamlined shape of the **shed roof,** which is one-half of a gable roof, is popular for Contemporary houses.

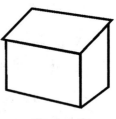

Shed roof

Saltbox

The **saltbox roof** looks like a lopsided triangle and is named after the boxes used to store salt in Colonial times. Saltbox roofs are seen on Colonial style and split-level houses.

Saltbox roof

Hip Roof

A **hip roof** slopes on all four sides, either from a ridge or from a single point at the top. Hipped roofs are often found on Ranch, French-inspired, American Foursquare, and a variety of Colonial style houses.

Pyramid-hipped roofs are used in single and two-story houses, as well as foursquare bungalows.

Hip roof

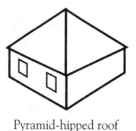

Pyramid-hipped roof

Mansard

With its nearly vertical sides and flat top, the **mansard roof** is the hallmark of the Second Empire style. Variations of this roof are also seen on Contemporary, Ranch, and French Colonial houses.

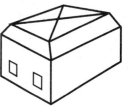

Mansard roof

Dormers

A **dormer** is a vertical window set in a framed window unit that projects from a sloping roof. Dormers are usually used in second story bedrooms or bathrooms. The variety of styles includes gable, hip, shed, and eyebrow.

Gabled Dormers: Colonial, Georgian, Queen Anne, Tudor, Craftsman

Shed Dormers: Colonial, Craftsman

Hipped Dormers: Prairie

Eyebrow Dormers: Queen Anne

Hipped dormers

Windows

Windows allow light into a house, improve airflow, and keep weather out. **Windowpanes** are held in place by window frames and sashes, which are made of wood, metal, vinyl, or fiberglass. Most windowpanes are conventional glass but some may be laminated glass, tempered glass, or even wired glass. Windows also come in single-glazed, dual-glazed, or even triple-glazed varieties.

A single house may use a variety of window types. Windows are described by their glazing patterns, shape, placement in the house, and the way they open.

Glazing Patterns

Glazing patterns refer to the way windowpanes are placed into a frame. Although many windows are made from a single sheet of glass, you may notice a variety of glazing patterns or windowpane arrangements. For example, a window with many small panes of glass would be found in a Colonial style house. A diamond-paned pattern is found in Tudor, English Cottage, and Prairie style houses. Leaded glass and stained glass designs can be found in any style of house.

Shape of the Windows

A house may have only square or rectangular windows, or it may utilize some of these popular styles as well:

A **Palladian window** is divided into three parts, with rectangular panes on each side of a wide arch. They are placed at the center of an upper story as a focal point in Colonial or Queen Anne houses. You may see them in modern houses with cathedral ceilings.

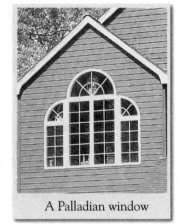

A Palladian window

Semi-circular windows and **oval windows** add accents to houses. These windows were popular in Colonial times and continued to be used through Victorian and into modern times.

Triangular windows and **angular windows** add drama to contemporary houses.

Gothic arch windows are characteristic of the Tudor style.

Window Placement

When defining architectural style, the placement of windows is as important as the shape of the windows.

Ribbon windows are several rectangular windows placed in a row with their frames abutting, and are a distinctive feature in Craftsman and Prairie style houses.

"Five-ranked" refers to the five rectangular windows equally spaced across the second story of Georgian Colonial-style houses.

Sidelights are tall, narrow windows flanking the entry door. These windows are characteristic of Greek Revival and are found in Neo-Eclectic houses.

Many houses today have semi-circular **fanlights** or **sunburst lights** above the entry door; these are characteristic of the Colonial Revival and Adam style.

Bay windows and oriel windows, which jut out from the side of the house, were popularized during the Victorian era. A **bay window** is a window or series of windows that protrudes from the exterior of a building, leaving a recess within. An **oriel window** is a smaller bay window on an upper story and is supported by decorative brackets. A **bow window** is made with curved glass. These window styles are found on Queen Anne, Tudor, and Neo-Eclectic styles.

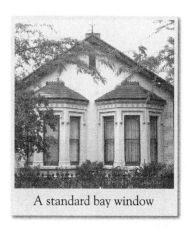

A standard bay window

How Windows Open

Most decorative and picture windows are fixed windows. **Fixed windows** do not open or move at all. **Skylights** are a type of fixed window. Skylights are estimated to let five times more light into a house than another window of the same size. They also add value to the house and help a space to look much larger.

A skylight with glass brick windows

Windows that open have either a traverse sliding mechanism or hinges. **Traverse windows** slide from side to side and are found in Ranch and other modern style houses. Sliding glass doors are simply large, traverse windows. **Single-hung windows** are commonplace in Ranch and modern style houses. The bottom portion slides up. **Double-hung windows** are a traditional style found in all Colonial style houses. Both top and bottom parts move up and down. **Casement windows** have hinges on the sides and are opened with cranks. Dutch Colonial, Craftsman, Tudor, Mission, Ranch, and other modern style houses have casement windows. A French window is actually two casement windows placed side by side. An **awning window** is hinged at the top and opens out. A **transom window** is hinged at the top and opens into the room. A **hopper window** (or eyebrow) is hinged at the bottom and opens into the room. **Jalousie windows** do not slide or use a hinge, instead, they have narrow glass slats like Venetian blinds that are opened and closed with a crank.

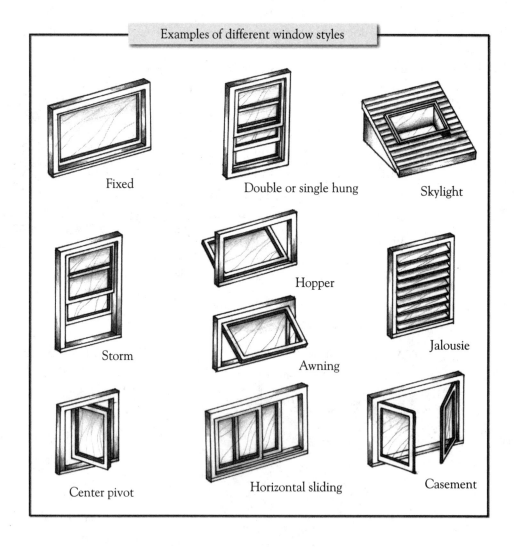

Examples of different window styles

Fixed

Double or single hung

Skylight

Storm

Hopper

Awning

Jalousie

Center pivot

Horizontal sliding

Casement

Doors

Doors come in solid, hollow, or paneled varieties. Typically, exterior doors are solid and interior doors are hollow. A decorative front door with attractive hardware invites a person to enter the house.

Traditional doors are hung with hinges on one side. **French doors** are double doors hinged at either side. **Sliding glass doors** can glide or roll on base tracks. **Pocket doors** can glide or roll on suspended or overhead tracks. Doors have different surfaces as well. They may be flush or level, glazed, paneled, or even louvered.

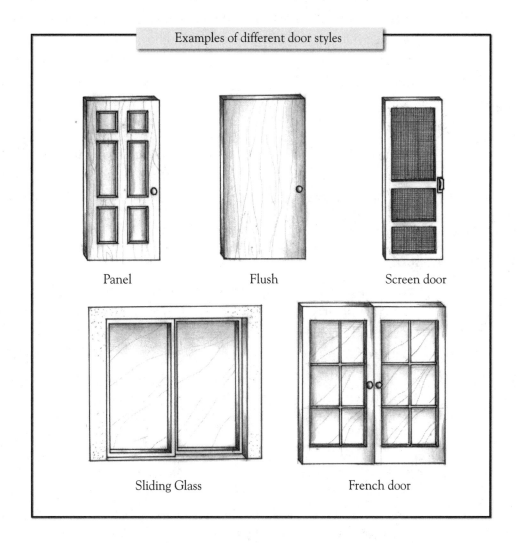

Examples of different door styles

Panel   Flush   Screen door

Sliding Glass   French door

Wall Material (Cladding)

Cladding includes the external protective skin of the exterior surfaces of a home (surface coatings, siding, doors, windows, trim, shutters, entryways, and flashings). The cladding for exterior walls includes surface coatings, such as paint and varnish, and all types of siding, stucco, brick, stone, adobe, concrete, metal panels, and plate glass with steel. The type of cladding chosen for the exterior finish provides clues to the architectural style of the house.

Siding

Siding refers to overlapping horizontal boards made from wood, vinyl, or aluminum that are applied to the house. Sometimes a house has "board and batten" which is an application of vertical boards with joints that are finished by thin vertical strips. Siding is found in a wide variety of styles including Cape Cod, Colonial, Queen Anne, Craftsman, Contemporary, and Ranch.

Shingles

Wood **shingles** are commonly used in combination with wood siding. Shingles can be plain or patterned and vary in shape from rectangular to diamond. Plain shingles are found in Craftsman style houses. Patterned shingles are found in Queen Anne and Tudor styles.

Stucco

Stucco is a mixture of cement, sand, and lime which is applied over a frame construction. It is found in buildings with Spanish or Mediterranean influences, as well as Ranch, Prairie, Art Deco, Art Moderne, and International houses. **Half-timbering** is a method of construction in which the wooden frame and principal beams of a structure are exposed, and the spaces between are filled with stucco, brick, or stone. This is found in Tudor, Craftsman, and Queen Anne styles.

Brick

Bricks are made in a variety of colors, and can be laid in many patterns to create a distinctive and pleasing appearance. **Bricks** are rectangular blocks of clay or shale baked dry by the sun or in a kiln.

Due to earthquake considerations, many houses in California have a brick veneer. Bricks are found in a range of styles, including Colonial, Craftsman, Bungalow, Prairie, and Ranch styles.

Adobe bricks are made with a mixture of clay and straw, formed into brick shapes, and dried in the sun rather than in a kiln. Adobe bricks are larger than standard bricks. Although very energy efficient, they do not withstand earthquakes, which is why you will find this material in Arizona and New Mexico rather than California. Adobe bricks are used in Spanish-Colonial, Monterey, Pueblo, and Santa Fe architectural styles.

Ornamental Details

Architectural style is also defined by the presence or absence of **ornamental details**. For example, a Victorian Queen Anne house has fancy scrollwork and gingerbread trim. However, an International style house made of glass and steel has no ornamentation at all.

Relationship Between Ornamental Details and Architectural Style

Dentil moldings	Federal
Garlands and flowers	Federal
Gingerbread scrollwork	Queen Anne
Little or no ornamentation	Cape Cod, National, International, Ranch, and Modern
Shutters	Cape Cod and other Colonials
Trapezoid porch supports	Craftsman, Prairie, Mission, and American Foursquare
Turned spindles	Queen Anne
Zigzags or chevrons	Art Deco

KNOW THE ARCHITECTURAL STYLES

As a professional real estate sales associate, you should understand the different **architectural styles** of the houses in your area because you will need to describe them in your listings. In some neighborhoods, only a few styles may be present. If the neighborhood is comprised of custom-built houses, a wide variety of architectural styles may be represented.

Trends occur in architecture and interior design as in anything else. As a result, the cute Craftsman in perfect condition may be "in" and sell very quickly, or "out" and you are desperate to find a buyer. In some newer developments, you may see houses that are "influenced" or "inspired" by one of the popular architectural styles such as Victorian, Tudor, Craftsman, or Bungalow. Fortunately, you do not need to know everything about each style, but it would be helpful to know the main style differences between a Victorian, Tudor, Mediterranean, or a Monterey style house.

Cape Cod Style

The twentieth century version of the **Cape Cod** style house is usually rectangular-shaped, one to one-and-one-half stories, and has a steeply pitched gable roof with a small overhang. Some Cape Cod houses also have small gable dormers. The roof is wood shingles and the exterior is wood siding or  stucco. The multi-paned windows with ornamental wood shutters are symmetrically placed on both sides of the front door. Masonry chimneys are usually located at the side. Aside from shutters, this style has very little ornamentation and no front porch. The garage is detached and placed at the back of the lot.

During the mid 1900s, the uncomplicated, rectangular-shaped Cape Cod was economically mass-produced in suburban areas. The upsurge in popularity was due to the return of service men and women from World War II who were able to purchase these houses with government guaranteed loans. Sometimes these houses were called the GI (Government Issued) houses.

Colonial Styles

Colonial styles are rectangular, symmetrical, two to two-and-one-half story houses with windows arranged in an orderly fashion around a central front door. Living areas are on the first floor, with bedrooms on the second floor. The windows usually have many small, equally sized square panes and decorative shutters. Typically, roofs are hip or gable.

Colonial style houses were popular in the 1600s and experienced a revival of interest in the 1900s, which led to the name Colonial Revival.

Colonial Revival

In 1876, the **Colonial Revival** style became popular after it appeared at the U.S. Centennial Exposition and it remained so until the mid-1950s. In the 1920s and 1930s, the Colonial Revival was the most popular revival house style in the United States.

These houses are large, with two or more stories. They feature wood exteriors with tall wood columns that are typically painted bright white with dark green or black shutters. On occasion, this type of house may have a brick exterior. Colonial Revival houses are known for their graceful symmetry and elegant center entry hall.

Georgian Colonial Revival

The **Georgian** style, with its formal, symmetrical lines, was favored by the well-to-do and became a symbol of the owner's financial standing in the community. It has paired chimneys (one on each side) and five windows across the front of the second story.

Regency

The **Regency** style is very similar to the Georgian except it has an octagonal window over the front door, double-hung windows, and a chimney on the far left or right side of the house.

Federal

The **Federal** style is similar to the Georgian except it has more ornamentation, dentil moldings, decorative garlands, Palladian-style windows, and fanlights.

Dutch Colonial Revival

Like all of the colonial styles, the **Dutch Colonial Revival** houses are one to two-and-one-half stories with shed-like dormers. They are easily identified by a distinctive gambrel roof. The front door may be a **Dutch door**, which is a horizontally divided double door.

Spanish Colonial Revival

Typical to the colonial style, the **Spanish Colonial Revival** houses are rectangular, symmetrical, and two stories high. They have low-pitched gable roofs with ceramic tiles, eaves with little or no overhang, stucco walls, wrought iron, and windows and doorways with round arches.

Victorian Styles

The term **"Victorian"** describes many styles built between the 1830s and early 1900s. For the first time since the beginning of the Industrial Revolution, machines could mass-produce affordable, ornamental building materials such as moldings, columns, brackets, spindles, and patterned shingles. As

a result, architects and builders eagerly incorporated the elaborate bric-a-brac, excessive gingerbread, trim work, and other ornamentation in Victorian style houses. Although the last true Victorian houses were built in the early 1900s, contemporary builders borrow Victorian ideas, creating "Neo-Victorians". Three more popular Victorian styles are the Second Empire, Queen Anne, and Folk Victorian.

Second Empire (Mansard)

Second Empire style houses were inspired by Parisian designs during the reign of Napoleon III. The houses are symmetrical, boxy, vertical, and two-to-three stories. Typical ornamentation includes paired columns and elaborate wrought iron along the rooftop. However, the most striking feature is the high, boxy mansard roof. The mansard roof has a trapezoid shape. It slopes almost straight up to the top, where it abruptly flattens. The boxy roof shape allows more usable living space in the upper story. The windows are tall and

narrow with no shutters. The exterior walls are usually stucco, brick, or wood siding.

Queen Anne

When people think of a Victorian house, they usually picture the highly imaginative and elaborate **Queen Anne** style. During the second half of the 19th century, for the first time, emerging middle-class homeowners had access to affordable, mass-produced finished windows, doors, turned spindles, brackets, and decorative scrollwork. Prior to the advanced manufacturing techniques, these decorative ornamental details were a luxury that only wealthy people could afford. The builders used every conceivable manufactured ornamental trim that was available to create these elaborate styles.

The houses were built with multiple stories with projecting wings, a complicated roof line with very steep cross-gabled roofs, towers, turrets, vertical windows and balconies, multiple chimneys with decorative chimney pots, scrollwork, bric-a-brac, gingerbread, and gingerbread with frosting. A

chimney pot is a round or octagonal "pot" on the top of each flue. Queen Anne style houses usually have several wide porches with turned posts and decorative railings. The wood siding is painted white or pastel with contrasting trim and it probably has a round tower or enormous round bay windows.

Folk Victorian

The **Folk Victorian** style is the affordable version of the Queen Anne house. They are asymmetrical, rectangular, or L-shaped, with white wood siding, steep gabled roofs, and a front porch with turned spindles. They are adorned with flat jigsaw cut trim in a variety of shapes and patterns.

These practical houses are found in small towns and on farms across the United States. Today, the farmhouse style is characterized by a rectangular or boxy, two-story shape with a steep gabled or cross-gabled roof. Most have siding, shutters, and the distinctive wraparound porch with turned spindles, jigsaw cut trim, and brackets under the eaves.

Bungalow Styles

Bungalows are one of the most common houses found in older neighborhoods and are characterized by simplicity and emphasis on horizontal rather than vertical lines.

The economical bungalow started on the East Coast, became popular in California, and quickly spread across the nation. In fact, between 1890 and the mid-1900s, they became so popular that Sears, Roebuck & Co., and Montgomery Ward offered mail-order pre-cut "kit" houses that were assembled at the building site. Before World War I, a small bungalow could be built for $900, while a much larger one cost about $3,500. Because they were so affordable, the bungalow symbolized homeownership to thousands of people.

These homes were ideal for the first-time homebuyer—small, inexpensive to build, and often included built-in furniture. The living room fireplace was usually large with a mantel and surrounds of brick, natural stone, or tiles. These features created a warm, homey atmosphere.

Different Styles of Bungalows

As the bungalow style spread across the United States, regional designers—Charles and Henry Greene in California and Gustav Stickley and Frank Lloyd Wright in Chicago—created variations to the style. Gustav Stickley is known for the Craftsman style and Frank Lloyd Wright is known for the

Prairie style. In California, it is typical to see bungalows with Craftsman lines or in a Spanish Colonial motif. In Chicago, bungalows are mostly brick and boxy with Prairie influences.

The bungalow style remains one of the most popular styles even today and can be seen influencing new residential developments.

California Bungalow

The Greene brothers helped popularize the **California Bungalow** and inspired other architects and designers to build simple one-and-one-half story bungalows. The California Bungalow has a low profile, with one to one-and-one-half stories, a square shape, with a low slung gable or hip roof, an offset entry with a wide front porch, and exterior walls finished with stucco and natural stone. These smaller, affordable bungalows were very popular between 1900 and the mid-1920s. Currently, this look is incorporated into modern houses.

Craftsman Bungalow

The **Craftsman Bungalow**, promoted by Gustav Stickley in his magazine, *The Craftsman*, has a tendency to be larger than the traditional California Bungalow. Other differences include rows of high, small "ribbon" windows, full-width porches framed by tapered columns, and overhanging eaves with exposed rafters. Stickley was a furniture designer and most of his plans for Craftsman Bungalows included built-in furniture throughout the house, such as kitchen cabinets, window seats, and buffets in

Traditional Craftsman Bungalow

Modern Craftsman Bungalow

dining rooms. Partial walls with bookshelves are frequently used as room dividers, as are chest-high cabinets topped by square, tapered pillars that reach to the ceiling. Leaded glass and stained glass in doors, cabinets, and windows are typically seen. The overall feeling is one of casual comfort.

Prairie Style

The **Prairie** style, designed by Frank Lloyd Wright and other Chicago architects, is an extension of the bungalow design in many ways, but it is much more expensive to build.

The Prairie style houses are much larger than the Craftsman Bungalows and are designed with low horizontal lines that require larger lots. They have low-pitched hip roofs with large overhanging eaves, casement windows, and rows of small, high windows. Due to the complexity of the designs, these houses require on-site architects and experienced builders. As a result, they are not marketed as pre-cut "kits" and are built primarily for the wealthier clientele.

American Foursquare

Although the Prairie style is very popular in the Midwest, a sub-style—the **American Foursquare**—has become one of the most common housing styles in the United States.

An updated version of an American Foursquare house

This practical style, based on the Prairie style, is sometimes called the **Prairie Box**. It is a very simple, space-efficient box shape, with a wide porch across the entire front of the house. The front door is centered with matching casement windows on either side. The pyramid-shaped hip roof has a large dormer centered in the front of the house.

Because they are symmetrical and uncomplicated, they were easier to build and cost less than the more complicated Victorians. This was another style sold by Sears, Roebuck & Co. as a mail order pre-cut "kit" house. Sears even sold a machine that could make the cement blocks on site that were used in the construction. This resulted in the American Foursquare spreading to residential neighborhoods throughout the United States. This style may still be found in older neighborhoods.

USonian

During the Depression, Frank Lloyd Wright modified the Prairie style to create a more affordable house, which he called **USonian**. They cost much less to build because they had no basements or attics and very little ornamentation. USonian style houses were built from the Depression until the mid 1950s. They became the model for early tract housing.

Period Styles

Period styles get their inspiration from the architectural styles of the past. In the early half of the 20th century, the trend was toward historical interpretations of European styles. Many styles existed, but seven period styles were very popular throughout the country.

Monterey

The first two-story **Monterey** style was built in 1853 when Thomas Larkin designed a house that blended the English Colonial with the single-story Spanish Colonial style, which was then prevalent in Monterey. The most distinguishing feature of the Monterey style is the second-story balcony on

the front of the house. The overhanging balcony creates a shaded, protected entry. These houses often have a courtyard and wrought iron trim and fencing. The roof is a shallow pitched gable or hipped roof with red tiles or wood shakes. Windows are often tall and in pairs with false shutters.

Mission

Since the **Mission** style house originated in California, the style is often called the California Mission style. These houses are easily recognized by the round parapets on the roof that resemble those found on early Spanish colonial churches. A **parapet** is a low wall projecting from the edge of a platform, terrace, or roof. They are one to two stories, rectangular shaped, and have flat roofs with red tile accents. The exterior walls are adobe or smooth stucco. Most Mission style houses have arched windows and a small courtyard entry with an arched front door. Some Mission style homes have quatrefoil (four-petal) decorative windows, an arcade style (multiple arches) entry porch, square or twisted columns on the second story, and even a bell tower.

Santa Fe

The thick, earth-colored adobe walls and flat roofs with rounded parapets of the **Santa Fe** style make these houses look chunky, but they are suitable

for hot, dry climates. Because of the thickness of the walls, the windows and heavy wooden doors are set into deep openings. Sometimes red clay tile accents on the roof and enclosed patios add a Spanish influence.

Another version of the Santa Fe is the **Pueblo Revival** style. This style is characterized by roof beams, called **vigas**, which protrude through the walls and help support the roof.

Typical of the **Territorial** style is a more angular look, with square corners replacing the round corners of the Santa Fe style. In addition, the windows of the Territorial style are framed with straight, unpainted, wooden moldings and brick detailing is present in the parapets.

Spanish Revival

California houses are influenced by a variety of Spanish styles, such as a two-story house with a Monterey style balcony, Mission style parapets,

Mediterranean style arches and tile roofs, or Pueblo-inspired rounded walls and flat roofs. Typically, the **Spanish Revival** will have red-tiled roofs, stucco siding, arched entryways and windows, and decorative tiles by the windows and doors.

Tudor Revival

The traditional **English Tudor** is a large, two-story masonry or stucco, steep-gabled house with a definite medieval feel. The **Elizabethan (Tudor Revival)** variation of this style is asymmetrical, has a very steep cross-gabled roof, a prominent chimney, and half-timbered exteriors. Both styles are characterized by patterned brick or stone walls, rounded doorways, and multi-paned casement windows. Inside, Tudor houses have intricate wood paneling or moldings. They feature arched entries, projecting oriel windows on the second floor, and large leaded-glass windows with stone mullions. Another characteristic is the massive chimney placed in a prominent location and often topped with a decorative chimney pot.

Initially, only very wealthy people could afford to build these large, elaborate mansions. They are expensive to build because of the various features such as the complex roof system with various gables of alternating heights, dormers, and large sculpted brick chimneys. However, many suburban houses are built today with Tudor influences, which make them accessible to mainstream America.

English (Cotswold) Country Cottage

The **English Cottage** style is patterned after the rustic cottages constructed in the Cotswold region of southwestern England since medieval times. Like their Tudor cousins, they are asymmetrical with an uneven sloping roof of slate or cedar that mimics the look of thatch. The exterior may have brick, stone, or stucco with half-timbering. The multi-pane casement windows and low entry door help create a cozy feeling. Many homes have a prominently placed chimney made of brick or stone.

French-Influenced Styles

Soldiers returning after World War I helped kindle an interest in French housing styles. French-inspired houses have some design elements in common, including distinctive hipped roofs with flared eaves, dormers, and multi-paned windows. In many French style houses, the tall second story windows break through the cornice and rise above the eaves. Some French style houses also have decorative half-timbering, and a round tower with an arched doorway as the entrance.

French Provincial

French Provincial style houses are large, square, symmetrical two-story houses with a distinctive steep, high, hip roof. The exterior is usually white brick or stucco. Windows and chimneys are symmetrical and perfectly balanced.

Frequently, tall second floor windows break through the cornice. They have balcony and porch balustrades; rectangular doors set in arched openings; and double French windows with shutters. Unlike French Normandy houses, French Provincial houses do not have towers.

French Normandy

The main characteristic of **French Normandy** style is the round stone tower topped with a cone-shaped roof. Sometimes the tower is the entrance to the house. In addition, vertical half-timbering (reminiscent of the Tudor style) adds height to the house. Unlike a Tudor, French Normandy houses have hip roofs, not cross-gabled roofs. The houses use stone, stucco, or brick as siding.

Modern Styles

In the early 1900s, some architects tiring of the excesses of the Victorian styles, looked to the future for their inspiration. Their concept of the future included clean lines, smooth surfaces, and little or no ornamentation. This resulted in the Art Deco, Art Moderne, and International styles.

Architects continued this trend, designing comfortable and practical houses that were affordable and relatively easy to build. These houses were purchased by returning World War II Veterans as quickly as the developers could build them. These styles included the California Ranch, Split-level, A-frame, Contemporary, Shed, and Mediterranean.

Art Deco

The **Art Deco** style is two or more stories and emphasizes the vertical lines of the house. It is angular and boxy with a flat roof and simple, clean, crisp lines. Glass blocks, metals, plastics, and other machine-made materials are used extensively. The walls are smooth texture stucco or stone. Geometric designs such as zigzags, chevrons, diamonds, and sunbursts are arranged in horizontal bands and painted or cut out near the roof line.

Art Moderne

The **Art Moderne** style is the precursor of future house design, displaying  extreme simplicity. It has a horizontal, cube-like shape with a flat roof and rounded corners. The exterior walls are smooth stucco with rounded corners. Casement windows are evenly spaced. Other than the use of glass brick, there is little or no ornamentation. Window and door trim and balustrades are made from polished aluminum and stainless steel.

International

The **International** style is modern, asymmetrical, and very practical in its use of concrete, glass, and steel to create sleek lines. With a flat roof and floor-to-ceiling "window walls", the design is avant-garde.

Ranch

Since its debut in San Diego in 1932, the **Ranch** style house, sometimes called the **California Ranch**, has become the most popular style in the country. Because Ranch style houses are found throughout the United States in suburban tracts, some critics say they have "no style". However, this practical, informal, comfortable style obviously is popular with many Americans. Today, the eclectic Ranch style is influenced by other styles such as Tudor, Colonial, Mediterranean, and Bungalow.

Ranch style houses are one-story, rambling, rectangular, L-shaped or U-shaped, with a low-pitch gable or hipped roof, attached garage, stucco, wood, or brick exterior walls, picture windows, and sliding doors leading to patios. Due to the horizontal nature of the style, these houses need wide lots.

Split-Level Ranch

The **Split-Level Ranch** or Raised Ranch is a variation of the Ranch style. Instead of just a one-level floor plan, split-levels usually have three levels at varying heights. The **mid-level entry** has stairs leading to the other two

levels. The upper level is used for sleeping areas; the mid-level has the living room, dining room, and kitchen, while the lower level has the family room, hobby or game rooms, laundry area, and the garage. These houses are asymmetrical, with a rectangular, L-shaped, or U-shaped design. The low-pitched roof may be hipped or gabled. Any siding may be used, but the most common is stucco or wood siding with brick or rock trim. A variety of window types are used, including single-hung, picture, and sliding glass doors that lead to patios. Some houses have decorative shutters. Newer houses may have features from almost any other architectural style.

A-Frame

The **A-frame** style, introduced in 1957 by the architect Andrew Geller, is ideal for cold, snowy regions. Instead of piling up on top of the roof, the snow slides down the steep slope of the A-frame roof. The triangular-shaped roof has deep-set eaves and goes all the way to the ground on two sides of the house. The large picture windows and doors are situated at the front and back of the house.

Contemporary

Contemporary style houses are characterized by attractive, simple, clean lines and the combination of stone, glass, masonry, and wood in the exterior.

These asymmetrical houses can be one or more stories with a roof that is flat or very low-pitched. Windows are often an odd shape because they follow the roof line. Sometimes the roof extends from a higher level down over a lower level. Ornamentation is simple with a verticalorientation.

Shed

The **Shed** style is another modern style characterized by its asymmetrical style and multiple roofs sloping in different directions. Typically, exterior walls are stucco or wood, with small windows and recessed doorways.

Mediterranean

One of the most common styles found in Southern California is the blend of the Italian, Moorish, Byzantine, and the early California mission styles to create a **Mediterranean** style. This style is very popular in all price ranges and house sizes. Look for white or light-colored stucco on the exterior and a red tiled gable roof with very little or no overhanging eaves. Additional features include arched doorways and windows, courtyard entrances, patios, ornamental tile, and wrought iron ornamentation.

This is a single story Ranch with Mediterranean influences (low pitch, red tile roof, arched, recessed entry to resemble a courtyard).

This house has a red tile roof and stucco as seen in the Mediterranean style.

This house exemplifies the mixed look of the Mediterranean style.

Postmodern Styles

As we have seen, housing styles continuously change. In the late 1970s, architects and developers moved away from the Modern style with its clean lines and lack of ornamentation. They became interested in traditional styles to gain inspiration for new developments. Most houses built since the late 1970s do not fall into a single category. Instead, designers and builders incorporate decorative details and features from many of the previous historic styles. Sometimes only one style is used to influence the house. Other times, the ideas are taken from more than one architectural source and create an eclectic mixture that is difficult to categorize. Whether one or more features are chosen, the result alludes to, but does not mimic, the historic styles. These styles are called Postmodern or Neo-Eclectic. Neo means new and eclectic refers to combining a variety of details from different styles to produce a harmonious look.

Some critics are not pleased with the mix and match Neo-Eclectic look, and describe these houses as oversized, pretentious, and without style. These houses do have a style, but it is not a traditional, set style.

Today, homeowners are still attracted to the traditional Colonial style. Builders combine the classic, clean lines of the Colonial with modern building materials and contemporary floor plans to create comfortable houses. A new two-story, rectangular-shaped house with gabled roofs, and vinyl or brick veneer siding, symmetrically placed windows, and decorative shutters is

The large front porch of the house is reminiscent of the Folk Victorian farm-house. The balanced symmetry of the facade and shutters are borrowed from the Colonial style.

reminiscent of the Colonial style. These new Colonials may borrow the wide porches from Queen Anne or Bungalow styles as well.

If a new house has an asymmetrical shape, very steep gabled roofs, and curved towers, it has Victorian or Tudor influences. Comfortable country homes are frequently a combination of Victorian Cottage, California Bungalow, and Ranch styles.

Housing styles continue to be inspired by French details such as the mansard roof, French doors, and wrought iron balconies that extend across the entire second story.

ASSIGNING A STYLE TO A HOUSE

Sometimes it is easy to assign a specific architectural style to a house, and sometimes it can be a challenge. The purpose of learning the different architectural styles and their components is so that you will be able to describe a property when you advertise a listing. In addition, you will be able to paint verbal pictures to prospective buyers to help them envision properties they might like to see.

You may have older houses or custom-built houses that are exact examples of the architectural styles. However, it is more likely that you will see houses that have features commonly found in those styles. For example, a house may have a gable roof and shutters as in the Cape Cod style, Queen Anne flourishes, Tudor detailing, or Mediterranean accents.

Try to determine which style is described in the example below. Remember, the components of architectural style (roofs, dormers, windows, doors, siding, and ornamental details) combine to create the entire architectural style of a house.

Example: If a seller described his or her house as a two-story, rectangular shape, with a symmetrical facade you would be able to eliminate any styles that are asymmetrical (Queen Anne, Tudor, French Normandy, Contemporary). However, from this information alone, can you tell which style it is? Probably not, so you would ask the seller for more details. You find out that it has a low gable roof, shutters, and virtually no exterior ornamentation. Still not enough information? The seller says the house is stucco and the roof has red tile accents. This information tells you that the house is Spanish or Mediterranean style... but which is it? Finally, the seller says the house has a second-story balcony. With that last piece of information, you know that the style in question is a Monterey or a Monterey-inspired house.

SUMMARY

Trends occur in architecture and interior design as in anything else. As a result, the houses in your neighborhoods will reflect these trends. In order to list and show property you must know the neighborhoods in your area. Whether the homes and amenities in each neighborhood are older, newer, custom-built, or tract-built, buyers have preferences regarding the neighborhood they choose. Older neighborhoods have mature landscaping, established businesses, and amenities. Newer neighborhoods have larger houses with updated floor plans and desirable amenities. In addition, the houses are built with safer materials and are energy efficient. In order to help buyers choose the neighborhood that best suits them, you need to know the neighborhoods in your community.

Architectural styles are defined by the number of stories, the shape of the house, the type of roof, dormers, windows, doors, siding, and ornamental details. As a professional real estate sales associate, you need to know about the different **architectural styles** of the houses in your area in order to describe them in your listings. In the United States, five basic types of housing exist. They are one-story, one-and-one-half story, two-story, split-level, and multiple-story houses.

The chart on the next two pages summarizes architectural styles you may find in real estate listings.

Housing Styles Quick Reference Guide

Architectural Style	No. Stories	Shape of House	Symmetrical	Roof Style	Roof Pitch	Cladding	Windows	Ornate	Special Features	Courtyard or Porch Entry
A-frame	1 to 2 1/2	Vertical, A-shaped	Yes	Gable	Very Steep	Wood, Shingles	Picture	No		Extension of Roofline Covers
American Foursquare	2 to 2 1/2	Boxy	Yes	Hip	Low	Stucco, Wood, Brick	Symmetrical Casement Windows	No	Large, Centered Dormer	Wide Porch Across Front
Art Deco	2 to 2 1/2	Vertical, Rectangular	Yes	Flat	Flat	Smooth Stucco	Square, Rectangular	No	Zigzags, Chevrons Glass Blocks	
Art Moderne	1 to 1 1/2	Square With Rounded Corners	No	Flat	Flat, No Overhang	Smooth Stucco	Evenly Spaced Casement Windows	No	Glass Blocks, Plastics, Metals	
Bungalow California	1 to 1 1/2	Boxy	No	Gable, Hip	Very Low	Wood, Brick, Stone	Square, Rectangular	No		Wide Porch Across Front
Bungalow Craftsman	1 to 1 1/2	Rectangular	No	Gable, Hip	Very Low	Wood, Brick, Stone	Ribbon	No	Exposed Rafters	Trapezoid Porch Supports
Cape Cod	1 to 1 1/2	Rectangular	Yes	Gable	Very Steep	Stucco, Wood	Multi-Paneled	No	Shutters	
Colonial – Dutch	1 1/2 to 2 1/2	Rectangular	Yes	Gambrel	Moderate	Wood, Brick	Square, Rectangular	No	Dutch Door	
Colonial – Georgian	2 to 2 1/2	Rectangular	Yes	Gable, Hip	Moderate	Wood, Brick	5 ranked	No	Paired Chimneys	
Colonial – Revival	2	Rectangular	Yes	Gable, Hip	Moderate	Wood, Brick	Square, Rectangular	No	Shutters	
Contemporary	1 to Multiple	Mixture of shapes	No	Flat, Shed	Flat, Very Low	Stucco, Concrete Wood, Brick	Triangle or Trapezoid	No	Simple Clean Lines	
English Cottage	1 to 1 1/2	Boxy	No	Gable	Uneven, Sloping	Stucco	Diamond Paned	No	Rustic, Thatch-Look Roof	Arched Entry With Low Door
French Normandy	2 to 2 1/2	Rectangular	No	Hip	Very Steep	Stucco, Brick, Stone	Square, Rectangular	No	Round Stone Tower With Cone-Shaped Roof	Sometimes Tower Is Entrance
French Provincial	2 to 2 1/2	Rectangular	Yes	Hip	Very Steep, No Overhang	White Stucco or Brick	French Windows	No	Balcony, Porch Balustrades	
International	Multiple	Boxy	No	Flat	Flat, No Overhang	Stucco, Concrete Steel	Floor to Ceiling "Window Walls"	No	Avant-Garde Sleek Lines	
Mediterranean	1 to 2	Multiple Rectangles	No	Gable, Hip, Red Tile	Low to Moderate, Slight Overhang	Light-Colored Stucco	Arched Palladian	Moderate	Decorative Tiles, Wrought Iron	Arched Doorways, Courtyard Entrance

Housing Styles Quick Reference Guide (Continued)

Architectural Style	No. Stories	Shape of House	Symmetrical	Roof Style	Roof Pitch	Cladding	Windows	Ornate	Special Features	Courtyard or Porch Entry
Mission	1 to 2	Rectangular	No	Flat, Red Tile	Flat	Adobe, Smooth, Stucco	Arched, Quatrefoil	Yes	Parapets, Bell Tower	Enclosed Courtyard
Monterey	2	Rectangular	Yes	Gable, Red Tile	Low	Adobe, Stucco	Narrow Paired	No	Second Story Balcony	Courtyard Wrought Iron Trim and Fencing
Prairie Style	1 to 1 1/2	Horizontal Rectangular	No	Hip	Very Low	Stucco, Wood, Brick	Rows of Small, High Windows	No	Large Overhanging Eves	Trapezoid Porch Supports
Pueblo/Santa Fe	1	Rectangular With Rounded Corners	Often	Flat, Red Tile	Flat	Adobe, Stucco	Small Paned, Palladian	No	Vigas	Low Adobe Wall Encloses Courtyard
Ranch	1	Horizontal, L-shaped, Rectangular	No	Gable, Hip	Very Low	Stucco, Wood, Brick	Picture	No	Attached Garage	Extension of Roofline Covers Small Front Porch
Shed	2	Rectangular	No	Shed	Moderate	Stucco, Wood	Small	No	Multiple Roofs Sloping in Different Directions	Recessed Doorway
Spanish Revival	1	Rectangular	No	Gable, Red Tile	Low	Stucco	Arched	No	Decorative Tiles Around Doors and Windows	Arched Entryway
Tudor Revival	Multiple	Rectangular	No	Cross Gable With Dormers	Very Steep	Half-Timbering, Patterned Brick Walls	Diamond Paned	Yes	Prominent Chimney	Arched Entryway
Victorian – 2nd Empire	Multiple	Boxy	Yes	Mansard	Very Steep Sides With Flat Top	Stucco, Wood, Brick	Tall and Narrow	Yes	Wrought Iron On Rooftop	Paired Columns
Victorian – Folk	1 to 2 1/2	L-shaped	No	Cross-Gable	Steep	Wood	Bay	Moderate	Shutters, Spindles, Jigsaw Cut Trim	Distinctive Porch
Victorian – Queen Anne	Multiple	Complicated	No	Gable, Hip	Very Steep	Shingles	Narrow, Vertical Circular, Bay	Very	Gingerbread Scrollwork	Wide, Wraparound Porch

UNIT 4 REVIEW

▢ Matching Exercise

Instructions: Write the letter of the matching term on the blank line before its definition. Answers are in Appendix A.

Terms

A. amenities

B. casement windows

C. cladding

D. dormers

E. Dutch doors

F. floor plan

G. French doors

H. glazing

I. jalousie windows

J. "kit" houses

K. Mansard roofs

L. Palladian windows

M. pitch

N. Postmodern

Definitions

1. _____ Glass panes used in windows and doors

2. _____ Steepness of a roof

3. _____ Roof with almost vertical sides and a flat top

4. _____ Vertical window set in a framed window unit that projects from a sloping roof

5. _____ Window that is divided into three parts, with rectangular panes on each side of a wide arch

6. _____ Windows with hinges on the sides, and opened with cranks

7. _____ Double doors that are hinged at either side

8. _____ Any protective finish material applied to the exterior surface of the house

9. _____ A horizontally divided double door

10. _____ Mail-order pre-cut houses that were assembled at the building site

▪ Multiple Choice Questions

Instructions: Circle your response and go to Appendix A to read the complete explanation for each question.

1. The selling points for houses in new neighborhoods include:
   a. larger floor plans.
   b. energy efficiency.
   c. being built to stringent safety codes.
   d. all of the above.

2. A buyer who is interested in conserving energy would want which of the following features in a house?
   a. Dual or triple-glazed windows
   b. Energy Star® appliances
   c. Increased insulation in walls and roofs
   d. All of the above

3. A _____ roof is pitched with two sloping sides.
   a. hip
   b. gambrel
   c. gable
   d. mansard

4. Several rectangular windows placed in a row with their frames abutting are called:
   a. sidelights.
   b. ribbon windows.
   c. oriel windows.
   d. bay windows.

5. Which popular style of house was called the G.I. house?
   a. Cape Cod
   b. Colonial
   c. Queen Anne
   d. Mediterranean

6. The most distinctive feature of the Georgian style is the:

   a. mansard roof.

   b. gambrel roof and Dutch doors.

   c   diamond-paned windows and half-timbering.

   d. five symmetrical windows across the front of the second story.

7. When people think of a Victorian house, they usually picture the highly imaginative, ornate, and elaborate_____ style.

   a. Bungalow

   b. Queen Anne

   c. International

   d. Mediterranean

8. Which style is described as having a low profile, with one to one-and-one-half stories, a square shape, a low-slung gabled roof, an offset entry with a wide front porch, rows of high, small "ribbon" windows, and built-in furniture included throughout the house?

   a. Craftsman Bungalow

   b. Art Deco

   c. Folk Victorian

   d. Ranch

9. The second-story balcony on the front of the house is the most distinguishing feature of the_____ style.

   a. French Normandy

   b. Craftsman

   c. Monterey

   d. Ranch

10. Which style is a blend of Italian, Moorish, Byzantine, and early California mission influences?

   a. Monterey

   b. Mediterranean

   c. Mission

   d. Santa Fe

11. Which style is described as a large, two-story masonry or stucco, steep-gabled house with a definite medieval feel? It is asymmetrical, has a very steep cross-gabled roof, a prominent chimney, and half-timbered exteriors.

    a. Cape Cod

    b. Spanish Colonial

    c. Art Moderne

    d. Tudor Revival

12. The main characteristic of French Normandy style is the:

    a. floor-to-ceiling "window walls".

    b. the five symmetrical windows across the front of the second story.

    c. red tiled gable roof with very little or no overhanging eaves.

    d. round stone tower topped with a cone-shaped roof.

13. Painted geometric designs such as zigzags, chevrons, diamonds, and sunbursts are a characteristic of the _____ style.

    a. Art Moderne

    b. Art Deco

    c. International

    d. A-frame

14. The _____ style is the most popular style in the U.S. since its debut in 1932.

    a. Cape Cod

    b. Craftsman

    c. Shed

    d. Ranch

15. Post modern is also known as:

    a. Colonial

    b. Tudor

    c. Mediterranean

    d. Neo-Eclectic

Completing the Seller's Forms

Unit 5

INTRODUCTION

Real estate transactions require a variety of forms. As a new licensee, you need to know which forms to use when obtaining a listing or writing an offer. In addition, you must know how to fill out and explain the paperwork used when dealing with sellers or buyers including agency disclosures, listings and sales contracts, and other disclosure forms. The more you know, the more you should earn.

This unit focuses on the seller's forms and disclosures. Unit 6 will cover the buyer's forms and disclosures. A case study is presented at the beginning of this unit, and the remainder of the unit provides examples of all the forms that you, as a salesperson, will use. The example forms have been filled out based on this unit's case study.

Learning Objectives

After reading this unit, you should be able to:

- identify the common forms included in a Seller Listing Package.
- name the steps in disclosing agency relationships.
- complete typical seller forms.
- recall the importance of real estate property disclosures.

CASE STUDY

The information in this case study is used to complete the typical seller's forms covered in this unit.

The Sellers

The Spring Family

Fred and Jan Spring own a single-family detached home in the Hillside Ranch subdivision located at 1652 Hill Street, Any City, Apple County, California 90000. The property's legal description is Lot 2 of Block 30 of Hillside Ranch, as shown on page 875 of book 465, records of Apple County. The assessor's parcel number is PQ9856.

The seller's telephone number is (555) 321-9876. Fred's e-mail is fred@speedy.xyz and Jan's e-mail is jan@speedy.xyz.

Since it is part of a planned community with common areas, the Springs currently pay $209 monthly as homeowners' association dues. The annual property taxes are $3,360 and are paid current by the seller. The current loan balance on the property is $155,485.00.

Due to a change in his career, Fred Spring and his family will be selling their home and moving to another state. Because they are moving out-of-state, they decided to include the side-by-side refrigerator and gas range in the sale.

Based on the amount other homes sold for in their neighborhood, Fred and Jan think theirs should sell for about $435,000.

Seller's Broker

Pat Green is a sales associate working for Tom Baker who is the broker-owner of Sunshine Real Estate. Sunshine Real Estate is located at 1234 Mountain Road, Any City, CA 90000. The phone number is 555-123-4567, fax is 555-123-4568, and the e-mail is baker@sunshinere.xyz. Pat wants to get a listing on the Springs' home. Pat is familiar with the homes in the Hillside Ranch area and has had many recent sales in the area. In fact, there is a strong demand for homes in this neighborhood, because over 95% of the homes are owner-occupied. Most homes here sell within two to five months. Before going to the listing appointment, Pat prepared a competitive market analysis (CMA) for the Springs, which indicated the recent sales activity in the area. Pat will use this information to help the Springs set an appropriate listing price.

Hillside Ranch has 150 single-family homes ranging in value from $350,000 to $450,000, with an average sales price of $425,000. After researching recent sales and current market activity, Pat determined that the Spring's home should list for $410,000 to $425,000. Since the Springs need to move as soon as possible, they decide to give the broker, Tom Baker, a 3-month listing on their home for $415,000 with a 6% commission. As an additional incentive, the Springs will pay Tom an additional 1% if he brings in an offer for the exact terms of the listing and closes within 30 days of the listing date. Since the home is in excellent condition, they decide to limit the amount they will pay for minor repairs not to exceed $1,000.

Remember, the Springs have an agency relationship with the broker, Tom Baker, not the salesperson, Pat Green. Pat is representing Tom. Tom is the broker and he will get the commission when escrow closes. Tom, in turn, will pay Pat Green his commission based on their agreed-upon commission split.

Description of the Property

The 1,750 square foot home, built in 1990, is in excellent condition. It has four bedrooms, two full baths, living room, formal dining room, kitchen, and a family room off the kitchen. The unfinished attic is accessible from the master bedroom closet.

The Spring's house measures 50 feet wide by 35 feet deep. It is located on a cul-de-sac lot measuring 70 feet by 160 feet, which is average for the neighborhood. Although some homes in Hillside Ranch have wonderful views of the valley, this home has no appreciable view.

Property Features

- Gas range
- Side-by-side refrigerator
- Built-in dishwasher
- Garbage disposal
- Aluminum gutters and downspouts (good condition)
- Washer/dryer hookups
- Smoke detectors
- Gas central forced-air furnace
- Central air conditioning
- Concrete and brick patio (25 feet wide by 15 feet deep)
- Fully fenced backyard with concrete block wall
- In-ground, heated spa. Currently the solar spa heater needs to be repaired and it has no locking safety cover.
- Attached two-car garage, with 220 volt wiring and poured concrete driveway.
- Public utilities: gas, sewer, water, electricity
- Exhaust fans in kitchen and bathrooms (good condition)
- Aluminum-framed window screens (fair condition). Three screens are missing and the frame of the back screen door is bent.
- Stone-faced, gas-fired fireplace located in the living room. The Springs have not used it in over a year and do not know its current condition.
- Concrete tile roof surface (excellent condition)
- Concrete slab foundation (excellent condition)
- Exterior walls are painted stucco (excellent condition)
- Dual-pane windows with aluminum framing (good condition)
- Interior walls are painted drywall with standard painted molding and trim (good condition)
- Floors consist of vinyl flooring and wall-to-wall carpeting (both in excellent condition)
- Water heater in garage (not anchored or braced)

The seller is not aware of any physical deficiencies or adverse conditions that would affect the value of this property. The property is not located in a FEMA Special Flood Hazard Area. The property complies with its zoning classification of R-1-10000 (single-family residential with a minimum lot size of 10,000 square feet).

Neighborhood Information

Hillside Ranch is comprised of single-family detached homes with several parks and common areas. An elementary school and a junior high school are located one mile south of the subdivision, and the high school is less than three miles west. Several houses of worship are located within one mile of the neighborhood. Several small retail centers are located in  the community, with larger centers located within a five-mile radius. The public, asphalt streets are typical for the area. Freeway access is three miles south, allowing for greater privacy and seclusion. Public transportation is available along the major thoroughfares that run through the neighborhood.

AGENCY RELATIONSHIPS AND DISCLOSURE

Every agency relationship has a principal, an agent, and a third party. In a real estate transaction the **principal** (buyer or seller), **agent** (real estate broker), and **third party** (customer) are bound together in a legal relationship, with all the duties and rights that go with that connection.

Usually, the principal is a seller who employs an agent to find a buyer for his or her property. Sometimes the principal is a buyer who employs an agent to locate a property.

The Broker is the Agent

The agent for the seller or buyer is always a licensed real estate broker, never a salesperson. Salespeople work on the behalf of their broker. A sales associate is the agent of his or her employing broker and must deal fairly with the broker's customers. Sales associates are not agents of the buyer or seller in a real property transaction, even though a buyer or seller may refer to the salesperson as "my agent".

When a broker represents only the buyer or the seller in the transaction, it is called **single agency**. **Dual agency** exists if one broker represents both principals (buyer and seller) in the transaction.

Broker Obtaining the Listing

The broker who gets the listing always acts as the seller's agent.

Listing Agent

A **listing agent** is a broker who obtains a listing from a seller to act as an agent for compensation. A **listing** is a contract between an owner of real property and an agent who is authorized to obtain a buyer.

Broker Obtaining the Offer

The broker obtaining an offer is often called the **cooperating broker** or selling agent. A **selling agent** is the broker who finds a buyer and obtains an offer for the real property. Depending on the agency relationship, the selling agent may represent the seller, the buyer, or both.

Buyer's Agent

A **buyer's agent** is a broker employed by the buyer to locate a certain kind of real property. This broker represents the buyer.

Subagent

A **subagent** is a broker delegated by the listing agent (if authorized by the seller) who represents the seller in finding a buyer for the listed property.

Dual Agent

A **dual agent** is a broker who represents both the seller and the buyer in the same transaction. This situation frequently occurs when two sales associates working for the same broker have the listing and selling side of the transaction.

Review - Agency Relationships		
Agent (Broker)	**Principal** (Client)	**Third Party** (Customer)
Listing Agent	Seller	Buyer
Subagent	Seller	Buyer
Buyer's Agent	Buyer	Seller
Dual Agent	Seller & Buyer	No Third Party

(Remember, the salesperson has an agency relationship with his or her employing broker, not the seller or buyer.)

Disclosing Agency Relationships

The **Agency Relationship Disclosure Act** has been in effect since January 1, 1988. Its purpose is to clarify the agency relationships between sellers, agents, and buyers and applies to every residential property transaction of one-to-four units. The agency disclosure is probably one of the most important documents available to the consumer. The law is finally clear about who is legally representing whom. Buyers or sellers can be confident that their best interests are being represented by an agent on their side in the negotiations.

As a licensee, you must use the "Disclosure Regarding Real Estate Agency Relationships" form explaining the nature of agency. The law is very clear about your responsibility for full disclosure. Misunderstanding or ignorance of the law is not a defense. A real estate license may be revoked or suspended for violation of the agency disclosure law. This disclosure must be made prior to taking a listing or writing an offer.

Disclosure Process

The steps in the disclosure process are: disclose, elect, and confirm.

Disclose the Relationship

The "**Disclosure Regarding Real Estate Agency Relationships**" form describes the obligations of an agent as "seller's agent", "buyer's agent", or "dual agent". At this point, all parties are made aware that they do have a choice of who is to represent them as their own agent.

A written disclosure must be presented by a:

- listing agent (or his or her sales associate) who must deliver the form to the seller before entering into a listing agreement.

- selling agent (who may also be the listing agent) who must provide the form to the buyer before the buyer makes an offer to purchase.

- selling agent (if different from the listing agent) who must provide the form to the seller before the offer to purchase is accepted.

Elect the Agency

The second part of the agency disclosure form requires all parties involved to confirm that they understand the agent's role. In other words, the first part of the disclosure reveals that the agent may represent only the buyer, only the seller, or both. All parties acknowledge their understanding at this point.

Confirm the Agency

All parties to the transaction (buyer, seller, and agents) are required to acknowledge that they understand who is representing whom, and sign the agency confirmation form. The agency relationship will be confirmed again in the sales contract, which is signed by all parties.

> ### Review - Disclosure of Agency Law
> - An agent is either the agent of the seller, the buyer, or both buyer and seller.
>
> - A selling broker may represent the buyer, seller, or both.
>
> - A dual agent may not tell the seller that the buyer is willing to pay more, nor may a dual agent tell the buyer that the seller will accept less without the express written consent of the parties.
>
> - An agency relationship can exist even though no compensation is received from the party with whom the agency relationship is established.

DISCLOSURE REGARDING
REAL ESTATE AGENCY RELATIONSHIP
(Listing Firm to Seller)
(As required by the Civil Code)
(C.A.R. Form AD, Revised 11/09)

When you enter into a discussion with a real estate agent regarding a real estate transaction, you should from the outset understand what type of agency relationship or representation you wish to have with the agent in the transaction.

SELLER'S AGENT

A Seller's agent under a listing agreement with the Seller acts as the agent for the Seller only. A Seller's agent or a subagent of that agent has the following affirmative obligations:
To the Seller: A Fiduciary duty of utmost care, integrity, honesty and loyalty in dealings with the Seller.
To the Buyer and the Seller:
   (a) Diligent exercise of reasonable skill and care in performance of the agent's duties.
   (b) A duty of honest and fair dealing and good faith.
   (c) A duty to disclose all facts known to the agent materially affecting the value or desirability of the property that are not known to, or within the diligent attention and observation of, the parties. An agent is not obligated to reveal to either party any confidential information obtained from the other party that does not involve the affirmative duties set forth above.

BUYER'S AGENT

A selling agent can, with a Buyer's consent, agree to act as agent for the Buyer only. In these situations, the agent is not the Seller's agent, even if by agreement the agent may receive compensation for services rendered, either in full or in part from the Seller. An agent acting only for a Buyer has the following affirmative obligations:
To the Buyer: A fiduciary duty of utmost care, integrity, honesty and loyalty in dealings with the Buyer.
To the Buyer and the Seller:
   (a) Diligent exercise of reasonable skill and care in performance of the agent's duties.
   (b) A duty of honest and fair dealing and good faith.
   (c) A duty to disclose all facts known to the agent materially affecting the value or desirability of the property that are not known to, or within the diligent attention and observation of, the parties.
An agent is not obligated to reveal to either party any confidential information obtained from the other party that does not involve the affirmative duties set forth above.

AGENT REPRESENTING BOTH SELLER AND BUYER

A real estate agent, either acting directly or through one or more associate licensees, can legally be the agent of both the Seller and the Buyer in a transaction, but only with the knowledge and consent of both the Seller and the Buyer.
In a dual agency situation, the agent has the following affirmative obligations to both the Seller and the Buyer:
   (a) A fiduciary duty of utmost care, integrity, honesty and loyalty in the dealings with either the Seller or the Buyer.
   (b) Other duties to the Seller and the Buyer as stated above in their respective sections.
In representing both Seller and Buyer, the agent may not, without the express permission of the respective party, disclose to the other party that the Seller will accept a price less than the listing price or that the Buyer will pay a price greater than the price offered.
The above duties of the agent in a real estate transaction do not relieve a Seller or Buyer from the responsibility to protect his or her own interests. You should carefully read all agreements to assure that they adequately express your understanding of the transaction. A real estate agent is a person qualified to advise about real estate. If legal or tax advice is desired, consult a competent professional.
Throughout your real property transaction you may receive more than one disclosure form, depending upon the number of agents assisting in the transaction. The law requires each agent with whom you have more than a casual relationship to present you with this disclosure form. You should read its contents each time it is presented to you, considering the relationship between you and the real estate agent in your specific transaction.
This disclosure form includes the provisions of Sections 2079.13 to 2079.24, inclusive, of the Civil Code set forth on page 2. Read it carefully.
I/WE ACKNOWLEDGE RECEIPT OF A COPY OF THIS DISCLOSURE AND THE PORTIONS OF THE CIVIL CODE PRINTED ON THE BACK (OR A SEPARATE PAGE).

☐ Buyer ☒ Seller ☐ Landlord ☐ Tenant ___*Fred Spring*___ Date __4/1/20XX__

☐ Buyer ☒ Seller ☐ Landlord ☐ Tenant ___*Jan Spring*___ Date __4/1/20XX__

Agent ___Tom Baker___ DRE Lic. # __00001234__

By __*Pat Green*__ Real Estate Broker (Firm) DRE Lic. # __00098765__ Date __4/1/20XX__
   (Salesperson or Broker-Associate)

AGENCY DISCLOSURE COMPLIANCE (Civil Code §2079.14):
- When the listing brokerage company also represents Buyer/Tenant: The Listing Agent shall have one AD form signed by Seller/Landlord and a different AD form signed by Buyer/Tenant.
- When Seller/Landlord and Buyer/Tenant are represented by different brokerage companies: (i) the Listing Agent shall have one AD form signed by Seller/Landlord and (ii) the Buyer's/Tenant's Agent shall have one AD form signed by Buyer/Tenant and either that same or a different AD form presented to Seller/Landlord for signature prior to presentation of the offer. If the same form is used, Seller may sign here:

     (SELLER/LANDLORD: DO NOT SIGN HERE)   **(SELLER/LANDLORD: DO NOT SIGN HERE)**
Seller/Landlord _____ Date _____ Seller/Landlord _____ Date _____

Published and Distributed by:
REAL ESTATE BUSINESS SERVICES, INC.
a subsidiary of the California Association of REALTORS®
525 South Virgil Avenue, Los Angeles, California 90020

Reviewed by _____ Date _____

EQUAL HOUSING
OPPORTUNITY

AD REVISED 11/09 (PAGE 1 OF 2)
DISCLOSURE REGARDING REAL ESTATE AGENCY RELATIONSHIP (AD PAGE 1 OF 2)

Agent: Tom Baker   Phone: (555) 123-4567   Fax: (555) 1234568   Prepared using zipForm® software
Broker: Sunshine Real Estate 1234 Mountain Road, Any City, CA 90000

RESIDENTIAL LISTING AGREEMENT – EXCLUSIVE

The listing agreement is a written employment contract between the broker and the seller. The listing agreement must be filled out correctly and signed by the necessary parties. At the time any exclusive listings are signed, the listing broker must give the seller a copy.

The most commonly used listing agreement is the **Residential Listing Agreement—Exclusive** (Exclusive Authorization and Right to Sell), where the broker is the sole agent and has the right to a commission. The broker has the sole right to obtain a purchaser for a property. If, during the listing term, a buyer is found by anyone, including the owner, the seller must pay the listing broker a commission if the property is sold within the time limit. By law, all exclusive listings must have a termination date. The property may be sold by the listing broker, any other broker, or the owner. From the broker's point of view, this type of listing is the most desirable.

Step–by–Step Examination of the Listing Agreement

An agency relationship may be created by agreement, with or without a written contract. However, a real estate agreement must be in writing to be enforceable in a court of law. The two common ways to create agency with a written real estate contract are through a listing agreement or a buyer representation agreement. The listing agreement is an exclusive authorization and right to sell because of the words "exclusive" and "irrevocable".

A "Residential Listing Agreement—Exclusive" listing is an exclusive contract that states that the seller must pay the listing broker a commission if the property is sold by the listing broker, any other broker, or even by the owner within the time limit. If the broker brings the seller a "**mirror offer**", (an offer that matches all terms in the listing), the seller does not have to accept the offer, but under the terms of the listing, the seller must pay the broker a commission. In this listing, the phrase "right to sell" means "right to find a buyer." It does not authorize the broker the right to convey any property belonging to the seller unless the agent has a power of attorney to do so. Every exclusive listing must specify a definite termination date.

As you go through each section of the form, refer to the numbered sections on the following pages for assistance or explanation.

1. Exclusive Right to Sell

Enter the full, legal name of the owner and the real estate office or broker receiving the listing. If someone other than the broker, such as a salesperson, takes the listing, the salesperson should write his or her employing broker's name.

> Enter the time period after the broker's name. The time period should include the beginning date April 01, 20xx and the termination date June 30, 20xx.

Enter the location of the property. Identify the property's location by city, county, and a specific address within the city. The location of the property by lot, block, and tract, or a metes-and-bounds legal description may also be given. In some cases, it may be necessary to sign and attach a legal description to the listing.

> Seller(s): Fred Spring and Jan Spring
> Broker: Tom Baker
> Listing Period: April 1, 20xx to June 30, 20xx
> Address: 1652 Hill Street, Any City, Apple County, California, 90000
> Assessor's Parcel No.: PQ9856
> Property Description: Single-family detached house

The salesperson completing the form should sign his or her name at the bottom of the form.

2. Items Excluded and Included

Items of real or personal property excluded from or included in the purchase are listed here. Listing the items the seller intends to include in the sale helps prevent future problems.

> Additional Items Included: Gas Range and Side-by-Side Refrigerator

3. Listing Price and Terms

A. Write the listing price in words and in numerals.

> Listing Price: Four Hundred Fifteen Thousand Dollars and Zero Cents
> ($415,000.00)

B. Extra space is provided to write the exact terms the owner requires when selling the property, such as financial arrangements or date of closing. If the broker presents an offer at the exact price and terms in the listing, the broker has earned the commission.

4. Compensation to Broker

The bold-faced type is a notice regarding commission. It states that the amount of commission a broker receives is not set by law and is negotiable.

A. The dollar amount or percentage rate of commission that will be paid if the property is sold is indicated here.

> ☑ 6% (six percent) of the listing price

(1) Regardless of who produces a potential buyer, a commission is due. The purchase offer must either meet the price and terms of the agreement (see Paragraph 2) or include a different price and terms that are acceptable to the seller. The offer must also be made during the listing period (see Paragraph 1).

OR

(2) This is the **safety clause** that protects the listing broker's commission. It states that if the owner personally sells the property to someone who had previously been shown the property or made an offer during the term of the listing the broker still receives a commission.

When the listing is signed, the seller and broker need to agree on a length of time for the protection period. The protection clause applies only if the broker has given the seller a list containing the names of the "protected" buyers within three (3) calendar days of expiration of the listing. This prevents the seller from waiting for a listing to end before accepting an offer and then refusing to pay a commission to the original broker.

> 30 (thirty) calendar days

OR

(3) The seller agrees to pay a commission if the seller sells, leases, or rents the property; withdraws it from the market without the broker's consent; or renders the property otherwise unavailable for sale before the expiration date.

B. If the sale is unable to be completed because of a party other than the seller, and damages are collected, then the total commission is to be the lesser of the commission due under Paragraph 4A, or one-half of the damages recovered after expenses are deducted.

C. Additional seller compensation, such as other broker expenses or MLS, is provided for here. Many brokerage firms charge sellers a fee for document preparation or transactions. Additional charges to the seller should be made clear in the listing contract.

> In addition, the seller agrees to pay the listing broker an additional 1% (one percent) commission if, within thirty (30) days of the listing date, an offer is brought meeting the exact terms of the listing agreement and escrow closes.

D. The broker advises the seller of the broker's policy regarding cooperating with and sharing compensation with other brokers.

   (1) If the seller authorizes the broker to cooperate with and compensate brokers through the multiple listing service (MLS), check either box to show the percentage or dollar amount to be paid. Notice that the amount is based on the purchase price, not the listing price.

> ☑ 3% (three percent) of the purchase price

   (2) The broker may cooperate and divide commission with brokers operating inside or outside the MLS.

E. The seller irrevocably assigns the broker his or her compensation from the seller's proceeds. This assignment agreement protects the broker's fee. Prior to this agreement, it was possible for the seller to notify an escrow not to pay the broker, but to turn the funds over to the seller instead.

F. The next three clauses protect the broker's commission. Since the broker will expend time, effort, and money in marketing the property, they want to be sure they will be paid for their successful efforts.

   (1) If the home had been listed before, enter that information here.

   (2) The owner is not required to pay anyone a commission, other than the broker, if the property is sold during the listing period (with the exception of listed prospective buyers).

   (3) If listed buyer purchases the property when seller is still obligated to pay another broker, the new listing broker is not entitled to a commission and is not obligated to represent seller in the transaction.

5. Ownership, Title, and Authority

The seller(s) are usually on title to the property and have the authority to sign the listing agreement and sell the property. The person selling the property could be different from the sellers. An example would be an attorney-in-fact who is authorized to list and sell a property on behalf of the owners. It's a good idea to ask the sellers to get out their grant deed because it shows who holds title (**vesting**) and how it was taken. Remember, either a husband or wife may list community property, but both must actually sign the purchase offer.

6. Multiple Listing Service

A **Multiple Listing Service** (MLS) is a networking system or cooperative listing service conducted by a group of brokers, usually members of a real estate association. Listings are submitted by the listing broker to a central bureau where they are made available by computer or printout to the members. Any MLS member may view the listings and obtain offers from buyers for these properties even if he or she is not the listing broker. A listing should be submitted to the MLS within 48 hours after the listing agreement is signed. However, the broker does not have to submit this listing to the MLS if the seller instructs the broker to withhold the listing. Instead, the broker would submit a form entitled "Seller Instruction to Exclude Listing from the Multiple Listing Service" signed by the seller(s).

7. Seller Representations

The listing broker would not want to waste time and money advertising a property that is subject to a lawsuit, foreclosure, or anything that would not allow the seller to complete the sale. This clause affirms that the seller is unaware of a notice of default recorded against the property; delinquencies due under loans; bankruptcy, insolvency, or other proceedings affecting the property as well as any litigation pending or threatened that could affect the seller's ability to sell. If the seller becomes aware of any of the above during the listing, the seller agrees to notify the agent immediately.

8. Broker's and Seller's Duties

The broker agrees to use diligence in achieving the purpose of the listing agreement. This is particularly important in an exclusive agency agreement because the seller is allowing one broker to market the property to the exclusion of other brokers. There are many cases where the seller sues for breach of contract because the listing broker did not actively advertise or use reasonable effort when marketing the property. Assuming the listing broker has done his or her part, the seller agrees to make the property available for showing. In addition, the seller agrees to consider offers received in good faith and to hold the broker harmless for claims resulting from incorrect information supplied or the failure to disclose information to the broker.

9. Deposit

The listing agent is authorized, on behalf of the seller, to accept and hold any deposits that will be applied toward the purchase price. Sometimes, the seller does not authorize the broker to accept deposits on his or her behalf. If the listing broker accepts a deposit without the seller's authorization, then the broker is responsible to the buyer for the deposit.

10. Agency Relationships

This is another reminder that you must disclose your agency relationship to the seller prior to signing this listing agreement, if the property is a residential property of one-to-four units.

A. Disclosure

You should have already given them the Disclosure Regarding Real Estate Agency Relationships form, and disclosed, elected, and confirmed the agency. This disclosure is required by law and pertains to sales, exchanges, installment land sale contracts, leases with the option to purchase, any other options to purchase, or ground leases coupled with improvements.

B. Seller Representation

Upon signing, this listing agreement creates a single agency wherein the broker represents the seller. The broker will not be the agent of the buyer.

C. Possible Dual Agency With Buyer

Sometimes, the listing broker finds the buyer. If that happens, the broker could act as a dual agent for both seller and buyer, but only with the written consent of both parties.

D. Other Sellers

Even though this listing agreement is an exclusive agency, it does not mean that the broker cannot represent other sellers or buyers as well.

E. Confirmation

Again, part of the Disclosure Regarding Real Estate Agency Relationships form, is the confirmation. Agency is to be confirmed, in writing, prior to or concurrent with the execution of a listing agreement.

11. Security and Insurance

Although the property will only be shown to prospective buyers in the presence of the listing broker (includes sales associates) or cooperating brokers (includes sales associates), the listing broker is not responsible for damage to or loss of personal property, even if a lockbox is present. Valuables should be locked up or removed from the premises and the seller must obtain insurance to protect against these risks.

12. Keysafe/Lockbox

If sellers want the most access to their home, they should authorize the listing broker to put a lockbox on the property. A lockbox makes the property more available for showing by other agents in the MLS. The agent is not liable to the owner for loss or damage resulting from access via the lockbox. If the seller chooses to have the property shown by appointment only, then the listing agent may not want to use a lockbox. The seller checks the box only if he or she does not want a lockbox.

13. Sign

The seller needs to authorize the agent to place a "For Sale" or "Sold" sign on the property. The seller checks the box only if he or she does not want a sign. Be sure to find out about and follow any signage rules for condominium developments, gated communities, or master-planned communities.

14. Equal Housing Opportunity

Sellers and brokers must abide by the federal and state fair housing laws. This statement affirms that the property is offered in compliance with anti-discrimination laws. The seller may not reject an offer on the property because of discrimination based on race, color, creed, etc.

15. Successors and Assigns

This agreement shall be binding upon the seller and seller's successors and assigns. This would not apply in the event of death or incapacity of either the principal or broker, because the agency relationship is a personal one between the principal and agent, and would terminate upon death or incapacity.

16. Management Approval

The broker is the agent of the principal and is responsible for his or her sales associates. When an associate-licensee signs a listing agreement, the broker or manager may cancel the agreement if he or she does not agree to the terms. The cancellation must be in writing, within five (5) days of its execution.

17. Additional Terms

This space is provided for additional owner-broker agreements or terms. In our case study, the Springs offer to pay Tom Baker more if he can close an escrow within 30 days of the listing.

> (1%) One percent more to the listing broker if an offer for the exact terms of the listing closes within 30 (thirty) days of the listing date.

18. Attorney's Fees

Hopefully, the transaction will have no problems; however, if a disagreement arises between the seller and the broker, and they go to court or arbitration, the loser in either incident must pay the costs. This paragraph tends to help reduce frivolous lawsuits.

19. Entire Agreement

Do not rely on any oral promises or other written documents that are not included in this agreement.

Remember, to be enforceable real estate contracts need to be in writing. Any verbal promises (if not included in the written contract) do not have to be honored. This clause reminds sellers to be sure the contract states what they expected in the listing agreement with the broker.

20. Dispute Resolution

This section explains two methods for resolving any misunderstandings that may arise regarding the listing agreement—mediation and arbitration.

A. Mediation

Mediation is a dispute resolution process. A neutral third party (the mediator) helps parties resolve a dispute. The mediator does not have authority to impose a settlement on either party. This clause states that the broker and seller agree to the mediation process. However, the broker and seller are not required to resolve the dispute through mediation. .

B. Arbitration of Disputes

In arbitration, the parties hire a neutral person (arbitrator) to listen to each side of the dispute. The main difference between mediation and arbitration is that the arbitrator may award a binding decision on all parties to the dispute. The decision is final, binding, and legally enforceable. Arbitration awards are final, and the courts will not re-hear the case. An arbitration award can be challenged in court if the arbitrator was corrupt, exceeded his or her power, or the award was procured by fraud, corruption, or other undue means.

Do not tell the sellers how to handle this clause. They need to read the clause, and if they are confused, tell them to consult their legal advisor.

(1) By initialing, all parties agree to neutral binding arbitration of any dispute, thus giving up rights to have the dispute litigated in the courts.

(2) Matters excluded from mediation and arbitration include foreclosure proceedings, unlawful detainer actions, mechanics' liens, matters within court jurisdiction, and tort injuries from latent or patent defects to the property.

Signatures

The seller acknowledges that he or she has read, understands, and accepts the agreement. The seller acknowledges receipt of a copy of the agreement as well.

There are lines for seller's and broker's signature, address, and telephone number. Remember to give a copy of the listing agreement to the seller at the time of signing.

CALIFORNIA
ASSOCIATION
OF REALTORS®

RESIDENTIAL LISTING AGREEMENT
(Exclusive Authorization and Right to Sell)
(C.A.R. Form RLA, Revised 11/11)

1. **EXCLUSIVE RIGHT TO SELL:** Fred Spring and Jan Spring _____ ("Seller")
   hereby employs and grants ____Tom Baker of Sunshine Real Estate____ ("Broker")
   beginning (date) April 01, 20XX and ending at 11:59 P.M. on (date) June 30, 20XX ("Listing Period")
   the exclusive and irrevocable right to sell or exchange the real property in the City of ____Any City____,
   County of ____Apple____, Assessor's Parcel No. ____PO98856____
   California, described as: 1652 Hill Street _____ ("Property").

2. **ITEMS EXCLUDED AND INCLUDED:** Unless otherwise specified in a real estate purchase agreement, all fixtures and fittings that are attached to the Property are included, and personal property items are excluded, from the purchase price.
   ADDITIONAL ITEMS EXCLUDED: _____
   ADDITIONAL ITEMS INCLUDED: Gas Range, Side-by-Side Refrigerator _____
   Seller intends that the above items be excluded or included in offering the Property for sale, but understands that: **(i)** the purchase agreement supersedes any intention expressed above and will ultimately determine which items are excluded and included in the sale; and **(ii)** Broker is not responsible for and does not guarantee that the above exclusions and/or inclusions will be in the purchase agreement.

3. **LISTING PRICE AND TERMS:**
   A. The listing price shall be: Four Hundred Fifteen Thousand Dollars and Zero Cents
   _____ Dollars ($ 415,000).
   B. Additional Terms: _____
   _____

4. **COMPENSATION TO BROKER:**
   Notice: The amount or rate of real estate commissions is not fixed by law. They are set by each Broker individually and may be negotiable between Seller and Broker (real estate commissions include all compensation and fees to Broker).
   A. Seller agrees to pay to Broker as compensation for services irrespective of agency relationship(s), either ☒ Six (6) percent of the listing price (or if a purchase agreement is entered into, of the purchase price), or ☐ $ _____
   AND _____, as follows:
   (1) If during the Listing Period, or any extension, Broker, cooperating broker, Seller or any other person procures a buyer(s) who offers to purchase the Property on the above price and terms, or on any price or terms acceptable to Seller. (Broker is entitled to compensation whether any escrow resulting from such offer closes during or after the expiration of the Listing Period, or any extension).
   OR **(2)** If within ____30____ calendar days **(a)** after the end of the Listing Period or any extension; or **(b)** after any cancellation of this Agreement, unless otherwise agreed, Seller enters into a contract to sell, convey, lease or otherwise transfer the Property to anyone ("Prospective Buyer") or that person's related entity: **(i)** who physically entered and was shown the Property during the Listing Period or any extension by Broker or a cooperating broker; or **(ii)** for whom Broker or any cooperating broker submitted to Seller a signed, written offer to acquire, lease, exchange or obtain an option on the Property. Seller, however, shall have no obligation to Broker under paragraph 4A(2) unless, not later than **3 calendar days** after the end of the Listing Period or any extension or cancellation, Broker has given Seller a written notice of the names of such Prospective Buyers.
   (3) If, without Broker's prior written consent, the Property is withdrawn from sale, conveyed, leased, rented, otherwise transferred, or made unmarketable by a voluntary act of Seller during the Listing Period, or any extension.
   B. If completion of the sale is prevented by a party to the transaction other than Seller, then compensation due under paragraph 4A shall be payable only if and when Seller collects damages by suit, arbitration, settlement or otherwise, and then in an amount equal to the lesser of one-half of the damages recovered or the above compensation, after first deducting title and escrow expenses and the expenses of collection, if any.
   C. In addition, Seller agrees to pay Broker: See page 3 of 4 #17 for "Additional Terms" ____
   D. Seller has been advised of Broker's policy regarding cooperation with, and the amount of compensation offered to, other brokers.
   (1) Broker is authorized to cooperate with and compensate brokers participating through the multiple listing service(s) ("MLS") by offering to MLS brokers out of Broker's compensation specified in 4A, either ☐ _____ percent of the purchase price, or ☒ $ ____Three(3)____.
   (2) Broker is authorized to cooperate with and compensate brokers operating outside the MLS as per Broker's policy.
   E. Seller hereby irrevocably assigns to Broker the above compensation from Seller's funds and proceeds in escrow. Broker may submit this Agreement, as instructions to compensate Broker pursuant to paragraph 4A, to any escrow regarding the Property involving Seller and a buyer, Prospective Buyer or other transferee.
   F. **(1)** Seller represents that Seller has not previously entered into a listing agreement with another broker regarding the Property, unless specified as follows: _____
   (2) Seller warrants that Seller has no obligation to pay compensation to any other broker regarding the Property unless the Property is transferred to any of the following individuals or entities: _____
   _____
   (3) If the Property is sold to anyone listed above during the time Seller is obligated to compensate another broker: **(i)** Broker is not entitled to compensation under this Agreement; and **(ii)** Broker is not obligated to represent Seller in such transaction.

Seller's Initials (FS)(JS)
Reviewed by _____ Date _____

EQUAL HOUSING
OPPORTUNITY

RLA REVISED 11/11 (PAGE 1 OF 4)

RESIDENTIAL LISTING AGREEMENT - EXCLUSIVE (RLA PAGE 1 OF 4)

Agent: Tom Baker   Phone: (555) 123-4567   Fax: (555) 123-4568   Prepared using zipForm® software
Broker: Sunshine Real Estate 1234 Mountain Road, Any City, CA 90000

Property Address: 1652 Hill Street, Any City, Apple County, CA 90000   Date: 4/01/20XX

5. **OWNERSHIP, TITLE AND AUTHORITY:** Seller warrants that: **(i)** Seller is the owner of the Property; **(ii)** no other persons or entities have title to the Property; and **(iii)** Seller has the authority to both execute this Agreement and sell the Property. Exceptions to ownership, title and authority are as follows: __None__

6. **MULTIPLE LISTING SERVICE:** All terms of the transaction, including financing, if applicable, will be provided to the selected MLS for publication, dissemination and use by persons and entities on terms approved by the MLS. Seller acknowledges that Broker is required to comply with all applicable MLS rules as a condition of entry of the listing into the MLS and Seller authorizes Broker to comply with all applicable MLS rules. MLS rules require that the listing sales price be reported to the MLS. MLS rules allow MLS data to be made available by the MLS to additional Internet sites unless Broker gives the MLS instructions to the contrary. MLS rules generally provide that residential real property and vacant lot listings be submitted to the MLS within 48 hours or some other period of time after all necessary signatures have been obtained on the listing agreement. However, Broker will not have to submit this listing to the MLS if, within that time, Broker submits to the MLS a form signed by Seller (C.A.R. Form SEL or the locally required form).

   Information that can be excluded:
   A. Internet Display;
      (1) Seller can instruct Broker to have the MLS not display the Property on the Internet. Seller understands that this would mean consumers searching for listings on the Internet may not see information about the Property in response to their search; **(2)** Seller can instruct Broker to have the MLS not display the Property address on the Internet. Seller understands that this would mean consumers searching for listings on the Internet may not see the Property's address in response to their search.
   B. Features on MLS Participant and Subscriber Websites;
      (1) Seller can instruct Broker to advise the MLS that Seller does not want visitors to MLS Participant or Subscriber Websites that display the Property listing to have **(i)** the ability to write comments or reviews about the Property on those sites; or **(ii)** the ability to hyperlink to another site containing such comments or reviews if the hyperlink is in immediate conjunction with the Property. Seller understands **(i)** that this opt-out applies only to Websites of MLS Participants and Subscribers who are real estate broker and agent members of the MLS; **(ii)** that other Internet sites may or may not have the features set forth herein; and **(iii)** that neither Broker nor the MLS may have the ability to control or block such features on other Internet sites. **(2)** Seller can instruct Broker to advise the MLS that Seller does not want MLS Participant or Subscriber Websites that display the Property listing to operate **(i)** an automated estimate of the market value of the Property; or **(ii)** have the ability to hyperlink to another site containing such automated estimate of value if the hyperlink is in immediate conjunction with the Property. Seller understands **(i)** that this opt-out applies only to Websites of MLS Participants and Subscribers who are real estate brokers and agent members of the MLS; **(ii)** that other Internet sites may or may not have the features set forth herein; and **(iii)** that neither Broker nor the MLS may have the ability to control or block such features on other Internet sites.

   Seller acknowledges that for any of the above opt-out instructions to be effective, Seller must make them on a separate instruction to Broker signed by Seller (C.A.R. Form SEL or the locally required form). Information about this listing will be provided to the MLS of Broker's selection unless a form instructing Broker to withhold the listing from the MLS is attached to this listing Agreement.

7. **SELLER REPRESENTATIONS:** Seller represents that, unless otherwise specified in writing, Seller is unaware of: **(i)** any Notice of Default recorded against the Property; **(ii)** any delinquent amounts due under any loan secured by, or other obligation affecting, the Property; **(iii)** any bankruptcy, insolvency or similar proceeding affecting the Property; **(iv)** any litigation, arbitration, administrative action, government investigation or other pending or threatened action that affects or may affect the Property or Seller's ability to transfer it; and **(v)** any current, pending or proposed special assessments affecting the Property. Seller shall promptly notify Broker in writing if Seller becomes aware of any of these items during the Listing Period or any extension thereof.

8. **BROKER'S AND SELLER'S DUTIES: (a)** Broker agrees to exercise reasonable effort and due diligence to achieve the purposes of this Agreement. Unless Seller gives Broker written instructions to the contrary, Broker is authorized to **(i)** order reports and disclosures necessary, **(ii)** advertise and market the Property by any method and in any medium selected by Broker, including MLS and the Internet, and, to the extent permitted by these media, control the dissemination of the information submitted to any medium; and **(iii)** disclose to any real estate licensee making an inquiry the receipt of any offers on the Property and the offering price of such offers. **(b)** Seller agrees to consider offers presented by Broker, and to act in good faith to accomplish the sale of the Property by, among other things, making the Property available for showing at reasonable times and referring to Broker all inquiries of any party interested in the Property. Seller is responsible for determining at what price to list and sell the Property. **Seller further agrees to indemnify, defend and hold Broker harmless from all claims, disputes, litigation, judgments and attorney fees arising from any incorrect information supplied by Seller, or from any material facts that Seller knows but fails to disclose.**

9. **DEPOSIT:** Broker is authorized to accept and hold on Seller's behalf any deposits to be applied toward the purchase price.

RLA REVISED 11/11 (PAGE 2 OF 4)

Seller's Initials (_FS_) (_JS_)
Reviewed by _____ Date _____

RESIDENTIAL LISTING AGREEMENT - EXCLUSIVE (RLA PAGE 2 OF 4)

Property Address: <u>1652 Hill Street, Any City, Apple County, CA 90000</u>   Date: <u>4/01/20XX</u>

10. **AGENCY RELATIONSHIPS:**
   A. **Disclosure:** If the Property includes residential property with one-to-four dwelling units, Seller shall receive a "Disclosure Regarding Agency Relationships" form prior to entering into this Agreement.
   B. **Seller Representation:** Broker shall represent Seller in any resulting transaction, except as specified in paragraph 4F.
   C. **Possible Dual Agency With Buyer:** Depending upon the circumstances, it may be necessary or appropriate for Broker to act as an agent for both Seller and Buyer, exchange party, or one or more additional parties ("Buyer"). Broker shall, as soon as practicable, disclose to Seller any election to act as a dual agent representing both Seller and Buyer. If a Buyer is procured directly by Broker or an associate licensee in Broker's firm, Seller hereby consents to Broker acting as a dual agent for Seller and such Buyer. In the event of an exchange, Seller hereby consents to Broker collecting compensation from additional parties for services rendered, provided there is disclosure to all parties of such agency and compensation. Seller understands and agrees that: **(i)** Broker, without the prior written consent of Seller, will not disclose to Buyer that Seller is willing to sell the Property at a price less than the listing price; **(ii)** Broker, without the prior written consent of Buyer, will not disclose to Seller that Buyer is willing to pay a price greater than the offered price; and **(iii)** except for (i) and (ii) above, a dual agent is obligated to disclose known facts materially affecting the value or desirability of the Property to both parties.
   D. **Other Sellers:** Seller understands that Broker may have or obtain listings on other properties, and that potential buyers may consider, make offers on, or purchase through Broker, property the same as or similar to Seller's Property. Seller consents to Broker's representation of sellers and buyers of other properties before, during and after the end of this Agreement.
   E. **Confirmation:** If the Property includes residential property with one-to-four dwelling units, Broker shall confirm the agency relationship described above, or as modified, in writing, prior to or concurrent with Seller's execution of a purchase agreement.

11. **SECURITY AND INSURANCE:** Broker is not responsible for loss of or damage to personal or real property, or person, whether attributable to use of a keysafe/lockbox, a showing of the Property, or otherwise. Third parties, including, but not limited to, appraisers, inspectors, brokers and prospective buyers, may have access to, and take videos and photographs of, the interior of the Property. Seller agrees: **(i)** to take reasonable precautions to safeguard and protect valuables that might be accessible during showings of the Property; and **(ii)** to obtain insurance to protect against these risks. Broker does not maintain insurance to protect Seller.

12. **KEYSAFE/LOCKBOX:** A keysafe/lockbox is designed to hold a key to the Property to permit access to the Property by Broker, cooperating brokers, MLS participants, their authorized licensees and representatives, authorized inspectors, and accompanied prospective buyers. Broker, cooperating brokers, MLS and Associations/Boards of REALTORS® are **not** insurers against injury, theft, loss, vandalism or damage attributed to the use of a keysafe/lockbox. Seller does (or if checked ☐ does not) authorize Broker to install a keysafe/lockbox. If Seller does not occupy the Property, Seller shall be responsible for obtaining occupant(s)' written permission for use of a keysafe/lockbox (C.A.R. Form KLA).

13. **SIGN:** Seller does (or if checked ☐ does not) authorize Broker to install a FOR SALE/SOLD sign on the Property.

14. **EQUAL HOUSING OPPORTUNITY:** The Property is offered in compliance with federal, state and local anti-discrimination laws.

15. **SUCCESSORS AND ASSIGNS:** This Agreement shall be binding upon Seller and Seller's successors and assigns.

16. **MANAGEMENT APPROVAL:** If an associate-licensee in Broker's office (salesperson or broker-associate) enters into this Agreement on Broker's behalf, and Broker or Manager does not approve of its terms, Broker or Manager has the right to cancel this Agreement, in writing, within **5 Days** After its execution.

17. **ADDITIONAL TERMS:** ☐ REO Advisory Listing (C.A.R. Form REOL) ☐ Short Sale Information and Advisory (C.A.R. Form SSIA)

   <u>One (1%) percent more to listing broker if offer for exact terms of listing closes within 30 days</u>
   <u>of listing date.</u>

18. **ATTORNEY FEES:** In any action, proceeding or arbitration between Seller and Broker regarding the obligation to pay compensation under this Agreement, the prevailing Seller or Broker shall be entitled to reasonable attorney fees and costs from the non-prevailing Seller or Broker, except as provided in paragraph 20A.

19. **ENTIRE AGREEMENT:** All prior discussions, negotiations and agreements between the parties concerning the subject matter of this Agreement are superseded by this Agreement, which constitutes the entire contract and a complete and exclusive expression of their agreement, and may not be contradicted by evidence of any prior agreement or contemporaneous oral agreement. If any provision of this Agreement is held to be ineffective or invalid, the remaining provisions will nevertheless be given full force and effect. This Agreement and any supplement, addendum or modification, including any photocopy or facsimile, may be executed in counterparts.

Seller's Initials (*FS*) (*JS*)
Reviewed by _____ Date _____

Property Address: <u>1652 Hill Street, Any City, Apple County, CA 90000</u>   Date: <u>4/01/20XX</u>

20. DISPUTE RESOLUTION:

    A.   MEDIATION: Seller and Broker agree to mediate any dispute or claim arising between them out of this Agreement, or any resulting transaction, before resorting to arbitration or court action, subject to paragraph 20B(2) below. Paragraph 20B(2) below applies whether or not the arbitration provision is initialed. Mediation fees, if any, shall be divided equally among the parties involved. If, for any dispute or claim to which this paragraph applies, any party commences an action without first attempting to resolve the matter through mediation, or refuses to mediate after a request has been made, then that party shall not be entitled to recover attorney fees, even if they would otherwise be available to that party in any such action. THIS MEDIATION PROVISION APPLIES WHETHER OR NOT THE ARBITRATION PROVISION IS INITIALED.

    B.   ARBITRATION OF DISPUTES: (1) Seller and Broker agree that any dispute or claim in law or equity arising between them regarding the obligation to pay compensation under this Agreement, which is not settled through mediation, shall be decided by neutral, binding arbitration, including and subject to paragraph 20B(2) below. The arbitrator shall be a retired judge or justice, or an attorney with at least 5 years of residential real estate law experience, unless the parties mutually agree to a different arbitrator, who shall render an award in accordance with substantive California law. The parties shall have the right to discovery in accordance with California Code of Civil Procedure §1283.05. In all other respects, the arbitration shall be conducted in accordance with Title 9 of Part III of the California Code of Civil Procedure. Judgment upon the award of the arbitrator(s) may be entered in any court having jurisdiction. Interpretation of this agreement to arbitrate shall be governed by the Federal Arbitration Act.

        (2) EXCLUSIONS FROM MEDIATION AND ARBITRATION: The following matters are excluded from mediation and arbitration: (i) a judicial or non-judicial foreclosure or other action or proceeding to enforce a deed of trust, mortgage, or installment land sale contract as defined in California Civil Code §2985; (ii) an unlawful detainer action; (iii) the filing or enforcement of a mechanic's lien; and (iv) any matter that is within the jurisdiction of a probate, small claims, or bankruptcy court. The filing of a court action to enable the recording of a notice of pending action, for order of attachment, receivership, injunction, or other provisional remedies, shall not constitute a waiver of the mediation and arbitration provisions.

        "NOTICE: BY INITIALING IN THE SPACE BELOW YOU ARE AGREEING TO HAVE ANY DISPUTE ARISING OUT OF THE MATTERS INCLUDED IN THE 'ARBITRATION OF DISPUTES' PROVISION DECIDED BY NEUTRAL ARBITRATION AS PROVIDED BY CALIFORNIA LAW AND YOU ARE GIVING UP ANY RIGHTS YOU MIGHT POSSESS TO HAVE THE DISPUTE LITIGATED IN A COURT OR JURY TRIAL. BY INITIALING IN THE SPACE BELOW YOU ARE GIVING UP YOUR JUDICIAL RIGHTS TO DISCOVERY AND APPEAL, UNLESS THOSE RIGHTS ARE SPECIFICALLY INCLUDED IN THE 'ARBITRATION OF DISPUTES' PROVISION. IF YOU REFUSE TO SUBMIT TO ARBITRATION AFTER AGREEING TO THIS PROVISION, YOU MAY BE COMPELLED TO ARBITRATE UNDER THE AUTHORITY OF THE CALIFORNIA CODE OF CIVIL PROCEDURE. YOUR AGREEMENT TO THIS ARBITRATION PROVISION IS VOLUNTARY."

        "WE HAVE READ AND UNDERSTAND THE FOREGOING AND AGREE TO SUBMIT DISPUTES ARISING OUT OF THE MATTERS INCLUDED IN THE 'ARBITRATION OF DISPUTES' PROVISION TO NEUTRAL ARBITRATION."

By signing below, Seller acknowledges that Seller has read, understands, received a copy of and agrees to the terms of this Agreement.

| Seller's Initials _____ / _____ | Broker's Initials _____ / _____ |

Seller <u>Fred Spring</u>   Date <u>4/01/20XX</u>
Address <u>1652 Hill Street</u>   City <u>Any City</u>   State <u>CA</u>   Zip <u>90000</u>
Telephone <u>(555) 321-9876</u>   Fax _____   E-mail <u>fred@speedy.xyz</u>

Seller <u>Jan Spring</u>   Date <u>4/01/20XX</u>
Address <u>1652 Hill Street</u>   City <u>Any City</u>   State <u>CA</u>   Zip <u>90000</u>
Telephone <u>(555) 321-9876</u>   Fax _____   E-mail <u>jan@speedy.xyz</u>

Real Estate Broker (Firm) <u>Sunshine Real Estate</u>   DRE Lic. # <u>00001234</u>
By (Agent) <u>Pat Green</u>   DRE Lic. # <u>000098765</u> Date <u>4/01/11</u>
Address <u>1234 Mountain Road</u>   City <u>Any City</u>   State <u>CA</u>   Zip <u>90000</u>
Telephone <u>(555) 123-4567</u>   Fax <u>(555) 123-4568</u>   E-mail <u>baker@sunshinere.xyz</u>

| Reviewed by _____ Date _____ |

RLA REVISED 11/11 (PAGE 4 OF 4)

RESIDENTIAL LISTING AGREEMENT - EXCLUSIVE (RLA PAGE 4 OF 4)

ESTIMATED SELLER'S PROCEEDS

This worksheet estimates the seller's approximate costs and proceeds from the sale of a property. Closing costs vary from county to county, but your broker should have estimates for you to use in your area. Typically, the commission, title, recording, escrow, inspection, property tax proration, home warranty, and repairs are calculated. Once this number is deducted from the expected sales price, the seller can deduct the balance of any loans on the property.

> In addition to information from the Case Study, use the "typical seller's costs for Any City, California" when completing the Estimated Seller's Proceeds form.
>
> Brokerage Fee - $24,900.00 ($415,000 x 6%)
>
> Taxes are paid twice per year and the seller has paid them current through June 30th. Depending on the date of closing, the seller may be credited a portion of the prepaid taxes, so allow up to $560.00 as a seller's credit.
>
> Documentary Transfer Tax: $456.50 ($415,000 divided by 1,000 x $1.10)
>
> **Inspections and Repairs:**
>
> Natural Hazard Disclosure Report - $125.00
> Corrective Work/Other Repairs - $1,000.00
> Pest Control Inspection - $150.00
> Roof Certification - $250.00
>
> **Standard Fees in Any City:**
>
> Demand and Reconveyance Fee - $160.00
> Escrow Fee - $800 (50/50)
> HOA Transfer Fees - $45.00
> Home Protection Policy - $450.00
> Reconveyance Deed - $85.00
> Recording/Notary Fees - $175.00
> Title Insurance Policy - $550.00

SELLER INSTRUCTION TO EXCLUDE LISTING FROM THE MULTIPLE LISTING SERVICE

The Exclude Listing from the Multiple Listing Service form is an addendum to the listing agreement used when the seller does not submit the listing to the MLS. The form discloses the benefits of submitting a listing to the MLS, the effects of exclusion of property from MLS, and authorization to exclude the listing from the MLS. Both seller and broker sign the form. The form may be used to satisfy local MLS documentation requirements.

Some sellers sign this form because they only want their broker to handle the sale of their home. Fred and Jan Spring do not sign the MLS exclusion form because they need to sell their home as soon as possible.

> These sellers want as much exposure for the property as possible so they would not sign this form.

CALIFORNIA
ASSOCIATION
OF REALTORS®

ESTIMATED SELLER PROCEEDS
(C.A.R. Form ESP, Revised 4/06)

SELLER: ___FRED SPRING AND JAN SPRING_____ DATE: __4/1/20XX__

PROPERTY ADDRESS: _1652 HILL STREET, ANY CITY, APPLE COUNTY, CALIFORNIA 90000_

This estimate is based on costs associated with _____CONVENTIONAL_____ type of financing.

PROJECTED CLOSING DATE: _____   PROPOSED SALE PRICE: $ _____415,000____

Current Annual Property Taxes: $ _$5,187.50___ Rate: ___1.25 %   Monthly Homeowners Dues, if any: $ _____

CHARGES BY EXISTING LIEN HOLDERS			**ENCUMBRANCES (EXISTING LIENS)**		
Interest to payoff date (first loan)	# Days ____	$ FIRST TD +/-	First Loan Rate: ____ %	$	155,485.00
Interest (secondary financing)	# Days ____	$	Secondary Financing Rate: ____ %	$	
Interest on lines of credit or other financing		$	Secured Lines of Credit	$	
Prepayment penalty		$	Bonds, Liens, etc.	$	
Demand and Reconveyance fees		$ 160.00	Other _____	$	
Other lender fees (wire transfers, courier, etc.)		$ FIRST TD +/-	**TOTAL ENCUMBRANCES**	$	155,485.00

ESCROW AND TITLE CHARGES

GROSS EQUITY $ 259,515.00

Escrow Fee ☐ including any Exchange Fees	$	400.00
Title Insurance Policy	$	550.00
Drawing, Notary and Recording Fees	$	175.00

(Expected sale price less encumbrances)

OTHER EXPENSES & PRORATIONS

ESTIMATED CREDITS

Brokerage -Listing ☐Amount $_____ or ☒ _6_ % $ 24,900.00
Fee   -Selling ☐Amount $_____ or ☐ ___ % $ 456.50

Prorated Property Taxes # Days ____	$ +/-	560.00
Prorated Homeowners Dues # Days ____	$ +/-	
Other _HOA MONTHLY FEES_	$ +/-	
Other _____	$	

Transfer Tax-County Rate per $1,000 $_____ $ _____
        -City   Rate per $1,000 $_____ $ _____

Property Taxes	# Days ____	$ SEE CREDITS	**TOTAL ESTIMATED CREDITS** $ 560.00
Homeowners Dues	# Days ____	$	

PROCEEDS RECAP

Buyer's Closing Costs	$	Expected Sale Price $ 415,000.00
Natural Hazard Disclosure and/or other Reports	$ 125.00	LESS Total Encumbrances - 155,485.00
Wood Destroying Pest and/or other Inspection Fees	$ 150.00	LESS Total Estimated Expenses - 28,761.50
Corrective Work and/or other Repairs	$ 1,000.00	PLUS Total Estimated Credits + 560.00
Home Warranty Program	$ 550.00	
Rents and Security Deposits	$	**ESTIMATED TOTAL SELLER PROCEEDS** $ 231,313.50
VA/FHA Discount Points and Fees	$	
HOA Transfer and/or Move-Out Fees	$ 45.00	LESS any Note Carried by Seller - _____
Other _ROOF CERTIFICATION_	$ 250.00	LESS any Federal/State Withholding - _____
	$	

TOTAL ESTIMATED EXPENSES $ 28,761.50   **ESTIMATED SELLER CASH PROCEEDS** $ 231,313.50 +/-

This estimate, based upon the above sale price, type of financing and projected closing date, has been prepared to assist Seller in estimating costs and proceeds. Amounts will vary depending upon differences between actual and estimated repairs that may occur in the transaction, unpaid loan balances, assessments, liens, impound accounts, charges by lenders, escrow companies, title insurers and other service providers and other items. Not all liens may yet have been identified. Neither Broker nor Agent guarantee these figures represent the actual, or only, amounts and charges.
By signing below Seller acknowledges that Seller has read, understands and received a copy of this Estimated Seller Proceeds.

Seller _Fred Spring_____ Date _4/1/20XX_

Seller _____Jan Spring_____ Date _4/1/20XX_

Real Estate Broker (Firm) _SUNSHINE REAL ESTATE_____ DRE Lic. # _00001234_

By (Agent) _PAT GREEN_____ DRE Lic. # _00098765_ Date _4/1/20XX_

Address _1234 MOUNTAIN ROAD_____ City _ANY CITY_ State _CA_ Zip _90000_

Telephone _(555) 123-4567_ Fax _(555) 123-4568_ E-mail _baker@sunshinere.xyz_

Published and Distributed by:
REAL ESTATE BUSINESS SERVICES, INC.
a subsidiary of the California Association of REALTORS®
525 South Virgil Avenue, Los Angeles, California 90020

Reviewed by _____ Date _____

EQUAL HOUSING
OPPORTUNITY

ESP REVISED 4/06 (PAGE 1 OF 1)   ESTIMATED SELLER PROCEEDS (ESP PAGE 1 OF 1)

Agent: Tom Baker	Phone: 555.123.4567	Fax: 555.123.4568	Prepared using zipForm® software
Broker: Sunshine Real Estate 1234 Mountian Road Any City, CA 90000			

SELLER INSTRUCTION TO EXCLUDE LISTING
FROM THE MULTIPLE LISTING SERVICE OR INTERNET
(C.A.R. Form SEL, REVISED 4/12)

This is an addendum ("Addendum") to the ☐ Residential Listing Agreement-Exclusive, ☐ Residential Listing Agreement-Agency, ☐ Residential Listing Agreement - "Open", ☐ Other ("Agreement") dated _____ on property known as _____ ("Property"), in which _____ is referred to as Seller and _____ is referred to as Broker.

1. **MULTIPLE LISTING SERVICE:** Broker is a participant/subscriber to the _____ Multiple Listing Service (MLS). The MLS is a database of properties for sale that is available and disseminated to and accessible by all other real estate agents who are participants or subscribers to the MLS. Property information submitted to the MLS also describes the price, terms and conditions under which the Seller's property is offered for sale (including but not limited to the listing broker's offer of compensation to other brokers). It is likely that a significant number of real estate practitioners in any given area are participants or subscribers to the MLS. The MLS may also be part of a reciprocal agreement to which other multiple listing services belong. Real estate agents belonging to other multiple listing services that have reciprocal agreements with the MLS also have access to the information submitted to the MLS.

2. **EXPOSURE TO BUYERS THROUGH MLS:** Listing property with an MLS exposes a seller's property to all real estate agents and brokers who are participants or subscribers to the MLS, all real estate agents and brokers receiving access to the MLS by way of an MLS reciprocal agreement, and potential buyer clients of those agents and brokers. The MLS may further transmit the MLS database to Internet sites that post property listings online, including national compilations of properties for sale (such as Realtor.com) and possibly even international compilations of properties for sale (such as worldproperties.com).

3. **MANDATORY SUBMISSION TO MLS:** The MLS generally requires brokers participating in the service to submit all exclusive right to sell and exclusive agency listings for residential real property or vacant lots to the MLS within 2 (or ☐ _____) days of obtaining all necessary signatures of the seller(s) on the listing agreement. However, Broker does not need to submit the listing to the MLS or can exclude this listing or certain information from it from appearing on the internet even if the listing is on the MLS if within that same period Broker submits to the MLS such an instruction signed by Seller (such as C.A.R. form SEL or a similarly required multiple listing service form).

4. ☐ **SELLER OPT-OUT - EXCLUSION OF PROPERTY FROM MLS:** Seller advises Broker that Seller elects to exclude the Property from the MLS. Seller understands and acknowledges that if this option is checked **(a)** real estate agents and brokers from other real estate offices, and their buyer clients, who have access to that MLS may not be aware that Seller's Property is offered for sale, **(b)** Seller's Property will not be included in the MLS's download to various real estate Internet sites that are used by the public to search for property listings, and **(c)** real estate agents, brokers and members of the public may be unaware of the terms and conditions under which Seller is marketing the Property.

   If this option is checked, Seller certifies that Seller understands the implications of not submitting the Property to the MLS. Seller instructs Broker not to submit the Property to the MLS (Check one): ☐ for a period of _____ calendar days from the commencement of the listing, ☐ until _____ (date) or,☐ during the listing period provided for in the Agreement.

Reviewed by _____ Date _____

SEL REVISED 4/12 (PAGE 1 OF 2)

SELLER INSTRUCTION TO EXCLUDE LISTING FROM MLS OR INTERNET (SEL PAGE 1 OF 2)

Agent:	Phone:	Fax:	Prepared using zipForm® software
Broker:			

Property Address: _____ Date: _____

5. ☐ **SELLER OPT-OUT - EXCLUSION OF LISTED PROPERTY FROM THE INTERNET:** Seller advises Broker that Seller does not want the Property to be displayed on the Internet. Seller understands and acknowledges that if this option is checked, a consumer who searches for listings on the Internet will not see information about the Property in response to their search.

6.   SELLER OPT-OUT - INTERNET FEATURE EXCLUSIONS:

   A. ☐ **Exclusion of Property Address from the Internet:** Seller advises Broker that Seller does not want the address of the Property to be displayed on the Internet; **and/or**

   B. ☐ **Exclusion of Comment or Property Review Feature from the Internet:** Seller advises Broker that Seller does not want visitors to Internet sites displaying the Property listing to have the ability to write comments or reviews about Seller's Property on those sites or the ability to hyperlink to another site containing such comments or reviews if the hyperlink is in immediate conjunction with Seller's Property; **and/or**

   C. ☐ **Exclusion of Automated Estimate of Property Value Feature from the Internet:** Seller advises Broker that Seller does not want visitors to Internet sites displaying the Property listing to display an automated estimate of the market value of the Property or the ability to hyperlink to another site containing such automated estimate of market value if the hyperlink is in immediate conjunction with Seller's Property.

By signing below, Seller acknowledges that Seller has read, understands, accepts and has received a copy of this Addendum.

Seller _____ Date _____
Address _____ City _____ State _____ Zip _____
Telephone _____ Fax _____ E-mail _____

Seller _____ Date _____
Address _____ City _____ State _____ Zip _____
Telephone _____ Fax _____ E-mail _____

Real Estate Broker (Firm) _____
By (Agent) _____ Date _____
Address _____ City _____ State _____ Zip _____
Telephone _____ Fax _____ E-mail _____

Published and Distributed by:
REAL ESTATE BUSINESS SERVICES, INC.
a subsidiary of the California Association of REALTORS®
525 South Virgil Avenue, Los Angeles, California 90020

| Reviewed by _____ Date _____ |

SEL REVISED 4/12 (PAGE 2 OF 2)
SELLER INSTRUCTION TO EXCLUDE LISTING FROM MLS OR INTERNET (SEL PAGE 2 OF 2)

SELLER'S ADVISORY

The Seller's Advisory form alerts sellers to the various disclosures they need to make regarding the condition of their home and its surroundings. The advisory explains the obligation to follow state and federal tax laws, comply with retrofit standards (if not exempt), and follow state and federal fair housing laws. The advisory also helps a seller with ideas about how to market his or her property effectively.

Disclosures

Sometimes the seller will need to fill out and sign a standard form; other times the seller (or broker) may meet requirements by giving the buyer informational booklets. Sellers must disclose, in writing, any and all known facts that materially affect the value of their property whether the buyer asks or not. Even if a home is sold "as is", the seller must disclose any observable (**patent**) defects as well as any hidden (**latent**) defects. The term "as is" means that the seller is not going to fix any of the problems.

In addition, you must also visually inspect the accessible parts of the home. If you notice something that could indicate a problem, you must let both the seller and any prospective buyer know. During the process of selling a home, the seller will need to prepare the **Transfer Disclosure Statement** (TDS) and **Natural Hazard Disclosure Statement** (NHD) as soon as possible. In addition, the seller will need to disclose if the property is subject to lead-based paint, military ordnance, commercial zone, or Mello-Roos tax. This disclosure information should be given to prospective buyers before they submit an offer. If they are provided to the buyer after acceptance of the offer, the buyer has three (3) days to terminate the offer. Remember, you cannot fill out these forms for the seller.

Depending on the age and type of construction of the property, sellers can receive limited legal protection by providing buyers with booklets titled *The Homeowners Guide to Earthquake Safety, The Commercial Property Owner's Guide to Earthquake Safety, Protect Your Family From Lead in Your Home,* and *Environmental Hazards: A Guide for Homeowners and Buyers.* If the booklet on lead is to be supplied, disclosure of any known lead-based paint and its hazards must be made to the buyer on a separate form.

Many buyers consider **death on real property** to be a material fact. However, the California Civil Code Section 1710.2 states that a seller has no disclosure duty "where a death has occurred more than three (3) years prior to the date that the transferee offers to purchase, lease, or rent the real property, or that an occupant of that property was afflicted with, or died from **HIV/LAV.**" This information should also be indicated on the "Supplemental Statutory and Contractual Disclosures" form.

If the property is a condominium, townhouse, or other property in a common interest subdivision, the seller must provide the buyer with copies of the governing documents, the most recent financial statements distributed, and other documents required by law or contract of the homeowners' association. This information should be affirmed on the "Homeowner Association Information Request" form.

Contract Terms and Legal Requirements

When the seller receives an offer from a prospective buyer, the seller may be asked to pay for repairs to the property and other items. Every situation is different; sometimes it will make sense to pay for all or part of a requested repair, and sometimes it will not.

Unless an "Affidavit of Nonforeign Status and California Withholding Exemption" form is completed and signed, the buyer must withhold a portion of the purchase price from the seller's sale proceeds for tax purposes. If not exempt, the seller must comply with government retrofit standards.

Since selling property may have legal, tax, insurance, title, or other implications, remind the seller to seek professional advice. Remember, you cannot give legal or tax advice to sellers or buyers.

Marketing Considerations

Advise the seller to prepare his or her home for sale by scheduling a professional home inspection. The seller should be aware of and correct any defects or problems.

Tell the seller about a home protection/warranty plan to cover problems that occur after the sale is complete.

Since many people will be viewing the seller's home, he or she should maintain insurance and take all necessary precautions to protect all property and people from injury, theft, loss, vandalism, damage, or other harm.

Remind the seller that he or she, not the broker, is responsible for the fees and costs needed to comply with the duties and obligations to the buyer. Show the seller the tentative costs on the "Estimated Seller's Proceeds" (seller's net sheet) discussed earlier in this unit.

Other Items

Anything not previously addressed should be entered in this section.

Signature Lines and Date

The "Seller's Advisory" should be signed and dated by the seller after complying with all of the disclosures indicated. The broker will sign and date this form as well, and a copy should be given to the seller.

It is important to have the seller sign and date the Seller's Advisory form

CALIFORNIA
ASSOCIATION
OF REALTORS®

SELLER'S ADVISORY
(C.A.R. Form SA, Revised 11/11)

Property Address: 1652 Hill Street, Any City, Apple County, California 90000 _____ ("Property")

1. **INTRODUCTION:** Selling property in California is a process that involves many steps. From start to finish, it could take anywhere from a few weeks to many months, depending upon the condition of your Property, local market conditions and other factors. You have already taken an important first step by listing your Property for sale with a licensed real estate broker. Your broker will help guide you through the process and may refer you to other professionals as needed. This advisory addresses many things you may need to think about and do as you market your Property. Some of these things are requirements imposed upon you, either by law or by the listing or sale contract. Others are simply practical matters that may arise during the process. Please read this document carefully and, if you have any questions, ask your broker or appropriate legal or tax advisor for help.

2. **DISCLOSURES:**

   A. **General Disclosure Duties:** You must affirmatively disclose to the buyer, in writing, any and all known facts that materially affect the value or desirability of your Property. You must disclose these facts whether or not asked about such matters by the buyer, any broker, or anyone else. This duty to disclose applies even if the buyer agrees to purchase your Property in its present condition without requiring you to make any repairs. If you do not know what or how to disclose, you should consult a real estate attorney in California of your choosing. Broker cannot advise you on the legal sufficiency of any disclosures you make. If the Property you are selling is a residence with one to four units except for certain subdivisions, your broker also has a duty to conduct a reasonably competent and diligent visual inspection of the accessible areas and to disclose to a buyer all adverse material facts that the inspection reveals. If your broker discovers something that could indicate a problem, your broker must advise the buyer.

   B. **Statutory Duties:** (For one-to-four Residential Units):

   (1) You must timely prepare and deliver to the buyer, among other things, a Real Estate Transfer Disclosure Statement ("TDS"), and a Natural Hazard Disclosure Statement ("NHD"). You have a legal obligation to honestly and completely fill out the TDS form in its entirety. (Many local entities or organizations have their own supplement to the TDS that you may also be asked to complete.) The NHD is a statement indicating whether your Property is in certain designated flood, fire or earthquake/seismic hazard zones. Third-party professional companies can help you with this task.

   (2) Depending upon the age and type of construction of your Property, you may also be required to provide and, in certain cases you can receive limited legal protection by providing, the buyer with booklets entitled "The Homeowner's Guide to Earthquake Safety," "The Commercial Property Owner's Guide to Earthquake Safety," "Protect Your Family From Lead in Your Home" and "Environmental Hazards: A Guide For Homeowners and Buyers." Some of these booklets may be packaged together for your convenience. The earthquake guides ask you to answer specific questions about your Property's structure and preparedness for an earthquake. If you are required to supply the booklet about lead, you will also be required to disclose to the buyer any known lead-based paint and lead-based paint hazards on a separate form. The environmental hazards guide informs the buyer of common environmental hazards that may be found in properties.

   (3) If you know that your property is: **(i)** located within one mile of a former military ordnance location; or **(ii)** in or affected by a zone or district allowing manufacturing, commercial or airport use, you must disclose this to the buyer. You are also required to make a good faith effort to obtain and deliver to the buyer a disclosure notice from the appropriate local agency(ies) about any special tax levied on your Property pursuant to the Mello-Roos Community Facilities Act, the Improvement Bond Act of 1915, and a notice concerning the contractual assessment provided by section 5898.24 of the Streets And Highways Code (collectively, "Special Tax Disclosures").

   (4) If the TDS, NHD, or lead, military ordnance, commercial zone or Special Tax Disclosures are provided to a buyer after you accept that buyer's offer, the buyer will have 3 days after delivery (or 5 days if mailed) to terminate the offer, which is why it is extremely important to complete these disclosures as soon as possible. There are certain exemptions from these statutory requirements; however, if you have actual knowledge of any of these items, you may still be required to make a disclosure as the items can be considered material facts.

   C. **Death and Other Disclosures:** Many buyers consider death on real property to be a material fact in the purchase of property. In some situations, it is advisable to disclose that a death occurred or the manner of death; however, California Civil Code Section 1710.2 provides that you have no disclosure duty "where the death has occurred more than three years prior to the date the transferee offers to purchase, lease, or rent the real property, or [regardless of the date of occurrence] that an occupant of that property was afflicted with, or died from, Human T-Lymphotropic Virus Type III/Lymphadenopathy-Associated Virus." This law does not "immunize an owner or his or her agent from making an intentional misrepresentation in response to a direct inquiry from a transferee or a prospective transferee of real property, concerning deaths on the real property."

   D. **Condominiums and Other Common Interest Subdivisions:** If the Property is a condominium, townhouse, or other property in a common interest subdivision, you must provide to the buyer copies of the governing documents, the most recent financial statements distributed, and other documents required by law or contract. If you do not have a current version of these documents, you can request them from the management of your homeowner's association. To avoid delays, you are encouraged to obtain these documents as soon as possible, even if you have not yet entered into a purchase agreement to sell your Property.

Seller's Initials (_FS_)(_JS_)

Reviewed by _____ Date _____

EQUAL HOUSING
OPPORTUNITY

SA REVISED 11/11 (PAGE 1 OF 2)

SELLER'S ADVISORY (SA PAGE 1 OF 2)

Agent: Tom Baker	Phone: (555) 123-4567	Fax: (555) 123-4568	Prepared using zipForm® software
Broker: Sunshine Real Estate 1234 Mountain Road, Any City, CA 90000			

Property Address: 1652 Hill Street, Any City, Apple County, California 90000   Date: 4/1/20XX

3. **CONTRACT TERMS AND LEGAL REQUIREMENTS:**
   A. **Contract Terms and Conditions:** A buyer may request, as part of the contract for the sale of your Property, that you pay for repairs to the Property and other items. Your decision on whether or not to comply with a buyer's requests may affect your ability to sell your Property at a specified price.
   B. **Withholding Taxes:** Under federal and California tax laws, a buyer is required to withhold a portion of the purchase price from your sale proceeds for tax purposes unless you sign an affidavit of non-foreign status and California residency, or some other exemption applies and is documented.
   C. **Prohibition Against Discrimination:** Discriminatory conduct in the sale of real property against individuals belonging to legally protected classes is a violation of the law.
   D. **Government Retrofit Standards:** Unless exempt, you must comply with government retrofit standards, including, but not limited to, installing operable smoke detectors, bracing water heaters, and providing the buyer with corresponding written statements of compliance. Some city and county governments may impose additional retrofit standards, including, but not limited to, installing low-flow toilets and showerheads, gas shut-off valves, tempered glass, and barriers around swimming pools and spas. You should consult with the appropriate governmental agencies, inspectors, and other professionals to determine the retrofit standards for your Property, the extent to which your Property complies with such standards, and the costs, if any, of compliance.
   E. **EPA's LEAD-BASED PAINT RENOVATION, REPAIR AND PAINTING RULE:** The new rule requires that contractors and maintenance professionals working in pre-1978 housing, child care facilities, and schools with lead-based paint be certified; that their employees be trained; and that they follow protective work practice standards. The rule applies to renovation, repair, or painting activities affecting more than six square feet of lead-based paint in a room or more than 20 square feet of lead-based paint on the exterior. Enforcement of the rule begins October 1, 2010. See the EPA website at www.epa.gov/lead for more information.
   F. **Legal, Tax and Other Implications:** Selling your Property may have legal, tax, insurance, title or other implications. You should consult an appropriate professional for advice on these matters.

4. **MARKETING CONSIDERATIONS:**
   A. **Pre-Sale Considerations:** You should consider doing what you can to prepare your Property for sale, such as correcting any defects or other problems. Many people are not aware of defects in or problems with their own Property. One way to make yourself aware is to obtain professional home inspections prior to sale, both generally, and for wood destroying pests and organisms, such as termites. By doing this, you then have an opportunity to make repairs before your Property is offered for sale, which may enhance its marketability. Keep in mind, however, that any problems revealed by such inspection reports or repairs that have been made, whether or not disclosed in a report, should be disclosed to the buyer (see "Disclosures" in paragraph 2 above). This is true even if the buyer gets his/her own inspections covering the same area. Obtaining inspection reports may also assist you during contract negotiations with the buyer. For example, if a pest control report has both a primary and secondary recommendation for clearance, you may want to specify in the purchase agreement those recommendations, if any, for which you are going to pay.
   B. **Post-Sale Protections:** It is often helpful to provide the buyer with, among other things, a home protection/warranty plan for the Property. These plans will generally cover problems, not deemed to be pre-existing, that occur after your sale is completed. In the event something does go wrong after the sale, and it is covered by the plan, the buyer may be able to resolve the concern by contacting the home protection company.
   C. **Safety Precautions:** Advertising and marketing your Property for sale, including, but not limited to, holding open houses, placing a keysafe/lockbox, erecting FOR SALE signs, and disseminating photographs, video tapes, and virtual tours of the premises, may jeopardize your personal safety and that of your Property. You are strongly encouraged to maintain insurance, and to take any and all possible precautions and safeguards to protect yourself, other occupants, visitors, your Property, and your belongings, including cash, jewelry, drugs, firearms and other valuables located on the Property, against injury, theft, loss, vandalism, damage, and other harm.
   D. **Expenses:** You are advised that you, not the Broker, are responsible for the fees and costs, if any, to comply with your duties and obligations to the buyer of your Property.

5. **OTHER ITEMS:** _____
   _____
   _____

Seller has read and understands this Advisory. By signing below, Seller acknowledges receipt of a copy of this document.

Seller _Fred Spring_____ Date _4/1/20XX_____
Print Name _____FRED SPRING_____

Seller _Jan Spring_____ Date _4/1/20XX_____
Print Name _____JAN SPRING_____

Real Estate Broker _TOM BAKER/SUNSHINE RE_____ By _Pat Green_____
                                                        (Agent)
Address _1234 Mountain Road_____ City _Any City____ State _CA_ Zip _90000__
Telephone _(555)123-4567____ Fax _(555)123-4568_ E-mail _baker@sunshinere.xyz_

Published and Distributed by:
REAL ESTATE BUSINESS SERVICES, INC.
a subsidiary of the California Association of REALTORS®
525 South Virgil Avenue, Los Angeles, California 90020

Reviewed by _____ Date _____

SA REVISED 11/11 (PAGE 2 OF 2)   **SELLER'S ADVISORY (SA PAGE 2 OF 2)**

REAL ESTATE TRANSFER DISCLOSURE STATEMENT (TDS)

As mentioned in the "Seller's Advisory", when selling or transferring residential property (one-to-four units), sellers are required by law to disclose any defects that materially affect the value of a property. The form used to disclose the condition of the property is the "Transfer Disclosure Statement" (TDS). Remember, the seller must complete and sign this form.

First, identify the property's location by city, county, and a specific address within the city. Then date the form with the current date.

1. Indicate any substituted disclosure forms used in place of the TDS.

2. Seller's Information:

    Part A lists several items that the property may have. The seller checks the item and states at the bottom of the page whether any of the items do not operate. If any of the items do not operate, the problem is described.

    Part B discusses the condition of the structure and systems. This time the seller only checks an item if it has a significant defect or malfunction. A brief description is included for anything that is checked.

    Part C discusses things that are not physical defects of the property, but other things such as environmental hazards or contaminated soil, shared property, changes made without required building permits, soil problems, earthquake zone, zoning violations, homeowners' association obligations, deed restrictions, neighborhood nuisances and pending lawsuits.

    The seller checks the "Yes" or "No" boxes and explains any "yes" item.

    Part D states that the property will be in compliance with the Health and Safety Code regarding smoke detectors and water heater bracing.

The seller should certify that the information is true and correct to the best of their knowledge by signing and dating the form where indicated.

The last page of the disclosure is reserved for statements and signatures of the listing and the selling brokers after completing a reasonably competent and diligent visual inspection of the accessible areas of the property.

Both buyer and seller may obtain advice and/or inspections of the property. Since the TDS is not part of any contract between the seller and buyer, anything the buyer wants repaired based on an inspection or information in the TDS must be included in the original offer or subsequent addendum.

Be sure to have the buyer sign and date the TDS when it is received because a buyer who receives the TDS after submitting an offer may rescind a purchase contract up to three (3) days after delivery of the TDS disclosure.

CALIFORNIA ASSOCIATION OF REALTORS®

REAL ESTATE TRANSFER DISCLOSURE STATEMENT
(CALIFORNIA CIVIL CODE §1102, ET SEQ.)
(C.A.R. Form TDS, Revised 11/11)

THIS DISCLOSURE STATEMENT CONCERNS THE REAL PROPERTY SITUATED IN THE CITY OF
___Any City___ , COUNTY OF ___Apple___ , STATE OF CALIFORNIA,
DESCRIBED AS ___1652 Hill Street___ .
THIS STATEMENT IS A DISCLOSURE OF THE CONDITION OF THE ABOVE DESCRIBED PROPERTY IN COMPLIANCE WITH SECTION 1102 OF THE CIVIL CODE AS OF (date) ___April 1, 20XX___ . IT IS NOT A WARRANTY OF ANY KIND BY THE SELLER(S) OR ANY AGENT(S) REPRESENTING ANY PRINCIPAL(S) IN THIS TRANSACTION, AND IS NOT A SUBSTITUTE FOR ANY INSPECTIONS OR WARRANTIES THE PRINCIPAL(S) MAY WISH TO OBTAIN.

I. COORDINATION WITH OTHER DISCLOSURE FORMS

This Real Estate Transfer Disclosure Statement is made pursuant to Section 1102 of the Civil Code. Other statutes require disclosures, depending upon the details of the particular real estate transaction (for example: special study zone and purchase-money liens on residential property).

Substituted Disclosures: The following disclosures and other disclosures required by law, including the Natural Hazard Disclosure Report/Statement that may include airport annoyances, earthquake, fire, flood, or special assessment information, have or will be made in connection with this real estate transfer, and are intended to satisfy the disclosure obligations on this form, where the subject matter is the same:

☐ Inspection reports completed pursuant to the contract of sale or receipt for deposit.
☒ Additional inspection reports or disclosures: ___Homeowner Association Information Request___
   ___"Hillside Ranch Community Association"___

II. SELLER'S INFORMATION

The Seller discloses the following information with the knowledge that even though this is not a warranty, prospective Buyers may rely on this information in deciding whether and on what terms to purchase the subject property. Seller hereby authorizes any agent(s) representing any principal(s) in this transaction to provide a copy of this statement to any person or entity in connection with any actual or anticipated sale of the property.

THE FOLLOWING ARE REPRESENTATIONS MADE BY THE SELLER(S) AND ARE NOT THE REPRESENTATIONS OF THE AGENT(S), IF ANY. THIS INFORMATION IS A DISCLOSURE AND IS NOT INTENDED TO BE PART OF ANY CONTRACT BETWEEN THE BUYER AND SELLER.

Seller ☒ is ☐ is not occupying the property.

A. The subject property has the items checked below: *

☒ Range	☐ Wall/Window Air Conditioning	☐ Pool:
☒ Oven	☐ Sprinklers	☐ Child Resistant Barrier
☐ Microwave	☐ Public Sewer System	☐ Pool/Spa Heater:
☒ Dishwasher	☐ Septic Tank	☐ Gas ☐ Solar ☐ Electric
☐ Trash Compactor	☐ Sump Pump	☒ Water Heater:
☒ Garbage Disposal	☐ Water Softener	☒ Gas ☐ Solar ☐ Electric
☒ Washer/Dryer Hookups	☒ Patio/Decking	☐ Water Supply:
☒ Rain Gutters	☐ Built-in Barbecue	☒ City ☐ Well
☐ Burglar Alarms	☐ Gazebo	☐ Private Utility or
☐ Carbon Monoxide Device(s)	☐ Security Gate(s)	Other _____
☒ Smoke Detector(s)	☒ Garage:	☒ Gas Supply:
☐ Fire Alarm	☒ Attached ☐ Not Attached	☒ Utility ☐ Bottled (Tank)
☐ TV Antenna	☐ Carport	☒ Window Screens
☐ Satellite Dish	☐ Automatic Garage Door Opener(s)	☐ Window Security Bars
☐ Intercom	☐ Number Remote Controls _____	☐ Quick Release Mechanism on
☒ Central Heating	☐ Sauna	Bedroom Windows
☒ Central Air Conditioning	☒ Hot/Tub Spa:	☐ Water-Conserving Plumbing Fixtures
☐ Evaporator Cooler(s)	☐ Locking Safety Cover	

Exhaust Fan(s) in ___Kitchen, Baths___   220 Volt Wiring in ___Garage___   Fireplace(s) in ___Living Room___
☒ Gas Starter ___Fireplace___   ☒ Roof(s): Type: ___Concrete Tile___   Age: ___Built in 1990___ (approx.)
☒ Other: ___Refrigerator (side-by-side)___

Are there, to the best of your (Seller's) knowledge, any of the above that are not in operating condition? ☒ Yes ☐ No. If yes, then describe. (Attach additional sheets if necessary): ___Solar spa heater not working, no locking spa cover, 3 missing screens,___
   ___water heater not braced.___
(*see note on page 2)

Buyer's Initials (_____)(_____)   Seller's Initials (_FS_)(_JS_)

TDS REVISED 11/11 (PAGE 1 OF 3)   Reviewed by _____ Date _____

REAL ESTATE TRANSFER DISCLOSURE STATEMENT (TDS PAGE 1 OF 3)

EQUAL HOUSING OPPORTUNITY

Agent: Tom Baker   Phone: (555) 123-4567   Fax: (555) 123-4568   Prepared using zipForm® software
Broker: Sunshine Real Estate   1234 Mountain Road, Any City, CA 90000

Property Address: <u>1652 Hill Street, Any City, Apple County, California 90000</u>   Date: <u>4/1/20XX</u>

B. Are you (Seller) aware of any significant defects/malfunctions in any of the following? ☐ Yes ☐ No. If yes, check appropriate space(s) below.

☐ Interior Walls ☐ Ceilings ☐ Floors ☐ Exterior Walls ☐ Insulation ☐ Roof(s) ☐ Windows ☐ Doors ☐ Foundation ☐ Slab(s) ☐ Driveways ☐ Sidewalks ☐ Walls/Fences ☐ Electrical Systems ☐ Plumbing/Sewers/Septics ☐ Other Structural Components
(Describe: _____

_____

_____)

If any of the above is checked, explain. (Attach additional sheets if necessary.): _____

_____

_____

*Installation of a listed appliance, device, or amenity is not a precondition of sale or transfer of the dwelling. The carbon monoxide device, garage door opener, or child-resistant pool barrier may not be in compliance with the safety standards relating to, respectively, carbon monoxide device standards of Chapter 8 (commencing with Section 13260) of Part 2 of Division 12 of, automatic reversing device standards of Chapter 12.5 (commencing with Section 19890) of Part 3 of Division 13 of, or the pool safety standards of Article 2.5 (commencing with Section 115920) of Chapter 5 of Part 10 of Division 104 of, the Health and Safety Code. Window security bars may not have quick-release mechanisms in compliance with the 1995 edition of the California Building Standards Code. Section 1101.4 of the Civil Code requires all single-family residences built on or before January 1, 1994, to be equipped with water-conserving plumbing fixtures after January 1, 2017. Additionally, on and after January 1, 2014, a single-family residence built on or before January 1, 1994, that is altered or improved is required to be equipped with water-conserving plumbing fixtures as a condition of final approval. Fixtures in this dwelling may not comply with section 1101.4 of the Civil Code.

C. Are you (Seller) aware of any the following:

1. Substances, materials, or products which may be an environmental hazard such as, but not limited to, asbestos, formaldehyde, radon gas, lead-based paint, mold, fuel or chemical storage tanks, and contaminated soil or water on the subject property . . . . ☐ Yes ☒ No
2. Features of the property shared in common with adjoining landowners, such as walls, fences, and driveways, whose use or responsibility for maintenance may have an effect on the subject property . . . . ☐ Yes ☐ No
3. Any encroachments, easements or similar matters that may affect your interest in the subject property . . . . ☐ Yes ☒ No
4. Room additions, structural modifications, or other alterations or repairs made without necessary permits. . . . . . . ☐ Yes ☒ No
5. Room additions, structural modifications, or other alterations or repairs not in compliance with building codes. . . . ☐ Yes ☒ No
6. Fill (compacted or otherwise) on the property or any portion thereof . . . . ☐ Yes ☒ No
7. Any settling from any cause, or slippage, sliding, or other soil problems . . . . ☐ Yes ☒ No
8. Flooding, drainage or grading problems . . . . ☐ Yes ☒ No
9. Major damage to the property or any of the structures from fire, earthquake, floods, or landslides . . . . ☐ Yes ☒ No
X 10. Any zoning violations, nonconforming uses, violations of "setback" requirements . . . . ☐ Yes ☒ No
11. Neighborhood noise problems or other nuisances . . . . ☐ Yes ☒ No
12. CC&R's or other deed restrictions or obligations . . . . ☒ Yes ☐ No
13. Homeowners' Association which has any authority over the subject property . . . . ☒ Yes ☐ No
14. Any "common area" (facilities such as pools, tennis courts, walkways, or other areas co-owned in undivided interest with others) . . . . ☒ Yes ☐ No
15. Any notices of abatement or citations against the property . . . . ☐ Yes ☒ No
16. Any lawsuits by or against the Seller threatening to or affecting this real property, including any lawsuits alleging a defect or deficiency in this real property or "common areas" (facilities such as pools, tennis courts, walkways, or other areas, co-owned in undivided interest with others) . . . . ☐ Yes ☒ No

If the answer to any of these is yes, explain. (Attach additional sheets if necessary.): <u>HOA Hillside Ranch Community</u>
<u>Homeowners' Association monthly dues: $209.00.   No pending assessments due as of April 1st 20XX.</u>

_____

_____

D. 1. The Seller certifies that the property, as of the close of escrow, will be in compliance with Section 13113.8 of the Health and Safety Code by having operable smoke detector(s) which are approved, listed, and installed in accordance with the State Fire Marshal's regulations and applicable local standards.

2. The Seller certifies that the property, as of the close of escrow, will be in compliance with Section 19211 of the Health and Safety Code by having the water heater tank(s) braced, anchored, or strapped in place in accordance with applicable law.

Seller certifies that the information herein is true and correct to the best of the Seller's knowledge as of the date signed by the Seller.

Buyer's Initials (_____)(_____)

TDS REVISED 11/11 (PAGE 2 OF 3)

| Reviewed by _____ Date _____ |

EQUAL HOUSING
OPPORTUNITY

REAL ESTATE TRANSFER DISCLOSURE STATEMENT (TDS PAGE 2 OF 3)

Property Address: 1652 Hill Street, Any City, Apple County, California 90000   Date: 4/1/20XX

Seller Fred Spring _____   Date 4/1/20XX

Seller Jan Spring _____   Date 4/1/20XX

III. AGENT'S INSPECTION DISCLOSURE
(To be completed only if the Seller is represented by an agent in this transaction.)

THE UNDERSIGNED, BASED ON THE ABOVE INQUIRY OF THE SELLER(S) AS TO THE CONDITION OF THE PROPERTY AND BASED ON A REASONABLY COMPETENT AND DILIGENT VISUAL INSPECTION OF THE ACCESSIBLE AREAS OF THE PROPERTY IN CONJUNCTION WITH THAT INQUIRY, STATES THE FOLLOWING:

☐ See attached Agent Visual Inspection Disclosure (AVID Form)
☐ Agent notes no items for disclosure.
☒ Agent notes the following items: The property has a few paint chips on the walls, a broken tile near the stove, and the back screen door frame appears bent. The fireplace has not been used by the sellers in over one (1) year.

Agent (Broker Representing Seller) _____ Tom Baker _____   By ___ Pat Green ___   Date 4/1/20XX
                                        (Please Print)   (Associate Licensee or Broker Signature)

IV. AGENT'S INSPECTION DISCLOSURE
(To be completed only if the agent who has obtained the offer is other than the agent above.)

THE UNDERSIGNED, BASED ON A REASONABLY COMPETENT AND DILIGENT VISUAL INSPECTION OF THE ACCESSIBLE AREAS OF THE PROPERTY, STATES THE FOLLOWING:

☐ See attached Agent Visual Inspection Disclosure (AVID Form)
☐ Agent notes no items for disclosure.
☐ Agent notes the following items: _____

Agent (Broker Obtaining the Offer) _____   By _____   Date _____
                                        (Please Print)   (Associate Licensee or Broker Signature)

V. BUYER(S) AND SELLER(S) MAY WISH TO OBTAIN PROFESSIONAL ADVICE AND/OR INSPECTIONS OF THE PROPERTY AND TO PROVIDE FOR APPROPRIATE PROVISIONS IN A CONTRACT BETWEEN BUYER AND SELLER(S) WITH RESPECT TO ANY ADVICE/INSPECTIONS/DEFECTS.

I/WE ACKNOWLEDGE RECEIPT OF A COPY OF THIS STATEMENT.

Seller _____ Fred Spring _____   Date 4/1/20XX   Buyer _____   Date _____

Seller _____ Jan Spring _____   Date 4/1/20XX   Buyer _____   Date _____

Agent (Broker Representing Seller) _____ Tom Baker _____   By ___ Pat Green ___   Date 4/1/20XX
                                        (Please Print)   (Associate Licensee or Broker Signature)

Agent (Broker Obtaining the Offer) _____   By _____   Date _____
                                        (Please Print)   (Associate Licensee or Broker Signature)

SECTION 1102.3 OF THE CIVIL CODE PROVIDES A BUYER WITH THE RIGHT TO RESCIND A PURCHASE CONTRACT FOR AT LEAST THREE DAYS AFTER THE DELIVERY OF THIS DISCLOSURE IF DELIVERY OCCURS AFTER THE SIGNING OF AN OFFER TO PURCHASE. IF YOU WISH TO RESCIND THE CONTRACT, YOU MUST ACT WITHIN THE PRESCRIBED PERIOD.

A REAL ESTATE BROKER IS QUALIFIED TO ADVISE ON REAL ESTATE. IF YOU DESIRE LEGAL ADVICE, CONSULT YOUR ATTORNEY.

R E B S | I N C
Published and Distributed by:
REAL ESTATE BUSINESS SERVICES, INC.
a subsidiary of the California Association of REALTORS®
® 525 South Virgil Avenue, Los Angeles, California 90020

Reviewed by _____ Date _____

EQUAL HOUSING OPPORTUNITY

TDS REVISED 11/11 (PAGE 3 OF 3)
REAL ESTATE TRANSFER DISCLOSURE STATEMENT (TDS PAGE 3 OF 3)

SUPPLEMENTAL STATUTORY AND CONTRACTUAL DISCLOSURES

Some brokers use this form in addition to the Transfer Disclosure Statement. The form includes the following representations made by the seller, which are not representations of the agents.

A. Has there been the death of an occupant of the property upon the property within the last three (3) years?

B. Has an order been issued by a government health official stating that the property is contaminated by methamphetamine?

C. Has there been the release of an illegal controlled substance on or beneath the property?

D. Is the property located in or adjacent to an "industrial use" area?

E. Is the property located within one (1) mile of a former federal or state ordnance location?

F. Is the property a condominium or located in a planned unit development or other common interest subdivision?

G. Are there insurance claims affecting the property within the past five (5) years?

H. Are there matters affecting title of the property?

I. Are there any material facts or defects affecting the property not otherwise disclosed to the buyer?

J. Are there any material facts or defects affecting the property not otherwise disclosed to the buyer?

When the seller signs and dates the disclosure, he or she affirms that the information is true and correct to the best of the seller's knowledge.

The buyer, the seller's agent, and the buyer's agent should acknowledge also with their respective signatures and dates, and affirm that the buyer has received, read, and understands the form.

Methamphetamine Contamination Notice

You should include a "Methamphetamine Contamination Notice" form in your seller's package. Although you may not need to use it, commencing January 1, 2006, a property owner must complete this disclosure form if a local health official has issued an order prohibiting the use or occupancy of the property. The property owner must either clean up or pay for the clean up and remediation of any contamination caused by meth lab activity. For more information, see Assembly Bill 1078.

CALIFORNIA
ASSOCIATION
OF REALTORS®

SUPPLEMENTAL STATUTORY
AND CONTRACTUAL DISCLOSURES
(C.A.R. Form SSD, Revised 11/09)

1. Seller makes the following disclosures with regard to the real property or manufactured home described as
   __1652 Hill Street_____ , Assessor's Parcel No. __PQ9856_____ ,
   situated in __Any City_____ , County of __Apple_____ , California, ("Property").

2. **THE FOLLOWING ARE REPRESENTATIONS MADE BY THE SELLER AND ARE NOT THE REPRESENTATIONS OF THE AGENT(S), IF ANY. THIS DISCLOSURE STATEMENT IS NOT A WARRANTY OF ANY KIND BY THE SELLER OR ANY AGENT(S) AND IS NOT A SUBSTITUTE FOR ANY INSPECTIONS OR WARRANTIES THE PRINCIPAL(S) MAY WISH TO OBTAIN. A REAL ESTATE BROKER IS QUALIFIED TO ADVISE ON REAL ESTATE TRANSACTIONS. IF SELLER OR BUYER DESIRE LEGAL ADVICE, CONSULT AN ATTORNEY.**

3. **Are you (Seller) aware of any of the following? (Explain any "yes" answers below.)**
   A. Within the last 3 years, the death of an occupant of the Property upon the Property. . . . . ☐ Yes ☒ No
   B. An Order from a government health official identifying the Property as being contaminated by
      methamphetamine. (If yes, attach a copy of the Order.) . . . . ☐ Yes ☒ No
   C. The release of an illegal controlled substance on or beneath the Property . . . . ☐ Yes ☒ No
   D. Whether the Property is located in or adjacent to an "industrial use" zone . . . . ☐ Yes ☒ No
      (In general, a zone or district allowing manufacturing, commercial or airport uses.)
   E. Whether the Property is affected by a nuisance created by an "industrial use" zone . . . . ☐ Yes ☒ No
   F. Whether the Property is located within 1 mile of a former federal or state ordinance location . . ☐ Yes ☒ No
      (In general, an area once used for military training purposes that may contain potentially explosive munitions.)
   G. Whether the Property is a condominium or located in a planned unit development or other
      common interest subdivision . . . . ☒ Yes ☐ No
   H. Insurance claims affecting the Property within the past 5 years . . . . ☐ Yes ☒ No
   I. Matters affecting title of the Property . . . . ☐ Yes ☒ No
   J. Material facts or defects affecting the Property not otherwise disclosed to Buyer . . . . ☐ Yes ☒ No
   Explanation, or ☐ (if checked) see attached; _____
   __The property is located in the Hillside Ranch Community Association Homeowner's_____
   __Association (HOA)_____
   _____
   _____
   _____
   _____

4. Seller represents that the information herein is true and correct to the best of Seller's knowledge as of the date signed by Seller. Seller hereby authorizes any agent(s) representing any principal(s) in this transaction to provide a Copy of this statement to any person or entity in connection with any actual or anticipated sale of the Property.

   Seller _*Fred Spring*_____ Date __4/01/20XX_____

   Seller _____*Jan Spring*_____ Date _4/01/20XX_____

5. By signing below, Buyer acknowledges Buyer has received, read, and understands this Supplemental Statutory and Contractual Disclosures form.

   Buyer _____ Date _____

   Buyer _____ Date _____

Published and Distributed by:
REAL ESTATE BUSINESS SERVICES, INC.
a subsidiary of the California Association of REALTORS®
525 South Virgil Avenue, Los Angeles, California 90020

Reviewed by _____ Date _____

EQUAL HOUSING OPPORTUNITY

SSD REVISED 11/09 (PAGE 1 OF 1)

SUPPLEMENTAL STATUTORY AND CONTRACTUAL DISCLOSURES (SSD PAGE 1 OF 1)

Agent:	Tom Baker	Phone: 555.123.4567	Fax: 555.123.4568	Prepared using zipForm® software
Broker:	Sunshine Real Estate 1234 Mountain Road Any City, CA 90000			

METHAMPHETAMINE CONTAMINATION NOTICE
(C.A.R. Form MCN, 1/06)

This Methamphetamine Contamination Notice relates to the
☐ Residential Purchase Agreement,
☐ Residential Lease or Month to Month Rental Agreement ("Agreement")
dated _____
on property known as _____
_____ ("Property") in which _____
_____ is referred to as ☐ Buyer/ ☐ Tenant and
_____
is referred to as ☐ Seller/ ☐ Landlord.

1. Owner of the Property hereby notifies Buyer/Tenant that Owner has received an Order from a governmental health official identifying the Property as being contaminated by methamphetamine and a remediation lien has been recorded against the Property. The Order prohibits use or occupancy of the Property until the Owner receives a notice from the health official that no further action is needed.

2. A copy of the Order is attached to this Methamphetamine Contamination Notice.

By signing below, the undersigned acknowledges that each has received, read and understands this Methamphetamine Contamination Notice and the attached Order. If the undersigned is a Tenant, this Notice and attached Order have been attached to the Lease or Rental Agreement and this Notice and attached Order have been reviewed prior to signing the Lease or Rental Agreement.

Buyer/Tenant _____

Buyer/Tenant _____

Published and Distributed by:
REAL ESTATE BUSINESS SERVICES, INC.
a subsidiary of the California Association of REALTORS®
525 South Virgil Avenue, Los Angeles, California 90020

Reviewed by _____ Date _____

MCN 1/06 (PAGE 1 OF 1) Print Date

METHAMPHETAMINE CONTAMINATION NOTICE (MCN PAGE 1 OF 1)

| Agent: | Phone: | Fax: | Prepared using zipForm® software |
| Broker: | | | |

NATURAL HAZARD DISCLOSURE STATEMENT (NHD)

It was mandated in March 1998 that sellers of many residential properties would give prospective buyers the "Natural Hazard Disclosure Statement" form. This statement warns prospective buyers that certain "hazards may limit your ability to develop the real property, to obtain insurance, or to receive assistance after a disaster". These hazards include:

- a **Special Flood Hazard** area designated by the Federal Emergency Management Agency.

- an **Area of Potential Flooding** in the event of a dam failure, designated by the state Office of Emergency Services.

- a **Very High Fire Hazard Severity Zone** designated by the California Department of Forestry and Fire Protection.

- a **Wildland Fire Area** that may contain substantial forest fire risks and hazards, designated by the State Board of Forestry.

- an **Earthquake Fault Zone** designated by the State Geologist.

- a **Seismic Hazard Zone** designated by the State Geologist.

- the local natural hazard zones (including land sliding, liquefaction, etc).

The statement also advises buyers and sellers that they "may wish to obtain professional advice regarding these hazards". Since most sellers are not soils engineers or geologists, it is a good idea to advise them to hire a professional to prepare the natural hazard statement.

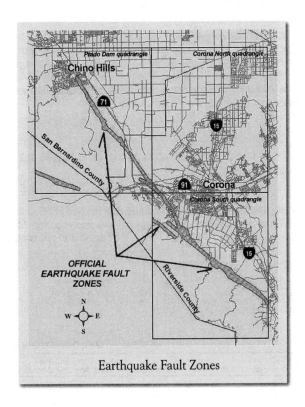

Earthquake Fault Zones

NATURAL HAZARD DISCLOSURE STATEMENT
(C.A.R. Form NHD, Revised 10/04)

This statement applies to the following property: _____

The transferor and his or her agent(s) or a third-party consultant disclose the following information with the knowledge that even though this is not a warranty, prospective transferees may rely on this information in deciding whether and on what terms to purchase the subject property. Transferor hereby authorizes any agent(s) representing any principal(s) in this action to provide a copy of this statement to any person or entity in connection with any actual or anticipated sale of the property.

The following are representations made by the transferor and his or her agent(s) based on their knowledge and maps drawn by the state and federal governments. This information is a disclosure and is not intended to be part of any contract between the transferee and transferor.

THIS REAL PROPERTY LIES WITHIN THE FOLLOWING HAZARDOUS AREA(S):

A SPECIAL FLOOD HAZARD AREA (Any type Zone "A" or "V") designated by the Federal Emergency Management Agency.
Yes _____   No _____   Do not know and information not available from local jurisdiction _____

AN AREA OF POTENTIAL FLOODING shown on a dam failure inundation map pursuant to Section 8589.5 of the Government Code.
Yes _____   No _____   Do not know and information not available from local jurisdiction _____

A VERY HIGH FIRE HAZARD SEVERITY ZONE pursuant to Section 51178 or 51179 of the Government Code. The owner of this property is subject to the maintenance requirements of Section 51182 of the Government Code.
Yes _____   No _____

A WILDLAND AREA THAT MAY CONTAIN SUBSTANTIAL FOREST FIRE RISKS AND HAZARDS pursuant to Section 4125 of the Public Resources Code. The owner of this property is subject to the maintenance requirements of Section 4291 of the Public Resources Code. Additionally, it is not the state's responsibility to provide fire protection services to any building or structure located within the wildlands unless the Department of Forestry and Fire Protection has entered into a cooperative agreement with a local agency for those purposes pursuant to Section 4142 of the Public Resources Code.
Yes _____   No _____

AN EARTHQUAKE FAULT ZONE pursuant to Section 2622 of the Public Resources Code.
Yes _____   No _____

A SEISMIC HAZARD ZONE pursuant to Section 2696 of the Public Resources Code.
Yes (Landslide Zone) _____   Yes (Liquefaction Zone) _____
No _____   Map not yet released by state ____

NHD REVISED 10/04 (PAGE 1 OF 2)

Buyer's Initials (___*FS*___)(___*JS*___)
Seller's Initials (_____)(_____)
Reviewed by _____ Date _____

EQUAL HOUSING
OPPORTUNITY

NATURAL HAZARD DISCLOSURE STATEMENT (NHD PAGE 1 OF 2)

Agent: Tom Baker   Phone: (555) 123-4567   Fax: (555) 123-4568   Prepared using zipForm® software
Broker: Sunshine Real Estate   1234 Mountain Road, Any City, CA 90000

Property Address: <u>1652 Hill Street, Any City, Apple County, CA 90000</u>   Date: _____

THESE HAZARDS MAY LIMIT YOUR ABILITY TO DEVELOP THE REAL PROPERTY, TO OBTAIN INSURANCE, OR TO RECEIVE ASSISTANCE AFTER A DISASTER.

THE MAPS ON WHICH THESE DISCLOSURES ARE BASED ESTIMATE WHERE NATURAL HAZARDS EXIST. THEY ARE NOT DEFINITIVE INDICATORS OF WHETHER OR NOT A PROPERTY WILL BE AFFECTED BY A NATURAL DISASTER. TRANSFEREE(S) AND TRANSFEROR(S) MAY WISH TO OBTAIN PROFESSIONAL ADVICE REGARDING THOSE HAZARDS AND OTHER HAZARDS THAT MAY AFFECT THE PROPERTY

Signature of Transferor(s) ___*Fred Spring*_____ Date ____4/1/20XX_____

Signature of Transferor(s) ___*Jan Spring*_____ Date ____4/1/20XX_____

Agent(s) ___*Pat Green*_____ Date ____4/1/20XX_____

Agent(s) _____ Date _____

Check only one of the following:

☑ Transferor(s) and their agent(s) represent that the information herein is true and correct to the best of their knowledge as of the date signed by the transferor(s) and agent(s).

☐ Transferor(s) and their agent(s) acknowledge that they have exercised good faith in the selection of a third-party report provider as required in Civil Code Section 1103.7, and that the representations made in this Natural Hazard Disclosure Statement are based upon information provided by the independent third-party disclosure provider as a substituted disclosure pursuant to Civil Code Section 1103.4. Neither transferor(s) nor their agent(s) (1) has independently verified the information contained in this statement and report or (2) is personally aware of any errors or inaccuracies in the information contained on the statement. This statement was prepared by the provider below:

Third-Party Disclosure Provider(s) _____ Date _____

Transferee represents that he or she has read and understands this document. Pursuant to Civil Code Section 1103.8, the representations made in this Natural Hazard Disclosure Statement do not constitute all of the transferor's or agent's disclosure obligations in this transaction.

Signature of Transferee(s) _____ Date _____

Signature of Transferee(s) _____ Date _____

SURE TRAC
The System for Success™

Published and Distributed by:
REAL ESTATE BUSINESS SERVICES, INC.
a subsidiary of the California Association of REALTORS®
525 South Virgil Avenue, Los Angeles, California 90020

Reviewed by _____ Date _____

EQUAL HOUSING OPPORTUNITY

NHD REVISED 10/04 (PAGE 2 OF 2)
NATURAL HAZARD DISCLOSURE STATEMENT (NHD PAGE 2 OF 2)

CALIFORNIA
ASSOCIATION
OF REALTORS®

LEAD-BASED PAINT AND LEAD-BASED PAINT HAZARDS DISCLOSURE, ACKNOWLEDGMENT AND ADDENDUM
For Pre-1978 Housing Sales, Leases, or Rentals
(C.A.R. Form FLD, Revised 11/10)

The following terms and conditions are hereby incorporated in and made a part of the: ☐ California Residential Purchase Agreement, ☐ Residential Lease or Month-to-Month Rental Agreement, or ☐ Other: _____ _____, dated _____ , on property known as: _____ ("Property") in which _____ is referred to as Buyer or Tenant and _____ is referred to as Seller or Landlord.

LEAD WARNING STATEMENT (SALE OR PURCHASE) Every purchaser of any interest in residential real property on which a residential dwelling was built prior to 1978 is notified that such property may present exposure to lead from lead-based paint that may place young children at risk of developing lead poisoning. Lead poisoning in young children may produce permanent neurological damage, including learning disabilities, reduced intelligent quotient, behavioral problems and impaired memory. Lead poisoning also poses a particular risk to pregnant women. The seller of any interest in residential real property is required to provide the buyer with any information on lead-based paint hazards from risk assessments or inspections in the seller's possession and notify the buyer of any known lead-based paint hazards. A risk assessment or inspection for possible lead-based paint hazards is recommended prior to purchase.

LEAD WARNING STATEMENT (LEASE OR RENTAL) Housing built before 1978 may contain lead-based paint. Lead from paint, paint chips and dust can pose health hazards if not managed properly. Lead exposure is especially harmful to young children and pregnant women. Before renting pre-1978 housing, lessors must disclose the presence of lead-based paint and/or lead-based paint hazards in the dwelling. Lessees must also receive federally approved pamphlet on lead poisoning prevention.

EPA'S LEAD-BASED PAINT RENOVATION, REPAIR AND PAINTING RULE: The new rule requires that contractors and maintenance professionals working in pre-1978 housing, child care facilities, and schools with lead-based paint be certified; that their employees be trained; and that they follow protective work practice standards. The rule applies to renovation, repair, or painting activities affecting more than six square feet of lead-based paint in a room or more than 20 square feet of lead-based paint on the exterior. Enforcement of the rule begins October 1, 2010. See the EPA website at www.epa.gov/lead for more information.

1. **SELLER'S OR LANDLORD'S DISCLOSURE**
   I (we) have no knowledge of lead-based paint and/or lead-based paint hazards in the housing other than the following:
   _____
   _____
   _____
   _____

   I (we) have no reports or records pertaining to lead-based paint and/or lead-based paint hazards in the housing other than the following, which, previously or as an attachment to this addendum have been provided to Buyer or Tenant:
   _____
   _____
   _____

   I (we), previously or as an attachment to this addendum, have provided Buyer or Tenant with the pamphlet *"Protect Your Family From Lead In Your Home"* or an equivalent pamphlet approved for use in the State such as *"The Homeowner's Guide to Environmental Hazards and Earthquake Safety."*

   For Sales Transactions Only: Buyer has 10 days, unless otherwise agreed in the real estate purchase contract, to conduct a risk assessment or inspection for the presence of lead-based paint and/or lead-based paint hazards.

I (we) have reviewed the information above and certify, to the best of my (our) knowledge, that the information provided is true and correct.

_____
Seller or Landlord   Date

_____
Seller or Landlord   Date

FLD REVISED 11/10 (PAGE 1 OF 2)

Buyer's Initials (_____) (_____)

| Reviewed by _____ Date _____ |

EQUAL HOUSING OPPORTUNITY

LEAD-BASED PAINT AND LEAD-BASED PAINT HAZARDS DISCLOSURE (FLD PAGE 1 OF 2)

| Agent: | Phone: | Fax: | Prepared using zipForm® software |
| Broker: | | | |

Property Address: _____ Date _____

2. LISTING AGENT'S ACKNOWLEDGMENT

Agent has informed Seller or Landlord of Seller's or Landlord's obligations under §42 U.S.C. 4852d and is aware of Agent's responsibility to ensure compliance.

I have reviewed the information above and certify, to the best of my knowledge, that the information provided is true and correct.

_____ By _____
(Please Print) Agent (Broker representing Seller or Landlord)   Associate-Licensee or Broker Signature   Date

3. BUYER'S OR TENANT'S ACKNOWLEDGMENT

I (we) have received copies of all information listed, if any, in 1 above and the pamphlet *"Protect Your Family From Lead In Your Home"* or an equivalent pamphlet approved for use in the State such as *"The Homeowner's Guide to Environmental Hazards and Earthquake Safety."* **If delivery of any of the disclosures or pamphlet referenced in paragraph 1 above occurs after Acceptance of an offer to purchase, Buyer has a right to cancel pursuant to the purchase contract. If you wish to cancel, you must act within the prescribed period.**

For Sales Transactions Only: Buyer acknowledges the right for 10 days, unless otherwise agreed in the real estate purchase contract, to conduct a risk assessment or inspection for the presence of lead-based paint and/or lead-based paint hazards; OR, (if checked) ☐ Buyer waives the right to conduct a risk assessment or inspection for the presence of lead-based paint and/or lead-based paint hazards.

I (we) have reviewed the information above and certify, to the best of my (our) knowledge, that the information provided is true and correct.

_____   _____
Buyer or Tenant   Date   Buyer or Tenant   Date

4. COOPERATING AGENT'S ACKNOWLEDGMENT

Agent has informed Seller or Landlord, through the Listing Agent if the property is listed, of Seller's or Landlord's obligations under §42 U.S.C. 4852d and is aware of Agent's responsibility to ensure compliance.

I have reviewed the information above and certify, to the best of my knowledge, that the information provided is true and correct.

_____ By _____
Agent (Broker obtaining the Offer)   Associate-Licensee or Broker Signature   Date

Published and Distributed by:
REAL ESTATE BUSINESS SERVICES, INC.
a subsidiary of the California Association of REALTORS®
525 South Virgil Avenue, Los Angeles, California 90020

Reviewed by _____ Date _____

FLD REVISED 11/10 (PAGE 2 OF 2)

LEAD-BASED PAINT AND LEAD-BASED PAINT HAZARDS DISCLOSURE (FLD PAGE 2 OF 2)

COMBINED HAZARDS BOOK

The *Combined Hazards Book* is comprised of three parts: (1) *Residential Environmental Hazards*, (2) *The Homeowner's Guide to Earthquake Safety*, and (3) *Protect Your Family From Lead* booklet. By giving the buyer this *Combined Hazards Book*, you will meet or exceed current disclosure requirements. Remember, even though you give buyers the disclosure booklets, the seller is still responsible to complete all disclosure forms honestly and accurately.

Combined Hazards Book

Residential Environmental Hazards

Increasingly, buyers are concerned about potential environmental hazards that may be present in a home they are considering to purchase. You may provide them with a booklet called *Residential Environmental Hazards: A Guide for Homeowners, Buyers, Landlords, and Tenants.* This booklet contains information regarding environmental hazards, which may affect residential property. You are not legally required to give the booklet to a buyer. However, the law does state that delivering the booklet to a buyer is considered to be giving adequate information regarding any environmental hazard described in the booklet. It is suggested that homeowners, homebuyers, landlords, and tenants seek professional assistance to determine how to handle these environmental hazards if they exist.

Homeowner's Guide to Earthquake Safety

If the home was built prior to 1960, the homeowner must give The *Homeowner's Guide to Earthquake Safety* booklet to buyers. This booklet has California earthquake maps, before and after pictures of homes damaged by earthquakes, how to use the gas shutoff valve, and other useful information.

Lead-Based Paint Hazards Disclosure

Always include the Lead-Based Paint Hazards Disclosure form and a pamphlet entitled *Protect Your Family From Lead in Your Home* in your listing package. A seller of any interest in residential real property built prior to 1978 is required to notify every purchaser that such property may present exposure to lead from lead-based paint. Exposure to lead-based paint may cause lead poisoning in young children and pregnant women.

WATER HEATERS, SMOKE DETECTORS, AND CARBON MONOXIDE DETECTORS

By the close of escrow, the seller must comply with state and local laws regarding **braced water heaters**. The seller must provide certification of having the water heater(s) braced, anchored, or strapped in place in accordance with those requirements by signing and dating this form. The buyer must acknowledge receipt of the form with his or her signature and date.

By the close of escrow, the seller must also comply with state and local laws regarding operable **smoke detectors**. The seller must have a certification of having operable smoke detector(s) approved and listed by the State Fire Marshal installed in accordance with the State Fire Marshal's regulations and in accordance with applicable local ordinance(s) by signing and dating this form. The buyer must acknowledge receipt of the form with his or her signature and date.

Effective July 1, 2011, the **Carbon Monoxide Poisoning Prevention Act** of 2010 requires that **carbon monoxide detectors** (CO detectors) must be installed in all dwelling units that contain a fossil fuel burning heater, appliance, or fireplace; or that have an attached garage. Carbon monoxide is an odorless gas produced whenever any fuel is burned. The Consumer Product Safety Commission recommends installing a CO detector in the hallway near every separate sleeping area of the home.

Sellers notify buyers on the Real Estate Transfer Disclosure Statement whether the property has carbon monoxide devices installed. No separate compliance certification is required. If the property does not have carbon monoxide devices, the buyer may negotiate with the seller for their installation as a condition of sale. [Health & Safety Code §13260 & §17926]

HOMEOWNER ASSOCIATION INFORMATION REQUEST

This form is used when purchasing types of common interest developments (condominium, community apartment projects stock cooperative, or planned development). Information required on this form should be obtained from the specified homeowner association. The seller should also acknowledge that he or she has read, understands, and has received a copy of this request.

WATER HEATER AND SMOKE DETECTOR
STATEMENT OF COMPLIANCE
(C.A.R. Form WHSD, Revised 11/10)

Property Address: 1652 Hill Street, Any City, Apple County, California 90000

NOTE: A seller who is not required to provide one of the following statements of compliance is not necessarily exempt from the obligation to provide the other statement of compliance.

WATER HEATER STATEMENT OF COMPLIANCE

1. **STATE LAW:** California Law requires that all new and replacement water heaters and existing residential water heaters be braced, anchored or strapped to resist falling or horizontal displacement due to earthquake motion. "Water heater" means any standard water heater with a capacity of no more than 120 gallons for which a pre-engineered strapping kit is readily available. (Health and Safety Code §19211d). Although not specifically stated, the statue requiring a statement of compliance does not appear to apply to a properly installed and bolted tankless water heater for the following reasons: There is no tank that can overturn; Pre-engineered strapping kits for such devices are not readily available; and Bolting already exists that would help avoid displacement or breakage in the event of an earthquake.
2. **LOCAL REQUIREMENTS:** Some local ordinances impose more stringent water heater bracing, anchoring or strapping requirements than does California Law. Therefore, it is important to check with local city or county building and safety departments regarding the applicable water heater bracing, anchoring or strapping requirements for your property.
3. **TRANSFEROR'S WRITTEN STATEMENT:** California Health and Safety Code §19211 requires the seller of any real property containing a water heater to certify, in writing, that the seller is in compliance with California State Law. If the Property is a manufactured or mobile home, Seller shall also file a required Statement with the Department of Housing and Community Development.
4. **CERTIFICATION:** Seller represents that the Property, as of the Close Of Escrow, will be in compliance with Health and Safety Code §19211 by having the water heater(s) braced, anchored or strapped in place, in accordance with those requirements.

Seller ___Fred Spring___ ___Fred Spring___ Date __4/1/20XX__
        (Signature)   (Print Name)

Seller ___Jan Spring___ ___Jan Spring___ Date __4/1/20XX__
        (Signature)   (Print Name)

The undersigned hereby acknowledges receipt of a copy of this document.

Buyer _____ _____ Date _____
        (Signature)   (Print Name)

Buyer _____ _____ Date _____
        (Signature)   (Print Name)

SMOKE DETECTOR STATEMENT OF COMPLIANCE

1. **STATE LAW:** California Law requires that **(i)** every single-family dwelling and factory built housing unit sold on or after January 1, 1986, must have an operable smoke detector, approved and listed by the State Fire Marshal, installed in accordance with the State Fire Marshal's regulations (Health and Safety Code §13113.8) and **(ii)** all used manufactured or mobilehomes have an operable smoke detector in each sleeping room.
2. **LOCAL REQUIREMENTS:** Some local ordinances impose more stringent smoke detector requirements than does California Law. Therefore, it is important to check with local city or county building and safety departments regarding the applicable smoke detector requirements for your property.
3. **TRANSFEROR'S WRITTEN STATEMENT:** California Health and Safety Code §13113.8(b) requires every transferor of any real property containing a single-family dwelling, whether the transfer is made by sale, exchange, or real property sales contract (installment sales contract), to deliver to the transferee a written statement indicating that the transferor is in compliance with California State Law concerning smoke detectors. If the Property is a manufactured or mobile home, Seller shall also file a required Statement with the Department of Housing and Community Development (HCD).
4. **EXCEPTIONS:** Generally, a written statement of smoke detector compliance is not required for transactions for which the Seller is exempt from providing a transfer disclosure statement.
5. **CERTIFICATION:** Seller represents that the Property, as of the Close Of Escrow, will be in compliance with the law by having operable smoke detector(s) **(i)** approved and listed by the State Fire Marshal installed in accordance with the State Fire Marshal's regulations Health and Safety Code §13113.8 or **(ii)** in compliance with Manufactured Housing Construction and Safety Act (Health and Safety Code §18029.6) located in each sleeping room for used manufactured or mobilehomes as required by HCD and **(iii)** in accordance with applicable local ordinance(s).

Seller ___Fred Spring___ ___Fred Spring___ Date __4/1/20XX__
        (Signature)   (Print Name)

Seller ___Jan Spring___ ___Jan Spring___ Date __4/1/20XX__
        (Signature)   (Print Name)

The undersigned hereby acknowledge(s) receipt of a copy of this Water Heater and Smoke Detector Statement of Compliance.

Buyer _____ _____ Date _____
        (Signature)   (Print Name)

Buyer _____ _____ Date _____
        (Signature)   (Print Name)

Published and Distributed by:
REAL ESTATE BUSINESS SERVICES, INC.
a subsidiary of the CALIFORNIA ASSOCIATION OF REALTORS®
525 South Virgil Avenue, Los Angeles, California 90020

Reviewed by _____ Date _____

WHSD REVISED 11/10 (PAGE 1 OF 1)

WATER HEATER AND SMOKE DETECTOR STATEMENT OF COMPLIANCE (WHSD PAGE 1 OF 1)

Agent: Tom Baker   Phone: (555) 123-4567   Fax: (555) 123-4568   Prepared using zipForm® software
Broker: Sunshine Real Estate 1234 Mountain Road, Any City, CA 90000

CALIFORNIA ASSOCIATION OF REALTORS®

HOMEOWNER ASSOCIATION INFORMATION REQUEST
AND CHARGES PER DOCUMENTS PROVIDED AS REQUIRED BY SECTION 1368
(C.A.R. Form HOA, Revised 4/12)

Property Address: 1652 Hill Street, Any City, Apple County, California 90000

Owner of Property: Fred and Jan Spring ("Seller")

Owner's Mailing Address: 1652 Hill Street, Any City, Apple County, California 90000
(If known or different from property address)

To: Homeowner Association Hillside Ranch Community Association ("HOA")

Pursuant to California Civil Code §1368 and the request of Seller (1) upon receipt of this request please provide on this form a written or electronic estimate of fees that will be assessed for providing the requested documents, and (2) within 10 calendar Days from the date of this request, please provide to Seller the items or information listed on page 2 at the mailing address indicated above, or (if checked) to ☐ _____

_____

_____ .

On page 2, please indicate whether the item is attached. If not attached, indicate if not available or not applicable.

Seller or Seller's Agent _Pat Green_ Date _4/1/20XX_

The documents and information provided by the HOA referenced above were provided by:

_____ Its _____
(print name) (title or position)

☐ Association or ☐ Agent Date: _____

By signing below, the undersigned acknowledge that each has read, understands and has received a copy of this Homeowner Association Information Request.

Seller _Fred Spring_ Date _4/1/20XX_

Seller _Jan Spring_ Date _4/1/20XX_

NOTE: Pursuant to California Civil Code § 1368 the requesting party has the option to receive the document in electronic form, if the association maintains the documents in electronic form. Fees charged must be reasonable and based upon the association's actual cost for procuring, preparing, reproducing or delivering the required documents. No additional fee may be charged for electronic delivery and fees charged for documents shall be distinguished from any other fee, fine or assessment billed as part of the transfer or sales transaction.

Reviewed by _____ Date _____

HOMEOWNER ASSOCIATION INFORMATION REQUEST (HOA PAGE 1 OF 2)

Agent: Tom Baker   Phone: (555) 123-4567   Fax: (555) 1234568   Prepared using zipForm® software
Broker: Sunshine Real Estate 1234 Mountain Road, Any City, CA 90000

Property Address: <u>1652 Hill Street, Any City, Apple County, California 90000</u>   Date: <u>4/1/20XX</u>

HOMEOWNER ASSOCIATION RESPONSE TO INFORMATION REQUEST FROM SELLER
FOR COMMON INTEREST DEVELOPMENTS

Document	Civil Codes	HOA Response — Attached or Not Available or Not Applicable		
Articles of Incorporation or statement that HOA not incorporated	1368(a)(1)	☐ Yes or	☐ N/AV	☐ N/APP
CC&R's	1368(a)(1)	☐ Yes or	☐ N/AV	☐ N/APP
Bylaws	1368(a)(1)	☐ Yes or	☐ N/AV	☐ N/APP
(Operating) Rules and Regulations	1368(a)(1)	☐ Yes or	☐ N/AV	☐ N/APP
Age restrictions, if any	1368(a)(2)	☐ Yes or	☐ N/AV	☐ N/APP
Pro Forma Operating Budget, or summary including reserve study	1365, 1368(a)(3)	☐ Yes or	☐ N/AV	☐ N/APP
Assessment and Reserve Funding Disclosure Summary	1365, 1368(a)(4)	☐ Yes or	☐ N/AV	☐ N/APP
Financial Statement Review	1365, 1368(a)(3)	☐ Yes or	☐ N/AV	☐ N/APP
Assessment Enforcement Policy	1365, 1368(a)(4)	☐ Yes or	☐ N/AV	☐ N/APP
Insurance Summary	1365, 1368(a)(3)	☐ Yes or	☐ N/AV	☐ N/APP
Regular Assessment	1368(a)(4)	☐ Yes or	☐ N/AV	☐ N/APP
Special Assessment	1368(a)(4)	☐ Yes or	☐ N/AV	☐ N/APP
Emergency Assessment	1368(a)(4)	☐ Yes or	☐ N/AV	☐ N/APP
Other unpaid obligations of Seller	1367.1, 1368(a),(4)	☐ Yes or	☐ N/AV	☐ N/APP
Approved changes to assessments	1365, 1368(a)(4), (8)	☐ Yes or	☐ N/AV	☐ N/APP
Settlement Notice Regarding Common Area Defects	1368(a)(6), (7), 1375.1	☐ Yes or	☐ N/AV	☐ N/APP
Preliminary list of defects	1368(a)(6), 1375, 1375.1	☐ Yes or	☐ N/AV	☐ N/APP
Notice(s) of Violations	1363, 1368(a)	☐ Yes or	☐ N/AV	☐ N/APP
Required statement of fees	1368(a)	☐ Yes or	☐ N/AV	☐ N/APP
Restriction of prohibition on renting or leasing	1368(a)(9)	☐ Yes or	☐ N/AV	☐ N/APP
Most recent 12 Months of HOA Minutes For regular meeting of Board of Directors	1368(a)(10)	☐ Yes or	☐ N/AV	☐ N/APP
Total fees for these documents	Fee $	☐ Yes or	☐ N/AV	☐ N/APP
Name of contact information of other HOAs governing the property		☐ Yes or	☐ N/AV	☐ N/APP
Pending or anticipated claims or litigation by or against HOA		☐ Yes or	☐ N/AV	☐ N/APP
Number of designated parking spaces		☐ Yes or	☐ N/AV	☐ N/APP
Location of parking spaces		☐ Yes or	☐ N/AV	☐ N/APP
Number of designated storage spaces		☐ Yes or	☐ N/AV	☐ N/APP
Location of storage spaces		☐ Yes or	☐ N/AV	☐ N/APP
Private Transfer Fees and/or Taxes		☐ Yes or	☐ N/AV	☐ N/APP
Pet Restrictions		☐ Yes or	☐ N/AV	☐ N/APP
Smoking Restrictions		☐ Yes or	☐ N/AV	☐ N/APP
Any other document required by law		☐ Yes or	☐ N/AV	☐ N/APP
Other		☐ Yes or	☐ N/AV	☐ N/APP

Left margin labels: REQUIRED BY CIVIL CODE SECTIONS 1368 AND PURCHASE AGREEMENT (rows above); REQUIRED BY PURCHASE AGREEMENT ONLY (lower rows)

The information provided by this form may not include all fees that may be imposed before the close of escrow. Additional fees that are not related to the requirements of Section 1368 may be charged separately.

HOA _____   Date _____

By _____   Title _____

Seller _____   Date _____

Seller _____   Date _____

I acknowledge receipt of a copy of each item checked above. This document may be executed in counterparts.

Buyer _____   Date _____

Buyer _____   Date _____

Reviewed by _____ Date _____   EQUAL HOUSING OPPORTUNITY

HOA REVISED 4/12 (PAGE 2 OF 2)

HOMEOWNER ASSOCIATION INFORMATION REQUEST (HOA PAGE 2 OF 2)

SELLER'S AFFIDAVIT OF NONFOREIGN STATUS AND/OR CALIFORNIA WITHHOLDING EXEMPTION

The Internal Revenue Code provides that a buyer (transferee) of a U.S. real property interest must withhold tax if the seller (transferor) is a "foreign person."

Completion of sections 1, 2, 3, 4, and 5 are required by law and the entire affidavit may be disclosed to the IRS and the California Franchise Tax Board by the seller. Any false statements made within the form may result in a fine, imprisonment, or both. Both the seller and buyer must sign and date this affidavit, and the buyer must receive a signed copy of the form.

**CALIFORNIA
ASSOCIATION
OF REALTORS®**

SELLER'S AFFIDAVIT OF NONFOREIGN STATUS AND/OR CALIFORNIA WITHHOLDING EXEMPTION
FOREIGN INVESTMENT IN REAL PROPERTY TAX ACT (FIRPTA) AND CALIFORNIA WITHHOLDING LAW
(Use a separate form for each Transferor)
(C.A.R. Form AS, Revised 4/12)

Internal Revenue Code ("IRC") Section 1445 provides that a transferee of a U.S. real property interest must withhold tax if the transferor is a "foreign person." California Revenue and Taxation Code Section 18662 provides that a transferee of a California real property interest must withhold tax unless an exemption applies.

I understand that this affidavit may be disclosed to the Internal Revenue Service and to the California Franchise Tax Board by the transferee, and that any false statement I have made herein may result in a fine, imprisonment or both.

1. **PROPERTY ADDRESS** (property being transferred): _1652 Hill Street, Any City, Apple County, CA 90000_ ("Property")
2. **TRANSFEROR'S INFORMATION:**
   Full Name _____ _Fred Spring and Jan Spring_ ("Transferor")
   Telephone Number _____
   Address _1652 Hill Street, Any City, Apple County, CA 90000_
   (Use HOME address for individual transferors. Use OFFICE address for an "Entity" i.e.: corporations, partnerships, limited liability companies, trusts and estates.)
   Social Security No., or Federal Employer Identification No. _____
   For a corporation qualified to do business in California, California Corporation No. _XXX-XX-XXXX_
   Note: In order to avoid withholding, IRC Section 1445 (b) requires that the Seller (a) provides this affidavit to the Buyer with the Seller's taxpayer identification number ("TIN"), or (b) provides this affidavit, including Seller's TIN, to a "qualified substitute" who furnishes a statement to the Buyer under penalty of perjury that the qualified substitute has such affidavit in their possession. A qualified substitute may be (i) an attorney, title company, or escrow company (but not the Seller's agent) responsible for closing the transaction, or (ii) the Buyer's agent.
3. **AUTHORITY TO SIGN:** If this document is signed on behalf of an Entity Transferor, THE UNDERSIGNED INDIVIDUAL DECLARES THAT HE/SHE HAS AUTHORITY TO SIGN THIS DOCUMENT ON BEHALF OF THE TRANSFEROR.
4. **FEDERAL LAW:** I, the undersigned, declare under penalty of perjury that, for the reason checked below, if any, I am exempt (or if signed on behalf of an Entity Transferor, the Entity is exempt) from the federal withholding law (FIRPTA):
   ☐ (For individual Transferors) I am not a nonresident alien for purposes of U.S. income taxation.
   ☐ (For corporation, partnership, limited liability company, trust and estate Transferors) The Transferor is not a foreign corporation, foreign partnership, foreign limited liability company, foreign trust or foreign estate, as those terms are defined in the Internal Revenue Code and Income Tax Regulations.
5. **CALIFORNIA LAW:** I, the undersigned, declare under penalty of perjury that, for the reason checked below, if any, I am exempt (or if signed on behalf of an Entity Transferor, the Entity is exempt) from the California withholding law.
   Certifications which fully exempt the sale from withholding:
   ☐ The total sales price for the Property is $100,000 or less.
   ☐ The Property qualifies as my principal residence (or the decedent's, if being sold by the decedent's estate) within the meaning of IRC Section 121 (owned and occupied as such for two of the last five years).
   ☐ The Property was last used as my principal residence (or the decedent's, if being sold by the decedent's estate) within the meaning of IRC Section 121 without regard to the two-year time period.
   ☐ The transaction will result in a loss or zero gain for California income tax purposes. (Complete FTB Form 593-E.)
   ☐ The Property has been compulsorily or involuntarily converted (within the meaning of IRC Section 1033) and Transferor intends to acquire property similar or related in service or use to be eligible for non-recognition of gain for California income tax purposes under IRC Section 1033.
   ☐ Transferor is a corporation (or an LLC classified as a corporation) that is either qualified through the California Secretary of State or has a permanent place of business in California.
   ☐ Transferor is a partnership (or an LLC that is not a disregarded single member LLC, classified as a partnership) and recorded title to the Property is in the name of the partnership or LLC. If so, the partnership or LLC must withhold from nonresident partners or members as required.
   ☐ Transferor is exempt from tax under California or federal law.
   ☐ Transferor is an insurance company, qualified pension/profit sharing plan, IRA or charitable remainder trust.
   Certifications which may partially or fully exempt the sale from withholding:
   ☐ The Property is being, or will be, exchanged for property of like kind within the meaning of IRC Section 1031.
   ☐ Payments for the Property are being made in installments, the transferor is a non-resident seller and withholding will be applied to each principal payment.
   ☐ As a result of the sale of the Property, Seller's tax liability, calculated at the maximum tax rate regardless of Seller's actual rate, will be less than the 3 1/3% withholding otherwise required. Seller will be required to sign a certification, under penalty of perjury, specifying the amount to be withheld. **(Not to be used for sales closing prior to January 1, 2007)**

By _Fred Spring and Jan Spring_ Date _4/1/20XX_
(Transferor's Signature) (Indicate if you are signing as the grantor of a revocable/grantor trust.)
FRED SPRING AND JAN SPRING
Typed or printed name   Title (If signed on behalf of Entity Transferor)

Buyer's unauthorized use or disclosure of Seller's TIN could result in civil or criminal liability.

Buyer _____ Date _____
(Buyer acknowledges receipt of a Copy of this Seller's Affidavit)
Buyer _____ Date _____
(Buyer acknowledges receipt of a Copy of this Seller's Affidavit)

Published and Distributed by:
REAL ESTATE BUSINESS SERVICES, INC.
a subsidiary of the California Association of REALTORS®
525 South Virgil Avenue, Los Angeles, California 90020

Reviewed by _____ Date _____

AS 4/12 (PAGE 1 OF 2)
SELLER'S AFFIDAVIT OF NONFOREIGN STATUS AND/OR CALIFORNIA WITHOLDING EXEMPTION (AS PAGE 1 OF 2)

Agent: Tom Baker   Phone: 555.123.4567   Fax: 555.123.4568   Prepared using zipForm® software
Broker: Sunshine Real Estate   1234 Mountain Road   Any City, CA 90000

UNIT 5 REVIEW

◼ Matching Exercise

Instructions: Write the letter of the matching term on the blank line before its definition. Answers are in Appendix A.

Terms

A. agent

B. arbitrator

C. buyer's agent

D. dual agency

E. dual agent

F. latent defect

G. listing agent

H. listing

I. mirror offer

J. Multiple Listing Service

K. patent defect

L. principal

M. selling agent

N. single agency

O. subagent

P. third party

Q. safety clause

R. vesting

Definitions

1. _____ The client (buyer or seller) in an agency relationship

2. _____ The customer in an agency relationship

3. _____ An agency in which the broker represents only the buyer or the seller in the transaction

4. _____ The broker who obtains a listing from a seller to act as an agent for compensation

5. _____ A contract between the property owner and the broker to place properties for sale with the brokerage

6. _____ The broker who finds a buyer and obtains an offer for the real property

7. _____ A broker employed by the buyer to represent him or her and locate a certain kind of real property

8. _____ A broker delegated by the listing agent (if authorized by the seller) who represents the seller in finding a buyer for the listed property

9. _____ A broker who represents both the seller and the buyer in the same transaction

10. _____ An offer that matches all terms in the listing

11. _____ A clause that protects the listing broker's commission if the owner personally sells the property to someone who had previously been shown the property or made an offer during the term of the listing

12. _____ How title to real property is held

13. _____ A neutral person hired to listen to each side of a dispute

14. _____ Observable defects

15. _____ Hidden defects

Multiple Choice Questions

Instructions: Circle your response and go to Appendix A to read the complete explanation for each question.

1. In order to help the seller set an appropriate listing price, a salesperson must prepare a(n):
   a. Seller Listing Package.
   b. Competitive Market Analysis.
   c. Agency Disclosure.
   d. none of the above.

2. Every single agency relationship has:
   a. an agent.
   b. a principal.
   c. a third party.
   d. all of the above.

3. Which of the following is a dual agency?
   a. A broker is representing only a buyer.
   b. A broker is representing only a seller.
   c. A broker is representing both the buyer and the seller.
   d. A principal is represented by a listing agent and a buyer's agent.

4. Salesperson Tom wants to get a listing from seller Fred. The meeting is going well and Tom is now ready to ask Fred to list his home. What should Tom do at this point in the meeting?

    a. Fill out a listing agreement
    b. Prepare a competitive market analysis
    c. Disclose the agency relationship
    d. Show Tom how much money he will make when the sale is complete

5. If a seller wishes to include a refrigerator in the sale of his or her property, on what part of the Residential Listing Agreement must the refrigerator be listed?

    a. Section 2.
    b. Section 3.A
    c. Section 4.B
    d. Section 4.F

6. In the unit's case study, the Springs will pay Tom Baker, their broker, an additional 1% if he brings in a "mirror" offer that closes within 30 days of the listing date. On what part of the Residential Listing Agreement is this information to be stated?

    a. Section 1.
    b. Section 3.B
    c. Section 4.C
    d. Section 4.D

7. What is the main difference between mediation and arbitration?

    a. The arbitrator makes suggestions, but does not create a binding decision on all parties to the dispute.
    b. Mediation is used for money damages and arbitration is only used for specific performance.
    c. Mediation awards are final, and the courts will not re-hear the case.
    d. Arbitration awards are final, and the courts will not re-hear the case.

8. Who signs the Residential Listing Agreement?

    a. Seller and selling agent
    b. Buyer and selling agent
    c. Seller and listing agent
    d. Buyer and listing agent

9. What is the purpose of the Estimated Seller's Proceeds form?
    a. It determines the sale price of a property.
    b. It estimates the seller's approximate costs and proceeds from the sale of a property.
    c. It discloses the seller's proceeds.
    d. None of the above

10. The *Combined Hazards Book* is comprised of:
    a. *Residential Environmental Hazards.*
    b. *Protect Your Family From Lead* booklet.
    c. *Homeowner's Guide to Earthquake Safety.*
    d. all of the above.

Completing the Buyer's Forms

Unit **6**

INTRODUCTION

Forms are a vital part of the real estate buying and selling process. To feel confident, you must know which forms to use, and how and when to use them. The seller's forms were covered in Unit 5. This unit covers the buyer's forms. One of the most important forms in the purchase and sale of real estate is the real estate **purchase agreement**. When signed by both buyer and seller, it is a legally binding written contract that indicates the terms and conditions of the purchase and sale of the piece of real estate.

Verbal promises should never be relied upon; all details of a verbal agreement should be included in your written real estate purchase agreement. Buyers and sellers will often ask for advice from a real estate agent or an attorney when working on a purchase and sale agreement.

No standard real estate purchase agreement will be suitable for all buyers and sellers. Therefore, in some cases buyers and sellers slightly modify, delete, or add parts to the purchase and sale agreement to satisfy their needs.

Learning Objectives

After reading this unit, you should be able to:

- identify the common forms used when working with buyers.
- name the steps in disclosing agency relationships.
- complete typical buyer forms.
- recall the importance of real estate property disclosures.

CASE STUDY

- The information in this case study is used to complete the typical buyer's forms covered in this unit.

The Buyers

Sam and Cindy Winter, a newly married couple currently living in Some Town, are looking at homes in the Hillside Ranch area of Any City, California, 90000. They found a single-family detached home with common areas located in Hillside Ranch, so on April 15, 20xx, the Winters signed an Offer to Purchase and Receipt for Deposit for the home. The address is 1652 Hill Street, Apple County, Any City, California, 90000.

Sam and Cindy Winter

The Winters offered $415,000. The buyers would like escrow to close in forty-five (45) days, or on June 30, 20xx. The buyers gave a check for $5,000 as an earnest money deposit. If the offer is accepted, they will increase the deposit to $41,500 when escrow is opened. Prior to close, the balance of the deposit, $41,500, will be deposited into escrow. The Winters plan to get a conventional 80%, fully amortized, 30-year loan, with a fixed interest rate not to exceed 5.75% and 2 points.

Based on this information, Linda Rose calculated that their estimated monthly payment will be $2,675.00 (principal and interest - $1,935.00, taxes - $430.00, insurance - $100.00, and association dues - $210.00).

The Winters will own and occupy the home and do not have to sell an existing home in order to purchase this home.

No loan charges or sales concessions will be paid on behalf of the borrower, which is typical of the local market.

Buyers' Broker

The Winters have buyer's representation with salesperson Linda Rose who works for Lisa Summers, broker of First Real Estate. The brokerage office is located at 1234 First Street, Any City, California, 90000. The phone number is 555-456-1234, fax is 555-456-9876, and e-mail is lisa@firstrealestate.xyz.

Remember, the Winters have an agency relationship with the broker, Lisa Summers, not the salesperson, Linda Rose. When escrow closes, the commission will be paid to Lisa Summers, the broker. Lisa, in turn, will pay Linda Rose her commission based on their agreed-upon commission split.

Description of the Property

The 1,750 square foot home, built in 1990, is in excellent condition. It has four bedrooms, two full baths, living room, formal dining room, kitchen, and a family room off the kitchen. The unfinished attic is accessible from the master bedroom closet.

The Spring's house measures 50 feet wide by 35 feet deep. It is located on a cul-de-sac lot measuring 70 feet by 160 feet, which is average for the neighborhood. Although some homes in Hillside Ranch have wonderful views of the valley, this home has no appreciable view.

Property Features
- Gas range
- Side-by-side refrigerator
- Built-in dishwasher
- Garbage disposal
- Aluminum gutters and downspouts (good condition)
- Washer/dryer hookups
- Smoke detectors

- Gas central forced-air furnace
- Central air conditioning
- Concrete and brick patio (25 feet wide by 15 feet deep)
- Fully fenced backyard with concrete block wall
- In-ground, heated spa. Currently the solar spa heater needs to be repaired and it has no locking safety cover.
- Attached two-car garage, with 220 volt wiring and poured concrete driveway
- Public utilities: gas, sewer, water, electricity
- Exhaust fans in kitchen and bathrooms (good condition)
- Aluminum-framed window screens (fair condition). Three screens are missing and the frame of the back screen door is bent.
- Stone-faced, gas-fired fireplace located in the living room. The Springs have not used it in over a year and do not know its current condition.
- Concrete tile roof surface (excellent condition)
- Concrete slab foundation (excellent condition)
- Exterior walls are painted stucco (excellent condition)
- Dual-pane windows with aluminum framing (good condition)
- Interior walls are painted drywall with standard painted molding and trim (good condition)
- Floors: vinyl flooring and wall-to-wall carpeting (both in excellent condition)
- Water heater in garage (not anchored or braced)

The seller is not aware of any physical deficiencies or adverse conditions that would affect the value of this property. The property is not located in a FEMA Special Flood Hazard Area. The property complies with its zoning classification of R-1-10000 (single-family residential with a minimum lot size of 10,000 square feet).

Neighborhood Information

Hillside Ranch is comprised of single-family detached homes with several parks and common areas. An elementary school and a junior high school are located one mile south of the subdivision, and the high school is less than three miles west. Several houses of worship are located within one mile of the neighborhood. Several small retail centers are located in the community, with larger centers located within a five-mile radius. The public, asphalt streets are typical for the area. Freeway access is three miles south, allowing for greater privacy and seclusion. Public transportation is available along the major thoroughfares that run through the neighborhood.

DISCLOSING THE AGENCY RELATIONSHIP

The Agency Relationship Disclosure Act has been in effect since January 1, 1988. Its purpose is to clarify the agency relationships between sellers, agents, and buyers and applies to every residential property transaction of one-to-four units. The law requires that an agent supply a written document, called Disclosure Regarding Real Estate Agency Relationships, explaining the nature of agency. This disclosure must be made prior to taking a listing or writing an offer.

Disclosure Process

The three steps in the disclosure process are disclose, elect, and confirm.

Disclose the Relationship

The Disclosure Regarding Real Estate Agency Relationships form describes the obligations of an agent as "seller's agent", "buyer's agent", or "dual agent". At this point, all parties are made aware that they do have a choice of who is to represent them as their own agent.

A written disclosure must be presented by a:

- listing agent (or his or her sales associate) who must deliver the form to the seller before entering into a listing agreement.
- selling agent (who may also be the listing agent) who must provide the form to the buyer before the buyer makes an offer to purchase.
- selling agent (if different from the listing agent) who must provide the form to the seller before the offer to purchase is accepted.

Elect the Agency

The second part of the agency disclosure form requires all parties involved to confirm that they understand the agent's role. In other words, the first part of the disclosure reveals that the agent may represent only the buyer, only the seller, or both. All parties acknowledge their understanding at this point.

Confirm the Agency

All parties to the transaction (buyer, seller, and agents) are required to acknowledge that they understand who is representing whom, and sign the agency confirmation form. One more time, the relationship will be confirmed in the sales contract, which is signed by all parties.

Review - Disclosure of Agency Law

- An agent is either the agent of the seller, the buyer, or both buyer and seller.

- A selling broker who is also the listing broker is a dual agent and may not be the agent for the buyer only.

- A dual agent may not tell the seller that the buyer is willing to pay more, nor may a dual agent tell the buyer that the seller will accept less without the express written consent of the parties.

- An agency relationship can exist even though no compensation is received from the party with whom the agency relationship is established.

CALIFORNIA
ASSOCIATION
OF REALTORS®

DISCLOSURE REGARDING
REAL ESTATE AGENCY RELATIONSHIP
(Listing Firm to Seller)
(As required by the Civil Code)
(C.A.R. Form AD, Revised 11/09)

When you enter into a discussion with a real estate agent regarding a real estate transaction, you should from the outset understand what type of agency relationship or representation you wish to have with the agent in the transaction.

SELLER'S AGENT

A Seller's agent under a listing agreement with the Seller acts as the agent for the Seller only. A Seller's agent or a subagent of that agent has the following affirmative obligations:
To the Seller: A Fiduciary duty of utmost care, integrity, honesty and loyalty in dealings with the Seller.
To the Buyer and the Seller:
    (a) Diligent exercise of reasonable skill and care in performance of the agent's duties.
    (b) A duty of honest and fair dealing and good faith.
    (c) A duty to disclose all facts known to the agent materially affecting the value or desirability of the property that are not known to, or within the diligent attention and observation of, the parties. An agent is not obligated to reveal to either party any confidential information obtained from the other party that does not involve the affirmative duties set forth above.

BUYER'S AGENT

A selling agent can, with a Buyer's consent, agree to act as agent for the Buyer only. In these situations, the agent is not the Seller's agent, even if by agreement the agent may receive compensation for services rendered, either in full or in part from the Seller. An agent acting only for a Buyer has the following affirmative obligations:
To the Buyer: A fiduciary duty of utmost care, integrity, honesty and loyalty in dealings with the Buyer.
To the Buyer and the Seller:
    (a) Diligent exercise of reasonable skill and care in performance of the agent's duties.
    (b) A duty of honest and fair dealing and good faith.
    (c) A duty to disclose all facts known to the agent materially affecting the value or desirability of the property that are not known to, or within the diligent attention and observation of, the parties.
An agent is not obligated to reveal to either party any confidential information obtained from the other party that does not involve the affirmative duties set forth above.

AGENT REPRESENTING BOTH SELLER AND BUYER

A real estate agent, either acting directly or through one or more associate licensees, can legally be the agent of both the Seller and the Buyer in a transaction, but only with the knowledge and consent of both the Seller and the Buyer.
In a dual agency situation, the agent has the following affirmative obligations to both the Seller and the Buyer:
    (a) A fiduciary duty of utmost care, integrity, honesty and loyalty in the dealings with either the Seller or the Buyer.
    (b) Other duties to the Seller and the Buyer as stated above in their respective sections.
In representing both Seller and Buyer, the agent may not, without the express permission of the respective party, disclose to the other party that the Seller will accept a price less than the listing price or that the Buyer will pay a price greater than the price offered.
The above duties of the agent in a real estate transaction do not relieve a Seller or Buyer from the responsibility to protect his or her own interests. You should carefully read all agreements to assure that they adequately express your understanding of the transaction. A real estate agent is a person qualified to advise about real estate. If legal or tax advice is desired, consult a competent professional.
Throughout your real property transaction you may receive more than one disclosure form, depending upon the number of agents assisting in the transaction. The law requires each agent with whom you have more than a casual relationship to present you with this disclosure form. You should read its contents each time it is presented to you, considering the relationship between you and the real estate agent in your specific transaction.
This disclosure form includes the provisions of Sections 2079.13 to 2079.24, inclusive, of the Civil Code set forth on page 2. Read it carefully.
I/WE ACKNOWLEDGE RECEIPT OF A COPY OF THIS DISCLOSURE AND THE PORTIONS OF THE CIVIL CODE PRINTED ON THE BACK (OR A SEPARATE PAGE).

☒ Buyer ☐ Seller ☐ Landlord ☐ Tenant _Sam Winter_____ Date __4/15/20XX____

☒ Buyer ☐ Seller ☐ Landlord ☐ Tenant _Cindy Winter_____ Date _4/15/20XX____

Agent _Lisa Summers, First Real Estate_____ DRE Lic. # __00931278_____
                Real Estate Broker (Firm)
By _Linda Rose_____ DRE Lic. # __00891254_____ Date _4/15/20XX____
     (Salesperson or Broker-Associate)

AGENCY DISCLOSURE COMPLIANCE (Civil Code §2079.14):
- When the listing brokerage company also represents Buyer/Tenant: The Listing Agent shall have one AD form signed by Seller/Landlord and a different AD form signed by Buyer/Tenant.
- When Seller/Landlord and Buyer/Tenant are represented by different brokerage companies: (i) the Listing Agent shall have one AD form signed by Seller/Landlord and (ii) the Buyer's/Tenant's Agent shall have one AD form signed by Buyer/Tenant and either that same or a different AD form presented to Seller/Landlord for signature prior to presentation of the offer. If the same form is used, Seller may sign here:

(SELLER/LANDLORD: DO NOT SIGN HERE)		**(SELLER/LANDLORD: DO NOT SIGN HERE)**	
Seller/Landlord	Date	Seller/Landlord	Date

R E B S
I N C

Published and Distributed by:
REAL ESTATE BUSINESS SERVICES, INC.
a subsidiary of the California Association of REALTORS®
525 South Virgil Avenue, Los Angeles, California 90020

| Reviewed by _____ Date _____ |

EQUAL HOUSING
OPPORTUNITY

AD REVISED 11/09 (PAGE 1 OF 2)

DISCLOSURE REGARDING REAL ESTATE AGENCY RELATIONSHIP (AD PAGE 1 OF 2)

Agent: Lisa Summers	Phone: (555) 456-1234	Fax: (555) 458-9876	Prepared using zipForm® software
Broker: First Real Estate 234 First Street, Any City, California 90000			

CIVIL CODE SECTIONS 2079.13 THROUGH 2079.24 (2079.16 APPEARS ON THE FRONT)

2079.13 As used in Sections 2079.14 to 2079.24, inclusive, the following terms have the following meanings:
(a) "Agent" means a person acting under provisions of title 9 (commencing with Section 2295) in a real property transaction, and includes a person who is licensed as a real estate broker under Chapter 3 (commencing with Section 10130) of Part 1 of Division 4 of the Business and Professions Code, and under whose license a listing is executed or an offer to purchase is obtained. **(b)** "Associate licensee" means a person who is licensed as a real estate broker or salesperson under Chapter 3 (commencing with Section 10130) of Part 1 of Division 4 of the Business and Professions Code and who is either licensed under a broker or has entered into a written contract with a broker to act as the broker's agent in connection with acts requiring a real estate license and to function under the broker's supervision in the capacity of an associate licensee. The agent in the real property transaction bears responsibility for his or her associate licensees who perform as agents of the agent. When an associate licensee owes a duty to any principal, or to any buyer or seller who is not a principal, in a real property transaction, that duty is equivalent to the duty owed to that party by the broker for whom the associate licensee functions. **(c)** "Buyer" means a transferee in a real property transaction, and includes a person who executes an offer to purchase real property from a seller through an agent, or who seeks the services of an agent in more than a casual, transitory, or preliminary manner, with the object of entering into a real property transaction. "Buyer" includes vendee or lessee. **(d)** "Dual agent" means an agent acting, either directly or through an associate licensee, as agent for both the seller and the buyer in a real property transaction. **(e)** "Listing agreement" means a contract between an owner of real property and an agent, by which the agent has been authorized to sell the real property or to find or obtain a buyer. **(f)** "Listing agent" means a person who has obtained a listing of real property to act as an agent for compensation. **(g)** "Listing price" is the amount expressed in dollars specified in the listing for which the seller is willing to sell the real property through the listing agent. **(h)** "Offering price" is the amount expressed in dollars specified in an offer to purchase for which the buyer is willing to buy the real property. **(i)** "Offer to purchase" means a written contract executed by a buyer acting through a selling agent which becomes the contract for the sale of the real property upon acceptance by the seller. **(j)** "Real property" means any estate specified by subdivision (1) or (2) of Section 761 in property which constitutes or is improved with one to four dwelling units, any leasehold in this type of property exceeding one year's duration, and mobile homes, when offered for sale or sold through an agent pursuant to the authority contained in Section 10131.6 of the Business and Professions Code. **(k)** "Real property transaction" means a transaction for the sale of real property in which an agent is employed by one or more of the principals to act in that transaction, and includes a listing or an offer to purchase. **(l)** "Sell," "sale," or "sold" refers to a transaction for the transfer of real property from the seller to the buyer, and includes exchanges of real property between the seller and buyer, transactions for the creation of a real property sales contract within the meaning of Section 2985, and transactions for the creation of a leasehold exceeding one year's duration. **(m)** "Seller" means the transferor in a real property transaction, and includes an owner who lists real property with an agent, whether or not a transfer results, or who receives an offer to purchase real property of which he or she is the owner from an agent on behalf of another. "Seller" includes both a vendor and a lessor. **(n)** "Selling agent" means a listing agent who acts alone, or an agent who acts in cooperation with a listing agent, and who sells or finds and obtains a buyer for the real property, or an agent who locates property for a buyer or who finds a buyer for a property for which no listing exists and presents an offer to purchase to the seller. **(o)** "Subagent" means a person to whom an agent delegates agency powers as provided in Article 5 (commencing with Section 2349) of Chapter 1 of Title 9. However, "subagent" does not include an associate licensee who is acting under the supervision of an agent in a real property transaction.

2079.14 Listing agents and selling agents shall provide the seller and buyer in a real property transaction with a copy of the disclosure form specified in Section 2079.16, and, except as provided in subdivision (c), shall obtain a signed acknowledgement of receipt from that seller or buyer, except as provided in this section or Section 2079.15, as follows: **(a)** The listing agent, if any, shall provide the disclosure form to the seller prior to entering into the listing agreement. **(b)** The selling agent shall provide the disclosure form to the seller as soon as practicable prior to presenting the seller with an offer to purchase, unless the selling agent previously provided the seller with a copy of the disclosure form pursuant to subdivision (a). **(c)** Where the selling agent does not deal on a face-to-face basis with the seller, the disclosure form prepared by the selling agent may be furnished to the seller (and acknowledgement of receipt obtained for the selling agent from the seller) by the listing agent, or the selling agent may deliver the disclosure form by certified mail addressed to the seller at his or her last known address, in which case no signed acknowledgement of receipt is required. **(d)** The selling agent shall provide the disclosure form to the buyer as soon as practicable prior to execution of the buyer's offer to purchase, except that if the offer to purchase is not prepared by the selling agent, the selling agent shall present the disclosure form to the buyer not later than the next business day after the selling agent receives the offer to purchase from the buyer.

2079.15 In any circumstance in which the seller or buyer refuses to sign an acknowledgement of receipt pursuant to Section 2079.14, the agent, or an associate licensee acting for an agent, shall set forth, sign, and date a written declaration of the facts of the refusal.
2079.16 Reproduced on Page 1 of this AD form.
2079.17 (a) As soon as practicable, the selling agent shall disclose to the buyer and seller whether the selling agent is acting in the real property transaction exclusively as the buyer's agent, exclusively as the seller's agent, or as a dual agent representing both the buyer and the seller. This relationship shall be confirmed in the contract to purchase and sell real property or in a separate writing executed or acknowledged by the seller, the buyer, and the selling agent prior to or coincident with execution of that contract by the buyer and the seller, respectively. **(b)** As soon as practicable, the listing agent shall disclose to the seller whether the listing agent is acting in the real property transaction exclusively as the seller's agent, or as a dual agent representing both the buyer and seller. This relationship shall be confirmed in the contract to purchase and sell real property or in a separate writing executed or acknowledged by the seller and the listing agent prior to or coincident with the execution of that contract by the seller.
(c) The confirmation required by subdivisions (a) and (b) shall be in the following form.

(DO NOT COMPLETE, SAMPLE ONLY)	is the agent of (check one): ☐ the seller exclusively; or ☐ both the buyer and seller.
(Name of Listing Agent)	
Lisa Summers, First Real Estate	is the agent of (check one): ☒ the buyer exclusively; or ☐ the seller exclusively; or
(Name of Selling Agent if not the same as the Listing Agent)	☐ both the buyer and seller.

(d) The disclosures and confirmation required by this section shall be in addition to the disclosure required by Section 2079.14.

2079.18 No selling agent in a real property transaction may act as an agent for the buyer only, when the selling agent is also acting as the listing agent in the transaction.

2079.19 The payment of compensation or the obligation to pay compensation to an agent by the seller or buyer is not necessarily determinative of a particular agency relationship between an agent and the seller or buyer. A listing agent and a selling agent may agree to share any compensation or commission paid, or any right to any compensation or commission for which an obligation arises as the result of a real estate transaction, and the terms of any such agreement shall not necessarily be determinative of a particular relationship.

2079.20 Nothing in this article prevents an agent from selecting, as a condition of the agent's employment, a specific form of agency relationship not specifically prohibited by this article if the requirements of Section 2079.14 and Section 2079.17 are complied with.

2079.21 A dual agent shall not disclose to the buyer that the seller is willing to sell the property at a price less than the listing price, without the express written consent of the seller. A dual agent shall not disclose to the seller that the buyer is willing to pay a price greater than the offering price, without the express written consent of the buyer. This section does not alter in any way the duty or responsibility of a dual agent to any principal with respect to confidential information other than price.

2079.22 Nothing in this article precludes a listing agent from also being a selling agent, and the combination of these functions in one agent does not, of itself, make that agent a dual agent.

2079.23 A contract between the principal and agent may be modified or altered to change the agency relationship at any time before the performance of the act which is the object of the agency with the written consent of the parties to the agency relationship.

2079.24 Nothing in this article shall be construed to either diminish the duty of disclosure owed buyers and sellers by agents and their associate licensees, subagents, and employees or to relieve agents and their associate licensees, subagents, and employees from liability for their conduct in connection with acts governed by this article or for any breach of a fiduciary duty or a duty of disclosure.

Buyer's/Tenant's Initials (*SW*) (*CW*)
Seller's/Landlord Initials (_____) (_____)

AD REVISED 11/09 (PAGE 2 OF 2)

| Reviewed by _____ Date _____ |

EQUAL HOUSING
OPPORTUNITY

DISCLOSURE REGARDING REAL ESTATE AGENCY RELATIONSHIP (AD PAGE 2 OF 2)

CALIFORNIA RESIDENTIAL PURCHASE AGREEMENT AND JOINT ESCROW INSTRUCTIONS

In most cases, a standard **California Residential Purchase Agreement and Joint Escrow Instructions (RPA-CA)** contract is used by real estate agents when a buyer makes an offer anywhere in California. It was created by the California Association of REALTORS® (C.A.R.®). The Department of Real Estate does not officially recommend this form; nor is any type of specific form required by law. Real estate agents do have an alternative, however, among the standard C.A.R.® forms, depending on the custom in their area of the state. Real estate practices differ significantly in different parts of California and some of those differences are not reflected in the commonly used deposit receipt. An alternate form, **Area Edition Residential Purchase Agreement (AERPA-11)** is available to real estate agents who desire features not included in the other form.

Step-by-Step Examination of the Agreement

The RPA-CA is probably the most important real estate document you—as a salesperson—will have to understand. Buyers rely on your knowledge, and your commission depends on your ability to explain a complex transaction. Become familiar with the entire document before writing the offer. As you go through each section of the form systematically, refer to the numbered sections below for assistance or explanation.

The offer covers more than just the purchase price and closing date. It covers contingencies, various inspections, mandatory disclosures, buyer's rights to investigate the property, how the buyer will take title, damages and dispute resolution, escrow instructions, compensation to the brokers and acceptance of the offer.

Title

The heading should read "California Residential Purchase Agreement and Joint Escrow Instructions". "California" refers to the fact that the form is available for use throughout the state. The words "and Joint Escrow Instructions" reflect that the form also has an instruction to the escrow holder by both the seller and the buyer. The form includes space for the escrow holder to sign for receipt of the document.

The first line on the contract to fill in is the date and place the buyer signs the contract.

Date

The date refers to the date the buyer signs the offer and the earnest money is received. Write out the date. Do not use abbreviations.

April 15, 20xx	not	4/15/20xx

1. Offer

This section shows the name of the buyer, describes the property to be purchased, the offered purchase price, and the closing date for escrow.

A. This Is an Offer From

This identifies the document as an offer from a specific buyer. List all buyers' names instead of using "nominee" or "assignee", even if not everyone has signed.

Sam Winter and Cindy Winter

B. The Real Property to Be Acquired

This section describes the property for purchase by address, legal description, and/or assessor's parcel number. It also indicates the city or county where the property is located.

A single-family detached home located at 1652 Hill Street, Any City, California. The property is located in Apple County.

The property's legal description is Lot 2 of Block 30 of Hillside Ranch Subdivision, as shown on page 875 of book 465, records of Apple County.

The assessor's parcel number is PQ9856.

C. The Purchase Price

The purchase price is the amount the buyer offers to pay the seller for the property. This amount does not include closing costs, any required funding fees, or insurance premiums.

Write the purchase price in words, and in numbers.

Four hundred fifteen thousand dollars and zero cents ($415,000.00)

D. Close of Escrow

Write a specific date for the close of escrow or choose a date that is a specific number of days after the offer is accepted. This sets the time for close of escrow in order to complete the transaction.

> June 30, 20xx   or   forty-five (45) days after acceptance of offer

2. Agency

A. Disclosure

In this paragraph, the buyer and seller acknowledge prior receipt of the Disclosure Regarding Real Estate Agency Relationships form (C.A.R. Form AD). This form must be presented to the buyer prior to signing a contract to purchase, the seller prior presenting the offer if the selling agent is not the listing agent as well, and the buyer prior to signing a contract to purchase.

B. Potentially Competing Buyers and Sellers

The seller and buyer are advised of and consent to the fact that either the buyer's broker or the seller's broker may represent other principals who may compete with the buyer or seller for purchase of the same property.

C. Confirmation

Confirmation of the agency relationship of the listing and selling agents is required under Civil Code Section 2079.17. No additional confirmation is needed if this is complete and accurate.

If the seller and the buyer do not agree to what is set forth in this confirmation or if this confirmation is blank or partially blank, a counteroffer will need to be written and a confirmation on a statutory form must be attached to the counteroffer.

Note: The selling broker who wrote this offer must sign and present a disclosure to the seller. This must be done before the offer is presented, even if the listing broker previously gave a written disclosure to the seller.

> Listing Agent – Sunshine Real Estate / Tom Baker, Broker
>
> Selling Agent – First Real Estate / Lisa Summers, Broker

3. Finance Terms

This section addresses the financing for the sale—whether the purchase will be an all cash offer or an offer based on obtaining financing. If the buyer must obtain financing to complete the transaction, the finance terms should state if the purchase of the property is contingent upon the buyer's ability to get financing.

The amounts of the initial deposit, any increased deposit, and the loans are listed and added to total the amount of the purchase price. Remember, any earnest money or deposits received by an agent are trust funds and handled as prescribed by the Commissioner's Real Estate Law and Regulations.

A. Initial Deposit

The initial deposit is given directly to the escrow holder or to the agent submitting the offer. This is usually the buyer's agent, but may be a seller's exclusive agent or dual agent if it is an in-house sale.

Funds received may not be commingled with a broker's personal funds. Funds must be deposited and disposed of within three business days after receipt unless otherwise instructed in writing. Indicate if the deposit will be placed into a broker's trust account or elsewhere.

Write the amount in the right-hand column. In some offices, it is a standard practice to write out the amount of the deposit on the dotted line that precedes the space in the right-hand column.

> Five Thousand Dollars and Zero Cents ($5,000.00)

B. Increased Deposit

Choose the amount of deposit and the number of days after acceptance that it will be paid. In order for the increased deposit to be included in the amount of liquidated damages, a separate receipt for the increased deposit must be included at the time it is paid.

Write the amount of the increased deposit in the right-hand column. In our case study, the Winters will increase the deposit to $41,500. Because their initial deposit was $5,000, they need to deposit an additional $36,500 to equal the $41,500.

> $36,500.00

C. Loans

This paragraph refers to the loans that will be used to finance the purchase.

(1) If the first loan will not use conventional financing, indicate whether it is FHA/VA, seller financing, assumed financing, or other financing. Write the amount of the first loan on the line provided in the righthand column. Then fill in the terms of the loan. Terms should be specific, not general or open to future interpretation. Fill in only the type of rate the buyer chooses (fixed or adjustable).

> $332,000.00 (on an 80/20 loan)
> 5.75% maximum interest rate
> 30 year term
> Points not to exceed two (2) percent of loan amount

(2) If the buyer is using a second loan to finance the purchase, this section will contain the terms of the second loan. Just like the instructions for the first loan, indicate the type of financing and write the amount of the loan on the line provided in the right-hand column. Fill in the specific terms of the loan and the type of rate the buyer chooses (fixed or adjustable).

Write the second loan terms in the space provided.

> N/A

(3) If the first or second loan is a FHA or VA loan, the buyer has at least 17 days after the acceptance to deliver to the seller any written notices of lender-required repairs or costs that the buyer wants the seller to cover. These requirements do not have to be met unless the seller agrees to them in writing.

D. Additional Financing Terms

This paragraph refers only to any additional terms that relate to financing.

Write the additional financing terms in the space provided.

> N/A

E. Balance of Purchase Price or Down Payment

The balance of the purchase price is deposited with the escrow holder within sufficient time to close.

Write the amount out in numbers in the right-hand column.

> (Forty-One Thousand Five Hundred Dollars and Zero Cents) $41,500.00

F. Total Purchase Price

Add sections 3A – E from the right-hand column and total. Be sure the total is correct.

Write the total amount in the right-hand column. In some offices, it is a standard practice to write out the amount of the deposit on the dotted line that precedes the space in the right-hand column.

> (Four Hundred Fifteen Thousand Dollars and Zero Cents) $415,000.00

G. Verification of Down Payment and Closing Costs

This paragraph requires the buyer to verify that he or she is able to pay the down payment and closing costs within seven days after acceptance, or the number of days inserted on the blank line.

H. Loan Terms

This paragraph outlines the loan requirements and contingencies for the purchase.

(1) Loan Applications

The buyer must provide a letter from a lender verifying that he or she is prequalified or preapproved for a loan. This must be done within seven days after acceptance, or the number of days inserted on the blank line.

(2) Loan Contingency

The buyer is required to exercise due diligence and act in good faith when obtaining a loan. The deposit, balance of the down payment, and closing costs are not contingencies in the purchase agreement.

(3) Loan Contingency Removal

This requires either the removal of the loan contingency or it specifies that the loan contingency will remain effective until the loan is funded.

(4) No Loan Contingency

This contingency is optional. If checked, it indicates that the offer is not contingent upon obtaining financing.

I. Appraisal Contingency and Removal

The buyer is not obligated to purchase the property if it appraises at less than the purchase price in paragraph 3F, even if a lender is willing to lend the amount specified in paragraph 3C. The buyer is able to check a box and opt out of this contingency.

J. All Cash Offer

The buyer indicates that the purchase will be all cash, with no loan, by checking this paragraph.

K. Buyer Stated Financing

This states that the seller is relying on the information provided by the buyer regarding the financing for the purchase. If the buyer wishes to pursue alternate financing, the seller does not have to cooperate with the buyer's efforts. In addition, the buyer must continue to adhere to the financing methods specified in the purchase agreement. If unable to obtain alternative financing, the buyer is not relieved of the obligation to purchase the property.

4. Allocation of Costs

The purchase of a property requires many inspections, reports, and tests; the cost of which must be allocated between buyer and seller. **Allocate** means to assign. Also, the buyer and seller must agree on allocation of payment for the escrow and title providers they select.

Check the appropriate box(es).

A. (1) – (6) Inspections and Reports

The parties identify who is responsible to pay for an inspection for wood destroying pests and which company should prepare the report. This section also identifies which party will pay for specified inspection reports, such as disposal systems, domestic wells, flood and fire zones, earthquake fault, seismic, etc.

B. (1) & (2) Government Requirements and Retrofit

The parties negotiate who will pay for smoke detector installation compliance, water heater bracing, and any other retrofits that may be required.

C. (1) & (2) Escrow and Title

The parties decide who will pay for the title policy and escrow fees, as well as who will provide those services. The seller must pay the entire escrow fee for VA transactions.

D. (1) – (8) Other Costs

The parties decide who will pay the fees for the enumerated costs as well as any other cost items.

5. Closing and Possession

This section covers the intent of the buyer to occupy the property as a primary residence, the date the seller (or tenant) will turn over possession of the property to the buyer, and whether the buyer is allowed to take possession of the property prior to close of escrow.

Sometimes a buyer wants early possession of the property, or the seller wishes to remain in possession after the close of escrow. In order to protect the rights of both seller and buyer, use an **Interim Occupancy Agreement**.

A. Buyer Occupancy

This paragraph states whether the buyer intends to occupy the premises. This is important because of matters such as liquidated damages, loan qualifications, rates, and terms.

Check the appropriate box.

B. Seller-Occupied or Vacant Property

This paragraph provides the date and time when the property will be turned over to the buyer.

If the buyer moves in early or the seller remains in the property, then the parties should enter into a written agreement to document that separate legal relationship. Occupancy is to be delivered to the buyer at the time specified on the close of escrow, or another specified date. Legal advisors and insurance companies should also be consulted.

C. Tenant-Occupied Property

Unless agreed otherwise, the tenant-occupied property must be vacant prior to the close of escrow. If this is not possible, the buyer and seller may check the following options:

(i) Property shall be vacant at least 5 or [ ] _____ days prior to Close of Escrow,

OR

(ii) Tenant to remain in possession: (C.A.R. Form PAA) should be used, and paragraph 3 checked.

D. Warranties

The seller provides the buyer with any assignable warranty rights and documentation. Third party warranties are automatically assigned by the contract on close of escrow. The broker does not determine the warranties to be assigned.

E. Keys

At time of possession, the seller must deliver keys and means of opening all locks.

6. Statutory Disclosures (Including Lead-Based Paint Hazard Disclosures) and Cancellation Rights

A seller is required by law to give a buyer several disclosures about the property and surrounding area, which might affect the buyer's decision to purchase the property.

A. Statutory Disclosures

(1) **Statutory disclosures** are those that are required by statute or law. This subparagraph summarizes the seller's statutory disclosure requirements to deliver to a buyer two mandated forms: a Transfer Disclosure Statement and a Natural Hazards Disclosure.

(2) The buyer must return the signed statutory and lead disclosures to the seller within the time indicated in Paragraph 14.

(3) The seller must give the buyer an amended written disclosure if the seller becomes aware of any adverse material condition before the close of escrow that the buyer did not know about.

(4) This subparagraph describes the buyer's cancellation rights if the disclosures are delivered after signing the offer.

(5) Neither buyer nor seller can waive their rights to receive these statutorily required disclosures.

B. Natural and Environmental Hazards

The seller must provide the buyer with the natural hazard disclosures specified in Paragraph 6 within the time specified in Paragraph 14. The form is required to make six natural hazard zone disclosures:

- Geologic, Earthquake, and Seismic Hazard Zones Disclosure
- Special Flood Hazard Areas
- Inundation Zone
- State (Fire) Responsibility Areas (SRA)
- Very High Fire Severity Zone
- Earthquake Safety

Note: The seller and broker must disclose known deficiencies in structure and earthquake hazards on all properties. The Environmental Hazard Booklet discusses common hazards.

C. Witholding Taxes

The seller must deliver to the buyer an affidavit that complies with the Foreign Investment in Real Property Tax Act and California tax withholding law by the date specified in paragraph 14A.

D. Megan's Law Data Base Disclosure

A seller is required by statute to inform a buyer that information is available from law enforcement officials regarding the location of registered sexual offenders.

7. Condominium/Planned Unit Development Disclosures

A. The seller will make known to the buyer that the property is part of a development where property is shared in common with other owners or is subject to certain rules along with other owners.

B. The seller must request and provide, within a specified number of days after acceptance, the contractually required documents from the homeowners' association.

8. Items Included In and Excluded From Purchase Price

If a buyer wants an item of personal property belonging to the seller such as drapes, bedspread, or washer and dryer; the deposit receipt must show that both the buyer and the seller agree to the transfer of the personal property.

A. Note to Buyer and Seller

The contract determines what is or is not included in the sale of the property; information from other sources is not determinative.

B. (1) – (5) Items Included In Sale

Unless personal property items are excluded in the listing agreement, the buyer may assume that what they see in the property is included in the sale. If additional items are to be included, list them here in detail.

> (3) The following additional items: Gas range and side-by-side refrigerator

C. Items Excluded From Sale

The seller and the buyer may specifically indicate items to be excluded from the sale. If additional items are excluded, list them here in detail.

9. Condition of Property

A. This paragraph instructs the seller to disclose all known material facts and defects that affect the property. This includes any known insurance claims on the property within the last 5 years.

B. This paragraph gives the buyer the right to inspect the property and cancel the agreement based upon the information discovered during those inspections or to request repairs or other action.

C. This paragraph strongly advises the buyer to investigate the property in its entirety.

10. Buyer's Investigation of Property and Matters Affecting Property

A. This paragraph gives the buyer the right to conduct an investigation of the property, within a specified period of time, and at the buyer's expense unless otherwise agreed. The inspections include the right to check for lead-based paint and wood destroying pests and organisms. The buyer must not make any invasive or destructive inspections on the seller's property. Inspections performed by government entities must have the seller's approval first.

B. The seller must make the property available for buyer inspections. After the inspection, the buyer may remove the contingency or cancel the agreement within the time specified in Paragraph 14. The buyer needs to give the seller copies of any inspections the buyer ordered.

C. The seller must have utilities turned on so the buyer can make the inspection(s).

D. The buyer cannot hold the seller liable for any damage done to the property as a result of inspections performed on the buyer's behalf. Anybody acting on the buyer's behalf during inspections must carry insurance or similar policies that protect the seller if any injuries or damages occur during the inspections.

11. Seller Disclosures; Addenda; Advisories; Other Terms

A. The seller must provide the buyer with a Seller Property Questionnaire or Supplemental Contractual and Statutory Disclosure within a specified time if any of these items are checked.

B. This paragraph includes any addenda that supplement the purchase agreement if checked.

C. This paragraph contains common advisories that will become part of the purchase agreement if checked.

D. Any other addenda, advisories, or other terms related to the purchase agreement can be included here.

12. Title and Vesting

The title and vesting is used for reviewing the preliminary title report with the buyer. Check for any undisclosed liens or easements that may affect the use of the property. Since the property is still owned by the seller, any existing trust deeds will be shown with the seller as the trustor. Once the property is sold, the new title insurance policy will show the buyer's loan. The manner in which a buyer takes title to real property (**vesting**) can have unforeseen legal and tax ramifications. Always direct the buyer to a legal and tax professional to get advice on vesting.

A. The buyer has a specified amount of time to review the preliminary report and give the seller a notice in writing to take corrective action.

B. All matters on the title, including easements and CC&Rs, will remain on the title unless otherwise indicated by the buyer in writing.

C. The seller must disclose all known title matters to the buyer, even those not recorded.

D. The title will be transferred by a grant deed at the close of escrow. An agent should never advise how to take title.

E. The buyer will receive a CLTA/ALTA Homeowner's Policy of Title Insurance.

13. Sale of Buyer's Property

Unless paragraph 13B is checked, sale of the buyer's property is not a contingency. A separate addendum called Contingent on Sale of Property (COP), must be attached if this matter is to be a contingency.

14. Time Periods; Removal of Contingencies; Cancellation Rights

Buyers and sellers are given specific amounts of time to meet the various conditions of the contract.

A. Seller Time Periods

Within seven days, or a specified number of days, the seller must deliver all reports and disclosures for which he or she is responsible.

B. Buyer Time Periods

(1) The buyer has 17 or a specified number of days after acceptance to complete all investigations and review of reports (may include reviewing lead-based paint and hazard disclosures, a home inspection, and investigating insurability). In addition, the buyer must deliver signed copies of the statutory disclosures in Paragraph 6A.

(2) Request that the seller make repairs. The seller may choose not to make the repairs.

(3) Within the time period specified in Paragraph 14B(1), the buyer must deliver the appropriate forms to the seller which either remove the contingency or cancel the agreement. If the seller does not deliver any government-mandated disclosures, which are required as a condition of closing, the buyer has five days after receipt of the disclosure, in writing, to remove any contingencies or cancel the agreement.

(4) The buyer retains the right to make requests of the seller, to remove contingencies, or to cancel the agreement until the seller exercises cancellation rights, even if this occurs after the expiration of time provided in Paragraph 14B(1).

C. Seller Right to Cancel

(1) If the buyer does not complete inspections or fulfill his or her obligations within the time specified in the purchase contract, the seller would prepare and give the buyer a **Notice Of Buyer To Perform**. After giving the buyer a Notice to Buyer to Perform, the seller may cancel the agreement and return the buyer's deposit if the conditions are still not met.

(2) The seller may cancel the agreement and return the buyer's deposit if the buyer does not meet certain obligations provided for in the contract, such as making a deposit, providing a prequalification or preapproved letter or signing a receipt for uninsured deposit. The seller must give the buyer a Notice to Buyer to Perform before a seller can cancel due to a buyer's failure to meet these obligations.

(3) The Notice to Buyer to Perform must be in writing and signed by the seller. It must also give the buyer at least 2 or a specified amount of days to take the appropriate action requested. The seller cannot deliver a Notice to Buyer to Perform earlier than 2 days before the expiration of time given for a buyer to remove a contingency.

D. Effect of Buyer's Removal of Contingencies

If the buyer removes any contingency or cancellation rights, in writing, the buyer will conclusively be deemed to have (i) completed all things pertaining to the contingency or cancellation; (ii) elected to proceed with the transaction; and (iii) assumed all responsibility for repairs or corrections pertaining to that contingency or cancellation right.

E. Close of Escrow

If either the seller or buyer fails to close escrow, a **Demand to Close Escrow** form must be given to the appropriate party before canceling the purchase agreement.

F. Effect of Cancellation on Deposits

The buyer and seller agree that if the agreement is cancelled, the buyer's deposit, less costs and fees, will be returned. The buyer and seller will sign a notice of cancellation and it will be given to the holder to release the deposit. This is not automatic.

15. Repairs

This paragraph requires that any repairs must be done with permits and in compliance with building codes. Repairs must be completed before the buyer's final verification of the condition of the property. The seller must obtain repair receipts, prepare a written statement of the repairs performed, and give them to the buyer.

16. Final Verification of Condition

This paragraph provides the buyer the right to conduct the final inspection, or **"walk-through"**, five days or a number specified, prior to close of escrow. This allows the buyer to verify the condition of the property as agreed upon, and that the seller has complied with repair and other contractual obligations.

17. Prorations and Property Taxes and Other Items

This informs escrow of the buyer's and seller's wishes regarding the proration of property tax, interest, assessments, and any other charge normally prorated in escrow. To **prorate** means to divide or distribute proportionately.

> As of the close of escrow, prorated items should be paid current by the seller or assumed by the buyer.

18. Selection of Service Providers

The broker does not guarantee the performance of any service providers. Buyers and sellers may select any company to provide escrow, title, inspection, finance, and certification services.

19. Multiple Listing Service (MLS)

The broker has the right to report the sale terms to an MLS service to be published. The release of this information by an agent, without such authorization, could breach the duty of confidentiality.

20. Equal Housing Opportunity

Under Federal law and California law, it is illegal to discriminate based on race, color, religion, sex, handicap, familial status, or national origin.

21. Attorney Fees

This paragraph relates to disputes between the buyer and seller only. The prevailing party is entitled to reasonable attorney's fees from the non-prevailing party in any court action or arbitration. If the parties decide to settle a dispute, attorney's fees may be one of the terms negotiated in the settlement.

22. Definitions

Certain terms of the agreement are defined here. The definitions of "Days", "Day after", and "Days prior" should be reviewed for the purposes of calendaring time.

23. Broker Compensation

The seller, buyer, or both agree to compensate the broker, which is specified in a separate, written agreement. The compensation will be paid at the close of escrow. If escrow does not close, the broker is paid according to the terms of a separate, written agreement with the seller or buyer.

24. Joint Escrow Instructions to Escrow Holder

A. This paragraph identifies which portions of the purchase agreement are instructions from the buyer and seller to the escrow holder. The escrow holder disburses the broker's compensation under separate compensation agreements provided for in Paragraph 23 or Paragraph D in the Real Estate Brokers section of the agreement.

B. Within three (3) business days, the parties agree to deliver the agreement to the escrow holder, unless there is a different agreed-upon time.

C. Brokers are parties to the agreement for compensation purposes only. Both buyer and seller agree irrevocably to assign any broker compensation provided for in Paragraph 23 or Paragraph D in the Real Estate Brokers section of the agreement.

D. Both buyer and seller agree to provide the escrow holder with a copy of any amendment affecting any paragraph that is also an escrow instruction. This must be done within 2 business days after the amendment is included.

25. Liquidated Damages

Parties to a contract may decide in advance the amount of liquidated damages that would be paid. **Liquidated damages** are the monies agreed upon by both parties to a contract that one will pay to the other upon backing out of the agreement. The purchase agreement, or sales contract, usually contains a printed clause that says the seller may keep the deposit as liquidated damages if the buyer backs out without good reason. In the event the buyer defaults on the contract, the liquidated damages cannot exceed 3% of the purchase price if the property is a single-family residence.

Note: In order for this clause to be included as an obligation, it must be initialed by the buyer and seller. If at least one, but not all parties initial, a counteroffer is required until an agreement is reached.

26. Dispute Resolution

Even with the most smoothly run or meticulous transaction, disputes may arise. To try to settle any disputes amicably, the contract offers both mediation and arbitration. Both buyer and seller must agree to be bound by mutual arbitration in order for the clause to be effective.

A. Mediation

This clause is not optional.

The buyer and seller must agree to mediation by a neutral mediator in the attempt to resolve disputes. Both parties must also agree to mediation for disputes that may arise with brokers. If any party does not attempt mediation before filing an arbitration or court action, they will not be entitled to be awarded attorney's fees even if they are the prevailing party.

B. Arbitration of Disputes

The buyer and seller agree to arbitration if a dispute cannot be resolved through mediation. This also applies to disputes with brokers. The arbitrator will be a retired judge with experience in real estate law or an arbitrator that the disputing parties mutually approve. This paragraph must be initialed by the buyer and seller. If at least one, but not all parties initial, a counteroffer is required until agreement is reached. Any exclusions to this arbitration agreement are outlined in Paragraph 26C(1).

C. Additional Mediation and Arbitration Terms

(1) This subparagraph lists the matters that are excluded from mediation and arbitration.

(2) A broker does not have to mediate or arbitrate with a buyer or seller unless he or she agrees to the terms in writing.

27. Terms and Conditions of Offer

This paragraph provides that the purchase agreement is an offer to purchase property on the terms and conditions set forth in the agreement. The offer will be revoked after the specified expiration date. The buyer, however, may revoke the offer any time prior to communication of seller's acceptance.

28. Time of Essence; Entire Contract; Changes

Time is often significant in a contract. The performance of a contract may be measured by the passage of time. By law, if no time is required by the contract, a reasonable time is allowed. If the act can be done instantly—as in the payment of money—it must be done at once.

Buyer and seller agree that any act should take place on the date and time stated. This agreement may only be changed in writing, and it incorporates all prior written and oral agreements.

29. Expiration of Offer

If the offer is not accepted by the seller within the time specified, the offer is revoked and any deposit is returned to the buyer. A deposit may be refunded by agreement, judgment, or arbitration. If other than the buyer, write the name of the person authorized to accept a copy of the signed offer. Write the date and time when the offer should be received.

> Buyer's Representative – First Real Estate
> April 16, 20xx at 5:00 p.m.

Write out the date and the name of the buyer(s) as well as the buyer(s) current home address.

> Sam Winter and Cindy Winter
> 901 Cherrywood Lane, Some Town, CA 90000

30. Acceptance of Offer

Once the deposit receipt is accepted and signed by the seller and the acceptance is communicated to the buyer, it becomes a legally binding contract. Death or incapacity does not automatically cancel a contract. If the seller dies or becomes incapacitated after acceptance of the offer, the seller's heir(s) must complete the sale.

Seller's Signature Section

By signing the agreement, the seller agrees to sell the property on the exact terms and conditions of the offer. The seller also confirms the agency relationships and agrees to pay the identified broker the amount of compensation for services set forth in a separate, written agreement.

Confirmation of Acceptance

A contract is formed when the seller's acceptance is received in person by the buyer or buyer's agent. This paragraph provides evidence of the date of acceptance.

Real Estate Brokers Section

The listing and selling brokers acknowledge they are not parties to the agreement. The selling broker signs to confirm the agency relationship and receipt of a deposit. The listing broker signs to confirm the agency relationship and agrees to pay the selling broker pursuant to the MLS offer of compensation (if the selling broker is a participant of that MLS or a reciprocal MLS) or pursuant to a separate written agreement.

Escrow Holder Acknowledgement

The escrow holder acknowledges receipt of the agreement and agrees to act as escrow holder.

Presentation and Rejection of Offer

The listing broker confirms that the offer was presented to the seller on the specific date indicated. If applicable, the seller will confirm that he or she rejected the offer on the specific date indicated.

CALIFORNIA
ASSOCIATION
OF REALTORS®

**CALIFORNIA
RESIDENTIAL PURCHASE AGREEMENT
AND JOINT ESCROW INSTRUCTIONS**
For Use With Single Family Residential Property — Attached or Detached
(C.A.R. Form RPA-CA, Revised 4/10)

Date ___4/15/20XX___

1. **OFFER:**
   A. **THIS IS AN OFFER FROM** __Sam Winter and Cindy Winter_____ ("Buyer").
   B. **THE REAL PROPERTY TO BE ACQUIRED** is described as __1652 Hill Street_____
      __Any City_____, Assessor's Parcel No. _____, situated in
      _____, County of __Apple_____, California, ("Property").
   C. **THE PURCHASE PRICE** offered is __Four Hundred Fifteen Thousand and Zero Cents_____
      _____ (Dollars $ ___415,000.00___).
   D. **CLOSE OF ESCROW** shall occur on ____June 30, 20XX_____ (date) (or ☐ _____ **Days** After Acceptance).

2. **AGENCY:**
   A. **DISCLOSURE:** Buyer and Seller each acknowledge prior receipt of a "Disclosure Regarding Real Estate Agency Relationships" (C.A.R. Form AD).
   B. **POTENTIALLY COMPETING BUYERS AND SELLERS:** Buyer and Seller each acknowledge receipt of a disclosure of the possibility of multiple representation by the Broker representing that principal. This disclosure may be part of a listing agreement, buyer representation agreement or separate document (C.A.R. Form DA). Buyer understands that Broker representing Buyer may also represent other potential buyers, who may consider, make offers on or ultimately acquire the Property. Seller understands that Broker representing Seller may also represent other sellers with competing properties of interest to this Buyer.
   C. **CONFIRMATION:** The following agency relationships are hereby confirmed for this transaction:
      Listing Agent __Sunshine Real Estate/Tom Baker_____ (Print Firm Name) is the agent
      of (check one): ☒ the Seller exclusively; or ☐ both the Buyer and Seller.
      Selling Agent __First Real Estate/Lisa Summers_____ (Print Firm Name) (if not the same as the
      Listing Agent) is the agent of (check one): ☒ the Buyer exclusively; or ☐ the Seller exclusively; or ☐ both the Buyer and Seller. Real Estate Brokers are not parties to the Agreement between Buyer and Seller.

3. **FINANCE TERMS:** Buyer represents that funds will be good when deposited with Escrow Holder.
   A. **INITIAL DEPOSIT:** Deposit shall be in the amount of .... $ ___5,000.00___
      (1) Buyer shall deliver deposit directly to Escrow Holder by personal check, ☐ electronic funds transfer, ☐ Other
      _____ within **3** business days after acceptance (or ☐ Other _____);
      OR (2) (If checked) ☒ Buyer has given the deposit by personal check (or ☐ _____)
      to the agent submitting the offer (or to ☐ _____),
      made payable to __Sunshine Real Estate_____ . The deposit shall be held
      uncashed until Acceptance and then deposited with Escrow Holder (or ☐ into Broker's trust account) within **3**
      business days after Acceptance (or ☐ Other _____).
   B. **INCREASED DEPOSIT:** Buyer shall deposit with Escrow Holder an increased deposit in the amount of .... $ ___36,500.00___
      within __3__ **Days** After Acceptance, or ☐ _____ .
      If a liquidated damages clause is incorporated into this Agreement, Buyer and Seller shall sign a separate
      liquidated damages clause (C.A.R. Form RID) for any increased deposit at the time it is deposited.
   C. **LOAN(S):**
      (1) FIRST LOAN: in the amount of .... $ ___332,000.00___
      This loan will be conventional financing or, if checked, ☐ FHA, ☐ VA, ☐ Seller (C.A.R. Form SFA),
      ☐ assumed financing (C.A.R. Form PAA), ☐ Other _____ . This loan shall be at a fixed
      rate not to exceed __5.75__ % or, ☐ an adjustable rate loan with initial rate not to exceed _____ %.
      Regardless of the type of loan, Buyer shall pay points not to exceed __2__ % of the loan amount.
      (2) ☐ SECOND LOAN: in the amount of .... $ ___N/A___
      This loan will be conventional financing or, if checked, ☐ Seller (C.A.R. Form SFA), ☐ assumed financing
      (C.A.R. Form PAA), ☐ Other _____ . This loan shall be at a fixed rate not to exceed
      _____ % or, ☐ an adjustable rate loan with initial rate not to exceed _____ %. Regardless of
      the type of loan, Buyer shall pay points not to exceed _____ % of the loan amount.
      (3) FHA/VA: For any FHA or VA loan specified above, Buyer has 17 (or ☐ _____) **Days** After Acceptance
      to Deliver to Seller written notice (C.A.R. Form FVA) of any lender-required repairs or costs that Buyer
      requests Seller to pay for or repair. Seller has no obligation to pay for repairs or satisfy lender requirements
      unless otherwise agreed in writing.
   D. **ADDITIONAL FINANCING TERMS:** __N/A_____
      _____
   E. **BALANCE OF PURCHASE PRICE OR DOWN PAYMENT:** in the amount of .... $ ___41,500.00___
      to be deposited with Escrow Holder within sufficient time to close escrow.
   F. **PURCHASE PRICE (TOTAL):** .... $ ___415,000.00___

Buyer's Initials (__SW__)(__CW__)

Seller's Initials (_____)(_____)

EQUAL HOUSING
OPPORTUNITY

RPA-CA REVISED 4/10 (PAGE 1 OF 8)

Reviewed by _____ Date _____

CALIFORNIA RESIDENTIAL PURCHASE AGREEMENT (RPA-CA PAGE 1 OF 8)

| Agent: Lisa Summers | Phone: 555.456-1234 | Fax: 555.456-9876 | **Prepared using zipForm® software** |
| Broker: First Real Estate 234 First Street, Any City, CA 90000 | | | |

Property Address: __1652 Hill Street, Any City, Apple County, CA 90000__   Date: ___4/15/20XX___

G. VERIFICATION OF DOWN PAYMENT AND CLOSING COSTS: Buyer (or Buyer's lender or loan broker pursuant to 3H(1)) shall, within **7 (or** ☐ _____) **Days** After Acceptance, Deliver to Seller written verification of Buyer's down payment and closing costs. (If checked, ☐ verification attached.)

H. LOAN TERMS:

(1) **LOAN APPLICATIONS:** Within **7 (or** ☐ _____) **Days** After Acceptance, Buyer shall Deliver to Seller a letter from lender or loan broker stating that, based on a review of Buyer's written application and credit report, Buyer is prequalified or preapproved for any NEW loan specified in 3C above. (If checked, ☐ letter attached.)

(2) **LOAN CONTINGENCY:** Buyer shall act diligently and in good faith to obtain the designated loan(s). Obtaining the loan(s) specified above **is a contingency** of this Agreement unless otherwise agreed in writing. Buyer's contractual obligations to obtain and provide deposit, balance of down payment and closing costs **are not contingencies** of this Agreement.

(3) **LOAN CONTINGENCY REMOVAL:**

(i) Within **17 (or** ☐ _____) **Days** After Acceptance, Buyer shall, as specified in paragraph 14, in writing remove the loan contingency or cancel this Agreement;

OR (ii) (if checked) ☐ the loan contingency shall remain in effect until the designated loans are funded.

(4) ☐ **NO LOAN CONTINGENCY** (If checked): Obtaining any loan specified above is NOT a contingency of this Agreement. If Buyer does not obtain the loan and as a result Buyer does not purchase the Property, Seller may be entitled to Buyer's deposit or other legal remedies.

I. APPRAISAL CONTINGENCY AND REMOVAL: This Agreement is (or, if checked, ☐ is NOT) contingent upon a written appraisal of the Property by a licensed or certified appraiser at no less than the specified purchase price. If there is a loan contingency, Buyer's removal of the loan contingency shall be deemed removal of this appraisal contingency (or, ☐ if checked, Buyer shall, as specified in paragraph 14B(3), in writing remove the appraisal contingency or cancel this Agreement within **17 (or** _____) **Days** After Acceptance). If there is no loan contingency, Buyer shall, as specified in paragraph 14B(3), in writing remove the appraisal contingency or cancel this Agreement within **17 (or** _____) **Days** After Acceptance.

J. ☐ **ALL CASH OFFER** (If checked): Buyer shall, within **7 (or** ☐ _____) **Days** After Acceptance, Deliver to Seller written verification of sufficient funds to close this transaction. (If checked, ☐ verification attached.)

K. BUYER STATED FINANCING: Seller has relied on Buyer's representation of the type of financing specified (including but not limited to, as applicable, amount of down payment, contingent or non contingent loan, or all cash). If Buyer seeks alternate financing, (i) Seller has no obligation to cooperate with Buyer's efforts to obtain such financing, and (ii) Buyer shall also pursue the financing method specified in this Agreement. Buyer's failure to secure alternate financing does not excuse Buyer from the obligation to purchase the Property and close escrow as specified in this Agreement.

4. ALLOCATION OF COSTS (If checked): Unless otherwise specified in writing, **this paragraph** only determines who is to pay for the inspection, test or service ("Report") mentioned; it **does not determine who is to pay for any work recommended or identified in the Report.**

A. INSPECTIONS AND REPORTS:

(1) ☐ Buyer ☒ Seller shall pay for an inspection and report for wood destroying pests and organisms ("Wood Pest Report") prepared by ___Happy Pest Service, Inc.___ a registered structural pest control company.

(2) ☐ Buyer ☐ Seller shall pay to have septic or private sewage disposal systems pumped and inspected _____ .

(3) ☐ Buyer ☐ Seller shall pay to have domestic wells tested for water potability and productivity _____ .

(4) ☐ Buyer ☒ Seller shall pay for a natural hazard zone disclosure report prepared by ___Seller___ .

(5) ☐ Buyer ☒ Seller shall pay for the following inspection or report ___Roof Certification___ .

(6) ☒ Buyer ☐ Seller shall pay for the following inspection or report ___Company of Buyer's Choice (Home Inspection)___ .

B. GOVERNMENT REQUIREMENTS AND RETROFIT:

(1) ☐ Buyer ☒ Seller shall pay for smoke detector installation and/or water heater bracing, if required by Law. Prior to Close Of Escrow, Seller shall provide Buyer written statement(s) of compliance in accordance with state and local Law, unless exempt.

(2) ☐ Buyer ☒ Seller shall pay the cost of compliance with any other minimum mandatory government retrofit standards, inspections and reports if required as a condition of closing escrow under any Law. _____ .

C. ESCROW AND TITLE:

(1) ☒ Buyer ☒ Seller shall pay escrow fee ___50/50___
Escrow Holder shall be ___Budget Escrow, Inc.___ .

(2) ☐ Buyer ☒ Seller shall pay for **owner's** title insurance policy specified in paragraph 12E _____
Owner's title policy to be issued by ___Harvard Title Company___
(Buyer shall pay for any title insurance policy insuring Buyer's **lender**, unless otherwise agreed in writing.)

D. OTHER COSTS:

(1) ☐ Buyer ☒ Seller shall pay County transfer tax or fee _____ .

(2) ☐ Buyer ☐ Seller shall pay City transfer tax or fee _____ .

(3) ☐ Buyer ☒ Seller shall pay Homeowner's Association ("HOA") transfer fee _____ .

(4) ☐ Buyer ☒ Seller shall pay HOA document preparation fees _____ .

(5) ☐ Buyer ☐ Seller shall pay for any private transfer fee _____ .

(6) ☐ Buyer ☒ Seller shall pay the cost, not to exceed $ ___450.00___ , of a one-year home warranty plan, issued by ___Homesafe Insurance Company___ , with the following optional coverages:
☐ Air Conditioner ☒ Pool/Spa ☐ Code and Permit upgrade ☐ Other: _____
Buyer is informed that home warranty plans have many optional coverages in addition to those listed above. Buyer is advised to investigate these coverages to determine those that may be suitable for Buyer.

(7) ☒ Buyer ☐ Seller shall pay for ___HOA transfer fees not to exceed $125.00___ .

(8) ☐ Buyer ☐ Seller shall pay for _____ .

Buyer's Initials (__SW__) (__CW__)

RPA-CA REVISED 4/10 (PAGE 2 OF 8)

Seller's Initials (_____) (_____)

Reviewed by _____ Date _____

EQUAL HOUSING
OPPORTUNITY

CALIFORNIA RESIDENTIAL PURCHASE AGREEMENT (RPA-CA PAGE 2 OF 8)

Property Address: ___1652 Hill Street, Any City, Apple County, CA 90000___   Date: ___4/15/20XX___

5. CLOSING AND POSSESSION:
   A. Buyer intends (or ☐ does not intend) to occupy the Property as Buyer's primary residence.
   B. **Seller-occupied or vacant property:** Possession shall be delivered to Buyer at 5 PM or (☐ _____ ☐ AM ☐ PM), on the date of Close Of Escrow; ☐ on _____ ; or ☐ no later than _____ **Days** After Close Of Escrow. If transfer of title and possession do not occur at the same time, Buyer and Seller are advised to: **(i)** enter into a written occupancy agreement (C.A.R. Form PAA, paragraph 2); and **(ii)** consult with their insurance and legal advisors.
   C. **Tenant-occupied property:**
      (i) **Property shall be vacant** at least **5 (or ☐ _____) Days** Prior to Close Of Escrow, unless otherwise agreed in writing. **Note to Seller: If you are unable to deliver Property vacant in accordance with rent control and other applicable Law, you may be in breach of this Agreement.**
      OR (ii) (if checked) ☐ **Tenant to remain in possession.** (C.A.R. Form PAA, paragraph 3)
   D. At Close Of Escrow, **(i)** Seller assigns to Buyer any assignable warranty rights for items included in the sale, and **(ii)** Seller shall Deliver to Buyer available Copies of warranties. Brokers cannot and will not determine the assignability of any warranties.
   E. At Close Of Escrow, unless otherwise agreed in writing, Seller shall provide keys and/or means to operate all locks, mailboxes, security systems, alarms and garage door openers. If Property is a condominium or located in a common interest subdivision, Buyer may be required to pay a deposit to the Homeowners' Association ("HOA") to obtain keys to accessible HOA facilities.

6. STATUTORY DISCLOSURES (INCLUDING LEAD-BASED PAINT HAZARD DISCLOSURES) AND CANCELLATION RIGHTS:
   A. **(1)** Seller shall, within the time specified in paragraph 14A, Deliver to Buyer, if required by Law: **(i)** Federal Lead-Based Paint Disclosures (C.A.R. Form FLD) and pamphlet ("Lead Disclosures"); and **(ii)** disclosures or notices required by sections 1102 et. seq. and 1103 et. seq. of the Civil Code ("Statutory Disclosures"). Statutory Disclosures include, but are not limited to, a Real Estate Transfer Disclosure Statement ("TDS"), Natural Hazard Disclosure Statement ("NHD"), notice or actual knowledge of release of illegal controlled substance, notice of special tax and/or assessments (or, if allowed, substantially equivalent notice regarding the Mello-Roos Community Facilities Act and Improvement Bond Act of 1915) and, if Seller has actual knowledge, of industrial use and military ordinance location (C.A.R. Form SPQ or SSD).
      (2) Buyer shall, within the time specified in paragraph 14B(1), return Signed Copies of the Statutory and Lead Disclosures to Seller.
      (3) In the event Seller, prior to Close Of Escrow, becomes aware of adverse conditions materially affecting the Property, or any material inaccuracy in disclosures, information or representations previously provided to Buyer, Seller shall promptly provide a subsequent or amended disclosure or notice, in writing, covering those items. **However, a subsequent or amended disclosure shall not be required for conditions and material inaccuracies** of which Buyer is otherwise aware, or which are **disclosed in reports provided to or obtained by Buyer or ordered and paid for by Buyer.**
      (4) If any disclosure or notice specified in 6A(1), or subsequent or amended disclosure or notice is Delivered to Buyer after the offer is Signed, Buyer shall have the right to cancel this Agreement within **3 Days** After Delivery in person, or **5 Days** After Delivery by deposit in the mail, by giving written notice of cancellation to Seller or Seller's agent.
      (5) **Note to Buyer and Seller: Waiver of Statutory and Lead Disclosures is prohibited by Law.**
   B. **NATURAL AND ENVIRONMENTAL HAZARDS:** Within the time specified in paragraph 14A, Seller shall, if required by Law: **(i)** Deliver to Buyer earthquake guides (and questionnaire) and environmental hazards booklet; **(ii)** even if exempt from the obligation to provide a NHD, disclose if the Property is located in a Special Flood Hazard Area; Potential Flooding (Inundation) Area; Very High Fire Hazard Zone; State Fire Responsibility Area; Earthquake Fault Zone; Seismic Hazard Zone; and **(iii)** disclose any other zone as required by Law and provide any other information required for those zones.
   C. **WITHHOLDING TAXES:** Within the time specified in paragraph 14A, to avoid required withholding, Seller shall Deliver to Buyer or qualified substitute, an affidavit sufficient to comply with federal (FIRPTA) and California withholding Law, (C.A.R. Form AS or QS).
   D. **MEGAN'S LAW DATABASE DISCLOSURE:** Notice: Pursuant to Section 290.46 of the Penal Code, information about specified registered sex offenders is made available to the public via an Internet Web site maintained by the Department of Justice at www.meganslaw.ca.gov. Depending on an offender's criminal history, this information will include either the address at which the offender resides or the community of residence and ZIP Code in which he or she resides. (Neither Seller nor Brokers are required to check this website. If Buyer wants further information, Broker recommends that Buyer obtain information from this website during Buyer's inspection contingency period. Brokers do not have expertise in this area.)

7. CONDOMINIUM/PLANNED DEVELOPMENT DISCLOSURES:
   A. **SELLER HAS: 7 (or ☐ _____) Days** After Acceptance to disclose to Buyer whether the Property is a condominium, or is located in a planned development or other common interest subdivision (C.A.R. Form SPQ or SSD).
   B. If the Property is a condominium or is located in a planned development or other common interest subdivision, Seller has **3 (or ☐ _____) Days** After Acceptance to request from the HOA (C.A.R. Form HOA): **(i)** Copies of any documents required by Law; **(ii)** disclosure of any pending or anticipated claim or litigation by or against the HOA; **(iii)** a statement containing the location and number of designated parking and storage spaces; **(iv)** Copies of the most recent 12 months of HOA minutes for regular and special meetings; and **(v)** the names and contact information of all HOAs governing the Property (collectively, "CI Disclosures"). Seller shall itemize and Deliver to Buyer all CI Disclosures received from the HOA and any CI Disclosures in Seller's possession. Buyer's approval of CI Disclosures is a contingency of this Agreement as specified in paragraph 14B(3).

8. ITEMS INCLUDED IN AND EXCLUDED FROM PURCHASE PRICE:
   A. **NOTE TO BUYER AND SELLER:** Items listed as included or excluded in the MLS, flyers or marketing materials are **not** included in the purchase price or excluded from the sale unless specified in 8B or C.
   B. **ITEMS INCLUDED IN SALE:**
      (1) All EXISTING fixtures and fittings that are attached to the Property;
      (2) EXISTING electrical, mechanical, lighting, plumbing and heating fixtures, ceiling fans, fireplace inserts, gas logs and grates, solar systems, built-in appliances, window and door screens, awnings, shutters, window coverings, attached floor coverings, television antennas, satellite dishes, private integrated telephone systems, air coolers/conditioners, pool/spa equipment, garage door openers/remote controls, mailbox, in-ground landscaping, trees/shrubs, water softeners, water purifiers, security systems/alarms; (If checked ☐ stove(s), ☐ refrigerator(s); and
      (3) The following additional items: ___Gas Range, Side-by-Side Refrigerator___ .
      (4) Seller represents that all items included in the purchase price, unless otherwise specified, are owned by Seller.
      (5) All items included shall be transferred free of liens and without Seller warranty.
   C. **ITEMS EXCLUDED FROM SALE:** Unless otherwise specified, audio and video components (such as flat screen TVs and speakers) are excluded if any such item is not itself attached to the Property, even if a bracket or other mechanism attached to the component is attached to the Property; and _____

Buyer's Initials (_SW_) (_CW_)   Seller's Initials (_____) (_____)

RPA-CA REVISED 4/10 (PAGE 3 OF 8)

Reviewed by _____ Date _____

CALIFORNIA RESIDENTIAL PURCHASE AGREEMENT (RPA-CA PAGE 3 OF 8)

Property Address: ___1652 Hill Street, Any City, Apple County, CA 90000___   Date: ___4/15/20XX___

9. **CONDITION OF PROPERTY:** Unless otherwise agreed: **(i) the Property is sold (a) in its PRESENT physical ("as-is") condition as of the date of Acceptance and (b) subject to Buyer's Investigation rights; (ii)** the Property, including pool, spa, landscaping and grounds, is to be maintained in substantially the same condition as on the date of Acceptance; and **(iii)** all debris and personal property not included in the sale shall be removed by Seller by Close Of Escrow.

   A. Seller shall, within the time specified in paragraph 14A, DISCLOSE KNOWN MATERIAL FACTS AND DEFECTS affecting the Property, including known insurance claims within the past five years, and make any and all other disclosures required by law.

   B. Buyer has the right to inspect the Property and, as specified in paragraph 14B, based upon information discovered in those inspections: **(i)** cancel this Agreement; or **(ii)** request that Seller make Repairs or take other action.

   C. **Buyer is strongly advised to conduct investigations of the entire Property in order to determine its present condition. Seller may not be aware of all defects affecting the Property or other factors that Buyer considers important. Property improvements may not be built according to code, in compliance with current Law, or have had permits issued.**

10. **BUYER'S INVESTIGATION OF PROPERTY AND MATTERS AFFECTING PROPERTY:**

   A. Buyer's acceptance of the condition of, and any other matter affecting the Property, is a contingency of this Agreement as specified in this paragraph and paragraph 14B. Within the time specified in paragraph 14B(1), Buyer shall have the right, at Buyer's expense unless otherwise agreed, to conduct inspections, investigations, tests, surveys and other studies ("Buyer Investigations"), including, but not limited to, the right to: **(i)** inspect for lead-based paint and other lead-based paint hazards; **(ii)** inspect for wood destroying pests and organisms; **(iii)** review the registered sex offender database; **(iv)** confirm the insurability of Buyer and the Property; and **(v)** satisfy Buyer as to any matter specified in the attached Buyer's Inspection Advisory (C.A.R. Form BIA). Without Seller's prior written consent, Buyer shall neither make nor cause to be made: **(i)** invasive or destructive Buyer Investigations; or **(ii)** inspections by any governmental building or zoning inspector or government employee, unless required by Law.

   B. Seller shall make the Property available for all Buyer Investigations. Buyer shall **(i)** as specified in paragraph 14B, complete Buyer Investigations and, either remove the contingency or cancel this Agreement, and **(ii)** give Seller, at no cost, complete Copies of all Investigation reports obtained by Buyer, which obligation shall survive the termination of this Agreement.

   C. Seller shall have water, gas, electricity and all operable pilot lights on for Buyer's Investigations and through the date possession is made available to Buyer.

   D. **Buyer indemnity and Seller protection for entry upon property:** Buyer shall: **(i)** keep the Property free and clear of liens; **(ii)** repair all damage arising from Buyer Investigations; and **(iii)** indemnify and hold Seller harmless from all resulting liability, claims, demands, damages and costs of Buyer's investigations. Buyer shall carry, or Buyer shall require anyone acting on Buyer's behalf to carry, policies of liability, workers' compensation and other applicable insurance, defending and protecting Seller from liability for any injuries to persons or property occurring during any Buyer Investigations or work done on the Property at Buyer's direction prior to Close Of Escrow. Seller is advised that certain protections may be afforded Seller by recording a "Notice of Non-responsibility" (C.A.R. Form NNR) for Buyer Investigations and work done on the Property at Buyer's direction. Buyer's obligations under this paragraph shall survive the termination or cancellation of this Agreement and Close of Escrow.

11. **SELLER DISCLOSURES; ADDENDA; ADVISORIES; OTHER TERMS:**

   A. **Seller Disclosures (if checked):** Seller shall, within the time specified in paragraph 14A, complete and provide Buyer with a:

☐ Seller Property Questionnaire (C.A.R. Form SPQ)	**OR**	☐ Supplemental Contractual and Statutory Disclosure (C.A.R. Form SSD)

   B. **Addenda (if checked):**   ☐ Addendum # _____   (C.A.R. Form ADM)

☐ Wood Destroying Pest Inspection and Allocation of Cost Addendum (C.A.R. Form WPA)	
☐ Purchase Agreement Addendum (C.A.R Form PAA)	☐ Septic, Well and Property Monument Addendum (C.A.R. Form SWPI)
☐ Short Sale Addendum (C.A.R. Form SSA)	☐ Other

   C. **Advisories (if checked):**

	☒ Buyer's Inspection Advisory (C.A.R. Form BIA)
☐ Probate Advisory (C.A.R. Form PAK)	☒ Statewide Buyer and Seller Advisory (C.A.R. Form SBSA)
☐ Trust Advisory (C.A.R. Form TA)	☐ REO Advisory (C.A.R. Form REO)

   D. **Other Terms:** Any/all pending/known HOA assessments to be paid by seller. Any/all repairs made to HOA compliance/standards.

12. **TITLE AND VESTING:**

   A. Within the time specified in paragraph 14, Buyer shall be provided a current preliminary title report, which shall include a search of the General Index. Seller shall within 7 Days After Acceptance give Escrow Holder a completed Statement of Information. The preliminary report is only an offer by the title insurer to issue a policy of title insurance and may not contain every item affecting title. Buyer's review of the preliminary report and any other matters which may affect title are a contingency of this Agreement as specified in paragraph 14B.

   B. Title is taken in its present condition subject to all encumbrances, easements, covenants, conditions, restrictions, rights and other matters, whether of record or not, as of the date of Acceptance except: **(i)** monetary liens of record unless Buyer is assuming those obligations or taking the Property subject to those obligations; and **(ii)** those matters which Seller has agreed to remove in writing.

   C. Within the time specified in paragraph 14A, Seller has a duty to disclose to Buyer all matters known to Seller affecting title, whether of record or not.

   D. At Close Of Escrow, Buyer shall receive a grant deed conveying title (or, for stock cooperative or long-term lease, an assignment of stock certificate or of Seller's leasehold interest), including oil, mineral and water rights if currently owned by Seller. Title shall vest as designated in Buyer's supplemental escrow instructions. THE MANNER OF TAKING TITLE MAY HAVE SIGNIFICANT LEGAL AND TAX CONSEQUENCES. CONSULT AN APPROPRIATE PROFESSIONAL.

   E. Buyer shall receive a CLTA/ALTA Homeowner's Policy of Title Insurance. A title company, at Buyer's request, can provide information about the availability, desirability, coverage, survey requirements, and cost of various title insurance coverages and endorsements. If Buyer desires title coverage other than that required by this paragraph, Buyer shall instruct Escrow Holder in writing and pay any increase in cost.

13. **SALE OF BUYER'S PROPERTY:**

   A. This Agreement is NOT contingent upon the sale of any property owned by Buyer.

   OR B. ☐ (If checked): The attached addendum (C.A.R. Form COP) regarding the contingency for the sale of property owned by Buyer is incorporated into this Agreement.

Buyer's Initials (_SW_)(_CW_)

RPA-CA REVISED 4/10 (PAGE 4 OF 8)

Seller's Initials (_____)(_____)

Reviewed by _____ Date _____

EQUAL HOUSING OPPORTUNITY

CALIFORNIA RESIDENTIAL PURCHASE AGREEMENT (RPA-CA PAGE 4 OF 8)

Property Address: 1652 Hill Street, Any City, Apple County, CA 90000   Date: 4/15/20XX

14. TIME PERIODS; REMOVAL OF CONTINGENCIES; CANCELLATION RIGHTS: The following time periods may only be extended, altered, modified or changed by mutual written agreement. Any removal of contingencies or cancellation under this paragraph by either Buyer or Seller must be exercised in good faith and in writing (C.A.R. Form CR or CC).

A. SELLER HAS: 7 (or ☐ _____) Days After Acceptance to Deliver to Buyer all Reports, disclosures and information for which Seller is responsible under paragraphs 4, 6A, B and C, 7A, 9A, 11A and B, and 12. Buyer may give Seller a Notice to Seller to Perform (C.A.R. Form NSP) if Seller has not Delivered the items within the time specified.

B. (1) BUYER HAS: 17 (or ☐ _____) Days After Acceptance, unless otherwise agreed in writing, to:
   (i) complete all Buyer Investigations; approve all disclosures, reports and other applicable information, which Buyer receives from Seller; and approve all other matters affecting the Property; and
   (ii) Deliver to Seller Signed Copies of Statutory and Lead Disclosures Delivered by Seller in accordance with paragraph 6A.

(2) Within the time specified in 14B(1), Buyer may request that Seller make repairs or take any other action regarding the Property (C.A.R. Form RR). Seller has no obligation to agree to or respond to Buyer's requests.

(3) Within the time specified in 14B(1) (or as otherwise specified in this Agreement), Buyer shall Deliver to Seller either (i) a removal of the applicable contingency (C.A.R. Form CR), or (ii) a cancellation (C.A.R. Form CC) of this Agreement based upon a contingency or Seller's failure to Deliver the specified items. However, if any report, disclosure or information for which Seller is responsible is not Delivered within the time specified in 14A, then Buyer has 5 (or ☐ _____) Days After Delivery of any such items, or the time specified in 14B(1), whichever is later, to Deliver to Seller a removal of the applicable contingency or cancellation of this Agreement.

(4) Continuation of Contingency: Even after the end of the time specified in 14B(1) and before Seller cancels this Agreement, if at all, pursuant to 14C, Buyer retains the right to either (i) in writing remove remaining contingencies, or (ii) cancel this Agreement based upon a remaining contingency or Seller's failure to Deliver the specified terms. Once Buyer's written removal of all contingencies is Delivered to Seller, Seller may not cancel this Agreement pursuant to 14C(1).

C. SELLER RIGHT TO CANCEL:
   (1) Seller right to Cancel; Buyer Contingencies: If, within time specified in this Agreement, Buyer does not, in writing, Deliver to Seller a removal of the applicable contingency or cancellation of this Agreement then Seller, after first Delivering to Buyer a Notice to Buyer to Perform (C.A.R. Form NBP) may cancel this Agreement. In such event, Seller shall authorize return of Buyer's deposit.
   (2) Seller right to Cancel; Buyer Contract Obligations: Seller, after first Delivering to Buyer a NBP may cancel this Agreement for any of the following reasons: **(i)** if Buyer fails to deposit funds as required by 3A or 3B; **(ii)** if the funds deposited pursuant to 3A or 3B are not good when deposited; **(iii)** if Buyer fails to Deliver a notice of FHA or VA costs or terms as required by 3C(3) (C.A.R. Form FVA); **(iv)** if Buyer fails to Deliver a letter as required by 3H; **(v)** if Buyer fails to Deliver verification as required by 3G or 3J; **(vi)** if Seller reasonably disapproves of the verification provided by 3G or 3J; **(vii)** if Buyer fails to return Statutory and Lead Disclosures as required by paragraph 6A(2); or **(viii)** if Buyer fails to sign or initial a separate liquidated damage form for an increased deposit as required by paragraphs 3B and 25. In such event, Seller shall authorize return of Buyer's deposit.
   (3) Notice To Buyer To Perform: The NBP shall: **(i)** be in writing; **(ii)** be signed by Seller; and **(iii)** give Buyer at least 2 (or ☐ _____) Days After Delivery (or until the time specified in the applicable paragraph, whichever occurs last) to take the applicable action. A NBP may not be Delivered any earlier than **2 Days** Prior to the expiration of the applicable time for Buyer to remove a contingency or cancel this Agreement or meet an obligation specified in 14C(2).

D. EFFECT OF BUYER'S REMOVAL OF CONTINGENCIES: If Buyer removes, in writing, any contingency or cancellation rights, unless otherwise specified in a separate written agreement between Buyer and Seller, Buyer shall with regard to that contingency or cancellation right conclusively be deemed to have: **(i)** completed all Buyer Investigations, and review of reports and other applicable information and disclosures; **(ii)** elected to proceed with the transaction; and **(iii)** assumed all liability, responsibility and expense for Repairs or corrections or for inability to obtain financing.

E. CLOSE OF ESCROW: Before Seller or Buyer may cancel this Agreement for failure of the other party to close escrow pursuant to this Agreement, Seller or Buyer must first give the other a demand to close escrow (C.A.R. Form DCE).

F. EFFECT OF CANCELLATION ON DEPOSITS: If Buyer or Seller gives written notice of cancellation pursuant to rights duly exercised under the terms of this Agreement, Buyer and Seller agree to Sign mutual instructions to cancel the sale and escrow and release deposits, if any, to the party entitled to the funds, less fees and costs incurred by that party. Fees and costs may be payable to service providers and vendors for services and products provided during escrow. **Release of funds will require mutual Signed release instructions from Buyer and Seller, judicial decision or arbitration award. A Buyer or Seller may be subject to a civil penalty of up to $1,000 for refusal to sign such instructions if no good faith dispute exists as to who is entitled to the deposited funds (Civil Code §1057.3).**

15. REPAIRS: Repairs shall be completed prior to final verification of condition unless otherwise agreed in writing. Repairs to be performed at Seller's expense may be performed by Seller or through others, provided that the work complies with applicable Law, including governmental permit, inspection and approval requirements. Repairs shall be performed in a good, skillful manner with materials of quality and appearance comparable to existing materials. It is understood that exact restoration of appearance or cosmetic items following all Repairs may not be possible. Seller shall: **(i)** obtain receipts for Repairs performed by others; **(ii)** prepare a written statement indicating the Repairs performed by Seller and the date of such Repairs; and **(iii)** provide Copies of receipts and statements to Buyer prior to final verification of condition.

16. FINAL VERIFICATION OF CONDITION: Buyer shall have the right to make a final inspection of the Property within 5 (or _____) Days Prior to Close Of Escrow, NOT AS A CONTINGENCY OF THE SALE, but solely to confirm: **(i)** the Property is maintained pursuant to paragraph 9; **(ii)** Repairs have been completed as agreed; and **(iii)** Seller has complied with Seller's other obligations under this Agreement (C.A.R. Form VP).

17. PRORATIONS OF PROPERTY TAXES AND OTHER ITEMS: Unless otherwise agreed in writing, the following items shall be PAID CURRENT and prorated between Buyer and Seller as of Close Of Escrow: real property taxes and assessments, interest, rents, HOA regular, special, and emergency dues and assessments imposed prior to Close Of Escrow, premiums on insurance assumed by Buyer, payments on bonds and assessments assumed by Buyer, and payments on Mello-Roos and other Special Assessment District bonds and assessments that are a current lien. The following items shall be assumed by Buyer WITHOUT CREDIT toward the purchase price: prorated payments on Mello-Roos and other Special Assessment District bonds and assessments and HOA special assessments that are a current lien but not yet due. Property will be reassessed upon change of ownership. Any supplemental tax bills shall be paid as follows: **(i)** for periods after Close Of Escrow, by Buyer; and **(ii)** for periods prior to Close Of Escrow, by Seller (see C.A.R. Form SPT or SBSA for further information). TAX BILLS ISSUED AFTER CLOSE OF ESCROW SHALL BE HANDLED DIRECTLY BETWEEN BUYER AND SELLER. Prorations shall be made based on a 30-day month.

Buyer's Initials (*SW*)(*CW*)

Seller's Initials (_____)(_____)

Reviewed by _____ Date _____

EQUAL HOUSING OPPORTUNITY

Property Address: 1652 Hill Street, Any City, Apple County, CA 90000   Date: 4/15/20XX

18. SELECTION OF SERVICE PROVIDERS: Brokers do not guarantee the performance of any vendors, service or product providers ("Providers"), whether referred by Broker or selected by Buyer, Seller or other person. Buyer and Seller may select ANY Providers of their own choosing.

19. MULTIPLE LISTING SERVICE ("MLS"): Brokers are authorized to report to the MLS a pending sale and, upon Close Of Escrow, the sales price and other terms of this transaction shall be provided to the MLS to be published and disseminated to persons and entities authorized to use the information on terms approved by the MLS.

20. EQUAL HOUSING OPPORTUNITY: The Property is sold in compliance with federal, state and local anti-discrimination Laws.

21. ATTORNEY FEES: In any action, proceeding, or arbitration between Buyer and Seller arising out of this Agreement, the prevailing Buyer or Seller shall be entitled to reasonable attorney fees and costs from the non-prevailing Buyer or Seller, except as provided in paragraph 26A.

22. DEFINITIONS: As used in this Agreement:

  A. **"Acceptance"** means the time the offer or final counter offer is accepted in writing by a party and is delivered to and personally received by the other party or that party's authorized agent in accordance with the terms of this offer or a final counter offer.

  B. **"C.A.R. Form"** means the specific form referenced or another comparable form agreed to by the parties.

  C. **"Close Of Escrow"** means the date the grant deed, or other evidence of transfer of title, is recorded.

  D. **"Copy"** means copy by any means including photocopy, NCR, facsimile and electronic.

  E. **"Days"** means calendar days. However, After Acceptance, the last **Day** for performance of any act required by this Agreement (including Close Of Escrow) shall not include any Saturday, Sunday, or legal holiday and shall instead be the next Day.

  F. **"Days After"** means the specified number of calendar days after the occurrence of the event specified, not counting the calendar date on which the specified event occurs, and ending at 11:59PM on the final day.

  G. **"Days Prior"** means the specified number of calendar days before the occurrence of the event specified, not counting the calendar date on which the specified event is scheduled to occur.

  H. **"Deliver", "Delivered"** or **"Delivery"**, regardless of the method used (i.e. messenger, mail, email, fax, other), means and shall be effective upon (i) personal receipt by Buyer or Seller or the individual Real Estate Licensee for that principal as specified in paragraph D of the section titled Real Estate Brokers on page 8; OR (ii) if checked, ☐ per the attached addendum (C.A.R. Form RDN).

  I. **"Electronic Copy"** or **"Electronic Signature"** means, as applicable, an electronic copy or signature complying with California Law. Buyer and Seller agree that electronic means will not be used by either party to modify or alter the content or integrity of this Agreement without the knowledge and consent of the other party.

  J. **"Law"** means any law, code, statute, ordinance, regulation, rule or order, which is adopted by a controlling city, county, state or federal legislative, judicial or executive body or agency.

  K. **"Repairs"** means any repairs (including pest control), alterations, replacements, modifications or retrofitting of the Property provided for under this Agreement.

  L. **"Signed"** means either a handwritten or electronic signature on an original document, Copy or any counterpart.

23. BROKER COMPENSATION: Seller or Buyer, or both, as applicable, agrees to pay compensation to Broker as specified in a separate written agreement between Broker and that Seller or Buyer. Compensation is payable upon Close Of Escrow, or if escrow does not close, as otherwise specified in the agreement between Broker and that Seller or Buyer.

24. JOINT ESCROW INSTRUCTIONS TO ESCROW HOLDER:

  A. The following paragraphs, or applicable portions thereof, of this Agreement constitute the joint escrow instructions of Buyer and Seller to Escrow Holder, which Escrow Holder is to use along with any related counter offers and addenda, and any additional mutual instructions to close the escrow: 1, 3, 4, 6C, 11B and D, 12, 13B, 14F, 17, 22, 23, 24, 28, 30, and paragraph D of the section titled Real Estate Brokers on page 8. If a Copy of the separate compensation agreement(s) provided for in paragraph 23, or paragraph D of the section titled Real Estate Brokers on page 8 is deposited with Escrow Holder by Broker, Escrow Holder shall accept such agreement(s) and pay out of Buyer's or Seller's funds, or both, as applicable, the respective Broker's compensation provided for in such agreement(s). The terms and conditions of this Agreement not specifically referenced above, in the specified paragraphs are additional matters for the information of Escrow Holder, but about which Escrow Holder need not be concerned. Buyer and Seller will receive Escrow Holder's general provisions directly from Escrow Holder and will execute such provisions upon Escrow Holder's request. To the extent the general provisions are inconsistent or conflict with this Agreement, the general provisions will control as to the duties and obligations of Escrow Holder only. Buyer and Seller will execute additional instructions, documents and forms provided by Escrow Holder that are reasonably necessary to close the escrow.

  B. A Copy of this Agreement shall be delivered to Escrow Holder within **3** business days after Acceptance (or ☐ _____). Escrow Holder shall provide Seller's Statement of Information to Title company when received from Seller. Buyer and Seller authorize Escrow Holder to accept and rely on Copies and Signatures as defined in this Agreement as originals, to open escrow and for other purposes of escrow. The validity of this Agreement as between Buyer and Seller is not affected by whether or when Escrow Holder Signs this Agreement.

  C. Brokers are a party to the escrow for the sole purpose of compensation pursuant to paragraphs 23 and paragraph D of the section titled Real Estate Brokers on page 8. Buyer and Seller irrevocably assign to Brokers compensation specified in paragraphs 23, respectively, and irrevocably instruct Escrow Holder to disburse those funds to Brokers at Close Of Escrow or pursuant to any other mutually executed cancellation agreement. Compensation instructions can be amended or revoked only with the written consent of Brokers. Buyer and Seller shall release and hold harmless Escrow Holder from any liability resulting from Escrow Holder's payment to Broker(s) of compensation pursuant to this Agreement. Escrow Holder shall immediately notify Brokers: **(i)** if Buyer's initial or any additional deposit is not made pursuant to this Agreement, or is not good at time of deposit with Escrow Holder; or **(ii)** if either Buyer or Seller instruct Escrow Holder to cancel escrow.

  D. A Copy of any amendment that affects any paragraph of this Agreement for which Escrow Holder is responsible shall be delivered to Escrow Holder within **2** business days after mutual execution of the amendment.

Buyer's Initials (_SW_)(_CW_)

RPA-CA REVISED 4/10 (PAGE 6 OF 8) Print Date

Seller's Initials (_____)(_____)

Reviewed by _____ Date _____

EQUAL HOUSING OPPORTUNITY

CALIFORNIA RESIDENTIAL PURCHASE AGREEMENT (RPA-CA PAGE 6 OF 8)

Property Address: ___1652 Hill Street, Any City, Apple County, CA 90000___   Date: ___4/15/20XX___

25. LIQUIDATED DAMAGES: If Buyer fails to complete this purchase because of Buyer's default, Seller shall retain, as liquidated damages, the deposit actually paid. If the Property is a dwelling with no more than four units, one of which Buyer intends to occupy, then the amount retained shall be no more than 3% of the purchase price. Any excess shall be returned to Buyer. Release of funds will require mutual, Signed release instructions from both Buyer and Seller, judicial decision or arbitration award. **AT TIME OF THE INCREASED DEPOSIT BUYER AND SELLER SHALL SIGN A SEPARATE LIQUIDATED DAMAGES PROVISION FOR ANY INCREASED DEPOSIT. (C.A.R. FORM RID).**

Buyer's Initials _____ / _____	Seller's Initials _____ / _____

26. DISPUTE RESOLUTION:

A. MEDIATION: Buyer and Seller agree to mediate any dispute or claim arising between them out of this Agreement, or any resulting transaction, before resorting to arbitration or court action. **Buyer and Seller also agree to mediate any disputes or claims with Broker(s), who, in writing, agree to such mediation prior to, or within a reasonable time after, the dispute or claim is presented to the Broker.** Mediation fees, if any, shall be divided equally among the parties involved. If, for any dispute or claim to which this paragraph applies, any party (i) commences an action without first attempting to resolve the matter through mediation, or (ii) before commencement of an action, refuses to mediate after a request has been made, then that party shall not be entitled to recover attorney fees, even if they would otherwise be available to that party in any such action. THIS MEDIATION PROVISION APPLIES WHETHER OR NOT THE ARBITRATION PROVISION IS INITIALED. **Exclusions from this mediation agreement are specified in paragraph 26C.**

B. ARBITRATION OF DISPUTES:
Buyer and Seller agree that any dispute or claim in Law or equity arising between them out of this Agreement or any resulting transaction, which is not settled through mediation, shall be decided by neutral, binding arbitration. Buyer and Seller also agree to arbitrate any disputes or claims with Broker(s), who, in writing, agree to such arbitration prior to, or within a reasonable time after, the dispute or claim is presented to the Broker. The arbitrator shall be a retired judge or justice, or an attorney with at least 5 years of residential real estate Law experience, unless the parties mutually agree to a different arbitrator. The parties shall have the right to discovery in accordance with Code of Civil Procedure §1283.05. In all other respects, the arbitration shall be conducted in accordance with Title 9 of Part 3 of the Code of Civil Procedure. Judgment upon the award of the arbitrator(s) may be entered into any court having jurisdiction. Enforcement of this agreement to arbitrate shall be governed by the Federal Arbitration Act. Exclusions from this arbitration agreement are specified in paragraph 26C.
   "NOTICE: BY INITIALING IN THE SPACE BELOW YOU ARE AGREEING TO HAVE ANY DISPUTE ARISING OUT OF THE MATTERS INCLUDED IN THE 'ARBITRATION OF DISPUTES' PROVISION DECIDED BY NEUTRAL ARBITRATION AS PROVIDED BY CALIFORNIA LAW AND YOU ARE GIVING UP ANY RIGHTS YOU MIGHT POSSESS TO HAVE THE DISPUTE LITIGATED IN A COURT OR JURY TRIAL. BY INITIALING IN THE SPACE BELOW YOU ARE GIVING UP YOUR JUDICIAL RIGHTS TO DISCOVERY AND APPEAL, UNLESS THOSE RIGHTS ARE SPECIFICALLY INCLUDED IN THE 'ARBITRATION OF DISPUTES' PROVISION. IF YOU REFUSE TO SUBMIT TO ARBITRATION AFTER AGREEING TO THIS PROVISION, YOU MAY BE COMPELLED TO ARBITRATE UNDER THE AUTHORITY OF THE CALIFORNIA CODE OF CIVIL PROCEDURE. YOUR AGREEMENT TO THIS ARBITRATION PROVISION IS VOLUNTARY."
   "WE HAVE READ AND UNDERSTAND THE FOREGOING AND AGREE TO SUBMIT DISPUTES ARISING OUT OF THE MATTERS INCLUDED IN THE 'ARBITRATION OF DISPUTES' PROVISION TO NEUTRAL ARBITRATION."

Buyer's Initials ___SW___ / ___CW___	Seller's Initials _____ / _____

C. ADDITIONAL MEDIATION AND ARBITRATION TERMS:
   (1) EXCLUSIONS: The following matters shall be excluded from mediation and arbitration: (i) a judicial or non-judicial foreclosure or other action or proceeding to enforce a deed of trust, mortgage or installment land sale contract as defined in Civil Code §2985; (ii) an unlawful detainer action; (iii) the filing or enforcement of a mechanic's lien; and (iv) any matter that is within the jurisdiction of a probate, small claims or bankruptcy court. The filing of a court action to enable the recording of a notice of pending action, for order of attachment, receivership, injunction, or other provisional remedies, shall not constitute a waiver or violation of the mediation and arbitration provisions.
   (2) BROKERS: Brokers shall not be obligated or compelled to mediate or arbitrate unless they agree to do so in writing. Any Broker(s) participating in mediation or arbitration shall not be deemed a party to the Agreement.

27. TERMS AND CONDITIONS OF OFFER:
   This is an offer to purchase the Property on the above terms and conditions. The liquidated damages paragraph or the arbitration of disputes paragraph is incorporated in this Agreement if initialed by all parties or if incorporated by mutual agreement in a counter offer or addendum. If at least one but not all parties initial such paragraph(s), a counter offer is required until agreement is reached. Seller has the right to continue to offer the Property for sale and to accept any other offer at any time prior to notification of Acceptance. If this offer is accepted and Buyer subsequently defaults, Buyer may be responsible for payment of Brokers' compensation. This Agreement and any supplement, addendum or modification, including any Copy, may be Signed in two or more counterparts, all of which shall constitute one and the same writing.

28. TIME OF ESSENCE; ENTIRE CONTRACT; CHANGES: Time is of the essence. All understandings between the parties are incorporated in this Agreement. Its terms are intended by the parties as a final, complete and exclusive expression of their Agreement with respect to its subject matter, and may not be contradicted by evidence of any prior agreement or contemporaneous oral agreement. If any provision of this Agreement is held to be ineffective or invalid, the remaining provisions will nevertheless be given full force and effect. Except as otherwise specified, this Agreement shall be interpreted and disputes shall be resolved in accordance with the laws of the State of California. **Neither this Agreement nor any provision in it may be extended, amended, modified, altered or changed, except in writing Signed by Buyer and Seller.**

Buyer's Initials (___SW___)(___CW___)

RPA-CA REVISED 4/10 (PAGE 7 OF 8)

Seller's Initials (_____)(_____)

Reviewed by _____ Date _____

CALIFORNIA RESIDENTIAL PURCHASE AGREEMENT (RPA-CA PAGE 7 OF 8)

Property Address: 1652 Hill Street, Any City, Apple County, CA 90000 _____ Date: _____ 4/15/20XX

29. EXPIRATION OF OFFER: This offer shall be deemed revoked and the deposit shall be returned unless the offer is Signed by Seller and a Copy of the Signed offer is personally received by Buyer, or by *Buyer's Representative - First Real Estate*, who is authorized to receive it, by 5:00 PM on the third Day after this offer is signed by Buyer (or, if checked, ☒ by 5:00 □ AM ☒ PM, on __April 16, 20XX__ (date)).

Buyer has read and acknowledges receipt of a Copy of the offer and agrees to the above confirmation of agency relationships.

Date __4/15/20XX__   Date __4/15/20XX__

BUYER *Sam Winter* _____   BUYER *Cindy Winter* _____
Sam Winter   Cindy Winter
(Print name)   **(Print name)**

         901 Cherrywood Lane, Some Town, CA 90000 _____
(Address)

☐ Additional Signature Addendum attached (C.A.R. Form ASA).

30. ACCEPTANCE OF OFFER: Seller warrants that Seller is the owner of the Property, or has the authority to execute this Agreement. Seller accepts the above offer, agrees to sell the Property on the above terms and conditions, and agrees to the above confirmation of agency relationships. Seller has read and acknowledges receipt of a Copy of this Agreement, and authorizes Broker to Deliver a Signed Copy to Buyer.

☐ (If checked) **SUBJECT TO ATTACHED COUNTER OFFER (C.A.R. Form CO) DATED:** _____

Date _____   Date _____

SELLER _____   SELLER _____

(Print name)   **(Print name)**

(Address)

☐ Additional Signature Addendum attached (C.A.R. Form ASA).

(___/___) **CONFIRMATION OF ACCEPTANCE:** A Copy of Signed Acceptance was personally received by Buyer or Buyer's authorized
(Initials) agent on (date) _____ at _____ ☐ AM ☐ PM. A binding Agreement is created when a Copy of Signed Acceptance is personally received by Buyer or Buyer's authorized agent whether or not confirmed in this document. Completion of this confirmation is not legally required in order to create a binding Agreement. It is solely intended to evidence the date that Confirmation of Acceptance has occurred.

REAL ESTATE BROKERS:
A. **Real Estate Brokers are not parties to the Agreement between Buyer and Seller.**
B. **Agency relationships are confirmed as stated in paragraph 2.**
C. If specified in paragraph 3A(2), Agent who submitted the offer for Buyer acknowledges receipt of deposit.
D. **COOPERATING BROKER COMPENSATION:** Listing Broker agrees to pay Cooperating Broker **(Selling Firm)** and Cooperating Broker agrees to accept, out of Listing Broker's proceeds in escrow: (i) the amount specified in the MLS, provided Cooperating Broker is a Participant of the MLS in which the Property is offered for sale or a reciprocal MLS; or (ii) ☐ (if checked) the amount specified in a separate written agreement (C.A.R. Form CBC) between Listing Broker and Cooperating Broker. Declaration of License and Tax (C.A.R. Form DLT) may be used to document that tax reporting will be required or that an exemption exits.

Real Estate Broker (Selling Firm) __First Real Estate, Lisa Summers__   DRE Lic. # __00931278__
By __Linda Rose__   DRE Lic. # __00891254__ Date _____
Address __234 First Street__   City __Any City__   State __CA__ Zip __90000__
Telephone __(555) 456-1234__ Fax __(555) 456-9876__ E-mail __lisa@firstrealestate.xyz__

Real Estate Broker (Listing Firm) _____   DRE Lic. # _____
By _____   DRE Lic. # _____ Date _____
Address _____   City _____   State _____ Zip _____
Telephone _____ Fax _____ E-mail _____

ESCROW HOLDER ACKNOWLEDGMENT:
Escrow Holder acknowledges receipt of a Copy of this Agreement, (if checked, ☐ a deposit in the amount of $ _____),
counter offer numbered _____ , ☐ Seller's Statement of Information and ☐ Other _____
_____ , and agrees to act as Escrow Holder subject to paragraph 24 of this Agreement, any
supplemental escrow instructions and the terms of Escrow Holder's general provisions if any.
Escrow Holder is advised that the date of Confirmation of Acceptance of the Agreement as between Buyer and Seller is _____ .
Escrow Holder _____
By _____   Escrow # _____
Address _____   Date _____
Phone/Fax/E-mail _____
Escrow Holder is licensed by the California Department of ☐ Corporations, ☐ Insurance, ☐ Real Estate. License # _____

PRESENTATION OF OFFER: (_____) Listing Broker presented this offer to Seller on _____ (date).
                              Broker or Designee Initials

REJECTION OF OFFER: (___) (___) No counter offer is being made. This offer was rejected by Seller on _____ (date).
                         Seller's Initials

Reviewed by _____
Broker or Designee _____ Date _____

REVISION DATE 4/10

CALIFORNIA RESIDENTIAL PURCHASE AGREEMENT (RPA-CA PAGE 8 OF 8)

ESTIMATED BUYER'S CLOSING COSTS

Many buyers think the down payment is the only money they need to pay for a house and are unprepared for the closing costs (additional costs needed to close escrow). Be sure to explain that these costs may be up to 1.5% of the purchase price, not including loan points. Closing costs vary from county to county, but your broker should have estimates for you to use for transactions in your area. It is better to estimate costs on the high side, because if the actual closing costs are less, the buyers are pleasantly surprised.

In addition to information from the Case Study, please use the following amounts when completing the Estimated Buyer's Costs form. These are typical buyer's costs for Any City, California.

Lender's prepaid interest (allow 15 days or $795.00) ($332,000 x 5.75% divided by 360 days x 15 days). The lender will charge a 2% loan origination fee for the first loan (332,000 x 2% = $6,640). The lender will also charge $350.00 as a processing and underwriting fee.

Your broker should have estimated buyer's closing costs for transactions in your area.

Impounds: Taxes are paid twice per year and the seller has paid them current through June 30th. Depending on the date of closing, the seller may be credited a portion of the prepaid taxes, so allow up to $560.00 as a buyer's expense. The buyer's first property tax payment will be November 1st. Therefore, three months impounds should be deposited into buyers' account with the lender. [$5,187.50 ($415,000 x 1.25%) divided by 12 = $432.29 per month x 3 months = $1,296.88. Round up to $1,300.00].

Sometimes insurance is prepaid for one year; other times it is paid in an impound account. Since the buyers want to use an impound account, $200.00 will be put into insurance impounds.

Standard Fees in Any City:

Appraisal Fee - $400.00
Document Preparation, Recording, Notary Fee - $485.00
Escrow Fee - $800.00 (50/50)
HOA Transfer Fee - $125.00
Physical Inspection Fee - $350.00

Sub-escrow Fee - $65.00
Tax Service - $75.00
Title Policy (lender) - $500.00
Transaction Fee - $100.00

The agent added an additional $450.00 to cover any miscellaneous fees and expenses. The total initial deposit from the buyers is $41,500.

ESTIMATED BUYER COSTS
(C.A.R. Form EBC, Revised 4/06)

CALIFORNIA ASSOCIATION OF REALTORS®

BUYER: Sam Winter and Cindy Winter   DATE: 4/15/20XX

PROPERTY ADDRESS: 1652 Hill Street, Any City, CA 90000

PROJECTED CLOSING DATE: June 30, 20XX   PROJECTED PURCHASE PRICE: $ 415,000.00

New First Loan: $ 332,000.00 Rate: 5.75 % ☒Fixed or ☐Adjustable ☐ Interest Only   Term: 30 years

New Second Loan: $ Rate: % ☐Fixed or ☐Adjustable ☐ Interest Only   Term: years

Current Annual Property Taxes: $ 5,187.50 Rate: 1.25 % If Rented, Current Monthly Rent $

FINANCING CHARGES

New First Loan Origination Fee/Points	2 %	$ 6,640.00
Secondary Financing Orig. Fee/Points	%	$
Prepaid Interest (First Loan)	# Days 15	$ 795.00
Prepaid Interest (Secondary Financing)	# Days	$
Impounds: - Property Taxes	# Months 3	$ 1,300.00
- Insurance	# Months	$ 200.00
Processing/Underwriting Fees		$ 350.00
Document Preparation Fees		$
Appraisal Fees		$ 400.00
Funding Fees		$
Other Lender Fees (Tax Service, Flood Certificates, etc.)		$ 75.00

ESCROW AND TITLE CHARGES

Escrow Fee ☒ including any Sub-Escrow Fee	$ 465.00
Owner's Title Insurance Policy	$
Lender's Title Insurance Policy	$ 500.00
Document Preparation, Recording, Notary & other Fees	$ 485.00

OTHER EXPENSES & PRORATIONS

Prorated Property Taxes	# Days 40	$ 560.00 +/-
Homeowners Dues	# Days	$
Transfer Tax (if charged to Buyer) Rate per $1,000 $		$
Buyer Brokerage Fee		$
Annual Insurance Premium (excluding flood & earthquake)		$
Home Warranty Program		$
Wood-Destroying Pest Inspection		$
Other Physical Inspection Fees Physical Inspection		$ 350.00
HOA Transfer and/or Move-In Fees		$ 125.00
Other Miscellaneous		$ 450.00
Transaction Fee		$ 100.00

TOTAL ESTIMATED EXPENSES $12,795.00

ESTIMATED CREDITS

Prorated Property Taxes	# Days	$ —
Prorated Rents	# Days	$ —
Tenant Security Deposits		$ —
Credit from Seller		$ —
Other		$ —
Total Estimated Credits		$

ESTIMATED CASH NEEDED TO CLOSE

Purchase Price	$	415,000.00
LESS Total Loans	-	332,000.00
Down Payment	=	83,000.00
PLUS Total Estimated Expenses	+	12,795.00
LESS Total Estimated Credits	-	
LESS Initial Deposits	-	41,500.00
Est. Cash Needed to Close Escrow	$	54,295.00

ESTIMATED MONTHLY PAYMENTS

New First Loan*	$ 1,935.00
Secondary Financing*	$
New Property Taxes	$ 430.00
Insurance (ex. flood & earthquake)	$ 100.00
Mortgage Insurance	$
Homeowners Dues	$ 210.00
Mello Roos	$
Other	$
Total Estimated Payment	$ 2,675.00

* Buyer is aware that with regard to adjustable rate loans, the monthly payments may increase at various times over the life of the loan. Buyer should confirm directly with lenders all terms and conditions of said loans.

This estimate, based upon the above proposed purchase price, type of financing and projected closing date, has been prepared to assist Buyer in computing costs. Amounts will vary depending upon differences between actual and estimated repairs that may occur in the transaction, assessments, liens, impound accounts, charges by lenders, escrow companies, title insurers and other service providers and other items. Not all liens may yet have been identified. Neither Broker nor Agent guarantee these figures represent the actual, or only, amounts and charges.

By signing below Buyer acknowledges that Buyer has read, understands and received a copy of this Estimated Buyer's Costs.

Buyer Sam Winter   Date 4/15/20XX
Buyer Cindy Winter   Date 4/15/20XX
Real Estate Broker (Firm) First Real Estate   DRE Lic. # 00931278
By (Agent) Linda Rose   DRE Lic. # 00891254   Date 4/15/20XX
Address 234 First Street   City Any City   State CA   Zip 90000
Telephone (555) 456-1234   Fax (555) 456-9876   E-mail lisa@firstrealestate.xyz

Reviewed by _____ Date _____

EQUAL HOUSING OPPORTUNITY

EBC REVISED 4/06 (PAGE 1 OF 1)   ESTIMATED BUYER COSTS (EBC PAGE 1 OF 1)

Agent: Lisa Summers   Phone: 555.456.1234   Fax: 555.456.9876   Prepared using zipForm® software
Broker: First Real Estate   234 First Street   Any City, CA 90000

BUYER'S INSPECTION ADVISORY

Generally, most real estate licensees are not qualified to evaluate the structural condition of a property, soil stability, environmental hazards, and other physical conditions that could affect the home. By giving this advisory to buyers, you are alerting them to get professional advice if they have any concerns about the property that an inspection might discover. The buyer is required to read and approve this two-page form, along with the Purchase Agreement.

A buyer may have to seek professional advice if there are concerns about the property in the home inspection report.

CALIFORNIA
ASSOCIATION
OF REALTORS®

BUYER'S INSPECTION ADVISORY
(C.A.R. Form BIA, Revised 10/02)

A. IMPORTANCE OF PROPERTY INVESTIGATION: The physical condition of the land and improvements being purchased is not guaranteed by either Seller or Brokers. For this reason, you should conduct thorough investigations of the Property personally and with professionals who should provide written reports of their investigations. A general physical inspection typically does not cover all aspects of the Property nor items affecting the Property that are not physically located on the Property. If the professionals recommend further investigations, including a recommendation by a pest control operator to inspect inaccessible areas of the Property, you should contact qualified experts to conduct such additional investigations.

B. BUYER RIGHTS AND DUTIES: You have an affirmative duty to exercise reasonable care to protect yourself, including discovery of the legal, practical and technical implications of disclosed facts, and the investigation and verification of information and facts that you know or that are within your diligent attention and observation. The purchase agreement gives you the right to investigate the Property. If you exercise this right, and you should, you must do so in accordance with the terms of that agreement. This is the best way for you to protect yourself. It is extremely important for you to read all written reports provided by professionals and to discuss the results of inspections with the professional who conducted the inspection. You have the right to request that Seller make repairs, corrections or take other action based upon items discovered in your investigations or disclosed by Seller. If Seller is unwilling or unable to satisfy your requests, or you do not want to purchase the Property in its disclosed and discovered condition, you have the right to cancel the agreement if you act within specific time periods. If you do not cancel the agreement in a timely and proper manner, you may be in breach of contract.

C. SELLER RIGHTS AND DUTIES: Seller is required to disclose to you material facts known to him/her that affect the value or desirability of the Property. However, Seller may not be aware of some Property defects or conditions. Seller does not have an obligation to inspect the Property for your benefit nor is Seller obligated to repair, correct or otherwise cure known defects that are disclosed to you or previously unknown defects that are discovered by you or your inspectors during escrow. The purchase agreement obligates Seller to make the Property available to you for investigations.

D. BROKER OBLIGATIONS: Brokers do not have expertise in all areas and therefore cannot advise you on many items, such as soil stability, geologic or environmental conditions, hazardous or illegal controlled substances, structural conditions of the foundation or other improvements, or the condition of the roof, plumbing, heating, air conditioning, electrical, sewer, septic, waste disposal, or other system. The only way to accurately determine the condition of the Property is through an inspection by an appropriate professional selected by you. If Broker gives you referrals to such professionals, Broker does not guarantee their performance. You may select any professional of your choosing. In sales involving residential dwellings with no more than four units, Brokers have a duty to make a diligent visual inspection of the accessible areas of the Property and to disclose the results of that inspection. However, as some Property defects or conditions may not be discoverable from a visual inspection, it is possible Brokers are not aware of them. If you have entered into a written agreement with a Broker, the specific terms of that agreement will determine the nature and extent of that Broker's duty to you. **YOU ARE STRONGLY ADVISED TO INVESTIGATE THE CONDITION AND SUITABILITY OF ALL ASPECTS OF THE PROPERTY. IF YOU DO NOT DO SO, YOU ARE ACTING AGAINST THE ADVICE OF BROKERS.**

E. YOU ARE ADVISED TO CONDUCT INVESTIGATIONS OF THE ENTIRE PROPERTY, INCLUDING, BUT NOT LIMITED TO THE FOLLOWING:

1. **GENERAL CONDITION OF THE PROPERTY, ITS SYSTEMS AND COMPONENTS:** Foundation, roof, plumbing, heating, air conditioning, electrical, mechanical, security, pool/spa, other structural and non-structural systems and components, fixtures, built-in appliances, any personal property included in the sale, and energy efficiency of the Property. (Structural engineers are best suited to determine possible design or construction defects, and whether improvements are structurally sound.)

2. **SQUARE FOOTAGE, AGE, BOUNDARIES:** Square footage, room dimensions, lot size, age of improvements and boundaries. Any numerical statements regarding these items are APPROXIMATIONS ONLY and have not been verified by Seller and cannot be verified by Brokers. Fences, hedges, walls, retaining walls and other natural or constructed barriers or markers do not necessarily identify true Property boundaries. (Professionals such as appraisers, architects, surveyors and civil engineers are best suited to determine square footage, dimensions and boundaries of the Property.)

3. **WOOD DESTROYING PESTS:** Presence of, or conditions likely to lead to the presence of wood destroying pests and organisms and other infestation or infection. Inspection reports covering these items can be separated into two sections: Section 1 identifies areas where infestation or infection is evident. Section 2 identifies areas where there are conditions likely to lead to infestation or infection. A registered structural pest control company is best suited to perform these inspections.

4. **SOIL STABILITY:** Existence of fill or compacted soil, expansive or contracting soil, susceptibility to slippage, settling or movement, and the adequacy of drainage. (Geotechnical engineers are best suited to determine such conditions, causes and remedies.)

BIA REVISED 10/02 (PAGE 1 OF 2)

Buyer's Initials (_SW_)(_CW_)
Broker's Initials (_____)(_____)
Reviewed by _____ Date _____

EQUAL HOUSING
OPPORTUNITY

BUYER'S INSPECTION ADVISORY (BIA PAGE 1 OF 2)

| **Agent:** Lisa Summers | **Phone:** (555) 456-1234 | **Fax:** (555) 456-9876 | **Prepared using zipForm® software** |
| **Broker:** First Real Estate | 234 First Street, Any City, California 90000 | | |

5. **ROOF:** Present condition, age, leaks, and remaining useful life. (Roofing contractors are best suited to determine these conditions.)
6. **POOL/SPA:** Cracks, leaks or operational problems. (Pool contractors are best suited to determine these conditions.)
7. **WASTE DISPOSAL:** Type, size, adequacy, capacity and condition of sewer and septic systems and components, connection to sewer, and applicable fees.
8. **WATER AND UTILITES; WELL SYSTEMS AND COMPONENTS:** Water and utility availability, use restrictions and costs. Water quality, adequacy, condition, and performance of well systems and components.
9. **ENVIRONMENTAL HAZARDS:** Potential environmental hazards, including, but not limited to, asbestos, lead-based paint and other lead contamination, radon, methane, other gases, fuel oil or chemical storage tanks, contaminated soil or water, hazardous waste, waste disposal sites, electromagnetic fields, nuclear sources, and other substances, materials, products, or conditions (including mold (airborne, toxic or otherwise), fungus or similar contaminants). (For more information on these items, you may consult an appropriate professional or read the booklets "Environmental Hazards: A Guide for Homeowners, Buyers, Landlords and Tenants," "Protect Your Family From Lead in Your Home" or both.)
10. **EARTHQUAKES AND FLOODING:** Susceptibility of the Property to earthquake/seismic hazards and propensity of the Property to flood. (A Geologist or Geotechnical Engineer is best suited to provide information on these conditions.)
11. **FIRE, HAZARD AND OTHER INSURANCE:** The availability and cost of necessary or desired insurance may vary. The location of the Property in a seismic, flood or fire hazard zone, and other conditions, such as the age of the Property and the claims history of the Property and Buyer, may affect the availability and need for certain types of insurance. Buyer should explore insurance options early as this information may affect other decisions, including the removal of loan and inspection contingencies. (An insurance agent is best suited to provide information on these conditions.)
12. **BUILDING PERMITS, ZONING AND GOVERNMENTAL REQUIREMENTS:** Permits, inspections, certificates, zoning, other governmental limitations, restrictions, and requirements affecting the current or future use of the Property, its development or size. (Such information is available from appropriate governmental agencies and private information providers. Brokers are not qualified to review or interpret any such information.)
13. **RENTAL PROPERTY RESTRICTIONS:** Some cities and counties impose restrictions that limit the amount of rent that can be charged, the maximum number of occupants; and the right of a landlord to terminate a tenancy. Deadbolt or other locks and security systems for doors and windows, including window bars, should be examined to determine whether they satisfy legal requirements. (Government agencies can provide information about these restrictions and other requirements.)
14. **SECURITY AND SAFETY:** State and local Law may require the installation of barriers, access alarms, self-latching mechanisms and/or other measures to decrease the risk to children and other persons of existing swimming pools and hot tubs, as well as various fire safety and other measures concerning other features of the Property. Compliance requirements differ from city to city and county to county. Unless specifically agreed, the Property may not be in compliance with these requirements. (Local government agencies can provide information about these restrictions and other requirements.)
15. **NEIGHBORHOOD, AREA, SUBDIVISION CONDITIONS; PERSONAL FACTORS:** Neighborhood or area conditions, including schools, proximity and adequacy of law enforcement, crime statistics, the proximity of registered felons or offenders, fire protection, other government services, availability, adequacy and cost of any speed-wired, wireless internet connections or other telecommunications or other technology services and installations, proximity to commercial, industrial or agricultural activities, existing and proposed transportation, construction and development that may affect noise, view, or traffic, airport noise, noise or odor from any source, wild and domestic animals, other nuisances, hazards, or circumstances, protected species, wetland properties, botanical diseases, historic or other governmentally protected sites or improvements, cemeteries, facilities and condition of common areas of common interest subdivisions, and possible lack of compliance with any governing documents or Homeowners' Association requirements, conditions and influences of significance to certain cultures and/or religions, and personal needs, requirements and preferences of Buyer.

> Buyer acknowledges and agrees that Broker: **(i)** Does not decide what price Buyer should pay or Seller should accept; **(ii)** Does not guarantee the condition of the Property; **(iii)** Does not guarantee the performance, adequacy or completeness of inspections, services, products or repairs provided or made by Seller or others; **(iv)** Does not have an obligation to conduct an inspection of common areas or areas off the site of the Property; **(v)** Shall not be responsible for identifying defects on the Property, in common areas, or offsite unless such defects are visually observable by an inspection of reasonably accessible areas of the Property or are known to Broker; **(vi)** Shall not be responsible for inspecting public records or permits concerning the title or use of Property; **(vii)** Shall not be responsible for identifying the location of boundary lines or other items affecting title; **(viii)** Shall not be responsible for verifying square footage, representations of others or information contained in Investigation reports, Multiple Listing Service, advertisements, flyers or other promotional material; **(ix)** Shall not be responsible for providing legal or tax advice regarding any aspect of a transaction entered into by Buyer or Seller; and **(x)** Shall not be responsible for providing other advice or information that exceeds the knowledge, education and experience required to perform real estate licensed activity. Buyer and Seller agree to seek legal, tax, insurance, title and other desired assistance from appropriate professionals.

By signing below, Buyer and Broker each acknowledge that they have read, understand, accept and have received a Copy of this Advisory. Buyer is encouraged to read it carefully.

Sam Winter	4/15/20XX	*Cindy Winter*	4/15/20XX
Buyer Signature	Date	Buyer Signature	Date

Broker Signature	Date	Broker Signature	Date

Published and Distributed by:
REAL ESTATE BUSINESS SERVICES, INC.
a subsidiary of the California Association of REALTORS®
525 South Virgil Avenue, Los Angeles, California 90020

Reviewed by _____ Date _____

SURE TRAC The System for Success™

EQUAL HOUSING OPPORTUNITY

UNIT 6 REVIEW

▣ Matching Exercise

Instructions: Write the letter of the matching term on the blank line before its definition. Answers are in Appendix A.

Terms

A. allocate

B. closing costs

C. Interim Occupancy Agreement

D. liquidated damages

E. Notice Of Buyer To Perform

F. prorate

G. purchase agreement

H. purchase price

I. RPA-CA

J. statutory disclosures

K. vesting

L. walk-through

Definitions

1. _____ When signed by both buyer and seller, the legally binding written contract that indicates the terms and conditions of the purchase and sale of the piece of real estate

2. _____ Standard contract created by the California Association of REALTORS® (C.A.R.®) that is used by real estate agents when a buyer makes an offer anywhere in California

3. _____ The amount the buyer offers to pay the seller for the property

4. _____ An agreement used if a buyer wants early possession of the property, or the seller wishes to remain in possession after the close of escrow

5. _____ To assign

6. _____ Disclosures that are required by law

7. _____ A notice sent to a buyer who does not complete inspections or fulfill his or her obligations within the time specified in the purchase contract

8. _____ The buyer's right to conduct the final inspection of the property a few days before escrow closes

9. _____ The money agreed upon by both parties to a contract that one would pay to the other upon backing out of the agreement

10. _____ Costs, in addition to the down payment that must be paid in order to close escrow

▣ Multiple Choice Questions

Instructions: Circle your response and go to Appendix A to read the complete explanation for each question.

1. Which of the following statements is true regarding the purchase agreement?
    a. The California Department of Real Estate requires a specific form.
    b. The Real Estate Law promulgates specific forms that are required by law.
    c. The California Residential Purchase Agreement and Joint Escrow Instructions (RPA-CA) contract is used by real estate agents when a buyer makes an offer anywhere in California.
    d. The RPA-CA form was created by the California Department of Real Estate.

2. On the "California Residential Purchase Agreement and Joint Escrow Instructions" form, to what do the words "and Joint Escrow Instructions" refer?
    a. The form is available for use throughout the state.
    b. The form has an instruction to the escrow holder by both the seller and the buyer.
    c. The form includes space for the lender to sign for receipt of the document.
    d. None of the above is correct.

3. Upon receipt of the initial deposit, the salesperson should:
    a. commingle it with the broker's personal funds.
    b. give it to his or her broker to deposit within three business days after receipt into the trust account.
    c. give it to the seller.
    d. hold on to it until escrow asks for the funds.

4. The section of the deposit receipt that indicates the date the sellers will turn over possession of the property is the _____ clause.
    a. allocation of costs
    b. title and vesting
    c. closing and occupancy
    d. liquidated damages

5. Both buyer and seller must agree on who will be responsible for paying for any inspection costs. Which of the following costs typically is prorated instead of allocated?
    a. Termite inspection
    b. Property tax
    c. Escrow fee
    d. Retrofit – water heater bracing

6. The seller's property was built in 1995. Which of the following is a disclosure that a seller does not have to make to the buyer regarding the property?
    a. Lead-based paint
    b. Data base disclosure
    c. Special flood hazard area
    d. Transfer Disclosure Statement

7. Buyers and sellers are given specific amounts of time to meet the various conditions of the contract. Which of the following statements is incorrect?
    a. Within 7 days, or a specified number of days, the seller must deliver all reports and disclosures for which he or she is responsible.
    b. Within 7 days, or a specified number of days, the seller must deposit the increased deposit into escrow.
    c. Within 17 days, or a specified number of days, the buyer must complete any investigations and review of reports.
    d. Within 17 days, or a specified number of days, the buyer must remove any contingencies or cancel the agreement.

8. The offer to purchase usually contains a printed clause that says the sellers may keep the deposit as:
    a. liquidated damages.
    b. personal property.
    c. equity.
    d. an action in foreclosure.

9. If the sellers do not accept an offer before its expiration:
    a. the offer may be revoked.
    b. any deposit is returned to the buyer.
    c. the buyers can create a counteroffer.
    d. both (a) and (b) may occur.

10. When purchasing a home, buyers need money for the:
    a. down payment only.
    b. down payment and closing costs.
    c. down payment, closing costs, and MLS fees.
    d. closing costs only.

How Will You Get Your Business?

Unit 7

INTRODUCTION

As with any business, success in real estate depends upon effective prospecting for new clients. **Prospecting** is the process of identifying potential customers. It is a positive, professional way to market yourself and your business.

If you want people to come to you, you must first perform some type of prospecting activity to let them know you are in the real estate profession. The following pages cover various prospecting activities that have proven effective with successful real estate sales associates. Find a few activities that you enjoy doing and then focus on pursuing and accomplishing those activities. Feeling anxious about prospecting is normal, but you should realize that successful people perform the activities that unsuccessful people are usually too afraid to attempt. With time and practice, however, prospecting does become easier.

Whenever real estate solicitation involves the use of the telephone, cell phone, fax, or email, you must comply with applicable federal and state Do Not Call and CAN-SPAM laws. You may still telephone, fax, and email potential clients, but you must follow certain procedures, which will be discussed later in this unit.

Learning Objectives

After reading this unit, you should be able to:

- identify qualified prospects.
- recall the laws pertaining to prospecting.
- recognize prospecting activities used by real estate sales associates.

WHO ARE LIKELY PROSPECTS?

Your most likely prospects will include people in your current sphere of influence, homeowners in your geographic target market, FSBOs, individuals in your demographic target markets, and prospects who call or come to the office while you have floor time.

A real estate prospect can be anyone needing to buy or sell a house.

Warm and Cold Prospects

The first thing to do as you begin your real estate sales career is to create a **contact list** using the contact management software on your computer. Each contact record should include information, such as name, address, telephone number, occupation, birthday, anniversary, and other family data.

Warm Prospects

The contact list should include everyone you know—family members, friends, teachers, former colleagues, and members of associations to which you belong. They are in your **sphere of influence** and are considered **warm prospects**. Successful sales associates make regular contact with people in their sphere of influence as part of their prospecting efforts. New real estate sales associates often start their careers by prospecting in their own communities, where knowledge of the local neighborhoods is a distinct advantage. Use of the sphere of influence approach widens the number of prospects to whom a salesperson might appeal. A new salesperson will benefit from contacts at local schools, churches, or other social groups.

> **Possible Warm Prospects**
>
> - Family members
> - Friends, neighbors, and acquaintances
> - Members of club(s) to which you belong
> - Members of the church to which you belong
> - Teachers and instructors
> - Professional contacts (doctor, dentist, lawyer, CPA)
> - People you see frequently (mail carrier, hairdresser, dry cleaner, store clerks)

Cold Prospects

Cold prospects are potential clients and customers who are not in your sphere of influence, but who may want to buy or sell real estate. Therefore, you should contact anyone and everyone you believe to be a buyer or seller in need of a real estate professional. While prospecting, however, it is important to make sure you are calling the right people. Just as some people are looking to buy a new home, others are looking to sell their property. Defining whether they are buyers or sellers will determine how you present your services.

> **Possible Cold Prospects**
>
> - Homeowners
> - Landlords
> - Renters
> - Newlyweds
> - New parents
> - Growing families
> - Empty nesters
> - Recent retirees
> - Real estate investors
> - Corporate transferees

Choose a Target Market

Rather than scatter your energies in all directions, it is useful to focus your attention and marketing dollars in one or two specific areas, or target markets. A **target market** is the defined group of properties or individuals with similarities. Your target market can be broad as in geographic markets or highly focused as in a niche market. A **niche market** consists of consumers with the same specialized needs.

Geographic Markets. A good example of a geographic target market is the traditional farm area that brokers have promoted for their agents for decades. A **farm area** is a geographic area where a salesperson specializes. Geographic markets are broad target markets and can be further segmented. For example, a 300-home farm area could be segmented into one-story homes versus two-story homes. Maybe this is a retirement area and main floor master bedrooms (for health reasons) are in high demand. The point being is that you have to analyze the market to discover these types of niches.

Property Type Markets. Markets are defined by the type of property—single-family homes, condominiums, lofts, vacation homes, golf course properties, etc. Again, these groups can be further segmented by price ranges, amenities, location, or age to name just a few variations.

Demographic Markets. People are often grouped into demographic markets by their shared experiences or social and economic characteristics. Age, language, marital status, income level, or just about any grouping could characterize demographic markets. Any demographic group could be further differentiated. For example, you could market to singles who are first-time homebuyers, single mothers, or older singles whose spouse has passed away. All of these are readily identifiable niches although not all can necessarily be cost effectively reached with your marketing message.

Buyer/Seller Types. Examples of these might be first time homebuyers, investors, pre-foreclosures, etc. First-time homebuyers might be segmented into groups that need special assistance programs and groups with good incomes but no down payment moneys. Investors could be segmented by property types in which they are interested. A segment of sellers would include FSBOs. **FSBOs (For Sale By Owner)** are properties that the owner has not listed with a real estate broker.

Psychographic Markets. Psychographics are any attributes relating to personality, values, attitudes, interests, or lifestyles. Examples of this segment are horse lovers, golfers, NASCAR fans, boat owners, and the like. Horse lovers might be further segmented by those who board their horses and those who want acreages on which to live and raise their horses. Boat owners could be segmented by those who want lake or ocean access. Possibly the person simply wants to live full-time onboard anchored in a marina.

As you can see, there is a variety of markets to serve. However, you may be able to identify a market and find a niche that your competition has not yet uncovered.

Qualified Prospects

As you become more proficient in prospecting, you will have a sizeable group of prospects. Do not prospect the wrong people. Prospect only those people who are ready to close a transaction. Remember, you do not have time to work with everyone; so spend your time and effort on motivated prospects—those who are ready and able to buy or sell.

If the prospects' answers reveal they are ready to take action, continue to work with them and transform them into clients. However, if it becomes apparent that they are not ready to move, then you must be ready to let them go. Do not waste time working with people who spend too much time deciding their actions rather than moving forward. Keep those people in your database, but focus your efforts on more active prospects.

Qualifying Questions

Seller

- How soon would you like to sell?
- How long have you been thinking of selling?
- If we agree upon a plan to market your property, will you be ready to list your home?

Buyer

- How soon would you like to buy?
- How long have you been looking?
- If you found a home that met your needs, what would you do?

PROSPECTING LAWS

One of the challenges real estate licensees constantly face is finding new clients and customers. Therefore, successful salespeople prospect constantly to create new leads and generate more sales. However, before exploring prospecting activities, it is important to review the prospecting laws.

Anytime real estate solicitation involves the use of the telephone, cell phone, fax, or email, you must comply with applicable federal and state Do Not Call, Do Not Fax, and anti-spam laws. These laws were passed to give consumers an opportunity to limit the amount of telemarketing calls and spam emails received.

Do Not Call

In 1991, Congress passed the Telephone Consumer Protection Act (TCPA). In 2003, the FCC established, together with the Federal Trade Commission (FTC), a national Do Not Call Registry. This registry is nationwide in scope, applies to all telemarketers (with the exception of certain non-profit organizations), and covers both interstate and intrastate telemarketing calls. You cannot make unauthorized calls to people whose names are on the registry, subject to certain exceptions. Today there are millions of numbers on that list.

Do Not Call rules apply to calls containing a commercial solicitation (most cold calls). The rules do not apply to calls made if an established business relationship already exists. With an **established business relationship**, the caller had a transaction with the receiver within the last 18 months; or the customer has made an inquiry or submitted an application with the caller's firm in the last 3 months. Because you can call individuals that have given you permission, use any opportunity to secure that permission—for example, when conducting open houses, presenting agency disclosures, and securing listing agreements.

Generally, to make a cold call, the real estate licensee must scrub the number against the national Do Not Call list and the real estate company's internal Do Not Call list. If the number does not appear on either list, the licensee may call.

Do Not Call Rules

- Real estate licensees may make calls between 8:00 a.m. and 9:00 p.m.
- Licensees must identify themselves before making the solicitation, must identify that the call is a solicitation, and disclose all material information related to the solicited service.
- Licensees may not use caller ID blocking.
- Telemarketers must scrub their contact lists against the national Do Not Call registry every month.

An **auto dialer** (automatic telephone dialing system) refers to equipment that can generate and dial telephone or cell phone numbers randomly or sequentially. When using an auto dialer, follow these simple rules. First, the auto dialer can place calls only between 8:00 a.m. and 9:00 p.m. Secondly, if a sales associate or broker uses an auto dialer, the call must connect to a live sales associate within 2 seconds after the recorded greeting has finished.

All real estate licensees are subject to the legislation. If a telephone number is on the national Do Not Call Registry (DNC) list, you may not make an unsolicited telephone call to that number. The fines for violations range from $500 up to $11,000.

Do Not Fax

The Telephone Consumer Protection Act of 1991 (TCPA) created the rules and regulations regarding unsolicited faxes. The TCPA prohibits the sending of faxes containing unsolicited advertisements. **Unsolicited advertisements** are defined as any material advertising the commercial availability or quality of any property, goods, or services that is transmitted to any person without that person's prior express invitation or permission. The penalties for violating the TCPA are $500 per fax with treble damages for willful violations.

Summary of the TCPA Rules

- Sender must have an established business relationship with the recipient or written consent from the recipient prior to sending unsolicited advertising faxes.
- Sender must have voluntarily received recipient's fax number.
- Sender must provide the recipient with the right to opt-out of receiving future unsolicited advertising faxes. Opt-out procedures should be clear and conspicuous on the fax.
- Sender must honor opt-outs received from recipients within 30 days of receipt.
- Bulk faxing has been largely eclipsed by email but the rules are still in place and enforceable.

Anti-SPAM

The **CAN-SPAM Act of 2003** (Controlling the Assault of Non-Solicited Pornography and Marketing Act) establishes requirements for those who send commercial email. It also gives consumers the right to ask emailers to stop sending them emails. The Act pertains to commercial email messages. A **commercial email message** is "any electronic mail message with the primary purpose of which is the commercial advertisement or promotion of a commercial product or service." Emails sent as part of an ongoing commercial transaction, called **transactional email messages**, are exempt from the Act.

Exempt Transactional Email Messages

- Facilitating or confirming an existing commercial transaction, such as an existing listing or sales transaction
- Sending purely informational messages, such as a newsletter without advertisements
- Giving notice about product updates or upgrades
- Providing notice about certain changes in a subscription, membership, account, or loan
- Providing warranty information, product recall information, or safety or security information with respect to a commercial product or service used or purchased by the recipient
- Providing information directly related to an employment relationship in which the recipient is currently involved

An unsolicited email message sent by a real estate agent to people on a mailing list to offer that agent's services is a commercial email message.

Items Required in a Commercial Email Message

- A legitimate return email and a physical postal address
- A clear and conspicuous notice of the recipient's opportunity to opt-out or decline to receive any future messages
- Opt out mechanism active for at least 30 days after the transmission of the message
- Clear and conspicuous notice that the message is an advertisement or solicitation

PROSPECTING STRATEGY

The purpose of prospecting is to find qualified buyers and sellers. To accomplish this, you need to have a prospecting strategy. A **prospecting strategy** describes the activities you will use—direct marketing, personal selling, and networking—to contact prospective clients and customers.

Although there are many ways to prospect, only choose the methods with which you are comfortable and that are within your planned budget. As part of your prospecting strategy, you will list the tactics you plan to use. The sales associate who persuades the prospect that he or she is the best person for the job will get the business. Many prospecting activities are highly effective if you are diligent and consistent. The measure of prospecting success will depend on talent, initiative, and good fortune.

Direct Marketing

Direct marketing refers to making phone calls and mailing or emailing promotional materials directly to potential customers as opposed to through mass media. Direct marketing is also known as **push marketing** because you send information to potential customers to attract the few who may have interest in you or your listings.

Direct marketing has advantages and disadvantages. The benefit is that your marketing pieces and messages are sent directly to your target market. However, unwanted telephone calls may be blocked, unsolicited marketing pieces may be considered junk mail, and unwanted email messages may be considered spam.

To get the best results when promoting yourself, always approach prospective clients with pleasant conversation, a positive attitude, and a presentable, professional appearance. Disregard any techniques that may feel unnatural, such as dull scripts, outrageous claims, and high-pressure tactics. Be conscientious of your personal appearance, whether you are in the office or out. Keep projecting a "can do" attitude.

There are a variety of direct marketing tactics including telemarketing, direct mail, email, and other types of electronic marketing.

Telemarketing

Telemarketing is a form of direct marketing that uses the telephone to reach potential customers. It is a useful way to contact potential sellers. You must call people to let them know you are in the real estate business. Although they may not be ready to buy or sell, they may give you a referral for someone who is ready. People are more likely to refer their friends and associates who are thinking about buying or selling if your name is fresh in their minds.

Two types of telephone prospecting are warms calls and cold calls. **Warm calls** are to people you already know and **cold calls** are to people you do not know. Warm calling may seem easier than cold calling because you are contacting people you know. Although, it is also the most efficient use of your prospecting time, many salespeople resist calling people they know because they do not want to appear pushy. Cold calling involves contacting individuals you do not know in order to sell a service or product. The effective use of cold calling skills can lead to success, increased income, and control of sales. However, without the proper mindset and skills, cold calling can be exhausting and self-defeating.

Most salespeople hate telemarketing because they associate it with negative images and rejection. One way to get past the fear of rejection is to make it your goal to call 15 contacts who say "NO" before you can introduce yourself and your service or product. Keep calling until you get 15 "NO" responses. For those contacts who do not hang up the telephone or say "NO" immediately, give them your best presentation, and really listen to what they say and what they need. Then, after each call, note what worked and what did not, and alter your approach for the next cold call.

Telephone Techniques

A good first impression will help you build your real estate business. Good first impressions are created by using proper telephone etiquette, speaking clearly with a "smile" in your voice, and being enthusiastic, sincere, and respectful. If the prospect raises any concerns, in addition to offering practical advice and assistance, you should be empathetic. This will make the first impression positive and will build the prospect's confidence in you and your company.

Plan Before Calling

Gather the facts before you dial the telephone. Get organized and think the call through. Use a bulleted fact sheet or brief notes to remember key points you would like to make during the call, so the conversation will flow logically. Keep the number of points to ten or less.

Be sure to have information about properties currently listed in the area. Typical information includes the age of the properties, sales history, typical marketing time, floor plans, neighborhood photos, and neighborhood information. In addition, make a point to attend the weekly tour of homes, or caravans. Although virtual tours of homes give you a brief look of a home, they do not take the place of an actual visit.

Be Positive

Treat every call as if it were the first one of the day. Project a fresh and upbeat image vocally, even if you are having a bad day. Positive energy is contagious and if you are feeling good, the prospect may feel the same, which could lead to a sale. When you enjoy what you are doing, you attract others and they will refer their friends and family to you.

Identify Yourself

Always identify yourself using a friendly tone of voice and give a brief purpose of the call.

"Is It a Good Time?"

Be sensitive to the prospect's busy life. Always ask the prospect if it is a good time to talk. If it is, ask the prospect for a few minutes of his or her time and state approximately how long the call will take. Be sure to stick to that time. Of course, the prospect may extend the conversation if necessary, but do not allow yourself to do so. If the prospect is busy, ask for a convenient time to call back.

Most prospects appreciate that you respect them by valuing their time. You should take only as much time as needed to achieve your goal. If the goal is to set an appointment, do so and end the call. If you sense the conversation winding down or a period of extended silence occurs, it is time to end the call. Thank them for their time and leave your contact information so they know how to get in touch with you.

Avoid Scripts

Telemarketing succeeds with conversations, not scripts, because most scripts sound stilted and insincere. Avoid reading scripts and do not launch into a monologue. Concentrate on bringing your prospect into the conversation. Ask a relevant question to get your prospect involved. Remember to give the prospects time to think and respond.. Be interested in what your prospect has to say.

Be an Expert

Become an expert in your field and stay up-to-date with industry news and developments. When you call a prospect for the first time, remember that you are introducing yourself. Let prospects know you are able to help them— then offer to work with them to sell their home. Even though you may have more knowledge than the prospect, you should use non-technical language. If prospects do not understand what you are saying, you will end up alienating or losing them.

Focus on the Prospect

Do not focus solely on what you are trying to sell. Instead, make the prospect the focus of your call. By doing so, you will sound more natural and relaxed, which will relax your prospects. Assess your prospect's level of interest by listening to his or her tone of voice as well as his or her actual words. Then, adapt your presentation to the prospect's interests.

Be Consistent

Each time you speak with a prospect update your contact management system with current information. Stay in touch with former customers and clients. Call each prospect quarterly, reintroducing yourself as the expert real estate professional in the area.

Direct Mail

Direct mail is a common form of direct marketing. However, people who are not ready to buy or sell property may consider your flyers, brochures, and other marketing pieces **junk mail**. Direct mail is most efficient when you are marketing a specific property or working your target market. Send a cover letter and a flyer or color brochure detailing the amenities and benefits of the property to prospective buyers who already are in your database. Or, schedule an open house and send appealing invitations.

Leaving flyers at homes in the neighborhood of an open house, listing or recent sale is similar to direct mail without the cost of stamps and envelopes. In addition, you may have an opportunity to introduce yourself and turn a passive marketing activity into a face-to-face sales opportunity. However, when delivering printed materials, it is important to know that the U.S. Code prohibits individuals, other than employees of the Postal Service, from depositing any type of unstamped mail in mailboxes.

Direct Mail Techniques

While prospecting, the direct mail pieces should support personal contact between you and the homeowner. The successful mailing piece will direct your prospects' attention to you.

Here is your chance to market yourself in a way that makes you stand out from your competitors. Create a postcard or newsletter to advertise your name and state that you specialize in real estate in the area. Then personalize it by adding your own slogan, photo, and a short personal note that is friendly and to the point. Every time you send any marketing piece, use the same format, design, and features in order to build name recognition.

Monthly mailings should be a ritual. Many sales associates stop sending out regular mailings because they are disappointed when their telephone does not immediately ring after the mailing. The amounts of effort and money expended, as well as the lack of immediate return, easily discourage some sales associates when they start a direct mail campaign.

Working your target market is one of the most effective prospecting tools. As listings in your target market increase, you will reap the benefit of inquiries generated by your For Sale signs. A For Sale sign with your name and telephone number is round-the-clock advertising because neighbors see your name every day when they drive by the sign. As you get more listings, you will become recognized as the specialist in your target market.

Building a reputation takes time. Nevertheless, the effort can pay off with area loyalty and many new leads. The key is consistency. If you are consistently making contact with your prospects, they will remember you when considering buying or selling property.

Tips for Direct Mail

- Place your name, telephone number, and email address in a prominent place on the marketing piece
- Include potential value of a seller's home
- Give details on any active, pending, or sold properties in the neighborhood
- State your recent sales or listings in the area to establish your professionalism in the neighborhood
- Include positive statements from former customers and clients
- Send pieces consistently at least once a month
- Be patient – building a reputation takes time

Email

Email is an effective way to keep in touch with your clients, customers, and prospects. Targeted mailings may include email groups that you set up to indicate special interests, such as repeat customers, first-time buyers, future buyers or sellers, or a specific demographic group. Because they are similar to business letters, email should reflect your status as a real estate professional. They should be well written, brief, and to the point.

Email allows you to create and distribute a newsletter or an ezine electronically to large numbers of people in less time than a traditional printed marketing piece and at virtually no cost. To quote Wikipedia®, "an **ezine** is a periodic publication distributed by email or posted on a website." Ezines, short for electronic magazines, are typically dedicated to one specific topic, such as real estate trends. They come in all varieties including a full-fledged magazine that notifies you when the current copy has been published, a weekly newsletter that comes via email, or a link in an email to a downloadable PDF. Most of them are intended to provide information on a specific topic while promoting the company and its services.

Aspects of an Ezine

- Someone has to create and write the material.
- You have to develop and maintain a distribution list (email addresses).

Ideally, your distribution list is your target market. Here is a case in which you will have to develop print advertising to secure the email addresses of your target market. Once collected, the email addresses are entered into your database, updated, and maintained on a regular basis.

Effective Email Hints

You want the reader of your email to know immediately that you are an informed real estate professional. Use the following guidelines to help you write more effective and professional emails.

Email Guidelines

- The reason for your email should be brief and clearly written in the subject line.
- Every email should include your electronic signature or information on how to contact you: your name, brokerage, telephone number, cell phone number, fax number, email address, and website address.
- You can send reports, acknowledge incoming email, and save an inquirer's email address with an auto-responder. Many email programs feature an auto-responder option that automatically sends a response to email inquiries.
- Check your email on a regular basis to take advantage of the quick responses you are likely to receive.
- Allow readers to access your website quickly by including a direct link in your email.

- Always get permission before sending an email to a prospect.
- Include any request for action from the reader in the second sentence so you can make sure you have their attention.
- Use the proper salutation, grammar, and a friendly close.
- Only send attachments if you are sure they will be welcomed.

While email is a convenient and efficient way to communicate, be sure to use it correctly and follow the CAN-SPAM rules. Email is great for communicating across time zones, transmitting printed materials and photos, confirming details, replacing some types of regular mail, and transferring computer files. It is not a good idea to use email when you need a personal touch, an urgent response, or with prospects who have limited email access. Use email only as a supplement to these activities because there is no substitution for face-to-face interaction or a personal telephone call.

Work Expired Listings with Direct Marketing

Expired listings are another great source of business. An **expired listing** is a property listing that did not sell during the specified period with the listing broker. Simply run an MLS report at the beginning of each week and pick out the listings that will expire the next week. The MLS report also will provide you with everything necessary to work the listing: the owner's name, address, telephone number, the size and age of the home, the current asking price, and any price reductions.

Because the owner is already open to using professional services to sell the property, you only have to convince the owner to re-list the property with you. Ideally, this can be done if you get the property owner's attention with a creative and effective pursuit of expired listings.

Contact the Owner

First, call the owners on the day their listing expires, or deliver a pre-listing package to the property and then follow up with a call. Include a letter of introduction in your package that tells them you would like to discuss marketing strategies for their property. The letter should also have a picture of their property. Include your resume, testimonials, and a list of your sales for the year along with samples of your advertising. You and your marketing techniques need to stand out from the crowd. Put your package in a bright, eye-catching plastic bag to hang on the door, or use other packaging that is different from that of your competitors.

Follow up

When you follow up with the owners, introduce yourself and tell them you noticed their expired listing. Ask if they have re-listed. If the answer is yes, the call is over. Move on to the next one. If they answer no, ask if they are still interested in selling their property. If they are still interested, briefly suggest the possible reasons why their property did not sell. Ask if you could see their home and visit with them for a few minutes to discover why their property did not sell. Let them know what you can do to ensure that it sells this time.

Get the Listing

While you are touring the home, ask the owners about their previous listing experience to discover why the listing failed. Was it: price, condition, timing, marketing, or the inability of the buyer to get suitable financing? Most listings expire because they are overpriced. If the property was not overpriced, there may be another problem.

Examine the condition of the seller's property. If the condition appears to be a problem, address it. If it is in good condition and the marketing was aggressive, the property may have been overpriced. Discuss pricing with the owners and try to get a listing exactly at or a little below market value. If you cannot get it priced correctly, then do not take the listing.

Personal Selling

Personal selling is any form of direct communication (usually face-to-face) between a salesperson and a customer. Personal selling opportunities can occur at any time, such as working an open house, making a listing presentation to a seller, showing properties to a prospective buyer who has come into the office while you have floor time, or contacting FSBOs.

Floor Time Opportunities

Floor time refers to the set hours that a sales associate must be in the brokerage office to answer incoming phone calls and handle inquiries from walk-ins. Some brokerage offices assign floor time and others do not. Currently, floor time is not as popular with real estate agents as it once was because agents have Internet access with smart phones and laptops. They can work out of their own homes and have little or no need to come into the brokerage office, except for meetings or to pick up sales materials.

However, floor time may be an opportunity for new sales associates to get leads. New sales associates tend to work with buyers more often than with sellers because buyers are more likely to call the brokerage in response to an advertisement, or stop into the office asking to speak to a sales associate who can show them properties.

Most of the floor time inquiries are in response to your brokerage's advertising. Therefore, stay current on your company's listed properties and other listings on the market. You also want to have back-up properties from different locations and price ranges to discuss with your prospects in case they appear disinterested in the property in question. It is important to prepare for the typical questions your prospects will ask about the real estate market.

Floor time is an opportunity to obtain leads and be productive in the office. Do not sit around the office waiting for the telephone to ring or for someone to walk in the door. You can work on other important tasks such as making outgoing calls, previewing properties on the Internet, preparing your marketing materials, or catching up on important paperwork.

Working with FSBOs

FSBOs (For Sale By Owner) properties can be an excellent source of business for real estate associates. Many sales associates believe FSBOs are unwilling to consider listing with a real estate brokerage; however, about 80% eventually do list with someone.

An excellent source of new business is For Sale By Owner.

When dealing with FSBOs you should make a personal visit to the owners. This will give you a competitive edge over sales associates who do not take time to visit in person. Most FSBOs will ignore direct mail from sales associates and may become annoyed by prospecting calls. However, after they meet you, they may be more likely to respond to mail, email, or telephone calls. Do not expect to list the property the first time you contact the owner.

Your first contact should be only to introduce yourself. Simply let the owners know you are available if they should require your assistance. If the home has not sold within four weeks, it may not sell at all. Unfortunately, it may take owners several additional weeks to come to that conclusion, so you must be patient during that time. If they have given you permission, send regular emails delivering valuable tips and advice for selling their homes.

Periodically stop by and inquire about a FSBO's progress. The owner may begin to think about the lack of progress and be interested in listing with a sales associate. Be ready to present your marketing plan when asked. It is important to highlight the differences between what an owner can do and what you can do.

Continued, yet non-intrusive, contact with FSBOs may lead them to the conclusion that they could benefit from your help. They may call you to list their property simply because they have received your ongoing personal contact, telephone calls, and emails.

Networking

Networking is the practice of making contact and exchanging information with other people of groups. Networking is one of the most profitable activities in which you can engage. Networking can be done by joining groups and associations and physically attending functions or through social media.

It pays to network in person, not only to meet new people, but also to keep your vital communication skills sharp. Practice making friendly conversation, even if no relationship develops with that person, he or she will likely remember you, if asked about you at some point in the future. Always have business cards with you to give to prospective customers. This friendly approach is equally applicable to every form of networking, whether the encounter takes place in person or online.

Social Networking

The Internet has changed prospecting to a certain extent. Instead of outgoing calls and direct marketing (the "push" model), using the Internet effectively "pulls" the customer to your website. **Pull marketing** attracts customers to you. A good example is advertising that draws visitors to your website

when they are actively seeking the services or products you provide. Your marketing should be designed to pull potential customers and clients to you.

Sometimes new technology is intimidating at the very least. Your challenge is to make sense of these opportunities and incorporate them into your prospecting and marketing plan. The good news is that there is no right or wrong way. The "secret" is to start small.

> For example, you can create a blog with only your time involved and not a whole lot of technology beyond your PC and a high-speed Internet connection. Or, join one of the social media sites. Just a few clicks and you are in. You will be surprised at who finds and claims you for a friend. You probably already own a digital camera (or phone) that shoots video. Go ahead, shoot a video, and post it to YouTube®. Just load the video file on your PC and upload it to YouTube®, and you are a movie producer on the World Wide Web!

The overriding principles to follow are innovating, testing, checking the results, and trying again. Keep in mind that what works today might not necessarily work tomorrow. Some new technology may come along that displaces a strategy that has worked well for you in the past.

Social Media

Social media is any form of online publication or presence that allows end users to engage in multi-directional conversations in or around the content on the website. The Internet provides a sense of community (a pull environment) through social media, such as MySpace®, wikis, such as Wikipedia®, and blogs.

This online network encourages communication between you and your customers and even your customers communicating with each other. Ultimately, real estate brokerage is about relationships. The Internet gives you the tools and therefore the ability to create and maintain relationships like never before.

Facebook®, MySpace®, YouTube®, LinkedIn®, MeetUp®, Squidoo®, and Trulia Voices® are just a sampling of some of the more popular social networking sites on the 'Net. Social networking is about relationships, friendships, and communication. Social networking connects people-to-people, people to businesses, businesses to people, experts to neophytes, garage sales to collectors, singles to singles, causes to constituencies, candidates to voters, and car parts to antique cars.

Each network tries to differentiate itself. MySpace® is a place for friends. They do not allow commercialization. Facebook®, on the other hand, is business friendly. They encourage the promotion of your websites and targeted marketing. YouTube® is an ideal place for your home tours and personal promotion and, in addition, the YouTube® videos can be embedded on your site. Squidoo® provides you a platform to demonstrate your "expertness" on certain topics. It provides an individual "lens" to present your view of the world. Popular lens creators become "go to" experts on Squidoo®. Social media, properly fashioned, can drive traffic to your blog and to your website. Are you seeing some marketing opportunities here? In addition, social media integrated into your entire marketing plan raises brand awareness and positively affects your rankings in search engines.

Blogs

The word **blog** is a contraction formed from the words we**b** **log**. A blog is a personal, online diary or journal that reaches out to millions of people on the World Wide Web. Unlike a paper diary, a blog is also two-way conversation. It gives you the ability to connect and to form cyber relationships that may well develop into business relationships.

Typical Blog Attributes

- Blogs represent the opinion and expertise of the author. They are typically written in an informal style in the first person.
- Readers have the ability to respond to the entry.
- Postings to the blog are in reverse chronological order with the newest entries on the top of the page.
- Readers can be informed of new additions to the blog by subscribing to the blog's news feed.

Blogging Hints

- Write something that you are passionate about. If you are not passionate about real estate, do not write about it. If you are passionate about golfing and your niche is golf communities, write about golfing.
- Be friendly, conversational, and humorous.
- Use a simple format and a clean layout. Your time to capture the initial reader is very, very short.
- Do not start a blog unless you are dedicated to its success, otherwise it is like sending a one-time mailing to your target market.

- Update your blog on a regular basis. There is nothing worse than a site that is not current. To keep it current, you will need to spend time. Regardless of when you update your blog, be consistent. Blogging requires an ongoing commitment to be successful and profitable.

- Provide an RSS (Really Simple Syndication) feed for your blog to provide notification when new content has been added.

- If you cannot write passionately about a topic, do not steal other people's material. Add a link to their site if their information is relevant.

One of the advantages of a blog is that it can help raise your website ranking in the search engines. As new content is added and your blog links out to other sites including your own website, the search engines will recognize that and give your site a higher placement for relevant searches. The key is adding relevant information on a regular basis.

Twitter

Twitter is a great tool for quickly communicating a message to a group of people. **Twitter** is a website, owned and operated by Twitter Inc., which offers a micro blogging and social networking service. The micro blogs are called **tweets**—text-based posts of up to 140 characters displayed on the user's profile page. Users may subscribe to other author tweets—known as following. The subscribers are known as followers. All users can send and receive tweets.

Podcasting

Podcasting is a free service that allows Internet users to pull audio files (typically MP3s) from a podcasting Web site to listen to on their computers or personal digital audio players. The word, **podcasting**, is a contraction formed from the words i**Pod** and broad**casting**. However, an iPod is not required to listen to a podcast—any portable media player or your computer plays a podcast.

You could create a podcast to educate prospective clients. For example, you could create a podcast that walks a first-time homebuyer through the buying process or a podcast that explains what a home inspector does.

Advantages of Podcasting

- It is another chance to tailor or target your message to a specific market.
- It is a very low cost delivery platform.
- Podcasts are downloadable, played at the user's convenience, and shared with other interested individuals.
- Podcasts will differentiate you from the competition.

Video Casting

Studies have shown that Americans, primarily between the ages of 25 and 35 (Generation Y and the Millennial Generation), view more than 10 hours of online video a month and that number is climbing. Video podcasting is similar to podcasting with the exception that you are broadcasting video in addition to audio. YouTube® is a great resource for publishing your video podcasts to the Internet. Many licensees have put virtual business cards and video listings of homes on the site.

Video casting is a powerful tool that can pull traffic to your website and engage the visitors once they are there.

Some Uses for Video Podcasting

- Tour of your properties.
- Tour of the neighborhood.
- "Show and tell" of what is included in an actual home inspection.

Social Bookmarking

Have you ever been to a website or blog and seen the following links: Add to del.icio.us or Digg This! Both of the services fall under the broad category of social bookmarking. **Social bookmarking** enables the user to bookmark a site on a web page as opposed to their browser. Those bookmarks can then be categorized, shared, and even rated for popularity.

For example, when you "**Digg This!**" your selected page, podcast, blog, video will appear in Digg's upcoming stories. As other Digg members discover the site, it raises in Digg's popularity ranking and if that submission hits the jackpot, it migrates to Digg's homepage.

Del.icio.us (delicious) enables you to bookmark a site to your own delicious web page and then categorize and share those sites as you see fit. Google™ and Yahoo!® among others offer this service or a variation of it. Your marketing challenge is to create content that is interesting and relevant to your target market.

ALWAYS ASK FOR REFERRALS

The goal of prospecting and networking is to cultivate new clients and expand your business. Therefore, always ask for referrals to build a referral database. A **referral** is a recommendation.

The first step in building a referral-rich business is to provide great service from the beginning. If your performance is not exceptional, your clients will not refer you to their friends and associates. One of the most important factors in customer satisfaction is communication. If your clients feel you have communicated with them clearly and regularly, their level of satisfaction increases. Clients may overlook minor errors, but lack of communication is rarely tolerated.

Actively seek out referrals. If you make it known that you are seeking referrals, people are more likely to think of you first. Call former clients and send out a mailing asking for referrals. Make telephone calls to everyone you know. When you finish with your entire list, start the whole process over. Most of your clients may report that they liked the job you did for them, but many may not remember your name. Make sure they remember you.

Your referral database tends to have more qualified leads that are usually serious prospects intent on closing a transaction. Therefore, it is important that the people in your referral database hear from you regularly via mail, telephone, email, and personal contact. Even if none of these people ever list a house with you, it is very likely that they may refer you to someone who will. Organize your referral names into a software program that can automate prospecting activities such as mail merging, providing reminders to make necessary telephone calls, and sending out mailings.

When asking for referrals, keep your questions open-ended. For instance, do not ask, "Do you know of anyone who is moving?" Instead, ask, "Which of your friends, associates, neighbors, etc. do you think will be the next to move?" Those in your referral network are more likely to think for a moment and give you a name or two. Ask for names and ask if they would mind if you contacted their friend, associate, neighbor, etc. Also, ask if they would mind if you told the new lead that they suggested you call him or her. Then take the initiative to make the calls yourself. Be sure to thank everyone who sends you a referral.

SUMMARY

Successful salespeople prospect constantly to create new leads and generate more sales. **Prospecting** is the process of identifying potential customers. Your most likely prospects will include people in your current sphere of influence, homeowners in your geographic target market, FSBOs, individuals in your demographic target markets, and prospects who call or come to the office while you have floor time. Family members, friends, teachers, former colleagues, and members of associations to which you belong are in your **sphere of influence** and are considered **warm prospects**. **Cold prospects** are potential clients and customers who are not in your sphere of influence, but who may want to buy or sell real estate. A **target market** is the defined group of properties or individuals with similarities. Your target market can be broad as in geographic markets or highly focused as in a niche market. A **niche market** consists of consumers with the same specialized needs.

When prospecting, be sure to comply with applicable federal and state Do Not Call, Do Not Fax, and anti-spam laws.

The purpose of prospecting is to find qualified buyers and sellers. To accomplish this, you need to have a prospecting strategy. A **prospecting strategy** describes the activities you will use—direct marketing, personal selling, and networking—to contact prospective clients and customers.

Direct marketing is also known as **push marketing** because you send information to potential customers to attract the few who may have interest in you or your listings. **Telemarketing** is a form of direct marketing that uses the telephone to reach potential customers. **Direct mail** is a common form of direct marketing. **Email** is an effective way to keep in touch with your clients, customers, and prospects. **Personal selling** is any form of direct communication (usually face-to-face) between a salesperson and a customer. **Networking** is the practice of making contact and exchanging information with other people of groups.

Remember! Always **ask for referrals**.

UNIT 7 REVIEW

☐ Matching Exercise

Instructions: Write the letter of the matching term on the blank line before its definition. Answers are in Appendix A.

Terms

A. Blog

B. cold prospects

C. direct marketing

D. expired listing

E. ezine

F. farm area

G. floor time

H. FSBOs

I. junk mail

J. networking

K. personal selling

L. prospecting

M. prospecting strategy

N. referral

O. social media

P. target market

Q. telemarketing

R. transactional email messages

S. tweets

T. warm prospects

Definitions

1. _____ Process of identifying potential customers

2. _____ Sphere of influence

3. _____ Potential clients and customers not in your sphere of influence

4. _____ Defined group of properties or individuals with similarities

5. _____ Geographic target market

6. _____ Properties that the owner has not listed with a real estate broker

7. _____ Emails sent as part of an ongoing commercial transaction

8. _____ Activities you will use to contact prospective clients and customers

9. _____ Making phone calls and mailing or emailing promotional materials directly to potential customers as opposed to through mass media

10. _____ Direct marketing that uses the telephone to reach potential customers

11. _____ Unwanted flyers, brochures, and other marketing pieces

12. _____   Periodic publication distributed by email or posted on a website

13. _____   Property that did not sell during the specified period with the listing broker

14. _____   Any form of direct communication (usually face-to-face) between a salesperson and a customer

15. _____   Set hours a sales associate must be in the brokerage office to answer incoming phone calls and handle inquiries from walk-ins

16. _____   Practice of making contact and exchanging information with other people of groups

17. _____   Any form of online publication or presence that allows end users to engage in multi-directional, online conversations

18. _____   Personal, online diary or journal

19. _____   Micro blogs

20. _____   Recommendation

◻ Multiple Choice Questions

Instructions: Circle your response and go to Appendix A to read the complete explanation for each question.

1. Of the following, which would not likely be a prospect?
   a. Blogs
   b. FSBOs.
   c. People in your target audience
   d. Sphere of influence

2. The commonality of family, friends, and acquaintances is that they are:
   a. in your sphere of influence.
   b. considered warm prospects.
   c. both (a) and (b).
   d. neither (a) nor (b).

3. Which federal law established a national Do Not Call Registry?

    a. Telephone Do Not Call Registry Act

    b. Telephone Consumer Protection Act

    c. Telephone Solicitation Act.

    d. CAN-SPAM Act

4. Which prospecting strategy should you use to find qualified buyers and sellers?

    a. Advertising

    b. Direct marketing

    c. Personal selling

    d. All of the above

5. Which statement is correct regarding direct marketing?

    a. Marketing pieces and messages are sent directly to your target market.

    b. Unsolicited marketing pieces may be considered spam.

    c. Unwanted email messages may be considered junk mail.

    d. All of the statements are correct.

6. What is the commonality of joining groups, attending functions, and using social media?

    a. Direct marketing

    b. Networking

    c. Personal selling

    d. Telemarketing

7. When prospecting or marketing online, the Internet:

    a. pulls the customer to your website.

    b. pushes the customer to your website.

    c. deflects customers from your website.

    d. does all of the above.

8. All of the following are tips for creating a successful blog, except:

    a. Be authentic. Write something that you are passionate about.

    b. Be aloof, reserved, and dull.

    c. Do not steal other people's material.

    d. Provide an RSS feed for your blog.

9. A free service that allows Internet users to pull audio files from a website to listen to on their computers or personal audio players is called:

    a. ezineing.

    b. infomercializing.

    c. podcasting.

    d. videocasting.

10. When prospecting or networking, you should always:

    a. ask for referrals.

    b. avoid signing up for floor time.

    c. use a script.

    d. do all of the above.

Advertising & Marketing Listings

Unit 8

INTRODUCTION

Homes do not sell magically. It takes consistent **property marketing** to create interest in a property, causing it to sell at a top price. This type of marketing requires skill, intuition, planning, and marketing strategies. Property marketing strategies include the tried-and-true methods, such as putting color flyers in a holder in front of a house, as well as an efficient marketing plan.

The different promotional methods are advertising, direct marketing, sales promotion, personal selling, and public relations. As a salesperson, you will use all of these methods in the course of promoting yourself and your listed properties. In marketing, this is called a **promotional mix**—the combination of the promotional methods to reach the target market and reach your goals.

You need to select which media—Internet, print, radio, or television—to use to attract business. Are newspaper ads or bus bench ads effective ways to advertise your business? What medium will you use to attract customers? How often will you deliver your marketing materials? This unit focuses on advertising.

Learning Objectives

After reading this unit, you should be able to:

- recall techniques for a successful marketing plan.
- specify elements of an effective ad.
- identify advertising media.

CREATE A PROPERTY MARKETING PLAN

A **property marketing plan** is a detailed schedule of everything done to market a property. A property marketing plan is a roadmap leading to the sale of a particular property. The plan should be tailored to your specific skills, personal qualities, and strengths. Attempting to follow a plan designed by another salesperson with a different personality may not produce the results you desire. You may use basic marketing activities, but you must decide, based on your special strengths, which methods are most effective.

Marketing efforts should be custom-designed for each property. To market a property successfully, be resourceful and creative. Not every property will be a designer model. Some properties are architecturally challenged, and others may need attention to details that would attract buyers. Put an emphasis on certain features that may attract buyers.

Techniques for Successful Marketing:

- Use attractive, creative photos of the property to create interest in its special features (exterior and interior).

- Choose the most desirable features of the house and promote those as the unique and exclusive benefits of the property.

- Promote the property's points of interest, accessibility to shops, proximity to schools, or other features regarding the desirability of the neighborhood.

- Plan marketing and promotional activities such as open houses, and stay on schedule.

- Make buyers aware of any special incentives such as seller financing or contribution to closing costs.

- Adequately expose the property by using advertising outlets such as classified ads, Internet listings, and MLS.

Marketing Plan to Sell Your Home

April 20XX

Sunday	Monday	Tuesday	Wednesday	Thursday	Friday	Saturday
30	**31** • Preview Home	**1** • Gather materials to prepare CMA	**2** • Prepare CMA	**3** • Prepare Seller Net	**4**	**5**
6 • Listing Appointments • Take photos of property • Signed Purchase Agreement	**7** • MLS Information • Preliminary flyer • Temporary "For Sale" sign	**8** • Notify main office • Contact top producer • Order final "For Sale" sign	**9** • Prepare the flyer	**10** • Obtain professional pictures • Order staging props/furniture	**11** • Place listing in local newspapers	**12** • Plan open house
13 • Plan open house	**14** • Collect agent cards • Call previewing agents	**15** • Mail postcards	**16** • Weekly Update	**17** • Plan open house	**18** • Prepare open house invitations	**19** • Plan open house
20 • Plan open house	**21** • Collect agent cards • Call previewing agents	**22** • Collect agent cards • Call previewing agents	**23** • Weekly Update	**24** • Monthly office meeting	**25** • Plan open house	**26** • Rerun listing in local newspapers • Run listing in magazines
27	**28** • Collect agent cards • Call previewing agents	**29** • Prepare open house invitations for mailing	**30** • Weekly Update • Plan open house	**1** • Prepare final outline for open house	**2** • Client preview of final open house plans	**3** • Send open house invitations

As real estate salespeople strive to gain customers in today's ultra-competitive environment, **target marketing**, or marketing to a precise group of consumers, is a necessity. Real estate professionals must quickly identify their highest-valued customers and prospects in order to succeed. With this insight, salespeople can then develop fine-tuned marketing strategies to draw these customers to their properties and win their business.

Demographics for Target Markets

- Employment
- Education
- Average age
- Average salary range
- Gender
- Occupation
- Number of children

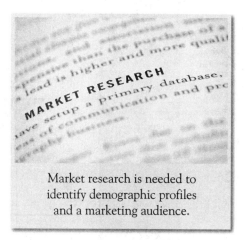

Market research is needed to identify demographic profiles and a marketing audience.

Other demographic information reflects social, economic, and housing characteristics. The information found in demographic profiles and your own evaluation of the property will determine the types of buyers to whom you will be marketing.

Your marketing strategy should highlight the factors that are most important to your target buyers. For example, if the property in question is an entry-level home, it will appeal to young professionals. An **entry-level home** is a type of home that appeals most to first-time buyers. A typical first-time buyer may be a new teacher or someone recently promoted to management, a recent college graduate, or a newly married couple whose parents are supplying the down payment. These buyers are attracted to convenient and available loan options, such as various down payment and mortgage payment programs.

The likely buyer of a **move-up home** may be a consumer who has outgrown the entry-level home and is looking for features that will be compatible with a growing family, larger income, or new interests.

Consumers who are attracted to **luxury homes** will most likely be experienced buyers who know what they want in their next home. Their children have grown up, moved out of the house, and they are now ready to purchase their dream home. On the other hand, they may have entered into an even higher paying position and are looking to upgrade their lifestyle. Luxury extras such as swimming pools, custom landscaping, custom architecture, spectacular views, and top-of-the-line appliances and fixtures would attract this type of buyer. Advertising should present the benefits of the home with professionally created color brochures that highlight the desirable amenities.

ADVERTISING

Advertising is an impersonal form of mass communication promoting a product or company that is paid for by the company. It involves spreading the word about your company and your listings.

The two main types of advertising are institutional advertising and product advertising. **Institutional advertising** is designed to create an image, enhance the reputation, and promote the person or company rather than a specific product. The Century 21® television ads are a good example of institutional advertising that reinforces the franchise brand. In addition, NAR uses institutional advertising effectively to promote the real estate industry. Often, NAR allows its affiliate member associations to customize the advertisements for use in their states and local areas. Unlike institutional advertising, **product advertising** is designed to promote a specific product or service. In real estate, the product is usually a listed property, so product advertising is used to market a specific home.

Advertising plays a large part in marketing, and first impressions can make or break your business. Once the marketing pieces and ads are written, it is time to get the word out with an advertising campaign. An **advertising campaign** is a plan with a common theme describing the mode and frequency through which someone communicates a marketing concept. The advertising campaign should be intensive, evenly paced, and scheduled to continue until the goals of the campaign are met.

Writing an Effective Ad

When writing an effective ad, remember that a person spends only about four seconds skimming an ad. The **AIDA formula** will help you write ads that attract the customer's attention and interest, create desire, and stimulate action.

Mnemonic — AIDA

Attention	First, get the customer's attention.
Interest	Give them benefits to create interest.
Desire	Make the offer irresistible to create desire.
Action	The customer must act in order for you to make a sale.

To be an effective marketer, it is your responsibility to get the customer to stop and read your ad in detail. Your ad should be visually appealing, descriptive, and factual.

AIDA Formula to Write an Ad for a Listing

Use the AIDA formula and the following tips to attract buyers' attention, spark their interest, create desire, and get them to act.

A   To start the ad, use a strong opening statement about the home.

I   In the first two sentences, mention a few key features of the home. Include the most important facts about the property. Focus on the strongest selling points of the home, and be careful not to crowd your ad with too many details. Avoid real estate jargon. The average consumer will appreciate clear, concise terminology.

D   Use appealing words that involve the readers' emotions and senses to create desire.

A   Complete the ad with a statement encouraging the prospect to contact you. Include your contact information— company name, telephone number, email address, and website address.

Sample Residential Advertisements

Prize Location! Enchanting 3br, 2ba, 2-car garage townhouse. Only 5 min from award-winning schools, large shopping mall, and easy freeway access. Gated community, central air, fireplace. Hurry! Call today! ABC Realty Group, Inc. (555) 555-5000 – ABCrealtygroup@xxxx.xyz – www.abcrealtygroup.xyz

Beautiful Colonial style 4br, 1 1/2ba, 2-story home on quiet cul-de-sac, lush park-like backyard, remodeled thru out, lg. kitchen, $250,000. ABC Realty Group, Inc. (555) 555-5000 – ABCrealtygroup@xxxx.xyz – www.abcrealtygroup.xyz

Like new! Ranch style 3br, 2ba home, updated kitchen, hardwood flrs, copper pipes, new paint. $540K. Open Sat/Sun 1-4pm, Tues. 12-1pm. 8300 W. 20th St. ABC Realty Group, Inc. (555) 555-0000 – ABCrealtygroup@xxxx.xyz – www.abcrealtygroup.xyz

Advertising Guidelines

Before you begin your marketing and advertising efforts, pay careful attention to the guidelines associated with the real estate profession. State and federal agencies regulate real estate advertising. By law, real estate brokers and sales associates must be honest and truthful when advertising property or services. If you make false statements or material omissions in any medium of advertising, you may be held liable for fraud, intentional misrepresentation, or negligent misrepresentation.

Advertising guidelines help real estate licensees avoid penalties and possible suspension or loss of license. You should avoid any advertising that can be interpreted a number of different ways, such as "half truths," inflated claims, and ambiguous or superlative terms.

Some of the marketing and advertising guidelines set forth in the real estate profession pertain to name and license status disclosures, use of words in advertisements, real estate signs, faxing, and emailing. In addition, there is a federal policy on real estate advertising, and the National Association of REALTORS® (NAR) has developed a code of ethics for real estate professionals. It is important to understand and follow these regulations in all your advertising efforts including electronic formats.

Federal Policy on Real Estate Advertising

The Federal Fair Housing Law requires that all residential real estate advertising have the Equal Housing Opportunity logotype and slogan. The logotype should be sufficiently large or visible. The logotype should be a clear sign or symbol of welcome to all potentially qualified buyers or renters regardless of race, color, etc. When the size of the logotype is so small that the facial features (ethnicities) of the people are not clearly distinguishable, then it is too small.

U.S. Department of Housing and Urban Development

**EQUAL HOUSING
OPPORTUNITY**

We Do Business in Accordance With the Federal Fair Housing Law

(The Fair Housing Amendments Act of 1988)

> # It is Illegal to Discriminate Against Any Person Because of Race, Color, Religion, Sex, Handicap, Familial Status, or National Origin

- In the sale or rental of housing or residential lots

- In advertising the sale or rental of housing

- In the financing of housing

- In the provision of real estate brokerage services

- In the appraisal of housing

- Blockbusting is also illegal

Anyone who feels he or she has been discriminated against may file a complaint of housing discrimination:
    1-800-669-9777 (Toll Free)
    1-800-927-9275 (TDD)

**U.S. Department of Housing and
Urban Development
Assistant Secretary for Fair Housing and
Equal Opportunity
Washington, D.C. 20410**

Previous editions are obsolete

form HUD-928.1A(8-93)

Be careful no to develop an advertising campaign that excludes a certain group. Certain kinds of advertising and the use of certain words or phrases can violate civil rights laws, even if the person who placed the advertisement had no intent to discriminate. It is illegal to advertise in such a way that indicates a preference, restriction, or intention to discriminate. This applies to all types of advertising media whether it is in print or on the Internet.

Advertising "Red Flags"

The use of certain terminology in an advertisement is often a red flag. For example, describing a certain neighborhood as exclusive, private, or restricted implies that certain applicants for sale or rental of such property might not be welcome. Likewise, using terms that are too specific are also potentially troublesome. Describing a house as "great for a single person" implies potential discrimination against married couples or "great for an active person" implies potential discrimination against a person with a disability. Even referring to the incidental presence of nearby religious, racial, ethnic, or similar landmarks, buildings, or monuments should be avoided because of the implication that specific buyers might be drawn to purchase because of those attractions.

> Example: Incorrect language might include "walk to nearby church," "down the street from Italian-American cultural center," or "close to the Mormon Temple."

In addition, if you use print or television advertising that depicts potential buyers or sellers by using models, be sure to vary the models according to age, sex, ethnicity, and social settings. Even consistently using members only of a minority group would potentially cause a problem here—e.g., using only persons of Hispanic background would be just as much of a problem as using only Caucasian models, because of the potential implications that steering one group is taking place. Recall *United States* v. *Real Estate One* in which potential Fair Housing Act violations were found from advertising in a strategically limited geographic area, or using particular editions of newspapers, to reach a certain segment of the community, or advertising only in small newspapers targeted to specific religious, racial, or ethnic groups.

Example: Ad using *inappropriate* words or phrases:

> ■ **Lovely 2Br, 2Ba Condo w/Garage**
> Near parks, hiking trails. Ideal for young, physically fit. New appliances. Hardwood floors. $95,000. Call Now! (555) 231-5564

Example: Ad using appropriate words or phrases:

> ■ **Lovely 2Br, 2Ba Condo w/garage**
> Near parks, hiking trails. New appliances. Hardwood floors. Must see! $95,000. Call Now! (555) 231-5564

Remember, when advertising a listing, you are advertising the characteristics of the property, so use words that focus on the most desirable qualities of the property and its surrounding area without being offensive. Before publicizing an advertisement, review it carefully for any words, phrases, or images that may be considered offensive to others.

NAR Code of Ethics

Standard of Practice 10-1

REALTORS® shall not volunteer information regarding the racial, religious, or ethnic composition of any neighborhood and shall not engage in any activity, which may result in panic selling. REALTORS® shall not print, display, or circulate any statement or advertisement with respect to the selling or renting of a property that indicates any preference, limitations, or discrimination based on race, color, religion, sex, handicap, familial status, or national origin (Adopted 1/94).

Article 12

REALTORS® shall be careful at all times to present a true picture in their advertising and representations to the public. REALTORS® shall also ensure that their professional status (e.g., broker, appraiser, property manager, etc.) or status as REALTORS® is clearly identifiable in any such advertising (Amended 1/93).

Standard of Practice 12-1

REALTORS® may use the term "free" and similar terms in their advertising and in other representations if all terms governing availability of the offered service or product are clearly disclosed at the same time (Amended 1/97).

Standard of Practice 12-2

REALTORS® may represent their services as "free" or without cost even if they expect to receive compensation from a source other than their client if the potential for the REALTOR® to obtain a benefit from a third party is clearly disclosed at the same time.

Standard of Practice 12-3

The offering of premiums, prizes, merchandise discounts, or other inducements to list, sell, purchase, or lease is not, in itself, unethical even if receipt of the benefit is contingent on listing, selling, purchasing, or leasing through the REALTORS® making the offer. However, REALTORS® must exercise care and candor in any such advertising or other public or private representations so that any party interested in receiving or otherwise benefiting from the REALTOR®'s offer will have clear, thorough, advance understanding of all the terms and conditions of the offer. The offering of any inducements to do business is subject to the limitations and restrictions of state law and the ethical obligations established by any applicable Standard of Practice.

ADVERTISING MEDIA

Now, how will you get the word out? What advertising media will you use to attract business? **Advertising media** are the different channels available to convey a message to a target market. In fact, any place that a company or individual pays for in order to deliver their message is an advertising media.

The major media channels are the Internet, print media, outdoor media, radio, and television (network, cable, and syndicated). Keep in mind that every advertising medium has characteristics that give it natural advantages and limitations. Your job is to find the advertising vehicle that most cost effectively communicates with your customers.

Internet

According to the NAR *Profile of Home Buyers and Sellers*, approximately 90% of all buyers use the Internet for home searches. This is a number that has been climbing every year since the inception of the Internet. Generally, Internet users are informed, anonymous, and in control. These buyers do their own research. Many Internet-savvy buyers will not approach a real estate agent until they are ready. These buyers are definitely not the buyers of 10-20 years ago. They know what they want, and they understand what to expect from a real estate broker and/or salesperson.

Internet Advertising

The Internet is becoming the primary source for information and advertising. In fact, many people think it is easier to find classified ads on the Internet than it is to find them in a newspaper. Consult your local newspaper about Internet classifieds, which are often sold independently of the newspaper's print ads. In addition, there are well-known websites, such as www.craigslist.org®, where you can place advertising at no cost.

> **Prized Location! - Church Ave.**
>
> Enchanting 3br, 2ba, 2-car garage townhome. Only 5 min. from great schools, large mall, and freeway access. Central air, fireplace. Hurry! Contact us today! ABC Realty Group (555) 505-0000   abc@abcrealtygroup.xyz   www.abcrealtygroup.xyz
>
> Details   Save   Contact   Email a Friend

Because Internet advertising and usage is growing daily, more people are being exposed to this medium, which in turn creates new markets and provides greater exposure for your message.

Benefits of Internet Advertising

- Internet Advertising Has A Lower Entry-Level Fee

  Internet advertising can be purchased on performance. You only pay when a visitor clicks on a banner that directs them to your site.

- Internet Advertising Can Be Targeted

  Advertises can focus their messages on their target market by using such programs as Google™, AdWords, and Google™ Ad-Sense.

- Internet Advertising Enables Conversion Tracking

  If you have ever tried to track the number of leads that you receive from a certain advertising medium, you realize how difficult a task that is. That is not the case on the Internet. Website traffic analytics enable you to precisely measure the number of visitors to your site and track the percentage that take a desired action, e.g., registering to use your search engine, signing up for your newsletter, or downloading your latest home buying or home selling tips. The ratio of actions taken to the number of total visitors is called the conversion ratio. The higher the conversion ratio, the greater the effectiveness of your site.

- Internet Advertising Is Inexpensive Based On Per Impression Cost

  Conversion rates tend to be better on the Internet due to the targeting possibilities that reduce your cost per lead. Another advantage of the Internet is low overhead. You do not have to pay for recurring costs like mailings, toner, postage, or spend time stuffing envelopes, etc. You can display all of your marketing materials effectively on your website at a very reasonable cost and with minimal effort.

- Internet Advertising Has Global Possibilities

  Since the Internet spans the globe, foreign buyers and sellers represent a market that previously was very expensive to reach. The Internet makes it as cost effective to reach your neighbors as to reach the rest of the world!

Types of Online Advertising

Advertising on the World Wide Web (web) is constantly changing. Common ways to advertise on the web include banner and sidebar ads, pop-ups (and pop-downs), floating ads, interstitial ads, unicast ads, and takeover ads.

A **banner ad** embeds an advertisement into a web page to attract traffic to a website by linking to the website of the advertiser. Companies try to put the banner ads on web pages that have interesting content, such as a newspaper article or an opinion piece. When the viewer clicks on the banner, the viewer is directed to the website advertised in the banner. This is called a click through. A **sidebar ad** is similar to a banner ad except that it is located on the side of the screen.

Pop-up ads try to attract web traffic or capture email addresses. **Web traffic** is the amount of data sent and received by visitors to a website. A **pop-down ad** is a variation on the pop-up ad. The pop-down ad opens a new browser window hidden under the active window and does not immediately interrupt the user. The pop-down ad is not seen until the covering window is closed.

Floating ads are so-named because they "float" over the page for five to 30 seconds. Floating ads appear when you first go to a web page. While they are floating on the screen, they obscure your view of the page you are trying to read, and they often block mouse input as well. Many people find these ads annoying because the ads appear each time that page is refreshed. Some advertisers prefer floating ads, because they grab the viewer's attention and are difficult to ignore. Sometimes they take up the entire screen. Therefore, from a branding standpoint, they are more powerful than banner and sidebar ads, yet users find them annoying.

Interstitial ads (*interstitial means in between*) are actually pages that appear between web pages that the user requests. Because interstitials load in the background, they are a preferred way of delivering ads that contain large graphics, streaming media, or applets.

A **unicast ad** is similar to a TV commercial except that it runs in the browser window and has similar branding power as a TV commercial. Unicast ads give the consumer the ability to click on the ad for more information. These ads are effective, with an average click-through rate of 5%.

A **takeover ad** is a large ad that appears when users first go to a site. The same message is reiterated throughout the site in the form of banners, sidebars, or buttons. The approach works very well for branding because the brand is visible to viewers throughout the visit to the site. Click-through rates are high.

Website

Today's website is yesterday's storefront. To compete, you must have a website. Your brokerage firm needs to have its own website with the company's branding, business philosophy, mission statement, and overview of what your company does for its clients. Your website does not give you a competitive advantage; it just puts you on par with your competitors. Providing you have a website, people could be "pulled" to it while they are searching online for homes.

To have a successful website, you must identify and focus on the target audience you are trying to attract. A mistake made by many sales associates is to assume that the only people looking at their website are potential buyers. To the contrary, many sellers and even FSBOs visit sites for a variety of reasons. Because of this, be careful not to exclude an important market segment. You can also brand your website to target smaller niche groups, such as retirees looking for a home in a gated community, golfers, or buyers looking for rural property.

It is pointless to push Internet buyers to move faster or to reveal themselves before they are ready. To be effective when working with Internet buyers, build relationships and offer services they cannot find elsewhere on the 'Net. Because Internet buyers and sellers spend time doing research, they have more real estate knowledge. The average purchaser of real estate services is in the market for a year before making a financial commitment. The best way to interact with Internet customers is to acknowledge that they are doing part of your work. Make them aware of the extra value you will bring to the transaction, such as interpreting data, answering questions, and writing and negotiating offers. To help buyers locate a property, discuss their price range and home preferences. Be especially perceptive of the buyer's expectations, and be ready to modify your services to get their business.

Online real estate brokerage has arrived, but the person-to-person relationships have not disappeared. It is every real estate broker's responsibility to make the buying and selling of real estate "high tech and high touch."

What to Include on Your Website

Structure is important. Use basic principles of design and flow. A visitor to your site should be able to navigate easily and find necessary information quickly. A well-designed website focuses on the needs of its readers and provides information, such as local points of interest, community pages, city history, maps, restaurants, shopping centers, local sports, etc. Links to lenders, home inspectors, termite inspectors, movers, and appraisers are always helpful. You could also offer answers to some of the most commonly asked questions about buying or selling a home.

Typical Questions about Home Buying and Selling

- How much can I afford to pay?
- Do I need a down payment?
- Should I rent or buy?
- Do I need to be pre-qualified or pre-approved for a mortgage?

Your homepage should reflect your brand and include your logo, company information and qualifications, contact information, and the services you offer. A **homepage** is the first web page that people will see when they visit your site. Customer testimonials are another way for prospects to learn more about your firm and build an early rapport. Give potential clients some type of incentive to contact you on your website, whether it is a particular property they want information about, a contest with a prize, or a sign-up for future mailings.

Property Web Page

You should create a web page for each of your listings. There are features exclusive to the Internet that a real estate broker should include along with all of the necessary information mentioned earlier in the unit.

Extra Items to Include

- Links for emailing the web page to clients
- Links for contacting the listing agent
- Printer-friendly brochures
- Online loan application

One very useful tool the real estate broker can include on a website is a virtual tour of the property. A **virtual tour** ensures that visitors to your website can imagine walking through the property and seeing it at its best twenty-four hours a day.

Print Media

There are many types of printed materials that real estate brokers can use to advertise their properties—newspapers, Yellow Pages™, homebuyer's guides, flyers and brochures, and outdoor signs.

Newspaper Advertising

The two types of newspaper advertising are classified and display ads. **Classified ads** are generally inexpensive text and are one of the most popular methods of advertising properties. Classified ads are found in a separate classified section of a newspaper and include ads of all types. Properties are listed under "Real Estate For Sale" and are generally arranged alphabetically by area or city.

Display ads use graphics and photographs. They are larger, more sophisticated, and more expensive. They are usually more visually appealing and have a greater impact on the reader than a classified ad.

All newspaper advertising should target a specific audience. A focused ad attracts attention by stating the benefits of the property. Residential display advertising focuses on desirability and image. The ads should list the location of the property, special features and amenities, and contact information. The advertising should give prospective buyers a reason to act quickly. This can be accomplished by offering an incentive, such as "seller will pay buyer's closing costs," if the property is sold within a certain timeframe.

Yellow Pages™

The Yellow Pages™ is still a good source for advertising. A real estate company should have its primary ad in a consumer directory. Choose the Yellow Pages™ directory in which the majority of businesses advertise—including the Internet, www.yellowpages.com™.

Homebuyer's Guides

In many areas, **homebuyer's guides** provide photos, amenities, and pricing of available properties. These publications are offered free to the public because you (and other brokers in the area) pay for them. This type of advertising reaches a large amount of people, is readily accessible, and is located prominently in racks at the entrances to stores and supermarkets. These guides may also be found in airports, train stations, and bus stations. The publisher guarantees the location and total number of magazines to be distributed. An ad can be placed for local distribution, or more ad dollars can be spent to cover a larger distribution area.

Many guides also provide online versions that are easy to use and contain the same information. They include all of the same photos and information on the website that is in the printed magazine. This allows the real estate broker to reach potential buyers who primarily use the Internet.

Outdoor Advertising

Outdoor advertising is more than just billboards. Outdoor advertising includes various types of advertisements, from traditional highway billboards to inflatables. Outdoor advertising can be as high tech as illuminated buildings or as simple as the ubiquitous yard sign. Regardless of the style, all outdoor advertising is geared toward communicating a message to the public. The benefit of outdoor advertising is that the ad cannot be turned off or put down, unlike TV, radio, or print. With outdoor advertising, consumers cannot change the channel, close the browser, or turn it off.

The Outdoor Advertising Association of America (OAAA) classifies outdoor advertising into four broad categories — billboards, street furniture, transit, and alterative advertising.

Billboard Advertising

Billboard advertising is ancillary to other forms of advertising. Billboards are the most common form of outdoor advertising, with those seen along highways being the most popular. A **billboard** is a large outdoor sign (15 square feet or larger) used for advertising purposes. Billboard advertising is expensive and should be reserved for institutional advertising or for large residential or commercial projects. It has the best cost benefit when combined with an ongoing direct mail campaign and newspaper or Internet advertising. New developments benefit from this type of advertising. A billboard has greater value when placed at a visible location on a main transportation route with high traffic counts, especially alongside major traffic arteries in cities.

Yard Signs

The billboard category includes yard signs. Yard signs can be a very effective method of targeting buyers for a particular property or neighborhood. When people want to buy in a certain area, they will often drive through the area in search of homes for sale. Yard sign calls generate clients, and signage is relatively inexpensive. In fact, a sign  should be displayed on a property even while it is being prepared for sale. This type of planning may result in locating a buyer before the mass marketing for the listing kicks in, which saves advertising dollars.

When using signs continuously in a geographic area or "farm," you can build a good reputation in the local community, which will draw more buyers.

The United States Constitution protects the right to display real estate signs as a form of free speech. Even so, a city, county, or private entity, such as a homeowners' association may regulate the size of signs and how they are displayed.

Sign Regulations

- A city, county, or state may ban all signs on publicly owned property.
- A city, county, or state cannot completely ban signs on privately owned property.
- A city, county, or state may impose reasonable restrictions on the time, place, and manner of displaying signs regardless of whether it is on privately or publicly owned property.

Generally, private real estate signs are banned completely from public property. However, a homeowners' association cannot prohibit private owners from displaying real estate signs on their own property. The signs must be reasonably located in plain view of the public, be of reasonable dimension and design, and advertise the property for lease, or give directions to the property. The real estate sign may include the owner's name, along with an address and telephone number.

Street Furniture Category

The **street furniture** category includes benches, bus shelters, bicycle racks, parking structures, kiosks, shopping mall displays, and in-store advertising. Nearly every bus shelter has advertising and while sitting and waiting for a bus, most of us will read the ads and study the pictures repeatedly. Many real estate companies, rather than individual sales associates use this form of advertising.

Transit Advertising

Transit advertising involves advertising that is on vehicles as well as positioned in the public areas of transit stations (bus, train, and subway) and terminals (airport, train, ship, and ferry). Magnetic signs for car doors are a type of transit advertising. Those of you who  want something a little more innovative could advertise with a custom **car wrap**. Your entire car is wrapped with your eye-catching advertising message. Unlike a static billboard, your wrapped car is mobile and gets attention everywhere you go.

Alternative Media Advertising

The **alternative media advertising** category includes advertising that reaches consumers during specialized activities, such as scoreboards at sports stadiums. Even grocery shopping is considered an activity. For example, you may notice advertising on the shopping carts or on the parking bumpers.

Radio and Television Media

Radio and television are another advertising source. However, it is generally very expensive. Real estate radio and television advertising lends itself to developing brand recognition rather than generating leads. The one exception is the cable TV shows that highlight specific properties in an effort to generate leads.

Radio

Radio specifically targets a narrow market. Research the radio stations to determine which of the stations reaches your target market. When scripting a radio ad, repetition is effective. Run the ad frequently and offer an attention-getting incentive to visit the property. Capturing the listener's attention in the first five seconds is extremely important with a radio ad.

Sometimes, radio stations have remnants of time and will run ads in unsold minutes for a small fee. If a radio station has airtime that is not committed, it might agree to charge airtime based on an agreed upon fee for each person who responds to the radio ad.

Television

The cost of television advertising on the major networks during prime time is exorbitant. However, television does offer some low cost advertising options. Cable networks and small local stations sell a minute of time from a few hundred dollars to a few thousand dollars. Local stations reach target audiences in the local area.

Infomercials

An **infomercial** is a commercial in the format of a television program, usually with a time length of 30 minutes. Infomercials are also known as direct response television (DRTV) commercials or direct response marketing. The main objective in an infomercial is to create an impulse purchase, so that the consumer sees the presentation and then immediately buys the product through the advertised toll-free telephone number or website. A well-known company, National Recreational Properties, Inc., sold vacation property throughout the United States using infomercials hosted by celebrities Chuck Woolery and Eric Estrada.

SUMMARY

A salesperson uses a **property marketing plan** to reach the target market and reach his or her goals.

The two main types of advertising are **institutional advertising** and **product advertising**. Your **advertising campaign** should be intensive, evenly paced, and scheduled to continue until the goals of the campaign are met. When writing ads, use the **AIDA formula** and be sure to follow advertising guidelines.

Before you begin your marketing and advertising efforts, pay careful attention to the guidelines associated with the real estate profession. State and federal agencies regulate real estate advertising.

Advertising media are the different channels available to convey a message to a target market. The major media channels are the **Internet, print media, outdoor media, radio**, and **television** (network, cable, and syndicated).

Common ways to advertise on the web include **banner** and **sidebar ads, pop-ups** (and **pop-downs**), **floating ads, interstitial ads, unicast ads**, and **takeover ads**. The two types of newspaper advertising are **classified** and **display ads**. The **Yellow Pages**™ is still a good source for advertising. The Outdoor Advertising Association of America (OAAA) classifies outdoor advertising into four broad categories—**billboards, street furniture, transit**, and **alternative advertising**. An **infomercial** is a commercial in the format of a television program, usually with a time length of 30 minutes.

UNIT 8 REVIEW

Matching Exercise

Instructions: Write the letter of the matching term on the blank line before its definition. Answers are in Appendix A.

Terms

A. advertising campaign

B. advertising media

C. AIDA

D. billboard

E. classified ads

F. product advertising

G. promotional mix

H. property marketing plan

I. transit advertising

J. web traffic

Definitions

1. _____ Combination of the promotional methods to reach the target market and reach your goals

2. _____ Detailed schedule of everything done to market a property

3. _____ Advertising designed to promote a specific product or service

4. _____ Plan describing the mode and frequency through which someone communicates a marketing concept

5. _____ Formula used to write ads that attract the customer's attention and interest, create desire, and stimulate action

6. _____ Different channels available to convey a message to a target market

7. _____ Amount of data sent and received by visitors to a website

8. _____ Ads found in a separate classified section of a newspaper

9. _____ Large outdoor sign used for advertising purposes

10. _____ Advertising placed on vehicles as well as positioned in public areas of transit stations and terminals

▨ Multiple Choice Questions

Instructions: Circle your response and go to Appendix A to read the complete explanation for each question.

1. Which promotional method should a salesperson use to market a property?
    a. Advertising
    b. Direct marketing
    c. Personal selling
    d. All of the above

2. Which of the following would NOT be considered a technique for a successful marketing plan?
    a. Promote the least desirable features of the house
    b. Use attractive, creative photos of the property to create interest in its special features
    c. Plan marketing activities such as open houses
    d. Promote the property's points of interest

3. In the AIDA formula, the first step is to:
    a. get the customer's attention.
    b. give them benefits to create interest.
    c. make the offer irresistible to create desire.
    d. get the customer to act.

4. Advertising guidelines help real estate licensees avoid penalties and possible suspension or loss of license. Which of the following phrases should be avoided in advertising?
    a. Exclusive neighborhood
    b. Great for a single person
    c. Great for an active person
    d. All of the phrases should be avoided.

5. What is the commonality of banner ads, pop-ups, floating ads, and unicast ads?
    a. Internet advertising
    b. Print advertising
    c. Radio advertising
    d. Television advertising

6. Of the following, which must you a broker have just to be competitive in today's real estate market?

   a. County club membership
   b. Expensive car
   c. Physical office
   d. Website

7. What are the two types of newspaper advertising?

   a. Classified and display
   b. Cold and warm
   c. Institutional and product
   d. Pop-ups and pop-downs

8. Yard signs are included in what advertising category?

   a. Billboard advertising
   b. Transit advertising
   c. Newspaper advertising
   d. Alternative media advertising

9. Magnetic signs for car doors are what type of outdoor advertising?

   a. Alternative Media
   b. Billboard
   c. Street Furniture
   d. Transit

10. Of the following advertising media, which is usually the most expensive?

   a. Classified ads
   b. Internet
   c. Television
   d. Yard signs

The Listing Presentation

Unit 9

INTRODUCTION

When a real estate salesperson obtains a listing, the seller promises to pay a commission if the salesperson presents a "ready, willing, and able" buyer who meets all terms of the listing. The listing salesperson has a legal obligation to work in the best interest of the seller. The salesperson may offer suggestions as far as decision-making goes, but ultimately, the seller instructs the salesperson on what to do. Remember, the listing agreement is between the broker and the seller; however, a salesperson represents the broker in the transaction.

Usually, when a homeowner decides to sell their home, they call one or more real estate professionals. If you are contacted, you will go to the prospective seller's home for a listing appointment. The **listing appointment** is the salesperson's opportunity to get the listing from the prospective seller. Each salesperson gives a listing presentation to persuade the prospective seller that he or she is the specialist who will sell the home. The seller chooses one salesperson to market the property and represent the seller in negotiations with buyers.

Imagine that due to your prospecting efforts, you are one of three real estate sales associates to get a listing appointment with a potential seller. Perhaps the prospect lives in your farm area, enjoys receiving your monthly mailings, wants to list their home, but wants to learn more about you and other salespeople in the area. The seller calls to ask you to stop by their home for a listing presentation. How will you prepare? The following sections will cover the listing presentation.

Learning Objectives

After reading this unit, you should be able to:

- identify the steps in preparing for a listing appointment.
- name the reasons for using a competitive market analysis (CMA).
- indicate the procedure for taking a listing

PREPARING FOR THE LISTING APPOINTMENT

Once the listing appointment is set, start preparing and gathering the information you will need to make a comprehensive **listing presentation**. You will have only one opportunity to convince the seller of your ability. Therefore, be sure to prepare a thorough, professional presentation.

Prequalify the Seller

Prior to the listing appointment, ask sellers questions to help create a personalized presentation, avoiding generalities. Asking prequalifying questions will impress sellers and demonstrate your attention to detail and professional approach to listing their property. You will also learn if the sellers are serious about selling their home, and if it is worth your time to take the listing. Ask the following questions and pay attention to the sellers' responses.

- **Motivation for selling**—Are they serious about selling? Why are they selling? Are they selling because of foreclosure? Are they looking to list their property as a short sale? Which is more important, obtaining the highest price or moving quickly?
- **Timeframe**—How soon do they need or want to move?
- **Purchase of new home**—Have the sellers already bought another home? Do they need the proceeds from this sale to close the sale of the new home? Are the sellers realistic about the value of their home? How flexible are they on price?

- **Previous experiences**—Have the sellers had positive or negative experiences with other real estate salespeople? Listen carefully to evaluate what type of client they may be. Perhaps they have misconceptions that you will need to clarify.

- **Real estate experience**—What is the sellers' level of real estate knowledge? Have they ever sold a home? This information will determine your approach to the sale, because if they are first-time sellers, you should begin with the fundamentals of a home sale.

- **Technology**—Determine if the sellers are interested in or competent with technology. Do they use the Internet and e-mail? If not, give a traditional presentation and use your career book and other non-technical materials instead of your laptop. Do not challenge a seller's comfort zone.

To save time, ask the sellers to have the following information available at the listing appointment:

- Loan information (balance, prepayment penalty, assumable)
- Title policy
- CC&Rs (if applicable)
- Current tax bill
- Mello Roos information and any outstanding assessments
- Current utility bills
- House keys

Create a Listing Package

Most successful salespeople create a listing package for sellers prior to the listing appointment. A **listing package** should include information about the seller's property, professional details about you and your brokerage, samples of your advertising and marketing pieces, and all the forms necessary for listing the property. A carefully prepared listing package will help achieve a position of trust, accountability, and communication with the seller.

> **What to Include in a Listing Package:**
> - Property profile
> - Graph showing community pricing trends
> - CMA (including photographs)
> - Seller's net sheet
> - Property marketing plan
> - Advertising samples and flyers

- Standard forms including the agency relationship disclosure statement, a listing agreement, and disclosure forms such as the Transfer Disclosure Statement. In addition, note any environmental or other issues that might need disclosure to a buyer. These other issues may include special zoning, annual property taxes, income and expenses if the property is an apartment or commercial building, and any special property features such as a view, pool, or recent room addition.
- Your career book
- Checklists for the seller including things to do so that the property shows well, money-making tips on getting a house ready for sale, moving tips, or retrofit requirements
- Local maps and other visual aids
- Items such as pen and paper, business calculator, and tape measure

Prepare a Property Profile

Most title companies will give you information to help you prepare a property profile. A **property profile** is a report about a specific piece of property. It should include a short legal description, property characteristics (lot size, year built, square footage, number of bedrooms and bathrooms), most recent grant deeds, any open deeds of trust, an Assessor's Parcel Number (APN) map, and the current taxes and assessed value. Take a photograph with your digital camera of the house you want to list and place a print of the photo in the property profile. During the appointment when you present the property profile to the sellers, they will be able to picture their house "for sale".

Prepare Your Property Marketing Plan

Before meeting with the seller, prepare the marketing plan for their property. The **property marketing plan** is a detailed schedule that shows them everything you will do to market their property. You may follow the same timeline and activities in your property marketing plan for almost all of your listings. Visualize your property marketing plan by filling in the boxes of a calendar page with your marketing activities. For example, if you plan to install a lock box on the property and submit the listing to the MLS on the second day of the listing, write that information on the calendar in the second box after the day you take the listing.

Presenting a property marketing plan to sellers is a great way to show that you are prepared, know how to set goals for marketing a listing, and have a plan.

Show that you implement your marketing plan from the date of the listing by using a blank calendar page and filling in the appropriate dates for each new listing. The seller will see that you will begin marketing their property the day you take the listing.

When presenting your property marketing plan, you have the opportunity to show the different types of flyers or newspaper ads you will use in your plan. Bring samples of these marketing materials to show the seller. Include the dates that you will send out the materials so the sellers will know when to expect an ad to run in the newspaper or when flyers will be placed in their outdoor literature box.

Prepare a Competitive Market Analysis (CMA)

Any homeowner should be able to approximate the value of their home within a few thousand dollars. This is due in part to the information readily available to buyers and sellers on the Internet. Sellers can instantly determine the probable value of their home by visiting web sites, such as www.moveup.com, which are usually sponsored by neighborhood real estate agents. Sellers simply enter their name, address, e-mail, and phone number to receive information about recent comparable sales in their neighborhood. If they are sure of the value, why do they call a real estate salesperson to tell them what they already know? Even though the homeowner used the same method as the salesperson to determine the home's value, he or she still desires the educated opinion of a real estate professional who can confirm the accuracy of the research.

A **competitive market analysis (CMA)** by a real estate professional is not much different from the inventory of sold properties the homeowner accumulates. The CMA is a comparison analysis that real estate brokers use while working with a seller to determine an appropriate listing price for the seller's house. You will present the CMA during your listing presentation to establish the home value with the prospective sellers. For the homeowner, the CMA either indicates or confirms the probable value of the home. The CMA lays the foundation for setting a realistic listing price for the property. The **listing price** is the amount of money a seller agrees to accept from a buyer as stated in the listing agreement that may be negotiable during the listing period.

The principle of substitution is the basis for using a CMA to determine value. The **principle of substitution** affirms that the maximum value of a property tends to be set by the cost of acquiring an equally desirable and valuable substitute. An owner cannot expect to sell for more than someone would ordinarily pay for a similar property, under similar conditions.

The **sales comparison approach** is the most easily and commonly used appraisal approach used by real estate salespeople. It is best for single-family homes or condominiums and vacant lots because sales information is readily available and easily compared. The sales comparison approach uses the principle of substitution to compare similar properties by looking at the current selling price of a similar property and adjusting it for any differences to determine the market value for the subject property. The **selling price** is the price a buyer actually pays for a property that may or may not be the same as the listing price. The **market value** is the highest price a property would bring if freely offered on the open market, with both a willing buyer and a willing seller.

How to Prepare a CMA

To prepare a CMA for a property, collect data on at least three comparable properties that are as similar to the property in question as possible. **Comparables**, or **comps**, are similar properties sold on the open market and offered for a reasonable length of time that are used to prepare a CMA for a subject property. Typical comparable categories include neighborhood location, view, size (comparable number of bedrooms/bathrooms as well as square footage), age, architectural style, financing terms, and the general price range. Most comps are taken from the Multiple Listing Service (MLS). The **MLS** allows you to find properties that match certain criteria you enter into the computerized database.

The salesperson will research comparable sales to discover any special circumstances influencing those sales, such as a seller bankruptcy or foreclosure. Only those similar properties—sold on the open market with approval of the seller, and offered for a reasonable length of time— are used for comparables. In addition, if possible, use only those properties that have

Research on comparable properties produces data that is used to develop a CMA.

sold within the past six months. Typically, comparables older than six months are less reliable. Features in either the property or the transaction itself are elements that may cause values to vary. Estimates of value may vary because of differences in the financing terms, time of sale, sale conditions, location, physical features, and investment income amounts. Those properties that have less similar features are excluded, and greater weight is given to the comparable sales most similar to the subject property. The salesperson arrives at a range of value for the property in question using the compatible comparables to indicate the estimated value and price for the subject property.

If you have a digital camera, take photographs of the properties used as comps. Use the microphone component of your camera to state the address and sales information as you take the photographs. If possible, create a PowerPoint® slide show presentation for your prospective seller, of all the homes. You can do the same thing with comparable listed properties and expired listings as you go through your listing presentation.

Items to Include on the Competitive Market Analysis:
- All listed comparable properties in the neighborhood
- All comparable properties that have sold within the last six months
- All comparable listings in the neighborhood that have expired within the last six months
- Local pricing trends in the real estate market over the last year
- A summary of the average number of days on the market for comparable homes within the last year
- Sold properties and days on the market, active listings, and pending sales
- Comparative sold and competing active properties with color photos (download from the MLS)
- All active listings, pending sale, under contract, withdrawn, and expired listings
- The number of days on the market for all categories
- A color-pricing chart that reflects current market conditions
- Full-color market charts reflecting current market from MLS or company
- All available property information including tax info, plats, recent sales history or mortgage, etc.
- A market absorption analysis that includes how many similar homes are for sale and historically how long it will take to absorb or sell that amount of homes

Prepare a Net Sheet

The seller's **net sheet** shows the approximate net amount of money sellers can expect to receive for a specified sales price. It is a line-by-line description of the fees associated with the sale of their home, including commission. The price of the home is based on the figures you calculated when you prepared your CMA for the property. Use your recommended listing price in the net sheet to determine the estimated cash proceeds. The figures you place in the net sheet are estimates you have arrived at based on usual and customary escrow fees, proration, inspections, and title insurance fees, to name a few. You may need to perform some research by calling your local title and escrow company, or asking your broker to help you calculate the costs associated with selling a home.

THE LISTING PRESENTATION

You do not get a second chance to make a first impression, as the saying goes, and this holds true in the real estate profession as well. You must do what it takes to set yourself apart from the competition, especially at the listing appointment.

Be sensitive to the prospective client and flexible in your presentation. Not everyone responds to the same type of presentation because people process information in different ways. After talking with the sellers and observing their surroundings, you may decide to use technology, or you may choose to keep it simple and to the point. Some sellers want endless sales statistics, while others want to know only how quickly you can sell their house and for what price. Be prepared for all types of sellers and be flexible enough to accommodate various needs.

Ways that People Process Information

Visually: Information is processed through pictures or graphics. If you are talking to people who need to "see" the information to understand it, speak quickly in a higher-pitched voice and use phrases such as: "Do you see what I mean?"

Auditorily: Information is processed by sound or vocal clues. When talking to people who assimilate information by what they hear, speak soothingly and use phrases such as "How does that sound?"

Kinesthetically: Information is processed through feelings or emotions. If you are talking to people who rely on their "gut feelings" or emotional impact of information, speak slowly and quietly, and use phrases such as "Does this feel right to you?"

What to Bring

The following items should be brought with you to the listing presentation:

- a full-color personalized CMA.
- seller's net sheet describing the selling costs as well as bottom-line profit.
- a personalized cover letter reflecting your professionalism and experience.
- your resume including credentials, designations, awards, and achievements.
- your cumulative sales, highlighting any in their neighborhood.
- testimonials from past clients.
- a concise marketing plan to sell the home, including print, media, virtual tours, and web marketing.
- full-color flyers, "just-listed" postcards, marketing materials with the seller's home in color.
- web statistics from your website including your website placement.
- a listing pack with all forms filled out as much as possible.
- a seller's checklist to prepare the home for sale.

Steps to Follow

Sellers want to feel confident in your ability as a skilled real estate salesperson. These skills include preparing their home for sale, selling tips, marketing, advertising, and giving realistic expectations of the selling timeframe and costs. When you give a listing presentation, be sure it is so thorough and concise that you will be "sold" to the seller, and all competition will be eliminated. Keep in mind that what the seller desires to know may be different from what you plan to show them.

The Listing Appointment

- Confirm the appointment.
- Arrive on time.
- Turn your phone and pager off. Never take a call during a listing presentation. To do so would indicate to your prospects they are not important.
- Tour the home, take notes and evaluate all features, take photographs, show interest in the home.
- Use the dining room or kitchen table for presentation. Do not favor one person when speaking.
- Present your career book, personal references, and professional qualifications for the job.
- Show the marketing plan you created for the property.
- Explain the specific services you will provide.

- After presenting the competitive market analysis, discuss pricing and settle on the listing price for the property.

- Discuss the terms of the sale, including how soon the seller wants or needs to close, which items of personal property are included in the sale, etc.

- Ask the seller to sign the listing agreement after discussion of commission and terms of the listing.

- Complete the disclosure forms such as agency and transfer disclosure statement.

- Mention any repairs, painting, yard work, or general cleanup that should be done to the home.

- Explain MLS, lock box, and "for sale" sign.

- Ask the seller if he or she has any questions, and if so, answer each one clearly and concisely.

- The most important aspects of the sale are setting the price, selling your abilities, presenting the net sheet, and presenting the listing agreement.

Set the Price with the Seller

The purpose of the listing presentation is to get the listing and set the price of the home so that it will sell for the highest price in the shortest amount of time. Therefore, your presentation should focus on price, so that you will have an opportunity to secure a sale rather than just a listing. The objective is to get the contract signed, but in most cases, the sellers need the highest dollar amount for their home. The price is similar to the known variable in an algebra equation. All other potential issues or problems probably connect to the known issue, which is variable price. During a "buyer's market", by lowering the price, you can sell a property in poor condition, in a poor location, on a busy street; or one that is functionally obsolete.

You must tell the seller the truth about setting the price. Do not sugarcoat your words or be vague. Many salespeople avoid this conversation. The sellers' needs most likely relate to the price, so help them understand how the price you have arrived at after looking at the comparables is the closest estimate to market value. You can either deal with setting the price appropriately in the beginning, or do so later when it has become more difficult. Once the price or range of value has been determined, be sure the seller is comfortable with it. Do not continue if you and the seller do not agree on price.

Using the CMA to Help Set the Price

The right listing price is the secret to a fast sale. This is where the CMA you prepared prior to the listing presentation is helpful. After preparing a CMA for a property, the experienced real estate salesperson will know what the range of value is for the property in question, and will probably have a feeling about the final selling price.

One of the most important jobs a salesperson does during the presentation of the CMA is guide the seller in setting the listing price. As a basis for determining the listing price, there will be a range of value the salesperson and seller will use. This range will come from the highest and lowest comparable prices in your CMA. Variables that affect how high or low to set the price are supply and demand, the urgency of the seller's move, and the condition of the home.

- **Supply and demand**—If there is more supply than demand (**buyer's market**) a seller may have to price a property lower. If there is more demand (**seller's market**) than **inventory** (listed properties), the seller could consider pricing the home at the top of the range of value or higher.

- **Motivation**—If the seller is not in a hurry to move, the price could be set at the upper range of value. If the seller must move quickly, lower the price to the bottom range of value.

- **Condition**—This is the hardest part of estimating the value of a property. If due to the condition of the home a buyer would not be interested in it at the current market value, the salesperson must tactfully inform the seller that some repairs, paint, or hauling may be necessary to bring it up to value.

- **Odor**—If the home is odor-challenged, the salesperson must find a way to communicate that to the seller.

A salesperson must tactfully explain to the seller that odors in the home may present a problem or that repairs must be made in order to increase the selling price.

A professional real estate salesperson will have solutions to selling problems caused by a home in less-than-perfect condition and will be able to help a grateful seller get the top price he or she deserves. If a seller refuses to price the home realistically, one thing a salesperson can do is get a commitment from the seller to reduce the price incrementally, within 20 days, 30 days, or whatever is necessary.

Sell Your Abilities

Once you have resolved the pricing issue, you must convince the sellers that you are the salesperson for the job. Keep this brief and to the point. Most people do not want to listen to someone talk about how great they are at selling homes. Ask the sellers specific questions to determine the kind of services they want from their salesperson. Present your record of accomplishment and success, and then ask them if they are looking for a salesperson of your caliber. If you are new to real estate and do not have a record of accomplishment, sell your company's record. You may even need to sell a little of both.

This part of your presentation should last less than ten minutes unless they ask several questions. If you want to be the chosen salesperson, focus on the problem and the solution. Spending endless amounts of time on other subjects will only weaken your presentation.

Once you have settled the price and have proven the probability of the home selling, it is time to present the net sheet.

Present the Net Sheet

Present a net sheet to the sellers and work it out in front of them. The net sheet will itemize the expenses of the sale including the commission. By subtracting the expenses from the sales price, the seller will see the amount he or she will net after the closing. The sellers may not agree on a price until they have seen the total picture and can predict their probable net proceeds.

A good time to present your commission is while you are explaining the costs in the net sheet because you can redirect the sellers' attention to the real issue—what their check amount will be at the closing. It is easier for the seller to see the commission when it is presented as part of the overall costs involved in the sale.

At this point, you have carefully shown the seller how you will market their home for the maximum price, in minimum time, with as little inconvenience to them as possible.

Ask for the Listing

Asking for the listing should be simple. Ask them if they believe you could sell their home, or tell them all you need is their signature to start selling their home. If they say no, ask them to tell you why, and listen to their answer. Once you know what the objection is, address it, and ask for the listing again. Do not give up after the first setback. The average sale takes place after the fifth or sixth refusal. Be persistent; do not give up.

> **This is the proper procedure to follow when asking for the listing.**
> 1. Present the Agency Disclosure Statement
> 2. Present the Listing Agreement
> 3. Present the Seller's Advisory

Present the Agency Disclosure Statement

When selling residential property of four units or less, the law requires all real estate licensees to give a Disclosure Regarding Real Estate Agency Relationships, explaining the nature of agency to prospective sellers and buyers. The steps in the disclosure process are to disclose, elect, and confirm (DEC).

Disclose the Relationship

First, describe and disclose the obligations of an agent as "seller's agent", "buyer's agent", or "dual agent". At this point, all parties are made aware that they do have a choice of who is to represent them as their own agent. A written disclosure must be presented by a listing agent (or his or her sales associate) who must deliver the form to the seller before entering into a listing agreement.

Elect the Agency

The second part of the agency disclosure form requires all parties involved to confirm that they understand the agent's role. In other words, the first part of the disclosure reveals that the agent may represent only the buyer, only the seller, or both. All parties acknowledge their understanding at this point.

Confirm the Agency

Finally, all parties to the transaction (buyer, seller, and agents) are required to acknowledge that they understand who is representing whom, and sign the agency confirmation form. One more time, the relationship will be confirmed in the sales contract, which is signed by all parties.

Present the Listing Agreement

Now that you have properly disclosed the agency relationship, you may present the listing agreement. A **listing agreement** is a written contract by which a principal, or seller, employs a broker to sell real estate. When the seller signs a listing agreement, he or she is promising payment for service by the listing broker and the broker promises to "use due diligence" in finding a buyer. The listing agreement is a **bilateral contract**; a promise is given in exchange for a promise.

The listing agreement states that the seller promises to pay a commission upon presentation of a "ready, willing, and able" buyer who meets all terms of the listing. A **"ready, willing, and able"** buyer is prepared to enter into a purchase contract, truly wants to buy, and meets the financial requirements of purchase. A listing agreement gives the broker the right to be paid only after doing the job, or producing results. It is an employment contract between the seller and the broker.

Types of Listing Agreements

In California, the four commonly used listing agreements are exclusive right to sell listing, exclusive agency listing, open listing, and net listing.

The **California Association of REALTORS®** (C.A.R.), a dominant provider of real estate forms, has renamed its listing forms as follows:

- Residential Listing Agreement—Exclusive (Form RLA)
- Residential Listing Agreement—Agency (Form RLAA)
- Residential Listing Agreement—Open (Form RLAN)

The **Residential Listing Agreement—Exclusive** (formerly named Exclusive Authorization and Right to Sell Agreement) is an exclusive contract where the seller must pay the listing broker a commission if the property is sold within the time limit by the listing broker, any other broker, or even by the owner. If the broker brings the seller a "mirror offer", or an offer that matches all terms in the listing exactly, the seller does not have to accept the offer. However, under the terms of the listing, the seller must pay the broker a commission.

The **Residential Listing Agreement—Agency** (formerly named Exclusive Agency Listing Agreement) is an exclusive contract where the seller must pay the listing broker a commission if any broker sells the property. However, the seller has the right to sell the property without a broker, and pay no commission.

The **Residential Listing Agreement—Open** (formerly named Non-Exclusive "Open" Agency Residential Listing Agreement) is a listing agreement that gives any number of brokers the right to sell a property. It is not exclusive and may be given to any number of agents at the same time. The first broker to obtain a buyer who meets the terms of the listing, and whose offer is accepted by the seller, earns the commission. That agent is known as the procuring cause of the sale. **Procuring cause** refers to a broker who produces a buyer "ready, willing, and able" to purchase the property for the price and on the terms specified by the seller, regardless of whether the sale is completed. Unlike an exclusive listing agreement, an open listing does not require a specific termination date. The owner may sell the property without an agent, owing no commission.

A **net listing** is a listing agreement in which the commission is not definite. Instead, the broker receives all the money from the sale of the property that is in excess of the selling price set by the seller. The broker must disclose the selling price to both buyer and seller within 30 days after closing the transaction.

Present the Seller's Advisory

Along with the Disclosure of Real Estate Agency Relationships form and the Residential Listing Agreement, a Seller's Advisory form is now mandatory when a broker or sales associate takes a listing. The California Association of REALTORS® has developed a standard Seller's Advisory form that brokers and sales associates may attach to the listing agreement. This form advises the seller of legal requirements and practical matters that may arise during the selling process. At the same time, the Seller's Advisory protects the sales associate and broker by providing evidence of advising the seller of required disclosures.

TOP REASONS HOMES FAIL TO SELL

Price–The most common reason a home fails to sell is overpricing. A home priced at or below market value shows that the owners are serious about selling and should attract serious buyers. On the other hand, an overpriced home could convey to the buyer that the seller is not open to negotiation or serious about selling. The likely result will be buyers looking for the next comparable property that has a lower asking price.

A home may fail to sell because of its condition.

Condition–The next common reason a home fails to sell is because of its condition. A prospective buyer will think that the listing price of a property is too high after factoring in the necessary costs for repair. Improving the condition of the home will help the seller obtain the highest possible value. It is important that the pricing reflect the home's condition. Urge your sellers to fix up their homes to avoid discounting the price in the future to compensate for repairs.

Location–You hear it all the time, especially in real estate, "Location, location, location". Regardless of how attractive a home is, an undesirable location will cause buyers, especially families, to shun the property. Poorly ranked schools, unattractive buildings, high crime rates, and noisy conditions are all elements of an undesirable location. Unfortunately, the seller and salesperson have no control over these external factors. Therefore, this refers to proper pricing of a property according to its features, location, and comparable properties in the area.

Even the best location may not help sell this odd shaped house.

Listing Salesperson–A salesperson's reputation and marketing plan may contribute to the reasons why a home does not sell. If the salesperson is uncooperative with other salespeople, their listings will probably not get many showings. Salespeople will take their buyers elsewhere to avoid dealing with the salesperson's inconsideration and rudeness. The sales marketing plan, or lack thereof, also affects a property's exposure. The successful salesperson will market the property to attract as many buyers and salespeople as possible rather than wait for offers to come in without any serious marketing efforts.

NAR CODE OF ETHICS—LISTINGS

Article 1

When representing a buyer, seller, landlord, tenant, or other client as an agent, REALTORS® pledge themselves to protect and promote the interests of their client. This obligation to the client is primary, but it does not relieve REALTORS® of their obligation to treat all parties honestly. When serving a buyer, seller, landlord, tenant or other party in a non-agency capacity, REALTORS® remain obligated to treat all parties honestly. (Amended 1/01)

Standard of Practice 1-9

The obligation of REALTORS® to preserve confidential information (as defined by state law) provided by their clients in the course of any agency relationship or non-agency relationship recognized by law continues after termination of agency relationships or any non-agency relationships recognized by law. REALTORS® shall not knowingly, during or following the termination of professional relationships with their clients:

1. reveal confidential information of clients; or

2. use confidential information of clients to the disadvantage of clients; or

3. use confidential information of clients for the REALTOR®'s advantage or the advantage of third parties unless:

   a) clients consent after full disclosure; or

   b) REALTORS® are required by court order; or

   c) it is the intention of a client to commit a crime and the information is necessary to prevent the crime; or

   d) it is necessary to defend a REALTOR® or the REALTOR®'s employees or associates against an accusation of wrongful conduct.

Information concerning latent material defects is not considered confidential information under this Code of Ethics. (Adopted 1/93, Amended 1/01)

Article 2

REALTORS® shall avoid exaggeration, misrepresentation, or concealment of pertinent facts relating to the property or the transaction. REALTORS® shall not, however, be obligated to discover latent defects in the property, to advise on matters outside the scope of their real estate license, or to disclose facts that are confidential under the scope of agency or non-agency relationships as defined by state law. (Amended 1/00)

Standard of Practice 2-1

REALTORS® shall only be obligated to discover and disclose adverse factors reasonably apparent to someone with expertise in those areas required by their real estate licensing authority. Article 2 does not impose upon the REALTOR® the obligation of expertise in other professional or technical disciplines. (Amended 1/96)

Article 9

REALTORS®, for the protection of all parties, shall assure whenever possible that all agreements related to real estate transactions including, but not limited to, listing and representation agreements, purchase contracts, and leases are in writing in clear and understandable language expressing the specific terms, conditions, obligations and commitments of the parties. A copy of each agreement shall be furnished to each party to such agreements upon their signing or initialing. (Amended 1/04)

Article 12

REALTORS® shall be honest and truthful in their real estate communications and shall present a true picture in their advertising, marketing, and other representations. REALTORS® shall ensure that their status as real estate professionals is readily apparent in their advertising, marketing, and other representations, and that the recipients of all real estate communications are, or have been, notified that those communications are from a real estate professional. (Amended 1/08)

Standard of Practice 12-4

REALTORS® shall not offer for sale/lease or advertise property without authority. When acting as listing brokers or as subagents, REALTORS® shall not quote a price different from that agreed upon with the seller/landlord. (Amended 1/93)

Article 16

REALTORS® shall not engage in any practice or take any action inconsistent with exclusive representation or exclusive brokerage relationship agreements that other REALTORS® have with clients. (Amended 1/04)

SUMMARY

Obtaining listings is a major focus of real estate marketing and is the goal of prospecting. You must do what it takes to set yourself apart from the competition, especially at the listing appointment.

Once the **listing appointment** is established, start preparing and gathering the information you need to make a comprehensive **listing presentation**. Prepare a **career book, property marketing plan, CMA**, and **seller's net sheet** prior to the appointment.

The objective of the listing appointment is definitely to get the **listing contract** signed; however, in most cases, sellers need to get the highest dollar amount for their home. After preparing a CMA for a property, a real estate salesperson will know the range of value for the property. The most common reason a home fails to sell is overpricing. Once you have resolved the pricing issue, you must convince the seller that you are the salesperson for the job. Keep this discussion brief and to the point.

Present a net sheet to the sellers and work it out in front of them. The net sheet will itemize the expenses of the sale, including the commission. After you have summarized your points, present the sellers with a listing agreement. Asking for the listing should be simple. Ask them if they believe you can sell their home, or tell them all you need is their signature to start selling their home.

UNIT 9 REVIEW

Matching Exercise

Instructions: Write the letter of the matching term on the blank line before its definition. Answers are in Appendix A.

Terms

A. bilateral contract

B. buyer's market

C. Competitive Market Analysis (CMA)

D. comps

E. exclusive agency listing

F. inventory

G. listing agreement

H. listing appointment

I. listing price

J. market value

K. net listing

L. net sheet

M. open listing

N. option listing

O. principle of substitution

P. procuring cause

Q. property marketing plan

R. property profile

S. "ready, willing, and able"

T. sales comparison approach

U. seller's market

V. selling price

Definitions

1. _____ The opportunity a salesperson has to convince a prospective seller to list the home with that particular salesperson

2. _____ A report about a specific piece of property

3. _____ A detailed schedule of everything a real estate salesperson will do to market a property

4. _____ A comparison analysis that real estate salespeople use while working with a seller to determine an appropriate listing price for the seller's house

5. _____ The amount of money a seller agrees to accept from a buyer as stated in the listing agreement that may be negotiable during the listing period

6. _____ A means of comparing similar properties, which have recently sold, to a subject property

7. _____ The price a buyer actually pays for a property that may or may not be the same as the listing price

8. _____ Similar properties sold on the open market and offered for a reasonable length of time that are used to prepare a CMA for a subject property

9. _____ Shows the approximate net amount of money the seller can expect to receive for a specified sales price

10. _____ A market containing more supply than demand

11. _____ The available listed properties in an area

12. _____ A written contract by which a principal, or seller, employs a broker to sell real estate

13. _____ A buyer who is prepared to enter into a purchase contract, who really wants to buy, and who meets the financial requirements of purchase

14. _____ The broker who produces a buyer "ready, willing, and able" to purchase the property for the price and on the terms specified by the seller, regardless of whether the sale is completed

15. _____ A listing agreement in which the commission is not definite

Multiple Choice Questions

Instructions: Circle your response and go to Appendix A to read the complete explanation for each question.

1. A carefully prepared listing package:
    a. will include information about the sellers' property.
    b. has advertising and marketing samples.
    c. helps create trust and communication with the sellers.
    d. does all of the above.

2. The best way to convince a prospective seller that you are the specialist to hire for the job of selling the home is by:
    a. calling the seller and asking for the listing.
    b. arranging a listing appointment.
    c. telling a seller that you can sell the house for a higher price than other salespeople can.
    d. sending a listing agreement to the seller in the mail.

3. An effective listing presentation should:
    a. be the same for each seller.
    b. be personalized for each seller.
    c. focus mainly on the salesperson.
    d. focus on the listing agreement.

4. Which of the following statements is correct regarding property marketing plans?
    a. It is possible to follow the same timeline and activities for each listing.
    b. Only certain listings will need a property marketing plan.
    c. It is not recommended that you tell the seller about your property marketing plan.
    d. Salespeople should ask sellers to make their own flyers as part of the property marketing plan.

5. The purpose of a CMA is to:
    a. establish the salesperson's knowledge of the market.
    b. determine an appropriate listing price for the seller's house.
    c. confirm the actual selling price of the property.
    d. do all of the above.

6. Which of the following items describes a reliable comp?
    a. A listing that has sold because of a bankruptcy
    b. A listing that is older than six months
    c. A listing that is similar to the subject property
    d. A privately sold property

7. In order to prepare a CMA, a salesperson usually:
    a. calls each seller in order to obtain information about each property included in the CMA.
    b. visits each property to make sure it is similar to the subject property.
    c. researches comparable properties on the MLS.
    d. includes one other comparable property.

8. When listing a property that is in poor condition, it is best to:
    a. be honest and tell the seller that the property will never sell.
    b. convince the seller to lower the listing price.
    c. ask the seller to add a pool.
    d. submit the listing to the MLS without a photo.

9. The secret to a fast sale is:
    a. the correct listing price.
    b. a charismatic salesperson.
    c. lowering your commission.
    d. only taking listings that are in good neighborhoods.

10. During a buyer's market:
    a. the seller should consider pricing the home at the top end of the range of value or higher.
    b. there is more demand than inventory.
    c. a buyer will usually have to pay more for a property.
    d. a seller might have to lower the price of the property.

11. It is a good idea to present the commission amount:
    a. when you first arrive at the listing appointment.
    b. over the phone when you set the listing appointment.
    c. only when the seller asks about it.
    d. when you present the seller's net sheet.

12. The average sale takes place:
    a. the first time a salesperson asks for the sale.
    b. during the first five minutes of a sales presentation.
    c. after the fifth or sixth refusal.
    d. none of the above.

13. The first thing you should do when asking for the listing is present the:
    a. Listing Agreement.
    b. Seller's Advisory.
    c. Agency Disclosure Statement.
    d. commission agreement.

14. The listing agreement is made between the:
    a. broker and seller.
    b. salesperson and seller.
    c. salesperson and broker.
    d. salesperson and buyer.

15. The most common reason a home fails to sell is:
    a. overpricing.
    b. poor condition.
    c. poor location.
    d. a lazy salesperson.

Servicing the Listing

Unit 10

INTRODUCTION

Listings are the bread and butter of the real estate profession. The way you service your listings could make or break your career. Repeat and referral business are the rewards when you make a great impression and deliver superior customer service. Positioning yourself for the future business of your current clients is part of a successful strategy. Staging the home, marketing efforts, and a high level of communication build a perception of professionalism and ensure loyalty.

Learning Objectives

After reading this unit, you should be able to:

- outline the steps to servicing the listing.
- recall techniques used in staging a home.
- indicate the factors of holding successful open houses.

SERVICING THE LISTING

Because you do not operate in a vacuum, your clients will compare the service you give with services offered by the broker up the street. Your service—whether excellent or mediocre—will be determined by the perception of the client. Therefore, find out what your current clients consider great customer service. Ask what they expect of you. What are their expectations regarding your communication with them? What other services can you provide? The answers you receive will enable you to exceed their expectations and provide exceptional service to all your clients.

Communication

Communication is a crucial element to servicing a listing effectively. Most clients equate consistency of communication with customer service. In fact, the most frequent complaint clients and customers have about real estate sales associates is the lack of communication. You need to maintain proactive communications with your clients, be highly accessible, and deliver quality as well as consistency in your communication and product. In order to meet your clients' expectations, set up a schedule of communication; agree to call them once a week to update them and then do it every week without fail. Even if you have nothing new to report, check in with them.

Your clients will appreciate when you keep your promise to contact them. Keep in touch with your clients with e-mails, letters, phone calls, or personal visits. High-performance Internet capabilities may help to streamline your communication. You need communication systems that provide customers with easy access to the resources they need.

Maintaining a high level of communication in the first few weeks of the listing gives the impression of service and activity. Many salespeople send a series of letters every three days during the first month, as well as courtesy calls, and a monthly update. Produce weekly and monthly reports. Follow up after the first 30 days of the listing, and maintain regular, consistent contact. If there is a low level of interest in the property, begin sending the sellers informational material that will condition them for price adjustments. It is almost impossible to communicate too much.

STEPS IN SERVICING THE LISTING

There are several steps to take when marketing a home, and the sellers need to know what to expect. Typically the steps include inputting the property information in the MLS, getting keys from the seller and installing the lockbox on the property, preparing marketing pieces, placing classified ads, putting up the "For Sale" sign, staging the home, scheduling a caravan, holding open houses, and counseling the sellers about offers they receive.

Multiple Listing Service (MLS)

The majority of listings sell through the MLS and other salespeople. As you have learned, an MLS is a cooperative listing service conducted by a group of brokers, usually members of a real estate association. Sales associates and brokers submit listings to a central bureau, where the listings are entered into a computerized system available for all members to see. In the past, brokers and sales associates had to search through books of listings when using the MLS. Today, the Internet has provided a more efficient and convenient method of submitting and searching listings.

An MLS is operated by a board of REALTORS®, or can also be privately operated. The benefits of joining an MLS affiliated with a board of REALTORS® include training and education as well as the advantage of working with real estate professionals held accountable by the board of REALTORS®. Your broker must be a REALTOR® in order for you to apply for membership status.

If you choose to join your local association of REALTORS®, you also have the option of joining that association's MLS. You may join as many local associations throughout California as you wish and in turn have access to each of their multiple listing services. For example, a licensee living in Orange County, California, may choose to join the Orange County Association of REALTORS® (OCAR). This licensee also has the option of paying dues to become a member of the Southern California MLS (SoCalMLS). He or she can then list properties on the MLS and view all properties listed by other REALTORS®.

Sample Listing

SFR Detached RES Closed Sale	Residential	Fri, Jul 22, 2005 03:45 PM	

	Residential		
SFR Detached RES Closed Sale	2468 Mountain Trail	Coto De Caza (CDC)	Price $5,400,000
	Coto De Caza (CC)	Zip 92679-	TGNO
	Orange County (OR)	XSTS	Aerial Map ✈

S351197	Media: 10	Builder Tract	
Bed 8		Model Custom	
Baths 9.5		Stories Two Levels	HOA Dues $ 277 + $ 0
View View			Land Fee $
ASqFt 10,280 Other		YrBlt 1987 Other	
ALotSize 81,859 Estimated		Dim	Acres 1.92

Prkng Gated Parking, Golf Cart Garage, Parking Space, Garage Attached, Garage Door Opener
Garage 6 A   Rem   Spc 4   Cprt 0   RV Acc   Range $: No

Spectacular Tuscan Estate On Apprx 2 Ac. 3-Building Compound W/ Main House (6br/7.5 Ba)+guest Hse(2br/2.5ba)+pool Hse(w/Kit&ba). Breathtaking 360 Deg Views Of Mtns And Coto Valley. This Property Has It All, Including, Sauna, 3 Kitchens, 2 Elevators, 2 Wet Bars, Master Retreat, Media Center, Gym, Beautiful Library, 4 Fireplaces

=Rooms=

Bedrooms Main Floor Bedroom, Master Bedroom Retreat, Dressing Area, Master Suite, Walk-In Closet
Other Family Room, Guest-Maid Quarters, Individual Laundry Room, Library, Wine Cellar, Workshop, Bonus Room, Den/Ofc, Separate Family Room

Living Rm Living Rm Entrance, Living Room
Dining Formal Dining Rm, Breakfast Counter/Bar, Breakfast Nook

=Amenities=

Pool Gunite, Heated & Filtered, Private Pool
Spa Gunite Spa
TV Cable TV
Firepl Family Room, Master Bedroom
Security Closed Circuit TV, Fire Sprinklers, Community with Guard, Security System
Appliances Convection Oven, Dishwasher, Freezer, Garbage Disposal, Gas/Elec Dryer Hook Up, Microwave, Refrigerator
Other Sauna Private, Vacuum Central, Wet Bar

=Interior/Exterior/Structural=

Heating Forced Air, Natural Gas
Roof Concrete Tile
Cond New Construction, No Additions/Alter
Structural Other Custom Built, 220V In Kitchen, 220V In Laundry, Termite Clearance

Cooling Central
Plumbing
Sprinklers Front, Side and Rear, Sprinkler Timer

Floors Hardwood, Marble, Wall-to-Wall Carpet
Patio Patio, Rock
Doors/Windows French Doors, French/Mullioned Windows

=Lot/Community/Association=

APNO		Zoning	Lot/Block/Tract
Lot Horse Property, Lot Over 40,000 SqFt			Mello Roos N
Sewer In, Connected & Paid	Legal Homeowners Association, No Special Study Area, Not In Flood Zone		
HS Dist Capistrano Unified School District Amenities	Water District	Yard Stucco Wall, Wrought Iron, Yard, Block Wall	
	Elemen WAGONWHEEL	Junior LAS FLORES	High Sch TESSORO
Units 2	HOA Dues $ 277 + $ 0		
Land Fee	Lse Trans $	Land Lse/Yr $	Lse Ren Lse Exp

=Financial Information=

Terms Cash, Cash To New Loan		Tax Amt $14243	Total Assessed Value $ 1,317,767	
1st TD $ Type Interest %	2nd TD $	Type	Interest % Seller Pnts	

=Listing Office/Agent Info=

List Office	Office	Fax	Res
List Agent	Pager	Cell	Primary
Agt E-Mail		Agt WSite	

Priv Rmks And Behind Private Gates W/Camera. Professional Landscaping & Hardscaping. No Need To Preview, Please Provide 24hr Notice.

Price Excl Coe +7
Occupant Owner   Occupant Name Owner

=Listing Activity=

List Date 5/5/2004	Date Added 5/7/2004	Tran Date 1/6/2005	DOM 245	COE: 12/8/2004	LP/SqFt $546.95
Org Price $ 5,685,000	Prev Price $ 5,685,000	Cur List Prc $5,400,000		Off market 12/8/2004	Comp 2.5%

=Pending/Sold Information=

List Price$5,685,000	Financing Conventional	Selling Terms	
Cont Price $		Begin Escrow 1/5/2005	Closed 12/8/2004
Sold Price $ 5,400,000	SP/SqFt $ 519.53	Sold/List 95%	DOM 245

=Selling Office/Agent Info=

Sell Office	Office	Fax	Res
Sell Agent	Pager	Cell	V-Mail
Agt E-Mail		Agt WSite	

Listing on the MLS

Submitting the listing to an MLS is the first marketing activity you should perform once the property is ready for showings. Each MLS will have a method for submitting a listing. Most of them require the listing agent to complete a form where the agent must list all details of the property. Be sure to include detailed and accurate information about the listing. MLS members have the option of downloading a limited number of photos available for online viewing. Be sure to include photos of the property because listings without photos do not attract buyers.

Lockbox and "For Sale" Sign

Install the lockbox (usually on the front door), put up an outdoor flyer holder with color flyers, and place "For Sale" signs at the front of the property. The "For Sale" sign is widely recognized as the number one marketing tool. It should be big enough for passersby to read easily, and it should always include your name and contact information. Develop distinctive signage that stands out. If the property is in an association, be sure to follow its rules regarding placement of signs.

The "For Sale" sign is the most widely recognized real estate marketing tool that is available 24/7.

Staging the Home

Most sellers are proud of their homes and may not see its flaws. If they choose not to make minor improvements to their property, there are other things that can be done to make the home more appealing to buyers. This process is referred to as **staging**. To help your sellers stage their home, walk around the property with them and help them view it from the buyers' eyes.

A good salesperson will inform sellers of areas of the home that need improvement. Highlighting attractive features of the home is also part of the staging process. Sellers who are serious about selling their home will listen to the salesperson's advice.

A clean house is important. It should not look like this.

Staging Tips

- The most important thing to buyers is that the home is spotlessly clean, both inside and outside. Kitchens and bathrooms should look and smell clean. Remove clutter from countertops and organize cupboards. New caulking around bathtubs, showers, and basins makes them look fresh and clean.

- The home must also smell clean. If the home has an offensive odor, buyers will not stay long enough to see its good points. If a home is odor-challenged, tactfully suggest ways to eliminate any odors. You might suggest burning candles, using an air purifier, cleaning the carpet, or painting.

- Buyers know that they are not looking at a model home, but they do not want to see dirty clothes, toys scattered around the room, unmade beds, or garden hoses snaking across the patio.

- Pack up personal items such as photo collections and knick-knacks. Buyers need to see how their own personal belongings will look in their new home.

- Sometimes rearranging furniture or storing excess pieces can make living areas appear more attractive and spacious.

- Remember to tell the sellers to lock up their valuables, jewelry, and money. Even though prospective buyers will be escorted by a salesperson, it is impossible to watch everyone all the time.

- **Curb appeal** is the first impression of a home when seen from the street. A home with good curb appeal invites people inside. If a home has manicured lawns and flowerbeds, sparkling windows, clean walkways and driveways, buyers will think the interior of the home is also clean and well maintained. A new front doormat is an excellent way to welcome prospective buyers.

Closet space is usually important to buyers, so make the closets appear more spacious by storing seasonal clothes and packing up any unused items.

How Would You Stage This Room?

Before

After

Entertainment Center: cabinet closed
Fireplace: clothing, pillows, books, CDs removed
Couch: clothing, book, toy, CD player and blanket removed, cushions straightened
Furniture: white chair and foot rest removed from room
Glass table: clutter removed and plant added
Walls: picture placed above couch, crayon mark removed
Floor: gym bag and cardboard boxes removed from room, rug straightened, floor cleaned

Marketing the Listing

Now that the listing is in the MLS and the property is staged and ready for showing, it is time to market the listing. The best marketing tools for selling a home are not complicated or expensive. You need to schedule a caravan for other real estate professionals, put the listing information online, place ads in the newspaper, prepare flyers, and hold open houses.

Schedule Previews of the Property

Remember to tell the sellers that salespeople will preview their home and hopefully return with serious buyers. Then, schedule a time for an office preview. The **office preview** is for the other salespeople in the office to preview the listing and get a "head start" on selling it. They may have buyers who are perfect for the listing. In addition, ask that the new listing is included in the weekly caravan. The **caravan** is similar to an office preview, but it is open to all the members of the MLS.

Online advertising is another method of marketing the listing.

Online Advertising

With the advent of the Internet, online advertising is no longer a luxury for sales associates but rather a necessity. Real estate information is readily available to buyers and sellers on the Internet. Brokers and sales associates have the opportunity to reach these prospects from across the globe. Post the property on your personal website or your company's website. Be sure to include at least one picture of the property and all the important information about the listing. You may even choose to include a virtual tour of the home. The **virtual tour** allows you to hold an open house online 24/7 and the property looks its best at all times.

Newspaper Advertising

Advertise in the large regional newspaper and any smaller local papers that carry real estate ads and have wide readership. Include information about your online listing so that buyers can access additional information and financing tools. You can even include your web page address.

Many buyers begin their search by looking at the classified ads and display ads in the real estate section of the newspaper. **Classified ads** are ads that use only text and are great when you first take a listing because they cost very little. **Display ads** are those including text and photos, and usually are placed by the brokerage company in the weekend real estate section. Call the local newspaper the day after taking a listing and put a three-line ad in the classified section to run for 3 or 4 days, or until the listing is added to the company brochure or a personal display ad.

Do not give too much away in your ad. Make the reader call you to find out more. Be sure to use the proper words for the property you are advertising. Know what style the property is before you name the style in your ad or brochure. For example, do not call a house with a red tile roof a Cape Cod home.

Make your ad appealing by painting a picture in the reader's mind of what the property is like. Writing successful ads begins and ends with emotions. Every good ad addresses the right brain (emotional) first and then the left-brain (logical). Research has shown that higher readership is due to ads that use figurative language (metaphors, puns, analogies, etc.) rather than literal wording (just the facts).

The following tips will help you write effective ads in less time:

- Categorize every home and buyer into two types—comfort or status. Does the house evoke images and feelings of comfort or status? If it is clearly one or the other, write the ad to that target audience.

- Does the home have a particular style, such as Tudor, Craftsman Bungalow, Ranch, or Cape Cod? Focus on the home's style.

- What does the home have that makes it better or different from comparable homes? Focus on the home's unique qualities.

- Play up any new features such as a new roof, appliances, paint, foundation, deck, etc.

- Ask the present owner what he or she loves best about the home and mention this in the ad.

Flyers

A **home flyer** is a property's "brochure". The purpose of this flyer is to provide quick facts and help buyers remember your property, so it should be clear and brief. Include all pertinent facts (address, price, number of bedrooms and bathrooms), highlight special features, provide your contact information, and include a picture of the property, if possible. Put flyers in a tube on your "For Sale" sign for people to pick up, and always provide one to anyone who views the property.

Some salespeople prepare a bound color brochure on each property, send it out to the top salespeople, and use it for the in-house marketing. They also include relocation information and school reports in the package.

Magazines

Many real estate brokerages run a monthly or quarterly magazine that features photos and descriptions of their listings, usually numbering about 50 at a time. These newsletters or magazines can reach prospects via direct mail, grocery store magazine stands, or newspaper "street boxes".

HOLDING A SUCCESSFUL OPEN HOUSE

Open houses draw serious buyers, as well as those just checking out the area. Holding an **open house** is a prospecting activity that markets the house and allows prospective buyers to visit the property spontaneously. The main purpose of having an open house is to find a buyer for that particular house as well as to attract other prospective buyers and sellers. Holding open houses is an ongoing activity that produces new business and usually leads to a long, successful real estate career.

Why Hold An Open House?

A listing agent may offer to hold a certain number of open houses for a seller as part of a listing presentation and marketing strategy. The seller's primary motivation for allowing the open house is to invite prospective buyers to visit the property and possibly make an offer to purchase the property. The reasons a listing agent should hold an open house are to market and sell the property as well as to meet prospective buyers and sellers.

Market and Sell the Open House

When marketing, remember the main objective of the open house is to sell the house! An open house can create a sense of urgency for a buyer because other people are looking at the house and may want to buy it. Buyers tune in to buying signals. One couple discussing the house may make another couple more interested in buying it.

Get Appointments

The primary goal when holding an open house is to sell the property. Another goal is to make appointments with prospective buyers and sellers. Appointments are made to make an offer on this or other properties, to show property, to prepare a market analysis on their current home, and to determine affordability.

Meet Prospective Buyers

One open house objective is to meet prospective buyers. Approximately 90% of the open house attendees who actually buy homes will purchase a different home than the one they visit. The house that is being held open rarely matches the requirements of prospective buyers, but it gives the sales associate an opportunity to discover what features prospective buyers like or dislike. For example, a prospective buyer may ask how many bedrooms the house has. Assuming it is a three-bedroom house, the answer should be, "Are you looking for a three bedroom home like this one?" If they say that they need four bedrooms, the sales associate will want to be able to discuss any available four-bedroom houses in the neighborhood. Therefore, the sales associate holding the open house must know inventory near the open house well.

In addition, if a sales associate has met prospective buyers but has not been able to make appointments with them, inviting them to the open house serves as an opportunity to build rapport.

Meet Prospective Sellers

Most sales associates do not think about prospective sellers when holding open houses. Some sales associates think that seeking buyers is their only job and often ignore the best clients who come to their open houses. Sales associates will often have a prospect come to an open house and say, "I'm just a neighbor", as they walk in. The sales associate should politely invite them in and say, "Feel free to look around", then go back to the door and wait for a buyer to come in. This "closet seller" may be the best prospect to enter the open house all day.

Greeting prospective sellers at an open house may lead to a new prospect.

Neighbors - The Hidden Prospect

Neighbors like to know the home values in their neighborhood. When they show up at the open house, they are checking out their competition and comparing it to their own home. If a neighbor drops by the open house, sales associates at the open house should make a mental note and at the first opportunity add the name and address of that neighbor to his or her list of prospective sellers. Having a laptop computer available would make it easy and quick to enter any information gathered by the focused sales associate. Your follow up with this contact might include a thank you note for attending the open house. Since potential sellers conduct informal interviews by visiting open houses to determine if they would feel comfortable with the sales associate as their representative, a sales associate should consider anyone who comes in the door as a potential prospect.

When speaking with neighbors, a sales associate should ask if they have given any thought to selling their home, or if they know friends or acquaintances who would be interested in a home like the one being held open. They may know of someone who could be a buyer for this home. Neighbors who come to the open house may not be thinking of selling soon, but are looking toward the future. If the sales associate asks if they are considering selling, they will probably say no. If the sales associate instead asks, "If you ever sold your house where would you move?" followed by, "And when would that be?" the sales associate is much more likely to discover their true motivation. If a neighbor tells the sales associate that he or she is planning to sell next year upon retirement, that neighbor's name should be put on a follow-up program. The program will allow personal contact with them at least once a month until they are ready to sell.

Who Holds the Open House?

Most seasoned sales associates list more than one property at a time and cannot hold all of their listings open themselves. This gives sales associates who have no listings, the opportunity to hold open houses for them. Ask successful sales associates in your brokerage if you can hold an open house for one of their listings. In many real estate offices, it is a standard practice to sign up for open houses at the weekly office meeting. A prudent sales associate, however, will be in touch with the top producers before the office meeting and get the OK a week or two in advance to hold the open house. The successful new sales associate, again, must be proactive and a step ahead to plan for success.

If the property sells because of the open house, both the listing sales associate and the sales associate who holds the open house are entitled to part of the commission. Remember, under the real estate agency law, if both sales associates work for the same broker, a dual agency is created providing both seller and buyer agree to it in writing.

Initially, sales associates should sign up to hold open houses in neighborhoods where they know the market. Sales associates holding open houses must be knowledgeable about the neighborhood inventory and be able to discuss the market with anyone who may ask. The house in which the open house is being held may not be quite right, but the house three doors down with the extra bedroom might be just what the visitors are looking for.

If a sales associate signs up for an open house that is not his or her listing, he or she should make sure the listing sales associate, as well as the seller, is aware that the house will be open on a certain date for certain hours. It is very embarrassing to show up at a seller's house on Sunday afternoon only to discover the sellers relaxing with no idea that the open house was scheduled. Speaking directly with the seller early in the week preceding the planned open house and prior to placing an ad is the most effective way of dealing with the date and time for the open house.

Signing Up to Hold an Open House

- **A house in the sales associate's farm.** A sales associate should use "Open House" signs with his or her name on them so that homeowners in the farm neighborhood begin recognizing the sales associate's name.

- **A house near the sales associate's farm**. If a sales associate is new and does not have any listings in his or her farm, a listed home nearby may be a good choice. The use of enough signs to guide buyers from the sales associate's farm area will indicate that he or she is hardworking.

- **A listing's first open house**. The first open house usually has the most visitors, especially by neighbors who could be possible sellers.

- **A well-priced property**. More buyers will visit the open house if they feel that the home is priced well for the neighborhood.

- **A well-located property**. If a house is in a neighborhood that is near or on major streets, more people will drive by the "Open House" signs. Properties that are easily accessible with "Open House" signs in clear view are more likely to receive potential clients and customers. Research in one city in California showed that 75% of the open house visitors stopped to see the house because they drove by the signs, even though all of the open houses in the study received good advertising in the local paper.

Promoting the Open House

First, select the dates and times for the open house. Usually, open houses are held on weekends, but they do not have to take place only on Saturdays and Sundays. Why not hold an open house from 4:00 p.m. to 6:00 p.m. on a weekday and catch people on their way home from work? These events also work well if you hold them during the lunch hour and serve food. Many prospects such as vacationers, job re-locaters, and retirees are available during the week to visit open houses.

Next, you need to make prospective buyers aware of the existence of the open house. The only way to attract visitors to an open house is to promote the open house effectively. Be sure to aggressively promote your open houses, especially the first few. The first open house after a property hits the market is the most important one. Be sure to promote the open house to neighbors in the area because they will be curious and some of them may be future buyers or sellers.

Advertise. Be sure that your office has placed an ad in the newspaper with the correct address, date, and hours of the open house.

Invite active sales associates in the area. A few days before the open house, send a personal invitation to active sales associates in the farm area where the open house is located. Include the open house information, and listing details along with a photograph of the house.

Coordinate with other sales associates. Coordinate with sales associates who also have listings in the neighborhood or surrounding area and are holding open houses on the same day. One broker suggested staggering the times of open houses in an area so that attendees will be guided adeptly from one listing to the next.

Deliver invitations to nearby neighbors. Prior to the open house, take brochures and open-house invitations personally to nearby neighbors.

Place Open House signs. A friendly way to make contact with possible prospects, either buyers or sellers, is by posting an open house sign on their property. Be sure to request permission before placing the sign on their property. Also, send a thank you note to the neighbor after the open house has taken place, thanking the homeowner for the use of his or her lawn. This could keep the lines of communication open and future business a possibility.

Placing an Open House sign on a neighbor's property is one way to make contact with a possible client. Be sure to get the neighbor's permission.

Telephone the homeowners in the area. Either prior to or during the open house, place calls using a reverse directory or the Internet to get telephone numbers to homeowners in areas outside of the neighborhood whose home values are 10-20% less than the open house. These homeowners may be ready to move up to a new neighborhood and would respond favorably to an invitation to the open house. Always refer to the Do Not Call Registry before making uninvited calls.

Communicate with other business prospects. Tell prospects, past clients, friends, and acquaintances about the open house and invite them to come for refreshments and to see the house.

Preparation for an Open House

When getting ready for an open house two things must be done: (1) prepare the sales associate and (2) prepare the house for showing.

Preparing the Sales Associate

The sales associate should wear appropriate professional attire to the open house. He or she will not get a second chance to create a favorable first impression, so use the opportunity to present a well-dressed, confident businessperson. The visitors should not have to guess who is in charge. An identifying name badge is helpful, as well as a stack of business cards with the sales associate's picture on each card.

Sales associates should wear appropriate professional attire at an open house.

The sales associate's vehicle should be parked away from the house, leaving the best parking spots, including the driveway, for visitors. In addition, the front or back window of the sales associate's parked car could be used to display additional signs pointing to the open house.

Visit the house prior to the first open house. The sales associate should know everything about the house that could be important to a buyer. A sales associate should know the size of the house, listing price, items included in the sale, number of bedrooms and baths, age of the roof, any special features, school district, neighborhood benefits, personal property excluded from the sale, and anything else that would be of interest to the buyer. In addition, the sales associate should know if the existing loan is assumable or if there is a prepayment penalty for an early payoff.

It cannot be stressed enough that a sales associate needs to know the neighborhood in which the open house is located. It is reasonable to believe that if a neighbor asks about other nearby sales or competitively priced properties, they are interested in the open house or are possibly potential sellers. The sales associate holding the open house needs to be able to discuss other available properties. Remember, the reason the sales associate is there is to create new business, and the only way to do that is to outshine the competition.

The sales associate should bring a net sheet prepared for a full-price offer, a copy of the listing, a blank offer to purchase, and a calculator or loan software program loaded onto a laptop computer to calculate financing options.

Preparing the Property for Showing

Part of the listing agent's duty is to prepare the owners and the property for the open house. Certain measures may be taken by the property owner to make the house more attractive.

The sales associate holding the open house should make sure the entire property looks inviting:

- Close the garage door and open the front door unless weather does not permit. If the front door must remain closed, place another large open house sign near the door.

- Sometimes sales associates may need to put dirty dishes into the sink or dishwasher and tidy up the rest of the rooms.

Clean up dirty dishes so the kitchen looks clean and inviting.

- If items appear strewn about on the patio, move them into a neat pile or a storage area where they are not in view.

- Leave all of the lights on in the house, even on a sunny day.

The home should smell inviting as well. A couple of drops of vanilla on some aluminum foil in a warm oven will give the impression of cookies baking in the kitchen. A house with unpleasant odors, such as pets, strong cooking smells, or lingering cigarette smoke, is difficult to sell. Encourage the owners to make the necessary changes to freshen up the home. The sensitive sales associate will approach this subject with tact and good judgment.

On cooler days, a fire in the fireplace can make a house much more inviting and "homier". A sales associate, however, should always get permission from the owner before using the fireplace to make sure it works properly. If the fireplace works fine and the owner gives permission, the sales associate can use one firelog, which will burn for about three hours, the typical length of an open house.

A fire in the fireplace on cooler days can make a home feel "homey".
Be sure to ask the homeowner if you may use the fireplace.

How Would You Create Curb Appeal for This House?

Before

After
- Replace shingles
- Repair down spout
- Paint house
- Replace door and sidewalk
- Remove antenna from roof
- Remove garbage can, lawn mower, toys, bike
- Landscape to include flowers, bushes, and lawn repair
- Relocate outside electrical outlet from beside front door

Review – Getting the Home Ready for the Open House

- **Boost curb appeal.** Mow the lawn, manicure the yard, or plant a few colorful flowers. Make sure the walkway and front porch are clear from clutter, debris, leaves, ice, or snow. Spruce up the front door with a fresh coat of paint, a seasonal wreath, or new hardware.

- **Clear the clutter.** Nothing turns away prospective buyers more than a messy house. Clear the counters, get rid of the knickknacks, limit the number of family photos and personal items on display, etc. If the sellers have too much furniture, put some in storage. If the closets are full, take some clothes out—the fewer clothes hanging in them, the larger the closets will appear.

- **Clean.** Dirt is the enemy. Be sure every nook and cranny is clean, from the kitchen to the laundry room to the kids' rooms. Do not forget the windows.

- **Music.** Turn on easy listening CDs or soft jazz to provide a peaceful setting.

- **Working order.** Make sure everything is working properly. Fix all squeaking hinges, loose knobs, and stuck drawers.

- **Pretty it up.** Place fresh flowers in several locations throughout the house for visual appeal and a pleasant aroma. If it is fall or winter, have a fire in the fireplace, with the permission of the seller.

- **Sellers gone.** Make sure the sellers are out of the house. Potential buyers want to take time to tour the entire house, and may feel rushed or uncomfortable if the sellers are there.

Showing the Home – The Open House

Finally, the day of the open house has arrived. A house crawling with eager prospects ready to do business is only a dream, but here are some tips that may turn that dream into a reality.

The Greeting

Greet visitors personally with warmth and relaxed friendliness. You may begin to gain the visitors' confidence by allowing them to talk about themselves and their reasons for stopping at the open house. Hand buyers a short survey when they come through the door. Ask them questions about why they came, what they thought about the house, what they thought about your service, and what they want in a house.

A quiet persuasion will elicit more information from a prospect than a non-stop deluge of words that only tend to speed the prospect toward the front door. Match your demeanor to that of the guest rather than forcing your personality on the visitor. For example, if the prospects are the quiet type, approach them thoughtfully, giving them a reasonable amount of time to become comfortable. By watching and listening, you will discover what prospects want and need to know. After discovering the visitors' motivation, either by words or by actions, you can begin working toward getting the appointment to work with them.

Signing the Guest Book

As visitors enter the home, guide them toward a guest book while mentioning that the owners would like to know who visited the house today. Have them sign in with their name, address, telephone number, and e-mail address. You will be much more successful at getting names and phone numbers if you ask for them up front. Offer them a property information brochure

Visitors can be potential clients. Guide them toward the guest book and ask them to sign in with their name, address, telephone number, and email address.

and one of your business cards. It is a good idea to have a unique business card designed for the open house. On a personal computer, create and print a special business card with typical personal information on one side (name, address, telephone, cell phone). On the other side, place a photo, and details of the home held open, and give them to all visitors.

When visitors sign the guest book, ask them to include their e-mail address. Offer to send them your monthly e-newsletter containing current sales and listings, as well as other local market conditions such as financing opportunities and interest rates.

If you have a digital camera, let visitors take photos of the parts of the home they especially like. Tell them you will e-mail the photos to them later that day so they can compare their memory of the home with the actual photos taken. This is also another opportunity to connect with the prospect.

Not all visitors to the open house will be local, and some will probably have questions about the area features, such as schools, markets, recreation, churches, and transportation. Create a virtual tour of the area, with a personal narrative, on your laptop computer, leaving it open and running during the entire open house. This is useful when several prospects arrive at the same time and you may be overwhelmed. Make multiple copies of this tour to give to visitors.

Escorting the Visitors

Escort visitors through the house and allow them to browse freely, only contributing information when necessary, such as pointing out the benefits of the property that may not be obvious to the visitors. Do not point out the obvious, such as "This is the living room" instead, say, "Is this living room  spacious enough for your lifestyle?", or "Is your present kitchen open to the family area like this one?" Pointing out particular features that the visitor may miss and discovering what they do or do not like about the house is the most beneficial way to show the house.

Sample Qualifying Questions

- "Does anything about the house specifically appeal to you?"

- "Do you live in the area?"

- "How long have you been looking for a home?"

- "Have you seen anything that you liked?" If yes, "Did you make an offer on it?" If no, "Why not?"

- "Do you need to sell your existing home to be able to buy a new one?"

- *"Do you want to buy this house?"* This is a fun question. Most people are somewhat shocked that you are that direct. However, why would you hold the open house if you do not want to know the answer from everyone in attendance.

Look For Buying Signals

Watch for buying signals. It is a matter of being sensitive to what the visitor needs before he or she can make the decision to become a buyer. If clients are lingering, offer to let them go through the house again.

Remember the purpose of the open house is to create new business. Ask qualifying questions to determine what the visitor's wants and needs are. For example, if the prospect asks, "How much is this house?" you would respond, "It is $325,000. Are you comfortable in that price range?"

Offer Lending Assistance

Have a lender on hand or on-call to prequalify buyers and answer questions about loans. It is a good idea to have information available on what the down payment and monthly mortgage payments would be. This is a beneficial service for buyers and an excellent way to be better than the competition.

Suggest Other Properties

As we have seen, most buyers do not find their dream home at an open house. Have information available about your other listings, as well as brochures and information about the property you are holding open. They are more likely to find the perfect house while working with a sales associate who listens to what they want and shows them several possibilities that would fit their requirements. A PowerPoint® presentation of homes in the area in other price ranges or with other amenities (more bedrooms, family room, and bigger kitchen) can be created on your laptop computer to show a visitor who is not interested in the open house, but is interested in the area.

If this property does not meet the buyers' needs, suggest other properties, without giving addresses. Statements to use include, "We have many properties for sale. Would you like to visit other homes so you can determine which one is best for you? I would be glad to make an appointment to show you some of the other properties. Would later this afternoon or tomorrow be better for you?"

After the Open House

Leave the house as you found it by turning off the lights, closing the windows, and locking the doors. If a door was unlocked when you arrived and there were no specific instructions to lock it or leave it unlocked, lock it. It is much easier to deal with locking out the owner than explaining how someone burglarized the house.

If you were diligent about getting the names, addresses, and phone numbers of all of the people who came to the open house, now is the time to capitalize on it. A personal thank you note and telephone call the next day make a good impression on potential clients. Do not forget to thank the listing sales associate if he or she provided you with the opportunity to hold the open house.

That evening or the next morning, call all prospects who visited the open house, ask if they saw any houses they liked well enough to take a second look, and offer to make appointments for showings. If they did not see anything of interest, find out exactly what type of property they are looking for and help them find it. Remember, as with all prospecting activities, the goal is to make an appointment with the client. You cannot sell them a house over the phone.

SUMMARY

Servicing listings is an area that can make or break your reputation. Preparing a home for maximum appeal to buyers is known as **staging**. A seller who is serious about selling his or her home will listen to the advice given to them by a real estate salesperson. Communication is a crucial element to effectively servicing a listing. Communicating the seller's expectations clearly and concisely is perhaps the single most important way you can foster trust and loyalty.

There are many ways to advertise in real estate. The majority of listings sell through the MLS and other salespeople. Offline advertising, flyers, open houses, and signs are also widely recognized marketing tools.

Holding open houses should be one of the ongoing activities to produce new business. The main reasons a sales associate should hold an open house are to take care of seller's interests, meet prospective buyers, meet prospective sellers, and to sell the open house. The primary goal when holding an open house is to close for an appointment. The reasons to make an appointment include making an offer, showing property, preparing a market analysis on their current home, and determining affordability.

UNIT 10 REVIEW

Matching Exercise

Instructions: Write the letter of the matching term on the blank line before its definition. Answers are in Appendix A.

Terms

A. caravan

B. classified ads

C. communication

D. curb appeal

E. display ads

F. home flyer

G. office preview

H. open house

I. staging

J. virtual tour

Definitions

1. _____ A crucial element to service a listing effectively

2. _____ Preparing a home for maximum appeal to buyers

3. _____ The first impression of a home when seen from the street

4. _____ An opportunity for all the members of the MLS to preview the listing

5. _____ An online video that allows you to show the interior of a home 24/7 without the hassle of holding an open house, and the property looks its best at all times

6. _____ Ads that use only text and are great when you first take a listing because they cost very little

7. _____ Ads that include text and photos, which are placed by the brokerage company in the weekend real estate section

8. _____ The property's "brochure"

▧ Multiple Choice Questions

Instructions: Circle your response and go to Appendix A to read the complete explanation for each question.

1. Since communication is important when servicing listings, how can salespeople meet their clients' expectations?
    a. Set up a schedule of communication
    b. Call them with weekly updates
    c. Both a and b
    d. Neither a nor b

2. The most effective way to service a listing is by:
    a. staging the home.
    b. heavily marketing the listing.
    c. maintaining a high level of communication.
    d. doing all of the above.

3. Which of the following statements is incorrect?
    a. Submitting the listing to an MLS is the first marketing activity you should perform once the property is ready for showing.
    b. Most listings sell without being placed on an MLS.
    c. The "For Sale" sign is widely recognized as the number one marketing tool.
    d. If the property is in an association, be sure to follow its rules regarding placement of property "For Sale" signs.

4. One way to prepare the home for sale is to:
    a. display photo collages of the seller's family.
    b. organize kitchen cupboards.
    c. hide unnecessary items in the closets.
    d. hire an interior decorator.

5. An effective advertisement contains:
    a. heavy verbiage.
    b. an emotional component.
    c. literal wording.
    d. both a and c.

6. One of the main reasons for a sales associate to hold an open house is to:
    a. sell the house at a higher price.
    b. meet prospective sellers.
    c. meet unqualified buyers.
    d. earn a commission faster.

7. Which of the following items should sales associates have at an open house?
    a. A net sheet prepared for a full price offer
    b. A spreadsheet showing their amount of the commission
    c. A completed offer to purchase
    d. All of the above

8. In order to improve the appearance of the property during an open house, a listing agent should:
    a. turn on the latest music with the volume up to attract attention.
    b. park an expensive vehicle on the driveway.
    c. clear any clutter to avoid a disorderly appearance.
    d. close all of the drapes and blinds.

9. While escorting visitors through an open house, sales associates should:
    a. allow them to browse freely.
    b. watch for and be sensitive to buying signals.
    c. have down payment and mortgage payment information available.
    d. do all of the above.

10. After the open house, sales associates should never:
    a. turn off all the lights.
    b. leave the doors unlocked and the windows open.
    c. let the sellers know the results of the open house.
    d. send a thank you note and call all visitors who came to the open house.

Working With Buyers

Unit 11

INTRODUCTION

Prospective buyers choose a real estate salesperson differently than sellers. Sellers typically establish an **exclusive agency relationship** with their listing broker and promise to pay a commission to that broker after the sale of the property. Buyers, however, do not have to work exclusively with one salesperson. In fact, buyers may work with as many salespeople as they wish.

Top producers know they must earn the trust and loyalty of a buyer before that buyer will work with them exclusively. Representing buyers requires familiarity with local property, knowledge of real estate law, disclosures, finance, agency, an understanding of consumer behavior, and the ability to write an offer to purchase.

This unit covers today's buyers, the influence of the Internet, and the different types of buyer representation. You will learn how to take a prospect through the buying process from your first contact to getting ready to write an offer.

Learning Objectives

After reading this unit, you should be able to:

- identify the different types of buyer representation.
- complete a list of important questions to ask a prospect before showing properties to them.
- describe why salespeople should view objections as a positive aspect of the sales process.

BUYER REPRESENTATION

Traditionally, no one had a clear legal responsibility to act in the buyer's interest. As time went by, the selling agent's position began to evolve and more light was shed on their specific duties. The law tends to look at the buyer-agent relationship in terms of a perceived obligation. In other words, if a salesperson or broker acts as if they represent the buyer, the law considers the agency a lawful fiduciary relationship. Therefore, boundaries exist that help distinguish the listing agent and the selling agent who both work in the best interest of their respective client.

Remember, California requires a **real estate agency disclosure** by a real estate broker working with a buyer or seller. The steps in the disclosure process (disclose, elect, confirm) are the same when working with buyers and sellers. In the course of their careers, most brokers alternate between representing the seller when listing a property and representing the buyer when showing properties to prospective homeowners. The important thing to remember when it comes to agency disclosure is who is representing whom.

If a buyer is working exclusively with a broker, the broker must first present a written disclosure regarding the agency relationship before entering into an agreement. If the buyer is not working with the broker exclusively, the selling agent (who may also be the listing agent) must provide a written disclosure regarding the agency relationship before the buyer makes an offer to purchase.

Types of Buyer Representation

Sellers may hire a listing agent who clearly represents them in the sale. On the other hand, a buyer has three possible choices of representation. When discussing the three types of buyer representation, "agent" refers to the broker. Remember, the salesperson is the agent of the broker, not the buyer or seller. The broker is the agent of the buyer or seller. In other words, the broker represents the buyer or seller because, even though the salesperson acts on the broker's behalf, the broker is the one who is ultimately responsible in all transactions. The buyer could be represented exclusively by a **buyer agency**, participate in a **dual agency** relationship with the seller, or have no representation at all.

Buyer Single Agency

The agent owes exclusive loyalty to a buyer, for an agreed-upon fee or commission, to be paid by the buyer. A **buyer's broker** is an agent who represents only the buyer and has a fiduciary duty to find the best house for the least money at the terms most favorable to his or her principal (the buyer). Real estate law requires a disclosure of agency with a buyer in every transaction, but does not require an exclusive agency with the buyer. A buyer's broker, however, requires the buyer to work only with him or her for a certain timeframe. Some buyer's brokers represent buyers exclusively and do not accept listings.

The benefit of this type of agreement to the salesperson is the certainty of a commission after spending time and effort to find the right property. The salesperson does not have to worry about buyers writing an offer with another salesperson. The benefit to buyers is that the salesperson is working diligently to find what they want. Buyer expectations are high because buyers are secure in the belief that the work ethic of their salesperson will produce the best fit for their needs. However, if buyers decide not to honor the agreement, buyers may still be responsible for paying a commission if buyers make an offer on a home with another salesperson that the buyers' broker previously showed them.

There is no set rule about who actually pays the buyer's broker a commission. The fee of the buyer's broker will be paid either by the buyer or by the seller. Remember, a seller agrees to pay the listing broker a certain percentage of the selling price as a commission. In a traditional transaction, the salesperson representing the buyer would earn 3% or half of a typical 6% commission. Customarily, the commission is part of the listed price as stated in the listing agreement. The buyer's broker must state, in the offer, how he or she intends to be paid. If the buyer has agreed to pay the broker, that amount may be deducted from the listed price. Some buyer's brokers work on an hourly basis or for a set fee that the broker negotiates with the client.

Dual Agency

In a dual agency, the selling agent is also the listing agent, representing both buyer and seller, requiring the knowledge and consent of both. The existence of the dual agency, with its implied conflict of interest, requires written disclosure prior to making an offer or as soon as practicable.

No Agency Relationship

The majority of buyers work with a salesperson (sometimes several) without the benefit of a legally binding agency relationship. Many buyers prefer this approach because it allows them to shop around for a salesperson. The buyers will settle for the agent who finds them a property to purchase. This arrangement does not require the buyer to sign an exclusive contract, nor does it require any loyalty on the part of the buyer to any agent. In this case, the broker or sales associate must have the buyer sign a written agency disclosure statement before writing the offer to purchase.

Consumers have had the opportunity to work exclusively with buyer's brokers since the 1980s, but for obvious reasons buyers have resisted the opportunity to work with only one salesperson. A lack of confidence in the professionalism and ability of a single salesperson is the primary reason a buyer chooses to work with several salespeople. Many of the larger brokerage firms, however, are training their new salespeople to work exclusively with buyers. It takes a confident, able, and strong-willed salesperson to convince a buyer of the benefits of an exclusive relationship.

PROSPECTING FOR BUYERS

Every sale starts with the challenge of finding a buyer. Whether it is through prospecting, referral, or as a response to an ad, you will have spent time and effort trying to attract the prospect. It is up to you to create a professional relationship with the buyer. The buyer must be confident of your abilities and knowledge of the market. The way to build buyers' confidence is to educate them about real estate transactions, especially if they are first-time buyers. Listen to their questions, be responsive to their needs, and always provide timely, professional service.

Many of the techniques you use in prospecting for sellers are equally effective in finding buyer clients. Never pass up the opportunity to work the up-desk for call-in and walk-in leads. Contact your sphere of influence to let them know you would like to help them or their friends find a home. Work open houses. Be sure that all visitors sign the guest book and, if possible, chat with them, not just about this listing, but also about their general buying needs.

Contact FSBOs, not for the purpose of listing their current home, but to assist them in finding a new home. Target renters who may be ready and able to buy a home. Obtain bridal registry lists from department stores. In a year or so, these newly married couples may be considering home ownership.

Put a buyers' section on your website with information on schools, shopping, and services in your marketing area. Include items such as a buyer checklist for evaluating a home. Get buyers' e-mail addresses and permission to contact them with market information and current listings.

Develop contacts with the human resources departments of any major employers in your area and offer your services for relocating employees. Offer home-buying or other real estate-related seminars to the public, organizations, and clubs. Many members may have interest in move-ups, second homes, or retirement communities.

Who Are Today's Buyers?

Not all buyers are the same. General demographic guidelines on the buying habits of different groups can provide you with a starting point when working with consumers.

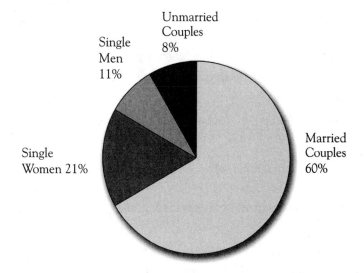

Real Estate Market Demographics (Buyers/Sellers)

Baby Boomers

Baby Boomers were born between 1946 and 1964 and are currently the largest generation in the history of the nation. Counting nearly 81 million people, with some 40 million households, baby boomers have a strong desire for home ownership. Many have bought and sold several properties, and are a ready market for upscale and second homes. Baby boomers are the dream customers of the real estate industry because they are stable, successful, financially secure, and retirement-ready.

> Home Buying Influence: Studies show that Baby Boomers have the desire and usually the financial ability to remain homeowners, but their preferences differ from the traditional single-family housing. They want housing that is easy to maintain and is close to shopping, recreational areas, and medical facilities.

Closing Baby Boomers:

- Listen to what type of features they want or need in their new home.
- Don't waste their time. Only show available properties that meet their criteria.
- Provide information to support your claims about home values, economic trends, and your qualifications.
- Add intelligent humor to some of your marketing and follow-up materials.
- Consider using uncluttered marketing pieces printed with a larger type.
- Strive to give professional service and exceed expectations.

Generation X

The next group of homebuyers, **Generation X**, was born between 1961 and 1981. The 44 million members of this group are prosperous, educated, and home ownership is a priority. With a high percentage of Generation X women in the workplace, these dual-income families purchase larger homes.

> Home Buying Influence: Generation X prefers homes with amenities such as gourmet kitchens, dressing rooms, whirlpool tubs, walk-in multi-faucet showers, and natural floor coverings such as stone, tile, or hardwood. To accommodate their vehicles and recreational toys, they need oversized garages.

Generation Y

Generation Y (also known as the Millennium Generation) are the children of Generation X. Born between 1982 and 2000, their numbers (more than 70 million) have led to growth in the housing market because some of them are old enough to buy homes. They are open to new ideas and are the most environmentally conscious generation since the Baby Boomers. Today, they are new first-time buyers. By 2015 to 2020, they may be trade-up buyers.

Home Buying Influence: Given that many from Generation Y are growing up in homes their parents own, it is reasonable to believe they will value home ownership. They will be the key first-time buyer market after 2010 and the key trade-up market after 2020.

Closing Generation Y:

- Generation Y relates to technology. Make sure your website is interactive with colors, lots of data, and a system for responding to inquiries.

- Keep up with and use changing technology. This group "cut their teeth" on computers, cell phones, and digital communication.

Generation Z

These are children of Generation Y, having been born after 2001. They will not be first-time buyers until around 2025. This generation is being raised on technology. It will be interesting to see what their taste in housing will be.

The Influence of the Internet

According to the *NAR Profile of Home Buyers and Sellers*, approximately 90% of all buyers use the Internet during their home searches. Generally, Internet users are informed, anonymous, and in control. These buyers do their own research. They will not approach a real estate agent until they are ready, and remain private for as long as they wish (or until they find a salesperson they trust). They definitely are not the buyers of 10-20 years ago. These Internet-savvy users know what they want, they understand what to expect from a real estate salesperson, and they will not settle for less. Online real estate brokerage has arrived.

NAR Technology Impact Survey Report

- Increasingly, buyers and sellers use the Internet as their primary source of information.

- Nearly all REALTORS® use e-mail and the Internet for business.

- Two-thirds of all REALTORS® have a personal web page or site for their real estate business.

It is pointless to push Internet buyers to move faster or to reveal themselves before they are ready. To be effective when working with Internet buyers, build relationships and offer services they cannot find on the Internet.

Because Internet buyers spend time researching properties, they have more real estate knowledge. Do not flood them with home buying basics. The best way to interact with Internet buyers is to acknowledge that they are doing part of your work. Make them aware of the extra value you will bring to the transaction such as interpreting data, answering questions, and writing offers. To help them locate a property, discuss their price range and home preferences. Be especially perceptive of the buyer's expectations, and be ready to modify your services and fees to get their business.

Internet Websites Frequented by Buyers

- **realtor.com**—Available listings.

- **homeseekers.com**—Available listings.

- **redfin.com**—Online brokerage for buying and selling homes. Provides real-time MLS updates, past sales records, and other data.

- **trulia.com**—Real estate search engine. Also allows users to access neighborhood statistics. Features blogs and advice from real estate professionals.

- **move.com**—Listings of available properties help buyers identify what they want and can afford. Also included are home buying tips, moving information, and links for related services.

- **realestate.com**—Home value tools and other real estate services.

- **zillow.com**—Real-time home value services.

- **mortgagebot.com**—Buyers can determine how much they can afford for a home.

- **forsalebyowner.com**—Listings by sellers without the assistance of a selling agent.

- **scorecard.org**—Zip code search for toxicities in a certain area.

- **ASHI.com**—The American Society of Home Inspectors lists inspectors by zip code and gives information on residential property inspections.

Turn Prospective Buyers into Clients

You know who your prospects are, but how do you convince them to use your services? Buyers do not know the "ins" and "outs" of buying a home because so much of what goes on is handled behind the scenes. You need to tell the buyers about all of the tasks that need to be done in order to buy the house. Let them decide if they have the time, knowledge, or expertise to handle the transaction. Usually they do not and look to you for help. At this point, give them a prepared list of all the things that you are capable of doing for them to make the process easier.

At this point, give them a prepared list of all the things that you are capable of doing for them to them to make the process easier.

Ask Your Buyers These Questions

* Do you have time to do residential housing market research?
* How do you find out which homes are available?
* Are you comfortable doing your own negotiating?
* Do you know how to find foreclosures or short sale listings?
* Do you have time to find a good lender?
* Do you know which type of title insurance to get?
* Have you chosen an escrow company?
* Do you know how to handle contingencies?
* Have you found a qualified home inspector?
* Are you aware of zoning regulations and building codes for the real estate area in which you are interested?
* Are you familiar with green technology and homes that incorporate energy efficiency?

QUALIFYING BUYERS

Before showing any properties, prequalify the buyers. To create a professional rapport with buyers, create a homebuyer's checklist and have prospects fill it out at their first opportunity.

Buyer's Profile

Many buyers know what they want, how much they can afford, and have a preapproval letter from a lender before they talk to a salesperson. Frequently, prospective buyers are completely unaware of financing options, real estate paperwork, and inspections—in short—almost everything about a real estate transaction.

A well-prepared salesperson will use a buyer's profile. A **buyer's profile** is a prepared list of questions used to determine the buyer's motivation and how much may be spent on a home. This questionnaire can be emailed to the buyer prior to meeting, or it can be completed at the initial interview.

While some consumers are reluctant to release personal information, it is the only reliable way that a salesperson can determine what the buyer can afford. The buyer's profile, along with the buyer's needs and wants serves as a guide in selecting homes that will fit the buyer.

Buyer's Profile

Name(s)_____

Current address:_____ City_____

_____ State_____ Zip_____

Telephone (　)_____ E-mail_____ Best time to contact: AM PM

Current homeowner? YES NO
Current monthly payment $_____
Renting? YES NO
Monthly rental payment　$_____
When are you planning to move to a new property?　under
　　　　　　　　　　　　　　　　　　　　　　　　　a month　1-2 months　3-6 months　1 year　Over 1 year

Motivation for moving?_____

How long have you been looking for a new home?　under
　　　　　　　　　　　　　　　　　　　　　　　　　a month　1-2 months　3-6 months　1 year　Over 1 year

Are you selling your home before buying another?　　Yes　　No

Will you be using your equity to purchase a home?　　Yes　　No

Convenient monthly payment for new home $_____

Amount of down payment $_____

Price range for new home? From $_____　To $_____

When are you available to view new properties?						
M	T	W	Th	F	Sat	Sun
Time:	Time:	Time:	Time:	Time:	Time:	Time:
AM PM	AM PM	AM PM	AM PM	AM PM	AM PM	AM PM

What type of property are you currently seeking:　Single Family Home　Condo/ Townhome　Multi-Unit (duplex, fourplex)　Manufactured Home

Describe your dream home (location, square feet, style, # of bedrooms, baths, single story, pool, large yard, etc.)

Do you have a preferred lender?　　　　　　　　Yes　　No
Do you have a prequalification letter?　　　　　Yes　　No
Is there a prepayment penalty in your current loan?　Yes　　No

What is your estimated FICO score?　　　below 500 500-550 551-559 600-650 651-700 701-750 Over 750

Involve a Lender

If your clients have not been in touch with a lender, you will want to place them in contact with one before you begin searching for homes. One of your most important presale tasks is getting buyers prequalified or preapproved by a lender for a specified loan amount. This keeps you from wasting any time previewing properties the buyers cannot afford.

It is better to get buyers preapproved rather than prequalified prior to submitting an offer. A **preapproval letter** is a written commitment from a lender to loan a certain amount based on a written application by the buyer, while **prequalification** is based on verbal information supplied by the buyer. The mortgage broker, lender, or loan officer will provide a written letter, stating the mortgage amount the buyer has been approved for and the terms of the loan. This letter will give buyers an advantage when submitting an offer. Sellers are more inclined to accept an offer that involves preapproved buyers who can actually obtain the financing necessary to complete the transaction.

Many brokerages have a preferred lender. You may have to network on your own and find one you trust before referring them to your clients.

Lenders make loans to consumers based on standardized guidelines, using the consumer's income and expenses to determine whether they qualify for the loan. The risk factor for the lender must fall within a certain range for them to approve the terms of any one of a number of types of loans.

A preferred way to qualify a prospect is to let the lender prequalify them by telephone from your office or before your appointment with them. You can set up a telephone appointment with a loan representative prior to meeting with your customer. The loan representative will be able to tell the buyers the highest sales price and mortgage they can afford, the best type of loan for their needs, and what they have to do to get qualified.

Homebuyer's Checklist

Based on the buyer's profile or preapproval letter, you know how much the buyer can spend. Have the prospective buyer fill out the **Homebuyer's Checklist** to describe his or her ideal home. These questions are less intrusive than those in the buyer's profile. Explain that you would like as much information as possible so that you can understand their needs. If they are opposed to filling out a questionnaire due to time constraints, ask the most important questions and write down their responses so you can reference them when searching for a property.

ABC Real Estate Company
123 Main Street
Any City, California, 92654

HOMEBUYER'S CHECKLIST

Need	Want	Don't Want	TYPE
			Single Family
			Townhouse
			Condo
			New
			Existing

Need	Want	Don't Want	LOCATION
			Central
			Suburbs
			Outlying
			Away from Heavy Traffic
			Rural

Need	Want	Don't Want	NEAR
			Job
			Schools
			Medical Facilities (Hospital, etc.)
			Parks
			Public Transportation
			Airport
			Expressway
			Neighborhood Shopping
			Regional Mall
			Entertainment/Restaurants/Theaters

Need	Want	Don't Want	CONDITION
			Well Kept
			Fixer Upper
			Needs Minor Work

Need	Want	Don't Want	STYLE
			Traditional
			Contemporary
			Ranch
			Two Story
			Tudor
			Victorian
			Split Level
			Colonial
			Cape Cod
			Other

Need	Want	Don't Want	EXTERIOR
			Brick
			Stucco
			Aluminum Siding
			Vinyl Siding
			Wood Frame

Need	Want	Don't Want	SYSTEMS
			Heating: Boiler, Furnace, Oil (circle one)
			Central Air Conditioning
			Security
			Internet/Cable Ready

Need	Want	Don't Want	FLOOR PLAN
			Basement
			Finished Basement
			Attic
			Formal Foyer
			Formal Living Room
			Great Room
			Family Dining Room
			Office
			Media Room/Rec Room
			Mud Room/Laundry Room

HOMEBUYER'S CHECKLIST (Con't)

Need	Want	Don't Want	BATHROOMS
			Number:
			Shower
			Tub
			Double Sinks
			Dressing Area

Need	Want	Don't Want	BEDROOMS
			Number:
			Master Suite
			First-Floor Master Suite
			Walk-In Closet

Need	Want	Don't Want	KITCHEN
			Countertop Materials:
			New Appliances
			Eating Area
			Desk Area
			Pantry
			Center Island

Need	Want	Don't Want	GARAGE/PARKING
			Size:
			Street Parking
			Paved Driveway
			RV/Motorhome/Boat Parking
			Reserved or Deed Spot (for condos)

Need	Want	Don't Want	SPECIAL FEATURES/INTERIOR
			Fireplace
			Vaulted Ceilings
			High Ceilings
			Wood Floors
			Built-In Cabinets
			Big Closets
			Extra Storage Space
			First/Second Floor Laundry

Need	Want	Don't Want	EXTERIOR
			Good View
			Natural Light
			Backyard
			Garden
			Play Area
			Screened Porch
			Patio/Deck
			Barbecue Area
			Outdoor Lighting
			Fenced Yard
			Mature Trees
			Mature Shrubs
			Maintenance provided by HOA

Need	Want	Don't Want	COMMUNITY/NEIGHBORHOOD
			Gated
			Homeowner's Association
			Mello-Roos
			Highly-Rated Schools
			Tennis Courts
			Golf Course
			Parks
			Park Programs/Activities
			Health Clubs
			Sidewalks
			Local University/College
			Equestrian

Need	Want	Don't Want	LIFESTYLE
			Child-Friendly Spaces
			Pet-Friendly Spaces
			Sport/Basketball Court
			Room for Guests/Entertaining

The Homebuyer's Checklist allows the salesperson to find out exactly what the buyer is looking for in a home. If you let each buyer know that you hear and understand what he or she wants, the result will be future sales and referrals.

SHOWING PROPERTIES

Now, with your completed buyer's profile and Homebuyer's Checklist, you can narrow down the inventory of properties to meet your buyer's needs. The process of showing qualified properties to buyers varies depending on how many properties are available that fit their needs. The number of homes you show will also depend on how well the buyers communicated their requirements to you. If buyers forget to tell you that they want a home with a pool or that they require a three-car garage, you will waste precious time showing properties that will never work for them.

Scorecard and Digital Camera

Provide the buyers with a **scorecard** or paper to note what they like (or dislike) about each house.

Loaning a digital camera to the buyers will benefit both of you. It allows them to photograph the front exterior and all the features they find appealing in the homes shown. At the end of the day, these photos can be printed and attached to the scorecard the buyers have created for each property. For example, if your buyers want a fireplace, encourage them to take pictures of every fireplace they see in each home they are shown. Usually, after looking at five to six homes in one day, the individual features of each home begin to blur or blend. Photographs make it easier to remember which home had the fireplace that the buyers have "been wanting for years". These photos also give you an idea of what the buyers did or did not like, which may affect your future showings considerably.

Loan an inexpensive digital camera to out-of-town buyers to help them in their search for a new home. While driving around on their own, they can record properties that they would like to see, as well as the amenities of the surrounding neighborhood. The return of the camera permits you to see them again, at which time you can assure them that the photos will be printed, emailed, or sent on a disk to them.

ABC Real Estate Company
123 Main Street
Any City, CA 92654
(123) 456-7890
www.abcsalesrealty.xyz

HOME BUYER'S SCORECARD
Information to Help You Find the Right House

Basic Information

Home Address_____

General Description_____

Asking Price_____

General Condition

Curb Appeal _____ ☐

Age of House_____ ☐

Kitchen

☐ Cabinets

☐ Countertops

☐ Eat-in Kitchen

☐ Breakfast Nook

☐ Stove/Oven

☐ Built-in Microwave

☐ Refrigerator

☐ Dishwasher

☐ Garbage Disposal

☐ Trash Compactor

Bedrooms #_____

☐ Master Bedroom

☐ Dressing Room

☐ Special Features_____

☐ Special Features _____

☐ **Bathroom(s) #_____**

☐ **Living Room**

☐ **Formal Dining Room**

☐ **Family Room**

☐ **Den**

Special Amenities

☐ Attic/Basement

☐ Laundry Area_____

☐ Fireplaces   #_____ Where_____

☐ Flooring: Wood _____ Carpeting_____

Tile _____   Linoleum _____

☐ Closets _____   ☐ Storage_____

Buying a home is an emotional roller coaster for most people, and the process is different for everyone. As a real estate professional, you can guide buyers toward making this important decision.

Listen to the buyers. Do not waste their time or yours by showing homes that are outside of their price range. Stay within an affordable price range, and show properties on both the high and low end of their range.

Get familiar with the properties you are showing by previewing them before your scheduled appointment with the buyers. Learn about the properties in order to answer typical questions from the buyers.

What Buyers Frequently Ask:
- Square footage of house and size of the property
- Number and size of rooms
- Age and condition of house
- Asking price, assumable loans, and financing terms
- Any special features of the home
- Why the sellers are selling
- Proximity of schools, shopping, recreation, etc.
- Typical cost of taxes, insurance, association fees, and utilities
- Any encumbrances: taxes, assessments, liens, easements, deed restrictions, zoning and nonconforming uses

Be honest, comply with all disclosure requirements, and be sure to advise the buyers if there are any obscure or hidden negative conditions.

Project a relaxed and calm appearance during the showing. The buyers will sense if you are anxious about the sale or try to hurry them into a decision. Your body language, a loud voice, compulsive or repetitive talking, or dominating personality will give the buyers the impression that this is all about you, not them. Instead, speak quietly, be interested in the house, and answer any questions from the buyers with knowledge and intelligence.

If you are working with a couple, remember that they have a personal and unique relationship. If your buyers have a conflict or disagreement, stay neutral and tactfully withdraw from their immediate area. If one of the partners is particularly dominant, he or she might be the decision-maker for buying the property. Be sure to give that person all the information he or she needs to make a decision. While being helpful to the decision-maker, however, do not alienate the other person; give both partners equal respect and consideration.

Drive together with the buyers in one car to establish rapport and learn their likes and dislikes about the homes they have seen.

Provide transportation for the buyers to the property, but make sure your car is clean, neat, and comfortable. This is a good time to set up anticipation for the next home on the tour, because you can discover what they like and do not like about the homes they have seen.

Tour the route as you drive to each property. Show off the amenities of each neighborhood as well as the approach to each property. If possible, allow the buyers to view each property from across the street by parking on the opposite side of the street.

Only select a few homes to view during one showing. Viewing five or more homes becomes a confusing blur to the buyers, thus making an offer on any of them nearly impossible. Many theories exist about when or in what sequence to show houses. Should you show the best one or the worst one first? Usually, the easiest way is to arrange them geographically and let the buyers make their likes and dislikes known. If you have not taken a preview photo of the house(s) you are showing, encourage the buyers to take a photograph of the exterior. These photos or those you made on a preview visit can be included in a binder or notebook with other information about each house. After leaving each home, ask the buyers to rate it on a scale of one to ten (ten being the best) on their scorecard.

The salesperson should let the buyers control how fast they view a home.

Allow the buyers to set their own pace while viewing a home. Do not rush buyers from room to room.

The worst mistake you can make is to try to "sell" the home. Let the property speak for itself. Your **listening skills** will help you handle any objections voiced by the buyers that prevent them from seeing the benefits or advantages of the property.

Do not oversell. Avoid the use of superlatives when describing the homes the buyers have just seen or that they are about to see. Encourage them to use the scorecards and the digital camera to literally and visually remind them of the features they like (or dislike) in each of the homes you show them. Do not contradict a buyer's opinion of a property or defend a specific property if what the buyers are saying now is contrary to what they said earlier about the property.

Although you may feel that a specific house is just the one for them, remember that the final choice is still that of the buyers. Allow them to experience the excitement of finding "just what they are looking for". At the end of the day, discuss with the buyers all the features (good and bad) of each viewed home. This will help determine which homes you will show them the next time.

When you have seen every property, review the homes, along with the ratings and comments from the buyer's personal scorecard. If the buyers seem particularly drawn to one home, show the favorite property a second time. Take your buyers back for another look. However, before going back for that second look, call the sellers. Let them know that you visited once already and would like to return for another look. Sellers rarely will say "no" because this is a second chance for them to reinforce the "good" first impression or visit.

BUYING SIGNS

Most people buy because they see themselves living in a new home, so it is easier to appeal to them emotionally rather than logically. A salesperson should know what kind of lifestyle the buyers enjoy. They can sell the benefits by pointing out emotional features such as ocean views with brilliant sunsets, old oak trees scattered across rolling hillsides, or a swimming pool of sparkling blue water in the backyard.

Pay attention to the verbal and nonverbal communication of the buyers when you are showing properties to them. Ultimately, the buying decision will be influenced more by emotions rather than by facts. Certain clues, or **buying signs,** will help you recognize when buyers are seriously considering a property. "Which bedroom is Katie's?" or "Is there enough room for Grandmother's antique highboy?" These buying signs (or questions) are a good indication of buyers' interest in a property.

Some of the common buying signs you can expect to encounter when showing desirable properties to buyers are:

- **Touching**—Often people will see something they like and just have to "touch it", whether it is a textured wall or satiny smooth granite countertop. This tactile perception usually helps to influence buyers' decisions about a specific property.

- **Lingering**—If people are comfortable, they tend to linger. If buyers enter a home and are not comfortable, they usually will leave quickly and go to the next one. If buyers are relaxed and at ease in a property, they will view it at length, lingering and looking at each room several times.

- **Asking specifics**—While lingering, buyers often ask specific questions such as, "What is the down payment on this home?" This generally indicates to the agent that the buyers truly are interested in the property. As the buyers move closer to making an informed decision, they will ask for more information and look to affirm their positive feelings about the property.

- **Visualizing possession** —"Our dining set would look great here." "This room is just the right size for Katie." If your buyers are visualizing living in the property and are talking of furniture placement and of assigning rooms to family members, you can be certain that they are interested in the property. This is a very popular and common buying signal.

- **Reviewing outside opinions**—When buyers are ready to make a serious decision about purchasing property, they will often ask for the opinions of trusted and valued friends, relatives, and associates. These opinions may or may not sway the buyers' feelings about the property or final decisions, but they are a definite indication that the buyers are considering the property.

- **Minor objecting**—In addition to the previously mentioned buying signals, buyers often will present minor objections when they are considering a property. These may seem to indicate that the buyers dislike a property, but actually are strong signals that the property is being seriously considered.

Overcoming Objections

When buyers raise objections during or after a property showing, it is wise for the salesperson to view the objections as a positive part of the sales process. Objections actually show the buyers' interest (whether large or small) in a property. Another way to think of it is that if the buyers do not raise any objections, they may not be interested in the property at all. In addition, salespeople should welcome objections because they provide feedback on how the buyers feel, and that gives the salesperson a chance to address the objections.

Buyers raise objections for various reasons. Sometimes they are simply seeking more information about the property. Other times, they may be confused and are seeking your guidance or clarification. Yet another reason may be that they are having trouble making a decision. Some people dislike making decisions on their own and look to others to assist them.

Five Question Sequence Method of Overcoming Objections:

1. "There must be a good reason for your hesitation. Do you mind if I ask what it is?"
2. "In addition to that, is there any other reason for not going ahead?"
3. "Supposing we did 'this or that', would you want to go ahead?"
4. "Then there must be some other reason. May I ask what it is?"
5. "What else do you need to move forward?"

You can be certain that your buyers will raise objections. The most common objections buyers raise are in the areas of price, terms, personal property, deposit amount, and financing. It is your duty to expect, appreciate, and handle objections as they come your way. When you are aware of the common objections and have a plan for how you will address them, your fear of objections will diminish.

ASK FOR THE SALE

When you witness buying signals and feel confident that the property in question is right for your buyers, it is imperative that you ask for the sale. If you never ask, you may never know if the buyers are seriously interested in a property. In addition, asking for the sale helps buyers clarify their thoughts and feelings about what they really want. Asking them to make a decision forces them to come to terms with how they feel about a property in question. There will be times when the buyers have found what they are looking for, but, due to fear, they are unable to commit to a "yes". It is your job as the salesperson to help guide the buyers in decision-making, and help them realize when the time has come to make those decisions.

Always be prepared to write up an offer. You have worked hard to get the buyers to commit, so be sure to have some blank deposit receipts and two or three blank counteroffers. Of course, you could fill out the offer electronically using ZipForms®. In addition, you should always have a Competitive Market Analysis (CMA), title rate sheet, financial calculator or loan amortization book, and a nice-looking pen with you when showing properties and trying to make a sale.

DUE DILIGENCE AND DISCLOSURE

Due diligence is the reasonable effort to provide accurate and complete information about a property. According to the Code of Ethics, "REALTORS® shall only be obligated to discover and disclose adverse factors reasonably apparent to someone with expertise in those areas required by their real estate licensing authority". The Code of Ethics requires a REALTOR® to "exercise reasonable care in the buyer's interest to obtain accurate information about a property". Buyers deserve the representation of a salesperson, as an informed professional, who takes all actions to discover and disclose anything that would cause a property to be less desirable to buyers.

For example, a salesperson would be expected to ask questions about the stability of a slope below a property in an area where landslides had occurred. Reasonable care would include a recommendation to the buyers to ask for a geological report on the site and surrounding area.

On the other hand, a salesperson does not have to disclose defects hidden from sight, such as foundation problems, damaged roof, poor drainage, water damage, termites, or damage to plumbing or electrical systems. It is common in most transactions, however, for a property inspection to take place before the closing to discover many of these problems if they do in fact exist.

Code of Ethics - Working with Buyers

Article 1

When representing a buyer, seller, landlord, tenant, or other client as an agent, REALTORS® pledge themselves to protect and promote the interests of their client. This obligation to the client is primary, but it does not relieve REALTORS® of their obligation to treat all parties honestly. When serving a buyer, seller, landlord, tenant or other party in a non-agency capacity, REALTORS® remain obligated to treat all parties honestly.

Standard of Practice 2-1

REALTORS® shall only be obligated to discover and disclose adverse factors reasonably apparent to someone with expertise in those areas required by their real estate licensing authority. Article 2 does not impose upon the REALTOR® the obligation of expertise in other professional or technical disciplines.

Article 6

REALTORS® shall not accept any commission, rebate, or profit on expenditures made for their client, without the client's knowledge and consent. When recommending real estate products or services (homeowner's insurance, warranty programs, mortgage financing, title insurance, etc.), REALTORS® shall disclose to the client or customer to whom the recommendation is made any financial benefits or fees, other than real estate referral fees, the REALTOR® or REALTOR®'s firm may receive as a direct result of such recommendation.

Article 9

REALTORS®, for the protection of all parties, shall assure whenever possible that all agreements related to real estate transactions including, but not limited to, listing and representation agreements, purchase contracts, and leases are in writing in clear and understandable language expressing the specific terms, conditions, obligations and commitments of the parties. A copy of each agreement shall be furnished to each party to such agreements upon their signing or initialing.

Article 10

REALTORS® shall not deny equal professional services to any person for reasons of race, color, religion, sex, handicap, familial status, or national origin. REALTORS® shall not be parties to any plan or agreement to discriminate against a person or persons on the basis of race, color, religion, sex, handicap, familial status, or national origin. REALTORS®, in their real estate employment practices, shall not discriminate against any person or persons on the basis of race, color, religion, sex, handicap, familial status, or national origin.

Standard of Practice 10-1

When involved in the sale or lease of a residence, REALTORS® shall not volunteer information regarding the racial, religious or ethnic composition of any neighborhood nor shall they engage in any activity which may result in panic selling, however, REALTORS® may provide other demographic information.

Article 11

The services which REALTORS® provide to their clients and customers shall conform to the standards of practice and competence which are reasonably expected in the specific real estate disciplines in which they engage; specifically, residential real estate brokerage, real property management, commercial and industrial real estate brokerage, land brokerage, real estate appraisal, real estate counseling, real estate syndication, real estate auction, and international real estate.

REALTORS® shall not undertake to provide specialized professional services concerning a type of property or service that is outside their field of competence unless they engage the assistance of one who is competent on such types of property or service, or unless the facts are fully disclosed to the client. Any persons engaged to provide such assistance shall be so identified to the client and their contribution to the assignment should be set forth.

SUMMARY

When it comes to choosing a salesperson, a buyer's experience is somewhat different from that of a seller's. Buyers do not have to work with one salesperson exclusively and can employ the services of as many salespeople as they choose.

The homebuyers of today come from a very broad timeframe. Among them are **Baby Boomers, Generation X,** and **Generation Y.**

With the advent of the **Internet,** a different breed of buyers has emerged. These technologically savvy individuals are well informed and have actively researched the home buying market. The salesperson of today should customize his or her approach when dealing with these buyers.

The buyer could be represented exclusively by a **buyer agency,** participate in a **dual agency** relationship with the seller, or have no representation at all. Before showing properties to the buyers, the salesperson should ask questions or have the buyers fill out a **Homebuyer's Checklist.** A salesperson should also qualify the buyers to find out what they can afford.

When showing properties, it is important for a salesperson to pay attention to **buying signals** that provide clues to buyers' interests. If any objections are raised, they should be viewed as a positive part of the sales process.

Ask the buyers if they are ready to make an offer on one of the homes you have shown them. Once the buyers agree to make an offer, discuss the terms as a way to convey serious interest in purchasing the property. Remember to follow the **Code of Ethics** when working with the buyers.

UNIT 11 REVIEW

Matching Exercise

Instructions: Write the letter of the matching term on the blank line before its definition. Answers are in Appendix A.

Terms

A. Baby Boomers

B. buyer's broker

C. buyer's profile

D. buying signs

E. due diligence

F. scorecard

G. Generation X

H. Homebuyer's Checklist

I. Generation Y

J. NAR Code of Ethics

K. preapproval letter

L. prequalification

M. real estate agency disclosure

Definitions

1. _____ For every residential property transaction of one to four units, the law requires that an agent supply this written document explaining the nature of agency to a seller before listing a property or to a buyer before writing an offer

2. _____ An agent who represents only buyers and has a fiduciary duty to get the best house for the least money at the terms most favorable to his or her principal (the buyer)

3. _____ Individuals born between 1946 and 1964 who make up the largest generation in the history of the United States

4. _____ Information regarding the buyer's financial resources

5. _____ A written commitment from a lender to loan a certain amount based on a written application by the buyer

6. _____ A written commitment from a lender to loan a certain amount based on a buyer's verbal information

7. _____ A detailed questionnaire about what a buyer is looking for in a home

8. _____ Verbal and nonverbal communication to determine if a buyer is ready to make an offer

9. _____ A group of homebuyers born between 1982 and 2000.

10. _____ To exercise reasonable effort in providing accurate and complete information about a property

Multiple Choice Questions

Instructions: Circle your response and go to Appendix A to read the complete explanation for each question.

1. In a transaction, what is required by real estate law concerning buyer representation?
    a. Exclusive agency
    b. Disclosure of agency
    c. Dual agency
    d. Non-exclusive agency

2. A buyer may choose to work with which of the following for representation?
    a. A buyer's broker
    b. A dual agent
    c. A non-exclusive agent
    d. All of the above

3. Which of the following represents the homebuyers of today?
    a. Baby Boomers
    b. Generation Y
    c. Generation X
    d. All of the above

4. The NAR Technology Impact Survey Report found that:
    a. most REALTORS® are not using e-mail and the Internet for business.
    b. buyers and sellers use the Internet to get real estate information.
    c. all REALTORS® have a personal website.
    d. buyers and sellers rarely use the Internet to get real estate information.

5. In order to qualify buyers, the salesperson has them fill out the:
    a. disclosure of agency.
    b. homebuyer's checklist.
    c. purchase agreement.
    d. buyer's profile.

6. To create professional rapport with buyers, a salesperson should perform one of the following before showing them properties.
    a. Create a homebuyer's checklist and have them fill it out after showing them properties.
    b. Ask buyers if they are able to afford the monthly payment.
    c. Create a homebuyer's checklist and have them fill it out at the first opportunity.
    d. Check buyers' credit scores.

7. As a real estate professional, you can guide the buyers toward making a decision by:
    a. avoiding conflict.
    b. selling the benefits of the home.
    c. being honest.
    d. doing all of the above.

8. What are some common buying signs that buyers exhibit when a salesperson shows a desirable property?
    a. Touching
    b. Talking about placing their furniture in the home
    c. Asking others for their opinion
    d. All of the above

9. When a buyer raises objections, a salesperson should view the objections as:
    a. a positive part of the sales process.
    b. the buyer showing some interest.
    c. a way to provide feedback.
    d. all of the above.

10. If a sales associate sees buying signals from the buyers, he or she should:
    a. ask the buyers to write up an offer on the property.
    b. show additional properties to the buyers.
    c. make an appointment for the next day to discuss writing the offer.
    d. ask the sellers to write up an offer on the property.

Writing and Presenting an Offer

Unit 12

INTRODUCTION

When writing an offer, you may be acting as a subagent for the sellers, or be the buyer's agent. The selling salesperson could be a subagent (representing the sellers), or a buyer's agent. If the selling salesperson is a subagent, remember to consider the buyers as a third-party customer. Giving advice or allowing buyers to believe that they are represented by you could result in a dual-agency. However, if you do represent the buyers, it is your job to get the buyers the best price and terms for the purchase of the property.

The majority of the information in this unit is from the perspective of a buyer's agent. When representing buyers, you need to help them decide how much to offer and what terms to include in the **purchase agreement**. The purchase agreement is also known as the **deposit receipt** and acts as the receipt for earnest money the buyers gives to secure an offer. Once signed by both parties, the purchase agreement becomes a legally binding contract between buyers and sellers.

The purchase agreement includes all terms of the sale, including agreements about financing. Buyers and sellers are bound by the contract when the buyers receive notification of the sellers' acceptance of the offer, without any changes. The purchase agreement may become the actual escrow instructions. **Escrow instructions** are written directions, signed by buyers and sellers, detailing the procedures necessary to close a transaction. Escrow instructions also give direction to the escrow agent on how to proceed.

If this is a buyer's first purchase of a home, they will rely heavily on your guidance through the stages of the purchase—from writing the offer to closing the escrow. This unit will focus mainly on how to write offers and handle counteroffers.

Learning Objectives

After reading this unit, you should be able to:

- recall the main clauses in the sales and purchase agreement.
- recall the steps in presenting an offer.
- determine how a sales associate can effectively handle counteroffers.

WRITING THE OFFER

Before writing the offer, try to find out as much as you can about the seller's motivation for listing the home. This knowledge will help you structure an offer and develop a strategy. If you know the seller's motivation, you will be able to present an offer that is close to what the seller needs and wants.

For example, if the property has been on the market for an extended period, the sellers may be in a vulnerable position and might be more apt to accept an offer that is below the listing price. As the selling salesperson, you can find out how long the house has been on the market by checking the MLS. Contact the listing salesperson to find out when the listing expires and what the seller's motivation is for listing the property. This information will help you obtain greater negotiating power when presenting the offer.

Purchase Price and Initial Deposit

Once the buyers decide to buy a property, you need to write up their purchase offer. Always be careful when completing forms. Make sure the names of the buyers and the property address are correct and spelled properly.

The first items to discuss are the price and terms of the offer and the amount of the earnest money deposit. A large initial deposit and quick closing combined with loan pre-approval are part of a good offer, even if the purchase price is not the highest.

If an offer is not full price, especially if the listing price is reasonably set, counsel the buyers to expect a counteroffer from the sellers. Work closely with your buyers, and have them nearby in another office or close to the location where you are presenting the offer. In this way, you will be able to respond to a counteroffer quickly because the buyers are prepared.

Before writing an offer for buyers, keep in mind the answers to these questions.

Writing and Presenting an Offer

- What is the most the buyers will pay?
- Which is more important to the buyers— price or terms?
- Are the buyers prepared for a counteroffer from the sellers?
- Are there any buyers' contingencies that must be part of the transaction?
- Is there a critical timeframe for the buyers to close the transaction?

Purchase Price

If buyers want their offers taken seriously, the suggested price must be close to reality. This is where your current CMA on the property will come in handy. Instead of using many words to convince the buyers to make a decent offer, use the CMA statistics as a guide for setting the amount of the offer. If the desired property appears to have more value than a similar property, the buyers' offer should be higher. However, the offer should be lower if the desired property is perceived to have less value. Based on the CMA, and with your help, buyers can decide what offer to make to purchase the property. Remember, there is always a chance that sellers may counter or even reject the offer if it does not meet their needs.

Initial Deposit

Upon writing a purchase agreement for real property, buyers usually give an **earnest money deposit** (consideration) as a sign that they are serious about making the offer. **Consideration** is a buyers' deposit in the form of cash, a personal check, cashier's check, promissory note, money order, or other form usually for 1-3% of the purchase price of the property. Some salespeople find it awkward to ask for the deposit. Remember, the deposit should be 1-3% of the purchase price to indicate a serious interest in purchasing the property. If the buyers object, you must let them know that if they are seriously interested in the property, they need to show the sellers evidence by placing an earnest money deposit before making the official offer.

Consideration is something promised, given, or done that has the effect of making an agreement a legally enforceable contract. The check is payable to an escrow company or the listing broker. The salesperson representing the buyers holds the check until the sellers either reject or accept the offer. If the sellers reject the offer, the earnest money deposit will be returned to the buyers. If the sellers accept the offer, the buyers' check is deposited into an escrow account or into the broker's trust account within three business days after receiving it.

Finance Terms

Once the purchase price and initial deposit are determined, you need to ask the buyers if they plan to pay all cash, obtain financing, assume a loan, or take title "subject to" an existing loan. If the buyers want to assume the loan, does it contain acceleration clauses or prepayment penalties? If so, have the buyers approved the terms?

All cash transactions close very quickly because the buyers do not have to complete the loan qualification process. In addition, the sellers do not have to be concerned about the buyers obtaining financing. For these reasons, the sellers may welcome an all-cash offer. However, buyers who submit an all-cash offer have greater negotiating power because all-cash buyers are more financially qualified than those buyers who must obtain financing. Frequently, all-cash buyers try to use their negotiating power to obtain a price that is lower than the listed price. The all-cash buyers are also in a fortunate position in terms of avoiding mortgage interest and other associated costs involved in obtaining financing. However, the all-cash buyers lose many of the tax advantages available to homeowners with conventional loans.

Common Contingencies

As you may recall, **contingencies** are statements that define the terms of an agreement and give the other party cause to void an offer if the terms are not met. Usually, they benefit the buyers rather than the sellers. Buyers want to make sure they get what they pay for and that no surprises will surface that would affect their decision to buy.

Become familiar with the common contingencies to prepare for the "deal killers" that can occur even after you have opened escrow. Remember, escrow is the period during which all terms of the contract, including any contingencies, must be met. Therefore, if these contingencies are not met escrow cannot close.

Residential real estate contingencies are written clauses in the purchase contract that require certain events to take place before closing. If these events do not take place within the time specified in the purchase contract, the party who has requested the actions of the other party can back out of the contract without any penalties. Common contingencies involve financing, title, condition of the property, sale of another property, easements, land use, sewer access, water rights, appraisals, and deed guarantees.

Financing Contingency

A very common contingency is the dependency on the buyers' ability to obtain financing at favorable terms. The purchase contract should reflect the type of financing the buyers are willing to accept and include a clause that allows the buyers to back out if the financing cannot be obtained. Currently, most buyers are pre-qualified or pre-approved for financing before they submit an offer on a property. If the buyers' offer includes a financing contingency, but they cannot obtain financing, they can withdraw from the contract and escrow will return the deposit.

Title to Property and Its Use

Contingencies that affect title include Covenants, Conditions, and Restrictions (CC&Rs); rights; stipulations; and agreements or other conditions of record that affect the property such as the existence of a common wall, encroachments, and easements.

If buyers are concerned that a neighbor allows access to a right of way across their property (an easement), they may request an **easement contingency**. For example, if the contract states that the sale is contingent upon negative findings of an easement and an easement is found to exist, this contingency could allow the buyers to back out of the offer.

Condition of Property

Currently, one of the most common reasons why a home sale falls apart is because of adverse property conditions discovered during inspections. When the buyers are unwilling to correct the problem themselves, the purchase contract is subject to negotiations. The buyers present the sellers with a condition to correct the problem or grant a price reduction for expenses the buyers may incur after fixing the problem. If the sellers agree, the deal is still good; if the sellers disagree, the deal falls apart and the house is back on the market.

Transfer Disclosure Statement (TDS)

A Transfer Disclosure Statement is a specific written disclosure that should be made and given to prospective buyers of one-to-four dwelling units. It should disclose facts about the particular piece of property that could materially affect the property's value and desirability.

Home Inspections

Another common type of contingency is the "contingent upon satisfactory completion of inspection". The most commonly requested inspections include those for hidden defects, pest inspections, water and sewage system inspections, and the presence of radon or mold. The contingency should outline the inspections the buyers want performed, the dates of completion, and outlined consequences if a problem is found.

A home inspection report is commonly requested by buyers.

Pest Inspections

If a structural pest inspection report and certification are to be furnished, who will pay the cost? Who will pay for any required work? Will multiple reports be required? These questions should be addressed to both the sellers and the buyers and decided by mutual agreement.

Contingent on the Sale of Another Home

Buyers and sellers can create contingencies on the sale of a home other than the subject property. Buyers can make an offer on another property contingent upon the sale of the current home. On the other hand, it is possible for sellers to create a contingency based on their ability to find a suitable replacement property to live in after the sale of their current home.

If buyers make an offer contingent upon the sale of their home, the buyers usually need to fund the financing for the new property with the proceeds from the sale of their current property. The buyers cannot act on the sale until their current home sells, and if the sellers accept the offer, the sellers will usually continue to market their property to other buyers. Most buyers will request an extended escrow period with their offer to give them adequate time to sell their current home.

Some sellers will not accept an offer with this type of contingency. However, if the sellers accept the offer, they usually will include a clause giving the buyers a set timeframe to close the sale.

If a transaction is contingent upon the sellers' ability to purchase a suitable replacement property, the sellers can accept an offer from buyers, but the sellers will not be able to complete the sale until they purchase another home. If the sellers are not able to purchase a suitable replacement property, they can withdraw from the sale. Most buyers will not accept this type of contingency because they do not have any type of guarantee that the sellers will perform. An option for the buyers would be to include a clause that allows the buyers to withdraw from the contract if the buyers find another property.

Escrow

Discuss with your buyers the numerous charges and fees that are inherent in any real estate transaction. The buyers, sellers, or both can pay these fees. Who will pay for the title policy, escrow services, and other customary charges? Ask if there are any special costs or unusual charges to be adjusted through escrow. If so, who would pay for them? Ask your buyers if they have an escrow company that they would like to use. If they do not know of anyone, suggest a few reputable companies. Both buyers and sellers should agree on this.

Proration

Proration is the process of distributing or dividing the expenses or income between the sellers and the buyers usually up to the date of closing or the date of possession. The most common items that are prorated include real property taxes, interest on loans, insurance premiums, rent or assessments, and sewer charges. If prorations are not made as of the date escrow closes, what date is to be used?

**CALIFORNIA
ASSOCIATION
OF REALTORS®**

CONTINGENCY FOR SALE OR PURCHASE
OF OTHER PROPERTY
(C.A.R. Form COP, Revised 11/08)

This is an addendum to the ☐ California Residential Purchase Agreement, ☐ Counter Offer, ☐ Other _____
_____ ("Agreement"), dated _____ ,
on property known as _____ ("Seller's Property"),
between _____ ("Buyer")
and _____ ("Seller").

A. ☐ **(If checked) SALE OF BUYER'S PROPERTY:**
  1. **(a)** The Agreement is contingent on the close of escrow of Buyer's property, described as: _____
_____ ("Buyer's Property").
  (b) If Buyer's Property does not close escrow by the earliest of: **(i)** the scheduled close of escrow of Seller's Property; **(ii)** the
  date specified in paragraph A3; or **(iii)** Other ☐ _____ , then either Seller,
  after first giving Buyer a Notice to Buyer to Perform (C.A.R. Form NBP), or Buyer may cancel the Agreement in writing.
  2. ☐ **(If checked)** Buyer's Property is **not** now in escrow and (check boxes as applicable):
  (a) ☐ is not yet listed for sale.
  (b) ☐ is listed for sale with _____ company and is
  offered for sale in the _____ MLS, # _____ .
  (c) Buyer shall, within **17** (or ☐ _____) **Days** After Acceptance, provide Seller with Copies of the contract, escrow instructions
  and all related documents ("Escrow Evidence") for the sale of Buyer's Property showing that Buyer's Property has entered
  escrow.
  3. ☐ **(If checked)** Buyer's Property **is in escrow** with _____
  escrow holder, (escrow # _____) scheduled to close escrow on _____ (date).
  Buyer shall, within **5 Days** After Acceptance, deliver to Seller Escrow Evidence that Buyer's Property is in escrow.
  4. If Buyer fails to provide to Seller Escrow Evidence within the time specified in A2(c) or A3, Seller, after first giving Buyer a Notice
  to Buyer to Perform, may cancel the Agreement in writing.
  5. If Buyer's Property is in or enters escrow, Buyer shall give Seller written notice if either party to that escrow gives notice to the
  other of intent to cancel. In such event, either Buyer or Seller may cancel the Agreement in writing.
  6. After Acceptance, Seller shall have the right to continue to offer the Property for sale for Back-up Offers. If Seller accepts a
  written back-up offer:
  (a) Immediate Right to Notify Buyer to Remove Sale of Property Contingency: Seller shall have the right to immediately
  give written notice to Buyer to, in writing: **(i)** remove this contingency; **(ii)** remove the loan contingency, if any; **(iii)** provide
  verification of sufficient funds to close escrow without the sale of Buyer's Property; and **(iv)** comply with the following
  additional requirement(s): _____
  If Buyer fails to complete these actions within **72** (or ☐ _____) **hours** after receipt of such notice, Seller may
  then immediately cancel the Agreement in writing.
  OR (b) ☐ **(If checked) Delayed Right to Notify Buyer:** Seller shall not invoke the notice provisions in paragraph A6(a): **(i)**
  within the first **17** (or ☐ _____) **Days** After Acceptance; or **(ii)** (if checked) ☐ during the term of the Agreement.

B. ☐ **(If checked) SELLER'S PURCHASE OF REPLACEMENT PROPERTY:**
  1. The Agreement is contingent on Seller entering a contract to acquire replacement property.
  2. Seller shall, within **17** (or ☐ _____) **Days** After Acceptance, remove this contingency or cancel the Agreement.
  If Seller does not remove this contingency in writing within that time, Buyer, after giving Seller a Notice to Seller to Perform
  (C.A.R. Form NSP), may cancel the Agreement in writing.
  3. **(a)** Time periods in the Agreement for inspections, contingencies, covenants and other obligations shall begin: **(i)** as
  specified in the Agreement; **(ii)** (if checked) ☐ the day after Seller delivers to Buyer a written notice removing this
  contingency; or **(iii)** (if checked) ☐ Other _____
  (b) Buyer and Seller agree that Seller may, by providing Buyer written notice at the time Seller removes this contingency, extend
  the Close Of Escrow date for a maximum of _____ additional Days or until ☐ _____ (date).
  4. Even after the expiration of the time specified in B2, Seller retains, until Buyer cancels pursuant to B2, the right to remove in
  writing this contingency or cancel the Agreement. Once Buyer receives Seller's written removal of this contingency, Buyer may
  not cancel pursuant to B2.

By signing below, Buyer and Seller each acknowledge that they have read, understand, accept and have received a copy of this Addendum.

Date _____   Date _____

Buyer _____   Seller _____

Buyer _____   Seller _____

Reviewed by _____ Date _____

COP REVISED 11/08 (PAGE 1 OF 1)   **CONTINGENCY FOR SALE OR PURCHASE OF OTHER PROPERTY (COP PAGE 1 OF 1)**

Agent:	Phone:	Fax:	Prepared using zipForm® software
Broker:			

Early Move-In

An **early move-in** allows the buyers to take possession of the property prior to the close of escrow. This should be carefully evaluated to avoid the risk of possible lawsuit due to inadequate insurance coverage, mechanics' liens, and/or "buyers' remorse". A written early occupancy agreement (Interim Occupancy Agreement—Form IOA) should be completed and signed by the sellers (as landlord), the buyers (as tenant), the listing agent (representing the sellers) and the selling agent (representing the buyers). The real estate brokers are not a party to the agreement between landlord and tenant, and agency relationships are confirmed within the agreement.

Expiration of Offer

Discuss with your buyers how much time they will allow the sellers to consider the buyers' purchase agreement. Some salespeople like to give sellers 24 hours to reply to the offer. Others expect an answer or counteroffer upon presentation.

Buyers are in a strong bargaining position if they are well-qualified, have financing in place, and do not have to sell their current home. They are able to select from a variety of homes that will meet their needs. Under these circumstances, a short time for the sellers to accept the offer is reasonable. The short acceptance time allows the buyers to go on to the next deal. If the buyers were in a weaker bargaining position, it would be advisable to not annoy or irritate the sellers with an unrealistic offer. Either way, the time for responding to an offer should be specified in the offer.

Sign the Contract

Be sure the signatures of all buyers, sellers, and salespeople are on the contract. Also, every purchase contract prepared or signed by a real estate salesperson must be reviewed, initialed, and dated by the salesperson's broker within five working days after preparation or signing by the salesperson, or before the close of escrow, whichever occurs first. Remember that the offer is not a contract until the broker accepts it.

PRESENTING THE OFFER

Presenting an offer requires tremendous skill and care. Ideally, the most effective way to present an offer is to meet face-to-face with the listing salesperson and the sellers. However, sometimes this is not feasible due to time constraints and location. If you cannot meet with them in person, fax or mail a copy of the offer, and follow up with a telephone presentation to the

INTERIM OCCUPANCY AGREEMENT
Buyer in Possession Prior to Close of Escrow
(C.A.R. Form IOA, Revised 1/06)

_____ ("Seller/Landlord")
and _____ ("Buyer/Tenant")
have entered into a purchase agreement for the real property described below. Close of escrow for the purchase agreement is scheduled to occur on
_____ (date). Seller, as Landlord, and Buyer, as Tenant, agree as follows:

1. **PROPERTY:**
   A. Landlord rents to Tenant and Tenant rents from Landlord, the real property and improvements described as: _____
   _____ ("Premises").
   B. The Premises are for the sole use as a personal residence by the following named persons **only**: _____
   _____
   C. The personal property listed in the purchase agreement, maintained pursuant to paragraph 11, is included.

2. **TERM:** The term begins on (date) _____ ("Commencement Date") and shall terminate
   at _____ ☐ AM/ ☐ PM on the earliest of: **(a)** the date scheduled for close of escrow of the purchase agreement as specified above, or as modified in writing; or **(b)** mutual cancellation of the purchase agreement. Tenant shall vacate the Premises upon termination of this Agreement, unless: **(i)** Landlord and Tenant have signed a new agreement, **(ii)** mandated by local rent control law, or **(iii)** Landlord accepts Rent from Tenant (other than past due Rent), in which case a month-to-month tenancy shall be created which either party may terminate pursuant to California Civil Code § 1946.1. Rent shall be at a rate agreed to by Landlord and Tenant, or as allowed by law. All other terms and conditions of this Agreement shall remain in full force and effect.

3. **RENT:** "Rent" shall mean all monetary obligations of Tenant to Landlord under the terms of this Agreement, except security deposit.
   A. Tenant agrees to pay $ _____ per month for the term of this Agreement.
   B. Rent is payable in advance on the **1st (or** ☐ _____ **)** day of each calendar week, and is delinquent on the next day; or ☐ in full at close of escrow; or ☐ _____
   C. PAYMENT: The Rent shall be paid by ☐ personal check, ☐ money order, ☐ cashier's check, ☐ through escrow (per escrow instructions), or ☐ other _____ , to (name) _____
   (phone) _____ at (address) _____
   (or at any other location subsequently specified by Landlord in writing to Tenant) between the hours of _____ and _____ , on the following days: _____ . If any payment is returned for non-sufficient funds ("NSF") or because tenant stops payment, then, after that: **(i)** Landlord may, in writing, require Tenant to pay Rent in cash for three months and **(ii)** all future Rent shall be paid by ☐ money order, or ☐ cashier's check.

4. **SECURITY DEPOSIT:**
   A. Tenant agrees to pay $ _____ as a security deposit. Security deposit will be ☐ transferred to and held by Seller; ☐ held in Seller's Broker's trust account; or ☐ held in escrow (per escrow instructions).
   B. **(1)** If the tenancy is terminated due to the close of escrow by Buyer under the purchase agreement, the full amount of the security deposit, less any deductions below, shall be credited to Buyer's down payment on the purchase (or, if checked ☐ returned to Buyer from Seller's proceeds in escrow). If required by lender for closing, Seller shall place the security deposit into escrow prior to the signing of loan documents by Buyer.
      (2) All or any portion of the security deposit may be used, as reasonably necessary, to: **(i)** cure Tenant's default in payment of Rent (which includes Late Charges, NSF fees or other sums due); **(ii)** repair damage, excluding ordinary wear and tear, caused by Tenant or by a guest or licensee of Tenant; **(iii)** clean Premises, if necessary, upon termination of the tenancy; and **(iv)** replace or return personal property or appurtenances. **SECURITY DEPOSIT SHALL NOT BE USED BY TENANT IN LIEU OF PAYMENT OF LAST MONTH'S RENT.** If all or any portion of the security deposit is used during the tenancy, Tenant agrees to reinstate the total security deposit within 5 Days after written notice is delivered to Tenant.
      (3) Within 21 days after Tenant vacates the Premises, Landlord shall: **(i)** furnish Tenant an itemized statement indicating the amount of any security deposit received and the basis for its disposition; and **(ii)** return any remaining portion of the security deposit to Tenant.
   C. **Except when escrow closes, security deposit will not be returned until all Tenants have vacated the Premises. Any security deposit returned by check shall be made out to all Tenants named on this Agreement, or as subsequently modified.**
   D. No interest will be paid on security deposit unless required by local Law.
   E. If the security deposit is held by Seller, Tenant agrees not to hold Broker responsible for its return. If the security deposit is held in Seller's Broker's trust account, **and** Broker's authority is terminated before expiration of this Agreement, **and** security deposit is released to someone other than Tenant, **then** Broker shall notify Tenant, in writing, where and to whom security deposit has been released. Once Tenant has been provided such notice, Tenant agrees not to hold Broker responsible for the security deposit.

5. **MOVE-IN COSTS RECEIVED/DUE:** Move-in funds made payable to _____ shall be
   paid by ☐ personal check, ☐ money order, ☐ cashier's check, or ☐ through escrow (per escrow instructions).

Category	Total Due	Payment Received	Balance Due	Date Due
Rent from _____ to _____ (date)				
*Security Deposit				
Other _____				
Other _____				
Total				

*The maximum amount Landlord may receive as security deposit, however designated, cannot exceed two months' Rent for unfurnished premises, or three months' Rent for furnished premises.

Tenant's Initials (_____) (_____)
Landlord's Initials (_____) (_____)

Reviewed by _____ Date _____

IOA REVISED 1/06 (PAGE 1 OF 6)

INTERIM OCCUPANCY AGREEMENT (IOA PAGE 1 OF 6)

Agent: Tom Baker	Phone: (555) 123-4567	Fax:	(555) 123-4568	Prepared using WINForms® software
Broker: Sunshine Real Estate	1234 Mountain Road, Any City, CA 92655			

Premises: _____   Date: _____

6. **LATE CHARGE; RETURNED CHECKS:**
   A. Tenant acknowledges either late payment of Rent or issuance of a returned check may cause Landlord to incur costs and expenses, the exact amounts of which are extremely difficult and impractical to determine. These costs may include, but are not limited to, processing, enforcement and accounting expenses, and late charges imposed on Landlord. If any installment of Rent due from Tenant is not received by Landlord within **5 (or ☐ _____) calendar days** after the date due, or if a check is returned, Tenant shall pay to Landlord, respectively, an additional sum of $ _____ or _____ % of the Rent due as a Late Charge and $25.00 as a NSF fee for the first returned check and $35.00 as a NSF fee for each additional returned check, either or both of which shall be deemed additional Rent.
   B. Landlord and Tenant agree these charges represent a fair and reasonable estimate of the costs Landlord may incur by reason of Tenant's late or NSF payment. Any Late Charge or NSF fee due shall be paid with the current installment of Rent. Landlord's acceptance of any Late Charge or NSF fee shall not constitute a waiver as to any default of Tenant. Landlord's right to collect a Late Charge or NSF fee shall not be deemed an extension of the date Rent is due under paragraph 3 or prevent Landlord from exercising any other rights and remedies under this Agreement and as provided by law.

7. **PARKING: (Check A or B)**
   ☐ A. Parking is permitted as follows: _____
   _____ The right to parking ☐ is ☐ is not included in the Rent charged pursuant to paragraph 3. If not included in the Rent, the parking rental fee shall be an additional $ _____ per month. Parking space(s) are to be used for parking properly licensed and operable motor vehicles, except for trailers, boats, campers, buses or trucks (other than pick-up trucks). Tenant shall park in assigned space(s) only. Parking space(s) are to be kept clean. Vehicles leaking oil, gas or other motor vehicle fluids shall not be parked on the Premises. Mechanical work or storage of inoperable vehicles is not permitted in parking space(s) or elsewhere on the Premises.
   OR ☐ B. Parking is not permitted on the Premises.

8. **STORAGE: (Check A or B)**
   ☐ A. Storage is permitted as follows: _____
   The right to storage space ☐ is ☐ is not included in the Rent charged pursuant to paragraph 3. If not included in the Rent, storage space fee shall be an additional $ _____ per month. Tenant shall store only personal property Tenant owns, and shall not store property claimed by another or in which another has any right, title or interest. Tenant shall not store any improperly packaged food or perishable goods, flammable materials, explosives, hazardous waste or other inherently dangerous material, or illegal substances.
   OR ☐ B. Storage is not permitted on the Premises.

9. **UTILITIES:** Tenant agrees to pay for all utilities and services, and the following charges: _____ except _____ , which shall be paid for by Landlord. If any utilities are not separately metered, Tenant shall pay Tenant's proportional share, as reasonably determined and directed by Landlord. If utilities are separately metered, Tenant shall place utilities in Tenant's name as of the Commencement Date. Landlord is only responsible for installing and maintaining one usable telephone jack and one telephone line to the Premises. Tenant shall pay any cost for conversion from existing utilities service provider.

10. **CONDITION OF PREMISES:** Tenant has examined Premises, all furniture, furnishings, appliances, landscaping, if any, and fixtures, including smoke detector(s).
    (Check all that apply:)
    ☐ A. Tenant acknowledges these items are clean and in operable condition, with the following exceptions: _____
    _____
    ☐ B. Tenant's acknowledgment of the condition of these items is contained in an attached statement of condition (C.A.R. Form MIMO).
    ☐ C. Tenant will provide Landlord a list of items that are damaged or not in operable condition within **3 (or ☐ _____) Days** after Commencement Date, not as a contingency of the Agreement but rather as an acknowledgment of the condition of the Premises.
    ☐ D. Other: _____

11. **MAINTENANCE:**
    A. Tenant shall properly use, operate and safeguard Premises, including if applicable, any landscaping, furniture, furnishings and appliances, and all mechanical, electrical, gas and plumbing fixtures, and keep them and the Premises clean, sanitary and well ventilated. Tenant shall be responsible for checking and maintaining all smoke detectors and any additional phone lines beyond the one line and jack that Landlord shall provide and maintain. Tenant shall immediately notify Landlord, in writing, of any problem, malfunction or damage. Tenant shall be charged for all repairs or replacements caused by Tenant, pets, guests or licensees of Tenant, excluding ordinary wear and tear. Tenant shall be charged for all damage to Premises as a result of failure to report a problem in a timely manner. Tenant shall be charged for repair of drain blockages or stoppages, unless caused by defective plumbing parts or tree roots invading sewer lines.
    B. ☐ Landlord ☐ Tenant shall water the garden, landscaping, trees and shrubs, except: _____
    _____
    C. ☐ Landlord ☐ Tenant shall maintain the garden, landscaping, trees and shrubs, except: _____
    _____
    D. ☐ Landlord ☐ Tenant shall maintain _____

IOA REVISED 1/06 (PAGE 2 OF 6)

Tenant's Initials (_____)(_____)
Landlord's Initials (_____)(_____)

Reviewed by _____ Date _____

EQUAL HOUSING OPPORTUNITY

INTERIM OCCUPANCY AGREEMENT (IOA PAGE 2 OF 6)

Premises: _____ Date: _____

   E. Tenant's failure to maintain any item for which Tenant is responsible shall give Landlord the right to hire someone to perform such maintenance and charge Tenant to cover the cost of such maintenance.

   F. The following items of personal property are included in the Premises without warranty and Landlord will not maintain, repair or replace them: _____.

12. NEIGHBORHOOD CONDITIONS: Tenant is advised to satisfy him or herself as to neighborhood or area conditions, including schools, proximity and adequacy of law enforcement, crime statistics, proximity of registered felons or offenders, fire protection, other governmental services, availability, adequacy and cost of any speed-wired, wireless internet connections or other telecommunications or other technology services and installations, proximity to commercial, industrial or agricultural activities, existing and proposed transportation, construction and development that may affect noise, view, or traffic, airport noise, noise or odor from any source, wild and domestic animals, other nuisances, hazards, or circumstances, cemeteries, facilities and condition of common areas, conditions and influences of significance to certain cultures and/or religions, and personal needs, requirements and preferences of Tenant.

13. PETS: Unless otherwise provided in California Civil Code § 54.2, no animal or pet shall be kept on or about the Premises without Landlord's prior written consent, except: _____.

14. RULES; REGULATIONS:
   A. Tenant agrees to comply with all Landlord rules and regulations that are at any time posted on the Premises or delivered to Tenant. Tenant shall not, and shall ensure that guests and licensees of Tenant shall not, disturb, annoy, endanger or interfere with other tenants of the building or neighbors, or use the Premises for any unlawful purposes, including, but not limited to, using, manufacturing, selling, storing, or transporting illicit drugs or other contraband, or violate any law or ordinance, or commit a waste or nuisance on or about the Premises.

   B. (If applicable, check one:)
       ☐ **(1)** Landlord shall provide Tenant with a copy of the rules and regulations within _____ Days or _____.
   OR ☐ **(2)** Tenant has been provided with, and acknowledges receipt of, a copy of the rules and regulations.

15. ☐ **(If checked) CONDOMINIUM; PLANNED UNIT DEVELOPMENT:**
   A. The Premises is a unit in a condominium, planned unit development or other common interest subdivision governed by a homeowners' association ("HOA"). The name of the HOA is _____.
   Tenant agrees to comply with all HOA covenants, conditions and restrictions, bylaws, rules and regulations and decisions. Tenant shall reimburse Landlord for any fines or charges imposed by HOA or other authorities, due to any violation by Tenant, or the guests or licensees of Tenant.

   B. (Check one:)
       ☐ **(1)** Landlord shall provide Tenant with a copy of the HOA rules and regulations within _____ Days or _____.
   OR ☐ **(2)** Tenant has been provided with, and acknowledges receipt of, a copy of the HOA rules and regulations.

16. ALTERATIONS; REPAIRS: Unless otherwise specified by law or paragraph 27C or pursuant to the purchase agreement, without Landlord's prior written consent, **(i)** Tenant shall not make any repairs, alterations or improvements in or about the Premises including: painting, wallpapering, adding or changing locks, installing antenna or satellite dish(es), placing signs, displays or exhibits, or using screws, fastening devices, large nails or adhesive materials; **(ii)** Landlord shall not be responsible for the costs of repairs, alterations or improvements made by Tenant; **(iii)** Tenant shall not deduct from Rent the costs of any repairs, alterations or improvements; and **(iv)** any deduction made by Tenant shall be considered unpaid Rent. Tenant shall immediately notify Landlord if Tenant, individually or by or through others, commences any work on the Premises. Tenant shall be charged for any costs Landlord incurs to post and record a Notice of Non-Responsibility for any such work. Upon completion of any such work, Tenant shall notify Landlord. Tenant shall be charged for any costs Landlord incurs to post and record a Notice of Completion relating to any such work. Tenant agrees to indemnify, defend and hold harmless Landlord for any mechanic's lien attaching to the Premises or other claim resulting from any work ordered by Tenant.

17. KEYS; LOCKS:
   A. Tenant acknowledges receipt of (or Tenant will receive ☐ prior to the Commencement Date, or ☐ _____):
       ☐ _____ key(s) to Premises,   ☐ _____ remote control device(s) for garage door/gate opener(s),
       ☐ _____ key(s) to mailbox,   ☐ _____,
       ☐ _____ key(s) to common area(s),   ☐ _____.
   B. Tenant acknowledges that locks to the Premises ☐ have, ☐ have not, been re-keyed.
   C. If Tenant re-keys existing locks or opening devices, Tenant shall immediately deliver copies of all keys to Landlord. Tenant shall pay all costs and charges related to loss of any keys or opening devices. Tenant may not remove locks, even if installed by Tenant.

18. ENTRY:
   A. Tenant shall make Premises available to Landlord or Landlord's representative for the purpose of entering to make necessary or agreed repairs, decorations, alterations, or improvements, or to supply necessary or agreed services, or to show Premises to prospective or actual purchasers, tenants, mortgagees, lenders, appraisers, or contractors.
   B. Landlord and Tenant agree that 24-hour written notice shall be reasonable and sufficient notice, except as follows. 48-hour written notice is required to conduct an inspection of the Premises prior to the Tenant moving out, unless the Tenant waives the right to such notice. Notice may be given orally to show the Premises to actual or prospective purchasers provided Tenant has been notified in writing within 120 Days preceding the oral notice that the Premises are for sale and that oral notice may be given to show the Premises. No notice is required to **(i)** enter in case of an emergency; **(ii)** if the Tenant is present and consents at the time of entry or **(iii)** the Tenant has abandoned or surrendered the Premises. No written notice is required if Landlord and Tenant orally agree to an entry for agreed services or repairs if the date and time of entry are within one week of the oral agreement.

Tenant's Initials (_____) (_____)
Landlord's Initials (_____) (_____)
| Reviewed by _____ Date _____ |

INTERIM OCCUPANCY AGREEMENT (IOA PAGE 3 OF 6)

Premises: _____ Date: _____

C. ☐ (If checked) Tenant authorizes the use of a keysafe/lockbox to allow entry into the Premises and agrees to sign a keysafe/lockbox addendum (C.A.R. Form KLA).

19. SIGNS: Tenant authorizes Landlord to place FOR SALE/LEASE signs on the Premises.

20. ASSIGNMENT; SUBLETTING: Tenant shall not sublet all or any part of Premises, or assign or transfer this Agreement or any interest herein, without Landlord's prior written consent. Unless such consent is obtained, any assignment, transfer or subletting of Premises or this Agreement or tenancy, by voluntary act of Tenant, operation of law or otherwise, shall at the option of Landlord, terminate the Agreement. Any proposed assignee, transferee or sublessee shall submit to Landlord an application and credit information for Landlord's approval and, if approved, sign a separate written agreement with Landlord and Tenant. Landlord's consent to any one assignment, transfer or sublease, shall not be construed as consent to any subsequent assignment, transfer or sublease and does not release Tenant of Tenant's obligations under this Agreement.

21. JOINT AND INDIVIDUAL OBLIGATIONS: If there is more than one Tenant, each one shall be individually and completely responsible for the performance of all obligations of Tenant under this Agreement, jointly with every other Tenant, and individually, whether or not in possession.

22. ☐ **LEAD-BASED PAINT (If checked):** Premises was constructed prior to 1978. In accordance with federal law, Landlord gives and Tenant acknowledges receipt of the disclosures on the attached form (C.A.R. Form FLD) and a federally approved lead pamphlet.

23. ☐ **MILITARY ORDNANCE DISCLOSURE:** (If applicable and known to Landlord) Premises is located within one mile of an area once used for military training, and may contain potentially explosive munitions.

24. ☐ **PERIODIC PEST CONTROL:** Landlord has entered into a contract for periodic pest control treatment of the Premises and shall give Tenant a copy of the notice originally given to Landlord by the pest control company.

25. ☐ **METHAMPHETAMINE CONTAMINATION:** Prior to signing this Agreement, Landlord has given Tenant a notice that a health official has issued an order prohibiting occupancy of the property because of methamphetamine contamination. A copy of the notice and order are attached.

26. DATABASE DISCLOSURE: Notice: Pursuant to Section 290.46 of the Penal Code, information about specified registered sex offenders is made available to the public via an Internet Web site maintained by the Department of Justice at www.meganslaw.ca.gov. Depending on an offender's criminal history, this information will include either the address at which the offender resides or the community of residence and ZIP Code in which he or she resides. (Neither Landlord nor Brokers, if any, are required to check this website. If Tenant wants further information, Tenant should obtain information directly from this website.)

27. POSSESSION:

A. Tenant is not in possession of the premises. If Landlord is unable to deliver possession of Premises on Commencement Date, such Date shall be extended to the date on which possession is available to Tenant. If Landlord is unable to deliver possession within **5 (or** ☐ _____ **) calendar days** after agreed Commencement Date, Tenant may terminate this Agreement by giving written notice to Landlord, and shall be refunded all Rent and security deposit paid. Possession is deemed terminated when Tenant has returned all keys to the Premises to Landlord.

B. ☐ Tenant is already in possession of the Premises.

28. TENANT'S OBLIGATIONS UPON VACATING PREMISES: If the tenancy is terminated due to any reason other than close of escrow by Buyer under the purchase agreement, upon termination of this Agreement:

A. Tenant shall: **(i)** give Landlord all copies of all keys or opening devices to Premises, including any common areas; **(ii)** vacate and surrender Premises to Landlord, empty of all persons; **(iii)** vacate any/all parking and/or storage space; **(iv)** clean and deliver Premises, as specified in paragraph C below, to Landlord in the same condition as referenced in paragraph 10; **(v)** remove all debris; **(vi)** give written notice to Landlord of Tenant's forwarding address; and **(vii)** _____ .

B. All alterations/improvements made by or caused to be made by Tenant, with or without Landlord's consent, become the property of Landlord upon termination. Landlord may charge Tenant for restoration of the Premises to the condition it was in prior to any alterations/improvements.

C. Right to Pre-Move-Out Inspection and Repairs as follows: (i) After giving or receiving notice of termination of a tenancy (C.A.R. Form NTT), or before the end of a lease, Tenant has the right to request that an inspection of the Premises take place prior to termination of the lease or rental (C.A.R. Form NRI). If Tenant requests such an inspection, Tenant shall be given an opportunity to remedy identified deficiencies prior to termination, consistent with the terms of this Agreement. **(ii)** Any repairs or alterations made to the Premises as a result of this inspection (collectively, "Repairs") shall be made at Tenant's expense. Repairs may be performed by Tenant or through others, who have adequate insurance and licenses and are approved by Landlord. The work shall comply with applicable law, including governmental permit, inspection and approval requirements. Repairs shall be performed in a good, skillful manner with materials of quality and appearance comparable to existing materials. It is understood that exact restoration of appearance or cosmetic items following all Repairs may not be possible. **(iii)** Tenant shall: **(a)** obtain receipts for Repairs performed by others; **(b)** prepare a written statement indicating the Repairs performed by Tenant and the date of such Repairs; and **(c)** provide copies of receipts and statements to Landlord prior to termination.

29. BREACH OF CONTRACT; EARLY TERMINATION: In addition to any obligations established by paragraph 27, in event of termination by Tenant prior to completion of the original term of the Agreement, Tenant shall also be responsible for lost Rent, rental commissions, advertising expenses and painting costs necessary to ready Premises for re-rental. Landlord may withhold any such amounts from Tenant's security deposit.

Tenant's Initials (_____)(_____)
Landlord's Initials (_____)(_____)

Reviewed by _____ Date _____

EQUAL HOUSING OPPORTUNITY

INTERIM OCCUPANCY AGREEMENT (IOA PAGE 4 OF 6)

Premises: _____   Date: _____

30. **TEMPORARY RELOCATION:** Subject to local law, Tenant agrees, upon demand of Landlord, to temporarily vacate Premises for a reasonable period, to allow for fumigation (or other methods) to control wood destroying pests or organisms, or other repairs to Premises. Tenant agrees to comply with all instructions and requirements necessary to prepare Premises to accommodate pest control, fumigation or other work, including bagging or storage of food and medicine, and removal of perishables and valuables. Tenant shall only be entitled to a credit of Rent equal to the per diem Rent for the period of time Tenant is required to vacate Premises.

31. **DAMAGE TO PREMISES:** If, by no fault of Tenant, Premises are totally or partially damaged or destroyed by fire, earthquake, accident or other casualty that render Premises totally or partially uninhabitable, either Landlord or Tenant may terminate this Agreement by giving the other written notice. Rent shall be abated as of the date Premises become totally or partially uninhabitable. The abated amount shall be the current monthly Rent prorated on a 30-day period. If this Agreement is not terminated, Landlord shall promptly repair the damage, and Rent shall be reduced based on the extent to which the damage interferes with Tenant's reasonable use of Premises. If damage occurs as a result of an act of Tenant or Tenant's guests, only Landlord shall have the right of termination, and no reduction in Rent shall be made.

32. **INSURANCE:** Tenant's or guest's personal property and vehicles are not insured by Landlord, manager or, if applicable, HOA, against loss or damage due to fire, theft, vandalism, rain, water, criminal or negligent acts of others, or any other cause. **Tenant is advised to carry Tenant's own insurance (renter's insurance) to protect Tenant from any such loss or damage.** Tenant shall comply with any requirement imposed on Tenant by Landlord's insurer to avoid: **(i)** an increase in Landlord's insurance premium (or Tenant shall pay for the increase in premium); or **(ii)** loss of insurance.

33. **WATERBEDS:** Tenant shall not use or have waterbeds on the Premises unless: **(i)** Tenant obtains a valid waterbed insurance policy; **(ii)** Tenant increases the security deposit in an amount equal to one-half of one month's Rent; and **(iii)** the bed conforms to the floor load capacity of Premises.

34. **WAIVER:** The waiver of any breach shall not be construed as a continuing waiver of the same or any subsequent breach.

35. **NOTICE:** Notices may be served at the following address, or at any other location subsequently designated:
Landlord: _____   Tenant: _____
_____   _____
_____   _____

36. **TENANT ESTOPPEL CERTIFICATE:** Tenant shall execute and return a tenant estoppel certificate delivered to Tenant by Landlord or Landlord's agent within 3 Days after its receipt. Failure to comply with this requirement shall be deemed Tenant's acknowledgment that the tenant estoppel certificate is true and correct, and may be relied upon by a lender or purchaser.

37. **TENANT REPRESENTATIONS; CREDIT:** Tenant warrants that all statements in Tenant's rental application are accurate. Tenant authorizes Landlord and Broker(s) to obtain Tenant's credit report periodically during the tenancy in connection with modification or enforcement of this Agreement. Landlord may cancel this Agreement: **(i)** before occupancy begins; **(ii)** upon disapproval of the credit report(s); or **(iii)** at any time, upon discovering that information in Tenant's application is false. A negative credit report reflecting on Tenant's record may be submitted to a credit reporting agency if Tenant fails to fulfill the terms of payment and other obligations under this Agreement.

38. **MEDIATION:**
   A. Consistent with paragraphs B and C below, Landlord and Tenant agree to mediate any dispute or claim arising between them out of this Agreement, or any resulting transaction, before resorting to court action. Mediation fees, if any, shall be divided equally among the parties involved. If, for any dispute or claim to which this paragraph applies, any party commences an action without first attempting to resolve the matter through mediation, or refuses to mediate after a request has been made, then that party shall not be entitled to recover attorney fees, even if they would otherwise be available to that party in any such action.
   B. The following matters are excluded from mediation: **(i)** an unlawful detainer action; **(ii)** the filing or enforcement of a mechanic's lien; and **(iii)** any matter within the jurisdiction of a probate, small claims or bankruptcy court. The filing of a court action to enable the recording of a notice of pending action, for order of attachment, receivership, injunction, or other provisional remedies, shall not constitute a waiver of the mediation provision.
   C. Landlord and Tenant agree to mediate disputes or claims involving Listing Agent, Leasing Agent or property manager ("Broker"), provided Broker shall have agreed to such mediation prior to, or within a reasonable time after, the dispute or claim is presented to such Broker. Any election by Broker to participate in mediation shall not result in Broker being deemed a party to this Agreement.

39. **ATTORNEY FEES:** In any action or proceeding arising out of the Agreement, the prevailing party between Landlord and Tenant shall be entitled to reasonable attorney fees and costs, except as provided in paragraph 37A.

40. **C.A.R. FORM:** C.A.R. Form means the specific form referenced or another comparable form agreed to by the parties.

41. **OTHER TERMS AND CONDITIONS; SUPPLEMENTS:** ☐ Interpreter/Translator Agreement (C.A.R. Form ITA); _____
   ☐ Keysafe/Lockbox Addendum (C.A.R. Form KLA); ☐ Lead-Based Paint and Lead-Based Paint Hazards Disclosure (C.A.R. Form FLD)
   The following ATTACHED supplements are incorporated into this Agreement: _____
   _____
   _____

42. **TIME OF ESSENCE; ENTIRE AGREEMENT:** Time is of the essence. All understandings between the parties are incorporated in this Agreement. Its terms are intended by the parties as a final, complete and exclusive expression of their Agreement with respect to its subject matter, and may not be contradicted by evidence of any prior agreement or contemporaneous oral agreement. If any provision of this Agreement is held to be ineffective or invalid, the remaining provisions will nevertheless be given full force and effect. Neither this Agreement nor any provision in it may be extended, amended, modified, altered or changed except in writing. This Agreement is subject to California landlord-tenant law and shall incorporate all changes required by amendment or successors to such law. The Agreement and any supplement, addendum or modification, including any copy, may be signed in two or more counterparts, all of which shall constitute one and the same writing.

Tenant's Initials   (_____) (_____)
Landlord's Initials (_____) (_____)

Reviewed by _____ Date _____

INTERIM OCCUPANCY AGREEMENT (IOA PAGE 5 OF 6)

Premises: _____   Date: _____

43. AGENCY:

    A. CONFIRMATION: The following agency relationship(s) are hereby confirmed for this transaction:

        Listing Agent: (Agent representing the Seller in the purchase agreement)

        (Print firm name) _____

        is the agent of (check one): ☐ the Landlord exclusively; or ☐ both the Landlord and Tenant.

        Selling Agent: (Agent representing the Buyer in the purchase agreement)

        (Print firm name) _____

        (if not same as Listing Agent) is the agent of (check one): ☐ the Tenant exclusively; or ☐ the Landlord exclusively; or ☐ both the Tenant and Landlord.

    B. DISCLOSURE: ☐ (If checked): The term of this lease exceeds one year. A disclosure regarding real estate agency relationships (C.A.R. Form AD) has been provided to Landlord and Tenant, who each acknowledge its receipt.

44. ☐ **INTERPRETER/TRANSLATOR:** The terms of this Agreement have been interpreted for Tenant into the following language: _____ . Landlord and Tenant acknowledge receipt of the attached interpretator/translator agreement, (C.A.R. Form ITA).

45. FOREIGN LANGUAGE NEGOTIATION: If this Agreement has been negotiated by Landlord and Tenant primarily in Spanish, Chinese, Tagalog, Korean, Vietnamese or pursuant to the California Civil Code, Tenant shall be provided a translation of this Agreement in the language used for the negotiation.

46. RECEIPT: If specified in paragraph 5, Landlord or Broker, acknowledges receipt of move-in funds.

Landlord and Tenant acknowledge and agree Brokers: **(a)** do not guarantee the condition of the Premises; **(b)** cannot verify representations made by others; **(c)** cannot provide legal or tax advice; **(d)** will not provide other advice or information that exceeds the knowledge, education or experience required to obtain a real estate license. Furthermore, Brokers: **(e)** do not decide what rental rate a Tenant should pay or Landlord should accept; and **(f)** do not decide upon the length or other terms of tenancy. Landlord and Tenant agree they will seek legal, tax, insurance and other desired assistance from appropriate professionals.

Tenant/Buyer _____ Date _____

Address _____ City _____ State _____ Zip _____

Telephone _____ Fax _____ E-mail _____

Tenant/Buyer _____ Date _____

Address _____ City _____ State _____ Zip _____

Telephone _____ Fax _____ E-mail _____

Landlord/Seller _____ Date _____

Landlord/Seller _____ Date _____

Landlord Address _____ City _____ State _____ Zip _____

Telephone _____ Fax _____ E-mail _____

REAL ESTATE BROKERS:

A. Brokers are not a party to the Agreement between Landlord and Tenant.

B. Agency relationships are confirmed as above.

Real Estate Broker _____ License # _____

    (Agent representing the Buyer in the purchase agreement)

By (Agent) _____ License # _____ Date _____

Address _____ City _____ State _____ Zip _____

Telephone _____ Fax _____ E-mail _____

Real Estate Broker _____ License # _____

    (Agent representing the Seller in the purchase agreement)

By (Agent) _____ License # _____ Date _____

Address _____ City _____ State _____ Zip _____

Telephone _____ Fax _____ E-mail _____

Published and Distributed by:
REAL ESTATE BUSINESS SERVICES, INC.
a subsidiary of the California Association of REALTORS®
525 South Virgil Avenue, Los Angeles, California 90020

SURE TRAC
The System for Success™

IOA REVISED 1/06 (PAGE 6 OF 6)

Reviewed by _____ Date _____

EQUAL HOUSING OPPORTUNITY

INTERIM OCCUPANCY AGREEMENT (IOA PAGE 6 OF 6)

x zfx

listing salesperson. Under no circumstances should you think that you have done your job by writing up the offer and simply mailing or faxing it to the listing salesperson.

Prepare for the Presentation

After you have filled out the offer, call the listing salesperson to arrange a presentation. If you are a subagent of the sellers, discuss the offer with the listing salesperson prior to meeting with the sellers. This gives you a chance to communicate with the listing salesperson and get his or her cooperation before negotiations begin. However, if you represent the buyer, you may not want to disclose the terms of the offer prior to the presentation. The presentation of the offer should be a face-to-face meeting with you, the sellers, and the listing salesperson. Do not bring the buyer with you, but have him or her waiting somewhere nearby or available via telephone while you present the offer.

Prepare a cover letter including the buyer's job history, income statement, credit information, and anything else that supports the buyer's qualifications and seriousness of intent. This reminds the sellers that they are dealing with real people and not just numbers and figures.

As a real estate professional, you should always carry plenty of your business cards, a financial calculator, and a nice pen. In your presentation folder, include the cover letter for the offer, the signed deposit receipt, the earnest money deposit, the buyer's pre-approval letter from the lender, and a copy of the deposit receipt or escrow instructions if the buyer's home is in escrow. To help you substantiate the buyer's offer, remember to take the Competitive Market Analysis (CMA) you prepared.

The Presentation

The following suggestions will help you have a successful face-to-face listing presentation when you meet with the listing salesperson and the sellers.

- Arrive on time. If the listing salesperson has not arrived and you are alone with the sellers, avoid the possibility of violating agency relationship by keeping conversation topics general. Do not discuss the offer or enter into negotiations without the listing salesperson present.

- Establish rapport with the sellers. Try to relate the presentation to the sellers' interests. You want to gain their trust and build up to the actual offer.

- Talk about the buyers in a way the sellers can relate. Include the buyers' motivation, what they liked about the house, what they do for a living, how many children they have, etc. You want to create an emotional attachment to the buyers.

- Present the offer and highlight the benefits. Treat the presentation as if you must present evidence that the offer is worth accepting. Discuss the deposit and all terms of the offer, including personal property issues, possession, down payment, and financing.

- It is common for sellers to raise objections at this point. Remain calm and sensitive to the sellers' feelings. Review the section on negotiating in this unit.

- After you have presented all terms of the offer, ask the sellers and the listing salesperson to review the points you have made and ask for their approval. At this point, the sellers' options are to accept, counteroffer, or reject the offer. Remain silent while the sellers consider the offer.

If you are the listing salesperson, you need to be prepared for the presentation and know your sellers' boundaries. This will help you determine what to do when the selling salesperson presents the offer or other information. Remember, if you are the listing salesperson, you must present all offers or potential offers at one time. If multiple offers are made, a suggestion from the listing salesperson might be to ask for loan prequalification letters from all potential buyers. The primary goal is to get the best possible offer from the most qualified buyers. It is ultimately up to the sellers whether to accept, reject, or counter an offer but they will look to you for guidance when making a decision.

COUNTEROFFERS

Salespeople who are focused on their clients, skilled in negotiation, and goal-oriented toward a successful closing, are able to effectively guide buyers and sellers through the maze of residential buying and selling.

Getting the offer accepted usually involves the art of **negotiating**, or communicating successfully. As the selling salesperson, your job is to present the buyers in the best light possible and convince the sellers that the buyers' offer is in their best interest. Ideally, your goal is to have the offer accepted by the sellers. In most cases, however, unless your offer is full price, sellers will be reluctant to agree to the buyers' proposal and you must be prepared to negotiate through the sellers' objections. The art of persuasion, a developed skill, is what convinces sellers of the benefits of an offer.

Sometimes it will not be possible to get an offer accepted as it stands. If you are the listing salesperson and your sellers cannot agree to any or all terms of an offer, a rejection or counteroffer may be necessary. It is rare that a salesperson recommends an outright rejection. A counteroffer is a more plausible reaction because it is an attempt to arrive at the terms of the sellers. A **counteroffer** is an offer made in return by someone rejecting an unsatisfactory offer.

Counseling Sellers

If you feel that the offer is fair, caution the sellers of the repercussions of countering rather than accepting the offer as it stands. Remind the sellers to consider the following:

- The counteroffer supersedes any previous offers made by the buyers.

- When you present the counteroffer, it becomes the buyers' option to accept, reject, or counter.

- The buyers could decide to target another property, especially if the offer was fair and they presented evidence of strong financial backing.

- The buyers have had time to think about aspects of the purchase with which they are uncomfortable, such as the monthly payments. Buyers remorse is a known deal killer.

Remember, all counteroffers must be in writing. When drawing up a counteroffer, avoid making any changes to the purchase contract and use a different form such as the C.A.R.® Form CO. Using a separate form will help ensure clarity. In addition, when several counteroffers are made, it may be difficult to assess what the current offer is if the purchase contract was used to reflect each subsequent counteroffer.

Counseling Buyers

The selling salesperson's responsibility is to present the sellers' counteroffer to the buyers. If you have maintained strong communication and negotiations with the listing salesperson and sellers, their counteroffer should be fair. As the salesperson of the buyers, when presenting the sellers' counteroffer, remember to review the following with your buyers:

- The sellers' concessions
- The buyers' motivation
- The benefits of home ownership to the buyers
- How the counteroffer will affect the monthly payments, length of escrow, etc.
- The CMA to show average sales prices
- The additional monies that may be needed

**CALIFORNIA
ASSOCIATION
OF REALTORS®**

COUNTER OFFER   No. _____
For use by Seller or Buyer. May be used for Multiple Counter Offer.
(C.A.R. Form CO, Revised 11/12)

Date _____

This is a counter offer to the: ☐ California Residential Purchase Agreement, ☐ Counter Offer, or ☐ Other _____ ("Offer"),
dated _____, on property known as _____ ("Property"),
between _____ ("Buyer") and _____ ("Seller").

1. **TERMS:** The terms and conditions of the above referenced document are **accepted subject to the following:**
   A. Paragraphs in the Offer that require initials by all parties, but are not initialed by all parties, are excluded from the final agreement unless specifically referenced for inclusion in paragraph 1C of this or another Counter Offer.
   B. Unless otherwise agreed in writing, down payment and loan amount(s) will be adjusted in the same proportion as in the original Offer.
   C. ☐ If checked, Buyer's deposit will be adjusted in the same proportion as in the original offer.
   D. _____
      _____
      _____
      _____
      _____
      _____
      _____

   E. The following attached addenda are incorporated into this Counter Offer: ☐ Addendum No. _____
      ☐ _____   ☐ _____

2. **RIGHT TO ACCEPT OTHER OFFERS:** If this is a Seller Counter Offer, (i) Seller has the right to continue to offer the Property for sale or for another transaction, and to accept any other offer at any time prior to Acceptance, as described in paragraph 3 and (ii) Seller's acceptance of another offer prior to Buyer's Acceptance of this Counter Offer, shall revoke this Counter Offer.

3. **EXPIRATION:** This Counter Offer shall be deemed revoked and the deposits, if any, shall be returned unless this Counter Offer is signed by the Buyer or Seller to whom it is sent and a Copy of the signed Counter Offer is personally received by the person making this Counter Offer or by _____, who is authorized to receive it, by 5:00 PM on the third Day After the later date specified in paragraph 5 or, (if checked) by ☐ _____ (date), at _____ AM/PM. This Counter Offer may be executed in counterparts.

4. ☐ **(If checked:) MULTIPLE COUNTER OFFER:** Seller is making a Counter Offer(s) to another prospective buyer(s) on terms that may or may not be the same as in this Counter Offer. Acceptance of this Counter Offer by Buyer shall **not** be binding unless and until it is subsequently re-Signed by Seller in paragraph 7 below and a Copy of the Counter Offer Signed in paragraph 7 is personally received by Buyer or by _____, who is authorized to receive it, by 5:00 PM on the third Day After the later date specified in paragraph 5 or, (if checked) by ☐ _____ (date), at _____ AM/PM. Prior to the completion of all of these events, Buyer and Seller shall have no duties or obligations for the purchase or sale of the Property. **NOTE TO SELLER: Sign and date in paragraph 5 to make this Counter Offer.**

5. **OFFER: BUYER OR SELLER MAKES THIS COUNTER OFFER ON THE TERMS ABOVE AND ACKNOWLEDGES RECEIPT OF A COPY.**
   _____ Date _____
   _____ Date _____

6. **ACCEPTANCE: I/WE** accept the above Counter Offer **(If checked ☐ SUBJECT TO THE ATTACHED COUNTER OFFER)** and acknowledge receipt of a Copy.
   _____ Date _____ Time _____ AM/PM
   _____ Date _____ Time _____ AM/PM

7. **MULTIPLE COUNTER OFFER SIGNATURE LINE:** By signing below, Seller accepts this Multiple Counter Offer. NOTE TO SELLER: Do NOT sign in this box until after Buyer signs in paragraph 6. (Paragraph 7 applies only if paragraph 4 is checked.)
   _____ Date _____ Time _____ AM/PM
   _____ Date _____ Time _____ AM/PM

8. (_____/_____) (Initials) **Confirmation of Acceptance:** A Copy of Signed Acceptance was personally received by the maker of the Counter Offer, or that person's authorized agent as specified in paragraph 3 (or, if this is a Multiple Counter Offer, the Buyer or Buyer's authorized agent as specified in paragraph 4) on (date) _____ at _____ AM/PM. **A binding Agreement is created when a Copy of Signed Acceptance is personally received by the maker of the Counter Offer, or that person's authorized agent (or, if this is a Multiple Counter Offer, the Buyer or Buyer's authorized agent) whether or not confirmed in this document. Completion of this confirmation is not legally required in order to create a binding Agreement; it is solely intended to evidence the date that Acceptance has occurred.**

Published and Distributed by:
REAL ESTATE BUSINESS SERVICES, INC.
a subsidiary of the California Association of REALTORS®
525 South Virgil Avenue, Los Angeles, California 90020

Reviewed by _____ Date _____

CO REVISED 11/12 (PAGE 1 OF 1)   Print Date

At this point, the buyers may accept the sellers' counteroffer, completely reject the counteroffer, or submit yet another counteroffer. If the buyers decide to submit another counteroffer, the entire counter-offering process starts again and all previous offers are void. If the buyers reject the counteroffer, the property in question goes back on the market and your buyers may or may not decide to look for another property. If the buyer accepts the counteroffer, you have achieved your objective.

Accepting a Counteroffer

The accepting party must notify the offeror of acceptance so that the offer or counteroffer will be valid. Up until the point of notification of the sellers' acceptance, the buyers are free to withdraw the offer. It is important that the party who created the offer receive a signed copy of the other party's written acceptance for it to be valid. If possible, personally deliver the acceptance to the offeror. However, you may also mail, or fax the acceptance. Proof of mailing or a confirmed fax transmittal report should be kept on file.

AFTER ACCEPTANCE

Once the sellers agree to the offer and the buyers are informed of the sellers' acceptance, the deposit receipt is a valid, non-rescindable, binding contract. Once all parties **execute**, or sign, the deposit receipt, it becomes a bilateral contract. A **bilateral contract** is an agreement in which each person promises to perform an act in exchange for another person's promise to perform.

Once the excitement of negotiating the sale is over, the following week or two is a busy time for buyers, sellers, and their salespeople. Depending on the agreement in the contract, your buyers need to order a home inspection to evaluate the mechanical and structural dependability of the home. Any other inspections that have been agreed upon between buyers and sellers, such as radon, lead, or other environmental issues should also be made. You may give the buyers a list of specialists in each of the inspection areas and they will choose whom to hire. The buyers also complete financing arrangements for the loan during this time.

After both the buyers and sellers have reached an agreement and have signed all required documents, either the listing or selling salesperson will take the paperwork to the escrow company chosen by the buyers and sellers. Depending on the complexity of the contract, the escrow period or timeline may vary. Salespeople should keep a list of the clauses in the deposit receipt where "time is of the essence". It is your job to supervise and follow through with these timelines and deadlines for the parties to the escrow.

SUMMARY

Part of a salesperson's job when representing buyers is to help the buyers decide how much they want to offer and what terms they want to include in the **purchase agreement**. The **deposit receipt** includes all terms of the sale, including agreements about financing.

The offer covers more than just the purchase price and closing date. It covers **contingencies**, various inspections, mandatory disclosures, buyers' right to investigate the property, how the buyers will take title, damages and dispute resolution, **escrow instructions**, compensation to the brokers, and acceptance of the offer.

Upon writing a purchase agreement for real property, buyers may give some **consideration** such as a personal check, commonly for 1-3% of the purchase price, as a sign that they are serious about making the offer. The selling salesperson must consider certain items carefully when preparing the purchase agreement and before going to escrow.

After filling out the offer, call the listing salesperson immediately to arrange a face-to-face presentation. As the selling salesperson, your job is to present your buyers in the best light possible and convince the sellers that the buyers' offer is in their best interest. If an offer is not full price, especially if the listing price is reasonably set, you should counsel the buyers to expect a **counteroffer** from the sellers.

The accepting party must notify the offeror of acceptance for the offer or counteroffer to be valid. Once the sellers agree to the offer and the buyers are informed of the sellers' acceptance, the deposit receipt is a valid, non-rescindable, binding contract. After both the buyers and sellers have reached an agreement and have signed all required documents, either the listing or selling salesperson will take the paperwork to the escrow company that the buyers and sellers have chosen.

UNIT 12 REVIEW

■ Matching Exercise

Instructions: Write the letter of the matching term on the blank line before its definition. Answers are in Appendix A.

Terms

A. all-cash transaction
B. bilateral contract
C. consideration
D. contingencies
E. counteroffer
F. deposit receipt

G. early move-in
H. easement
I. escrow instructions
J. execute
K. purchase agreement
L. proration

Definitions

1. _____ An agreement that is also known as the deposit receipt

2. _____ Contract that acts as the receipt for earnest money given by the buyers to secure an offer, as well as being the basic agreement, between the buyers and sellers. Also known as the purchase agreement

3. _____ The written directions, signed by buyers and sellers, detailing the procedures necessary to close a transaction and direct the escrow agent on how to proceed

4. _____ A buyers' deposit in the form of cash, a personal check, cashier's check, promissory note, money order, or other form usually for 1-3% of the purchase price of the property

5. _____ Statements that define the terms of an agreement and give the other party to the agreement cause to void an offer if the terms are not met

6. _____ A clause that allows the buyers to take possession of the property prior to the close of escrow

7. _____ An offer made in return by one who rejects an unsatisfactory offer

8. _____ An agreement stating that each person promises to perform an act in exchange for another person's promise to perform

Multiple Choice Questions

Instructions: Circle your response and go to Appendix A to read the complete explanation for each question.

1. The document that may become the actual escrow instructions is the:
   a. deposit receipt.
   b. counteroffer.
   c. earnest money deposit.
   d. disclosure statement.

2. Before writing an offer, the selling salesperson should know:
   a. how much the buyers are willing to offer.
   b. whether price or terms are more important to the buyers.
   c. if there are any contingencies that must be included in the offer.
   d. all of the preceding.

3. The financial terms under which a property will be purchased must be included:
   a. in the purchase agreement.
   b. after submitting the purchase agreement.
   c. any time during escrow.
   d. only in a counteroffer.

4. The best way to present an offer is:
   a. over the telephone.
   b. by fax.
   c. in person.
   d. by mail.

5. An important item for a salesperson to bring when presenting an offer is:
   a. the cover letter.
   b. the deposit receipt.
   c. the earnest money deposit.
   d. all of the above.

6. If the sellers do not want to accept an offer because they feel the price offered is a little too low, they should:

    a. reject the offer.

    b. give the buyers a counteroffer.

    c. ignore the offer.

    d. wait for another offer.

7. When counseling sellers regarding a counteroffer, a salesperson should tell the sellers that:

    a. the counteroffer supersedes any previous offers made by the buyers.

    b. the sellers must verbally explain the counteroffer to the buyers.

    c. the sellers will have to put the home back on the market if a counteroffer is submitted.

    d. an outright rejection is a better idea.

8. Which of the following statements are true regarding counteroffers?

    a. They are illegal in California.

    b. They must be in writing.

    c. If the counteroffer is not accepted, the seller may sign the original purchase offer and create a binding contract.

    d. Counteroffers can only be written by sellers.

9. If sellers submit a counteroffer and the buyers accept it, the counteroffer is valid:

    a. at the time the buyers accept the counteroffer.

    b. as long as the buyers tried to fax the acceptance.

    c. unless the sellers withdraw the counteroffer after notification of acceptance.

    d. once the sellers receive notification of the buyers' acceptance.

10. Salesperson Spring has set up an appointment to present Pat's purchase agreement for Sally's split-level home. If Sally accepts the offer and Pat is informed of Sally's acceptance, the deposit receipt:

    a. is a valid, non-rescindable, binding contract.

    b. is a unilateral contract.

    c. needs to be executed.

    d. forms the basis for the title insurance policy.

Financing the Purchase

Unit 13

INTRODUCTION

A home usually is the largest purchase people make. Financing allows sellers to sell and buyers to buy. Therefore, some type of financing is at the center of nearly all real estate transactions.

The task of applying for and getting the necessary loan to purchase property can be overwhelming. Often, borrowers do not understand the jargon used by lenders, such as FICO® score, debt-to-income ratio, escrow fee, buy-down points, and trust deed. Since financing the purchase of a home is new to many buyers, be sure you can explain the steps in the loan process.

In this unit, you will learn about many aspects of real estate financing. These steps will better equip you to guide a buyer through the loan process. You will begin with the fundamentals of real estate finance to give you an understanding of the foundation of borrowing money to purchase real estate. Next, you will learn about promissory notes and security instruments, types of repayment plans, terms found in financing instruments, and different types of loans currently available to buyers. Then, you will learn the important aspects of the loan process, from choosing a lender to getting a credit report, underwriting the loan, and approving and funding the loan.

Learning Objectives

After reading this unit, you should be able to:

- recognize financing fundamentals.
- name financing instruments.
- identify types of repayment plans.
- identify conventional and government-backed loans.

FUNDAMENTALS OF REAL ESTATE FINANCE

Grasping the concepts of real estate finance requires an understanding of loan fundamentals. When a loan is made, the borrower signs a promissory note that states a certain amount of money has been borrowed. The **promissory note**, then, is the evidence of the debt. Lenders want collateral from borrowers as well as their promise to repay the loan. **Collateral** is the security pledged for repayment of a loan. The property being purchased is used as the security, or collateral, for the debt.

In California, the most common security instrument for the promissory note is a trust deed. A **security instrument** is a recorded legal document given by the borrower to the lender, which pledges the title of the property as insurance to the lender for the full payment of the loan. After signing the promissory note, the borrower is required to **execute** (sign) a trust deed, which is the security guaranteeing loan repayment. The borrower (**trustor**) has possession of the property, but transfers the naked legal title to a third party (**trustee**). The lender holds the original promissory note and the trust deed until the loan is repaid. Once the loan has been repaid, title to the property is returned to the borrower using a **deed of reconveyance.**

Terms Used in Real Estate Loans

- The **principal** is the actual amount of the loan or outstanding balance that the borrower owes the lender.
- The **interest rate** is simply the cost incurred when borrowing money and usually is expressed as a percentage.
- The **term** is the timeframe in which to repay the loan. Most mortgage loans primarily are 15 or 30 years in length. The longer the term of the loan, the lower the monthly payment will be, but more interest accrues over the years.

> - **Amortization** is the breakdown of the monthly payments from the start of the repayment plan all the way to the finish. Once the final payment is completed, the loan is fully amortized.
>
> - An **impound account** is a trust account set up for funds that are set aside for future, recurring costs relating to a property such as property taxes and insurance.

Understanding Promissory Notes

A promissory note serves as evidence of the debt and is a written agreement between a lender and a borrower to document a loan. It is a promise to pay back a certain sum of money at a specified interest, and at an agreed-upon time. Sometimes it is called "the note" or "a debt repayment contract".

In addition to showing the amount borrowed (principal), a promissory note sets the terms of the loan, such as the interest rate, repayment plan, and an acceleration clause in the event of default. With that information, you can calculate the payments using a financial calculator, printed amortization schedule, or software.

Types of Repayment Plans

A promissory note may be unsecured or secured by either a trust deed or mortgage. The promissory note, however, is the prime instrument, and if there are conflicts in the terms of the note and trust deed or mortgage, generally the terms of the note are controlling.

The promissory note terms create the basis for the repayment plan. There are several types of repayment plans, each with a different kind of obligation made clear by the terms of the note. The terms of the note include interest, repayment plan, and default. Some repayment plans are: (1) a single payment of principal and interest at the end of the loan term, (2) interest-only payments, (3) partially amortized with a balloon payment, and (4) fully amortized payments.

Unsecured Loan

Some borrowers who need a small loan to fix their car, buy a new appliance, or take a trip, choose a closed-end, unsecured loan instead of using their credit cards or getting a home equity loan. An **unsecured loan** is one in which the lender receives a promissory note from the borrower, without any security for payment of the debt, such as a trust deed or mortgage. The only recourse is a lengthy court action to force payment. This is the traditional I.O.U.

Single Payment of Principal and Interest

Some loans have no regular payments of interest and/or principal. Instead, the loan is paid off all at once, at a specified future date. This payment includes the entire principal amount and the accrued interest.

Interest-Only Payments

An interest-only loan offers borrowers greater purchasing power, increased cash flow and is a very popular alternative to traditional fixed rates loans. The **interest-only loan** is called a **straight loan** or **term loan**. It has regular interest payments during the term of the note. The interest rate is generally higher on a straight note and the principal does not decrease. A large payment is made at the end of the term to repay the principal and any remaining interest. This type of loan works well for people who only want to stay in a home for a few years. If the borrower plans to live in the house for only three to five years, an interest-only loan may be the right choice. With a conventional 30-year mortgage, most of the payment is applied directly to the interest of the loan with very little applied to the principal. With an interest-only loan, the borrower will have a lower payment and have almost the same principal balance at the end of three to five years as if a conventional loan had been selected.

Partially Amortized (Installment) Payments

This type of repayment schedule is used to create lower payments. The **partially amortized installment note** calls for regular, level payments on the principal and interest during the term of the loan. Since the loan does not fully amortize over the original term, there is still a remaining principal loan balance. The last installment, a **balloon payment**, includes all of the remaining principal and interest. Balloon payments can have extra risks because the borrower may need to refinance the property—possibly at higher interest rates.

INSTALLMENT NOTE - INTEREST INCLUDED
(Balloon Payment)

$ _____ _____, California _____, 20___

FOR VALUE RECEIVED, we, or either of us, promise to pay in lawful money of the United States of America, to

_____

_____

or order, at place designated by payee, the principal sum of _____

_____ dollar

with interest in like lawful money from _____, 20_____ at _____ per cei

per annum on the amounts of principal sum remaining unpaid from time to time.

Principal and interest payable in _____ installments of _____

_____

or more each, on the _____ day of each and every _____ beginning on th

_____ day of _____, 20____ and continuing until _____

at which time the entire unpaid balance of principal and interest hereunder shall be due and payable.

Each payment shall be credited first on interest then due and the remainder of principal; and interest shall thereupo cease upon the principal so credited. Should default be made in payment of any installment of principal or intere: when due the whole sum of principal and interest shall become immediately due at the option of the holder of th note. If action be instituted on this note I promise to pay such sum as the Court may fix as attorney's fees. Th note is secured by a Deed of Trust in which the maker of this note is referred to as "Trustor".

THE FOLLOWING PARAGRAPH IS ONLY APPLICABLE ON ONE TO FOUR RESIDENTIAL UNITS:

This note is subject to Section 2966 of the Civil Code, which provides that the holder of this note shall give writte notice to the Trustor, or his successor in interest, of prescribed information at least 90 and not more than 150 day before any balloon payment is due.

_____ _____

_____ _____

DO NOT DESTROY THIS NOTE

When paid, this note, with Deed of Trust securing same, must be surrendered to Trustee for cancellation befor reconveyance will be made.

FD-30C (Rev. 4/94)   INSTALLMENT NOTE - INTEREST INCLUDED (BALLOON PAYMENT)

Amortized (Installment) Payments

With **installment payments**, the loan is repaid in equal payments, typically monthly, until the loan has been repaid in full. The principal and interest are calculated for the term of the loan, and payments are determined by dividing the total by the number of payments in the term of the loan. Regular, periodic payments to include both interest and principal are made, which pay off the debt completely by the end of the term. This type of loan is **fully amortized** because the loan and interest are paid off when the last payment is made.

Negative amortization occurs if a borrower makes lower payments than should be made on a fully amortized loan. The difference between what should be paid and what is actually paid is added to the principal balance of the loan and the principal increases instead of decreases.

Fixed-Rate Fully Amortized Note

A **fixed-rate fully amortized note** is a loan with an interest rate that is fixed and payments that are level for the life of the loan. This note is common with institutional lenders. It is characterized by regular, periodic payments of fixed amounts, to include both interest and principal, which pay off the debt completely by the end of the term.

> **Review - Two Features of Fixed-Rate Fully Amortized Loans**
> - Interest rate remains fixed for the life of the loan.
> - Payments remain level for the life of the loan and repay the loan at the end of the loan term.

Adjustable-Rate Mortgage (ARM)

Lenders have created alternative payment plans such as the adjustable-rate mortgage, which allow borrowers to qualify for larger loans and at the same time help maintain the lender's investment return. An **adjustable-rate mortgage** (ARM) is a note with an interest rate that is tied to a movable economic index. The **index** is the overall average of market interest rates that a lender will use to determine the rate of an ARM. The interest rate in the note varies upward or downward over the term of the loan, depending on the agreed-upon index. To protect the borrower from wild swings in interest rates, there is usually a limit on how much the interest rate can change on an annual basis, as well as a lifetime cap. A **cap** is a limit on changes in interest rate.

A lender may offer several choices of interest rates, terms, payments, or adjustment periods to a borrower with an ARM. The initial interest rate, or **qualifying rate**, is determined by the current rate of the chosen index. Then, a margin is added to the index, which might be anywhere from one to three percentage points. The **margin** is the spread or markup that a lender charges on the loan in order to earn a profit. It is added to the initial interest rate to determine the actual beginning rate the borrower will pay. The margin does not change for the life of the loan. The interest rate may change, however, as the chosen index changes, depending on economic conditions.

The borrower's payment will stay the same for a specified time, which might be six months or a year, depending on the agreement with the lender. At the agreed-upon time, the lender re-evaluates the loan to determine if the index has changed, either upward or downward, and calculates a new payment based on the changed interest rate plus the same margin.

Generally, adjustable-rate financing benefits the bankers because it allows for an inflow of extra cash during times of higher interest rates. In other words, the borrower's payments will increase because the interest rate will go up, therefore more money will flow into the financial institution.

Understanding Security Instruments

The claim a lender (**creditor**) has in the property of a borrower (**debtor**) is called a security interest. The **security interest** allows certain assets of a borrower to be set aside so that a lender can sell them if the borrower defaults on the loan. Proceeds from the sale of that property can be taken to pay off the debt. The rights and duties of lenders and borrowers are described in documents called **security instruments**, which are used to secure promissory notes. The security instruments used to secure the interest for the lender are the deed of trust, mortgage, and contract for sale.

Deed of Trust

In California, the deed of trust (or trust deed) is the most commonly used security instrument in real estate finance. A **trust deed** is a security instrument that conveys title of real property from a trustor to a trustee to hold as security for the beneficiary for payment of a debt. The three parties to a trust deed are the borrower (**trustor**), lender (**beneficiary**), and a neutral third party called a **trustee**.

WHEN RECORDED MAIL TO:

_____ [Space Above This Line For Recording Data] _____

State of California   **DEED OF TRUST**   FHA Case No.

THIS DEED OF TRUST ("Security Instrument") is made on
The Trustor is

("Borrower").

The trustee is

("Trustee").

The beneficiary is

which is organized and existing under the laws of   ,
and whose address is

("Lender").

Borrower owes Lender the principal sum of

Dollars (U.S. $). This debt is evidenced by Borrower's note
dated the same date as this Security Instrument ("Note"), which provides for monthly payments, with the full debt, if not
paid earlier, due and payable on   . This Security Instrument secures to Lender:
(a) the repayment of the debt evidenced by the Note, with interest, and all renewals, extensions and modifications of the
Note; (b) the payment of all other sums, with interest, advanced under paragraph 7 to protect the security of this Security
Instrument; and (c) the performance of Borrower's covenants and agreements under this Security Instrument and the Note.
For this purpose, Borrower irrevocably grants and conveys to Trustee, in trust, with power of sale, the following described
property located in   County, California:

TOGETHER WITH all the improvements now or hereafter erected on the property, and all easements, appurtenances,
and fixtures now or hereafter a part of the property. All replacements and additions shall also be covered by this Security
Instrument. All of the foregoing is referred to in this Security Instrument as the "Property."

Initials _____
FHA California Deed of Trust 10/95

The trustor (borrower) signs the promissory note and the trust deed and gives them to the beneficiary (lender) who holds them for the term of the loan. Under the trust deed, the trustor has **equitable title** and the trustee has "bare" or "naked" legal title to the property.

The trustee acts as an agent for the beneficiary and has only two obligations. The first is to foreclose on the property if there is a default on the loan and the second is to reconvey the title to the borrower when the debt is repaid in full. When the debt is fully repaid, the beneficiary signs a **Request for Full Reconveyance**, which is a document that states a borrower has completely paid off the loan and can now own free and clear title to the property. The request is sent to the trustee ordering them to reconvey title to the borrower. The trustee signs and records a **Deed of Reconveyance**, which is a document that shows the debt has been repaid, and clears the lien from the property.

Mortgage

In the early 1900s, the deed of trust virtually replaced the note and mortgage when financing real estate. The promissory note shows the obligation of the debt and the mortgage is a lien against the described property until the debt is repaid.

The two parties in a mortgage are a **mortgagor** (borrower) and a **mortgagee** (lender). The mortgagor receives loan funds from a mortgagee and signs a promissory note and mortgage. Once signed by the borrower, both the note and mortgage are held by the lender until the loan is paid. Unlike a trust deed, under a mortgage both title and possession remain with the borrower.

Contract of Sale

The **contract of sale** is the financing instrument with many names. It may be called an installment sales contract, an agreement of sale, a conditional sales contract, a contract for deed, or a land sales contract.

Within this contract, the seller (**vendor**) becomes the lender to the buyer (**vendee**). The vendor pays off the original financing while receiving payments from the vendee on the contract of sale. The vendor and vendee's relationship is like that of a beneficiary and a trustor in a trust deed. The buyer, (vendee) has possession and use of the property even though legal title is held by the seller (vendor). In a contract of sale, the vendor retains legal ownership of the property and the vendee holds what is known as equitable title. When all the terms of the contract are met, the vendor will pass title to the vendee.

Land contracts are used in CalVet loans under the California Veterans Farm and Home Purchase Plan (discussed later in the unit). The state of California is the vendor who has legal title, and the veteran is the vendee who has equitable title.

Terms Found in Finance Instruments

When a borrower signs a note promising to repay a sum, the lender usually will include some specific requirements in the note regarding repayment. In addition to the terms in the note, the trust deed lists several covenants (promises) regarding the relationship of the borrower and the lender. These special clauses protect the lender and the lender's interests.

Prepayment Clauses

Occasionally, a trust deed will include a **prepayment clause**. This is a penalty fee that a borrower is responsible for if a loan is paid off too early. When lenders make loans, they calculate their return over the term of the loan. If a loan is paid off ahead of time, the lender gets less interest; therefore, the borrower has to make it up by paying a penalty.

"Or More" Clause

An **"or more" clause** allows a borrower to pay off a loan early, or make higher payments without penalty.

Late Payments

Lenders may not impose a late charge on a payment until after the payment is ten days late.

Acceleration Clause

An **acceleration clause** allows a lender to call the entire note due, on occurrence of a specific event such as default in payment, taxes, insurance, or sale of the property. In addition, a lender may use the acceleration clause to call the entire note due if the borrower sells the property. In order to pay off the outstanding loan, a lender will foreclose on the loan.

Alienation Clause

The **alienation** or **due-on-sale clause** is a type of acceleration clause. A lender may call the entire note due if the original borrower transfers (alienates) ownership of the property to someone else. If the note contains an acceleration clause, the trust deed must mention this clause in order to enforce the contract. This clause protects the lender from an unqualified, unapproved buyer taking over a loan. Justifiably, the lender fears possible default, with no control over who is making the payments.

Usually a lender will want the existing loan paid off if a property owner transfers the property to someone else. However, under certain circumstances, a property owner may transfer responsibility for the loan to the buyer when he or she sells the property to another party. A buyer may "assume" an existing loan, or may buy a property "subject to" an existing loan.

Loan Assumption

An **assumption clause** allows a buyer to assume responsibility for the full payment of the loan with the lender's knowledge and consent. When a property is sold, a buyer may assume the existing loan. Usually with the approval of the lender, the buyer takes over primary liability for the loan, with the original borrower secondarily liable if there is a default. What that means is that even though the original borrower is secondarily responsible, according to the loan assumption agreement, no actual repayment of the loan may be required of that person.

The original borrower (seller) can avoid any responsibility for the loan by asking the lender for a **substitution of liability (novation)**, relieving the seller of all liability for repayment of the loan. In most cases, a buyer assumes an existing loan with the approval of the underlying lender. However, an alienation clause in the note would prevent a buyer from assuming the loan.

"Subject To"

A buyer may also purchase a property "subject to" the existing loan. A **"subject to" clause** allows a buyer to take over a loan, making the payments without the knowledge or approval of the lender. The original borrower remains responsible for the loan, even though the buyer takes title and makes the payments. In this case, the property remains the security for the loan. In the case of default, the property is sold and the proceeds go to the lender, with no recourse to the original buyer other than the foreclosure going against the borrower's credit.

When a buyer takes a property "subject to" the existing loan, the underlying lender may not always be informed. The buyer simply starts making the payments and the seller hopes he or she is diligent and does not default.

Escrow No. _____   Title Order No. _____

(DUE ON SALE CLAUSE)

$ _____, California _____, 20_____

_____ after date, for value received

I promise to pay to _____

_____ or order, at

_____

the sum of _____ DOLLARS

with interest from _____ until paid at the

rate of _____ per cent per annum, payable _____

_____

_____

Principal and interest payable in lawful money of the United States of America. should default be made in payment of interest when due the whole sum of principal and interest shall become immediately due at the option of the holder of this note and after said breach, said obligation shall continue to accrue interest at the rate of _____% per annum. If action be instituted on this note I promise to pay such sum as the Court may fix as Attorney's Fees. This note is secured by a Deed of Trust of even date herewith.

In the event the herein described property or any part thereof, or any interest therein which has been given as security for the payment of this obligation is sold, agreed to be sold, conveyed or alienated by the Trustor, or by the operation of the law or otherwise, all obligations secured by this instrument, irrespective of the maturity dates expressed therein, at the option of the holder hereof and without demand or notice shall immediately become due and payable.

_____   _____

_____   _____

_____   _____

DO NOT DESTROY THIS NOTE
When paid, this note, if secured by Deed of Trust, must be surrendered to Trustee for cancellation before reconveyance will be made.

FD-30G (Rev. 2/95)   STRAIGHT NOTE (DUE ON SALE CLAUSE)

The occurrence of "subject to" sales is relative to economic and market conditions. In a seller's real estate market, where more buyers than sellers exist, a homeowner does not need to sell "subject to" his or her loan.

Types of Loans

Loans are classified according to their loan terms and whether they have government backing. First, all of the various loans are classified by their terms— fixed-rate loans or adjustable-rate loans and their combinations. Second, loans are classified by whether they are conventional or have government backing.

Some lenders specialize in only conventional conforming loans, whereas full service lenders offer a wide selection of loan programs including conventional, government-sponsored FHA and VA loans, and non-conforming loans.

Conventional Loans

A **conventional loan** is any loan made by lenders without any governmental guarantees. The basic protection for a lender making conventional loans is the borrower's equity in the property. A low down payment will mean greater risk for the lender and a higher interest charged to the borrower. Conventional loans may be conforming or non-conforming.

Conforming Loans

Conforming loans have terms and conditions that follow the guidelines set forth by the Federal National Mortgage Corporation (Fannie Mae) and the Federal Home Loan Mortgage Corporation (Freddie Mac). These loans are called **"A" paper loans**, or **prime loans**, and can be made to purchase or refinance homes (one to four residential units). Fannie Mae and Freddie Mac guidelines establish the maximum loan amount, borrower credit and income requirements, down payment, and suitable properties. Fannie Mae and Freddie Mac announce new loan limits every year. This limit is reviewed annually and, if needed, modified to reflect changes in the national average price for single-family homes.

Private Mortgage Insurance (PMI)

When the loan exceeds 80% of the value of the property, lenders usually require **private mortgage insurance** (PMI) on conventional loans. Usually borrowers pay for this insurance as part of the monthly payment. Conventional lenders usually require private mortgage insurance on low down payment loans for protection if borrowers fail to make their payments. A few companies provide this insurance.

Non-Conforming Loans

Sometimes either the borrower's creditworthiness or the size of the loan does not meet conventional lending standards; these loans are **non-conforming loans** and include jumbo subprime loans.

Jumbo Loans

Loans that are above the maximum loan limit set by Fannie Mae and Freddie Mac are called **jumbo loans**. Because jumbo loans are not funded by these government-sponsored entities, they usually carry a higher interest rate and some additional underwriting requirements.

Subprime Loans

Subprime loans were developed to help higher risk borrowers obtain a mortgage. Loans that do not meet the borrower credit requirements of Fannie Mae and Freddie Mac are called **subprime loans** or "B" and "C" paper loans as opposed to "A" paper conforming loans. Subprime loans are offered to borrowers who may have recently filed for bankruptcy or foreclosure, or have had late payments on their credit reports. The purpose of these loans is to offer temporary financing to applicants until they can qualify for conforming "A" financing. Due to the higher risk associated with lending to borrowers who have a poor credit history, subprime loans typically require a larger down payment and a higher interest rate.

Government Participation in Real Estate Finance

Two federal agencies and one state agency help make it possible for people to buy homes they would never be able to purchase without government involvement. The two federal agencies that participate in real estate financing are the Federal Housing Administration (FHA) and the Veterans Administration (VA). The California Veterans' Farm and Home Purchase Program, or CalVet loan is a state program that helps eligible veterans.

The Federal Housing Administration and the Veterans Administration are two federal agencies that help make it possible for veterans to buy homes.

Federal Housing Administration (FHA)

The **Federal Housing Administration** (FHA) does not make loans; it insures lenders against loss. Loans are made by authorized lending institutions such as banks, savings banks, and independent mortgage companies. The borrower applies directly to the FHA-approved lender (mortgagee), not the FHA, for a loan.

As long as FHA guidelines are used in funding the loan, the FHA, upon default by the borrower, insures the lender against loss. If the borrower does default, the lender may foreclose and the FHA will pay cash up to the established limit of the insurance. The FHA guidelines encourage home ownership by allowing 100% of the down payment to be a gift from family or friends and by allowing closing costs to be financed to reduce the up front cost of buying a home. The down payment on FHA loans varies with the amount of the loan.

The FHA maximum loan amounts vary from one county to another. It is important that the total loan amount, including financed closing costs, not exceed the maximum limit set by the FHA for the county in which the property is located. There are no income limits on FHA loans and an FHA loan will be based on the selling price when it is lower than the appraisal. There are no alienation or prepayment penalty clauses allowed in FHA loans.

The lender is protected, in case of foreclosure, by charging the borrower a fee for an insurance policy called **Mutual Mortgage Insurance** (MMI). The insurance requirement is how the FHA finances its program. The premium may be financed as part of the loan or paid in cash at the close of escrow.

Popular FHA Loan Programs

Any qualified resident of the United States may obtain an FHA loan as long as the property will be the borrower's principal residence and is located in the United States. There is a variety of FHA loan programs.

Section 203(b)

The FHA 203(b) loan offers financing on the purchase or construction of owner-occupied residences of one to four units. This program offers 30-year, fixed-rate, fully amortized mortgages with a down payment requirement as low as 3.5%, allowing financing of up to 96.5% of the value of the home.

Section 203(k)

A purchase rehabilitation loan (purchase rehab) is a great option for buyers who want to improve their property immediately upon purchase.

This mortgage loan provides the funds to purchase the home and the funds to complete the improvement project all in one loan, one application, one set of fees, one closing, and one convenient monthly payment.

Section 245(a) Graduated Payment Mortgage

A **Graduated Payment Mortgage** (GPM) has a monthly payment that starts out at the lowest level and increases at a specific rate. Payments for the first five years are low, and cover only part of the interest due, with the unpaid amount added to the principal balance. After that time, the loan is recalculated, with the new payments staying the same from that point on. In this loan, the interest rate is not adjustable and does not change during the term of the loan. What actually changes is the amount of the monthly mortgage payment.

A GPM is offered by the FHA to borrowers who might have trouble qualifying for regular loan payments, but who expect their income to increase. This loan is for the buyer who expects to be earning more after a few years and can make a higher payment at that time.

Section 255 Home Equity Conversion Mortgage

Home Equity Conversion Mortgage (HECM) is a type of reverse annuity mortgage. It is a program for homeowners 62-years old and older who have paid off their mortgages or have only small mortgage balances remaining. The program has three options for homeowners: (1) borrow against the equity in their homes in a lump sum, (2) borrow on a monthly basis for a fixed term or for as long as they live in the home, or (3) borrow as a line of credit. Borrowers are not required to make payments as long as they live in the home because the loan is paid off when the property is sold.

VA Loan

The **Department of Veterans Affairs** (VA) does not make loans. It guarantees loans made by an approved institutional lender, much like the FHA. Both programs were created to assist people in buying homes when conventional loan programs did not fit their needs. The main differences between the two government programs are (1) only an eligible veteran may obtain a VA loan and (2) the VA does not require a down payment up to a certain loan amount, which means qualified veterans, could get 100% financing. As with FHA loans, there are no alienation or prepayment penalty clauses allowed with VA loans.

VA loans are made by a lender, such as a mortgage company, savings and loan, or bank. The VA's guaranty on the loan protects the lender against loss if the payments are not made, and is intended to encourage lenders to offer veterans loans with more favorable terms.

California Veteran Loans (CalVet)

The **California Department of Veterans Affairs** (CA VA) administers the CalVet loan program to assist California veterans in buying a home or farm. Unlike other government financing, the CalVet program funds and services its own loans through the sale of State General Obligation Bonds. The CA VA sells bonds to purchase homes and then sells the homes to qualified California veterans using a land sale contract.

An eligible California veteran applies for the loan and makes loan payments directly to the Department of Veterans Affairs. Upon application for a CalVet loan and approval of the borrower and property, the Department of Veterans Affairs purchases the property from the seller, takes title to the property, and sells it to the veteran on a contract of sale. The department holds legal title, with the veteran holding equitable title, until the loan is paid off. The veteran has an obligation to apply for life insurance, with the Department of Veterans Affairs as beneficiary, to pay off the debt in case of the veteran's death.

Junior Loans

A lender uses strict standards about the amount of equity required in a property before loaning money, and particularly for a junior loan. The reason is simple. All lenders want is to get their money back in a timely manner, along with the calculated return on the investment. Care must be taken, in case of a decrease in the value of the subject property, to make sure there is enough of a margin between the total amount owed and the value of the property. If the property is sold at a foreclosure sale, the lender will be assured of getting the money back. By only loaning up to 75%-90% of the property value, the lender leaves some room for loss. Typical junior loans include home equity loans, home equity lines of credit, and seller financing.

Home Equity Loan

In a **home equity loan**, the borrower gets the entire loan balance at one time. It is a fixed-rate second mortgage with principal and interest payments remaining the same over the life of the loan. **Equity** is the difference between the value of the property and any outstanding loans or the initial down payment. Assuming there is enough equity, a homeowner can apply for a cash loan for any purpose. Being a homeowner can be advantageous, especially if there is built-up equity in a house, townhouse, duplex, or condominium. The equity can pay for home improvements, bill consolidation, or college tuition.

Home Equity Line of Credit

A **home equity line of credit** (HELOC) is a type of junior loan that taps into a property owner's equity and creates a revolving credit line. With a HELOC, the borrower takes money, as it is needed, up to the credit limit. It has a low starting interest rate with a variable monthly rate based on the outstanding balance. More and more lenders are offering home equity lines of credit. By using the equity in their home, borrowers may qualify for a sizable amount of credit, available for use when and how they please, at a relatively low interest rate. Furthermore, under the California tax law—depending on the borrowers' specific situation—they may be allowed to deduct the interest because the debt is secured by their home.

A home equity line is a form of revolving credit in which a borrower's home serves as collateral. Because the home is likely to be a borrower's largest asset, many homeowners use their credit lines only for major items such as education, home improvements, or medical bills.

Seller Financing: 2nd Trust Deed

Another common source for secondary financing of a sale is the seller. If the seller is going to be the lender, he or she agrees to carry back, or act as a banker, and make a loan to the buyer for the needed amount. That loan is secured by a trust deed, in favor of the seller, recorded after the first trust deed. With a seller carry-back loan, the seller acts as the beneficiary and the buyer is the trustor.

When a seller carries the paper on the sale of his or her home, it is also called a **purchase money loan**, just like the loan made by an outside lender. If a seller receives a substantial amount from the proceeds of a first loan, plus the buyer's down payment, it may be in the seller's interest to carry a second trust deed— possibly for income or to reduce tax liability by accepting installment payments.

Example: Dave made an offer on a house owned by John, who accepted an offer of $375,000 with $37,500 as the down payment. The buyer, Dave, qualified for a new first loan in the amount of $318,750, and asked John to carry a second loan in the amount of $18,750 to complete the purchase price.

When the seller extends credit in the form of a loan secured by a **second trust deed,** the note may be written as a straight note, with interest-only payments, or even no payments. Alternatively, it could be an installment note with a balloon payment at the end, or fully amortized note with equal payments until it is paid off. The term of the loan is decided by the buyer and seller. The instructions of the buyer and seller regarding the seller financing are usually carried out through escrow.

If a trust deed held by the seller is sold to an outside party, usually a mortgage broker, the note and trust deed will be discounted. **Discounting a note** is selling a note for less than the face amount or the current balance. Even though the seller receives a reduction in value by the mortgage broker, it is one way a seller can get cash out of a trust deed that was carried back.

Example: Bob and Todd owned a house together as investors. After several years, they put the house on the market for $550,000 and hoped to get a full-price offer so they could go their separate ways with the profit from the house.

After a short time, they did get a full-price offer. The buyer offered to put $110,000 down, get a $385,000 new first loan and asked Bob and Todd to carry $55,000 for five years, as a second trust deed. Bob and Todd would have turned the offer down if their salesperson had not suggested they accept and sell the second trust deed after the close of escrow. Even though it would be discounted, it was one way they could get most of the cash out of their investment.

If the second trust deed were sold at a discounted 20%, or $11,000, Bob and Todd would end up with $55,000, less $11,000, or $44,000. In that way they would get the cash out of the sale, though they would be netting less than they originally planned because of the discount. They followed their salesperson's suggestion, and were satisfied with the result.

Whenever there is seller financing in a real estate transaction, the law requires the buyer and seller to complete a Seller Financing Disclosure Statement. It is a document that gives both the seller and buyer all the information needed to make an informed decision about using seller financing to complete the sale.

By looking at the buyer's income, and whether the buyer has a good credit history, the seller can see from the disclosure whether the buyer has the ability to pay off the loan. The buyer can see what the existing loans are, as well as such things as due date and payments on existing loans that would be senior to the loan in question.

Seller Financing: All-Inclusive Trust Deed (AITD)

The **all-inclusive trust deed** (AITD), or **wrap-around mortgage**, is a type of seller financing. It is used in a transaction between buyer and seller to make the financing attractive to the buyer and beneficial to the seller as well. Instead of the buyer assuming an existing loan and the seller carrying back a second trust deed, the AITD can accomplish the same purpose with greater benefit to both parties. At the closing, the buyer receives title to the property.

An AITD (wrap-around mortgage) wraps an existing loan with a new loan, and the borrower makes one payment for both. In other words, the new trust deed (the AITD) includes the present encumbrances, such as first, second, third, or more trust deeds, plus the amount to be financed by the seller.

THE LOAN PROCESS

Getting a loan is an integral part of the real estate transaction since very few people have the amount of ready cash to buy a home with no financing. The first step in getting a loan is for the borrower to fill out a loan application. Once the lender has the borrower's completed application, the underwriting process can begin. **Underwriting** is the process of evaluating a borrower's risk factors before the lender will make a loan. The lender will determine the ability of a borrower to pay the loan and determine if the value of the property is sufficient to repay the loan in the event of a default by the borrower. The purpose of underwriting is to determine if the borrower and the property meet the minimum standards established by the primary lender and the secondary market investor. Once both the borrower and the property qualify, the loan process continues until it closes.

Steps in Getting a Loan
- Choose a lender
- Get a credit report
- Complete a loan application and provide required documentation
- Process and underwrite the loan
- Approve and fund the loan

Choose a Lender

Prospective borrowers have individual requirements; therefore, they may choose one lender over another for many reasons.

- **Variety of Products** – Choose a lender that offers a variety of products. Thirty years ago, a borrower generally had a choice of a 30-year, fixed-rate loan, or no loan. A competitive lender will be one who offers the most loan products or types of loans (ARMs, interest-only, etc.).

- **Low Interest Rates and Fees** – Shop around for a loan with few or no points, sometimes called the loan fee, and competitive interest rates. Most real estate loans are **simple interest**—the interest is paid only on the principal owed. The **effective interest rate** is the rate the borrower is actually paying, commonly called the "**annual percentage rate**" (APR). Lenders receive compensation for their risk in the form of interest rates. If the lender thinks the borrower is a high risk, the lender will charge a higher interest rate for the privilege of borrowing the lender's money. The lower the interest rate, the more you can pay down the principal.

- **Convenience** – Choose a lender who will help fill out the paperwork. Some lenders will go to the borrower's home or will take the application via the telephone or Internet.

- **Reputation** – It is one thing to offer low interest rates, and another to fund a loan according to the promises made to the buyer. A lender's reputation in the business community is another of the standards that a prospective borrower will use in selecting a loan provider.

What Lenders Look For

Lenders make loans to borrowers based on standardized guidelines. They look for an ability to repay debt and a willingness to do so—and sometimes for a little extra security to protect their loans. They speak of the Three Cs of credit: capacity, character, and collateral.

> **The Three Cs of Credit**
> - Capacity
> - Character
> - Collateral

Capacity: Can the borrower repay the debt? Lenders ask for employment information such as the borrower's occupation, how long he or she has worked there, and for what earnings. They also want to know what the borrower's expenses are: how many dependents there are, whether the borrower pays alimony or child support, and the amount of any other obligations.

Character: Will the borrower repay the debt? Lenders will look at the borrower's credit history, including the amount of money owed, the frequency of borrowing, the timeliness of paying bills, and a pattern of living within one's means. Lenders also look for signs of stability such as how long the borrower has lived at the present address, whether he or she owns or rents the home, and the length of present employment.

Collateral: Is the lender fully protected if the borrower fails to repay? Lenders want to know what the borrower may have that could be used to back up or secure a loan, and any other resources the borrower has for repaying debt other than income, such as savings, investments or property.

Lenders require collateral to fully protect a loan. Property can be used as collateral.

Credit Report

The lender requests a credit report from one of the credit-reporting agencies: Experian, Equifax, or TransUnion. These companies research the credit records of borrowers and memorialize the findings in a factual **credit report**. They have access to databases that store credit information on most borrowers in the country. Additionally, they search the public records for derogatory items that may have been filed against a borrower, such as judgments, bankruptcies, and liens.

The credit report indicates a credit score for the loan applicant. **Credit scoring** is an objective, statistical method that lenders use to assess the borrower's credit risk. The score is a number that rates the likelihood that a borrower will repay a loan. Credit scores only consider the information contained in the credit profile. They do not consider income, savings, down payment amount, or demographic factors such as gender, nationality, or marital status.

Credit scores are determined by past delinquencies, derogatory payment behavior, current debt level, length of credit history, types of credit, and number of inquiries. Establishing a good track record of making payments on time will raise the credit score, but late payments will lower the score.

Scores range from 350 (high risk) to 950 (low risk). There are a few types of credit scores; the most widely used are **FICO® scores**, which were developed by Fair Isaac Corporation. The FICO® scores run from 400 to 620 for the applicants who are late in paying bills and between 700 to above 800 for those applicants who always pay bills on time.

Paying bills on time affects your FICO® score.

Under the Fair Credit-Reporting Act, a person who has been denied credit, housing, or employment may receive a free copy of his or her credit report by contacting one of the credit-reporting agencies directly.

Building a Good Record

A borrower's first attempt to get credit may prove frustrating—sometimes it seems a borrower already has to have credit to get credit. Some lenders will look only at a borrower's salary, job, and the other financial information on the application. However, most want to know how reliably the person has repaid past debts. They turn to the records kept by credit bureaus or credit-reporting agencies, whose business is to collect, store and report information about borrowers that is routinely supplied by many lenders. These records include the initial credit amount and its repayment.

Ways to Build Good Credit

- Open a checking account or a savings account or both. These accounts may be checked as evidence that the borrower has money and knows how to manage it. Cancelled checks can be used to show that a borrower pays utilities or rent bills regularly, a sign of reliability.

- Apply for a major credit card. Initially, the lender may ask for funds to be deposited with the financial institution to serve as collateral for a credit card. Some institutions will issue a credit card with a credit limit no greater than the amount on deposit.

- Apply for a department store credit card.

- Paying credit card bills and financial obligations on time is a plus in credit histories.

Maintaining Complete and Accurate Credit Records

Mistakes on a borrower's credit record can cloud future credit. A borrower's credit rating is so important, the individual should be sure that credit bureau records are complete and accurate. The Fair Credit-Reporting Act says that a borrower must be told what is in the credit file and have any errors corrected.

Negative Information

If a lender refuses a borrower credit because of unfavorable information in his or her credit report, a borrower has a right to get the name and address of the agency that keeps the report. Then, a borrower may either request information from the credit bureau by mail or in person. The borrower may not get an exact copy of the file, but will learn what is in the report. The law also says that the credit bureau must help a borrower interpret the data in the report, because the raw data may take experience to analyze. If a borrower is questioning a credit refusal made within the past 60 days, the bureau cannot charge a fee for explaining the report.

If a borrower notifies the bureau about an error, generally the bureau must investigate and resolve the dispute within 30 days after receiving the notice. The bureau will contact the lender who supplied the data and remove any information that is incomplete or inaccurate from the credit file.

A borrower who disagrees with the findings may include a short statement (100 words) in the record, giving the borrower's side of the story. Future reports to lenders must include this statement or a summary of it.

Old Information

Sometimes credit information is too old to give a good picture of a borrower's financial reputation. There is a limit on how long certain information may be kept in the file.

Bankruptcies must not be reported after 10 years. However, information about any bankruptcies at any time may be reported if a borrower applies for life insurance with a face value over $150,000, for a job paying $75,000 or more, or for credit with a principal amount of $150,000 or more.

Lawsuits and judgments paid, tax liens, and most other kinds of unfavorable information must not be reported after seven years.

A borrower's credit record may not be given to anyone who does not have a legitimate business need for it. Stores to which a borrower is applying for credit may examine the record; curious neighbors may not. Prospective employers may examine a borrower's record with his or her permission.

Complete the Loan Application

Once the borrower has chosen a lender, the next step is to fill out a loan application. Filling out the application form, which asks for detailed information about the borrower, the employment record, and information regarding the address of the property desired is the first step toward obtaining a loan. The lender will need documentation to substantiate the information in

After filling out the loan applications, buyers will find out whether they are preapproved for a loan.

the application, such as recent pay stubs, bank statements, verifications of employment, deposit and rent or mortgage, tax returns, appraisal, purchase agreement, divorce decrees, bankruptcy papers and any other information the lender may need.

A recent convenience is being able to complete the loan application online. Computer access to credit information allows a lender to give a preliminary qualification to a borrower within minutes based on the borrower's income and credit score.

By filling out the loan application, buyers will find out whether they are preapproved for the loan. Remember, prequalification relies on verbal representations made by the buyer to the lender. Preapproval is based on documentation that verifies verbal representations. If the buyer is preapproved for the loan, the lender will create a letter that outlines the approved financing so that the buyer can submit this preapproval letter with the earnest money deposit and offer.

The standard form for residential mortgage loan applications, the **FHLMC/ FNMA 1003** form **(Uniform Residential Loan Application)**, makes it possible for lenders to sell their loans on the secondary money market. Lenders who want to keep their mortgage loans within their own house, have adopted the Uniform Residential Loan Application to make sure the loans conform to the required standards of the secondary market, should they want to sell the loans at a future time.

> **Uniform Residential Loan Application**
> - Type of mortgage and terms of loan
> - Property information and purpose of loan
> - Borrower information
> - Employment verification
> - Monthly income and combined housing expense information
> - Assets and liabilities
> - Details of transaction
> - Declaration
> - Acknowledgement and agreement
> - Information for government monitoring purposes

Before filling out the form, the borrower needs the following information: Social Security number, current and previous employers and residences, most recent pay stubs, copies of credit card and loan statements, copies of bank statements and asset information (stocks, pension, and retirement funds).

Type of Mortgage and Terms of Loan

The first section of the loan application is a request for a specific type of mortgage loan by the prospective borrower, listing the amount and terms of the anticipated loan. The lender usually fills in this part of the application.

Property Information and Purpose of Loan

The second section lists the address and legal description of the desired property, purpose of the loan, how title will be held, and source of the down payment. Fill in the address of the property only if the borrower's offer on the property has been accepted. If no property has been selected, just fill out the purpose of the loan (purchase or refinance); type of property; the name(s) in which the title will be held; how the title will be held; and the source of down payment. Usually, cash is the source of the down payment on a purchase.

Borrower/Co-Borrower Information

Borrower information helps the lender decide whether the borrower has the ability and willingness to repay the loan. This section asks for name, Social Security number, marital status, number of dependents and their ages, phone number, age, years in school, and address (current and former).

Employment Verification

Evidence that borrowers are able to pay back the loan is shown by their employment status. This section asks for the name and address of the borrower's employer. It also asks for the borrower's position and the length of time the borrower has been employed.

Monthly Income and Combined Housing Expense Information

This section informs the lender about the borrower's current income and housing expenses, as well as the proposed income and housing expenses if the loan is funded. This income information can be found on the borrower's pay stubs.

Assets and Liabilities

Assets include checking and savings accounts, stocks and bonds, life insurance, real estate owned, retirement funds, net worth of a business owned, automobiles owned and any other items of value. **Liabilities** are listed as credit card accounts, pledged assets, alimony or child support owed, job-related expenses and any other amounts that may be owed. The information needed to fill out this section comes from bank statements, credit card and loan statements. Only fill in information about credit cards that have a balance, because these are the only numbers that are considered when calculating the debt-to-income ratios.

Details of Transaction

This section includes a detailed listing of the purchase price, the loan amount, as well as other costs of obtaining the loan for the benefit of borrower and lender. Most borrowers do not know this information, so the loan agent usually fills it out.

Declaration

This section includes a list of questions the borrower must answer regarding judgments, bankruptcies, foreclosures, lawsuits, or any other voluntary or involuntary legal obligations. The borrower needs to answer the questions and declarations.

Acknowledgement and Agreement

This section contains a final declaration by the borrower regarding the statements and information made in the application as well as an acknowledgement of the borrowers' awareness of their obligation regarding the loan. The borrower and co-borrower must sign and date this section.

Information for Government Monitoring Purposes

This section is optional and may or may not be completed by the borrower. It includes the disclosure that the lender is held liable for complying with state and federal fair housing laws and home mortgage disclosure laws.

Review the Commitment Letter – Be sure you understand any conditions of the loan offer that are stated in the lender's commitment letter. Be sure all conditions have been met before closing. For example, if the home you are buying has been found to be in violation of a building code or zoning regulations, the lender may specify that those problems must be corrected before the closing. If the sellers have agreed to make repairs required by the lender, you need to make sure the work is finished and done properly before closing.

Inquire about Mortgage Insurance – Mortgage Insurance (MI) helps protect the lender in case of a foreclosure. **Foreclosure** is the legal process that a lender may use to take ownership of your home if you fail to make your monthly payments. Typically, the lender will require this insurance if your down payment is less than 20% of the purchase price of the property.

The lender orders MI from a mortgage insurance company after your loan is approved. You may be required to pay the full first year's premium at closing. Renewal premiums will be added to the monthly mortgage payments made to your lender after closing, and will be put into an escrow account. Many MI companies offer programs that require no upfront payment at closing, but they may require a slightly higher monthly payment.

Process and Underwrite the Loan

Processing a loan is probably the most time-consuming, yet most important part of the loan procedure. All pertinent information must be gathered and evaluated to determine whether a loan fits certain guidelines, along with risk analysis to prevent loss to investors. Underwriting typically involves qualifying the borrower for a certain loan amount and qualifying the property for the loan amount in question.

Lenders use different combinations of these facts to reach their decisions. Some set unusually high standards; others simply do not make certain kinds of loans. Lenders also use different rating systems. Some rely solely on their own instinct and experience. Others use a "credit-scoring" or statistical system to predict whether the borrower is a good credit risk. They assign a certain number of points to each of the various characteristics that have proved to be reliable signs that a borrower will repay. Then they rate the borrower on this scale.

Different lenders may reach different conclusions based on the same facts. One may find the applicant an acceptable risk, whereas another may deny the loan.

To figure the mortgage payment, the lender will begin by asking for the loan amount. Lenders determine the maximum loan amount by the value of the property and the borrower's personal financial condition. To estimate the value of the property, the lender will ask a real estate appraiser to give an opinion about its value, which can be important in determining whether the borrower qualifies for the size of mortgage.

The mortgage industry uses **electronic underwriting systems** that predict multiple-risk factors in a loan application. Approximately 98% of mortgage companies use some form of automated underwriting with about 60% using either **Fannie Mae's Desktop Underwriter** or **Freddie Mac's Loan Prospector.** Fannie Mae offers its lenders electronic loan processing with its Desktop Underwriter system. Users receive an analysis of the borrower's credit, estimate of the property's value, and an opinion of the risk involved. This information is prepared from the data submitted on the loan application and is available in a matter of minutes. The use of a common automated underwriting standard will simplify the electronic mortgage application process and reduce its cost.

Qualifying the Borrower

Lenders make loans using the borrowers' income and expenses to determine whether they qualify. To determine a borrowers' maximum mortgage amount, lenders use guidelines called **debt-to-income ratios.** This is simply the percentage of a borrowers' monthly gross income (before taxes) that the borrower uses to pay monthly debts. Because there are two calculations, there is a "front" ratio and a "back" ratio. This ratio generally follows this format: 28/36.

The **front ratio** is the percentage of the borrowers' monthly gross income (before taxes) that is used to pay housing costs, including principal, interest, taxes, insurance, mortgage insurance (when applicable), and homeowners' association fees (when applicable). The **back ratio** is the same thing, but it also includes the borrowers' monthly borrower debt. Borrower debt includes car payments, credit card debt, installment loans, and similar expenses. Auto or life insurance is not taken into consideration as part of the borrowers' debt. Borrowers' housing costs should consume no more than 28% of their monthly income. The borrowers' monthly debt and housing costs added together should take no more than 36% of the monthly income.

The guidelines are flexible. If a borrower makes a small down payment, the guidelines are more rigid. If a borrower has marginal credit, the guidelines are more rigid. If a borrower makes a larger down payment or has sterling credit, the guidelines are less rigid. The guidelines also vary according to loan program. FHA guidelines state that a 31/43 qualifying ratio is acceptable. VA guidelines do not have a front ratio at all, but the guideline for the back ratio is 41.

Example: If a borrower makes $5,000 a month, with 28/36 qualifying ratio guidelines, the maximum monthly housing cost should be around $1,400. Including the borrower's debt, the monthly housing, and credit expenditures should be around $1,800 as a maximum.

Qualifying the Property

The lender's first line of defense in being repaid on the loan is the borrower's creditworthiness. However, the underlying security for the loan is the property; therefore, an accurate valuation of the property is important. The lender will require an appraisal to determine fair market value of the property prior to making a loan.

Once the appraised value is determined, the lender will calculate the loan amount. Most lenders want an 80% loan-to-value ratio. **Loan-to-value** is the percentage of appraised value to the loan. An 80% loan would require the borrower to make a 20% down payment. Loans made with less than a 20% down payment will require mortgage insurance. If the appraisal is below the asking price of the home, the lender may require a larger down payment to make up the difference between the price of the house and its appraised value.

Approve and Fund the Loan

If the borrower has met the lender's financial guidelines and the property appraises for the amount necessary to fund the loan, the lender approves the loan. The lender will then process the loan papers and prepare all of the necessary documents. Instructions will be given to the escrow and title companies by the lender so that additional documents needed to close the loan can be drawn up. Closing statements, security instruments, and the promissory note are all included in the loan package. Once all of the documents are in order, the borrower signs them and the loan is ready to be funded. The signing of loan documents involves a great deal of paperwork and buyers will appreciate guidance and support from their salesperson. The loan usually takes two to three days to be funded after all documents have been signed. Two or three days after the loan funds, all of the necessary documents are recorded with the county. After the loan has been recorded, the transaction is complete and the lender will begin servicing the loan.

WHAT IF A LOAN IS DENIED?

Laws now require fair and equal treatment of all borrowers; therefore, more people are able to buy their own homes than any other time in history. These laws set a standard for how individuals are to be treated in their financial dealings. They contain the concepts of "fair" and "equal" credit, prohibit unfair discrimination in credit transactions, require that borrowers be told the reason when credit is denied, let borrowers find out about their credit records, and set up a way for borrowers to settle billing disputes.

If the lender turns down the loan application, federal law requires the lender to tell the borrower, in writing, the specific reasons for denial. Factors that may affect the loan decision include the borrower's financial standing, or issues with appraising the property to meet the lending requirements. It may be that the lender thinks the borrower has requested more money than can be repaid from current income. It may be that a borrower has not worked or lived long enough in the community. If a prospective buyer does not have strong enough credit to qualify for the loan, maybe someone will cosign the loan application.

If a borrower is turned down, find out why and try to resolve any misunderstandings. A borrower can discuss terms with the lender and ways to improve creditworthiness.

Remember, a borrower's gender or race may not be used to discourage the individual from applying for a loan. In addition, lenders may not hold up or otherwise delay an application on those grounds. Under the Equal Credit Opportunity Act, a borrower must be notified within 30 days after making an application whether or not the loan has been approved. If credit is denied, this notice must be in writing, and it must explain the specific reasons that a borrower was denied credit, or tell the borrower of the right to ask for an explanation. A borrower has the same rights if an active account is closed.

Laws require that borrowers be told the reason when credit is denied. Borrowers can discuss terms with the lender to improve their credit rating.

Fair Credit Reporting Act (FCRA)

One of the most important laws protecting a borrower's identity and credit information is the **Fair Credit Reporting Act**. Designed to promote the accuracy, fairness and privacy of the information collected and maintained by credit-reporting agencies, the FCRA gives borrowers specific rights.

The Fair Credit Reporting Act establishes procedures for correcting mistakes on a person's credit record and requires that a borrower's record only be provided for legitimate business needs. It also requires that the record be kept confidential. A credit record may be retained seven years for judgments, liens, suits, and other adverse information except for bankruptcies, which may be retained ten years.

Borrowers may sue any credit-reporting agency or lender for breaking the rules about who may see their credit records or for not correcting errors in a credit file. Again, a borrower is entitled to actual damages, plus punitive damages that the court may allow if the violation is proved to have been intentional. In any successful lawsuit, a borrower will also be awarded court costs and attorney's fees. A person who obtains a credit report without proper authorization or an employee of a credit-reporting agency who gives a credit report to unauthorized people may be fined up to $5,000 or imprisoned for one year or both.

Borrowers must be told if personal credit information is used against them. If a borrower is denied credit, employment, or insurance because of information in the credit report, the denying party must alert the borrower and provide the name, address and phone number of the credit-reporting agency used to support the denial.

Borrowers have access to their files. Upon request, a credit-reporting agency must give a borrower the information in the file and a list of everyone who has requested it, once during any 12-month period without charge to the borrower. In addition to the free annual credit report, there is no charge if the borrower has been denied credit, employment, or insurance because of items in the file (if a request is made within 60 days). In addition, a borrower is entitled to one free report every 12 months if unemployed or on welfare, or if the report is inaccurate.

A borrower can dispute inaccurate information. A credit-reporting agency must investigate items that a borrower reports as inaccurate. The borrower will receive a full copy of the investigation report. If the dispute is not settled satisfactorily, the borrower may add a statement to the report. Inaccurate information must be corrected or deleted. Credit-reporting agencies are required to remove or correct inaccurate or unverified information. They are not required to remove accurate data unless it is outdated.

Access to a borrower's file is limited. Only people and institutions with needs recognized by the FCRA may legally gain access to a file. This normally includes lenders, government agencies, insurers, employers, landlords, and some businesses.

Borrowers can remove their names from credit-reporting agency lists used for unsolicited credit and insurance offers. Unsolicited offers must include a toll-free phone number where borrowers can call to be removed from credit-reporting agency lists.

Equal Credit Opportunity Act (ECOA)

Credit is used by millions of borrowers to finance an education or a house, remodel a home, or get a small business loan. The **Equal Credit Opportunity Act** (ECOA) does not guarantee that an applicant will get credit. The borrower must still pass the lender's tests of creditworthiness. However, the lender must apply these tests fairly and impartially. The act bars discrimination based on age, gender, marital status, race, color, religion, and national origin. The act also bars discrimination because the applicant receives public income, such as veteran's benefits, welfare, or Social Security.

The law protects a borrower when dealing with any lender who regularly extends credit, including banks, small loan and finance companies, retail and department stores, credit card companies, and credit unions. Anyone involved in granting credit, such as real estate brokers who arrange financing, is covered by the law. Businesses applying for credit also are protected by the law.

Remedy for Discrimination

If borrowers can prove that lenders have discriminated against them for any reason prohibited by this act, they may sue—but as an individual—for actual damages plus punitive damages; that is—damages of up to $10,000 for the fact that the law has been violated. In a successful lawsuit, the court will award the borrower court costs and a reasonable amount for attorney's fees. Class action suits are also permitted.

Equal Credit Opportunity Act—Regulation B

Regulation B was issued by the Board of Governors of the Federal Reserve System to implement the provisions of the Equal Credit Opportunity Act (ECOA). The law was enacted in 1974 to make it unlawful for lenders to discriminate in any aspect of a credit transaction because of sex or marital status. In 1976, through amendments to the Act, it became unlawful to discriminate because of race, color, religion, national origin, age, receipt of public assistance, and the good faith exercise of rights under the Borrower Credit Protection Act.

The primary purpose of the ECOA is to prevent discrimination in the granting of credit by requiring banks and other lenders to make extensions of credit equally available to all creditworthy applicants with fairness, impartiality and without discrimination on any prohibited basis. The regulation applies to borrower and other types of credit transactions.

Real Estate Settlement Procedures Act (RESPA)

The federal **Real Estate Settlement Procedures Act** (RESPA) protects borrowers from abuses during the residential real estate purchase and loan process. It enables them to be better-informed shoppers by requiring disclosure of costs of settlement services.

RESPA requires that borrowers receive disclosures at various times. Some disclosures spell out the costs associated with the settlement, outline lender servicing and escrow account practices, and describe business relationships between settlement service providers.

Disclosures at the Time of Loan Application

- A **Special Information Booklet**, which contains borrower information on various real estate settlement services.

- A **Good Faith Estimate** of settlement costs, which estimates the charges the buyer will pay at settlement and states whether the lender requires the buyer to use a particular settlement service.

- A **Mortgage Servicing Disclosure Statement**, which tells the buyer if the lender plans to keep the loan or to transfer it to another lender for servicing, and also gives information about how the buyer can resolve complaints.

Disclosures Before Settlement (Closing) Occurs

- An **Affiliated Business Arrangement Disclosure** is required whenever a settlement service refers a buyer to a firm with which the service has any kind of business connection.

- A **preliminary copy of a HUD-1 Settlement Statement** is required if the borrower requests it 24 hours before closing. This form gives estimates of all settlement charges that will need to be paid, by both buyer and seller.

Disclosures at Settlement

- The **HUD-1 Settlement Statement** is required to show the actual charges at settlement.

- An **Initial Escrow Statement** is required at closing or within 45 days of closing. This itemizes the estimated taxes, insurance premiums, and other charges that will need to be paid from the escrow account during the first year of the loan.

Truth-in-Lending Act— Regulation Z

The **Truth-in-Lending Act** (TILA), Title I of the Borrower Credit Protection Act, promotes the informed use of borrower credit by requiring disclosures about terms and costs. The Truth-in-Lending Act requires disclosure of the finance charge and the annual percentage rate—and certain other costs and terms of credit. TILA helps borrowers to compare the cost of cash versus credit transaction and the difference in the cost of credit among different lenders.

The Federal Reserve Board and the Federal Home Loan Bank Board have published a book entitled *Borrower Handbook on Adjustable-Rate Mortgages* to help borrowers understand the purpose and use of adjustable-rate mortgage loans. Regulation Z requires that lenders offering adjustable-rate mortgage loans make this booklet, or a similar one, available to borrowers.

Home Equity Loan Borrower Protection Act

The **Home Equity Loan Borrower Protection Act** requires lenders to disclose terms, rates, and conditions (APRs, miscellaneous charges, payment terms, and information about variable rate features) for home equity lines of credit with the applications and before the first transaction under the home equity plan. If the disclosed terms change, the borrower can refuse to open the plan and is entitled to a refund of fees paid in connection with the application. The act also limits the circumstances under which lenders may terminate or change the terms of a home equity plan after it is opened.

SUMMARY

Traditionally, **fixed-rate** residential loans were the only choice offered by commercial banks, and savings and loans. However, no single type of financing is suitable for everyone because there are different kinds of lenders and borrowers, all in need of credit to buy houses. In an attempt to offer alternatives to borrowers and renew their faith in their ability to borrow money for homes, lenders found new ways to make loans borrower friendly. Loan programs include numerous purchase and **home equity loans**.

Today, many "alphabet soup" loan programs are available to serve borrowers. The right type of mortgage for a borrower depends on many different factors, such as:

- current financial situation and future expectations.
- length of time expected to own the home.
- comfort level of changing mortgage payments.
- ability to qualify for a conventional loan.
- amount of down payment.
- ability to qualify for a VA loan.
- desire to take advantage of FHA-insured loans.
- credit rating of the borrower.
- purpose of the loan: home purchase, refinance, equity loan.

As we have seen, various loan programs are determined by the terms in the promissory note—primarily interest rate and repayment schedule. The borrower's creditworthiness affects the interest rate quoted by the lender. Make yourself knowledgeable about real estate financing and become familiar with the home loan process. The basic components of a loan consist of the **principal**, **interest rate**, **term**, and **amortization**.

When a loan is made, a borrower signs a **promissory note**, which is an unconditional written promise to pay back a certain sum of money. In addition, there are certain requirements that make a valid promissory note. Within the promissory note are the **repayment plans** which can come in different types such as interest-only, fixed rate, and adjustable rate to name a few.

A **security instrument** is a recorded document that pledges title to property as **collateral** in paying back a loan. In California, the most common type of security instrument is the **deed of trust**. This involves three parties: the **trustor** (borrower), the **beneficiary** (lender), and the **trustee** (a neutral third party).

Loans can be either **conventional** or **government-backed**. Conventional loans do not contain any governmental guarantees for the lender. They can include **conforming loans**, which follow guidelines by **Fannie Mae** and **Freddie Mac;** or **non-conforming loans**, which do not meet conventional lending standards. Government-backed loans insure lenders against loss via the Federal Housing Administration (**FHA**). Popular government loans are the graduated payment mortgage, the reverse annuity mortgage, **VA** loans, and **CalVet** loans.

Alternative financing solutions can include secondary financing such as home equity lines of credit (HELOCs), seller financing, and a variety of other loan options.

The loan process begins with the **Uniform Residential Loan Application** (FHLMC/FNMA 1003 form). It asks for specific information about a borrower's current financial situation when applying for a loan. In order to determine affordability, lenders will use debt-to-income ratios that compare the borrower's monthly debt to their gross monthly income. If the borrower has met the lender's financial guidelines and the property appraises for the amount necessary to fund the loan, the lender approves the loan.

Currently, there are several laws requiring fair and equal treatment of all borrowers, which set standards for how individuals are to be treated in their financial dealings. They prohibit unfair discrimination in credit transactions, require that borrowers be told the reason when credit is denied, let borrowers find out about their credit records, and set up a way for borrowers to settle billing disputes.

UNIT 13 REVIEW

☐ Matching Exercise

Instructions: Write the letter of the matching term on the blank line before its definition. Answers are in Appendix A.

Terms

A. acceleration clause

B. adjustable-rate mortgage

C. amortization

D. beneficiary

E. conforming loan

F. contract of sale

G. conventional loan

H. equitable title

I. fixed-rate mortgage

J. Home Equity Line of Credit (HELOC)

K. interest rate

L. mortgagor

M. non-conforming loan

N. prepayment clause

O. principal

P. promissory note

Q. security instrument

R. term

S. trust deed

T. Uniform Residential Loan Application (1003 form)

Definitions

1. _____ The actual amount of the loan or outstanding balance that the borrower owes the lender

2. _____ The amount charged to borrow money, which is usually expressed as a percentage

3. _____ The timeframe given to repay a loan

4. _____ The breakdown of the monthly mortgage payments throughout its term from the start of the repayment plan all the way to the finish

5. _____ The evidence of debt, which states the amount of the money borrowed and the terms of repayment

6. _____ A recorded legal document given by the borrower to the lender, which pledges the title of the property as insurance to the lender for the full payment of the loan

7. _____ A type of repayment plan that is characterized by an interest rate that is fixed and payments that are level for the life of the loan

8. _____ A type of repayment plan with an interest rate based on a movable economic index

9. _____ A security instrument that conveys title of real property from a trustor to a trustee to hold as security for the beneficiary for payment of a debt

10. _____ A contract in which the seller becomes the lender to the buyer. The seller retains ownership to the property while the buyer makes payments and occupies the property. Once all the terms of the contract are met, the seller passes title to the buyer

11. _____ A penalty fee that a borrower is responsible for if a loan is paid off early

12. _____ Any loan made by lenders without any governmental guarantees

13. _____ A loan with terms and conditions that follow guidelines set forth by the Federal National Mortgage Corporation (Fannie Mae) and the Federal Home Loan Mortgage Corporation (Freddie Mac)

14. _____ A loan that does not meet the standards of Fannie Mae and Freddie Mac

15. _____ A standardized form for residential mortgage applications

◼ Multiple Choice Questions

Instructions: Circle your response and go to Appendix A to read the complete explanation for each question.

1. Which of the following statements is correct?
   a. The interest rate is the actual amount of the loan or outstanding balance that the borrower owes the lender.
   b. The term is simply the cost incurred when borrowing money and usually expressed as a percentage.
   c. The principal is the timeframe in which to repay the loan.
   d. Amortization is the breakdown of the monthly payments from the start of the repayment plan all the way to the finish.

2. Which of the following is not a basic component of a promissory note?
    a. Principal
    b. Interest
    c. Collateral
    d. Term

3. What type of repayment plan consists of regular interest payments during the term of the note?
    a. Interest-only loan
    b. Straight loan
    c. Term loan
    d. All of the above

4. What is a key feature of a fixed-rate fully amortized loan?
    a. The interest rate is based on a movable economic index.
    b. Payments remain level for the life of the loan.
    c. It is the least common note with institutional lenders.
    d. It comes with a 50-year term.

5. Which of the following is a characteristic of an adjustable rate mortgage?
    a. Payments remain level for the life of the loan.
    b. The interest rate does not follow a movable economic index.
    c. The qualifying rate is determined by the current rate of a chosen index.
    d. Interest rate remains fixed for the life of the loan.

6. The three parties involved in a deed of trust are:
    a. trustor, trust deed, and beneficiary.
    b. mortgagor, lender, and trustee.
    c. mortgagor, mortgagee, and beneficiary.
    d. trustor, trustee, and beneficiary.

7. What obligation does the trustee have when acting as an agent for the beneficiary?
    a. Foreclosing on the property if there is a default on the loan
    b. Reconveying the title to the borrower when the debt is repaid in full
    c. Collecting monthly loan payments on behalf of the beneficiary
    d. Both (a) and (b)

8. Which of the following is a type of conventional loan?

    a. Conforming loan

    b. FHA loan

    c. VA loan

    d. CalVet loan

9. What are loans that do not meet the borrower credit requirements of Fannie Mae and Freddie Mac?

    a. CalVet loans

    b. FHA loans

    c. Subprime loans

    d. VA loans

10. The difference between the value of the property and any outstanding loans or the initial down payment is known as:

    a. secondary financing.

    b. equity.

    c. deregulation.

    d. amortization.

11. When a seller carries the paper on the sale of his or her home, it is also called a _____ loan.

    a. CalVet

    b. construction

    c. bridge

    d. purchase money

12. What needs by borrowers should a lender take into consideration in order to attract customers?

    a. Low interest rates

    b. Variety of products

    c. Reputation

    d. All of the above

13. An objective, statistical method that lenders use to assess the borrower's credit risk is called:

    a. equity.

    b. credit scoring.

    c. credit report.

    d. credit profile.

14. Which of the following is not included on the Uniform Residential Loan Application?

    a. Employment verification

    b. Property information and purpose of the loan

    c. Completion of a salesperson's customer service survey

    d. Type of mortgage and terms of loan

15. To determine a borrower's maximum mortgage amount, lenders use guidelines called:

    a. debt-to-income ratios.

    b. loan-to-value.

    c. FICO® scores.

    d. asset monitoring.

16. Under the Equal Credit Opportunity Act a lender may use which of the following criteria to determine an applicant's creditworthiness?

    a. The applicant's age and marital status

    b. The applicant receives Social Security

    c. The applicant's FICO® score

    d. The applicant's national origin

From Acceptance to Close

Unit 14

INTRODUCTION

You have now come to the final stretch on your journey from acceptance to close. In a real estate transaction, **closing** is the process in which agreed-on costs are paid and legal title is transferred from seller to buyer in exchange for consideration—usually cash from the buyer. You should think about closing the transaction at your first meeting with a buyer or a seller. As you complete a listing agreement or purchase offer, review it for completeness and accuracy. Make sure that forms are properly filled out, required initials and signatures are in place, and that information is current, accurate, and consistent on all documents. Any discrepancies, inaccuracies, or a lack of information can cause undue delays during the closing process.

Closing may be handled by an attorney, title company, or escrow holder. In California, most people who buy and sell real property use an escrow company to transfer property from the seller to the buyer. The **escrow holder**, or escrow officer, is a neutral third party who carries out the provisions of an agreement between a seller and buyer, or a lender and a borrower if the transaction is a loan closing.

The seller and buyer always choose the escrow holder; if they do not know any, they may rely on their real estate broker or salesperson to make a recommendation. Either the buyer or seller may pay the fee, or share it equally. An escrow holder may be a bank, savings and loan, title insurance company, attorney, real estate broker, or an independent escrow company.

After escrow opens, the escrow holder follows the seller's and buyer's instructions and requests that all parties involved observe the terms and conditions of the contract. The escrow holder coordinates communication between the principals, the salespeople, and any other professionals such as the lender, title company, or pest control company.

The escrow process may take days, weeks, or even months to complete. Time extensions are often necessary to complete the process. Both listing and selling agents should check with the escrow holder regarding specific items. It is important to keep the process moving in a forward direction.

Learning Objectives

After reading this unit, you should be able to:

- identify the basic requirements for a valid escrow.

- recall the role of escrow instructions in a real estate transaction.

- indicate what each party involved in a real estate transaction does during escrow.

OPENING ESCROW

The first step in the closing process is to **open escrow**. This usually is done by the listing salesperson, who gives the escrow officer the signed purchase agreement along with the buyers' good faith deposit. The escrow officer needs to make sure the contract is complete, fully signed, and initialed by all parties before accepting it.

> What happens to the buyer's deposit after the offer is accepted? Since most deposit checks are made out to the escrow, the listing salesperson gives it to the escrow officer when escrow is opened. The escrow officer deposits it immediately into a trust account until the close of escrow.

What is Necessary for a Valid Escrow?

The basic requirements for a valid escrow include (1) a binding purchase agreement contract made between the parties, (2) conditional delivery of funds, and (3) conditional delivery of transfer documents.

The most important item needed for a valid contract is a binding purchase contract between the buyer and seller. Conditional delivery of funds means the buyers and/or the lender will deliver to escrow whatever funds are required to complete the sale. Sometime before the escrow closes, the sellers will sign a grant deed conveying title to the buyers. In a grant deed, the grantor warrants that he or she has not previously conveyed the property being granted, has not encumbered the property except as disclosed, and will convey to the grantee any title to the property acquired later. Because the sellers will sign over ownership to the buyers before getting the money, the escrow holder must hold the signed deed until funds from the buyers are deposited in escrow and all other terms of the escrow have been met. At this time, the sellers have made conditional delivery of the grant deed.

WHO DOES WHAT DURING ESCROW?

Since every real estate transaction is unique, escrow procedures may vary according to local custom. However, certain activities occur during the regular course of all escrows such as ordering and reviewing title, obtaining financing, appraising the property, inspecting the property, drawing deeds, obtaining insurance (including hazard, mortgage, title, and others), making needed repairs, removing all contingencies, prorating costs and fees, and preparing closing statements.

As a salesperson or broker, it is important to know the responsibilities of each party involved in the escrow process. For example, the escrow officer will order a preliminary title report for the buyer to review. The buyer's salesperson should be prepared to explain any of the easements or liens that might be shown on the report. There may be items that the seller will have to clear up before the buyer is satisfied that title is clear. Once the buyer is satisfied then he or she will remove the title contingency.

Your clients will have questions about what is expected of them, as well as what to expect from other parties involved in the transaction. Any required items that are not received in a timely manner could delay the closing of escrow. It is the salesperson's responsibility to communicate with buyers and sellers about what is expected of them. Remember to inform your clients that they should keep copies of all documents and instruments they sign, deliver, or receive regarding the real estate transaction.

Each party to the escrow—escrow holder, seller, buyer, and lender—have specific duties and obligations that must be satisfactorily completed in order for the escrow to close.

Escrow Holder

Upon receipt of the signed purchase agreement, the escrow holder's first responsibility is to open an escrow file and create escrow instructions. Once escrow is opened, the escrow holder will serve as a depository for documents and funds and will complete a variety of tasks until closing the escrow when title is transferred and funds are appropriately disbursed.

Prepares Escrow Instructions

The escrow officer must know all facts of the purchase to carry out the expectations of all parties to the transaction. The principals must establish all agreements of a sale before signing escrow instructions. All information given to the escrow officer should reflect the agreement by the principals in the purchase contract. Escrow instructions will vary from transaction to transaction. The escrow officer gathers the purchase agreement and other important information, and draws up escrow instructions in detail to describe how the escrow holder will complete the transaction.

Although there is no set format for escrow instructions, the California Association of REALTORS® (C.A.R.) created a form known as the California Residential Purchase Agreement and Joint Escrow Instructions (RPA-CA) that seems to simplify escrow. The form combines the offer to purchase and escrow instructions into one contract. Using the signed purchase agreement to create escrow instructions ensures that escrow reflects that agreement.

Usually within a day or two after opening escrow, computer-generated escrow instructions are ready for the sellers and buyers to sign. The **escrow instructions** are the written authorization to the escrow holder or title company to carry out the directions of the parties involved in the transaction. The instructions, as you recall, reflect the agreement between the sellers and buyers as seen in the offer to purchase (deposit receipt) and usually include all disclosures required by law.

What are escrow instructions?

Escrow instructions outline all terms required to complete the transaction. The escrow holder is the only one authorized to perform the activities specified in the escrow instructions.

Escrow instructions are either **unilateral**, where the buyers sign one set of instructions and the sellers sign another, or **bilateral**, where the sellers and buyers sign the same set of instructions.

Escrow instructions state any conditions that both parties must satisfy in order to close the deal, such as who will pay for what, how the escrow holder disburses monies, and what documents are recorded at the close of escrow.

If any changes in the original instructions are required, the escrow officer must draw up an amendment for each change. Perhaps the sellers want to close escrow later than the original date agreed upon, or maybe the buyers want to get an adjustable loan rather than a fixed rate as previously stated in the offer to purchase. No matter how small the detail, if it differs from the original agreement, all parties to the escrow must agree to the change by signing an amendment.

Northern vs. Southern California

In Northern California, title companies conduct escrows. In Northern California, the escrow officer prepares the instructions at the end of the escrow period. In addition, after receiving loan approval and the terms of the loan have been approved by the buyers, the lender sends the legal documents to the escrow officer to hold for the buyers' signature just prior to the closing. Unilateral escrow instructions are then drawn and the closing process begins.

Title companies conduct escrows in Northern California.

In Southern California, escrow companies or banks conduct escrows. In Southern California, the responsible parties send the instructions, required deeds, purchase money encumbrances, and notes to the escrow company designated to handle the transaction. Escrow sends copies of the same document to both sellers and buyers (bilateral instructions) or the respective salesperson for both parties to deliver them. Once both sides sign the escrow instructions, a valid contract exists and the escrow officer prepares the title for closing, and follows any lender instructions.

Escrow companies or banks conduct escrows in Southern California.

Orders a Title Search

When the sellers and buyers reach an agreement about the sale of the property, they also select a title company. One of the jobs of the escrow officer, after escrow opens, is to order a title search and prepare a preliminary title report for the property.

Preliminary Title Report

The **preliminary title report** (prelim) is prepared to verify the legal ownership of the property. This report indicates whether the seller currently holds title to the property and includes a list of the previous owners, purchase dates, and sale dates to make sure the chain of title is correct. The **chain of title** is the public record of prior transfers and encumbrances affecting the title of a parcel of land. If there is a missing connection in a property's history or ownership, or if a deed was recorded in error or is incomplete, it **clouds the title**. The prelim also lists any liens or claims against the property such as property taxes, income taxes, mortgage payments, or other unpaid debts. Any problems that arise should be corrected during the escrow period so the title is clear for the new owner.

The buyers have a certain number of days to approve this preliminary title report. Buyers' approval is important to eliminate surprises regarding the title as the escrow progresses. The escrow holder should prepare an addendum that notifies the sellers and buyers if there is any difference in the preliminary report and the escrow instructions. If the sellers cannot provide clean title and eliminate certain exceptions prior to closing, the buyers have the right to accept or reject the prelim and back out of the transaction. Some of these exceptions include easements, liens, and encumbrances.

Example: The Clarks and the Marshalls instructed their escrow holder to order a preliminary title search. The Marshalls had three days to approve the report, as a contingency of the sale. However, when they examined it, they found there was an undisclosed bond for street repairs against the property.

The bond was for a lien of $3,500. The buyers would not approve the preliminary title report until an agreement of payment was settled. New instructions would be given to the escrow officer to prepare an amendment for the buyers' and sellers' signatures stating who would pay the bond.

Title Insurance Policy

The goal of title insurance companies is to insure the clear, marketable title of property. A **marketable title** would be accepted as clear and free from likely challenges–reasonably free from risk of litigation over possible defects.

Title insurance protects real estate owners from challenges to their property titles. It protects against loss due to errors in searching records and in reporting the status of title and guarantees that the property is free of liens. In addition, title insurance protects the lender against loss or damage due to defects in the property's title, and the buyer from unpredictable factors such as human error or forgery. The main benefit is that it extends protection against matters of record and many non-recorded types of risks, depending on the type of policy purchased.

The title insurance policies used throughout California are standardized forms prepared by the **California Land Title Association®** (**CLTA**) or the **American Land Title Association** (**ALTA**). The two types of title insurance policies normally used are standard and extended coverage.

The **standard policy** of title insurance issued to homebuyers only covers matters of record. No physical inspection of the property is required and the buyers obtain protection against all recorded matters, and certain risks such as forgery and incompetence. The title company does not do a survey or check boundary lines when preparing a standard title insurance policy.

The **extended coverage policy** of title insurance covers everything that a standard policy covers, plus other unrecorded hazards, such as outstanding mechanic's liens, unrecorded physical easements, facts a properly conducted survey would show, certain water claims, and rights of parties in possession—including tenants and owners under unrecorded deeds. The American Land Title Association offers an owner extended coverage policy known as ALTA Owner's Policy that includes the same coverage as a standard policy, with the following additions: (1) protection against claims of parties in physical possession of the property but no recorded interest, (2) reservations in patents, and (3) unmarketability of title.

Receives and Holds All Funds

The escrow coordinates the receipt and disbursement of all funds, whether from the buyer or a lender. In addition, the escrow holder coordinates the payoff or assumption of the seller's existing loans on the property, as well as any new loans the buyer is arranging for the purchase of the property.

Seller's Loans

The escrow officer must verify any existing loans on the subject property. If proceeds from the sale will pay off existing loans, the escrow officer requests a payoff demand from the lender holding the note and trust deed. The **payoff demand** shows the unpaid principal balance, the daily interest rate, and any other amounts due. The lender must disclose the exact amount of the loan payoff so the escrow officer's accounting will be correct at the closing.

If an existing loan is going to be assumed, or taken subject to, a **beneficiary statement** that sets forth the unpaid balance of the loan amount and the condition of the debt is requested from the lender by the escrow holder.

Buyer's New Loan Instructions and Documents

Escrow accepts loan documents or instructions about financing the subject property and completes them as directed. The escrow officer gets the buyers' approval of and signature on loan documents then receives and disburses loan funds as instructed.

Accepts Documents and Inspection Reports

The parties to an escrow may request reports regarding the condition of the property. Therefore, the escrow holder accepts and holds reports such as the structural pest control report (termite report), property inspection report, soil condition report, or environmental report. The reports are given to the person who needs to approve them and remove any contingency. Then the escrow holder accepts those approvals that remove contingencies from the buyers on title insurance, pest control reports, and other inspections.

Prorates and Allocates Costs

A real estate transaction closes by prorating any expenses between the buyers and the sellers. This ensures that they are responsible for their share of expenses such as taxes, homeowner's dues, rental income, or fire insurance on the property during the tenure of his or her ownership. The escrow holder prorates insurance, taxes, rents, etc. and prepares a final statement for each party indicating the amount to be disbursed for services and any other amounts necessary to close escrow.

Property Taxes. Homeowners usually pay annual property taxes in December and April. The escrow company will prorate the taxes for the closing date to ensure that neither the buyers nor the sellers overpay.

Hazard Insurance. The buyer and seller will have agreed on hazard insurance and will instruct the escrow officer accordingly. **Hazard insurance** protects the borrower and the lender against loss due to fire, windstorm, vandalism, and other hazards. The escrow holder will accept, hold, and deliver any policies and will follow instructions about transferring them. A lender will require hazard insurance to cover the outstanding loan on the property and will expect the escrow holder and the buyers to be accountable for either a new policy or the transfer of an existing one.

Some costs and expenses are allocated (assigned) to the buyer or seller in escrow. Typical costs that are allocated include escrow fees, title costs, inspection reports, home warranty fees, transfer tax, and retrofit costs.

How to Calculate the Documentary Transfer Tax. A **documentary transfer tax** is charged to the owner of the property whenever real property transfers to another person. The county recorder places stamps (doc stamps) on the recorded grant deed to indicate the amount of the documentary transfer tax paid. In most cases, it is based on $.55 per $500 of purchase price, or $1.10 per $1,000 of purchase price. The money goes to local government, either city or county.

The tax assessment is based upon the full price of the property at the rate specified above if the sale is all cash, or if a new loan is involved, where the sellers get all cash. The tax is levied only on the equity transferred (or consideration) if the buyers assume an existing loan. When the deed records or when escrow closes, the responsible party then pays the documentary transfer tax.

Example: If the buyers purchased a home for $300,000 assuming an existing loan of $200,000, the tax would be based on the $100,000 the buyers paid as a down payment, or the new money put into the transaction. $100,000 divided by $1,000 equals 100; therefore, 100 times $1.10 equals $110.00 for the tax.

Prepares and Records Deeds

The escrow holder prepares the grant deed and sends it to the seller. The seller needs to sign the grant deed in front of a notary public and return it to escrow before the closing date. At close, the escrow holder records the deed and other documents.

Prepares Final Closing Statements

One of the escrow officer's main jobs is to present the obligations of each party in a personalized closing statement. The **closing statement** is an accounting of funds made to the sellers and buyers individually, and it is required of the escrow holder at the completion of every real estate transaction. The sellers and buyers are both credited and debited for their agreed-upon share of costs.

The debit and credit columns on the closing statement are marked sellers/ lender or buyers/borrower, depending on whether it describes a sale or loan escrow.

The closing statement outlines the flow of consideration through escrow, as well as the adjustments and disbursements that reflect the prior agreement of the parties.

Seller's Statement

The seller's statement is a record of the financial proceeds the sellers will receive upon the transaction's closing.

Seller's Credit
- Amount of the total consideration, or sales price, debit the buyers.
- Any property taxes paid, debit the buyers.
- Monthly homeowners' association dues, debit the buyers.
- Interest on loan if paid in advance (from recordation to date of next loan payment).

Seller's Debits

Loan payoff on existing loan plus any interest charges

- Selling commission
- Title insurance including title policy premium, reconveyance fee, and documentary transfer tax
- Recording fee (reconveyance)
- Escrow fee (seller's share)
- Legal fees
- Prepayment penalty
- State or local transfer tax
- Pest control inspection fee
- Pest control work
- Recording fee
- FHA or VA points
- Termite report

Seller's Proceeds

Buyer's Statement

The buyer's statement is a record of costs and credits incurred for the purchase of the property.

Buyer's Credits

- Down payment
- Amount of new loan
- Prorated taxes
- Prorated rents
- Security deposits held by sellers

Buyer's Debits for Non-Recurring Costs

- Title insurance (buyers' share)
- Escrow fee (buyer's share)
- Legal fees
- Loan application fee
- Underwriting fee
- Tax service
- Recording fees
- Courier fee
- Verification fee
- Warehousing fee
- Loan fee
- Appraisal fee
- Credit report
- Notary fee
- Pest control inspection (according to agreement with sellers)
- Document preparation fee
- Review fee

> **Buyer's Debits for Recurring Costs**
> - Hazard insurance
> - Trust fund or impound account
> - Prorated taxes (if prepaid by sellers beyond recordation)
> - Prorated interest (if charged in arrears)

Closes Escrow

The final responsibility of the escrow holder is to close escrow. Escrow cannot close until all financial and legal items have been completed. A refinance and the purchase of a property that includes financing will require a **financial closing**. Steps must be taken in the financial closing to ensure that funds are distributed appropriately. The escrow officer follows instructions regarding financing the property, and prepares any documents necessary to close escrow. These might be a note and trust deed, or assumption papers. In the purchase of property, there is a transfer of ownership from the sellers to the buyers, which involves a **legal closing**. Care must be taken to ensure a legal transfer of ownership.

The escrow holder orders the title company to record all transactional documents as instructed by the sellers and buyers. Documents that may require recording include the grant deed, trust deed, contract of sale, or option. Recording occurs after a final check of the title company records to be sure nothing has changed since the preliminary title search. Then the title company issues a policy of title insurance to insure the buyers' title.

Upon closing, the escrow officer delivers all documents to the proper parties, disburses all monies, and gives closing statements to sellers and buyers. The sellers get a check for the proceeds of the sale minus escrow fees, real estate commissions, or any other costs of selling, and any pertinent documents; and the buyers get a grant deed. The original deed is mailed directly to the buyers at the new property by the county recorder's office. This usually takes several weeks, sometimes longer.

Seller

When the seller receives the escrow instructions, plan to be available to answer any questions. Remind the seller to read the escrow instructions before signing them because it is important to verify that the escrow instructions accurately state the terms of the purchase agreement.

Escrow will prepare a grant deed transferring title from the seller to the buyer. Be sure the seller signs the grant deed before a notary public and return the grant deed to escrow.

Depending on the terms of the transaction, there may be several required inspections. The seller will rely on your expertise to get the various inspections scheduled, any required repair work completed, and proper certifications made. Typically, these include pest, roof, and septic inspections and certifications. You must also check smoke detectors and appropriate water heating bracing. Send all certifications to escrow immediately. The seller would not want a delay in the closing due to improper delivery of the certifications.

If the buyer is financing the purchase, his or her lender will require an appraisal of the property. Work with the buyer's agent to schedule a time that the property will be available to the appraiser.

Some items will be prorated in escrow. Tell the seller to give the latest property tax bill, homeowner's assessment, and mortgage statement to the escrow holder. If the buyer plans to assume the seller's fire insurance policy, remind the sellers to provide the policy to escrow so the premium can be prorated.

Make sure the seller provides escrow information about anything that will be paid off through escrow, such as outstanding liens, judgments, security agreements, or loans. Unless assumed by the buyer, any tax liens, judgments, loans, or mechanic's liens against the property are usually paid with the proceeds from the sale of the property.

If the seller plans to sell any personal property outside of escrow, prepare an inventory sheet. Usually escrow will prepare the bill of sale for the personal property. The seller should not release possession of the personal property or execute the bill of sale until he or she has received the agreed-upon payment.

If the property is a rental, remind the seller to give escrow a copy of the lease and a statement showing the amount of security deposit. Provide assignment to the buyer of all leases affecting the property.

Property Address 1652 Hill Street, Any City, Apple County, California 90000

File Number _____ Date Opened 4/1/20XX

SERVICING YOUR LISTING DURING THE ESCROW PERIOD

DATE COMPLETED   **ACTIVITIES/DISCLOSURE**

_____   Be sure Residential Purchase Contract, any applicable Contract Addenda (e.g., "Contingency for Sale or Purchase of Other Property - Form COP, "Interim Occupancy Agreement (Buyer in Possession Prior to Close of Escrow) - Form IOA, "Purchase Agreement Addendum - Form PAA, "Residential Lease After Sale (Seller in Possession After Close of Escrow) - Form RLAS, "Wood Destroying Pest Inspection and Allocation of Cost Addendum - Form WPA) and all Counter Offers (Form CO) are signed/initialed by all parties.

_____   Buyer's Good Faith Deposit Check - Log into Trust Account Transaction Log - Broker Trust Account? Escrow?

_____   Deliver all the above forms (purchase contract and all addenda) to Escrow.

_____   Give the Buyer the completed "Transfer Disclosure Statement" (Form TDS).

_____   Give the Buyer the "Combined Hazards Book" and the completed "Lead-Based Paint and Lead-Based Paint Hazards Disclosure, Acknowledgement and Addendum for Pre-1978 Sales" (Form FLD).

_____   Giver Buyer the "Property Transaction Booklet." Obtain a signed copy of the "Disclosure Regarding Real Estate Agency Relationships" (Form AD) signed by the Seller and the Buyer's Agent.

_____   Report Sale to Broker/Manager. Report Sale to MLS as Pending.

_____   Buyer's Increased Deposit? Have Buyer Complete "Receipt for Increased Deposit/Liquidatd Damages" (Form RID)

_____   Obtain Buyer's loan prequalification.   Report/Letter Delivered to Seller? _____

_____   Order Preliminary (Title) Report.   Report Delivered to Buyer?   _____

_____   Order Structural Pest Control Inspection.   Report Delivered to Buyer?   _____

_____   Receive Pest Control Certification Report.   Report Delivered to Buyer?   _____

_____   Order City/County Retrofit Report, if applicable.   Report Delivered to Buyer?   _____

_____   Buyer's "Request for Repair" (Form RR)?   Report Delivered to Seller?   _____

_____   Have Seller Give Written Response.   Report Delivered to Buyer?   _____

_____   Subsequent Repair on Property?   Report Delivered to Buyer?   _____

_____   Seller Financing? "Seller Financing Addendum and Disclosure" (Form SFA) to be completed by Buyer's Agent.

_____   Have Seller complete "Notice to Buyer to Perform" (Form NBP) if Buyer has not timely removed contingencies.
                   Receive Lender Approval?   1TD _____   2TD _____

_____   Loan documents sent to Escrow/Title.

_____   Buyer's final verification of property condition performed. Have Buyer complete "Verification of Property Condition" (Form VP)

_____   ALL DISCLOSURE BOOKLETS/FORMS GIVEN TO BUYER? Signed Receipts?

                   Can use "Receipt for Reports (Form RFR) to obtain signed acknowledgments from Buyer.
                   (Use Checklist Provided On Next Page of Folder)

FOR YOUR LEGAL PROTECTION

**Document All Telephone and Personal Conversations
Related to the Transaction**

Buyer

When the buyer receives the escrow instructions, plan to be available to answer any questions. Remind the buyer to read the escrow instructions before signing them because it is important to verify that the escrow instructions accurately state the terms of the purchase agreement. Compare the terms of the purchase contract, escrow instructions, title report, and deed to make sure there are no discrepancies in the transaction documents.

The salesperson should plan to be available to answer the buyer's escrow questions.

When escrow opened, the initial earnest money was deposited. If the contract calls for an increased deposit be sure to remind the buyer to deposit any additional funds required.

Arranges for Financing

Most buyers are preapproved so the loan is already in process. However, if buyers need to arrange financing, give them the names of a few reputable lenders who will help complete a loan application. Remind buyers to review carefully all new loan documents prior to signing them. Once the loan is reviewed and there are no outstanding conditions, the lender will send the buyers' loan funds directly to escrow.

In order to close escrow, buyers must deposit sufficient funds to cover escrow and closing costs. Sometimes the escrow will use the term "good funds". **Good funds** include cashier's checks, certified checks, or wired funds. A personal check is not considered "good funds" because it may take several days for the check to clear. If buyers plan to use a personal check, remind them to send it at least ten days before the close of escrow.

The lender will require the buyers to have various kinds of insurance. The hazard insurance coverage should be equal to the cost of replacing the structure. If the property is located in a flood zone or near a body of water, the buyers may need to purchase flood insurance. Equally important to consider for California residents is the purchase of earthquake insurance. Personal liability insurance (covering injuries to persons on the property) and personal property coverage (covering loss and damage to personal property by theft or other means) are other policies that buyers should consider purchasing. Provide buyers with the names of several insurance companies from whom they can get quotes and compare rates for the various insurances they may need. Usually lenders require the payment of the first year's insurance premium to be paid at or before closing.

If the down payment is less than 20%, the lender may require that the hazard insurance premium and a payment for property tax be added to the monthly payments. The insurance and property tax portion of the payments will be kept in an **impound account** (reserve account). In this way, the lender pays the insurance and property tax bills when they come due.

Property Condition

Depending on the terms of the transaction, there may be several required inspections. Typically, these include pest, roof, and septic inspection and certifications as well as compliance with smoke detectors and water heating bracing certifications. Buyers have a set number of days to approve or disapprove these inspections. Make sure your buyers respond in a timely manner regarding all inspections and contingencies.

Title

Explain to the buyers that escrow will order a title search and that they will receive a preliminary title report. The preliminary title report (prelim) verifies the legal ownership, shows any liens against the property, and describes any easements or CC&Rs. Be prepared to go over it with them. Help them check for any unusual easements, taxes, or anything that would affect use and title of the property. Review and approve any Conditions, Covenants, and Restrictions (CC&Rs), whether of record or not.

Review Closing Statement

Review and approve any items to be prorated in escrow including property taxes, interest, fire insurance, and rents (if applicable). Before close, escrow will send the buyers a summary of the estimated closing costs. Frequently they will have questions about the charges.

Walk-Through

Just before the actual closing (generally within five days before the close of escrow), schedule a final **walk-through** of the property to be certain it is in the same condition as when the purchase offer was made. Make sure that any required work is satisfactorily completed. Recheck for any undisclosed items that might affect the property's use, such as party walls, access roads to other properties, common drives, irrigation canals or ditches, or people in occupancy or possession of the property, which county records would not disclose.

There is a reason for the final walk-through before escrow closing. The pull-out stove was sold with the house. During the final walk-through, the buyers and salesperson discovered the stove was removed from the house.

Possession

Now that escrow is nearly closed, remind buyers to set up accounts for utilities, phone, cable, garbage, and other services. They will also need to arrange to have those same accounts closed at their current home.

Once the transaction records and closes, call the buyers and let them know they are new homeowners. Let them know how and when to get the keys so they can take possession of their new home. Sometimes the escrow instructions allow the sellers a day or two after closing to move out of the home. The buyers may be able to move in immediately, or wait a few days until the sellers have actually moved out.

Lender

The lender plays a huge role in closing the purchase because most people are unable to pay all cash for a home. In fact, financing is so important, most prospective buyers get preapproved by a lender prior to house hunting. Once the offer is accepted, the buyer will complete a loan application to start the loan process.

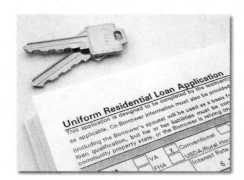

During the loan origination phase, the lender orders all employment, income, and deposit verifications, orders an appraisal, orders a credit report, and prepares the loan for underwriting.

If the lender approves the loan, it is underwritten, and the funds are wired to the escrow or title company. When the deed and loan documents are recorded, escrow may disburse the funds.

Property Address 1652 Hill Street, Any City, Apple County, California 90000

File Number _____ Date Opened 4/1/20XX

AFTER THE ESCROW HAS CLOSED – DOCUMENTS FOR YOUR FILE

DATE COMPLETED

ACTIVITIES/DISCLOSURE

Keys Delivered to the Buyer
Sign Removed from Property
Lock Box Removed from Property
Reported to MLS as Closed
Sale Reported to Broker/Manager

DISCLOSURE FORMS - CONTRACTS (not all may be applicable or necessary):

Agency Confirmation (AC-6 for change of agency during escrow)
Agency Disclosure (AD)
Agent's Inspection Statement (AIS when no TDS required)
Buyer's Investigation Advisory (BIA)
Cancellation of Contract, Release of Deposit and Joint Escrow Instruction (CC)
"Combined Hazards Book" (includes Environmental Hazards Booklet, Lead Paint Booklet,
   Homeowners Earthquake Guide)
Contingency Removal (CR)
Contract of Sale (Purchase Contract, Counter Offers and Addenda - various forms available)(e.g.
   RPA-CA)
Cooperating Broker Compensation and Escrow Instruction (CBC)
Earthquake Guide: Commercial Property Owner's Guide
Estoppel Certificate (Tenants)
Exclusive Authorization and Right to Sell (Form RLA) or other Listing Contract
FIRPTA/Buyer's Affidavit (AB) (not required if AS completed by Seller)
FIRPTA-California Withholding/Seller's Affidavit (AS)
HUD Home Inspection Notice (HID)
Industrial Use Zone Location (SSD or other)
Interim Occupancy Agreement (IOA) or Residential Lease After Sale (RLAS)
Lead Paint Notice (FLD)
Local Disclosures
Lock Box Authorization Addendum (LBA-11)
Megan's Law Disclosure (If language is not on purchase contract, use Form DBD)
Mello-Roos Tax and 1915 Bond Act Assessment Notice (Govt. form or on substituted NHD)
Military Ordnance Location (SSD or other)
Mold Disclosure (RGM)
Natural Hazard Disclosure Statement (NHD or substituted disclosure)
Pest Control Report
Smoke Detector Compliance (SDS)
Transfer Disclosure Statement (TDS)
Verification of Property Condition (VP)
Water Heater Bracing (WHS)

SUBDIVISION - CONDOMINIUM DISCLOSURES:

Homeowner Association Information Request (HOA)
Articles of Incorporation/Association
Blanket Encumbrance Release (new subdivision)
Bylaws
Current Financial Statement
CC&Rs (Restrictions)
List of Defects
Minutes of Board/Membership Meetings
Operating Budget
Public Report (Conditional, Preliminary, or Final) (new subdivision)
Rules & Regulations
Statement of Assessment and Fees
Statement of Residency Restriction Based on Age
Study of Reserves

ADDITIONAL BROKER/OFFICE REQUIREMENTS:

_____
_____
_____

> **Place All Documents Related to the Transaction
> Into a File and Save for 3 Years**

SUMMARY

To have a smooth closing, make sure that forms are properly filled out, required initials and signatures are in place, and that information is current and accurate, and consistent on all documents. Any discrepancies, or a lack of information can cause undue delays during the closing process.

The **escrow holder** may be a bank, savings and loan, title insurance company, attorney, real estate broker, or an independent escrow company. The basic requirements for a valid escrow are a binding purchase agreement contract made between the sellers and the buyers, and conditional delivery of transfer documents and funds.

Escrow procedures may vary according to local custom. The escrow instructions usually list any conditions that both parties must satisfy in order to close the deal. The law does not set the format for escrow instructions as long as all parties approve.

An escrow cannot close until all financial and legal items have been completed. In the sale of property, a transfer of ownership from the sellers to the buyers involves a legal closing. During both a refinance and the sale of a property, a financial closing takes place and the escrow officer must make sure that funds are distributed appropriately.

The final responsibilities of the escrow holder are to close the escrow and give closing statements to sellers and buyers; disburse all money; and deliver all documents to the proper parties after confirming all documents have been recorded by the title company. Full performance, by satisfying all the conditions set in escrow, terminates the escrow.

UNIT 14 REVIEW

Matching Exercise

Instructions: Write the letter of the matching term on the blank line before its definition. Answers are in Appendix A.

Terms

A. beneficiary statement

B. bilateral instructions

C. chain of title

D. closing

E. closing statement

F. contingencies

G. documentary transfer tax

H. escrow holder

I. escrow instructions

J. extended coverage policy

K. good funds

L. hazard insurance

M. impound account

N. marketable title

O. payoff demand

P. preliminary title report

Q. standard policy

R. title insurance

S. unilateral instructions

T. walk-through

Definitions

1. _____ The process in which agreed-on costs are paid and legal title is transferred from seller to buyer in exchange for consideration

2. _____ Acts as a neutral agent of both seller and buyer

3. _____ Written directions, signed by a seller and buyer, detailing the procedures necessary to close a transaction and directing the escrow officer how to proceed

4. _____ Escrow instructions in which the buyers sign one set of instructions and the sellers sign another

5. _____ Escrow instructions in which the sellers and buyers sign the same set of instructions

6. _____ Chronological summary of all useful documents discovered in a title search regarding the ownership of a property

7. _____ Good or clear saleable title reasonably free from risk of litigation over possible defects

8. _____ A title insurance policy issued to homebuyers that only covers matters of record

9. _____ The amount of the unpaid principal balance, the daily interest rate, and any other amounts due on a loan payoff so the escrow officer's accounting will be correct at the closing

10. _____ A property insurance policy that protects the owner and lender against fire, windstorm, vandalism, and other hazards

11. _____ A tax collected on all transfers of real property located in the county. The amount of the payment is entered on the face of the deed

12. _____ An accounting of funds made to the seller and buyer separately. Required by law to be made at the completion of every real estate transaction

13. _____ Funds that have already cleared the bank such as cashier's checks, certified checks, or wired funds

14. _____ A trust account set up for funds set aside for future costs relating to a property

15. _____ The buyer's final viewing of the property prior to closing to be certain it is in the same condition as when the purchase offer was made

▪ Multiple Choice Questions

Instructions: Circle your response and go to Appendix A to read the complete explanation for each question.

1. The seller signs a grant deed conveying title to the buyer:
    a. before going to escrow.
    b. after escrow closes.
    c. after funds from the buyer are deposited in escrow.
    d. before escrow closes.

2. The person who commonly opens escrow is the:
    a. buyer.
    b. seller.
    c. listing salesperson.
    d. lender.

3. Which statement regarding escrow procedures is correct?

    a. Escrow procedures may vary according to local custom.

    b. Escrow procedures are the same in every locality.

    c. Only escrow companies may conduct escrows.

    d. Buyers and sellers need a representing salesperson in order to use an escrow holder.

4. Which statement regarding escrow instructions is false?

    a. Escrow instructions may be unilateral.

    b. Escrow instructions may be bilateral.

    c. The purchase agreement may become the escrow instructions.

    d. Law sets the format for escrow instructions.

5. Hazard insurance protects:

    a. the lender.

    b. the buyer.

    c. the escrow holder.

    d. both (a) and (b).

6. What document outlines the flow of consideration through escrow, as well as adjustments and disbursements?

    a   The closing statement

    b. The escrow instructions

    c. The purchase agreement

    d. The grant deed

7. In escrow, a seller is commonly credited for:

    a. the down payment.

    b. the documentary transfer tax.

    c. the sales price.

    d. title insurance policy premiums.

8. Costs that are recurring for the buyer are:

    a. notary fees.

    b. appraisal fees.

    c. hazard insurance premiums.

    d. title insurance premiums.

9. What type of insurance covers errors such as a missing connection in a property's history or ownership?

    a. Hazard insurance

    b. Homeowner's insurance

    c. Title insurance

    d. Recording insurance

10. The salesperson's main responsibility during escrow is to:

    a. review and approve the preliminary title report.

    b. sign the escrow instructions.

    c. follow up with all parties on escrow conditions.

    d. disburse funds to complete the real estate transaction.

Putting it all Together

Unit 15

INTRODUCTION

This unit is an accumulation of the information from previous units. There are four sections: (1) Working with Sellers, (2) Working with Buyers, (3) Required Transaction Documents, and (4) Required Disclosures. Concise checklists are provided for each important phase - from your initial meeting with a prospect, to closing the transaction. Since these topics are from earlier units, if additional information is needed, reference the corresponding unit.

The real estate industry is constantly changing. Although it is important to keep abreast of market changes, it is also important to keep up with new **disclosures**, contracts, real estate laws, and regulations. The websites of the California Department of Real Estate and the California Association of REALTORS® offer valuable information.

Learning Objectives

After reading this unit, you should be able to:

- recall the steps when working with sellers.
- identify the ways to work with buyers.
- specify the documents required in a sales transaction.
- designate the disclosures required in a sales transaction.

WORKING WITH SELLERS

Obtaining **listings** is very important to real estate sales associates and brokers. You need to cover all of the important aspects of the **listing appointment** to gain the prospect's trust and confidence. After obtaining the listing, take the appropriate steps in servicing the listing: Are you prepared to handle an offer and/or submit a counteroffer? What happens after acceptance of an offer? Do you remember what tasks are required of the sales associate upon closing the sale? How can you ensure referrals after you close the transaction? The following checklists will help you keep track of each transaction.

Preparing for the Listing Appointment

During the listing appointment, convince the prospective sellers that you are the best person to list their home. Preparation and a stunning first impression will set you apart from the competition. Consider the following when preparing for the listing appointment:

Convincing the sellers that you are the best person to sell their home is the goal of the listing appointment.

- ❑ Prequalify the seller
- ❑ Send a **pre-listing package**
- ❑ Prepare a **career book**
  - Prepare your **property marketing plan**
  - Prepare a **CMA**
  - Prepare a **net sheet**

The Listing Presentation

During the listing presentation, convince the seller of pricing, terms, and your ability. For a professional and winning listing presentation, do the following:

- ❑ Bring the following items:
  - CMA
  - Net sheet
  - Cover letter
  - Resume
  - Your cumulative sales
  - Testimonials
  - Property marketing plan
  - Advertising samples
  - Listing pack with forms and disclosures

- ❑ Set the price with the seller
- ❑ Sell your abilities
- ❑ Present the net sheet
- ❑ Ask for the listing
- ❑ Disclose the **agency relationship**
- ❑ Elect the agency relationship with the seller
- ❑ Confirm the agency relationship with the seller
  - Have the seller sign the appropriate **listing agreement**
  - Have the seller sign the Seller's Advisory

Servicing the Listing

Your responsibilities begin when you get the listing. You must be prepared to stage the home, market the listing, and exceed your client's customer service expectations. Properly servicing listings will build your reputation and help ensure future business. To service the listing effectively, discuss the following:

An open house is part of the marketing plan to sell a house.

- ❑ **Staging** the home with the seller.
- ❑ The seller's property disclosure statements and related forms (see end of section for list of required/if applicable disclosures)
- ❑ **Marketing** considerations:
    - **Advertising**/signs
    - **Open houses**
    - Virtual tours
    - Promotional flyers/brochures
    - Closing time
    - **MLS** exposure
- ❑ How showings will be arranged through the listing office.
- ❑ Contact person.
    - Who the contact person will be if listing agent is sick, out of town, or otherwise unavailable.
- ❑ The **electronic lock box key system**.
- ❑ How offers will be handled:
    - Seller availability for potential time-sensitive issues such as inspections or removal of contingencies.
    - Does the seller prefer offers to be faxed or a face-to-face presentation?
    - Will an attorney be reviewing offers?
    - Did you discuss the pros and cons of accepting or rejecting offers that include contingencies, and what the seller will allow?
    - Did you discuss the importance of buyer prequalification/ pre-approval?
    - Did you discuss the requirements for a binding purchase agreement? (must be executed - oral agreements are not binding)

Handling Offers/Counteroffers

Communication with your client will prepare you for handling offers and counteroffers. Are you prepared to represent your client's needs and desires when you receive an offer? Do you know what the seller's boundaries are? Have you counseled the seller regarding the offer/counteroffer process? When handling offers and counteroffers, consider the following:

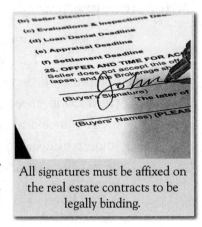

All signatures must be affixed on the real estate contracts to be legally binding.

❑ Analyze the offer with the seller. What is flexible, what is not? Consider the following:

- Earnest money deposit amount
- Purchase price
- Personal property issues
- Contingencies
- Inspections (what can happen as a result of the inspection)
- Closing date
- Possession/Move-in Agreements
- Multiple offers
- Appraisal and underwriting approval
- Net proceeds

❑ Counsel the seller regarding countering or accepting a particular offer

❑ Obtain proper signatures

❑ Provide copies to seller

After Acceptance

Your job is not complete upon acceptance of an offer. **Escrow** can be lengthy or complicated, depending on the type of transaction. Your client will look to you for guidance and assistance to ensure a smooth transaction. After acceptance of an offer, consider the following:

Buyers have a right to a walk-through prior to closing.

- ❑ Follow through and stay on top of all aspects
- ❑ Discuss inspection timeframes and work orders
- ❑ Verify appraisal has been ordered
- ❑ Locate and provide title to **title company**
- ❑ Schedule closing date, time, and location, and provide all necessary documents
- ❑ Provide lender with necessary documents
- ❑ Remind seller that the buyer has a right to a walk-through prior to closing
- ❑ Obtain and verify mortgage information and payoff requirements
- ❑ Counsel seller about what to expect at closing:
  - What to bring (photo ID, Social Security numbers, previous addresses)
  - Review net proceeds and financial information

Closing the Sale

Closing time can be exciting and stressful for your client. Continue your guidance and assistance to the very end and consider the following:

- ❏ Attend the closing
- ❏ Match estimated proceeds with **closing statements**
- ❏ Make sure to address **Home Warranty Program** issues
- ❏ Exchange keys, garage door openers, and final information about the property
- ❏ Verify possession date and time

Closing the sale includes exhanging keys, garage door openers, and final information about the property.

After Closing

The chances are great that your client or someone they know will need the help of a real estate professional in the future. To ensure referrals and future business, consider the following:

- ❏ Follow-up with questions, problems, or concerns
- ❏ Assess your customer service
- ❏ Send a thank you note and/or gift

Follow-up with a thank you note and/or gift to your client after the closing.

WORKING WITH BUYERS

Every sale starts with the challenge of finding a buyer. Buyers do not have to work exclusively with one broker or sales associate. How will you build their confidence and trust in you? How will you learn of their needs and desires? Do you know how to write an offer and negotiate its terms in your buyer's best interest? Here is a review of what you have learned about working with buyers.

The Initial Meeting

The goal of your initial meeting with a buyer is to build trust and learn as much as possible about the buyer's needs. Some buyers are new to the home-buying process and will depend on you to guide them through the entire process. Most buyers will come to you with knowledge of the real estate market and will already have an understanding of the home-buying process. Offering all buyers exceptional, personal service will give you the competitive edge you need. At the initial meeting, consider the following:

The initial meeting with a buyer is to build trust and learn as much as possible about their needs.

- ❑ Ask the buyers if they are working with another agent
- ❑ Explain and discuss agency relationships
- ❑ Have the buyer sign applicable forms (Agency Relationships, Buyer-Broker Agreement if applicable)
- ❑ Determine the buyer's expectations
- ❑ Describe the home-buying process
- ❑ Determine the buyer's housing needs (**Homebuyer's Checklist**)
- ❑ Qualify the buyer
- ❑ Get the buyer in touch with a lender
- ❑ Find out which method of communication the buyer prefers

Previewing Properties

Now that you know what the buyers are looking for and how much they can afford, you can begin researching and previewing available properties. When previewing properties with buyers, consider the following:

When previewing properties, offer personal service and look for signs of buyer interest.

- ❑ Research properties according to buyer's needs and wants
- ❑ Evaluate and analyze the differences in properties
- ❑ Narrow the choices with the buyer and address all objections
- ❑ Use due diligence and disclose all pertinent information
- ❑ Look for signs of buyer interest
- ❑ Ask for an offer when applicable

Writing the Offer

When the buyer has chosen a home, you need to help them decide how much they want to offer and what terms they want to include in the offer to purchase. Before writing the offer with the buyer, consider the following:

- ❑ Explain the offer/counteroffer process
- ❑ Consult the buyer regarding the **purchase contract** and discuss
  - **Contingencies**
  - Clauses
  - **Earnest money deposit**
  - Price
  - Inspections
  - Closing date
  - Possession
- ❑ Discuss how the offer will be presented
- ❑ Obtain all signatures
- ❑ Provide copies for the buyer

From Acceptance to Closing

Once you have received acceptance of an offer from a seller, be sure you meet all terms of the purchase contract in a timely fashion.

Arrange for the property inspections in a timely fashion.

- ❏ Arrange for property inspections
- ❏ Follow-up on all inspections and contingencies
- ❏ Follow-up with the lender:
  - • Provide all documents to lender
  - • Verify **appraisal** has been ordered
  - • Make sure Good Faith Estimate is provided
- ❏ Explain **title insurance**
- ❏ Arrange closing date, time, and location
- ❏ Verify title work is complete
- ❏ Arrange for and attend final walk-through
- ❏ Counsel buyers on what to expect and what to bring at closing:
  - • Photo ID
  - • Social Security numbers
  - • Previous residence addresses
  - • Additional monies
  - • Verify good funds
- ❏ Verify that parties have met all terms of the purchase contract

Closing the Sale

As mentioned earlier, closings are an exciting yet stressful time for buyers and sellers. It is important to show your support, professionalism, and efficiency while performing the following:

Buyers will appreciate your support, professionalism, and efficiency during the closing process.

- ❏ Attending the closing
- ❏ Handling any last minute issues
- ❏ Exchanging keys, garage door openers
- ❏ Verifying possession date and time

After Closing

Ensure future business by utilizing your customer service skills beyond the transaction closing. Consider performing the following tasks:

Customer service includes sending your client a thank you note and/or a gift.

- ❑ Ask if buyers have any questions, concerns, or problems
- ❑ Assess your customer service
- ❑ Send a thank you note and/or gift

REQUIRED TRANSACTION DOCUMENTS

In this section, the mandatory transaction documents in residential real estate sales are listed. Also listed are optional and strongly recommended transaction documents. Depending on the type of transaction, you may need to use the documents listed as "If Applicable". For example, if your sellers or buyers are listing or purchasing a property contingent upon the sale of their homes, you will need a form that outlines these terms. Remember, the more you confirm agreements in writing, the more you are practicing risk management.

You may use your own form or a standard form. Standard forms usually are available through an association. This textbook uses C.A.R.®'s standard forms in the examples. When you join C.A.R®, you will be able to access standard forms through either zipForm® Professional Edition (web-based) or zipForm® Standard Edition (downloadable software).

The Listing

The listing agent must provide the following documents upon taking a listing. The type of listing agreed upon by the listing agent and seller will dictate which listing agreement to use.

Mandatory (Listing Agent to provide):

1. AD: Disclosure of Real Estate Agency Relationships
2. RLA: Residential Listing Agreement – Exclusive
   RLAA: Residential Listing Agreement – Agency
   RLAN: Residential Listing Agreement – Open
3. SA: Seller's Advisory

If Applicable:

4. SEL: Sellers Instruction to Exclude Listing from MLS

5. Any permits or invoices that the seller provides

From Offer to Closing

Once the selling agent procures a buyer and writes an offer on a property, the following forms are applicable:

Optional (Selling Agent to provide):

1. BBE: Buyer-Broker Agreement – Exclusive

2. BBNE: Buyer-Broker Agreement – Non-Exclusive

3. BBNN: Buyer-Broker Agreement – Non-Exclusive/Not for Compensation

Mandatory (Selling Agent to provide):

4. AD: Disclosure of Real Estate Agency Relationship

5. RPA-CA: Residential Purchase Agreement

6. BIA: Buyer's Inspection Advisory

If Applicable:

7. COP: Contingency for Purchase or Sale of Other Property

8. IOA: Interim Occupancy Agreement

9. RLA: Residential Lease After Sale

10. Counter Offer(s), if any

Strongly Recommended

11. WPA: Wood Destroying Pest Inspection and Allocation of Costs

12. RDN: Receipt and Delivery of Notices to Perform

13. CC: Cancellation of Contract (decide what happens to money if escrow cancels)

14. CBC: Cooperating Broker Commission Agreement

REQUIRED DISCLOSURES

As the business of buying and selling real estate becomes more complex, so do the required disclosures. The following is a concise list of the disclosures required in the sale of residential property. The required real estate disclosures are constantly changing and therefore brokers and sales associates should include a disclosure course as part of their continuing education.

Disclosures Required of a Seller and/or Real Estate Agent

1. Disclosures Upon Transfer of Real Property
   a. Real Estate Transfer Disclosure Statement
   b. Local Option Real Estate Transfer Disclosure Statement
   c. Natural Hazards Disclosure
   d. Mello-Roos Bonds and Taxes
   e. Ordnance Location
   f. Window Security Bars
2. Earthquake Guides
3. Water Heater and Smoke Detector Statement of Compliance
4. Disclosure Regarding Lead-Based Paint Hazards
5. California's Environmental Hazards Pamphlet
6. Delivery of Structural Pest Control Inspection and Certification Reports
7. Energy Conservation Retrofit and Thermal Insulation Disclosures
8. Foreign Investment in Real Property Tax Act
9. Notice and Disclosure to Buyer of State Tax Withholding of Disposition of California Real Property
10. Furnishing Controlling Documents and a Financial Statement
11. Notice Regarding the Advisability of Title Insurance
12. Data Base – Locations of Registered Sex Offenders

Disclosures Required of Both Real Estate Agents in the Transfer of Residential Real Property

1. Visual Inspection
2. Agency Relationship Disclosure
3. Disclosure of the Negotiability of Real Estate Commissions
4. No Disclosure Required for Manner/Occurrence of Death; Affliction of Occupant with AIDS
5. Disclosure of Sale Price Information

SUMMARY

Obtaining **listings** is very important to real estate sales associates and brokers. Be sure to cover all important aspects of the listing appointment to gain the prospect's trust and confidence. When working with sellers remember to **service the listing, handle offers** and **counteroffers**, and **provide customer service** before and after the closing.

Every sale begins with the challenge of finding a buyer. Offering all buyers a unique and personal service will give you the competitive edge you need to earn their trust and loyalty. When working with buyers, pay careful attention to the various tasks involved in the initial meeting, previewing properties, writing the offer, handling counteroffers, and the **transactional closing**. Be sure to continue your customer service efforts beyond the transactional closing to help ensure future business and referrals.

You may use your own or standard forms for real estate transactions. Certain forms are mandatory for each type of transaction, and depending on the terms of the purchase agreement, you may need additional applicable forms. There are also various highly recommended forms that may be used; the more agreements are in writing, the more you are practicing risk management.

As the business of buying and selling real estate gets more complex, so do the required disclosures. There are certain disclosures required only of the seller and/or listing agent, as well as disclosures that are required of both the listing and selling agent in the transfer of residential real estate. The required real estate disclosures are constantly changing and therefore brokers and sales associates should include a disclosure course as part of their continuing education.

UNIT 15 REVIEW

Matching Exercise

Instructions: Write the letter of the matching term on the blank line before its definition. Answers are in Appendix A.

Terms

A. advertising

B. agency relationship

C. appraisal

D. career book

E. closing statement

F. CMA

G. contingencies

H. disclosures

I. earnest money deposit

J. electronic lock box system

K. escrow

L. execute

M. Homebuyer's Checklist

N. home warranty program

O. listing agreement

P. listing appointment

Q. listings

R. marketing

S. MLS

T. net sheet

U. open house

V. pre-listing package

W. property marketing plan

X. purchase contract

Y. staging

Z. title company

AA. title insurance

Definitions

1. _____ Information that must be given to consumers about their financial dealings

2. _____ Owner agreements to place properties for sale with a brokerage

3. _____ The opportunity a salesperson has to convince a prospective seller to list the home with that particular salesperson

4. _____ A professional marketing piece sent to a prospective seller before a listing appointment that is designed to identify a salesperson and highlight his or her qualifications

5. _____ A marketing piece that reflects the personal history of a real estate salesperson's career

6. _____ A detailed schedule of everything a real estate salesperson will do to market a property

7. _____ A comparison analysis that real estate salespeople use while working with a seller to determine an appropriate listing price for the seller's house

8. _____ Shows the approximate net amount of money the seller can expect to receive for a specified sales price

9. _____ A special relationship of trust by which one person (agent) is authorized to conduct business, sign papers, or otherwise act on behalf of another person (principal). This relationship may be created by expressed agreement, ratification, or estoppel

10. _____ A written contract by which a principal, or seller, employs a broker to sell real estate

11. _____ Preparing a home for maximum appeal to buyers

12. _____ The process involved in promoting a product or service

13. _____ The mode and frequency through which a marketing concept is communicated

14. _____ A prospecting activity that advertises the house and allows prospective buyers to visit the property spontaneously

15. _____ A cooperative listing service conducted by a group of brokers, usually members of a real estate association

16. _____ The contract that outlines all the special terms of a transaction as agreed upon by the buyer and seller

17. _____ Statements that define the terms of an agreement and give the other party to the agreement cause to void an offer if the terms are not met

18. _____ To make valid by signing

19. _____ Down payment made by a purchaser of real estate as evidence of good faith A deposit or partial payment

20. _____ The estimation of property value

21. _____ The period during which all parties are held accountable for the terms in the purchase agreement

22. _____ A company that performs a title search on the property and issues a title policy for the lender and the purchaser to ensure that there is a valid mortgage lien against the property and title is clear

23. _____ A detailed questionnaire about what a buyer is looking for in a home

Multiple Choice Questions

Instructions: Circle your response and go to Appendix A to read the complete explanation for each question.

1. Which of the following statements about the real estate industry is true?
   a. The real estate industry is constantly changing.
   b. The real estate industry has remained the same over the last ten years.
   c. The real estate law rarely changes.
   d. Keeping current with new disclosures is not very important.

2. How can a sales associate prepare for an effective listing appointment?
   a. Prequalify the seller
   b. Send a pre-listing package
   c. Prepare a net sheet
   d. All of the above

3. Staging the home and marketing considerations should take place:
   a. when the transaction closes.
   b. as soon as possible after taking the listing.
   c. while previewing properties with the buyers.
   d. when filling out the offer to purchase.

4. To prepare for offers and counteroffers, a listing agent should:
   a. determine the seller's boundaries.
   b. tell the seller to counter every offer.
   c. decide on the purchase price for the seller.
   d. avoid asking the seller what they want because they are not qualified to answer.

5. What should sales associates take into consideration after an offer is accepted?

    a. Inspection timeframes and work orders
    b. Verification that appraisal has been ordered
    c. The closing date, time, and location
    d. All of the above

6. When should a sales associate follow-up with a client regarding questions and concerns?

    a. Up to the transaction closing
    b. When the client is wealthy
    c. Throughout the transaction and after the closing
    d. Only when the question or concern is of great importance

7. The first thing a selling agent should do during the initial meeting with a prospective buyer is to:

    a. ask the buyer to sign a Buyer-Broker agreement.
    b. ask the buyer if they are working with another agent.
    c. have the buyer fill out a loan application.
    d. discuss the earnest money deposit with the buyer.

8. It is important to discuss contingencies and the earnest money deposit:

    a. after going to escrow.
    b. before previewing any properties.
    c. before writing the offer to purchase.
    d. None of the above

9. Which of the following documents must the listing agent provide before taking a listing?

    a. Disclosure of Real Estate Agency Relationships
    b. Sellers Instruction to Exclude Listing from MLS
    c. Buyer-Broker Agreement
    d. Interim Occupancy Agreement

10. Which of the following disclosures is required of the buyer?

    a. Real Estate Transfer Disclosure Statement
    b. Natural Hazards Disclosure
    c. Visual Inspection
    d. None of the above

APPENDIX A: ANSWER KEY

Unit 1: Your Real Estate Career

Answers - Matching

1. N	6. P	11. V	16. M
2. Q	7. E	12. T	17. F
3. A	8. O	13. C	18. S
4. R	9. I	14. H	19. B
5. L	10. D	15. U	20. W

Answers - Multiple Choice

1. **d** A career in real estate offers real estate salespeople high earning potential, independence, career, and advancement opportunities, flexible work schedules, and an unlimited inventory. **Page 9**

2. **b** Instead of salaries, real estate agents earn commissions when transactions close. **Page 10**

3. **b** Commissions on sales are the main source of earnings for real estate salespeople and brokers. **Page 10**

4. **a** Commissions are based on a certain percentage of the sale price of a property. The amount is not set by law, and must be decided between the broker and the seller. **Page 24**

5. **c** An employee is someone who is under the control and direction of an employer. **Page 19**

6. **a** The term brokerage generally refers to an activity involving the sale of something through an intermediary who negotiates the transaction for payment. **Page 2**

7. **c** A listing agreement is a bilateral contract between the seller and the broker. Listings belong to brokers. **Page 7**

8. **b** Prospecting for listings and selling properties are the main activities of salespeople in a real estate brokerage. **Page 5**

9. **a** The listing coordinator manages all required paperwork for listings. Duties may include preparing a pre-listing package and competitive market analysis for each seller, communicating with sellers regarding the marketing of their property, following up with salespeople who show the property, arranging office and MLS previews, and completing any task required to take the listing from potential sale to closed transaction. **Page 29**

10. **b** During the escrow process, anything that needs to be resolved prior to closing is the responsibility of the escrow coordinator. This may include the buyer's approval of the property inspection, pest control inspection, geological report and other disclosures required by law or by agreement of the buyer and seller. **Page 29**

Unit 2: Prepare for Success

Answers - Matching

1.	I	4.	D	7.	M	10.	B
2.	O	5.	C	8.	E		
3.	H	6.	G	9.	A		

Answers - Multiple Choice

1. **d** Personal attributes, financial reserves, technology, and training are all extremely important factors to take into consideration before you enter the profession. **Page 37**

2. **a** A new real estate salesperson should set aside at least six months to a year of living expenses to allow enough time and money to build a substantial client base. **Page 37**

3. **b** Ongoing expenses recur every month like your cell phone bill, car maintenance, postage, printing, advertising, and insurance premiums. **Page 38**

4. **d** The first cost of doing business after passing the state exam will be to pay for your salesperson license. Remember, you must have your license before you can start to work as a sales associate in a brokerage. **Page 39**

5. **c** At one time typewriters were used to prepare forms. Today, most licensees access zipForm® from their computers to do this task. **Page 39**

6. **c** A well-designed website will focus on the needs of its readers. **Page 43**

7. **b** Busy real estate professionals can protect themselves against liability by documenting every event in a transaction. **Page 44**

8. **d** Your appearance is a powerful business tool, which helps you make a good first impression. **Page 45**

9. **c** One of the ways to improve your listening skills is to focus on the buyer's most important issues. **Page 51**

10. **b** When dealing with an upset client, listen carefully to the client's criticism, and try to work out the problem in the best possible way. **Page 52**

Unit 3: Goal Setting & Productivity

Answers - Matching

1.	D	4.	H	7.	J	10.	F
2.	G	5.	B	8.	A		
3.	E	6.	C	9.	I		

Answers - Multiple Choice

1. **d** Productivity management incorporates business planning techniques, personal marketing strategies, and time management skills. **Page 57**

2. **c** A business plan is not a static document. It is dynamic and changes while at the same time providing a road map of the business' direction. **Page 58**

3. **d** Goals should be SMART (specific, measurable, attainable, relevant, and timely). **Page 60**

4. **b** Short-term goals can be met in hours, days, or weeks. Closing one transaction is a stepping-stone to reaching the long-term financial goal. **Page 60**

5. **b** Break long-term goals into easier, short-term goals. A practical way to do this is to make daily activities consistent with the daily, weekly, and monthly goals. **Page 60**

6. **c** A personal marketing plan describes the marketing efforts you will make to reach your target market. **Page 65**

7. **c** Repeated mailings of a strong, direct-mail piece helps establish permanent name recognition, which will generate new and repeat business. **Page 65**

8. **c** For any marketing to be successful, sales associates must use a prospect management system to track the source of leads. **Page 70**

9. **d** The income funnel quantifies the number of prospects from each activity that must be contacted in order to complete a sale. Marketing activities that produce income are networking, regular mailings, floor time, website leads, open houses, referrals, repeat business, and other sources. **Page 72**

10. **c** The first step is to determine what time to start work each day. The highest priority activities and goals should be scheduled first. Schedule the business and prospecting activities for the week and items from the prioritized task list that need to be completed. Finally, block in some contingency time. **Page 73**

Unit 4: Product Knowledge

Answers - Matching

1. H	4. D	7. G	10. J
2. M	5. L	8. C	
3. K	6. B	9. E	

Answers - Multiple Choice

1. **d**   The obvious selling point for new neighborhoods is that everything is new, modern, and sought-after. The houses are larger with up-to-date floor plans and amenities. The houses are safer due to more stringent building safety codes, easier to maintain, and energy efficient. **Page 83**

2. **d**   New houses are designed and built to conserve energy. The use of dual and triple-glazed windows, increased insulation in walls and roofs, more efficient heating and cooling equipment, and Energy Star® appliances have helped to decrease energy consumption. These houses not only save the homeowner money, but they are less drafty and more comfortable. **Page 84**

3. **c**   A gable roof has a pitched roof with two sloping sides. A hip roof is a pitched roof with four sloping sides. A gambrel roof is a curbed roof with a steep lower slope with a flatter one above. A Mansard roof has four nearly vertical sides with a flat top. **Page 89**

4. **b**   Ribbon windows are several rectangular windows placed in a row with their frames abutting, and are a distinctive feature in Craftsman and Prairie style houses. **Page 93**

5. **a**   During the mid 1900s, the uncomplicated, rectangular-shaped Cape Cod was economically mass-produced in suburban areas. The upsurge in popularity was due to the return of service men and women from World War II who were able to purchase these houses with government guaranteed loans. Sometimes these houses were called the GI Government Issued houses. **Page 98**

6. **d**   The Georgian style has formal, symmetrical lines, paired chimneys, and five windows across the front of the second story. **Page 99**

7. **b**   When people think of a Victorian house, they usually picture the highly imaginative and elaborate Queen Anne style. **Page 101**

8. **a**   This describes the Craftsman Bungalow style. **Page 103**

9. **c**   The most distinguishing feature of the Monterey style is the second-story balcony on the front of the house. **Page 105**

10. **b**   The Mediterranean style of architecture is a blend of the Italian, Moorish, Byzantine, and the early California mission styles. This style uses white or light-colored stucco on the exterior and a red-tiled gable roof with very little or no overhanging eaves. Additional features include arched doorways and windows, courtyard entrances, patios, ornamental tile, and wrought iron. **Page 112**

11. **d** This is a classic description of the Tudor Revival style. **Page 107**

12. **d** The main characteristic of French Normandy style is the round stone tower topped with a cone-shaped roof. Sometimes the tower is the entrance to the house. **Page 108**

13. **b** Art Deco style is characterized by geometric designs such as zigzags, chevrons, diamonds, sunbursts, and painted or relief designs arranged in horizontal bands near the roofline. **Page 109**

14. **d** The Ranch style house has become the most popular style in the country since its debut in 1932 in San Diego. Ranch style houses are found throughout the United States in suburban housing tracts. **Page 110**

15. **d** Neo means new and eclectic refers to combining a variety of details from different styles to produce a harmonious look. **Page 113**

Unit 5: Completing the Seller's Forms

Answers - Matching

1.	L	5.	H	9.	E	13.	B
2.	P	6.	M	10.	I	14.	K
3.	N	7.	C	11.	Q	15.	F
4.	G	8.	O	12.	R		

Answers - Multiple Choice

1. **b** Before going to the listing appointment, Pat prepares a competitive market analysis (CMA) to show the Springs. This information will help them set an appropriate listing price. **Page 123**

2. **d** Every single agency relationship has a principal, an agent, and a third party. A dual agency would have one agent and two principals, but not a third party. **Page 125**

3. **c** A dual agency exists if one broker represents both principals (buyer and seller) in the transaction. **Page 125**

4. **c** A written agency disclosure must be presented by a listing agent (or his or her sales associate) who must deliver the form to the seller before entering into a listing agreement. **Page 127**

5. **a** This information is written on the lines provided in Section 2. **Page 139**

6. **c** This is written on the line provided in Section 4.C. **Page 139**

7. **d**   In arbitration, the parties hire a neutral person (arbitrator) to listen to each side of the dispute. The main difference between mediation and arbitration is that the arbitrator may award a binding decision on all parties to the dispute. The decision is final, binding, and legally enforceable. Arbitration awards are final, and the courts will not re-hear the case, unless the arbitrator was corrupt, exceeded his or her power, or the award was procured by fraud, corruption, or other undue means. **Pages 138**

8. **c**   The listing agreement is a contract between the seller and the listing agent, so both must sign it. Once signed, it becomes an enforceable, bilateral contract. **Page 138**

9. **b**   This form provides a worksheet to estimate seller's approximate costs and proceeds from the sale of a property. **Page 143**

10. **d**   The *Combined Hazards Book* is comprised of three parts: (1) Residential Environmental Hazards, (2) *Protect Your Family From Lead* booklet, and (3) *The Homeowner's Guide to Earthquake Safety*. By giving the buyer this *Combined Hazards Book*, you will meet or exceed current disclosure requirements. Remember, even though you give buyers the disclosure booklets, the seller is still responsible to complete all disclosure forms honestly and accurately. **Page 164**

Unit 6: Completing the Buyer's Forms

Answers - Matching

1.	G	4.	C	7.	E	10.	B
2.	I	5.	A	8.	L		
3.	H	6.	J	9.	D		

Answers - Multiple Choice

1. **c**   In most cases, a standard California Residential Purchase Agreement and Joint Escrow Instructions (RPA-CA) contract is used by real estate agents when a buyer makes an offer anywhere in California. It was created by the California Association of REALTORS® (C.A.R.). The Department of Real Estate does not officially recommend this form; nor is any type of specific form required by law. **Page 183**

2. **b**   The words "and Joint Escrow Instructions" reflect that the form also has an instruction to the escrow holder by both the seller and the buyer. The form includes space for the escrow holder to sign for receipt of the document. **Page 183**

3. **b**   Funds received may not be commingled with a broker's personal funds. Funds must be deposited and disposed of within three business days after receipt unless otherwise instructed in writing. Indicate if the deposit will be placed into a broker's trust account or elsewhere. **Page 186**

4. **c** The closing and occupancy section covers the intent of the buyers to occupy the property as a primary residence, the date the sellers (or tenant) will turn over possession of the property to the buyers and whether or not the buyers will take possession of the property prior to close of escrow. **Page 189**

5. **b** Because the purchase of a property requires many inspections, reports, and tests, it is important for both buyer and seller to agree on who will be responsible for payment of each one. Also, the buyer and seller must agree on allocation of payment for the escrow and title providers they select. Prepaid items such as property taxes and insurance are prorated in escrow. **Page 189**

6. **a** Sellers must complete the TDS and NHD and give them to buyers. The Lead-Based Paint disclosure must be given to buyers if the property was built prior to 1978. **Page 190**

7. **b** The contract specifies time periods for buyers and sellers. Choices (a), (c), and (d) are correct. In choice (b), the buyer, not the seller, deposits additional money for the downpayment. **Page 194**

8. **a** The purchase agreement usually contains a printed clause that says the sellers may keep the deposit as liquidated damages if the buyers back out without good cause. **Page 198**

9 **d** If the offer is not accepted by the seller within the time specified, the offer is revoked and any deposit is returned to the buyer. **Page 199**

10. **b** In addition to the down payment, the buyers will have to pay for their share of the closing costs. Advise the buyers that the closing costs may be up to 1.5% of the purchase price and are not financed. **Page 209**

Unit 7: How Will You Get Your Business?

Answers - Matching

1.	L	6.	H	11.	I	16.	J
2.	T	7.	R	12.	E	17.	O
3.	B	8.	M	13.	D	18.	A
4.	P	9.	C	14.	K	19.	S
5.	F	10.	Q	15.	G	20.	N

Answers - Multiple Choice

1. **a** Your most likely prospects will include people in your current sphere of influence, homeowners in your geographic target market, FSBOs, individuals in your demographic target markets, and prospects who call or come to the office while you have floor time. **Page 218**

2. **c** Family members, friends, teachers, former colleagues, and members of associations to which you are in your sphere of influence and are considered warm prospects. **Page 218**

3. **b** In 1991, Congress passed the Telephone Consumer Protection Act (TCPA). In 2003, the FCC established, together with the Federal Trade Commission (FTC), a national Do Not Call Registry. **Page 222**

4. **d** A prospecting strategy describes the activities you will use—direct marketing, personal selling, and networking—to contact prospective clients and customers. **Page 224**

5. **a** The benefit of direct marketing is that your marketing pieces and messages are sent directly to your target market. However, unsolicited marketing pieces may be irrelevant to the recipient and may be considered junk mail, and unwanted email messages are considered spam. **Page 225**

6. **b** Networking can be done by joining groups and associations and physically attending functions or through social media. **Page 234**

7. **a** The Internet has changed prospecting to a certain extent. Instead of outgoing calls and direct marketing (the "push" model), using the Internet effectively "pulls" the customer to your website. Pull marketing attracts customers to you. **Page 234**

8. **b** Write about something that you are passionate about. Do not steal other people's material. Link to them if their information is relevant. Be friendly, conversational, and humorous, and it does not hurt to be a little edgy occasionally. Provide an RSS feed for your blog. **Page 236**

9. **c** Podcasting is a free service that allows Internet users to pull audio files (typically MP3s) from a podcasting website to listen to on their computers or personal digital audio players. **Page 237**

10. **a** The goal of prospecting and networking is to cultivate new clients and expand your business. Therefore, always ask for referrals to build a referral database. **Page 239**

Unit 8: Advertising & Marketing Listings

Answers - Matching

1. G	4. A	7. J	10. I
2. H	5. C	8. E	
3. F	6. B	9. D	

Answers - Multiple Choice

1. **d** The different promotional methods are advertising, direct marketing, sales promotion, personal selling, and networking. As a salesperson, you will use all of these methods in the course of promoting yourself and your listed properties. **Page 245**

2. **a**   The sales associate should put emphasis on features that may attract buyers. **Page 246**

3. **a**   The "A" in the AIDA formula is for attention.   You must first get the customer's attention before anything else. **Page 250**

4. **d**   The use of certain terminology in an advertisement is often a red flag. Describing a certain neighborhood as exclusive, or a house as "great for a single person" or "great for an active person" implies potential discrimination. **Page 253**

5. **a**   Common ways to advertise on the web include banner and sidebar ads, pop-ups (and pop-downs), floating ads, interstitial ads, unicast ads, and takeover ads. **Page 257**

6. **d**   Today's website is yesterday's storefront. To compete, you company must have a website. Your website does not give you a competitive advantage; it just puts you on par with your competitors. **Page 258**

7. **a**   The two types of newspaper advertising are classified and display ads. **Page 260**

8. **a**   The billboard category includes yard signs. **Page 262**

9. **d**   Transit advertising involves advertising that is on vehicles as well as positioned in the public areas of transit stations and terminals. Magnetic signs for car doors are a type of transit advertising. **Page 263**

10. **c**   The cost of television advertising on the major networks during prime time is exorbitant. **Page 264**

Unit 9: The Listing Presentation

Answers - Matching

1. H	5. I	9. L	13. S
2. R	6. T	10. B	14. P
3. Q	7. V	11. F	15. K
4. C	8. D	12. G	

Answers - Multiple Choice

1. **d**   A listing package should include information about the seller's property, professional details about you and your brokerage, samples of your advertising and marketing pieces, and all of the forms necessary for listing the property. A carefully prepared listing package will help achieve a position of trust, accountability, and communication with the seller. **Page 271**

2. **b**   When a homeowner decides to sell his or her home, they generally call one or more real estate professionals. If you are the one they contact, you will come to the prospective seller's home for a listing appointment. Each salesperson gives a listing presentation and tries to convince the prospective seller that he or she is the specialist to sell the home. **Page 269**

3. **b** Develop a list of questions to ask the seller prior to the listing appointment that will help tailor your presentation to each particular seller. Everyone desires to be treated as an individual, and sophisticated sellers will know immediately if you use a standard presentation. **Page 270**

4. **a** It is possible to follow the same timeline and activities in your property marketing plan for any listing because certain recommended marketing activities will benefit any listing. **Page 272**

5. **d** You will present the CMA during your listing presentation to establish the home value with the prospective sellers. For the homeowner, the CMA either indicates or confirms the probable value of the home. For the real estate professional, the CMA establishes his or her knowledge of the market as well as laying the foundation for setting a realistic selling price for the property. **Page 273**

6. **c** Only those similar properties—sold on the open market, with approval of the seller, and offered for a reasonable length of time—are used for comparables. In addition, if possible, use only those properties that have sold within the past six months. Comparables older than six months are typically less reliable. **Page 274**

7. **c** To prepare a CMA for a property, collect data on at least three comparable properties (comps) that are as similar to the property in question as possible. The MLS allows you to find properties that match certain criteria you enter into the computerized database. **Page 274**

8. **b** During a "buyer's market" by lowering the price, you can sell a property that is functionally obsolete, in poor condition, in a poor location, or on a busy street. When advertising on the Internet, it is crucial you include pictures and even virtual tours. Potential buyers who encounter a listing with a "photo not available" will go elsewhere to find a home. **Page 278**

9. **a** The right listing price is the secret to a fast sale. A salesperson needs more than charisma to sell a property. Lowering your commission may help you obtain the listing, but it will not influence a salesperson's ability to procure a buyer. If the price is right, a home can sell in a poor neighborhood. **Page 278**

10. **d** If there is more supply than demand (buyer's market), a seller might have to lower the price of a property. If there is more demand (a seller's market) than inventory (listed properties), the seller could consider pricing the home at the top end of the range of value or higher. **Page 279**

11. **d** A good time to present your commission is while you are explaining the costs in the net sheet because you can redirect the sellers' attention to the real issue—what will their check amount be at the closing. It is easier for the seller to see the commission when it is presented as part of all of the costs involved in the sale. **Page 280**

12. **c** The average sale takes place after the fifth or sixth refusal. **Page 281**

13. **c**   The proper procedure to follow when asking for the listing is: (1) Present the Agency Disclosure Statement, (2) Present the Listing Agreement, and (3) Present the Seller's Advisory. **Page 281**

14. **a**   The listing agreement is between the broker and the seller, but a salesperson usually represents the broker in the transaction. **Page 269**

15. **a**   The most common reason a home fails to sell is overpricing. **Page 283**

Unit 10: Servicing the Listing

Answers - Matching

1.	C	3.	D	5.	J	7.	E
2.	I	4.	A	6.	B	8	F

Answers - Multiple Choice

1. **c**   Most clients equate consistency of communication with customer service. In fact, the most frequent complaint clients and customers have about real estate sales associates is the lack of communication. You need to maintain proactive communications with your clients, be highly accessible, and deliver quality as well as consistency in your communication and product. In order to meet your customer's expectations, set up a schedule of communication; agree to call them once a week to update them. **Page 292**

2. **d**   Staging the home, marketing efforts, and a high level of communication build a perception of professionalism and ensures loyalty. **Page 291**

3. **b**   The majority of listings sell through the MLS and other salespeople. Submitting the listing to an MLS is the first marketing activity you should perform once the property is ready for showings. The "For Sale" sign is widely recognized as the number one marketing tool. It should be big enough for passersby to read easily, and it should always include your name and contact information. Develop distinctive signage that stands out. If the property is in an association, be sure to follow its rules regarding placement of property "For Sale" signs. **Page 293**

4. **b**   To prepare a home for sale, the seller should remove huge photo collages, get rid of the clutter, clean closets, and organize kitchen cupboards. It is not necessary to hire an interior decorator. **Pages 296**

5. **b**   To write more effective ads in less time, keep your audience and their emotions in mind. Writing successful ads begins and ends with emotions. Every good ad addresses the right (emotional) brain first and then the left (logical) brain. Research has shown that higher readership is due to ads that used figurative language (metaphors, puns, analogies, etc.) rather than literal wording (just the facts). **Page 300**

6. **b**   The reasons a listing agent should hold an open house are to market and sell the property as well as to meet prospective buyers and sellers. **Page 301**

7. **a**   A net sheet prepared for a full price offer, a copy of the listing, and a blank offer to purchase are all items to bring in preparation for an open house. **Page 308**

8. **c**   One of the ways to improve the visual appearance of a property during an open house is to clear the clutter. **Page 312**

9. **d**   Escort visitors through the house and allow them to browse freely. Watch for buying signals. It is a matter of being sensitive to what the visitor needs before he or she can make the decision to become a buyer. It is a good idea to have information available on what the down payment and monthly mortgage payments would be. **Page 314**

10. **b**   Leave the house as you found it by turning off the lights, closing the windows, and locking the doors. If a door was unlocked when you arrived and there were no specific instructions to lock it or leave it unlocked, lock it. A personal thank you note and telephone call the next day makes a good impression on potential clients. **Page 316**

Unit 11: Working with Buyers

Answers - Matching

1.	M	4.	C	7.	H	10.	E
2.	B	5.	K	8.	D		
3.	A	6.	L	9.	I		

Answers - Multiple Choice

1. **b**   A disclosure of agency with a buyer is required by real estate law in every transaction. **Page 323**

2. **d**   A buyer can choose to work with a buyer's broker, dual agent, or non-exclusive agent. **Page 323**

3. **d**   Baby Boomers, Generation Y, and Generation X all represent today's homebuyers. **Page 326**

4. **b**   Increasingly, buyers and sellers are looking to the Internet as their primary source of information. **Page 327**

5. **d**   A buyer's profile provides information about the buyer's financial resources which helps qualify them. **Page 329**

6. **c**   One of the activities a salesperson should perform before taking a prospect on property showings is to create a homebuyer's checklist and have them fill it out at the first opportunity. **Page 329**

7. **d** Avoiding conflict, selling the benefits of the home, and being honest are a few of the several ways to help buyers make a decision. **Page 336**

8. **d** Touching, talking about placing their furniture in the home, and asking others for their opinion are all buying signs of a desirable property. **Page 339**

9. **d** Objections can be viewed as a positive part of the sales process—a buyer is showing interest, a way to provide feedback, and that the buyer requires further clarification. **Page 339**

10. **a** When salespeople witness buying signals and feel confident that the property in question is right for their buyers, it is imperative that they ask for the sale. If they never ask, they may never know if the buyers are seriously interested in a property. **Page 340**

Unit 12: Writing and Presenting an Offer

Answers - Matching

1.	K	3.	I	5.	D	7.	E
2.	F	4.	C	6.	G	8.	B

Answers - Multiple Choice

1. **a** The deposit receipt may become the actual escrow instructions or simply the basic agreement for escrow instructions when escrow opens. **Page 347**

2. **d** Before writing an offer for buyers, the selling salesperson should know how much the buyers are able to pay and if terms are more important than price. He or she should also know if the buyers are prepared for a counteroffer from the sellers, any contingencies, and the timeframe to close the transaction. **Page 349**

3. **a** Once the purchase price and initial deposit are determined, you need to ask the buyers if they plan to pay all cash, obtain financing, assume a loan, or take title "subject to" an existing loan. **Page 350**

4. **c** Some salespeople think that they have done their job by writing up the offer and simply faxing the offer to the listing salesperson. It is better to try to arrange a presentation with the listing salesperson and sellers. Generally, it is not a good idea to present an offer over the telephone because you cannot obtain a written acceptance over the telephone. **Page 362**

5. **d** In your presentation folder, include the cover letter for the offer, the signed deposit receipt, the earnest money deposit, the buyers' pre-approval letter from the lender, and a copy of the deposit receipt or escrow instructions if the buyers' home is in escrow. **Page 362**

6. **b**   Sometimes it will not be possible to get an offer accepted as it stands. If you are the listing salesperson and your sellers cannot agree to any or all terms of an offer, a rejection or counteroffer may be necessary. It is rare that a salesperson recommends an outright rejection. A counteroffer is a more plausible reaction because it is an attempt to arrive at the terms of the sellers. **Page 364**

7. **a**   It is your responsibility to caution the sellers of the repercussions of countering rather than accepting an offer as is. The counteroffer supersedes any previous offers made by the buyers. When you present the counteroffer, it is now the buyers' option to accept, reject, or counter. The buyers could decide to target another property, especially if the offer was fair and they presented evidence of strong financial backing. **Page 364**

8. **b**   Remember, all counteroffers must be in writing. **Page 364**

9. **d**   The accepting party must notify the offeror of acceptance so that the offer or counteroffer will be valid. Up until the point of notification of the sellers' acceptance, the buyers are free to withdraw the offer. It is important that the party who created the offer receive a signed copy of the other party's written acceptance for it to be valid. **Page 366**

10. **a**   Once the sellers agree to the offer and the buyers are informed of the sellers' acceptance, the deposit receipt is a valid, non-rescindable, binding contract. Once all parties execute, or sign, the deposit receipt, it becomes a bilateral contract. A bilateral contract is an agreement in which each person promises to perform an act in exchange for another person's promise to perform. **Page 366**

Unit 13: Financing the Purchase

Answers - Matching

1.	O	5.	P	9.	S	13.	E
2.	K	6.	Q	10.	F	14.	M
3.	R	7.	I	11.	N	15.	T
4.	C	8.	B	12.	G		

Answers - Multiple Choice

1. **d**   The principal is the actual amount of the loan or outstanding balance that the borrower owes the lender. The interest rate is simply the cost incurred when borrowing money and usually expressed as a percentage. The term is the timeframe in which to repay the loan. Amortization is the breakdown of the monthly payments from the start of the repayment plan all the way to the finish. **Page 372**

2. **c**   It is a promise to pay back a certain sum of money at specified interest terms, and at an agreed-upon time. Collateral is the security in a mortgage of trust deed. **Page 372**

3. **d**   The interest-only loan is called a straight loan or term loan. It has regular interest payments during the term of the note. **Page 374**

4. **b**   A fixed-rate fully amortized note is a loan with an interest rate that is fixed and payments that are level for the life of the loan. This note is common with institutional lenders. **Page 376**

5. **c**   The initial interest rate, or qualifying rate, is determined by the current rate of the chosen index. **Page 377**

6. **d**   The three parties to a trust deed are the borrower (trustor), lender (beneficiary), and a neutral third party called a trustee. **Page 377**

7. **d**   The trustee acts as an agent for the beneficiary and has only two obligations. The first is to foreclose on the property if there is a default on the loan and the second is to reconvey the title to the borrower when the debt is repaid in full. **Page 379**

8. **a**   A conventional loan is any loan made by lenders without any governmental guarantees. The basic protection for a lender making conventional loans is the borrower's equity in the property. A low down payment will mean greater risk for the lender and a higher interest charged to the borrower. Conventional loans may be conforming or non-conforming. **Page 383**

9. **c**   Loans that do not meet the borrower credit requirements of Fannie Mae and Freddie Mac are called subprime loans or "B" and "C" paper loans as opposed to "A" paper conforming loans. **Page 384**

10. **b**   Equity is the difference between the value of the property and any outstanding loans or the initial down payment. **Page 388**

11. **d**   When a seller carries the paper on the sale of his or her home, it is also called a purchase money loan, just like the loan made by an outside lender. **Page 388**

12. **d**   A prospective borrower may choose one lender over another for many reasons. Each borrower has individual requirements, but there are some basic needs that borrowers should take into consideration when choosing a lender. **Page 391**

13. **b**   By definition. **Page 392**

14. **c**   Filling out the application form, which asks for detailed information about the borrower, his or her employment record, and information regarding the address of the property desired is the first step toward obtaining a loan. The lender will need documentation to substantiate the information in the application, such as recent pay stubs, bank statements, verifications of employment, deposit and rent or mortgage, tax returns, appraisal, purchase agreement, divorce decrees, bankruptcy papers and any other information the lender may need. **Page 395**

15. **a** To determine a consumer's maximum mortgage amount, lenders use guidelines called debt-to-income ratios. This is simply the percentage of a consumer's monthly gross income (before taxes) that the borrower uses to pay his or her monthly debts. **Page 399**

16. **c** The applicant must still pass the lender's tests of creditworthiness. However, ECOA bars discrimination based on age, gender, marital status, race, color, religion, national origin, and whether the applicant receives public income, such as veteran's benefits, welfare, or social security. **Page 403**

Unit 14: From Acceptance to Close

Answers - Matching

1.	D	5.	B	9.	O	13.	K
2.	H	6.	C	10.	L	14.	M
3.	I	7.	N	11.	G	15.	T
4.	S	8.	Q	12.	E		

Answers - Multiple Choice

1. **d** Sometime before the escrow closes the seller will sign a grant deed conveying title to the buyer. Because the seller will sign over the ownership to the buyer before getting the money, the escrow holder must hold the signed deed until funds from the buyer are deposited in escrow and all other terms of the escrow have been met. **Page 415**

2. **c** The person who commonly opens escrow, if there is a real estate salesperson involved, is the listing salesperson. **Page 414**

3. **a** Every real estate transaction is unique. Escrow procedures may vary according to local custom. In some areas of California, such as Southern California, escrow companies or banks conduct escrows. In other areas, such as Northern California, title companies conduct escrows. The principals may go to the escrow office if there is no real estate salesperson involved, and tell the escrow officer to prepare instructions according to their agreement. **Page 415**

4. **d** Escrow instructions are unilateral or bilateral. The law does not set the format for escrow instructions so long as all parties approve. A new approach to conducting escrow is using the purchase agreement as escrow instructions. **Page 417**

5. **d** Lenders require hazard insurance that covers the outstanding loan on the property. Hazard insurance protects the borrower and the lender against loss due to fire, windstorm, and natural hazards. **Page 421**

6. **a**   The closing statement outlines the flow of consideration through escrow, as well as adjustments and disbursements reflecting the prior agreement of the parties. **Page 422**

7. **c**   The seller is credited for the amount of the total consideration, or sales price. The buyer is credited with the down payment. The title policy premiums and documentary transfer taxes are debited on the seller's closing statement. **Page 422**

8. **c**   Fees that are debited and non-recurring on the buyer's closing statement are notary fees, appraisal fees, and title insurance premiums. Hazard insurance premiums are debited and recurring for the buyer. **Page 423**

9. **c**   Title insurance was created in response to the need for reliable assurance of title combined with an insurance against loss caused by errors in searching records and reporting the status of title. Title insurance covers a missing connection in a property's history or ownership. **Page 419**

10. **c**   The salespersons' main responsibilities during escrow are maintaining contact with parties and following up on escrow conditions. **Page 415**

Unit 15: Putting it all Together

Answers - Matching

1.	H	7.	F	13.	A	19.	I
2.	Q	8.	T	14.	U	20.	C
3.	P	9.	B	15.	S	21.	K
4.	V	10.	O	16.	X	22.	Z
5.	D	11.	Y	17.	G	23.	M
6.	W	12.	R	18.	L		

Answers - Multiple Choice

1. **a**   The real estate industry is constantly changing. It is important to keep abreast of market changes, new disclosures, contracts, real estate laws, and regulations. **Page 437**

2. **d**   The salesperson should do all of the suggested actions. **Page 439**

3. **b**   Your responsibilities begin when you get the listing. You must be prepared to stage the home, market the listing, and exceed your client's customer service expectations. **Page 440**

4. **a**   Communicate with your sellers to find out what their boundaries are regarding offers and counteroffers. **Page 441**

5. **d**   Your client will look to you for guidance and assistance to ensure a smooth transaction. Be prepared to do all of the suggested actions. **Page 442**

6. **c**   Communicate with your clients throughout the escrow process and even after closing. They will refer business to you if you handle their transaction professionally. **Page 443**

7. **b**   The first thing a salesperson should do is ask if the prospective buyer is working with another agent. The other choices are not wrong, but they are not the first thing on the list. **Page 444**

8. **c**   In order to write up an offer, the sales associate must discuss the amount of the earnest money deposit with the buyer. **Page 445**

9. **a**   If the seller agrees to list the house, before preparing the listing agreement, the sales associate must prepare and give the seller the Disclosure of Real Estate Agency Relationships form. **Page 447**

10. **d**   The seller must complete and provide to the buyer the Real Estate Transfer Disclosure Statement and the Natural Hazards Disclosure statement. The real estate agents are required to visually inspect the property and disclose any material facts. The buyer should inspect the property, but has no requirement to make a disclosure regarding his or her inspection. **Page 449**

GLOSSARY

A-frame style
The triangular-shaped roof that goes all the way to the ground on two sides of the house gives this housing style its name. This style is ideal for cold, snowy regions.

acceptance
An unqualified agreement to the terms of an offer.

accrued
Accumulated over a period of time.

acknowledgment
A signed statement, made before a notary public, by a person who has signed an instrument which states that the signing was voluntary.

action plan
This lists the tasks you must perform to accomplish a particular goal.

activity chart
A daily chart listing every activity, including non-job related tasks.

addendum
Additional documents attached to and made part of a contract.

adobe bricks
Bricks made from a mixture of clay and straw, which were dried in the sun rather than in a kiln.

advertising
The mode and frequency through which someone communicates a marketing concept.

advertising coordinator
This person makes sure every listing gets its share of advertising time and creates flyers and brochures for team listings. This person must be creative as well as technically skilled.

after-the-fact-referral fees (ATFs)
Fees requested after a sales associate has established a relationship with a buyer or seller.

agency relationship
A special relationship of trust by which one person (agent) is authorized to conduct business, sign papers, or otherwise act on behalf of another person (principal).

agent
A person who acts for and in the place of another, called a principal, for the purpose of affecting the principal's legal relationship with third persons.

agreement
A mutual exchange of promises (either written or oral). Although often synonymous with a contract, technically it denotes mutual promises that fail as a contract for lack of consideration.

agreement of sale
A contract for the sale of real property where the seller gives up possession, but retains the title until the purchase price is paid in full. Also called contract for sale or land contract.

all-cash transaction
Transaction that closes quickly because the buyers do not have to complete the loan qualification process.

allocate
To assign or set apart for a specific purpose.

amenities
Features that add value to a property.

American Foursquare style
This practical housing style is a sub-style of the Prairie. They are simple, space-efficient, and box-shaped, with a wide porch across the entire front of the house.

appreciation
(1) An increase in the worth or value of property. (2) The increase in market value of real estate. (3) An increase in property value with the passage of time.

arbitrator
In a dispute, the parties hire a neutral person to listen to each side. The arbitrator may award a binding decision on all parties to the dispute.

Architectural style
Generally the appearance and character of a building's design and construction.

Art Deco style
This housing style was popular in the early 1900s. It is angular and boxy with a flat roof and simple, clean lines. Glass blocks, metals, and plastics are used extensively.

Art Moderne style
A simple housing style with a horizontal, cube-like shape and a flat roof and rounded corners. The exterior walls are smooth stucco with rounded corners.

GLOSSARY

"as is"
Term stating the property is being sold exactly as it is found, without seellar warranties.

associate licensee
Another term used for a licensed real estate salesperson employed by a licensed real estate broker.

assumption of mortgage
The taking of a title to property by a grantee wherein grantee assumes liability for payment of an existing note secured by a mortgage or deed of trust against the property, becoming a co-guarantor for the payment of a mortgage or deed of trust note.

attorney-in-fact
(1) The person holding the power of attorney. (2) A competent and disinterested person who is authorized by another person to act in his or her place in legal matters.

auto dialer (automatic telephone dialing systems)
Computerized or prerecorded messages and equipment that can generate and dial telephone or cell phone numbers randomly or sequentially.

awning window
A window that is hinged at the top and opens out.

Baby Boomers
Individuals born between 1943 and 1960. Currently the largest generation in the history of the nation.

bay window
A window that protrudes from the exterior of a building, leaving a recess within.

bilateral contract
An agreement in which each person promises to perform an act in exchange for another person's promise to perform.

bilateral instructions
One set of escrow instructions signed by both the seller and buyer.

blind advertising
Advertising that fails to disclose that the party is a licensee acting as an agent.

blockbusting
The illegal practice of telling people that property values in a neighborhood will decline because of a specific event, such as the purchase of homes by minorities.

bona fide purchaser
Bona fide means good faith, so a bona fide purchaser is one who pays fair value for property in good faith, and without notice of adverse claims.

bow window
A window made of curved glass and found on Queen Anne, Tudor, and Neo-Eclectic housing styles.

branding
Making yourself known to a specific area, group of people, or segment of the market.

breach of contract
A failure to perform on part or all of the terms and conditions of a contract.

broker
An agent who earns income by arranging sales and other contracts. A real estate broker is an individual licensed by the state of California to arrange the sale or transfer of interests in real property for compensation.

broker-owner
The broker who creates and sets all policies for the real estate brokerage firm.

broker's trust fund account
An account set up by a broker; withdrawals from this account may be made only by the broker.

brokerage
An activity involving the sale of something through an intermediary who negotiates the transaction for payment.

budget
A forecast of future income and expenses.

Bungalow style
A house style found in older neighborhoods, characterized by simplicity, with an emphasis on horizontal rather than vertical lines.

buyer's agent
A broker employed by the buyer to locate a certain kind of real property.

buyer's broker
An agent who represents only the buyer and has a fiduciary duty to find the best house for the least money at the terms most favorable to his or her principal (the buyer).

buyer's market
A market containing more supply than demand.

buyer's profile
A document indicating the buyer's motivation and how much he or she can afford to spend on a home.

buyer's statement
A record of costs and credits incurred for the purchase of the property.

buying signs
Certain clues that indicate when a buyer is seriously considering buying a property.

calendar year

Starts on January 1 and continues through December 31 of the same year.

California Bungalow style

A low profile house with one to one-and-one-half stories, a square shape, a low-slung gable or hip roof, an offset entry with a wide front porch, and exterior walls finished with stucco and natural stone.

California Fair Employment and Housing Act

State law that prohibits discrimination in the sale, rental or financing of practically all types of housing.

California Land Title Association

A trade organization of the state's title companies.

California Ranch style

One-story, rambling, rectangular, L-shaped or U-shaped, with a low-pitch gable or hipped roof, and attached garage.

"CAN-SPAM" laws

Federal and state laws regulating commercial e-mail messages.

Cape Cod style

A house that is usually rectangular and has one to one-and-one-half stories, with a steeply pitched gable roof and small overhang.

caravan

An opportunity for the other salespeople in the office and the members of the MLS to preview a new listing.

career book

A marketing piece that identifies a salesperson and highlights his or her qualifications. This marketing piece is solely about the salesperson's credentials and successes.

casement windows

These windows have hinges on the sides and are opened with cranks.

caveat emptor

"Let the buyer beware".

CC&Rs (See covenants, conditions and restrictions)

chain of title

A chronological summary of all useful documents discovered in a title search regarding the ownership of a property.

chimney pot

Round or octagonal "pot" on top of each flue in a Queen Anne style home.

cladding

The external protective skin of the exterior surfaces of a home (surface coatings, siding, doors, windows, trim, shutters, entryways, and flashings).

classified ads

Ads that use only text and cost very little.

client

The person who employs an agent to perform a service for a fee.

closing

Process by which all the parties to a real estate transaction conclude the details of a sale or mortgage. The process includes the signing and transfer of documents and distribution of funds.

closing costs

The miscellaneous expenses buyers and sellers normally incur in the transfer of ownership of real property over and above the cost of the property.

closing statement

An accounting of funds made to the buyer and seller separately. Required by law to be made at the completion of every real estate transaction.

cloud on title

Any condition that affects the clear title of real property or minor defect in the chain of title which needs to be removed.

Code of Ethics

A set of rules and principles expressing a standard of accepted conduct for a professional group and governing the relationship of members to each other and to the organization.

cold calling

The practice of making unsolicited calls to people you do not know in order to get new business.

Colonial Revival style

Houses that are large, with two or more stories, featuring dark green or black shutters and wood exteriors with tall wood columns that are typically painted bright white.

commercial e-mail message

Any electronic mail message whose primary purpose is the commercial advertisement or promotion of a commercial product or service.

commingling

The illegal practice of depositing client's funds in a broker's personal or general business account.

commission

A fee for services rendered usually based on a certain percentage of the sales price of a property.

commission split

The previously agreed-upon division of money between a broker and sales associate when the brokerage has been paid a commission from a sale made by the associate.

common area

An entire common interest subdivision except the separate interests therein.

common interest development

A common interest development combining the individual ownership of private dwellings with the shared ownership of common facilities of the entire project.

communication

The effective exchange of information.

communication skills

These may affect how you connect with the people who rely on you. If you are not connecting, then you are not communicating.

community property

All property acquired by a husband and wife during a valid marriage (excluding certain separate property).

community property with right of survivorship

Community property with the added tax benefit of a "double step-up in basis".

comparable sales (comps)

Recent selling prices of properties that are similar to the subject property. They are used to help set the selling price on a listing and determine property value in the appraisal process.

competitive market analysis (CMA)

A comparison analysis that real estate brokers use while working with a seller to determine an appropriate listing price for the seller's house.

complete escrow

When all terms of the escrow instructions have been met.

condominium

A housing unit consisting of a separate fee interest in a particular specific space, plus an undivided interest in all common or public areas of the development. Each unit owner has a deed, separate financing, and pays the property taxes for his or her unit.

consideration

A buyer's deposit in the form of cash, a personal check, cashier's check, promissory note, money order, or other form. Usually for 1-3% of the purchase price of the property.

Consumer Credit Protection Act

A federal law that includes the Truth-in-Lending Law.

contact list

A record of everyone you know—family members, friends, teachers, former colleagues, and members of associations to which you belong.

contact management software

A database program that allows real estate salespeople to manage and track all client information and activities, including names, phone numbers, addresses, websites, e-mail addresses, last meeting dates, and more.

Contemporary style

This asymmetrical housing style is characterized by attractive, simple, clean lines and the combination of stone, glass, masonry, and wood in the exterior.

contingencies

Statements that define the terms of an agreement and give the other party to the agreement cause to void an offer if the terms are not met.

contract

A legally enforceable agreement made by competent parties, to perform or not perform a certain act.

contract date

The date the contract is created. The contract is created when the final acceptance was communicated back to the offeror.

contract of sale

A contract for the sale of real property where the seller gives up possession but retains title until the total of the purchase price is paid off.

conversion

The appropriation of property or funds belonging to another; as in a broker using a client's money.

conveyance

The transfer of title to land by use of a written instrument.

cooperating agent

A selling agent who assists another broker by finding a buyer.

coordinators

People at a brokerage who keep the files of each transaction or listing current and active.

counteroffer

The rejection of an original purchase offer and the submission of a new and different offer.

covenants, conditions, and restrictions (CC&Rs)

Restrictions placed on certain types of real property that limit the activities of owners. Covenants and conditions are promises to do or not to do certain things.

Craftsman Bungalow style

This house is larger than the traditional California Bungalow and has rows of high, small, "ribbon" windows and a full-width porches framed by tapered columns.

credit

A bookkeeping entry on the right-hand side of an account, recording the reduction or elimination of an asset or an expense, or the creation of an addition to a liability or item of equity or revenue.

credit reporting agency

A company that researches the credit records of consumers and summarizes the findings in a factual credit report.

credit scoring
An objective, statistical method that lenders use to quickly assess the borrower's credit risk.

cul-de-sac lot
A lot found on a dead-end street with the same way for ingress and egress.

curb appeal
A phrase, implying an informal valuation of a property based on observation and experience.

customer
A prospective buyer of real estate; not to be confused with a property seller, who is the listing broker's client.

debt service
The sum of money needed for each payment period to amortize the loan or loans.

debt-to-income ratios
Guidelines used by lenders to determine a consumer's maximum mortgage amount.

Declaration of Restrictions
A written legal document which lists covenants, conditions and restrictions (CC&Rs). This document gives each owner the right to enforce the CC&Rs.

deed
A formal transfer by a party.

delivery
The unconditional, irrevocable intent of a grantor immediately to divest (give up) an interest in real estate by a deed or other instrument.

demand
The desire to buy or obtain a commodity.

demographic profiles
The statistical study of human populations, from a variety of sources used to create a broad profile of any community.

Department of Veterans Affairs (VA)
Offers loan programs to individuals qualified by military service or other entitlement.

deposit receipt
Contract that acts as the receipt for earnest money given by the buyer to secure an offer, as well as being the basic agreement, between the buyer and seller.

direct mail
A farming activity in which a sales associate sends marketing materials directly to the prospect's residence.

discharge of contract
The cancellation or termination of a contract.

disclosures
Information that must be given to buyers and borrowers regarding the financial and legal aspects of a real estate transaction.

display ads
Ads that include text and photos, and usually are placed by the brokerage company in the weekend real estate section.

"do not call"
Federal and state regulations regarding unsolicited telephone calls.

documentary transfer tax
A state enabling act allowing a county to adopt a documentary transfer tax to apply on all transfers of real property located in the county. Notice of payment is entered on the face of the deed or on a separate paper filed with the deed.

dormer
A vertical window set in a framed window unit that projects from a sloping roof. Dormers are usually used in second story bedrooms or bathrooms.

dual agency
An agency relationship in which the agent acts concurrently for both principals in a transaction.

dual agent
A broker acting as agent for both the seller and the buyer in the same transaction.

due diligence
The reasonable effort to provide accurate and complete information about a property.

Dutch Colonial Revival style
Houses that are one to two-and-one-half stories with shed-like dormers and a distinctive gambrel roof.

Dutch door
A horizontally divided double door.

early move-in
Allows the buyer to take possession of the property prior to the close of escrow.

earnest money deposits
Down payment made by a purchaser of real estate as evidence of good faith.

easement
The right to use another's land for a specified purpose, sometimes known as a right-of-way.

Elizabethan (Tudor Revival)
This asymmetrical housing style has a very steep cross-gabled roof, a prominent chimney, half-timbered exteriors, rounded doorways, and multi-paned casement windows.

employee
Someone who is under the control and direction of a broker.

employment agreement
This agreement is required by law and must state the important aspects of the employment relationship, including supervision of licensed activities, licensee's duties, and the compensation arrangement.

energy efficient ratio (EER)
A measurement of the efficiency of energy; used to determine the effectiveness of appliances.

English Cottage style
Asymmetrical housing style patterned after the rustic cottages in southwestern England. They have an uneven sloping roof of slate or cedar that mimics the look of thatch.

English Tudor style
This traditional housing style is large, two-stories, with masonry or stucco, and has steep-gabled roofs with a medieval feel. It is characterized by patterned brick or stone walls, rounded doorways, and multi-paned casement windows.

Equal Credit Opportunity Act (ECOA)
Federal act to ensure that all consumers are given an equal opportunity to obtain credit.

errors and omissions insurance (E&O)
A policy that covers various claims for errors, mistakes, neglect, or carelessness in the normal business activities of a real estate brokerage.

escrow
A small and short-lived trust arrangement.

escrow agent
The neutral third party holding funds or something of value in trust for another.

escrow holder
A company that acts as a neutral agent of both buyer and seller.

escrow coordinator
When a seller accepts an offer, the salesperson or the listing coordinator gives the file to this person who guides the transaction through to closing.

escrow instructions
Written directions, signed by a buyer and seller, detailing the procedures necessary to close a transaction and directing the escrow agent how to proceed.

ethics
A set of principles or values by which an individual guides his or her own behavior and judges that of others.

exclusive authorization and right-to-sell listing
An exclusive contract where the seller must pay the listing broker a commission if the property is sold within the time limit by the listing broker, any other broker, or even by the owner.

exclusive agency listing
An exclusive contract where the seller must pay the listing broker a commission if any broker sells the property.

execute
(1) To perform or complete. (2) To sign.

executed contract
All parties have performed completely.

executory contract
A contract in which obligation to perform exists on one or both sides.

expenses
Certain items which appear on a closing statement in connection with a real estate sale.

expired listing
A property listing that did not sell during the specified period with the listing broker.

extended coverage policy
An extended title insurance policy.

farm
A specific geographical location that an agent walks every month in order to obtain listings.

farming
One of the most effective prospecting tools. It is used to identify and cultivate new leads with the ultimate goal of gaining new business.

Federal Fair Housing Act
This law, amended in 1988, was created to provide fair housing throughout the United States.

Federal Home Loan Mortgage Corporation
A shareholder-owned corporation that purchases, secures and invests in home mortgages.

Federal Housing Administration
A federal government agency that insures private mortgage loans for financing of homes and home repairs.

Federal National Mortgage Association
"Fannie Mae" a quasi-public agency converted into a private corporation whose primary function is to buy and sell FHA and VA mortgages in the secondary market.

fictitious business name
A business name other than the name of the person who has registered the business. Also known as DBA or "doing business as."

fictitious trust deed
Recorded trust deed containing details which apply to later loan documents.

financial goal
Used to determine how much money a salesperson wants to make, and then a plan is created to achieve the goal.

finder's fee
Money paid to a person for finding a buyer to purchase a property or a seller to list property.

fiscal year
Starts on July 1 and runs through June 30 of the following year; used for real property tax purposes.

five-ranked windows
Five rectangular windows equally spaced across the second story of Georgian Colonial-style houses.

fixed rate mortgage (loan)
The most common type of loan. Regular payments of fixed amounts, to include both interest and principal are made. This payment pays off the debt completely by the end of the term.

fixed windows
Windows that do not open or move at all.

fixture
Personal property that has become affixed to real estate making it real property.

flat roof
This roof is popular in the Southwestern house styles, such as Pueblo and Spanish Eclectic, and modern styles such as International, Art Moderne, and Art Deco.

flood (100-year)
Boundary indicating areas of moderate flood hazards.

flood hazard boundary maps
Maps that identify the general flood hazards within a community.

floodplain
Low land adjacent to a river, lake, or ocean.

floor plan
Drawings that show the placement of the layout of rooms and their sizes in a building.

floor time
The daily rotating of salespeople to answer telephone calls from newspaper ads and real estate signs. During these scheduled periods, a specific salesperson is responsible for answering property inquiries asked by people who call or walk in.

Folk Victorian style
The affordable version of a Queen Anne house. Symmetrical, rectangular, or L-shaped with white wood siding, steep gabled roofs, and a front porch with turned spindles.

For Sale By Owner (FSBOs)
Properties that are for sale by owner.

franchise
A right or privilege awarded by law to operate a business using another company's name and products. In real estate, there are franchised brokerages.

fraud
An act meant to deceive in order to get someone to part with something of value.

French doors
Double doors hinged at either side.

French Normandy style
This housing style has a round stone tower topped with a cone-shaped roof. Sometimes the tower is the entrance to the house. In addition, vertical half-timbering adds height to the house.

French Provincial style
This style of house is large, square, symmetrical, and has two floors, with a distinctive steep, high, hip roof. Windows and chimneys are symmetrical and balanced.

gable roof
A pitched roof with two sloping sides.

gambrel roof
Typically seen in Dutch colonial architecture, it is a curbed roof with a steep lower slope with a flatter one above.

Generation X
The group of homebuyers born between 1961 and 1981.

Georgian style
A formal style house with symmetrical lines. It has paired chimneys (one on each side) and five windows across the front of the second story.

glazing
The process of installing glass panes into window sashes.

glazing patterns
The way windowpanes are placed into a frame.

global positioning system
A device that uses satellite technology to track your location and map out driving directions.

goal
The measurable accomplishment or outcome an individual strives to achieve.

goal setting
An activity that requires you to make a list of things you want to achieve, acquire, or attract in a certain amount of time.

good consideration
Gifts such as real property based solely on love and affection.

good funds
Funds that have already cleared the bank such as cashier's checks, certified checks, or wired monies.

half-timbering
A method of construction where the wooden frame and principal beams of a structure are exposed, and the spaces between are filled with stucco, brick, or stone.

hazard insurance
A property insurance policy that protects the owner and lender against physical hazards to property such as fire and windstorm damage.

hazardous household waste
Consumer products such as paints, cleaners, stains, varnishes, car batteries, motor oil, and pesticides that contain hazardous components.

hazardous waste
Materials—chemicals, explosives, radioactive, biological—whose disposal is regulated by the Environmental Protection Agency (EPA).

hip roof
A pitched roof with sloping sides and ends.

Holden Act
A law designed primarily to eliminate discrimination in lending practices based upon the character of the neighborhood in which real property is located. Also known as the Housing Financial Discrimination Act of 1977.

homebuyer's checklist
Completed by a prospective buyer to describe his or her ideal home. It allows the salesperson to find out exactly what the buyer is looking for in a home.

home flyer
An advertising piece used to sell a home.

home warranty program
A type of coverage that protects the buyer and seller on major property systems and built-in appliances.

homeowners' association
A group of property owners in a condominium or other subdivision neighborhood, who manage common areas, collect dues, and establish property standards.

homeowners' exemption
A $7,000 tax exemption available to all owner-occupied dwellings.

hopper window
A window that is hinged at the bottom and opens in the room. Also known as an eyebrow window.

hotspot
A WiFi enabled location offering public access.

HVAC
The acronym for heating, ventilation, and air conditioning.

impound account
A trust account set up for funds set aside for future costs relating to a property.

independent contractor
A person who is hired to do work for another person but who is not an employee of that person.

Independent firms
(1) Large independent firms do not have an affiliation with national franchises. They are usually owned by private parties or partnerships, and may have many offices in one area. (2) Small independent firms have one or two office locations and offer the greatest amount of flexibility for a new associate.

infill development
The development of vacant parcels in existing urban and suburban areas.

interest rate
The percentage charged for the use of money.

Interim Occupancy Agreement
A written agreement between a buyer and a seller that allows the buyer to take possession of the property before the closing date.

International style
This asymmetrical housing style is modern, and practical in its use of concrete, glass, and steel to create sleek lines. It has a flat roof and floor-to-ceiling "window walls".

inventory
The number of housing units available for sale in an area.

jalousie window
These windows do not slide and are not hinged. Instead, they have narrow glass slats like Venetian blinds that are opened and closed with a crank.

job outlook
A forecast for future jobs in any industry.

joint tenancy
When two or more parties own real property as co-owners, with the right of survivorship.

key lot
A lot that resembles a key fitting into a lock, is surrounded by the backyards of other lots. It is the least desirable because of the lack of privacy.

"kit" house
A "House-in-a-Box" complete with blue prints and all the materials needed to build a home.

land contract
A contract for the sale of real property where the seller gives up possession, but retains the title until the purchase price is paid in full. Also known as a contract of sale or agreement of sale.

latent defect
Defects in a home that may be hidden from a buyer, but known by a seller, and must be disclosed.

legal description
(1) A land description recognized by law. (2) A description by which property can be definitely located by reference to government surveys or approved recorded maps.

legal title
Title that is complete and perfect regarding right of ownership.

lien
A legal claim against a property for the payment of a debt.

limited liability company
An alternative business that has characteristics of both corporations and limited partnerships.

liquidated damages
Agreed upon money that one party to a contract will pay to the other upon backing out of the agreement.

liquidated damages clause
Clause in a contract that allows parties to the contract to decide in advance the amount of damages to be paid, should either party breach the contract.

listing
A contract between an owner of real property and an agent who is authorized to obtain a buyer.

listing agent
A broker who obtains a listing from a seller to act as an agent for compensation.

listing agreement
A written contract by which a principal, or seller, employs a broker to sell real estate.

listing appointment
The opportunity a salesperson has to convince the prospective seller to list the home with them.

listing coordinator
This person manages all required paperwork for listings, and performs other duties that help balance the jobs of other team members.

listing presentation
A thorough, professional presentation given by a salesperson to persuade the prospective seller that he or she is the specialist who will sell the home.

listing price
The amount of money a seller agrees to accept from a buyer as stated in the listing agreement. The listing price may be negotiable during the listing period.

loan to value ratio
The percentage of appraised value to the loan.

lockbox
A box that is hung on or near the front door of a listed property to hold the key to a listed property. Many real estate boards use electronic lockboxes.

logo
A mark or symbol used as an identifier for an individual, company, or organization.

long-term goals
These goals refer to the major areas of your life, such as career, family, and lifestyle.

love and affection
Consideration used in a gift deed.

Mansard roof
This roof has four nearly vertical sides with a flat top and is featured in Second Empire and other French-inspired housing styles.

manufactured home
A home built in a factory after June 15, 1976, which must conform to the U.S. government's Manufactured Home Construction and Safety Standards.

market value
The highest price a property would bring if freely offered on the open market, with both a willing buyer and a willing seller. Sometimes called objective value.

marketable title
Good or clear saleable title reasonably free from risk of litigation over possible defects.

marketing
The process involved in promoting a service or product.

marketing pieces
Business cards, stationery, flyers, door-hangers and brochures, promotional or giveaway items, newsletters, and presentation binders.

material fact

Any fact that would seem likely to affect the judgment of the principal in giving consent to the agent to enter into the particular transaction on the specified terms.

median home price

The price that is midway between the least expensive and most expensive home sold in an area during a given period of time.

median income

This is the middle income in a series of incomes ranked from lowest to highest.

Mediterranean style

One of the most common housing styles in Southern California. It consists of a blend of Italian, Moorish, Byzantine, and California mission styles. It is characterized by white or light-colored stucco on the exterior and a red tiled gable roof with very little or no overhanging eaves.

Mello Roos District

An area where a special tax is imposed on those real property owners within a Community Facilities District. Public services such as roads, sewers, parks, schools, and fire stations in new developments may be financed under this law.

Millennium Generation

The children of Generation X, born between 1982 and 2000. Also known as Generation Y.

mirror offer

An offer that matches all terms in the listing.

Mission style

This housing style has round parapets on the roof that resemble those found on Spanish colonial churches. They are one to two stories, rectangular-shaped, with flat roofs with red tile accents.

mobile home

A factory-built home manufactured prior to June 15, 1976, constructed on a chassis and wheels, and designed for permanent or semi-attachment to land.

mobile home park

Any area or tract of land where two or more mobile home lots are rented or leased or held out for rent or leased to accommodate manufactured homes or mobile homes used for human habitation.

Monterey style

The most distinguishing feature of the Monterey style house is the second-story balcony on the front of the house. These houses often have a courtyard, wrought iron trim, and fencing.

motivated prospects

People who are ready to close a transaction.

multiple listing service (MLS)

A cooperative listing service conducted by a group of brokers (usually members of a real estate association) to provide an inventory of all available properties in the area.

mutual mortgage insurance

A fee for an insurance policy charged the borrower to protect the lender under an FHA loan, in the event of foreclosure on the property.

mutual rescission

When all parties to a contract agree to cancel an agreement.

National Do-Not-Call Registry

A database that contains registered telephone numbers that cannot receive telemarketing calls.

negotiating

The art of persuasion, a developed skill, used to convince a seller of the benefits of an offer.

Neo-Eclectic style

A postmodern housing style combining a variety of details from different styles to produce a harmonious look.

net annual income

The amount of expenses for one year of operation subtracted from the salesperson's gross income.

net listing

A listing agreement in which the commission is not definite. The broker receives all the money from the sale of the property that is in excess of the selling price set by the seller.

net sheet

Line-by-line description of the fees associated with the sale of a home, including commission. Shows the approximate net amount of money the seller can expect to receive for a specified sales price.

newsletter

A personal marketing device created to advertise a person's name and services.

notary public

A licensed public officer who takes or witnesses the acknowledgement.

Notice of Buyer to Perform

A notice given to a buyer telling them that they need to complete one or more of the agreements in a contract. Non-compliance could be in breach of contract.

offer

A presentation or proposal for acceptance to form a contract.

offer to purchase
The proposal made to an owner of property by a potential buyer to purchase the property under stated terms.

offeree
The party receiving an offer.

offeror
The party making an offer.

office preview
It is an opportunity for the other salespeople in the office to preview a new listing.

one month
For escrow purposes, 30 days.

one year
For escrow and proration purposes, 360 days, 12 months, 52 weeks.

ongoing expenses
Expenses that recur at regular intervals—weekly, monthly, quarterly.

open house
A common real estate practice of showing listed homes to the general public during established hours.

open listing
A listing agreement that gives any number of brokers the right to sell a property.

optionor
The person who owns the property (seller, lessor).

"or more" clause
A clause in a mortgage or trust deed that allows a borrower to pay it off early with no penalty.

oriel window
A smaller bay window on an upper story, supported by decorative brackets.

orientation
The placement of a building on its lot in relation to exposure to sun, prevailing wind, traffic, and privacy from the street.

palladian window
A window that is divided into three parts, with rectangular panes on each side of a wide arch. They are placed at the center of an upper story as a focal point in Colonial or Queen Anne houses.

parapet
A low wall projecting from the edge of a platform, terrace, or roof.

patent defect
Observable defects in a home that must be disclosed by a seller.

payoff demand
A document prepared when a loan payoff is being considered that shows the current status of the loan account, all sums due, and the daily rate of interest.

personal marketing
Marketing yourself as the best possible salesperson for a prospect's real estate needs.

personal marketing plan
A plan that describes what you expect to accomplish, what you will do to reach your goals, and what marketing efforts you will make to reach your target group.

personal property
Anything movable that is not real property.

pitch
The slope, incline, or rise of a roof.

planned development
A planning and zoning term describing land not subject to conventional zoning to permit clustering of residences or other characteristics of the project which differ from normal zoning.

pocket doors
Doors that glide or roll on suspended or overhead tracks.

pocket listing
A list that is kept by the listing broker or salesperson, and is not shared with other brokers in the office or other multiple listing service members. This is discouraged by the real estate profession and is prohibited by many broker's offices.

points
Charges levied by the lender based on the loan amount. Each point equals one percent of the loan. Discount points are used to buy down the interest rate. Points can also include a loan origination fee, which is usually one point. (See Discount Points)

Postmodern style *(See Neo-Eclectic style)*

Prairie style
This housing style is much larger than the Craftsman Bungalows and is designed with low horizontal lines that require larger lots. These houses have low-pitched hip roofs with large overhanging eaves, casement windows, and rows of small, high windows.

preapproval letter
A written commitment from a lender to loan a certain amount based on a buyer's written application.

preliminary title report
An offer to issue a policy of title insurance in the future for a specific fee.

prelisting package

A professional marketing piece that identifies the salesperson and highlights his or her qualifications.

prepaid items of expense

Prorations of prepaid items of expense which are credited to the seller in the closing escrow statement.

prequalification

Based on verbal information supplied by the buyer.

principle of substitution

It is the basis for using a CMA to determine value. It affirms that the maximum value of a property tends to be set by the cost of acquiring an equally desirable and valuable substitute.

priority

The order in which deeds are recorded.

private mortgage insurance

Mortgage guarantee insurance available to conventional lenders on the first part of a high risk loan.

pro rata

(1) In proportion. (2) According to a certain percentage or proportion of a whole.

procuring cause

A broker who produces a buyer "ready, willing and able" to purchase the property for the price and on the terms specified by the seller, regardless of whether the sale is completed.

property management

A specialty in which real estate brokers manage homes and large real estate projects such as industrial complexes, shopping centers, apartment houses, and condominiums.

property marketing

Marketing efforts designed to create interest in a property, causing it to sell at a top price.

property marketing plan

A detailed schedule of everything a real estate salesperson will do to market a property.

property profile

A report about a specific piece of property usually provided by a title company.

property taxes

Taxes used to operate the government in general.

prorate

To divide and distribute expenses and/or income between the buyer and seller of property as of the date of closing or settlement.

prospecting

The process of identifying potential customers.

prospecting coordinator

An employee in a brokerage firm whose primary responsibility is to generate leads and set up appointments for the lead listing salesperson.

public record

A document disclosing all important facts about the property, its marketing, and the financing of the subdivision.

Pueblo Revival style

A version of the Santa Fe style, characterized by roof beams which protrude through the walls and help support the roof.

purchase agreement (purchase contract)

This contract must exist between the parties involved in an escrow. This contract forms when both seller and buyer sign the purchase agreement and the sellers inform the buyers of acceptance of the offer.

purchase offer

A written offer for the purchase of a property.

qualifying rate

The initial interest rate which is determined by the current rate of the chosen index.

Queen Anne style

A house with multiple stories, projecting wings, a complicated roofline with very steep cross-gabled roofs, towers, turrets, vertical windows and balconies, multiple chimneys with decorative chimney pots, scrollwork, bric-a-brac, gingerbread, and gingerbread with frosting.

RPA-CA

The abbreviation for the C.A.R. California Residential Purchase Agreement and Joint Escrow Instructions form used to make an offer on real property residential purchase agreement.

rate

The percentage of interest charged on the principal.

"ready, willing and able" buyer

A person who is prepared to enter into a purchase contract, really wants to buy, and meets the financing requirements of purchase.

real estate agency disclosure

For every residential property transaction of one to four units, the law requires that an agent supply this written document explaining the nature of agency to a seller before listing a property, or to a buyer before writing an offer.

real estate agent

A broker licensed by the Department of Real Estate who negotiates sales for other people.

real estate assistant

Individual who handles a major portion of a real estate transaction.

Real Estate Professional Assistant (REPA)

The designation of a real estate assistant who has completed the course offered by NAR.

real estate salesperson

A person with a real estate license who must be employed by a real estate broker in order to perform any of the activities that requires a license.

Real Estate Settlement Procedures Act

A federal law requiring disclosure to borrowers of settlement (closing) procedures and costs by means of a pamphlet and forms prescribed by the United States Department of Housing and Urban Development.

Real Estate Transfer Disclosure Statement

A document that the seller must provide to any buyer of residential property (one-to-four units).

recording

The process of placing a document on file with a designated public official for public notice.

red flag

Something that alerts a reasonably observant person of a potential problem.

referral

New prospects received by a real estate agent or broker from prior customers or other contacts in the real estate industry.

referral network

A group of people cultivated by real estate professionals to send them new clients and listings.

relocation company

A firm that administers all aspects of moving individuals to a new community.

remodeling

Changes the basic design or plan of the building to correct deficiencies.

residential brokerage

The business of helping homeowners sell and homebuyers purchase homes.

reverse directory

A directory from which you can obtain a subscriber's name and address when only a telephone number or e-mail address is known.

revocation

The canceling of an offer to contract by the person making the original offer.

revoke

Recall and make void.

R-value

A rating that measures how well insulation resists heat.

safety clause

Protects the listing broker's commission, if the owner personally sells the property to someone who was shown the property or made an offer during the term of the listing.

sales associate

A licensed real estate salesperson or broker whose license is held by an employing licensed broker.

sales comparison approach

One of the three classic approaches to value. It involves comparing similar properties that have recently sold, to the subject property.

sales contract

Contract by which buyer and seller agree to terms of a sale.

Santa Fe style

A housing style with thick, earth colored adobe walls and a flat roof with rounded parapets. Windows and heavy wooden doors are set into deep openings. The roof has red clay tile accents, and the enclosed patios add a Spanish influence.

scorecard

A checklist used by a buyer to note what they do or do not like about each property.

Second Empire style

Symmetrical, boxy, vertical two-to-three story houses. Typical ornamentation includes paired columns and elaborate wrought iron along the rooftop, and a high, boxy mansard roof with a trapezoid shape.

security deposit

Money given to a landlord to prepay for any damage other than just normal wear and tear.

seller's advisory form

A standard form that brokers and sales associates may attach to the listing agreement. It advises the seller of legal requirements and practical matters that may arise during the selling process.

seller's market

The market condition which exists when a seller is in a more commanding position as to price and terms because demand exceeds supply.

seller's statement
A record of the financial proceeds the sellers will receive upon the transaction's closing.

selling agent
The broker who finds a buyer and obtains an offer for the real property.

selling price
The actual price that a buyer pays for a property.

septic tank
A sewage settling tank which must be at least five feet away from the improvements.

shed roof
This roof has a streamlined shape which is one-half of a gable roof, and is popular for Contemporary styles.

Shed style
This housing style is modern and is characterized by its asymmetrical style and multiple roofs sloping in different directions.

shingles
Commonly used in combination with wood siding. They can be plain or patterned and vary in shape from rectangular to diamond.

short-term goals
These are the stepping stones used to meet long-term goals. These goals can be met in hours, days, or weeks.

sidelights
Tall, narrow windows that flank the entry door. These windows are characteristic of Greek Revival and are found in Neo-Eclectic houses.

siding
Overlapping horizontal boards made from wood, vinyl, or aluminum that are applied to the house.

simple interest
Interest computed on the principal amount of a loan only as distinguished from compound interest.

single-hung windows
The bottom portion of the window slides up; commonly found in Ranch and modern style houses.

skylights
A type of fixed window that lets five times more light into a house than another window of the same size.

slogan
(1) A phrase expressing the goals or nature of a business. (2) A motto.

smart growth
Reconciling the needs of development with the quality of life. Smart growth focuses on revitalizing older suburbs and older city centers.

Spanish Colonial Revival style
Houses that are rectangular, symmetrical, and two stories. They have low-pitched gable roofs with ceramic tiles, eaves with little or no overhang, and stucco walls, wrought iron, and windows and doorways with round arches.

specific performance
An action brought in a court to compel a party to carry out the terms of a contract.

sphere of influence
A group of individuals whom you already know, who may choose to give you their business, or may refer you to someone who is in need of your services.

Split-Level Ranch style
This housing style, also known as the Raised Ranch style, usually has three levels at varying heights. These houses are asymmetrical with a rectangular, L-shaped, or U-shaped design.

staging
Preparing a home for maximum appeal to buyers.

standard policy
A policy of title insurance covering only matters of record.

start-up costs
One time costs or expenses for your business—advertising, computer equipment, etc.

Statute of Frauds
A state law which requires that certain contracts must be in writing to prevent fraud in the sale of land or an interest in land.

Statute of Limitations
The period of time limited by statute within which certain court actions may be brought by one party against another.

statutory disclosures
Disclosures that are required by law.

steering
The illegal practice of only showing clients property in certain areas.

stigmatized property
Property in which buyers or tenants may avoid for reasons which are unrelated to its physical conditions or features. Common stignatized properties are those in which there have been murders, suicides, or criminal activity. Also known as psychologically impacted property.

stock cooperative
A corporation formed for the purpose of owning property.

stucco
A mixture of cement, sand, and lime which is applied over a frame construction.

subagent
A broker delegated by the listing agent (if authorized by the seller) who represents the seller in finding a buyer for the listed property.

subdivision
The division of land into five or more lots for the purpose of sale, lease, or financing.

"subject to" clause
A buyer takes over the existing loan payments, without notifying the lender. The buyer assumes no personal liability for the loan.

subprime loans
Loans that do not meet the borrower credit requirements of Fannie Mae and Freddie Mac. Also known as "B" and "C" paper loans.

substitution of liability (novation)
The substitution by agreement of a new obligation for an existing one. Also known as novation.

target marketing
Marketing to a precise group of consumers.

tax lien
When income or property taxes are not paid.

tender
An offer by one of the parties to a contract to carry out his or her part of the contract.

Territorial style
A housing style that is a more angular, with square corners. In addition, the windows of are framed with straight, unpainted, wooden moldings, and brick detailing is present in the parapets.

time management plan
Schedules all of the required activities necessary to reach your goals.

timely manner
An act must be performed within certain time limits described in a contract.

time is of the essence clause
A clause in a contract that emphasizes punctual performance as an essential requirement of the contract.

T-intersection lot
A lot that is fronted head-on by a street. The noise and glare from headlights may be detractors from this type of lot.

title
Evidence that the owner of land is in lawful possession.

title companies
Companies who perform a title search on the property and issue a title policy for the lender and the purchaser to ensure that there is a valid mortgage lien against the property and title is clear.

title insurance
An insurance policy that protects the named insured against loss or damage due to defect in the property's title.

title plant
The storage facility of a title company in which it has accumulated complete title records of properties in its area.

title report
A report which discloses condition of the title, made by a title company preliminary to issuance of title insurance policy.

"to do" list
This itemizes every task that must be done within a certain period. Different from an action plan because it combines all required activities into one list to prioritize tasks according to importance.

townhouse
One of a row of houses usually of the same or similar design with common side walls or with a narrow space between adjacent side walls.

transaction coordinator
This person must be organized and exhibit the ability to manage information in a timely manner. He or she has the skills that lead each transaction to a successful and timely close.

transaction sides
Each real estate transaction has two sides (buyer side and seller side).

transom window
A window that is hinged at the top and opens into the room.

traverse windows
Windows that slide from side to side.

trust account
An account separate and apart and physically segregated from the broker's own funds, in which the broker is required by law to deposit all funds collected for clients.

trust funds
Money or other things of value received from people by a broker to be used in real estate transactions.

Truth in Lending Act
A federal law that requires borrowers to be informed about the cost of borrowing money.

underwriting
The process of evaluating a borrower's risk factors before the lender will make a loan.

undue influence
Using unfair advantage to get agreement in accepting a contract.

Uniform Residential Loan Application (1003 form)
A standardized form for residential mortgage applications.

Unilateral instructions
In which the buyer signs one set of instructions and the seller signs another.

unilateral contract
A contract where a party promises to perform without expectation of performance by the other party.

unilateral rescission
Legal action taken to repeal a contract by one party when the other party has breached a contract.

up desk
Handling calls from prospects while at the front desk or reception area. A passive lead-generation technique used to answer calls about ads or questions about the purchase or sale of property.

urban sprawl
The unplanned and often haphazard growth of an urban area into adjoining areas.

USonian style
This housing style cost much less to build because there were no basements or attics and very little ornamentation. These houses were built from the Depression until the mid 1950s and became the model for early tract housing.

vesting
The way title will be taken.

Victorian style
A style of housing popular in the late 1800s, characterized by ornate embellishments.

vigas
Roof beams that protrude through the walls and help support the roof.

virtual tour
An online open house.

wainscoting
The bottom portion of a wall that is covered with wood siding; the top part is treated with another material.

walk-through
The buyer's final viewing of the property prior to closing to be certain that the property is in the same condition as when the purchase offer was made.

walk-in
Prospects who have sought out a brokerage due to advertising such as newspaper ads or a brokerage sign on the building.

walk-up
An apartment of more than one story with no elevator.

warm calling
The practice of making unsolicited calls to people you know in order to get new business.

water pressure test
Water pressure can be tested by turning on all faucets and flushing all toilets at the same time.

website
A place (address) an individual or company has on the World Wide Web.

WiFi
A computer feature that gives a person the ability to access the Internet wirelessly.

windowpanes
Pieces of glass that are held in place by window frames and sashes, which are made of wood, metal, vinyl, or fiberglass.

workers' compensation insurance
Injury compensation insurance that a broker must provide to all salespeople as well as any non-licensee employees of the firm.

"X"
A person who cannot write may execute a document by placing an "X" (his or her mark) where the signature is normally placed. Beneath the mark a witness then writes the person's name and signs his or her own name as a witness.

ZipForm®
A free software program that allows REALTORS® to download, complete, and print transaction forms from their computers.

zoning
The regulation of structures and uses of property within selected districts.

INDEX

acceleration clause 380

action plan 73

adjustable-rate mortgage (ARM) 376

adobe bricks 97

advertising 249

advertising guidelines 251

advertising media 255

A-frame 111

agency 185

agency disclosure 127, 128, 281

agency relationship 125, 135, 179, 439

Agency Relationship Disclosure Act 127

agent 18, 125

AIDA formula 249

alienation 380

allocation of costs 189

amenities 84

American Foursquare 104

amortization 373

annual percentage rate 391

Anti-SPAM 223

appointments 302

appraisal 400, 446

appraiser 4

arbitrator 138

architectural styles 86, 89, 97, 105, 113, 114

Art Deco 109

Art Moderne 109

ask for the listing 281

ask for the sale 340

assets 397

assumption clause 381

Baby Boomers 326, 327

back ratio 400

balloon payment 374

banner ad 257

bay window 93

beneficiary 377

beneficiary statement 420

bilateral 417

bilateral contract 282, 366

billboard 262

blog 236

Bluetooth 40

branding 66

bricks 96

brochures 71

broker 123, 125, 126, 131, 132, 134

brokerage 2

broker-owner 16

budget 37, 38

Bungalow Style 102, 103

business cards 69

buyer's agent 126, 127, 156

buyer's broker 323, 324

buyer's forms 175

Buyer Single Agency 323

Buyer's Inspection Advisory 211

buyer's market 279

buyer's profile 329, 331, 334

buyer's statement 423

buying signals 302, 315

buying signs 338

California Association of REALTORS® 39

California Bungalow 89, 103, 113

California Department of Veterans Affairs 387

California Ranch 110

California Residential Purchase Agreement and Joint Escrow Instructions (RPA-CA) 183

CalVet loan 387

cancellation 137

cap 376

Cape Cod 98

caravan 299

career book 67, 272, 439

car wrap 263

casement windows 94, 109

chain of title 418

cladding 96

classified ads 260, 300

close escrow 424

closing 413, 443, 446

closing statements 422, 443

Code of Ethics 254, 284, 341
cold calls 225
cold prospects 219
collateral 372
Colonial 98
Colonial Revival 99
Combined Hazards Book 164
commercial brokerage 4
commercial email message 223
commission disputes 26
commissions 25
commission split 25, 26
commitment letter 398
communication 40, 50, 53, 292
communication skills 50, 53
competitive market analysis (CMA) 273, 439
comps 274
conforming loans 383
consideration 349, 350
contact list 218
contact management software 41
Contemporary 111
contingencies 195, 350, 445
contract of sale 379
conventional loan 383
cooperating broker 126
coordinators 28
counseling buyers 364
counseling sellers 364
counteroffer 363, 364, 366, 441
Craftsman Bungalow 103, 119
credit 391, 392
creditor 377
credit report 392
credit scores 392
curb appeal 310, 312

death on real property 147
debtor 377
debt-to-income ratios 399
Deed of Reconveyance 372, 379
deed of trust 377
definite termination date 130
demographic 325
demographic markets 220
demographics for target markets 248
Department of Veterans Affairs 386
deposit receipt 347, 367, 368, 370

difficult clients 52
digital camera 43
direct mail 228
direct marketing 225
Disclosure of Agency Law 128
Disclosure Regarding Real Estate Agency
   Relationships 127, 135, 136
disclosures 190, 448
display ads 260, 300
dispute resolution 137, 198
documentary transfer tax 421
domain name 69
Do Not Call 222
Do Not Fax® 223
doors 95
dormer 91
double-hung windows 94
dual agency 125, 323, 324
dual agent 126, 127, 128, 135
due diligence 341
due-on-sale clause 380
Dutch Colonial Revival 100

early move-in 355
earnest money deposit 349, 445
earning potential 9, 30
electronic lockbox key 39, 54
Elizabethan (Tudor Revival) 107
email 40, 229
employee 18, 19, 26, 28
employment agreement 20, 25
energy efficient 84
Energy Star® 84
English Cottage 108
English Tudor 107
environmental hazards 164
Equal Credit Opportunity Act 403
Equal Housing Opportunity 251
equitable title 379
equity 388
errors and omissions insurance 45
escrow 8, 29, 353, 442
escrow holder 413
escrow instructions 197, 348, 416
established business relationship 222
estimated buyer's closing costs 209
estimated seller's proceeds 143
exclusive agency relationship 321

exclusive right to sell 131
execute 366, 372
expiration of offer 355
expired listing 231
extended coverage policy 419
ezine 229

Fair Credit-Reporting Act 402
farm area 219
Federal 99
Federal Housing Administration 385
FHA loan 385
FICO® scores 393
finance 372
finance terms 187, 350
financial closing 424
financial reserves 53
financing 43
FIRPTA 170
Five-ranked 93
fixed-rate fully amortized note 376
flat roof 89, 109, 110
floor plan 83
floor time 232
Folk Victorian 102
foreclosure 398
"for sale" signs 295
franchise 16, 17, 18
French Normandy 108
French Provincial 108
front ratio 400
FSBOs (For Sale By Owner) 220, 233, 325
fully amortized 376

gable roof 89, 90, 98, 112
gambrel roof 89, 90, 100, 119
Generation X 326
Generation Y 326
Generation Z 327
geographic markets 219
Georgian 99
glazing 85
glazing patterns 92
global positioning system (GPS) 38, 40, 44
goal 60
goal setting 61

good funds 427
gross domestic product (GDP) 1
guest book 313, 314

hazard insurance 421
hip roof 89, 91, 104, 108
homebuyer 42
Homebuyer's Checklist 331, 334
homebuyer's guides 261
home equity line of credit 388
home equity loan 388
Home Equity Loan Borrower Protection Act 406
home flyer 301
home inspections 352
homeowner association 165
homepage 259
hotspots 41
house types 87
housing styles 81, 113

impound account 373, 428
income funnel 72
independent contractor 10, 19, 20, 26, 29
index 376
infomercial 264
initial deposit 348, 349
installment payments 376
institutional advertising 249
insulation 85
insurance 44
interest-only loan 374
interest rate 372
Interim Occupancy Agreement 189
Internal Revenue Code 169
International 110
Internet 38, 40, 41, 42, 43, 234, 255, 327
Internet access 40
Internet advertising 256
interview 14, 30
inventory 279

jumbo loans 384
junior loan 387
junk mail 228

large independent firms 17
latent defects 147
lead-based paint 164
legal closing 424
lender 315
liabilities 397
lifestyle 50, 52
liquidated damages 197
listening 50, 51
listening skills 50, 338
listing 126
listing agent 126, 127, 135, 136
listing agreement 7, 127, 130, 282, 439
listing appointment 269, 438
listing package 271
listing presentation 270, 276
listing price 273
loan 373, 381, 383, 385, 390, 395
lockbox 39, 136, 295
lockbox key 440
long-term goals 60

magazine 301
mansard roof 89
margin 377
marketable title 419
marketing pieces 65, 70
marketing plan 68
marketing the listing 299
median income 36
Mediterranean 112
mentor 2
Methamphetamine Contamination Notice 156, 158
mid-level entry 110
mirror offer 130
Mission 105
Monterey 105
mortgage 379
mortgagee 379
mortgage loan agent 3
mortgagor 379
Multiple Listing Service (MLS) 10, 39, 134, 274, 293, 440
Mutual Mortgage Insurance 385

National Association of REALTORS® 1
Natural Hazard Disclosure Statement 147, 159
negative amortization 376
negotiating 363
neighbors 303
net listing 283
net sheet 276, 280, 439
networking 234
niche market 219
non-conforming loans 384
novation 381

offer 184
offer to purchase 367
office preview 299
ongoing business expenses 38, 53
online advertising 299
open escrow 414
open house 69, 301, 440
open house signs 304, 305, 306
ornamental details 97
outdoor advertising 261
overcoming objections 339
oversell 338

Palladian window 92
parapet 105
partially amortized installment note 374
patent defects 147
payoff demand 420
personal appearance 45, 48, 53
personal marketing 64
personal marketing plan 65
personal selling 232
pest inspection 352
PMI 383
Podcasting 237
postcards 71
Postmodern 112
Prairie 104
preapproval letter 331
preliminary title report 418
pre-listing package 439
prepare the owners 308

INDEX

preparing the property for showing 308
prepayment clause 380
prequalification 330, 331
prequalify the seller 270
presenting an offer 355
previewing properties 445
principal 125, 137, 372
print media 260
private mortgage insurance 383
procuring cause 283
product advertising 249
product knowledge 81
productivity management 57
productivity software 41
professional attitude 49
promissory note 372
promotional mix 245
property management 4
property marketing 245
property marketing plan 246, 272, 439
property profile 272
property taxes 421
property web page 260
prorate 420
proration 353
prospecting 6, 217, 324
prospecting laws 221
prospecting strategy 224
prospective buyers 302
prospective sellers 302
psychographics 220
Pueblo Revival style 106
pull marketing 234
purchase agreement 175, 347
purchase contract 445
purchase money loan 388
purchase offer 8
purchase price 348, 349
push marketing 225
Pyramid-hipped roofs 91

qualifying buyers 329
qualifying questions 221, 315
qualifying rate 377
qualifying the borrower 399
qualifying the property 400
quality business 58
Queen Anne 101

Ranch 110
ready, willing, and able 282
real estate agency disclosure 322
real estate agency law 304
real estate assistant 13
Real Estate Settlement Procedures Act 404
red flag 253
referral 239
Regency 99
Regulation B 404
Regulation Z 406
Request for Full Reconveyance 379
Residential brokerage 3
Residential Listing Agreement—Agency 282
Residential Listing Agreement—Exclusive 130, 282
Residential Listing Agreement—Open 282
Ribbon windows 93
roofs 89

safety clause 132
saltbox roof 90
Santa Fe 106
scheduling 73
scorecard 334
Second Empire 101
security instrument 372, 377
security interest 377
Seismic Hazard Zone 159
seller financing 388
Seller's Advisory 147, 283
seller's forms 121
seller's market 279
seller's statement 422
selling agent 126, 127
selling points 82-83
selling price 274
setting priorities 59
setting the listing price 279
shed roof 90
Shed Style 111
shingles 96, 98, 100
short-term goals 60
showing properties 334
sidelights 93
siding 96

single agency 125, 135

skylights 93

small independent firms 17

smartphones 40

smoke detectors 165

social bookmarking 238

social media 235

social networking 234

solicitation materials 65

Spanish Colonial Revival 100

Spanish Revival 107

sphere of influence 218, 325

Split-Level Ranch 110

square footage 83

staging 295, 440

standard policy 419

statutory disclosures 190

straight loan 374

street furniture 263

stucco 96

subagent 126

"subject to" clause 381

subprime loans 384

target market 65, 219

target marketing 248

task list 73

telemarketing 225

term 372

Territorial 106

third party 18

time management 57

time management plan 72, 73

title company 442

title insurance 419, 446

title insurance policies 419

transactional email messages 224

transaction coordinator 3, 29

transaction documents 447

Transfer Disclosure Statement 147, 152, 156, 352

transferee 148, 169

transferor 169

transit advertising 263

Traverse windows 93

trust deed 377

trustee 377

trustor 372, 377

Truth in Lending Act 405

tweets 237

Twitter 237

underwriting 390

unilateral 417

unsecured loan 373

unsolicited advertisements 223

USonian 105

valid escrow 415

VA Loan 386

vendee 379

vendor 379

vesting 134

Victorian 100

video casting 238

vigas 106

virtual tour 260, 299

walk-ins 232, 325

walk-through 196, 429

wardrobe 48

warm calls 225

warm prospects 218

water heater 165

website 42, 43, 69, 71, 258

windows 92

workers' compensation insurance 28

World Wide Web 257

writing the offer 348, 445

written disclosure 127

yard signs 262

Yellow Pages™ 261